M000281828

DEATH OF THE WEHRMACHT

MODERN WAR STUDIES

Theodore A. Wilson
General Editor

Raymond A. Callahan
J. Garry Clifford
Jacob W. Kipp
Jay Luvaas
Allan R. Millett
Carol Reardon
Dennis Showalter
David R. Stone
Series Editors

DEATH OF THE WEHRMACHT

The German Campaigns of 1942

Robert M. Citino

UNIVERSITY PRESS OF KANSAS

© 2007 by the University Press of Kansas
All rights reserved

Published by the University Press of Kansas (Lawrence, Kansas 66049), which was organized by the Kansas Board of Regents and is operated and funded by Emporia State University, Fort Hays State University, Kansas State University, Pittsburg State University, the University of Kansas, and Wichita State University

ISBN 978-0-7006-1531-5

Printed in the United States of America

To my wife, Roberta.
Fighter.
Survivor.

Contents

Illustrations

Maps

Photographs

Acknowledgments

No book is truly written alone, and I want to take the opportunity to acknowledge the many people who help to bring my projects to fruition. Many years have passed since my graduate years at Indiana University, but not the fondness with which I recall studying under my mentors there, Professors Barbara and Charles Jelavich. All of my books are, in a sense, a tribute to the education I received at their hands. My colleagues within the field also deserve recognition. Among the many whose kindness, friendship, and scholarly advice I have received gratefully over the years are Dennis E. Showalter (Colorado College), Geoffrey Wawro (North Texas State), Richard L. DiNardo (Marine Corps Command and Staff College), and the formidably hospitable James F. Tent (University of Alabama at Birmingham). I would also like to thank Gerhard L. Weinberg (University of North Carolina) and James S. Corum (U.S. Army Command and General Staff College) for their expert advice in the preparation of this manuscript.

A special thanks is also in order to all those at the new U.S. Army Military History Institute (MHI) in Carlisle, Pennsylvania. The collection of materials found there is nonpareil, and there is no more welcoming place in the profession than the MHI's reading room. The staff could not be more helpful to the visiting scholar: Conrad Crane, the director of the MHI, and Richard Sommers, the chief of patron services, have every reason to be proud. I would also like to mention archivist David A. Keough, who never fails to teach me something every time we talk, and chief librarian Louise Arnold-Friend, who must put in her share of twenty-five-hour days, based on the excellent condition of the materials I examined while I was there. I will confess that I was one of many who didn't think it would be possible to replace the old MHI, but my first five minutes in the new one dispelled any Luddite nostalgia I might have been harboring.

Closer to home, my colleagues at Eastern Michigan University have given me more in the past two years than I could ever hope to repay, with James Holoka, Stephen Mucher, Ronald Delph, and Mark Higbee deserving pride of place. And of course, to my family—my wonderful wife Roberta and my daughters Allison, Laura, and Emily—there are simply no words to thank you adequately for all the love.

DEATH OF THE WEHRMACHT

Introduction

Ponder for a moment this dramatic scene from the pages of German military history. It is 1942, a year of fate for the German army:

"Incredible," he muttered to himself, "absolutely overwhelming." Marshal Fedor von Bock stood at his hilltop observation post, just southeast of Lozovaia, shaking his head at the scene. The vista beneath him was one that few generals in history had ever been privileged to see: an entire enemy army surrounded in a tiny pocket just a few miles away. He focused his field glasses here, then there, flitting back and forth. The entire area couldn't have been more than two miles wide from east to east, perhaps ten miles from north to south, and every inch of it was seething with activity. Massed formations of dusty brown infantry, tank columns so dense you could probably walk from one vehicle to the other without touching the ground, guns of every shape and description—all milling about, moving hither and yon without apparent plan or purpose. Above them thundered hundreds of Luftwaffe ground attack aircraft, Richthofen's boys: Stukas and 109s and Ju-88s, bombing and strafing and herding. With so many men and tanks, guns and horses, packed into such a tight space, they were an impossible-to-miss target. The airmen were probably licking their chops, he thought, and the same went for his gunners. As he surveyed the scene, he could see artillery firing from all points of the compass into the helpless, writhing mass below him. There were explosions everywhere; every square inch of the pocket roiled with fire and smoke.

He thought of a term he had learned so many years ago as a cadet in the War Academy: *Kesselschlacht*, the "cauldron battle." It was the perfect term to describe what was going on below: an entire enemy army being boiled alive. He remembered studying the campaigns of the Great Elector, Frederick the Great, Blücher, and Moltke. They were the gamblers of their day: bold maneuvers, daring attacks from flank and rear, battles of encirclement. And he remembered another word: *Vernichtungsschlacht*, the "battle of annihilation."

There was a massive explosion in the killing fields below. Bock couldn't know it, but a single 500-pound bomb delivered from a Stuka had just struck a Soviet ammunition convoy. The explosions—both primary and secondary—had killed or wounded over 300 men. Were those screams he heard? Horses? Men? No matter. He was back to his reverie. He thought once more of those long-ago classes, the handsome, red-bound books. *Der Schlachterfolg*, they were called—"Success in Battle." They contained the battles and operations of all the great German captains, and they were required reading in the first-year course. The great cavalry commander Seydlitz, slashing across the march route of the hapless French army at Rossbach and destroying it in an hour. Yorck crossing the Elbe River at Wartenburg into the rear of Napoleon's army, the maneuver that trapped the emperor and led directly to his defeat at Leipzig. Hadn't the king given him a new title after that one? Yes, he thought, "Yorck von Wartenburg." Best of all, Moltke's elegant maneuver at Königgrätz, coolly risking the destruction of one army while waiting for another one to slam into the Austrian flank. Bock had long ago memorized the details of every one of these battles, could recite their orders of battle, could still diagram each one on a chalkboard from memory.

He was sixty-one, but he felt young again. Not one of those immortal battles, he suddenly realized, could rival what was happening beneath him at this very moment. For ease, for swiftness, for decisiveness, this might be the greatest victory in the history of the German army. "They'll be adding another name to that list," he chuckled. Maybe he'd even get a title, like old Yorck. He chuckled and rolled it from his tongue: "Fedor von Bock und Kharkov."

At Marshal Bock's feet, an enemy army was dying.

The above scene may seem strange. If 1942 means anything to the informed student of World War II, it means the turning point of the war,[1] the year of El Alamein and Stalingrad (and, in the Pacific, the year of Guadalcanal and Midway), the turning of the tide—the "hinge of fate," in Winston Churchill's memorable phrase.[2] It was the year in which the German army (the *Wehrmacht*) died and took German dreams of conquest along with it. But it was also a year that began with no fewer than five of the greatest victories in the long history of German arms: at Kerch, Kharkov, and Sevastopol in the Soviet Union, and at Gazala and Tobruk in North Africa. Here the Wehrmacht wrote a new chapter in its already impressive résumé of battlefield success.

On the strategic level, things had turned sour for Germany in December 1941. Germany, already at war with Great Britain, a conflict that it tried half-heartedly to end in the summer and fall of 1940, had done nothing but add enemies since then. In June 1941, with Britain still unconquered, it had launched Operation Barbarossa, an invasion of the Soviet Union. The early weeks of the campaign had seen the Wehrmacht smash one Soviet army after another: at Bialystok, at Minsk, at Smolensk, and especially at Kiev. As summer turned to fall, Barbarossa became Operation Typhoon, the drive on Moscow. The Germans were within sight of the Soviet capital by December when the Red Army launched a great counteroffensive that drove them back in some confusion. The next day, the Japanese bombed Pearl Harbor, and the German Führer, Adolf Hitler, decided to join them in their war on America. Earlier in the year, Germany had been at war with Britain alone. Now, just six months later, it was at war with an immense and wealthy enemy coalition, which Churchill, with a nod to his great ancestor the Duke of Marlborough, dubbed the "Grand Alliance."[3]

The Grand Alliance controlled most of the world's resources. It included the preeminent naval and colonial power (Britain), the largest land power (the Soviet Union), and the globe's financial and industrial giant (the United States)—more than enough potential power to smash Germany. Harnessing that dominating power, however, proved to be a difficult thing. The United States, in particular, had come into the war with only the barest idea of how it intended to fight it. It would become evident to all concerned that there was a world of difference between potentially beating Germany and actually defeating the German army on a field of battle.

The Problem: The German Way of War

Performing that feat would prove to be harder than anyone could have imagined. If there was one army in the world that was used to fighting from a position of material inferiority, this was the one. Since the earliest days of the German state, a unique military culture had evolved, a German way of war. Its birthplace was the kingdom of Prussia. Starting in the seventeenth century with Frederick William, the Great Elector, Prussia's rulers recognized that their small, relatively impoverished state on the European periphery had to fight wars that were *kurtz und vives* (short and lively).[4] Crammed into a tight spot in the middle of Europe, surrounded by states that vastly outweighed it in terms of manpower and resources, it could not win long, drawn-out wars of attrition. From the start, Prussia's military problem was to find a way to fight short, sharp wars that ended in a decisive battlefield victory. Its conflicts had to unleash a storm against the enemy, pounding it fast and hard.

The solution to Prussia's strategic problem was something the Germans called *Bewegungskrieg*, the "war of movement." This way of war stressed maneuver on the operational level. It was not simply tactical maneuverability or a faster march rate, but the movement of large units like divisions, corps, and armies. Prussian commanders, and their later German descendants, sought to maneuver these formations in such a way that they could strike the mass of the enemy army a sharp, even annihilating, blow as rapidly as possible. It might involve a surprise assault against an unprotected flank, or both flanks. On several notable occasions, it even resulted in entire Prussian or German armies getting into the rear of an enemy army, the dream scenario of any general schooled in the art. The goal was *Kesselschlacht:* literally, a "cauldron battle," but more specifically a battle of encirclement, one that hemmed in enemy forces on all sides before destroying them through a series of concentric operations.

This vibrant and aggressive operational posture imposed certain requirements on German armies: an extremely high level of battlefield aggression and an officer corps that tended to launch attacks no matter what the odds, to give just two examples. The Germans also found over the years that conducting an operational-level war of movement required a flexible system of command that left a great deal of initiative in the hands of lower-ranking commanders. It is customary today to refer to this command system as *Auftragstaktik* (mission tactics): the higher commander devised a general mission (*Auftrag*), and then left the means of achieving it to the officer on the spot. It is more accurate, however, to speak, as the Germans themselves did, of the "independence of the lower commander" (*Selbständigkeit der Unterführer*).[5] A commander's ability to size up a situation and act on his own was an equalizer for a numerically weaker army, allowing it to grasp opportunities that might be lost if it had to wait for reports and orders to climb up and down the chain of command.

It wasn't always an elegant thing to behold. Prussian-German military history is filled with lower-level commanders making untimely advances, initiating highly unfavorable, even bizarre, attacks, and generally making nuisances of themselves—at least from the perspective of the higher command. There were men like General Eduard von Flies, who launched one of the most senseless frontal assaults in military history at the battle of Langensalza in 1866 against a dug-in Hanoverian army that outnumbered him two to one[6]; General Karl von Steinmetz, whose impetuous command of the 1st Army in the Franco-Prussian War in 1870 almost upset the entire operational applecart[7]; and General Hermann von François, whose refusal to follow orders almost derailed the East Prussian campaign in 1914.[8] Although these events are nearly forgotten today, they represent the active, aggressive side of the German tradition, as opposed to the more thoughtful, intellectual approach of Karl Maria von Clausewitz, Alfred Graf von Schlieffen, or Helmuth von Molkte the Elder. Put differently, these hard chargers in the field tended to elevate the strength of the commander's will over a rational calculus of ends and means.

Indeed, although *Bewegungskrieg* may have been a logical solution to Prussia's strategic problem, it was hardly a panacea. The classic illustration of its strengths and weaknesses was the Seven Years' War (1756–1763). Frederick the Great opened the conflict with a classic front-loaded campaign, assembling an immense force, seizing the strategic initiative by invading the Austrian province of Bohemia, and pounding the Austrian army in front of Prague with a series of highly aggressive attacks. Unfortunately, he also pounded his own army in the process. When the Austrians sent an army to the relief of Prague, Frederick attacked it too, at Kolin.[9] It may have been his own fault, or it may have been due to an overambitious subordinate commander (a general named, of all things, von Manstein), but what Frederick intended as an attack onto the Austrian right flank turned into a frontal assault against a well-prepared enemy who outnumbered him 50,000 to 35,000. The Prussians were mauled and retreated in disarray.

Frederick was now in serious trouble. The Austrians were resurgent, the Russians advancing, if ponderously, from the east, and the French moving on him from the west. He retrieved the situation by some of the most decisive victories of the entire era. First he crushed the French at Rossbach (November 1757), where another ambitious subordinate, the cavalry commander Friedrich Wilhelm von Seydlitz (who, like Manstein, would also have a namesake general in World War II), played the crucial role, actually maneuvering his entire cavalry force across the march route of the French army.[10] Then, at Leuthen in December, Frederick's keen gift for operational maneuver resulted in the whole Prussian army dramatically appearing on the perpendicular against a weakly defended Austrian left flank and a shocked Austrian high command. Finally, in August 1758, he warded off the Russians at Zorndorf, a murderous and close-fought battle that saw him march his entire army clear around the Russian flank to attack it from the rear.

Frederick had saved himself, for the moment, with classic examples of short, lively campaigns. But with his enemies refusing to make peace with him, the overall situation remained dire. The alliance facing him was huge and had many times his own number of men, cannon, and horse. His only way out now was to fight from the central position,[11] holding secondary sectors with small forces (often commanded by his brother, Prince Henry[12]), rushing armies to whatever sector appeared most threatened in order to bring the enemy to battle there and crush him. Even while Prussia sat on the overall strategic defensive, however, the army's task was to remain a well-honed instrument of attack. It had to be ready for pounding marches, aggressive assaults, and then more pounding marches. It couldn't destroy Frederick's adversaries, either singly or collectively. What it had to do instead was to land such a hard blow against any one of them—France, let us say—that Louis XV might well decide that seeking another round with Frederick wasn't worth the money, time, or effort, and therefore decide to drop out of the war. It wasn't an easy mission for the Prussian army, especially because the incessant attacks it launched in the first two years of the war had dulled its edge, with casualties among the officers and elite regiments being especially high.

Prussia fought all its succeeding wars in similar fashion. It opened them by attempting to win rapid victories through the war of movement. Some, such as the October 1806 campaign against Napoleon, misfired horribly. Here the Prussian army deployed aggressively, far out on a limb to the west and south. It was an ideal spot to initiate offensive operations as Frederick the Great might have conceived them. Unfortunately, Frederick was long gone, his generals were in many cases well into their eighties, and they were now facing the Emperor of the French and his Grande Armée, two forces of nature in their respective primes. Prussia paid the price at the twin battles of Jena and Auerstädt. It was *Bewegungskrieg* of a sort. Unfortunately, all of the *Bewegung* was performed by the French.[13]

Other Prussian campaigns succeeded beyond their commanders' wildest dreams. In 1866, General Helmuth von Moltke's dramatic victory at the battle of Königgrätz essentially won the war with Austria just eight days after it began.[14] The main action in the war with France in 1870 was similarly brief. Prussian troops crossed the French border on August 4 and fought the climactic battle of St. Privat-Gravelotte two weeks later. Major operations in this war ended with an entire French army, and the emperor Napoleon III, bottled up in Sedan and smashed from all compass points simultaneously, perhaps the purest expression of the *Kesselschlacht* concept in history.

The year 1914 was the major test for the Prussian (and now the German) doctrine of making war. The opening campaign was an immense operation involving the mobilization and deployment of no fewer than eight field armies; it was the brainchild of Count Alfred von Schlieffen, the chief of the General Staff until 1906. Like all German commanders, he had set a general operational framework (usually labeled, incorrectly, the Schlieffen Plan).[15] What he most certainly did not do was to draw up any sort of detailed or prescriptive maneuver scheme. That, as always in the German way of war, was up to the commanders on the spot. The opening campaign in the west came within an inch of winning a decisive operational victory. The Germans smashed four of France's five field armies, nearly trapping the final one at Namur. They came far closer to winning the war than historians have generally assumed, but eventually came to grief at the battle of the Marne in September 1914.

The failure at the Marne was the decisive moment of World War I. For German staff officers and commanders alike, it felt as if they had returned to the time of the Seven Years' War. All the ingredients were there. There was the same sense of being surrounded by a coalition of powerful enemies. There was the same sense that the army would never be as powerful as it had been before the bloodletting of that first autumn. Its new commander, General Erich von Falkenhayn, went so far as to tell Kaiser Wilhelm II that the army was a "broken instrument" incapable of winning any sort of annihilating victory. Most problematic was the locking of the western front into trenches, barbed wire, machine guns, and a solid wall of backing artillery. This was no longer mobile *Bewegungskrieg*, but its exact opposite, what the Germans call *Stellungskrieg*, the static war of position. With both armies hunkered down in trenches and hurling shells at one another, it was by definition a war of attrition, and that was a conflict that Germany could never win.

Even now, however, there was a sense that Germany's only hope lay in driving one of its opponents out of the war. Although the Germans did indeed become experts at defensive war, warding off a nearly constant series of Allied offensives, they also launched repeated offensives of their own, attempting to restart the war of movement that German officers continued to view as normative. For the most part, these offensive operations targeted the Russians, although there were huge offensives in the west in both 1916 (against Verdun) and 1918 (the so-called *Kaiserschlacht*, or "Kaiser's battle," of the spring). There were also large-scale offensives against the Romanians in 1916 and the Italians at Caporetto in 1917. It is significant that the post-1918 professional literature of the German army, the weekly *Militär-Wochenblatt*, for example, spent almost as much time studying the Romanian campaign, a classic example of a rapid *Bewegungskrieg*, as it did the much larger campaigns of trench warfare in the west.[16] Those four long years of trench warfare exhausted the German army and eventually ground it down, but they did not change the way the German officer corps viewed military operations.

It should be clear by now that the Wehrmacht's situation after 1941, ringed by powerful enemies who vastly outnumbered it, was nothing particularly new in German military history. There were unique aspects of this war, such as Hitler's vast plans for European and world empire, his racialism and eagerness to commit genocide, and the willing participation of the Wehrmacht itself in the crimes of his regime. On the operational level, however, it was business as usual. The Wehrmacht, its staff, and its officer corps were all doing what the Prussian army had done under Frederick the Great and what the Kaiser's army had done under generals Paul von Hindenburg and Erich Ludendorff. Until the end of the war, it sought to land a resounding blow against one of its enemies—a blow hard enough to shatter the enemy coalition, or at least to demonstrate the price that the Allies would have pay for victory. The strategy failed, but it certainly did its share of damage in those last four years, and it retained enough sting to the very end to give British, Soviet, and American commanders alike plenty of premature gray hairs.

Although launching repeated offensives in order to smash the enemy coalition failed in the end, no one at the time or since has been able to come up with a better solution to Germany's strategic conundrum. A war-winning strategy? Not in this case, obviously. The optimal one for a Germany facing a world of enemies? Perhaps, perhaps not. An operational posture consistent with German military history and tradition as it had unfolded over the centuries? Absolutely.

The Work

In 1942, the Wehrmacht provided a characteristic answer to the question, "What do you do when the blitzkrieg fails?" by launching another one. The attempt to defeat the Soviet Union in a lightning campaign in 1941 had come to grief in front of Moscow, and the winter that followed was one of the worst periods in the history of the German army. It survived, but it suffered massive casualties (over 1 million) and losses in equipment and weapons that it had still not made good the following spring. Despite the low manpower and poor supply situation, the high command—Adolf Hitler, the staffs of the army command and armed forces command, and the chief of the General Staff, General Franz Halder—immediately began planning for another offensive round in the Soviet Union. They chose the southern sector, aiming for the oilfields of the Caucasus, a strategic target whose seizure would provide Germany with the fuel it needed to fight a war of almost indefinite duration and permanently cripple the Soviet war economy. Along the way, the army would have to block Soviet reinforcements from arriving in the sector by either masking or seizing the city of Stalingrad on the Volga River. Before this offensive, code-named Operation Blue, could begin, there also had to be certain preliminary operations: clearing Soviet forces out of the Crimea, for example, or cleaning up a number of jagged salients along the highly irregular front.[17] For an army that had barely survived the previous winter, it was a full operational plate. So large were the demands that it would place on the Wehrmacht that the high command had no choice but to rely on the allied and satellite nations for much of its manpower: Italians, Hungarians, and especially Romanians.

Although the mass of the Wehrmacht would be heading east this spring, a significant German force was already in contact with the British in North Africa. The "western desert" (as in "west of Egypt") was the highly unusual turf of General Erwin Rommel's Panzerarmee. It, too, was a coalition force: a pair of German Panzer Divisions (grouped together into the Afrika Korps); the German 90th Light Division, a motorized formation especially equipped and trained for desert conditions; and a mass of Italian divisions, a few of them motorized (Ariete armored division, for example), but most straight leg infantry. As May dawned, Rommel's army was facing a much larger and better-equipped British 8th Army, ensconced in a tough defensive position that stretched out into the desert south of Gazala. The operational problems of desert warfare were in many ways unique, but some things never change. Just as the Wehrmacht was marching off to attack a much larger and wealthier adversary in Operation Blue, so, too, did Rommel react to his situation, an entrenched enemy that outnumbered him, by doing the characteristic thing: launching an offensive at Gazala, Operation Theseus, that would mark the apogee of his career.

Death of the Wehrmacht is intended as a sequel to my previous book, *The German Way of War: From the Thirty Years' War to the Third Reich*. Where the former work covered 300 years of military history, this one will analyze roughly seven months in the operational life of the German army, starting with the decisions to launch Operations Blue and Theseus and ending with the destruction of the Panzerarmee at the battle of El Alamein and the encirclement of the German 6th Army at Stalingrad. It will provide a detailed account of German military operations in all theaters during those fateful months, both in the eastern and North African fronts. Starting with an overview of the campaigns of 1941 in both the Balkans and in the Soviet Union, we will turn to the renewed fighting in the east, the launching of what the Germans called the "second campaign."[18] The action will begin in the nearly isolated peninsula known as the Crimea, where General Erich von Manstein would write another chapter in his own personal résumé, first by smashing Soviet armies in the eastern Crimea in the highly mobile Kerch campaign, a decisive and improbable victory that is nearly forgotten today, and then launching a successful, although bloody, assault on what was at the time the strongest fortress in the world: Sevastopol.

From here, we move north. Operation Fridericus was one of the preliminary offensives to regularize the front in the east before the start of Blue. Directed at a sharp bulge jutting into the German lines between German-held Kharkov and Soviet-held Izyum (the "Izyum salient"), it was on the launching pad and ready to go when something unusual happened. The Red Army launched an offensive of its own, this one out of the Izyum salient toward Kharkov. It was a new model Soviet force, one that relied on tanks and more tanks, very different from the infantry horde that the Germans had come to expect from 1941. The clash of armor would be one of the largest in the war so far, and the result would be one of the greatest victories of annihilation in the history of the German army.

Just weeks after decisive victories at Kerch and Kharkov, Rommel would launch his own grand offensive at Gazala. The situation seemed particularly unpropitious for an offensive. Manpower levels, numbers of tanks and guns, the inherent strength of the defense—all these crucial factors tilted decisively toward the British. The Panzerarmee had something too: not only a skilled general, but a way of war that called for seeking the operational-level opening, one that scoffed at an "ordinary victory" in favor of an annihilating one. Rommel's solution to the Gazala problem was simple: march his entire mechanized army, in the dead of night and across a featureless desert, around the flank of his adversary. The British woke up to more than their morning tea: they found an entire tank army in the rear of their carefully constructed defensive line. When all was said and done, the 8th Army had been routed, Rommel had seized the fortress, Tobruk, that had eluded him the previous year, and the Panzerarmee was in Egypt, driving hard for Alexandria, the Nile River, and the Suez Canal.

It was an amazing May, but everyone in the Wehrmacht planning circles knew that the main event was yet to come. Operation Blue began well and ended badly, a microcosm of German operations in both world wars. With no fewer than five German armies (along with three, and later four, from the satellite countries) involved in the initial thrusts, it was a complex plan over which Hitler and Halder alike were determined to maintain a firm grip. Above all, they wanted to avoid the operational chaos that had arisen during the drive on Moscow the previous fall, a factor that had played no small role in the German failure.

The success of the opening assault seemed to bear them out. Blue slashed through the Soviet lines within days, heading east toward Voronezh and then swinging to the south, brushing the Don River with its sleeve on the left. The Red Army appeared to have been caught off balance. Most of its best formations were completely out of position, screening Moscow from the southwest against a thrust that never came. In front of the German assault, one Soviet formation after another simply vanished. Seen by some as a new, flexible operational approach on the part of the Soviet army and by others as simple flight, it was probably something in the middle: an order to retreat from higher command echelons that got lost in translation by the time it had reached the common riflemen in the field. At any rate, it was a process attended by a sense of chaos all its own.

From the German perspective, the Soviet flight, whether planned or spontaneous, was a development that threatened the entire operational sequence of Operation Blue. On two occasions, at Millerovo and then at Rostov, German armored pincers closed on what the high command believed were large Soviet concentrations—and came up empty. Like the proverbial tree falling in the forest without anyone to hear, the Wehrmacht had fought a *Kesselschlacht* without the enemy being present. Analysis of the German reaction to this failed maneuver scheme will form a major portion of the book. It is a disturbing picture: a sequence of fired generals and a raving Führer, hastily improvised operational plans, and in the background, a million-man army hurtling ever further from its bases of supply and communications. By September, it was stuck, with two strong arrowheads embedded firmly at Stalingrad and in the Caucasus, unable to reach its objectives and equally unable, or unwilling, to retreat. It was in southern Russia that *Bewegungskrieg* ground to a halt, giving way to the very type of war that the German army had historically tried to avoid: *Stellungskrieg*. At virtually the same time, the wheels at come off of Rommel's offensive as well, and he too found himself stuck fast against superior forces. The result in both theaters would be decisive and catastrophic defeat. After their promising starts, the German offensives of 1942 would give birth to twins: Stalingrad and El Alamein.

In the course of this survey, we will attempt to answer some fundamental questions about the Wehrmacht. How does a military force configured, armed, and trained for the offensive war of movement and quick victory cope with a military situation that suddenly turns sour? How much responsibility does Hitler bear for the catastrophe? How much should be shared by the General Staff and the field commanders? How much was it the result of individual decisions, and how much was the result of more impersonal, systemic factors, the complicated matrix of military culture, tradition, and history that comprise the German way of war? Indeed, how much of it was simply chance?

Throughout, I have tried to refrain from argumentation that attempts to show "how the German army could have won at Stalingrad" or "what the Wehrmacht should have done to win the war." This is a history book. It does not offer a series of perfect plans for 1942—as if it could make any difference at this point; nor does it purport to be a manual of lessons learned. These approaches, which praise this decision as "correct" and that one as "wrong" with all the assurance of a sixteenth-century reformer parsing Scripture,[19] are essentially ahistorical (as important as they may be to the training of soldiers and officers). They are akin to writing a history of the French Revolution that does nothing but tell Louis XVI how he could have avoided it. Operational history (that is, explaining what actually happened in the course of a campaign, and why) is complicated enough without spending time lecturing the historical actors on what they ought to have done.[20]

Admittedly, there are times when it is hard not to. Hitler's decision to split the offensive into two parts in late July 1942 and head simultaneously for Stalingrad and the Caucasus (Directive 45) is a classic example. Another was the decision, shared by all levels of authority, to send Rommel into Egypt with an unconquered Malta still choking off his supply lines. In both cases, however, the Germans came within an ace of victory anyway. The short distances, in some cases only hundreds of yards, that separated the Wehrmacht from its strategic objectives in Stalingrad, the Caucasus, and North Africa should give anyone pause about treating 1942 as a foregone Conclusion.

1

From Victory to Defeat

1941

In the opening years of World War II, the German army uncorked a run of victories that was quite unlike anything in living memory. In contrast to World War I, in which the front lines soon solidified and battlefield stalemate was the norm, this war saw the Germans move from one dramatic success to another. With their fearsome tank, or Panzer, formations as an apparently irresistible spearhead, and with a powerful air force (Luftwaffe) circling overhead, the Wehrmacht ran through, around, and over every defensive position thrown in its path. The opening campaign in Poland (which went by the operational name Case White) saw the Germans smash the Polish army in eighteen days, although a bit more fighting was necessary to reduce the capital, Warsaw.[1] Equally impressive was the invasion of Denmark and Norway (which went by the operational name Exercise Weser), which saw two enemy capitals, Oslo and Copenhagen, fall on the first day to a combination of ground forces, seaborne landings, and paratroopers.[2]

Still, there were those among the European general staffs who took comfort in the fact that up to now, the Wehrmacht was beating up on weaker, smaller neighbors. The great offensive in the West in May 1940 (Case Yellow) quickly disabused them of that notion. Here, the German Panzer formations met and smashed the cream of the French and British armies, destroying the former and booting the latter off the continent altogether in a hurried evacuation from one of the last ports still in British hands, Dunkirk. Even with most of the British army gone, the Germans took something like 2 million French, British, Dutch, and Belgian prisoners. Combined with the minimal nature of their own losses, Case Yellow was one of the most decisive military victories in history.[3]

The next year continued the pattern. A lightning drive into the Balkans in April 1941 overran both Yugoslavia and Greece. When a British army arrived to help defend the latter, the Germans drove it from position to position, then off the mainland altogether, forcing their hapless foe into its second forced evacuation in less than a year. The British destination this time was Crete, where they were hit by a true thunderbolt: Operation Mercury, the first all-airborne military operation in history.[4] It quickly seized the island from its British and Commonwealth defenders, who had to evacuate again, this time to Egypt. Indeed, in the opening period of the war, it sometimes seemed like the evacuation had become the characteristic British military operation. Certainly no other army in the world had as much practice at it.

Analysis of these German operations in World War II continues to paint them as somehow novel, as an example of a new method of warmaking called *blitzkrieg*, or "lightning war." Allegedly invented in the interwar era, blitzkrieg is said to have transformed warfare by mechanizing it.[5] In place of the foot soldier and the cavalry, there were now machines, especially tanks and aircraft. In place of the trench deadlock that had characterized World War I were vast campaigns of breakthrough, encirclement, and maneuver. In fact, the word itself is a misnomer. The German army didn't invent it, and they hardly ever used the word outside of quotation marks. It was a term that seems to have been kicked around international military circles in the 1930s to describe any rapid and decisive victory, in contrast to the long, horrible war of attrition that had just ended.

Even if they didn't invent the blitzkrieg, however, the Germans clearly did something in the interwar period. It had been a time of rethinking and experimentation for them, certainly, but we might say the same thing for all armies of the day. The British had invented the tank and were working on a radical Experimental Mechanized Brigade as early as 1928.[6] Likewise, if there was one military force in the world that seemed obsessed with the possibilities of tanks, aircraft, and paratroopers, it would had to have been the Red Army. What distinguished the activity of the interwar German army (the Reichswehr until 1934, then renamed the Wehrmacht) was that it was not trying to discover anything new. It felt that it already had a workable warfighting doctrine: *Bewegungskrieg*, the war of movement on the operational level.[7] This is where the Germans saw tanks and aircraft as making their contribution. These new weapons had to be used on the operational level—that is, in large units, from divisions on up. The result was the Panzer Division, a unit built around tanks but containing a full panoply of combined arms: infantry, artillery, reconnaissance, supply columns, bridging trains, and more, all of which had their mobility raised to the level of the tank. A Panzer Division was more than any contemporary army could handle from 1939 to 1941. It could assault and penetrate, smash through into the clear, pursue, and destroy any defensive position or formation that tried to stop it, then reform and do it all over again. It wasn't a wonder weapon or magic bullet, but it certainly might have looked that way to a Polish lancer or a Belgian antitank gunner.[8]

As important as the tank and the airplane was the Wehrmacht's highly articulated system of command and control. Some of this hearkened back to older German traditions, especially the notion of the independence of the lower commander, often referred to, incorrectly, as *Auftragstaktik*, or mission tactics.[9] Arising first out of the distinctive social contract in old Prussia—in which the king had only limited authority to intervene in the operations of his commanders, who were without exception of the noble, or Junker, caste—it had evolved over the centuries into the distinctive characteristic of command in the Prussian and German armies. In the eyes of Field Marshal Helmuth von Moltke, the victor in the wars of German unification, modern field operations had become far too complex to be tightly choreographed in advance. There were simply too many factors in play: huge forces, complex weaponry, and massive supply requirements, not to mention the friction and fog that were simply part of war in any era. Under Moltke, the Prussian army prided itself on providing general missions to lower levels of command, then allowing the lower commander to devise the best way to carry them out. On all levels of command, orders were to be short, snappy, and to the point. Ideally, they were to be delivered orally; the Prusso-German armies made more limited use of written orders than any other contemporary force. Finally, commanders were encouraged to forgo maps, if at all possible, and to deliver their orders by pointing to the actual terrain. The recipient was to listen, repeat the order out loud in the presence of his superior, and then go off and carry it out in the best possible way.

On its face, the Prussian command system might seem to be a recipe for chaos, a free-for-all in which each division, corps, and army commander fought his own private war. In fact, there were two circumstances that worked in its favor. The staff system was the first. While on campaign, each commander had a chief of the General Staff at his side, an operational advisor and confidante. He was not a co-commander, and in fact the formation commander always bore ultimate responsibility for his own decisions and the performance of his unit. The chief of staff, however, was an elite officer who had been taught the art of war in a highly selective school with a murderously difficult curriculum, the famous *Kriegsakademie*. Members of the staff tended to see operational problems in a similar way and to dispense remarkably similar advice to the commanders with whom they worked.

A second factor that made *Auftragstaktik* work was the highly aggressive nature of the Prussian-German officer corps. Throughout German military history, the officer corps's operational doctrine almost always consisted of one thing: making a beeline for the nearest enemy force and launching an attack on it. It rarely meant slacking or lying down on the job. Prussia-Germany had fought dozens of campaigns since the seventeenth century, and virtually all of them saw the army on the operational offensive, seeking to strike a sharp and unsettling blow against its opponents. The "short and lively war" demanded such an aggressive posture. Frederick the Great was the exemplar, perhaps the most aggressive commander of the entire eighteenth century, and certainly one of the top ten of all time. He didn't think war was all that complicated. "The Prussian army always attacks," he once said. During Prussia's difficult path through the Napoleonic wars, there was Marshal Gebhard Leberecht von Blücher, a septuagenarian oddball who wedded an innate battlefield drive and aggression to a visceral hatred of the French enemy. His art of war wasn't all that intellectual, either; his men nicknamed him *Marschall Vorwärts* (General Forward).[10] During the wars of unification, Moltke may have been the brains of the army, its doctrinal and administrative wizard. Its guts were army commanders like Frederick Charles, the Red Prince, who attacked an Austrian army that outnumbered him two to one to get the battle of Königgrätz rolling in 1866.[11] World War II hard chargers like Guderian and Manstein look far less unusual when we examine Prussian-German warmaking from the perspective of the *longue durée*. This spirit of aggression was not something that the German army invented one afternoon in 1935.

The preference for the "short and lively" war; *Bewegungskrieg* (the war of movement on the operational level); an officer corps that was allowed to handle matters in the field as it saw fit, without a great deal of interference from above, and that paid for that privilege in blood, some of its own and a great deal belonging to the men under its command; tanks and aircraft working in close harmony, commanded and controlled by the modern miracle of radio communications—these comprised the impressive and highly successful operational package the Germans brought to the table in the opening years of World War II. Like all military cultures, it was a unique combination of traits, a "distinctive language" spoken only by the Wehrmacht, as the leading German military journal of the day, the *Militär Wochenblatt*, put it.[12] As in all of Germany's wars, the main—indeed, the only—question was whether Germany's adversaries could learn to decipher it in time.

Bewegungskrieg in Full Stride: The Balkans, 1941

If war was a simple contest to see who could most completely humiliate an opponent in a first encounter, then the Wehrmacht would have won World War II, hands down. The Polish, Danish, Norwegian, French, Yugoslavian, Greek, British, and Soviet armies all learned this lesson the hard way. The first six armies did not survive to tell the tale, nor did the states they were called on to defend. British armies were smashed not just in their first encounter with the Wehrmacht (in France), but also in the next three, as well (in North Africa, in Greece, and then again in Crete). Britain managed to survive the experience thanks to the presence of the English Channel, a sturdy water barrier that has stopped many would-be invaders since 1066. Finally, the Soviet army was hammered as hard as any military force in history during that first awful campaigning season, from June to December 1941. It was an utterly hapless performance that saw it sustain the incredible total of 4 million casualties in six short months, most of them prisoners lost in one massive *Kesselschlacht* after another. And finally, lest we forget, the U.S. Army's first meeting with the Wehrmacht, on an obscure hunk of Tunisian rock known as the Kasserine Pass, was a humbling experience that should have made all Americans happy for the existence of the Atlantic Ocean.

The point is that first encounters with the Wehrmacht were inherently dangerous. This was an army that liked its campaigns front-loaded, meticulously planned, and designed for maximum impact. The corollary was that those who survived that first encounter had taken the best shot that the Germans had to offer. For the Wehrmacht, things were always going to go downhill after it delivered that first devastating blow. The advantage in sustainability was always going to lie with the Allies, especially after the entry of the United States into the war in 1941. As satisfying as it would be to blame the problem on individuals within the Nazi leadership, it was not due to poor planning on Hitler's part or to the General Staff's deep and documented disinterest in logistics. It was simply the way things were, the way they had been since the 1600s, and the way they would still be today, if Germany had survived World War II as a great military power. If there was still a German General Staff, there would still be war-fighting doctrine based on landing a knockout punch early through aggressive, mobile operations.

One of the classic examples of *Bewegungskrieg* in World War II was the German campaign in the Balkans in the spring of 1941.[13] Here the Germans fought the front-loaded campaign to perfection, with the German 2nd and 12th Armies launching two simultaneous operations into Greece and Yugoslavia on April 6. Operation Marita—the invasion of Greece—had been in the works for months, a response to the humiliating defeat suffered by the Italian army in its invasion of Greece in late 1940. Not only had the hardy Greeks stopped Italian forces at the border, but they also had gone on the offensive, driving into Albania and threatening to unhinge the entire Axis position in the Balkans. The invasion of Yugoslavia, by contrast, had been put together overnight, quite literally, as a response to a pro-Allied coup in Belgrade on the night of March 26–27, 1941. It was an improvisation, just the sort of thing that the Germans historically excelled at. The brief time span for conception and planning did leave a few loose ends here and there, and in fact, the undertaking would take place under the nearly anonymous designation of Operation 25.

It is easy to underestimate the significance of a campaign like this. After all, given its population and resource advantages, Germany should have been able to beat the Greek army, or the Yugoslav army, or both at the same time, without breaking a sweat. We might say the same thing about the Polish campaign in 1939, or the invasion of Denmark and Norway in 1940. Yet those who look at the Balkan campaign and see only a great power landing a hit on two of the war's weaker sisters miss the point entirely: the Wehrmacht's complete and rapid victory over the Greeks and Yugoslavs precisely mirrors the treatment it meted out in every first encounter of the war, without exception.

Operation 25: Yugoslavia

For centuries, the ideal of Prussian-German military operations had been the concentric attack, with converging columns coming at the defender from all directions and making it impossible for him to establish any sort of coherent position. In that sense, Operation 25 marks a culmination point in the German art of war. With Hungary, Romania, and Bulgaria all safely in the Axis camp by this time, the attacking force of German and German-allied (Hungarian and Italian) armies could be strung out over an immense crescent nearly 400 miles long, from Trieste on the Adriatic in the north to the Bulgarian-Yugoslav border in the south. Moving from right to left, there was Italian 2nd Army, German 2nd Army under General Maximilian von Weichs (consisting of XXXXIX Mountain Corps, LI and LII Corps, and XXXXVI Panzer Corps); Hungarian 3rd Army; an independent German XXXXI Panzer Corps; and, finally, 1st Panzer Group (Field Marshal Ewald von Kleist). With the Italians and Hungarians having to be cajoled into doing anything more than occupying a place in the line, the heavy lifting was the task of the three German formations. Weichs's army was deployed in the Austrian provinces of Carinthia and Styria, curling around the Slovenian-Croatian bend in northern Yugoslavia; XXXXI Panzer Corps was deployed in western Romania, near Timosoara; Kleist's Panzer group lay far to the south, in western Bulgaria.

The *Schwerpunkt*, or point of main effort, included no fewer than three mighty mechanized columns driving on the capital, Belgrade. On the right, XXXXVI Panzer Corps (2nd Army) would deploy in Nagykanizsa in Hungary, southwest of Lake Balaton. It would cross the Drava River into Yugoslavia, then wheel sharply southeast toward Belgrade. In the center, the independent XXXXI Panzer Corps under General Georg-Hans Reinhardt, including the 2nd S.S. Motorized Division, the Grossdeutschland Motorized Infantry Regiment, and the Hermann Göring Panzer Regiment, had the shortest hop to Belgrade, a straight shot heading almost due south. Finally, on the extreme left, 1st Panzer Group would send two corps (XIV Panzer and XI) across the Bulgarian border, head toward Nis, and then wheel sharply to the north. As always in German operations, the point of these multiple drives was not simply to seize the capital, but rather to threaten a strategic object that the Yugoslavs could not afford to lose and would therefore have to defend. As in the Franco-Prussian war in 1870, driving in the general direction of the capital was the best way to ensure a confrontation with the enemy's main field army.[14]

The Yugoslavs did what all of Germany's enemies had done in the first two years of the war. They tried to defend every inch of the country's borders, establishing what the Germans called a "cordon position" (*Kordonstellung*). The 1st Army Group stood in the north, consisting of 7th Army in Slovenia, facing the German and Italian frontiers, and the 4th Army along the Hungarian border. The 2nd Army Group stood to its right, with 2nd Army along the Danube and 1st Army in the western part of the Vojvodina. An independent 6th Army deployed to the east, along the Romanian border, defending the district known as the Banat as well as the northern approaches to Belgrade. Finally, a 3rd Army Group (5th and 3rd Armies) had to cover an immense stretch of southern Yugoslavia, with 5th Army along the Bulgarian border and 3rd Army standing watch against the Italians on the Albanian frontier. None of these "armies" was up to modern standards. They consisted, typically, of two to four weak infantry divisions, with an attached cavalry division or brigade. Reserve forces were grossly inadequate, as they are by definition in a cordon defense. The 3rd Army Group in the south, for example, had a single infantry division in reserve at Skoplje, and the entire Yugoslav reserve consisted of three infantry divisions and one cavalry division.[15] Although each army had some terrain feature in front of it (typically one of Yugoslavia's numerous rivers: the Drava, Sava, Morava, and Danube), the deployment offered no hope of operational maneuver. Strategic redeployment to respond to threats as they developed, always tricky in a linear defense, would simply be impossible in this case. Neither the road nor rail net would permit it.

It is interesting to note that this was still the orthodox response to the Wehrmacht's mobile operations. The Poles had done the same in September 1939, stringing their armies in a cordon over 875 miles long along the border with Greater Germany and Slovakia.[16] The French and British had also attempted a linear defense of western Europe in 1940, which was penetrated in three days. The Yugoslav army was not an insignificant force: it included seventeen active and twelve reserve infantry divisions, plus three cavalry divisions and a number of nondivisional brigades. When fully mobilized, it numbered nearly 10,000,000 men. Still, lining it up to defend 1,900 miles of border was to extend it far beyond its capabilities.

To be fair, the Yugoslav supreme commander, General Dušan Simović (who had also been one of the ringleaders of the coup that precipitated the German invasion), was faced with a number of equally bad alternatives. Analysts of the campaign both then and since have spoken of the advantages of a pullback from the borders and a concentrated defense of some central position, perhaps Belgrade itself, just as analysts of the Polish campaign tend to talk up a withdrawal to the river lines of the Narew, Vistula, and San. A cordon defense invited penetration and destruction by a mobile enemy, it is true, and given the almost complete absence of armor, antitank, or air assets in the Yugoslav military, it was made to order for the German approach of a high-speed mechanized *Bewegungskrieg*. But military historians need to admit that any strategy that advocates the immediate abandonment of over 90% of the national territory before a shot has even been fired is a nonstarter. It is a school exercise, in other words, utterly divorced from the reality of politics. No government in the modern era will ever do it, or could afford to.[17] Moreover, the situation within Yugoslavia was not all propitious for the success of any strategy. The state was riven by ethnic tension. Neither the Slovenes nor the Croats could generate much enthusiasm about fighting for a Serb-dominated regime which, in their opinion, treated them like second-class citizens. Under the urging of German propaganda broadcasts and leaflets, large numbers of Croats would desert once the shooting started.[18]

Operation 25 played out fairly predictably, given the balance of forces, the weaponry in play, and the imperatives of German doctrine. No campaign in Prussian or German history had a more pressing need to be wrapped up so quickly.[19] It had been designed overnight, the formations fighting it had to be dragged hither and yon from across Germany and the occupied territories into this remote and underdeveloped theater, and the Panzer units, at least, had to finish their business and then be ready for transfer to the east. Barbarossa was only two and a half months away. An army that habitually moved fast was about to kick the tempo up one more notch.

The campaign opened with a massive early-morning bombing raid against a nearly undefended Belgrade. It was April 6, the Orthodox Easter Sunday. In Operation Punishment, the Wehrmacht did something that many later military ventures have tried, yet none have been able to achieve: a "decapitation" of the enemy's command structure. The Luftwaffe came in three separate waves, some 500 sorties in all, flying mainly from bases in the Ostmark and western Romania. Not only did the Germans destroy the obsolete Yugoslav air force and Belgrade's weak antiaircraft screen, pound large chunks of the city into rubble, and kill thousands of civilians, they also destroyed the communication links between the Yugoslav high command and the field formations. It was an unprecedented event, an air power advocate's dream, that left virtually every operational unit in the army begging for direction and orders just at the moment that the Wehrmacht poured over the borders in strength. The Luftwaffe's losses amounted to just two aircraft. It is no exaggeration to say that Operation Punishment had won the Yugoslav campaign in the first twenty minutes. The raid, and especially the massive number of civilian deaths, would also be one of the war crimes included in the later indictment against General Alexander

Löhr, commander of Luftflotte 4; he would be executed in Belgrade in 1947.[20]

The land campaign now began, as 1st Panzer Group crossed the border in the south on April 8. With XIV Panzer Corps in the lead and XI Corps trailing, Kleist's forces headed for Nis. After breaking through the defenses of the Yugoslav 5th Army, the Germans took the city on April 9. As planned, the Panzers now wheeled north, driving rapidly along the valley of the Morava River toward Belgrade. Resistance was weak and getting weaker, and the high command soon decided to remove 5th Panzer Division from the main drive on the capital.[21] It peeled off in a southwesterly direction, making it one of the few formations to take part in both Operation 25 against Yugoslavia and Operation Marita against Greece. By April 12, 1st Panzer Group stood just 35 miles south of Belgrade; it was also deep in the rear of Yugoslav 6th Army, still deployed along the Romanian border.

The second element in the drive on Belgrade was XXXXVI Panzer Corps, part of 2nd Army. The original schedule called for 2nd Army's attack to begin on April 12, which had then been moved up to April 10. Some analysts still see this as a deliberate staggering of the initial thrusts to further confuse the enemy leadership as to the location of the main blow.[22] A better explanation was the difficulty the Germans were having in transporting the assault formations into position. The Yugoslav border was immense, and the entire region was vastly underserved by road and rail. The 2nd Army, in particular, was still arriving in the theater when the bombers appeared over Belgrade. Nonetheless, there were a series of small attacks by German units as they deployed, often undertaken on the initiative of the local commander. These included the seizure of a road bridge at Barcs and a rail bridge near Koprivnica.[23] Even before the start of formal hostilities, the sluggish Yugoslav response to these provocations, due no doubt to the large proportion of Croats in the Yugoslav 7th Army, the principal defender in this sector, showed the Germans that there was trouble in the enemy camp.

When XXXXVI Panzer Corps's actual attack opened on April 10, it blew a hole in the Yugoslav line almost immediately. Although most of the corps wheeled southeast to join in the drive on Belgrade, one division, the 14th Panzer, headed for the Croatian capital, Zagreb ("Agram" to the Germans). The drive on Zagreb was an epic in its own way. Rolling at top speed, moving so rapidly that it was out of radio communications with corps and army headquarters for much of

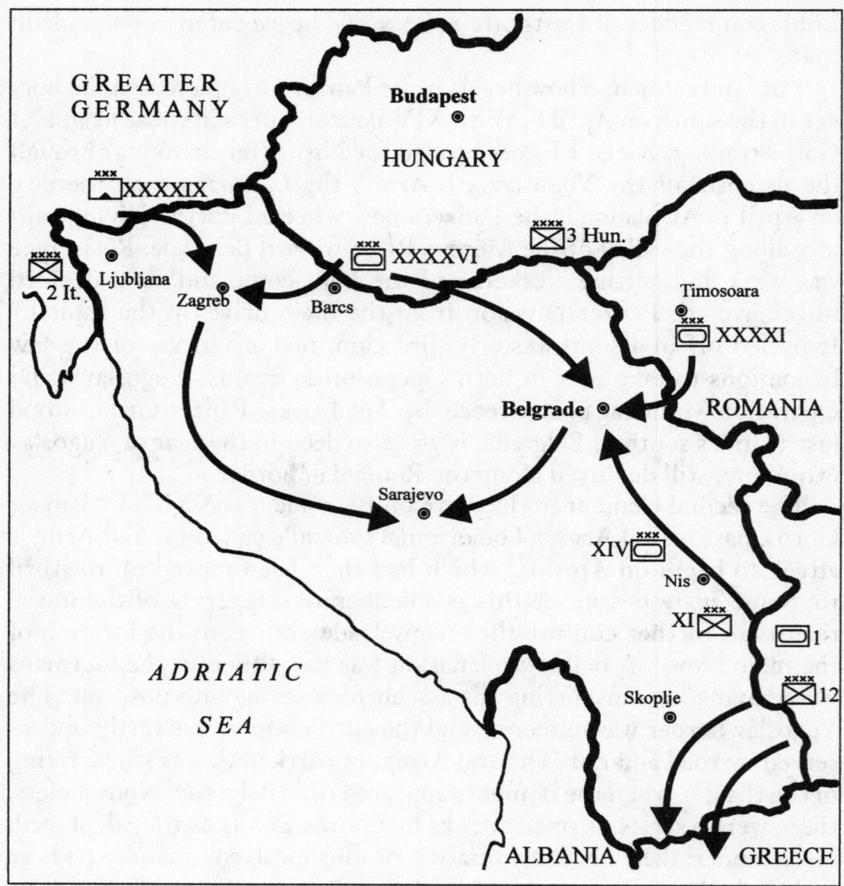

Map 1. Operation 25: concentric operations in Yugoslavia.

the day, it smashed through position after position, taking 15,000 prisoners, among them twenty-two Yugoslav generals. It reached Zagreb by nightfall after traveling almost one hundred miles since morning. It ended the day being feted by thousands of enthusiastic Croats who considered the arrival of the Germans as a day of liberation from Serb oppression.[24]

The third motorized drive on Belgrade was that of the XXXXI Panzer Corps. After crossing the Romanian-Yugoslav border south of Timosoara on April 11, Reinhardt's corps almost immediately broke through Yugoslav 6th Army and raced into the clear. The relatively weak force, consisting of little more than the Grossdeutschland Regiment and 2nd S.S. Motorized Infantry Division, drove halfway to Belgrade in a single day, reaching Pancevo by nightfall and preparing itself for a drive on the capital the next day. Already, the Yugoslav situation had deteriorated to the point that General Simović sent orders to his three army groups to "fight the enemy wherever you may be in contact with him in all directions, on your own initiative, without awaiting special orders from higher command echelons."[25]

Even today, it is difficult to say which German force arrived first in Belgrade. With all three sending mobile detachments ahead of the main body in a headlong rush, even the German high command wasn't exactly sure. Elements of the 2nd S.S. Motorized Infantry Division (XXXXI Panzer Corps) crossed into the city on rafts over the Danube in the early evening of April 12; patrols of 8th Panzer Division (2nd Army) entered at about the same time from the north; and 11th Panzer Division (1st Panzer Group) did the same from the south. Although none of these armored drives met with much opposition, they did have to negotiate some of Europe's most difficult terrain, and the exercise showed that there really isn't any such thing as "bad tank country" to a well-trained and aggressive armored force. Although sending flying armored columns into enemy territory might have been risky in a different context, here the principal problem was dealing with the hordes of Yugoslav soldiers wishing to surrender.

With the capital in German hands and the Yugoslav front broken everywhere, and with Italian and Hungarian troops finally crossing the Yugoslav border, all that remained was the final pursuit. There was some fear on the part of the German command that remnants of the defeated army would retreat into the mountain fastness of the southern part of the country, in particular Bosnia. To counter the threat, the Germans now redirected virtually all their mobile formations toward a drive on Sarajevo. One pursuit group, spearheaded by 14th Panzer Division, moved in from the west; another, with 8th Panzer Division in the van, approached the city from the east. The city fell to these converging drives on April 15, the tenth day of hostilities, signaling the end of major operations.[26] An armistice would be signed on April 17.

The Wehrmacht had overrun Yugoslavia in record time and with ease. It had dismantled a million-man army and taken at least 250,000 prisoners in this short campaign. Its own casualties were just 151 dead, 392 wounded, and 15 missing. The ingredients for the rout were obvious. On the German side, they included superior training and weaponry; total command of the air; and a high degree of mechanization, at least at the cutting edge. For the Yugoslavs, there was the lateness of the mobilization decree, which resulted in numerous units being overrun before they were fully prepared for combat; lack of air and armor; the decision to defend every inch of the country's long border; and, perhaps most importantly, the ethnic troubles inside the country, especially in the Croatian territories. One German staff officer called Operation 25 more of "a military parade" than a campaign,[27] and that is in many ways a fair assessment of this "twelve-day war."[28]

Still, there is more to it than that. The conquest of Yugoslavia was a distilled form of the German way of war as it had developed over the centuries. As one German source put it, after the breakthrough along the border fortifications, the Yugoslav army was "smashed in the open field, held in place by German infantry forced-marching in the pursuit, overtaken and encircled by the mobile troops, broken down by uninterrupted attack from the air while on the march and during rail transport."[29] It was a "lightning victory" (*Blitzsieg*), one that displayed every aspect of the German operational package. The assembly of massive force; a plan that included a violent blow from the very outset in the form of the vicious air raids on Belgrade; a maneuver scheme for the land forces that emphasized shock, rapidity, and a concentric advance against a crucial objective in the enemy's heartland—these had been the ingredients of *Bewegungskrieg* at least since the days of Moltke. Given the gross imbalance of force, the Wehrmacht should have beaten the Yugoslav army and swiftly overrun the country; that much is obvious. But as Prussian and German armies had shown other armies in other times and places, when the war of movement was working as it should, it could make many a campaign appear to be a "military parade."

There is one last aspect of the quick and almost painless victory in Yugoslavia that deserves mention, especially as it reflects on the German way of war. Despite the totality of the victory, this was a campaign with an extremely problematic aftermath. By the end of the operation, fighting had already broken out within Yugoslavia between Serbs and Croats in Mostar and other parts of Dalmatia. With German forces being redeployed rapidly to the East and the land occupied by relatively small forces, there was no one to stop it, even if the Germans had wanted to. Moreover, a quick look at the math of the campaign (250,000 prisoners taken out of an army that numbered almost 1 million when fully mobilized) would indicate that large forces had indeed escaped the German net. The Germans had advanced so far and so fast that they left numerous loose ends. Yugoslav soldiers cut off from their units soon took to the mountains to form resistance bands, and the Germans would find themselves conducting an anti-partisan campaign for the rest of the war.[30] There was no unanimity among these groups about the kind of Yugoslavia they wished to recreate once they had liberated the country, and they would spend as much time fighting each other as fighting the Germans. Royalist Chetniks under Colonel Draža Mihailović and the communist Partisans under Josip Broz, code-named Tito, would fight their own bloody war for the future of Yugoslavia, a tale outside our purview here. Nevertheless, there is something incomplete about a way of war that relies on the shock value of small, highly mobile forces and airpower, that stresses rapidity of victory over all, and that then has a difficult time putting the country it has conquered back together again.

Operation Marita: Greece

It was more of the same in Greece. Here the Wehrmacht encountered not just another weak army of a second-rate power, but British and Commonwealth forces as well. Operation Marita met Operation Lustre, the transfer of a British expeditionary force from North Africa to the Balkans.[31] Force W, as it was known, was utterly inadequate to fight the Germans, comprising two divisions (2nd New Zealand, 6th Australian), the 1st Tank Brigade (of 2nd Armored Division), and a small commitment of airpower. One German commentator called it "a drop in the ocean by the standards of continental warfare."[32] The commander of the expedition, General Henry Maitland Wilson, was placed in a nearly impossible position; he had to thrust forward a small force against an onrushing Wehrmacht coming at him from all directions.

The precise placement of the force was a thus a matter of crucial importance, as well as controversy, within the Allied camp. Essentially, the Greek supreme commander, General Alexander Papagos, wanted the British as far north as possible; Maitland Wilson preferred to stay as far south as he could manage.[33] Again, like the Yugoslavs, the Greeks were not at all enthusiastic about defending the country at the relatively narrow waist, Mount Olympus, perhaps, or points south—or any position that abandoned a large chunk of it to the invader. Indeed, Papagos was still thinking of the offensive, one last blow to shatter the Italians in Albania.

The plan that eventually evolved was, as is typical, the worst of both worlds. If the Germans had been advancing from Bulgaria alone, then the deployment of Force W to a defensive position stretching northwest-southeast along the Vermion Mountains and Aliakmon River (it was called the "Vermion line," grandiloquently, because there were no prepared works there at all) might have made sense. The operational situation that Maitland Wilson encountered as he marched north, however, was far different.

Once again, the Germans had planned a bold operational-level stroke, utilizing the mechanized formations of 12th Army. Although the infantry divisions of XXX Corps crossed the Rhodope Mountains into western Thrace and the XVIII Mountain Corps had the unenviable task of smashing through the well-fortified Metaxas Line along the Bulgarian frontier, 2nd Panzer Division would cross into Yugoslavia toward Strumica. From here it would wheel sharply south, pass just to the west of Lake Doiran on the Greek-Yugoslav border, then drive as rapidly as possible on the major port of Thessaloniki. Seizure of the city would be a strategic blow to the Greeks, cutting off their entire 2nd Army still fighting to the east.

Simultaneously, however, there would be an even more dramatic stroke, a westward drive into southern Yugoslavia by XXXX Corps (9th Panzer Division, *Leibstandarte Adolf Hitler* S.S. Motorized Infantry Regiment, and the 73rd Infantry Division). The corps would drive toward the Vardar River between Skoplje and Veles, then, once again, wheel sharply south, passing through the Monastir Gap and crossing into central Greece from the north. This would result in a linkup with the Italians and the isolation of the Greek 1st Army still fighting in Albania. The Albanian campaign still accounted for the lion's share of the Greek army, some twelve infantry divisions, a cavalry division, and three infantry brigades. Morever, the German maneuver would also fatally compromise the Allied defensive position, outflanking Force W no matter what line it happened to occupy.[34]

And so it went. As in Operation 25, there was a signal moment at the start of Marita. An April 6, at virtually the same moment that Belgrade was going up in flames, a Luftwaffe raid on the port of Piraeus scored a direct hit on the 12,000-ton ammunition ship S.S. *Clan Fraser*. It exploded spectacularly, triggering secondary explosions all over the harbor and destroying much of the port itself, along with twenty-seven craft docked there and a great deal of shore equipment. Windows were shattered seven miles away in Athens.[35] Within hours, German forces were across the Greek border in strength. On the far left, XXX Corps had fairly easy going because much of the Greek force in isolated western Thrace had been evacuated when German troops first entered Bul-

Map 2. Operation Marita: *Bewegungskrieg* in Greece, April 1941.

garia. In the center, XVIII Mountain Corps found the Metaxas Line, and the Greek infantry and gunners defending it, to be as tough as anything they'd yet encountered in this war. Losses were heavy here, with at least one regiment having to be pulled out of the line, but the attack on both sides of the Rupel Gorge, supported by massed artillery and nonstop attack by Stukas, finally chewed its way through the Greek wire, pillboxes, and concrete bunkers.[36]

The battle for the Metaxas Line soon became a moot point, however, as 2nd Panzer Division cut through light opposition to the west and reached Thessaloniki on April 9. In the course of its short hop south, it overran elements of the Greek 19th Division that were just moving up into position. The Greek formation was ostensibly "motorized," which meant in this case possessing a handful of Bren carriers and captured Italian tanks and trucks.[37] The fall of Thessaloniki made the entire Greek force to the east superfluous, and 2nd Army surrendered to the Germans on April 9.

The *Schwerpunkt* of this campaign, however, lay with XXXX Panzer Corps (General Georg Stumme). Jumping off at 5:30 A.M. on April 6, it encountered Yugoslav forces almost immediately (elements of the 5th Yugoslav Army). Brushing them aside, the mass of the corps reached its objective (the line Skoplje-Veles) the next day. Stumme's lead formations had made sixty miles in that one day and had to perform a major river crossing of the Vardar to boot. After passing through Prilep on April 8 and Monastir on April 9, the corps stood ready to invade Greece the next day. On April 10, XXXX Corps crossed the border, peeled off the 9th Panzer Division to link up with the Italians in Albania, and continued the drive to the south, toward the Greek town of Florina.[38]

It was not immediately apparent, but the drive on Florina and thence into central Greece had unhinged the entire Allied strategic position in the theater. Not only had the maneuver uncovered the communications of the Greek 1st Army in Albania, it had also inserted a strong mobile German force far into the rear of the original British defensive position along the Vermion line. Maitland Wilson could read a map. The news sent the entire Commonwealth force scurrying back down to the south from whence it had come, desperately trying to extricate itself from the jaws of two pursuing German pincers. Australian and New Zealand troops fought with their usual tenacity, and there was some gritty action of the rear guard variety, but on the operational level, the front line moved steadily southward. The original Vermion position became the Aliakmon Line (April 11), which gave way to the Mount Olympus position (April 16) and then the Thermopylae line (April 24), the last actually a crescent-shaped defensive position stretching across central Greece from Molos in the east to the Gulf of Corinth in the south.[39] The place-names make the after-action reports read like some lost essay by Herodotus, which lends the entire affair a certain epic aura that it does not at all deserve. In fact, the retreat was a nightmare, carried out under a nearly constant barrage of Stuka attacks. It had been the same in Norway and Dunkirk, and now it was more of the same in Greece.

Making good use of the difficult terrain and their 25-pounder guns, however, the Commonwealth rear guards did manage to hold up the Germans just long enough to allow the main body to escape, and that was no small feat. The Germans, for their part, managed to keep up the pressure only by sending light pursuit groups ahead of their main body. There certainly were not entire Panzer divisions in play during this portion of the campaign. But even the smaller pursuit groups found themselves limited by the difficulty of mountainous terrain. At one point they tried, unsuccessfully, to pass a column of tanks single file through the pass at Thermopylae—the original European tactical exercise, one might say.[40] Even the most celebrated incident of the campaign, the April 26 airdrop onto the isthmus of Corinth by two battalions of the 2nd Fallschirmjäger Regiment, failed to seal the deal. Indeed, it met with disaster when a lucky shot detonated charges on the canal bridge, dropping it and killing most of the German paratroopers crossing it, along with the German war correspondent filming the seizure of the bridge.[41] It did not matter one way or another. Most of Force W was off the mainland by this time, having already been evacuated from Rafina and Porto Rafti in Attica or from Monemvasia and Kalamata in the Peloponnesus.

Athens fell on April 27, and the onrushing Germans swiftly occupied the Peloponnesus on April 28 and 29. The fighting was over by April 30. General Wilhelm List's 12th Army had performed impressively. It had dismantled the Greek army and handed the British another humiliating defeat, driving them into another helter-skelter retreat and forcing them into yet another evacuation that saved the men only at the cost of abandoning virtually all of the equipment. Nor were British manpower losses inconsiderable: 11,840 men out of the 53,000-plus who had originally embarked for Europe. Both retreat and evacuation alike had taken place under nonstop German air attack, accounting for a large share of British casualties. Robert Crisp, a South African armored commander, describes what it was like:

> From dawn to dusk there was never a period of more than half an hour when there was not an enemy plane overhead. It was the unrelenting pressure of noise and the threat of destruction in every hour which accentuated the psychological consequences of continuous retreat, and turned so many men into nervous wrecks who leapt from their driving seats and trucks at the first distant hum—often without stopping their vehicles—and ran from the roads . . . not

> to stop running until the skies were clear and the explosions had ceased to echo in their minds. Then they would make their way slowly, fearfully, back and ride on for another few miles until the next raid, or threat of a raid, set them running again.[42]

In "tossing Tommy from the continent,"[43] German losses had been much heavier than in the Yugoslav campaign, yet still startlingly light overall, especially as they were fighting against one of their great power adversaries in this campaign: 1,100 killed and 4,000 wounded. The vast majority of the casualties had been sustained by XXX Corps's frontal assault on the Metaxas Line, a venture that even some German analysts argued could have been dispensed with altogether.

Bewegungskrieg and Its Weaknesses

The Balkan campaign was a classic demonstration of the German art of war. Once again, bold and rapid maneuver had led to decisive success. As we view the Wehrmacht standing on the eve of Barbarossa, however, it is appropriate to discuss the weaknesses of the approach. Today, it has become customary to argue that the German focus on maneuver represented a narrow, even crabbed vision of warfare, one that placed the German army at a serious disadvantage in both world wars.[44] World War II saw German staff officers planning ever more elegant maneuver schemes, ones that may well represent the acme of the art, while their enemies did much, much more: mobilizing a major portion of the world's resources, easily besting Germany in the battle of manpower, technical innovation, production, and logistics, and winning a decisive victory in the shadow war of intelligence and counterintelligence.[45]

Consider this point: in World War II, the Allies actually cracked the German encoding mechanism, the so-called Enigma machine.[46] They then spent the entire war deliberately underreacting to the intelligence they had gleaned from this coup, lest the Germans realize they'd been had and move to some new, more secure system. Even so, the Allies enjoyed as complete an intelligence advantage as any in military history. Likewise, the Allies employed an entire series of highly successful agents, from Richard Sorge in Tokyo to Juan Pujol Garcia to the "12 apostles"[47] dispatched by President Roosevelt to North Africa to prepare the ground for the Torch invasion. Even today, the story of Pujol Garcia seems to have been concocted by an overly imaginative Hollywood screenwriter. Code-named Garbo, he was ostensibly a German agent working in Britain, who fed false information to the very top of the Nazi intelligence chain, up to and including Hitler himself. For his intelligence reports before the Normandy invasion, he received the Reich's highest honors and decorations, including the Iron Cross.[48] The Germans managed nothing like a counterweight to Allied success in this area. Despite the Nazi reputation for fanaticism, the democracies and Soviet Russia were far more successful at producing men and women who were willing to go behind enemy lines and risk life and limb in the battle for information. The German military intelligence office, the Abwehr, by contrast, spent much of the war trying first to overthrow, and then to kill, Hitler. In this war, most of the true believers were on the side of the Allies.

The Wehrmacht, in other words, was a military force that cared a great deal for concentric operations but very little for long-term planning. German military planners gave little thought at all to strategic concerns, at least as they have traditionally been conceived in the rest of the world. Exactly how individual operational victories—even decisive ones—would actually lead to the surrender of their enemies received very little consideration. In May 1940, for example, the Germans smashed four enemy armies in short order and occupied the Netherlands, Belgium, and France. When Britain refused to surrender, or even to come to terms, Hitler and the entire German leadership were completely at sea about how to proceed. The Wehrmacht, in a sense, had conquered its way into a strategic impasse.

It knew it, and it spent the next year flailing around, searching for a way to move forward. The amount of paperwork generated by such indecision (shared by Hitler and the high command) was prodigious. In the year after Case Yellow, the staff produced plans for no fewer than fifteen major operations: Sea Lion (the invasion of England), Sunflower (the introduction of German forces to North Africa), Cyclamen (the occupation of Albania), Marita (an attack on Greece), Felix (the seizure of Gibraltar), Isabella (the occupation of Spain and Portugal), a possible invasion of Switzerland, operations against the Canary and Azore Islands, Operation 25 against Yugoslavia, Operation Mercury against Crete, plans to occupy Vichy France, and the establishment of military missions to Romania and Iraq.[49] It wasn't as if there was a lot of downtime in German planning circles during this period. All of this frenzied activity sat uneasily on top of planning the greatest operation in military history: Barbarossa. Nor are we talking about the Pentagon, with a gigantic bureaucratic hive churning out planning documents by the bushel. German planning staffs were small—tiny, in fact. The General Staff had always seen itself as the true German military elite, and keeping itself small was part of the institutional ethos.[50]

Although wars are won or lost on the strategic level, the Germans were literally sitting in a conceptual prison. It was all operations, all the time. This was not an issue of trying to think outside the box. German staff officers might not have even been conscious of the fact that there was a box. *Bewegungskrieg* had worked well enough over the centuries; the Germans actually seemed unaware that there might have been viable alternatives to it. It had become a default setting.

Barbarossa

It is axiomatic to say that the invasion of the Soviet Union was the ultimate test of operational-level *Bewegungskrieg*.[51] Here, a way of war that had been designed to win short, sharp campaigns in the cozy confines of western Europe, a prosperous region with a highly developed economy and communications infrastructure, found itself very far from home indeed. Here it faced a behemoth, one with room in which to retreat and a manpower pool that was, by German standards at least, limitless. Moreover, the road and rail net was utterly unsatisfactory for a mechanized army that relied so heavily on tanks and other vehicles.

It would be untrue to state that planners on the German General Staff were unaware of any of these things. They also knew that the campaign would have to end before the onset of winter. At the same time, however, it was nearly impossible for most of them to conceive of failure. The war was approaching its third year, and no land force had yet come close to stopping them. Although the postwar memoir literature of the German generals is filled with misgivings over Hitler's decision to go east, there was in fact little debate over the wisdom of the move at the time. Most of the staff felt that the overthrow of the Soviet Union would amount to little more than a "sand table exercise"—a war game.[52]

In fact, the Red Army very nearly got the Yugoslav treatment. On June 21, 1941, over 3 million German and Axis troops crossed the Soviet border. Organized into three great army groups (North, Central, and South, heading for Leningrad, Moscow, and the Ukraine, respectively), they had managed to assemble beneath the radar of Soviet intelligence and to achieve not just strategic or operational surprise, but actual tactical surprise as well. As a result, the opening of Operation Barbarossa saw the Wehrmacht pound the Red Army senseless, methodically encircling and destroying huge Soviet forces at Bialystok and Minsk. In this opening phase, the Germans fought the *Kesselschlacht* to perfection, taking hundreds of thousands of prisoners and overrunning a huge swath of territory as large as Great Britain. The operational plan for Barbarossa called for destroying as much of the Red Army as close to the border as possible before it could retreat into the endless depths of the country, and it could not have worked much better than it did. The disaster has no parallel in military history: the world's largest army was essentially destroyed and the richest portions of the world's largest country overrun.

Although by this time the Germans had the entire thing down to a well-practiced drill, we must recognize how much of the responsibility for their early triumphs has to lie at Stalin's feet. He ignored, quite literally, the pile of intelligence on his desk—from sources as diverse as the Yugoslav ambassador to Moscow and Winston Churchill—of a massive German buildup on the border. With a network of intelligence agents abroad unparalleled in size and motivation (this was the age in which communism was still a religion for many in the West), and with a steady stream of German deserters crossing the border before the operation, Stalin should at least have been able to alert the units at the border to the imminent German blow. The only trouble was that the *vozhd*, or Boss, as he liked to be called, didn't believe any of it. It was all a plot, he swore—either a western one to get him mixed up in a war with Germany, or a Nazi one to get him to move first and thus justify a German counterblow. "You cannot always trust the intelligence," he once snapped at General G. K. Zhukov, who was gingerly trying to talk sense into him.[53] The evidence mounted, but Stalin remained unmoved, and his aides learned to pull punches in their reports, hesitating to tell him things that they knew would only anger him. When Richard Sorge, his spymaster in Tokyo, tried to tell him the truth, Stalin dismissed him as "a little shit." When the commissar for state security, Merkulov, passed on inside reports of Luftwaffe preparations for the impending attack, Stalin blew up. "Comrade Merkulov," he hissed, "you can send your 'source' from the headquarters of German aviation to his —ing mother."[54] The Red Army not only had to fight the Germans in those early days, therefore, but also what one modern writer aptly calls the "staggeringly inept" nature of its own regime.[55]

The resulting level of confusion still boggles the mind. Communications between Moscow and the front broke down immediately, although perhaps it is more accurate to say that they were never really established.[56] Stalin's technological conservatism, shared by old civil war cronies like the greatly mustachioed cavalry officer Marshal Semen Budenny, ensured that the Red Army's communications net consisted almost entirely of cable rather than radio. A relative handful of German agents in the country were able to utterly disable it before the main body had even crossed the border. Likewise, it took months for something like a valid supply system to get up and running. Some Soviet soldiers in those terrible early days actually marched into battle with no food but anchovies, a particularly terrible thing in light of the heat and the lack of drinking water.[57] There is one moment that may stand as representative of the entire opening phase of Barbarossa: Soviet 8th Mechanized Corps trundling up the single road from Drogobych to Sambor and crashing into Soviet 13th Mechanized Corps, which was, unfortunately, moving from Sambor to Drogobych. The result, needless to say, was a traffic jam of epic proportions.[58] They might still be there, sorting themselves out, if the Germans hadn't destroyed them both.

As a result of all these factors, the initial German progress was dizzying. By now, the surprise air assault, launched in early morning hours of June 22, had become almost obligatory. It did enormous damage. It destroyed hundreds of planes on the ground and made short work of the few disorganized patrols that managed to get into the air. After wrecking the Red Air Force, the Luftwaffe turned its attention to other targets, interdicting Soviet road and rail movement, pounding enemy troop concentrations and thoroughly disrupting command and communication facilities. As German ground forces advanced, they would, as always up to this point in the war, have the advantage of operating under an irresistible umbrella of air power.

There was progress almost everywhere. Army Group North (Field Marshal Wilhelm Ritter von Leeb) blasted through the Soviet border defenses in the newly occupied Baltic states almost immediately and headed for Leningrad. With 4th Panzer Group under General Erich Hoepner acting as the armored spearhead, Leeb's army group actually covered half the distance to Leningrad within the first five days of the campaign.[59] Pride of place for the mobile formations has to go to LVI Panzer Corps, under General Erich von Manstein, which drove fifty miles into the Baltic states on the first day alone against thoroughly befuddled Soviet opposition. By the end of day 4, Manstein had not only covered the 185 miles to Dvinsk, but had seized the crucial bridges over the Dvina River there, one of the principal strategic barriers on the road to Leningrad. Manstein's neighbor on the left, the XXXXI

Panzer Corps, wasn't far behind. After fighting Soviet tanks north of Raseynyay soon after crossing the border, it closed up to the Dvina and established bridgeheads across it on June 30. Beyond Dvinsk lay the Ostrov-Pskov area, another 155 miles distant, the second intermediate position on the way to Leningrad. The Panzer spearheads captured Ostrov on July 4 and reached Pskov the next day. By July 14, XXXXI Panzer Corps stood on the lower Luga, with a bridgehead over the river at Sabsk. It was just 62 miles from Leningrad; it had covered 470 miles in three weeks. As ever, the point was not simply to seize the city, but to ensure that the Soviets would have to throw troops in front of it, which could then be subjected to a concentric attack in the classic style and destroyed. To that end, Leeb had his two other armies, the 18th (General Georg von Küchler) and 16th (General Ernst Busch), hustling along to the left and right of Hoepner's Panzers, respectively. Throughout Barbarossa, the ability of the 126 German infantry divisions to keep up with their brethren in the tanks would play a crucial role. It was a murderous pace for the infantry and artillery, not to mention the 300,000 horses with which the Wehrmacht invaded the Soviet Union.[60]

The Germans met even more dramatic success on the road to Moscow. Here, Army Group Center (Field Marshal Fedor von Bock) dealt out a series of hammer blows that would have felled virtually any army in the world except the one it happened to be facing. Bock was wielding a large bat indeed: the *Schwerpunkt* of the entire German effort in the east, containing half the armor committed to Barbarossa.[61] He had four large maneuver units in all: two armies (the 9th under General Adolf Strauss and the 4th under Field Marshal Günther von Kluge), plus two Panzer Groups (the 3rd under General Hermann Hoth, and the 2nd under the celebrated Panzer leader, General Heinz Guderian, and thus often called Panzer Group Guderian).[62] German armor tore a great gash in the Soviet line from the first day, with Hoth on the northern wing of the army group and Guderian on the southern. The Panzer leaders were aiming deep—all the way to the city of Minsk, in fact. Here they swung inward, Hoth coming down and Guderian moving up, and sealed off an immense pocket of Soviet forces. At the same, the infantry armies were carrying out an encirclement of their own, a shorter hook. With 9th Army on the left and 4th on the right, another huge Soviet pocket was formed at Bialystok. This was a new milestone in the German way of war. The tradition of concentric operations had become something much more deadly: actual physical encirclement of entire enemy armies. No army in the world had ever fought two simultaneous battles of encirclement, and certainly no army had ever taken the surrender of 417,000 prisoners in a single encounter.

Barely pausing for breath, Hoth and Guderian now set off even deeper into the interior. Once again they turned and sealed off a pocket, the third great *Kesselschlacht* of this opening phase, just west of Smolensk. A daring armored raid by Hoth's Panzers seized the city itself on July 16. It is often said that the Germans failed to seal off these encirclements, allowing sizable portions of the trapped forces to escape, either to make their way back to Soviet lines or to remain behind German lines as partisans. That is certainly true. In its haste to wrap things up as quickly as possible, the German way of war always left more than its share of loose ends. But the destruction wrought by the Wehrmacht certainly had been bad enough: by mid-August, there were at least 895,000 Soviet prisoners in German hands, a figure that seems as incredible today as it did then.[63]

Only in the south was there disappointment, at least temporarily. Here the Soviet force commitment was much stronger, their preparations carried out with at least some degree of foresight.[64] The terrain and the conformation of the border, too, conspired against Army Group South. The commander, Field Marshal Gerd von Rundstedt, had two armies (the 6th under Field Marshal Walter von Reichenau and the 17th under General Carl Heinrich von Stülpnagel), plus 1st Panzer Group under General Ewald von Kleist, fresh from his victory in Yugoslavia. All three formations, however, would have to slither through one of the border's most difficult bottlenecks: the tight squeeze between the Pripet Marshes in the north and the foothills of the Carpathian Mountains in the south. With deployment space at a premium, another army (the 11th under General Eugen von Schobert) had to begin the campaign in Romania. It would join up with Army Group South only after the main force was well into the Ukraine. Unfortunately, that took longer than anticipated. With the Soviets across his entire front in force and fighting hard from the first day, Rundstedt's operations were by necessity more deliberate. Not until June 30, in fact, did the key city of Lvov (Lemberg) fall to the Germans, allowing Rundstedt some freedom of maneuver as defending Soviet forces began to fall back into the vast Ukrainian interior.

A month into the campaign, the Germans could look with satisfaction on their progress. The Red Army seemed to be coming apart at the seams. Army Group Center stood at Smolensk, where the initial operational plan had called for a pause in order to rest, refit, and replenish for the drive on Moscow. Leningrad had not yet fallen, but Army

Group North had made such astonishing progress that it seemed to be a matter of time. German armored forces had penetrated the Ukraine, and it was going to be a long time before the retreating Soviets reached a good defensive position in such flat country. Indeed, General Franz Halder, the chief of the German General Staff, felt that it was all over. The July 3 entry in his war diary contains some of the most famous last words in military history:

> Looked at overall we can already say that we have carried out our job of smashing the bulk of the Russian Army this side of the Dvina and Dnieper. I believe that a certain captured Russian general was right when he said that east of the Dvina and Dnieper we have got only to deal with scattered forces which will not of themselves be strong enough to offer any serious resistance to German operations. I am therefore not exaggerating when I say that the campaign against Russia was won in fourteen days.

To be fair, he did go on to hedge his bets slightly, adding, "Of course, it is not over yet." Because of the sheer size of the theater and the "stubborn resistance of the enemy with all the means at his disposal," there would be weeks of mopping up. In the same diary entry, however, we find Halder discussing future moves in the war against England, the "preparation of an offensive against the land-bridge between the Nile and the Euphrates, coming out of Cyrenaica and down from Anatolia, and perhaps from the Caucasus against Iran."[65] These were clearly times for thinking big in the German high command.

Things only got better through July. The third great *Kessel* at Smolensk yielded up another 348,000 Soviet prisoners by the end of the month. Army Group North continued its drive toward the southern approaches to Leningrad, although the combination of difficult terrain—dense forests and swamps—as well as increasing Soviet pressure on the army group's open flank in the southeast was beginning to slow Leeb down. Army Group South had finally gotten into full stride, sealing off a sizable *Kessel* of its own near Uman.[66] In what was by now a depressingly familiar ritual, another 103,000 soldiers of the Red Army marched off into the horrors of Nazi captivity.

And yet it was at this very moment—with Soviet Russia seemingly on the ropes and the Red Army having apparently dissolved—that Barbarossa began to fall apart. As always, the Wehrmacht's maneuver scheme had been a thing of beauty, completely baffling Soviet attempts to counter it. Cooperation between the ground forces and the

Luftwaffe, likewise, had been as good as two years of highly successful practice could make it. Virtually every other aspect of Barbarossa was a mess. This was not at all like the earlier campaigns. The country was huge, and the initial objectives of the Army Groups were a long, long way from the border: Army Group North had 490 miles to Leningrad, for example, and Army Group Center 615 to Moscow. These were measurements as the crow flies, however, and do not take into account the arcs, parabolas, and doubling backs necessitated by a series of armored flanking maneuvers. Moreover, the roads were as bad as they were long, and the enormous distances involved led to heavy demands on the men and much more wear and tear on the equipment than, let us say, the 150-mile drive across northern France in Case Yellow. German preinvasion intelligence had been abysmal, even by its own normally low standards. It is an understatement to say that the Germans had "underestimated" the size of the Soviet army. It is much more accurate to say they missed it altogether. By the end of June, over 5 million Soviet reservists had received the call-up, and a few weeks after famously declaring the campaign ended, General Halder was writing an equally famous lament in his war diary entry for August 11:

> Overall it is clearer and clearer that we have underestimated the Russian colossus, which had prepared itself for war with an utter lack of restraint which is characteristic of the totalitarian state. This is as true in the area of organization as it is of the economy, the area of transport and communications, but above all to pure military power. At the start of the war, we reckoned on some 200 enemy divisions. Now we have already counted 360. These divisions are definitely not armed and equipped in our sense, and tactically they are in many ways badly led. But they are there.

Indeed, he went on, "if we destroy a dozen, the Russians put another dozen in their place," and all the while, "they are falling back on their sources of supply, while we are drawing ever further away from ours."[67]

Nor were these new formations merely defending passively. There was, for example, a series of sharp counterstrokes against the Germans near Smolensk in late July, involving Soviet 20th Army (General P. A. Kurochkin), 19th Army (General I. S. Konev), and 21st Army (General F. I. Kuznetsov).[68] They were hastily planned and badly coordinated, for the most part. In Konev's case, the men quite literally launched their assault as they dismounted from their troop trains. But these incessant counterattacks, as well as a particularly aggressive one against Guderian's bridgehead over the Desna River, at Yelnya, did take their toll on the Wehrmacht's Panzer forces.[69]

By now the Germans were astonished at the quality of Soviet equipment, especially their medium T-34 tank and the heavy KV-1. A single one of the latter broke into the rear of the German forces driving on Leningrad, parked itself athwart the main supply route, and cut off the motorized brigade of 6th Panzer Division for two full days. The Germans wheeled up everything they could find, batteries of 50mm antitank and then high-velocity 88mm antiaircraft guns, drilling the tank at point blank ranges. After a good long while, the infantry approached it and crawled on top of it: "Suddenly the gun barrel started to move again, and our soldiers dispersed in amazement. Quickly, the engineers took hand grenades and pushed them into the hole produced by the hit at the lower part of the turret. A dull explosion sounded, and the hatch lid flew open. In the interior of the tank lay the bodies of the brave crewmen, who before had apparently only fainted."[70] The T-34, too, was more than a match for any tank in the field, and would stay that way until the introduction of the German Mark V Panther tank, much later in the war. Virtually every period account from German soldiers uses the same language in describing the first encounter: the speed, the distinctive sloped armor, the shock at having antitank shells bounce off. Here is Hans Kissel, an antitank gunner of the 101st Light Infantry Division near Poltava at the start of October, meeting the T-34 for the first time:

> We could see our the tracer shells. Each shot seems to be a direct hit. What in the world? The shells bounce off and shatter as ricochets all over the place, some vertically into the air, others sideways. You could clearly see them with the naked eye. The fire doesn't bother the tanks in the least. They roll swiftly toward us without even noticing. Two-hundred meters away, by one or the collective farm's buildings, they leave the street and turn north. Then they plunge into our left flank, heading towards the center of the village. The antitank guns turn and open fire again. The same picture, however. . . .

With the 37mm guns described here nearly useless against the T-34, Kissel and his men called on the much more powerful 50mm gun. It, too, was found wanting, even when it was blasting round after round into one of the T-34s at a range of fifty meters. That tank might still be there if one of the 50mm guns hadn't gotten a rear shot at it, where its armor was relatively weaker.[71]

What it all added up to was that the Wehrmacht's losses in men and matériel, even in victory, were far heavier than they had been in previous campaigns.[72] As the front line moved further and further into the Soviet Union, making those losses good proved to be beyond German capability. Because of the insufficiencies of the road net, staff planners had assigned just two major road arteries per army group. The standard up to that point in the war had been a main artery for every corps; with eight to ten corps in an army group, the Germans weren't even coming close to keeping up with the supply requirements.[73] By late August, front line formations were running short of a laundry list of items crucial to modern, mechanized war: tanks, tank engines, trucks, prime movers. Moreover, it wasn't a good idea for any modern army to be operating 450 miles from its railhead, but with conversion of the Russian railways to the western European gauge moving so slowly, that was the exact situation for large parts of Army Group Center.

Logistics, intelligence, production, manpower: the Germans were having their difficulties in any number of areas by August. How they dealt with those problems should not surprise anyone even passably acquainted with the long-term pattern of German military operations. Rather than drastically beef up the logistical pipeline, ruthlessly draft every able-bodied man in the Reich, and bring some sense to an increasingly disordered economy, the Wehrmacht high command decided to do the traditional German thing: tinker with the maneuver scheme. During August, the Führer met with his top generals, both the staff and the various field headquarters, and decided that the real problem facing Barbarossa was that the drive on Moscow had outstripped those on the flanks. Leeb was still moving toward Leningrad, true, but between the lakes, the dense, trackless forests, endless swamps, and an increasingly long and vulnerable flank along the Volkhov River in the southeast, he was having his share of troubles. With only two Panzer Corps sharing three Panzer divisions between them, he lacked the concentrated armored punch to do much more than drive the Soviets back; large-scale encirclements were out of the question. After XXXXI Panzer Corps reached the Luga River, for example, just sixty miles from Leningrad, it sat, more or less immobilized, for three and a half weeks. It was waiting for its neighboring LVI Panzer Corps to extricate itself from far more difficult terrain on the right, which eventually happened; it was also waiting for enough infantry divisions to arrive to support a last lunge toward Leningrad, which didn't.[74] All along the front, Soviet resistance was growing, and Army Group North never did solve the problem of its exposed right flank. Likewise, Rundstedt was by now deep in the Ukraine, closing up to the Dnieper bend and doing damage, but it was apparent that he was vastly outnumbered and could not really expect to achieve any sort of decision on his own.

This was the genesis, then, of the decision to detach Guderian's 2nd Panzer Group from the drive on Moscow to help encircle Soviet forces in the Ukraine. With Kleist (1st Panzer Group) attacking out of his bridgehead across the Dnieper at Kremenchug on September 12, and with Guderian hurtling down from Roslavl in the north, the two great armored forces met at Lovitsa, forming what we can only call an *Über-Kessel* around Kiev. It trapped four complete Soviet armies, the 5th, 37th, 26th, and 21st, some 665,000 prisoners in all.[75] The number of Soviet prisoners in German hands was now close to 2 million.

There has been a mountain of historical literature written on the decision, virtually all of it highly condemnatory. The Kiev encirclement is one of those alleged turning points that lost the war for the Germans. Postwar accounts by General Staff officers, in particular, would point to it as Hitler's classic blunder. His amateurish grasp of strategy finally caught up with him, they argue. He wasted precious time on a sideshow into the Ukraine while the road to Moscow lay open to German forces.[76]

Although that certainly is a plausible case, there is another one to be made. The road to Moscow was certainly not wide open. The battles in front of Smolensk had been hard, and German forces had been sitting on the Desna River for two weeks awaiting supplies and replacements. Despite their ex post facto protests, there was a great deal of support from the staff and command echelons for the turn into the Ukraine. This should not be surprising. There was always a great deal of support within this officer corps for any bold move or one likely to bring glory to the victor. The payoff in front of Kiev had been stunning. From the perspective of the battle of annihilation—the only perspective most German officers had—Kiev was a master stroke, another in a long series of brilliant concentric operations, and one should be very careful in using the word *blunder* to describe any battle that takes an entire enemy army group prisoner. Indeed, in forcing Army Group Center and Army Group South to cooperate by converging on the principal concentration of enemy force still in the field, Hitler had brought a rare moment of operational coherence to an increasingly confused and scattered Barbarossa. It was the greatest victory in German history.

Typhoon: To Moscow

The slaughter at Kiev had finally cleared up the operational situation. There was no longer any debate. The Wehrmacht would head for Moscow, smash every Soviet army that it met along the way, and take the city before winter. This was Operation Typhoon, which touched off as soon as Guderian had gotten back from the Ukraine on September 30. It does not speak well for Soviet "operational art" that even after two months of preparing forces for the defense of Moscow and fortifying the approaches in every conceivable way, the Red Army suffered defeats in the opening phase of this operation that were every bit as painful as those of Barbarossa. For the Red Army, October was very much like June, only worse, because this debacle was happening directly in front of the capital.

Typhoon included three armies (9th, 4th, and 2nd, running north to south), as well as three Panzer Groups (3rd, 4th, and Guderian's 2nd, now formally renamed "2nd Panzer Army"). Here the Wehrmacht returned to the tried-and-true approach: a vast concentric crescent of armies bearing down on Moscow. Touching off in the south, Guderian's advance to the northeast bagged an enormous haul—three full Soviet armies (3rd, 15th, and 50th). Further north, the Wehrmacht finally achieved what German armies had been searching for since the days of Schlieffen: a perfect "Cannae." As always, it happened along the Minsk-Moscow highway. With 3rd Panzer Group coming down and 4th Panzer Group coming up, the pincers met to the east of Vyazma. Six more Soviet armies went into the bag (for the record, 19th, 24th, 29th, 30th, 32nd, and 43rd). The combined total for the Bryansk and Vyazma pockets: 750,000 more Soviet prisoners.[77]

Of course, this was almost the precise moment it began to rain. In central Russia, rain meant mud, and thus a halt to large-scale operations. By the time the Bryansk-Vyazma pocket had been liquidated, the already inadequate roads had been churned into a sea of mud. Bock, the commander of Army Group Center, complained on October 21, "The Russians are impeding us less than the wet and the mud!"[78] Indeed, how does one fight a war of movement when, as Bock noted on October 24, twenty-four horses were needed to move a single artillery piece?[79]

Winter was just weeks away now, and it might have made sense for the Germans to shorten their line, go into something approximating winter quarters, and try again in the spring. They didn't, of course, for reasons that must have made sense to them at the time. The rousing opening of Operation Typhoon had blown a 300-mile-wide hole in the

Soviet position in front of Moscow, and it was inconceivable to most German commanders that Stalin would be able to plug it before they were knocking on his office door in the Kremlin. Even the Soviet manpower pool had to have a limit. Moreover, the notion of calling a halt ran contrary to everything this officer corps believed: the importance of will and aggression, and especially the importance of finishing the war in a single campaign.

And so they kept going, lured forward as much by their own faith in the German way of war as by the shimmering mirage of Moscow on the horizon. They would push until they quite literally had fought themselves down to the last man, gun, and tank. In November, the freeze hit. Analysts often point to the fact that the freeze allowed the mechanized German army to get moving once again. But for everything it gave, it took away far more, especially in terms of front-line morale. Every educated German soldier, whether officer or enlisted man, knew what winter in Russia meant. It meant Napoleon. It also meant new things—like using ammunition to light watch fires and building a fire under the tank in the morning in order to melt the oil in the pan—that will never become standard operating procedures. Even now, however, the operation continued. Halder himself told Bock on November 18, "We must understand that things are going much worse for the enemy than for us and that these battles are less a questions of strategic command than a question of energy."[80]

The intense cold, dipping as low as -40°F, was just one reason for the defeat of Typhoon. The other was the increasingly chaotic nature of the operation itself. Since the origins of the Prussian army, the officer corps had resembled nothing so much as a pack of attack dogs, straining at any leash designed to limit their freedom of action and often snapping at each other when the prey was near. It had worked well enough over the years, certainly, although it had also led to its share of problems, even absurdities, on battlefields from Kolin to Tannenberg. By the end of November, Typhoon had degenerated into little more than a series of separate encounters without strategic coherence. On the right wing, Guderian was hammering at the gates of Tula. On the extreme left, Hoth was doing the same to Kalinin. Bock, commanding the army group, would have turned in his shoulder straps rather than call a halt on the way to Moscow. He had played second fiddle in Poland (to Rundstedt) and in France (to Rundstedt). His best armor had been taken away from him in September (once again to come to Rundstedt's aid). Moscow was going to be his entry into the German pantheon. Frankly, it is hard to think of a single German commander who would have thought any differently from Bock. That, in itself, was part of the problem.

The Wehrmacht was now in the worst possible place at the worst possible time. Front-line strength was at a fraction of what it should have been, there were no reinforcements, and replacements had dried up to a trickle. For nearly a month, the logistics pipeline had been privileging ammunition and fuel at the expense of everything else, like winter clothing or supplies. Just getting to Moscow had used up the army's last reserves of strength. Taking it was out of the question, and advancing beyond it was a fantasy. Six hundred miles inside the Soviet Union, the machine had broken down. The war of movement had ground to a halt.

The great Soviet counterstroke in the first week of December, then, was a separate act. The Germans had already lost the battle for Moscow, and had clearly failed in their attempt to destroy the Soviet Union in a single campaign. Even if they had taken Moscow, however, the campaign would almost certainly have gone on. By now, Stalin and his regime had recovered the equilibrium they had momentarily lost in June. A large portion of Soviet industry had relocated beyond the Urals, safely out of German reach. There were also many industrial areas in the European portions of the country that were still producing, even under German bombs and shells: those at Gorki and Stalingrad, for example, as well as Moscow. Even encircled, Leningrad was still churning out weapons, tanks, and shells. As 1941 drew to a close, the U.S.S.R. was a long way from being destroyed.

Still, the counteroffensive that opened on December 5 was an impressive recovery for an army that had been hit so hard since June. After having suffered the mind-boggling total of 4 million casualties, 2 million since the start of Typhoon, the Soviets still managed to assemble a massive force for the blow: four *fronts*, the Russian equivalent of army groups (Northwest, Kalinin, West, and Southwest) containing seventeen armies and two large cavalry corps (Cavalry Group Below and 11th Cavalry Corps).[81] Although the Soviets also had numerous units whose strength was well under their establishment, they were still able to amass an enormous advantage over the frozen, nearly immobile skeleton of the Wehrmacht.

Their commanders, too, were not the hapless incompetents of the summer, but a cadre of younger, active men (G. K. Zhukov in overall command, I. S. Konev of Kalinin Front, K. K. Rokossovsky of 16th Army) who had learned a great deal in the last six months. This was not simply some crude frontal assault, still the general popular stereotype of the Red Army in this period, but a solid operational combination of frontal and flank attacks. The goal was an encirclement of the German forces in front of Moscow. Kalinin Front was responsible for destroying the northern pincer threatening Moscow, the Klin salient. The 29th and 31st Armies attacked the northern side of the salient; 20th Army and 1st Shock Army attacked the point; and three more armies (20th, 16th, and 5th) hit its southern face. Mobile units (cavalry corps and small tank brigades, for the most past) charged into the gaps created by the infantry assaults. There was a second major thrust to the south, against Guderian's Panzer Group in front of Tula. Here 50th Army and a "Cavalry-Mechanized Group" rudely pushed back Guderian's force—once irresistible, now utterly fought out.[82] Under this inconceivable onslaught, the German line gave, and it broke altogether in several places. Stalin was emboldened by the signs of German collapse to extend the offensive to Northwest Front. It launched a series of thrusts seeking the far left flank and rear of the German position, driving deep toward Velikiye Luki and Smolensk. He also ordered a vain offensive to relieve Leningrad in the north and equally ill-fated ones to retake Orel and Kharkov to the south.[83] It was nothing less than a strategic offensive. German casualties in all this were enormous. Army Group Center stood on the brink of dissolution.

Where to Now? The Wehrmacht after Barbarossa

Of course, it did not dissolve, and for this Hitler deserves some share of the credit. His *Haltbefehl*, usually translated as "stand-fast order," ordered each German soldier and formation to hold their position and defend it to the last, even if bypassed or surrounded. It was almost certainly the right thing to do. Any attempt to retreat under such pressure, not to mention the winter conditions, would have been courting disaster, and once again the Napoleon comparisons are instructive: it wasn't the advance to Moscow that had destroyed the Grande Armée, but the retreat from it. It wouldn't have been a mobile retreat. Even the Panzer divisions were straight leg infantry by this time. Indeed, events would prove Hitler's intuition correct. By January 1942, Soviet momentum had worn down. It had neither the supply systems nor established procedures for command and control that would allow it to prosecute the offensive further. The Red Army was not yet ready to go deep on the Germans.

Even so, the Wehrmacht had suffered a devastating blow. Consider this passage from a November 1941 issue of the *Militär-Wochenblatt*. Even allowing for some of its hyperbole, it is a striking document:

> November 22nd marks five months since the German Wehrmacht moved against the threat of a Bolshevist attack from the east. In that time, it has occupied 1.7 million square kilometers of the territory of the Soviet Union, containing three quarters of its industry and 75 million of its inhabitants. It has simultaneously taken 3,792,600 prisoners and destroyed 389 divisions; including battle casualties, we may estimate total Soviet losses at over eight million soldiers. Materiel losses correspond to human ones: more than 22,000 tanks, 27,452 guns, 16,912 aircraft have been destroyed or captured. . . . It is a balance sheet that represents both a proud success for the German Wehrmacht and an annihilating defeat for the enemy.[84]

Indeed, by one estimate, the Germans had formed twelve great encirclements in the course of Barbarossa-Typhoon, from Bilaystok to Bryansk.[85] In the eastern campaign, the Germans had brought *Bewegungskrieg* to a destructive peak that it would never know again. It was as if it had fought and won Case Yellow twelve times over.

But it had achieved precisely nothing. Not only had the Germans been thwarted in front of Moscow, they'd nearly been destroyed. After the victory over France in 1940, Hitler had rewarded his generals by creating field marshals en masse. Now he fired them wholesale: all three Army Group commanders (Leeb, Bock, and Rundstedt) were soon gone, followed by such luminaries as "Hurryin' Heinz" Guderian, the man who more than any other was the public face of the German Panzer Corps. General Walter von Brauchitsch, the chief of the OKH (High Command of the Army) was gone as well. He'd suffered a heart attack, brought on as much by trying to mediate the battle between Hitler and the field commanders as by the stress of handling the Red Army. Ominously, Hitler himself now took Brauchitsch's spot, assuming personal command over army operations. It would be interesting to see what, if anything, the Führer could bring to the table in the future beyond his order to stand fast.

More than a campaign had been lost here. The German way of war itself, based on rapid, decisive victory and an independent-minded officer corps that handled situations as it saw fit, had suffered a grievous, perhaps mortal, blow. For the rest of the conflict, the officer corps would be fighting a two-front war all its own, one for Germany's future, but also one for its own. It was about to clash with the realities of life in the Third Reich, a *Führerstaat* where the leader's will was the law and that by definition was a strange matrix in which to sustain "the independence of the lower commander." It also had a conflict on its hands with a vast enemy coalition, especially after Hitler's declaration of war on the United States in December, a huge multiheaded beast that could never be subjected to a single knockout blow.

In fighting this war, the Wehrmacht's officer corps knew what it did not want to do, and that was to go over the defensive. That, they believed almost to a man, had been the fundamental mistake of World War I: assuming a passive *Stellungskrieg* and trying to fight a war of attrition that had eventually swallowed them all. As to what they did want to do, one model came readily to mind. In early 1942, at the very moment that the Soviet winter offensive was winding down and the German army in the East, although shaken, appeared to have survived to fight again, a new issue of the *Militär-Wochenblatt* appeared. The Friday arrival of the magazine—with its mixture of war reportage, analysis of campaigns both contemporary and historical, tactical exercises, and book reviews—was an eagerly awaited moment for members of the officer corps. Debate within its pages was always of a high scholarly tone, although undeniably vigorous at the same time, and its editorial pronouncements were important enough to be seen, at the very least, as semiofficial.

It was the January 23 issue.[86] There, on the cover, stood a reminder of the officer corps's tradition and greatness, and perhaps a way out of Germany's current dilemma. It was an image of a bewigged older gentleman wearing a simple dark tunic and an Order of the Black Eagle on his chest. The man's eyes were wide and intelligent, and his lips were pursed, perhaps in an inner tension, or perhaps in a kind of cynical half-smile. There was an identifying caption, but no German officer needed it, nor would he have any doubt as to why this portrait had been chosen for the cover of the magazine. It was an image of a man who had commanded German soldiers in a long, difficult war against a vast coalition, a general who never stopped attacking, one whose reputation as the most aggressive field commander of his day was well deserved; the man who, more than any other, had invented *Bewegungskrieg* as a solution to Prussia's strategic dilemma. He was a man who could safely wear the Black Eagle. After all, he had handed out his share of them. It was *der alte Fritz* himself, Frederick the Great, the man who had once summed up his art of war in the simple motto: "The Prussian army always attacks."

2

The Wehrmacht Reborn

The Crimean Campaign

For many in the German high command, 1942 was a "new start,"[1] a time to breathe deeply and savor the thrill of still being alive. In fact, it should have been a time for an agonizing reappraisal. The attempt in the summer of 1941 to smash the Soviet Union in one great campaign, Operation Barbarossa, had achieved tremendous early success and inflicted enormous damage on the Red Army. It had also failed. When an unusual set of circumstances actually allowed the Wehrmacht to reload the gun a second time, it launched Operation Typhoon, the drive on Moscow, in October. That too had done enormous damage and then failed. Indeed, it had ended disastrously in the face of the Red Army's great winter counteroffensive at the gates of the capital. In the first few months of the new year, the Wehrmacht, first Army Group Center, then the others as well, actually found themselves in survival mode as the Red Army launched a vast strategic offensive that eventually engulfed the entire eastern front. An army that prided itself on rapid campaigns of maneuver on the operational level had, for the time being, dissolved into small groups of weary infantrymen clinging desperately to whatever miserable piece of shelter they could find. They survived the winter, however, and now it was time to look ahead.

The strategic problem of 1942 was quite a bit different from that of the previous year. The Reich now faced a grand alliance of unprecedented power. Viewed from our own day, it is difficult to think of plausible scenarios in which Germany could have won this war, as anyone who has read much of the "alternate history" genre can testify.[2] It is important to remember, however, that real alternatives existed in 1942 as to the future course of the conflict. Theoretically, the Germans could have done any number of things. They could have gone over to a *guerre de course* against Allied shipping with ever more advanced submarine models[3]; they could have pursued the development of their own strategic bomber force, an effort they toyed with from time to time[4]; they could have gone into total war mode in late 1941, rather than 1943, after Stalingrad, when it was already too late.[5] With German armies in occupation of virtually all of Europe, including the lion's share of its industrial areas, and with the Reich itself yet to feel the pain from the Allied bombing offensive, the resources really did exist for any number of options. What would the impact have been by 1944, let us say, of a sizable increase in the production of antiaircraft guns in 1941? German flak was murderous enough as it was, and B-17 and B-24 crews paid the price in blood.[6] Or a production program that stressed U-boats over tanks? The Allied victory in the battle of the Atlantic was one of those near-run things that dot the landscape of military history, perhaps one of Hitler's lost opportunities. A bit more attention here, a nip and a tuck there, and Germany might well have won the war, or staved off defeat long enough that it might have seemed like victory.

So there were possibilities. In reality, however, expecting Germany to win the war, or even to better its position, through naval submarine warfare or defensive antiaircraft assets or better signals intelligence is to ignore history. The fundamental basis of German power had always been the army. With a central position in Europe, essentially open borders, and far fewer resources than its neighbors, Germany could not afford to pursue strategies that might, in the long term, result in victory. With far more serious dangers poised on the very border from day one of any potential war, Germany was an unlikely place to generate and fund a risky, long-term research program in the style of the Manhattan Project, no matter how many gifted nuclear physicists the country churned out. That is one reason that the Germans never really pursued the long-range bomber option; strategic bombing might work, but it would definitely take time. It is also the reason that the navy never pursued an antishipping war to its limit; for all the threat it might have posed to Britain in the long term, it was not a strategy designed to yield quick results. Only the army still held out the possibility of a victory decisive enough to pry apart the enemy coalition.

Germany faced serious strategic obstacles in early 1942. It was outnumbered on land and sea and in the air. It was surrounded by enemies. Its principal field army had just suffered a horrible, almost annihilating blow in the fighting before Moscow and during the winter. Its own casualty list in the east had just topped 1 million men. Nevertheless, what is perhaps most noticeable about German decision making in the spring is how little dissent there was to Hitler's decision to launch another great offensive in the Soviet Union. Viewed through the long-term lens of German military history, the Wehrmacht's seemingly hopeless situation left it only one option: attack.

Prelude: The Crimea

Convinced that it was winter, more than anything else, that had beaten them in 1941, and that in warm weather and on dry ground the Wehrmacht was still more than a match for the Red Army, Hitler and the high command ordered another great offensive for the summer of 1942. It would be known as Operation Blue. This time, the tiresome arguments during Operation Barbarossa about objectives, with Hitler demanding action on the flanks (Ukraine and Leningrad) and his generals by and large preferring Moscow, were a moot point. Most of those who had bickered with Hitler were gone from the service or were in temporary retirement. With few members of the staff eager for another crack at Moscow, and with the Leningrad front frozen into a *Stellungskrieg* in some of the Soviet Union's most difficult terrain, Operation Blue would take place in the south.

Before it could start, however, it was clear that the Wehrmacht first had to undertake a number of preliminary campaigns to clean up loose ends from the previous campaign. Predominant among them was the situation in the Crimea.[7] The German army couldn't really head east until the nettlesome Soviet resistance in the peninsula had been smashed once and for all. "The southern flank of such a far-reaching operation would have been extremely endangered as long as the Crimean peninsula was in enemy hands," wrote one German officer. "The enemy forces were in a position to conduct an exceedingly dangerous attack at any time from the Crimean peninsula toward the north, against the south flank or against the rear of Army Group South. Strong enemy formations on Crimea constituted a permanent threat to rear area communications and to the supply lines of the German units which were fighting north of the Sea of Azov."[8] Even if the narrow neck of the peninsula could be closed, leaving the Crimea in Soviet hands left open the danger of landing operations by amphibious forces based in the peninsula, in cooperation with the Black Sea fleet operating out of Sevastopol. In addition, Soviet aircraft flying out of the Crimea could pose a serious threat to the Romanian oil fields at Ploesti, one of the most vulnerable of Germany's supply nodes.[9]

The Crimean campaign was one of the most interesting and unusual in the history of modern war. It featured huge forces on both sides crammed into a tiny, self-contained package, and at times the unit densities beggared description. The German commander there, General Erich von Manstein, described it as "a campaign which, in ten months of incessant fighting, included both offensive and defensive battles, mobile warfare with full freedom of action, a headlong pursuit operation, landings by an enemy in control of the saw, partisan engagements and an assault on a powerfully defended fortress."[10] It also featured something that had once been common in the Prussian-German tradition, but was now increasingly rare: a force that "operated for over nine months with a measure of independence greater than that of any other army in the eastern theater."[11] As Manstein himself put it, it was "one of the few cases where an army was still able to operate independently in a segregated theater of war, left to its own devices and free of interference from the supreme command."[12]

Much of this was due to the peculiar nature of the peninsula itself. The main body of the Crimea is a rough square, with its corners approximating the four points of the compass: Perekop in the north, Ak-Mechet in the west, Sevastopol in the south, and Parpach in the east. The city of Simferopol sits nicely on the central point of the square. The peninsula appears to have been gouged out of the mainland by some-long ago cataclysm, and it connects with mainland Ukraine, just barely, at the arrow Perekop isthmus, a strip of land that is itself less than five miles wide, and that is further winnowed down by numerous lakes. To the west of the Perekop bottleneck sits the sea, to the east the "Sivash," a salty swamp that was nearly impassable to military forces. Another neck of land, little more than a spit in places, lay to the east, containing the railroad from Genichesk on the mainland to Simferopol. Sevastopol, the peninsula's key port, naval base, and fortress, perches on the peninsula's southwestern coast, and it would obviously be the operational objective of any campaign into the Crimea. Conquering Sevastopol was a problem that would have to wait, however. Simply getting into the Crimea would be difficult enough.

Adding to the geographical complexity, the Crimea also contained another narrow strip of land jutting out from the eastern point of the diamond. The Kerch peninsula, which stretches from Parpach in the west, points like an arrow toward the region known as the Kuban, from which it is separated by a narrow strait, barely more than three miles wide at its narrowest. Any force breaking into the Crimea from the north and heading for Sevastopol would have plenty to worry about on its flank and in its rear because the Strait of Kerch could function as a highway for enemy reinforcements into the Crimea, and the Kerch peninsula itself could serve as a kind of invulnerable sally port.

All told, the Crimea appears to have been designed by the god of war to present both attacker and defender with thorny problems of time and space. An attacker would first have to launch a deliberate breakthrough battle just to get access into the peninsula. Even if it succeeded, the defender could simply retreat in two divergent directions, south to Sevastopol and east into the vastness of Kerch peninsula. An attacker concentrating against Kerch lay open to a strike from Sevastopol, and vice versa. Neither was the defender completely safe: there would be a natural tendency to fortify oneself in either Sevastopol or Kerch, granting the attacker the advantage of interior lines and a free choice of target. And if by chance the attacker did manage to break into the Kerch peninsula, he had a convenient path across the strait into the Taman peninsula, the northwestern tip of the Caucasus and the deep rear of the Soviet strategic position in the south.

The Germans had tried, and failed, to conquer the Crimea in the fall.[13] With Army Group South driving east toward Rostov, it had diverted up one of its armies (the 11th, originally under the command of General Eugen von Schobert) for a drive south into the peninsula. Before he could carry out the maneuver, however, General von Schobert was killed when his Fieseler *Storch* command plane had the bad luck to touch down in a freshly laid Russian minefield.[14] The new commander, General von Manstein, was already a well-known figure within the officer corps. He had devised the operational plan for the highly successful 1940 campaign in the West, Case Yellow. It was a daring plan—some said at the time overdaring—that called for launching an immense armored thrust through the difficult terrain of the Ardennes Forest. With its dense woods, winding trails, and deep gorges, it was not at all good tank country, and as a result was nearly undefended by the French and Belgian armies. Manstein, then on the staff of General Gerd von Rundstedt's Army Group A, had a hard time selling the plan, and his intemperate manner and arrogance had ruffled more than a few feathers among the senior officers. It had been a tradition going back to the days of Moltke that General Staff officers should be nameless—that they should work only for the greater glory of their commander.[15] Hitler heard of it, however, and decided that Manstein's plan was just what he needed and what his hidebound, conservative generals were refusing to give him: a lighting and surprise blow against the powerful armies of the western powers, and the possibility of a decisive victory. It had worked like a dream, of course, although Manstein himself played a relatively small role in the campaign as commander of the XXXVIII Corps, an infantry formation.[16]

The start of Barbarossa brought him the armored command he had long coveted in the form of the LVI Panzer Corps. He had spearheaded the drive of Army Group North, smashing his way to Dvinsk in a headlong rush in the opening few days of the campaign. It was, he later wrote, "the fulfillment of all a tank-force commander's dreams."[17] But disappointment was to follow. At Dvinsk, he had received orders from his Panzer Group commander, General Erich Hoepner, to halt and wait for XXXXI Panzer Corps and the left wing of 16th Army to close up. The pause threw away the real advantage gained from the rapid thrust over the Dvina. It was not until July 2 that Mantein resumed his drive on Leningrad. It ran into tough resistance almost from the start because the Red Army had used the extra time to assemble its reserves and restore some semblance of a front. Further problems ensued: difficult terrain, a constantly shifting axis of attack, contradictory orders from Hoepner and the commander of Army Group North, General von Leeb, and above all, increasing Soviet strength, especially against the dangling southeastern flank of the army group.

With the drive on Leningrad stalled, therefore, Manstein was probably not at all disappointed to receive the call to command 11th Army after Schobert's death. Indeed, it was another dream assignment for any German officer: a more or less independent command, real opportunity for maneuver, and a long way from Berlin. He arrived at his new headquarters, at Nikolayev at the mouth of the Bug River, on September 17. He commanded the extreme southern wing of the Russian front and had simultaneous responsibility for the Crimea and for the lower Dneiper. He also had a responsibility that not every German commander had to worry about: working out liaison with Allied troops, in this case the Romanian 3rd Army under General Petre Dumitrescu.[18]

Ordered, like so many German formations that fell, to advance in two directions at once, Manstein decided from the moment he assumed his new command to give priority to the Crimea. His original plan had LIV Corps (46th and 73rd Infantry Divisions, under General Erich Hansen) serving as the assault force against the Perekop position.[19] The isthmus here is as flat as a pancake, a salt steppe without even a hint of cover, and the Soviets were manning a defensive zone echeloned some forty kilometers deep. The assault divisions would have heavy artillery support, as well as Stukas from Luftflotte 4. The latter were crucial because in the flat terrain, there would be virtually no means of artillery observation. Frankly, the infantry was going to need all the help it could get. It was a gamble, said one staff officer, "which was only justified by the repeatedly displayed superiority of troop leadership and by the bravery and offensive spirit of the German soldier."[20] It is easy to scoff at such rhetoric as overdone, even romantic, but it needs to be entered into the historical record. Whether it is true or not, the Wehrmacht's officer corps really did believe it.

Once the corps had made a breach, Manstein had two formations ready to exploit into the Crimea proper: the XXXXIX Mountain Corps (170th Infantry Division, plus the 1st and 4th Mountain Division, General Ludwig Kuebler) and the 1st S.S. Panzer Division (*Leibstandarte Adolf Hitler*). Meanwhile, to plug holes back on the mainland caused by the Crimean diversion, Manstein employed 3rd Romanian Army under General Dumitrescu. The Romanians were still at this time displaying considerable reluctance to cross the Dnieper River because Romania had already achieved its principal war aim, the return of the lost province of Bessarabia (later Soviet Moldavia, today's independent Republic of Moldova).

The operation, opening on September 24, ran into trouble from the start.[21] With 73rd Division on the right and 46th on the left, LIV Corps had to smash its way into and through the Perekop isthmus. Although it had strong backing from artillery, antiaircraft guns, and airpower, it was still a grinding fight that caused heavy losses to both sides, as this type of close positional fighting always will. The assault divisions were already exhausted from months of tough fighting in the Ukraine, and the Soviet position was a strong one, a series of concrete bunkers linked by a nearly invisible system of trenches. The two principal towns of the isthmus, Perekop and Preobrashenka, were actually linked by what one German combat engineer called "an amazing underground trench system that even connected one house with another."[22] Its existence was unknown to the Germans at the start of the battle. Finally, there was the Tartar Wall, a name given by the Germans to nearly every old fortification they met in the southern Soviet Union, an eighteenth-century trench that was ten to fifteen meters deep, running across the neck of the isthmus.[23] The Soviets would make it their principal line; it was defended by three rifle divisions, the 156th, 271st, and 276th.[24]

With the Soviet defenders fighting from prepared positions, then, the initial phases of the assault were largely in the hands of the engineers. They went in, laid down smoke, and employed demolition charges against the bunkers and hand grenades against the trenches. They also died in droves, along with many small unit commanders among the infantry. The first three days saw limited progress as the Germans slowly ground their way up to the Tartar Wall. It would take three more days to get past the wall and then chew their way through the Soviet defenders in front of Armyansk. By now Soviet resistance was softening as the Stukas took a toll on formations defending in what was essentially an open plain. One German source describes the bodies of dead Soviet soldiers "piled high" as a result of air attack.[25] There was a last-ditch Soviet attempt to shore up the position, an armored thrust by 5th Tank Regiment. It broke through the exhausted German front lines, recrossed the Tartar Wall to the north, and actually got into 73rd Division's rear. A weak and unsupported thrust by a single regiment was hardly enough to restore the situation, however, and the Soviet tanks also came under murderous fire from German artillery and from the Luftwaffe, which had by now won air superiority over this tiny front. The 5th Tank Regiment suffered heavy losses and had to retreat. It was the battle's turning point. At Armyansk, the broadening of the peninsula and slightly more open ground offered greater possibilities for maneuver. The Germans had gotten through the isthmus.

Unfortunately, they had done so to no purpose whatsoever. Manstein was in the embarrassing position of having no force in hand to exploit the hard-won gains of his infantry. The two formations originally intended for the pursuit were no longer around. He had intended to use 1st S.S. Panzer Division, for example, in a lightning drive on Sevastopol if the situation permitted. Unfortunately, the *Leibstandarte* had just received orders to hold itself in readiness for a transfer to Kleist's 1st Panzer Group for the drive on Rostov. Moreover, the losses sustained by the two lead divisions had been high, and both needed time to recuperate and assimilate replacements before thrusting any deeper into the Crimea.

In addition, while the infantry were battling grimly through Perekop, the Soviet Southern Front under General I. T. Cherevichenko had launched an offensive of his own against 11th Army to the north of the Sea of Azov.[26] He had three armies on line (the 12th, 18th, and 9th, moving from north to south), part of a wave of new infantry formations that would soon swamp Army Group South. The attack opened on September 26, slammed hard into the German lines, and made a number of penetrations so deep that a breakthrough appeared possible. Manstein's memoirs[27] blame the Romanian army alone, as German memoirs often do, and singled out the 4th Mountain Brigade in particular, but in fact the assault had shaken the entire 11th Army. Even Manstein admitted that "the situation became pretty tense" throughout the German XXX Corps sector.[28] In order to restore the situation, the German XXXXIX Mountain Corps, already more than halfway to Perekop, had to turn around. The reinsertion of the German mountain corps in the line soon stabilized the situation in the north. Even after their initial assault was stymied, however, the Soviets continued to launch repeated attacks against the same points in 11th Army's line, even after the previous ones had been repulsed bloodily. That too would be a pattern of the fighting on the eastern front for the next four years. The end result was to pin the three Soviet armies in place and to chew up all their reserves, two dangerous things to have happen when one was in contact with the Wehrmacht.

Indeed, the Soviets could not yet know it, but trouble was brewing from the north. Elements of Panzer Group Kleist were arriving on the scene. They poured out of their Dnieper bridgeheads at Zaporozhye and took a straight shot directly into the rear of Cherevichenko's Southern Front. Kleist's offensive opened on September 30, and the next day, his Panzers cut the principal supply route for Southern Front, the Kharkov-Zaporozhye railroad. Cherevichenko tried to restore the situation, desperately pulling his front back at an angle while pivoting on the coast, but nothing moved fast enough—not his orders, the response time of his individual armies' command structures, or the formations themselves. Nor did he have the reserves that might have stabilized the situation; he had already used them up in the attack. As 12th and 18th Armies tried to reestablish a defense line to the rear, Kleist's vanguard sliced through the seam between them. Combined with an attack along the northern coast of the Sea of Azov by the *Leibstandarte* and the XXXXIX Mountain Corps out of the Dnieper bridgehead at Berislav,[29] the Germans sealed off a sizable Soviet pocket, virtually all of 18th and 9th Armies, between Orekhov and the coastal town of Osipenko. On Southern Front's right flank, 12th Army managed to escape the trap, withdrawing to the northeast in order to maintain contact with the main body of Soviet forces. By the time the pocket was liquidated, the Germans took the surrender of 65,000 men.

Back in the Crimea, Manstein had some serious rethinking to do. He had taken Perekop, but he lacked the fresh formations to go any further. Although it says something about the quality of the Soviet army at this point in the war that it had been unable to defend itself even when plunked down in the middle of one of nature's most perfect bottlenecks, it was also clear to Manstein that there were a lot more Soviet divisions in the Crimea than he had been led to believe. Original reports had said three; there were at least seven by this time,[30] and another was on the way as the Soviets began to evacuate their forces by sea from besieged Odessa. The city would fall on October 16. The problem of force levels in the Crimea was, once again, an all-too-typical example of underperformance by German intelligence. Even worse, the map showed Manstein another bottleneck to the south of Armyansk, a series of finger lakes just north of the town of Ishun. The conformation of the terrain here would allow little more than single division assaults line abreast, without any mutual support between them or any kind of maneuver scheme. It was also clear by now that LIV Corps was a spent force. Losses in men and officers had been high, especially in the assault formations, and the commander of the corps, General Hansen, had seen signs of men and units cracking in the course of the battle.

The battle of the Sea of Azov and the fiasco at Perekop had at least made it clear to higher command echelons that 11th Army could either head east to Rostov or south to Crimea, but not both. Manstein now received unequivocal orders to enter the Crimea and clear out Soviet opposition there. The thrust toward Rostov would become the exclusive business of 1st Panzer Group, which now received the XXXXIX Mountain Corps as a permanent component formation.[31] Manstein's army, too, was beefed up for its new assignment. Along with XXX Corps (General Hans von Salmuth), which had been fighting along the Sea of Azov, and LIV Corps (now assigned an extra division, the 50th, but still en route from the successful fighting at Odessa), Manstein managed to wheedle another corps out of OKH (High Command of the Army), the XXXXII (consisting of the 24th and 132nd Infantry Divisions). He was equally successful with the Romanians, convincing Marshal Ion Antonescu to send the Romanian Mountain Corps (1st Mountain Brigade, 8th Cavalry Brigade, 19th Artillery Regiment) into the peninsula, although the transfer was only to take place once 11th Army had breached the northern bottleneck.[32]

It was therefore a greatly reinforced 11th Army that carried out Manstein's second attempt to break into and conquer the Crimea. The need to organize these new forces, as well as to amass supplies, meant that it did not begin until October 18. From the start, this was a murderous struggle that put the battle for Perekop in the shade. Manstein simply lined up three divisions abreast, 73rd and 46th (from LIV Corps) and 22nd (from XXX Corps), and sent them forward. The conformation of the terrain really wouldn't permit anything else. The rest of his divisions lay to the rear, not so much in support as simply in waiting for room to move. Under such unusual terrain conditions, there could be no real building of a *Schwerpunkt*, and the initial balance of forces (three attacking divisions against three defending ones) was typical of a purely frontal attack.

Soviet strength in the Ishun position now amounted to eight divisions and four cavalry brigades, and the Red Air Force was here in strength. Both were signs of how seriously Stalin took the threat to the Crimea. Soviet fighters and fighter-bombers made life miserable for the Wehrmacht in the first few days of the operation. Hastily dug rifle pits and trenches were the order of the day, not just for the front lines, but also for the rear echelons, even for the horses.[33] The Luftwaffe was there as well, in the form of Fliegerkorps IV, once again doing good work by pounding the Soviet front as well as supply lines, headquarters, and installations in the rear. Nevertheless, 11th Army was certainly not fighting with the air superiority to which Wehrmacht formations were accustomed.

Losses, once again, were far too heavy to sustain for long, especially among the officers. Manstein himself stated that he "was alarmed by the way fighting power deteriorated" and "whether the struggle for the narrow corridors could possibly succeed"[34] under such conditions. The reports from his divisional and regimental commanders were uniformly bad. Losses on the Soviet side, however, were just as high. This was narrow terrain, and German artillery took a heavy toll. The difficulty of positional fighting for the defender is often underestimated, but it can be murderous, especially if the enemy has superior artillery, and that was certainly the case here. As always, German advantages were not necessarily material—they had neither heavier guns nor longer range, for example—but were in areas such as flexibility, fire control, and liaison with the infantry.

There is no doubt the veteran German infantry had an advantage in this type of fight. It had, in a sense, been here before, in front of fortified lines like Modlin in Poland, the Maginot Line, or the Metaxas Line in Greece. Small unit tactics and unit cohesion had been well developed, and casualties had been light enough so far in the war that officers and men had bonded tightly, often for years. When company commanders were killed, sergeants calmly stepped in to take their place, and within a few days, several German battalions were actually being commanded by lieutenants.[35] The Soviet units in the Ishun position, by contrast, were hastily armed infantry levies that had neither the combat experience nor the cohesion that comes with it. Gradually, they began to wilt under superior German firepower and stronger small-unit fundamentals. The front line moved ever southward, hundreds of meters at a time, along what must have seemed to be little more than causeways.

By October 25, the German attack was nearly spent, but Soviet resistance was weakening perceptibly. The 51st Army had already fed its twelve divisions into the fight, and its reserves were gone. It was a typical sequence of events in a breakthrough battle of this sort. The Soviet front line had been under nearly constant bombardment from artillery and air, and its defensive positions between the lakes had nowhere near the strength of the fortifications along the Perekop line. Worst of all, each man and commander knew what lay behind him: a broad plain without a single intermediate position that the Germans could not immediately turn or bypass. This last factor, more than anything, may account for the absolute collapse of Soviet resistance in front of Ishun on October 28.

It had been a tough frontal assault, but Manstein had broken into the Crimea proper. During those agonizing twelve days, he had been ruthless in refusing to feed more divisions into the breakthrough phase. Although it had made the breakthrough perhaps more difficult than it might have been, it had also kept the other formations of 11th Army fresh for the pursuit phase.[36] German forces now set off on a swift, three-corps exploitation that rapidly overran the entire peninsula. On the left stood the newly arrived XXXXII Corps (170th, 73rd, and 46th Divisions), aiming toward the east, Feodosia, and eventually Kerch; in the center, XXX Corps (72nd and 22nd Divisions) drove almost straight south toward the Yaila Mountains and the coast[37]; on the right, LIV Corps (50th and 132nd Divisions) marched on Sevastopol. Progress was rapid. For the moment, Soviet command and control, not the Red Army's strong suit at this point of the war, had dissolved. Indeed, it wasn't entire German divisions carrying out the pursuit, but "small, improvised, motorized units"[38] that were nipping at the heels of Soviet formations as they fled south and east, and rain and muddy roads held them up far more than the Soviets. The centrally located city of Simferopol fell to a single motorized antitank (*Panzerjäger*) battalion on November 1, while another battalion took Eupatoria on the west coast.[39] The key southeastern port of Feodosia fell three days later. Kerch was taken on November 16, with the remnants of the retreating Russian 51st Army being evacuated by sea. With the exception of Sevastopol, Manstein had conquered the Crimea.

Of course, that was a big exception. In fact, taking Sevastopol was the *raison d'être* of the entire operation, and the campaign wouldn't be finished until it had fallen. Manstein's original operational plan had called for LIV Corps to carry out a coup de main, to "maintain the momentum of the pursuit, penetrate Sevastopol with the fleeing enemy, and take the fortress."[40] The rains and the softened roads prevented LIV Corps from generating enough speed or momentum to do the job, however, and the advance mobile detachments that had proven so effective at Simferopol and Eupatoria had nowhere near enough combat strength to blast though even a weakly held fortified line, which was the situation here in the last week of November. By November 8, LIV Corps's pursuit had come to a halt along a line some six miles north and east of the city. Both sides now began to reinforce, as Sevastopol became the focus of the campaign. German XXX Corps slid over from the east, throwing the Soviets back on Balaklava and tightening the ring around the city. The Soviets had already manned the outer works with tough marine detachments, and they were in the process of transferring forces into the fortress from Odessa and the Caucasus. By the time the siege proper began, the defenders numbered some 52,000 men and 170 guns, although many more were on the way.[41] It would take some time to form this fairly ragged horde of manpower into battle-ready units, but the Independent Coastal Army, as it was styled, had soon established a firm defense line around the Sevastopol perimeter.

Manstein reacted to his failure to seize Sevastopol on the fly by planning a deliberate assault. As 11th Army command was preparing for it, however, events intervened that probably doomed it from the start and should have led to its cancellation. First, there was the onset of winter, manifested in the Crimea by rains and then by icy cold and snow, the conditions that had been so ruinous to the Allied expeditionary force in 1854. The weather alone made it impossible to gather the artillery and launch the preliminary bombardment until mid-December. Second, events elsewhere on the front conspired to rob 11th Army of one of its divisions. Army Group South was then passing through its first real crisis of the campaign. The lead units of Kleist's 1st Panzer Group, the III Panzer Corps under General Eberhard von Mackensen, had captured Rostov, on the mouth of the Don, on November 19. Rostov was the gateway to the Caucasus, and the stakes were high for both sides. Mackensen almost immediately came under furious Soviet counterattacks, one of the first times the Red Army had been able to concentrate overwhelming combat power against a Ger-

On the surface, it was a master stroke for the Soviet command, who landed three complete armies under the very noses of the German garrison at Kerch. Certainly, it had been an impressive performance by a military establishment for whom the amphibious landing had never been a top priority. This wasn't simply a raid, or a diversion to draw the Germans away from Sevastopol. The Kerch-Feodosiya landing operation held a much higher priority for Stalin. It was part of the general Soviet counteroffensive that had begun in front of Moscow, but had gradually expanded to include the entire front, and it aimed at nothing less than the destruction of the German 11th Army and the reconquest of the entire Crimea.[50]

All that being said, the landings had been extremely confused affairs. This was years before Operation Overlord, and the Soviets possessed nothing in the way of the specialized equipment or techniques to make such complex operations run smoothly and safely. There were no dedicated landing craft for either infantry or tanks, nor had the Soviets ever given much thought to the sophisticated command and control techniques for making sure a land force was ready to fight once it got to shore. This was more like Gallipoli landing of 1915, with the main difference being the horrible weather: the Kerch landings had taken place in a Force 8 gale and the Feodosia operation in a Force 5, with temperatures of –20°C. It was all an improvisation, "astute, astonishing, and in parts brilliant,"[51] but an improvisation nonetheless, a deadly failing in an activity that requires precision planning and split-second timing. Soldiers and equipment were simply loaded onto anything that would float, including barges and naval vessels of various shapes and sizes, and then dropped off, quite often far from shore. Wading through icy water up to one's neck was a common experience, as was frostbite and even death by exposure. As a result, the soldiers comprising the first amphibious waves ashore did not exactly leap into action with a glint in their eyes. Mainly they shook themselves out into their formations, tried to stay warm, and huddled close to the shore. It is no surprise that of the ten landing sites for operation, local German garrison troops were able to smash all but four of them,[52] including a separate landing at Eupatoria that took place on January 5.[53]

Still, the Red Army was back in the peninsula in force. It had reconquered the Kerch peninsula, and its sudden arrival threw the German defenders in Kerch, the XXXXII Corps, into a panic. Its commander, General Hans von Sponeck, had just one division in the peninsula at the time (the 46th). Although he had been willing to hold his position against the Kerch landings and had a great deal of success containing them, the arrival of 44th Army at Feodosia, deep in his right rear and well placed to cut him off from home, cracked his nerve. He immediately radioed Manstein for permission to evacuate his exposed position. Manstein refused, ordering him to throw as many of the landings as he could back into the sea and to contain the rest. Three times Sponeck made his request, and three times Manstein refused. On his own initiative, Sponeck now ordered his command back to Parpach on the peninsula's narrow western neck. For 46th Division, it was an epic in its own way, a brutal forced march to the west in subzero temperatures and howling winds that resulted in thousand of frostbite casualties and necessitated the abandonment of virtually all of the heavy weapons and equipment. It nearly became a rout. December 29 was, according to chief of the German General Staff, General Franz Halder, "a very difficult day!"[54] The division survived the ordeal intact. Sponeck did not; he was immediately dismissed. Although he claimed the traditional prerogatives of a Prussian officer to make battlefield decisions as he saw fit, he was put on trial, found guilty of disobeying the explicit order of a superior officer, and sent to prison.[55]

Clearly, the assault on Sevastopol would have to be postponed until things cleared up in the east. Along with elements of the Romanian Mountain Corps and the 213th Infantry Regiment, which had to make a forced march of its own down from Genichesk, the 46th Division managed to establish a shaky defensive line west of Parpach, a position that stretched haphazardly on the diagonal from Stary Krim in the southwest to Ak-Monaj in the northeast. It was clearly untenable in the long run. Not only was it far too long and required too many troops to hold, but it also left Feodosiya, a good port that could be used to build up massive reinforcements, in Soviet hands. Manstein felt that it was necessary to launch an immediate counterattack with XXX Corps in order to reach a better line.

The two divisions of XXX Corps (132nd and 170th) now had to carry out yet another forced march. They crossed the Crimea from west to east in horrible weather and launched an assault on January 15. The attack caught the Soviets at the worst possible time, in the midst of preparing their own general offensive to break out of Kerch and reconquer the Crimea. The German attack drove them back in some confusion, retook Feodosiya on January 18, and won back the much shorter line of the Parpach bottleneck. It also caught the 44th Army commander, General Pervushin, out in the open during an air raid, wounding him seriously and killing several staff officers who happened to be with him.[56]

The situation in the Crimea was now a rough stalemate, with perhaps a slight advantage to the Soviets. The Germans still held the body of the peninsula and the Perekop and Parpach bottlenecks that governed access to it, but the Red Army held both strategic points on the periphery, Sevastopol and Kerch. Manstein still had Sevastopol under siege, but three Soviet armies now lay to the east, a large dagger preparing to strike him in the back. Although the Crimea clearly wasn't a place where "the issue of European hegemony" would be settled, as Hitler had once put it, it had come to occupy an increasingly important place in the strategic calculations of each side. For Stalin, this would be the first of the great annihilation battles in his plan to destroy the German invaders in 1942. For the Red Army, it would be another proof that the still relatively new doctrine of "deep battle," with attacks echeloned in depth, was a valid means of applying modern mechanized combat power. For the Germans, it was something else: an opportunity to prove, to themselves and to the rest of the world, the continuing vitality of their traditional way of war: *Bewegungskrieg*.

Both sides were therefore preparing new offensives, but the Soviets got theirs in first. With the Soviets making the short hop over from the Taman peninsula—the strait had frozen by now, so they simply marched by ice road—reinforcements continued to pour into Kerch, including tank brigades equipped with the T-34. Kozlov's orders were to achieve a breakout through Parpach toward Karasubazar, thirty miles west of Feodosiya, then follow it up with a deep strike into the rear of 11th Army, still concentrated against Sevastopol. Kozlov certainly had the necessary force for the job. He had a first echelon of two armies: 44th on his left (in the south) and 51st on the right (north), with 47th Army forming a second echelon in the junction behind them, ready to exploit wherever the first echelon had effected a breach. Once the German front had been penetrated, Kozlov was to "encircle and destroy the enemy Feodosiya grouping."[57] To stress the importance of the offensive, Stalin even dispatched one of his most trusted political cronies, Lev Mekhlis, to act as a formal Stavka representative. During his four-month stint in the Crimea, Mekhlis poked his nose into everything, ostentatiously wrote everything down (presumably to remind everyone that he was reporting to Stalin), and in general drove every officer in all three Soviet armies to distraction. That he was absolutely inept in battlefield matters, a "military illiterate,"[58] only made things worse. There would come a time in this war when Stalin allowed his generals to do their jobs, relatively free from political watchdogs, but that time was not yet.

On February 27, Kozlov launched his great offensive to the west. It went nowhere. Although no attack by three Soviet armies in such a narrow space could ever fail to do some damage, in operational terms, it gained nothing at all but high casualties and a seven-mile bulge in the northern portion of line. With Mekhlis urging him on, and no doubt uttering veiled threats against him, Kozlov tried again on March 13, and then again on March 26, and then again one final time on April 9, all to no avail. As the rest of the events in the spring would show, the Red Army was still feeling its way forward toward a greater professionalism, and there were moments of shocking incompetence. The April offensive in particular had been horrible, with tanks, guns, and trucks stuck in the mud and shells being carried forward by hand, with men and officers alike failing to take even the simplest precautions. Konstantin Simonov, the great *Krasnaya Zvezda* correspondent and one of the Soviet Union's best-known wartime writers, was shocked by what he saw in the 51st Army sector:

> Never before or since have I seen such a great number of people who were killed neither in battle nor in the attack, but rather in systematic artillery strikes. Without fail, every ten meters there was an individual subjected to that danger. The people were trampled and knew not what they were doing. There was neither a foxhole nor a slit trench around—nothing. Everything was taking place in these barren open spaces and mud, and it was absolutely open on all sides of the field.[59]

By April 15, Kozlov had withdrawn to his start line. Taking all three offensives together, his front had suffered a casualty rate of over 40 percent.

The German defenders, with XXXXII Corps on the left and XXX Corps on the right, had fought with their customary professionalism in the defense. Their Romanian allies, defending the extreme southern portion of the line, had also managed to hold firm. The perception of Romanian performance in the Crimea has been forever set in stone by the handful of pages devoted to the topic in Manstein's memoirs, *Lost Victories.* He describes them as primitive drones who had difficulty thinking for themselves and lived in constant fear of the Russians: "In difficult situations, this was liable to end in a panic."[60] In fact, they not only formed a major portion of 11th Army's fighting strength during the campaign, but they also performed quite credibly, and sometimes more than that. It was all the more impressive given another of Manstein's observations, this one accurate: their distressing lack of heavy weapons and antitank guns.

Manstein also had the Luftwaffe to thank for the defeat of the Soviet Kerch offensives. The German commitment of air power to the Crimea had grown steadily since the fall of 1941. It had expanded from a single understrength unit (Fliegerkorps IV under General Kurt Pflugbeil) to a dedicated improvised group, the Sonderstab Krim (Special Staff Crimea, under General Robert Ritter von Greim), and then to Fliegerführer Süd (Colonel Wolfgang von Wild).[61] Wild's command was on the spot during the Soviet offensives, and his aircraft (Ju-87 Stukas, Ju-88 and HE-111 bombers, and Bf-109 fighters) not only made the Soviets pay for every inch of ground taken, but also turned Soviet rear areas into an inferno. A crucial factor here was the extremely high density of the attacking Soviet force. Hitting a truck with a bomb, even from a Ju-87 dive bomber, is much easier when they are crammed bumper to bumper on an isolated supply road, and the same might be said of tanks fighting en masse in such tightly packed formations.[62]

Still, there were many anxious moments in the course of these three attacks. German troop strength was nowhere near large enough to guarantee success. On March 20, during Kozlov's second offensive, the situation looked grim enough for Manstein to commit the recently arrived 22nd Panzer Division in a counterattack to help shore up the faltering line. It was not only new to the theater, it was a newly formed unit equipped mainly with captured French equipment. It performed about as well as could be expected, rolling forward into battle unsupported by either neighboring infantry or airpower, getting stuck in the mud, and running into a buzz saw of Soviet fire: tank, antitank, and artillery. By the time it was pulled out of the line a few hours later, it had suffered a severe mauling, losing over thirty tanks. One bemused *Landser* of the 132nd Infantry Division had watched it drive by, with its men still wearing new, crisp uniforms and its tanks of French design. He dubbed it the "Eau de Cologne Division," because "it came from the west and evaporated quickly."[63] A chastened Manstein now did what he should have done when the division first arrived: he sent it to the rear for training and exercises.

Operation Trappenjagd: Clearing the Kerch Peninsula

Kozlov had failed, and now it was Manstein's turn. His task was no easier than that of his Soviet counterpart. In fact, it was exactly the same task—an unusual, perhaps unique, confluence of opposing missions. There have been any number of bottleneck battles like Parpach in the modern era. As rifles, machine guns, and rapid fire artillery came to dominate late nineteenth-century battlefields, the smartest thing a defender could do was to find some unflankable position, dig a line of trenches, and blast away at an onrushing enemy. These same Russians had occupied one of nature's most amazing choke points in May 1904, the Nanshan position, in the Russo-Japanese War.[64] They had eventually been turned out of it, but they had taken an immense toll on the Japanese assault force; indeed, a single regiment had held up and mauled the batter part of an army for three days. In the First Balkan War of 1912, the Bulgarian army had smashed the Turks at the battle of Kirk Kilisse, then pursued them in the direction of Constantinople. The Turks managed to recover their cohesion just in time to establish a defensive line at Chatalja, some twenty miles west of the great city. Fighting from entrenchments, and no longer needing to worry about a Bulgarian flanking maneuver—and Bulgarian infantry had proven themselves highly skilled at precisely that—the Turks managed to save their capital.[65]

The German task, then, was to do what the Soviets had failed to do: blast through the Parpach bottleneck. Given the force levels involved, with the Soviets outnumbering the Germans at least two to one in manpower and matériel, it should have been impossible. The position was strong up front and echeloned in great depth. The first obstacle an attacking force would hit was a great antitank ditch. The Soviets had dug it in 1941, and now they fortified it with concrete emplacements, not to mention a number of disabled tanks that were serving as protected machine gun posts.[66] Five miles behind it was a second position, the Nasyr Line, and behind that a third, the Sultanovka Line, based on an old fortification the Germans called the Turkish Wall, which guarded the peninsula at its widest point. Kerch was forty miles to the east of the front line—a long way indeed, given the strength of the Soviet defensive position in front of it.

Two factors need to be mentioned, however. First, with Hitler matching Stalin in his desire to clear the entire Crimea of enemy forces, German air strength here would eventually reach what we can only call startling heights. Hitler had taken a personal role in the dispositions by then, assigning all of Luftflotte 4 to the Crimea.[67] A Luftflotte was equivalent to a World War II American air force, and normally it took care of the airpower needs for an entire army group. It was an incredible mass of aircraft to devote to the tiny Kerch peninsula. The risk was obvious: while Manstein was attacking Kerch, Army Group South would be without any air support at all. Any Soviet offensive in the Ukraine could have serious consequences. As if deploying all of Luftflotte 4 weren't enough, Hitler also assigned Fliegerkorps VIII under General Wolfram von Richthofen to support the offensive in the Crimea. Richthofen, the cousin of Manfred (the world-famous Red Baron of World War I fame), was the Luftwaffe's recognized expert on ground support operations. His corps had formed the impenetrable umbrella of air power hovering over the Panzer divisions as they made their mad dash to the English Channel in May 1940. Since then, he had distinguished himself in the Balkans, as well as in the opening phases of Barbarossa. His ground attack aircraft would be sorely needed here, especially in the opening breakthrough phase, helping to "pull the infantry forward,"[68] in Manstein's own phrase, getting the assault divisions through a position they could never crack on their own.

The second advantage lay on the ground. Kozlov's offensives had ended with slight gains on the northern sector of the front, a bulge that pushed out toward the German lines. A practiced operational eye like Manstein's saw possibilities here. The Soviets would surely wish to protect their hard-won gains in the north. Aerial and ground reconnaissance soon confirmed that Kozlov had indeed deployed the mass of his forces here, leaving the southern portion of the bottleneck relatively weaker. Perhaps a breakthrough was possible in the south, and the more Manstein looked at the hundreds of aircraft landing in the Crimea, some operating from fields only miles behind his front, the better he liked his odds. Moreover, once a mobile force had broken through in the south, all that would be required was a two- to three-mile advance and then a short left hook to encircle the better part of two enemy armies: 51st, which had led Kozlov's assault in the north, and 47th, which had followed it up as the second echelon. With their front torn wide open and their best formations trapped in a *Kessel*, Manstein felt that the Soviets would simply fall apart. He had been in contact with them since the first day of Operation Barbarossa, and he knew that they were at their best in tightly controlled, highly choreographed operations. The rapid cut and thrust of maneuver in the open field wasn't their game, and if they tried it, they were in the peninsula in such densely packed masses that they'd probably just get in their own way. For all these reasons, Manstein went into the offensive with a certain amount of confidence, despite the gap in numbers. Opening on May 8, this was Operation Trappenjagd ("Bustard Hunt"), a reference to the harmless black game bird the inhabits the Crimea in great numbers. A U.S. general feeling the same way might have called it "Turkey Shoot."[69]

Trappenjagd was a well-planned operation, front-loaded and in that sense typically German. There was air power in abundance, and it had the elegant maneuver and the concentric nature that generations of German officers had considered the highest expression of *Bewegungskrieg*. Manstein's plan had XXXXII Corps (now under the command of General Franz Mattenklott) in the northern sector of the front. With only one German division (the 46th) and three Romanian ones, Mattenklott wasn't commanding the *Schwerpunkt* of the attack. In the days before May 9, however, the Germans had done a number of things to make it seem that he was, and to convince the Soviets to keep their right wing strong: fake artillery positions, obvious troop movements, false radio messages. It was in the south that the real blow fell. Here was the oversize XXX Corps under General Maximilian Fretter-Pico: the 28th Light Division, the 50th, 132nd, and 170th Infantry Divisions, and the by now much better drilled 22nd Panzer Division.[70] The plan was for the infantry to go in first, supported by heavy concentrations of air and artillery. It would cross the ditch and open a path for the Panzers. Once the 22nd Panzer Division had gotten past that first obstacle, it would wheel sharply to the left, heading north and driving to the coast, across the rear of the Soviet 51st and 47th Armies. The distances involved were so short that the Panzers could actually be accompanied by infantry every step of the way—another unusual aspect to this operation. If all went well, it would close the ring against the Soviet formations in the northern bulge on the second day of the offensive

Two last elements of Trappenjagd deserve mention. With 22nd Panzer Division and other elements of XXX Corps forming the *Kessel*, the danger existed that the Soviets would be able to reestablish a line at one of the defensive positions in the rear, either the Nasyr or the Sultanovka. To prevent that from happening, Manstein had formed a task force out of the 11th Army's few mobile units. Known as the Grodeck Brigade (for the colonel who commanded it), it contained a German reconnaissance battalion (the 22nd), the truck-mounted 6th Company from the Brandenburg Regiment, and the 560th Antitank Company, along with two complete Romanian motorized cavalry regiments (the Korne Detachment, also named for its commander, Colonel Radu Korne).[71] Its mission was the most exciting one of all. Once XXX Corps had made its wheel north, it was to peel off and drive as rapidly as possible to the east, breaking up any Soviet attempts to reinforce the

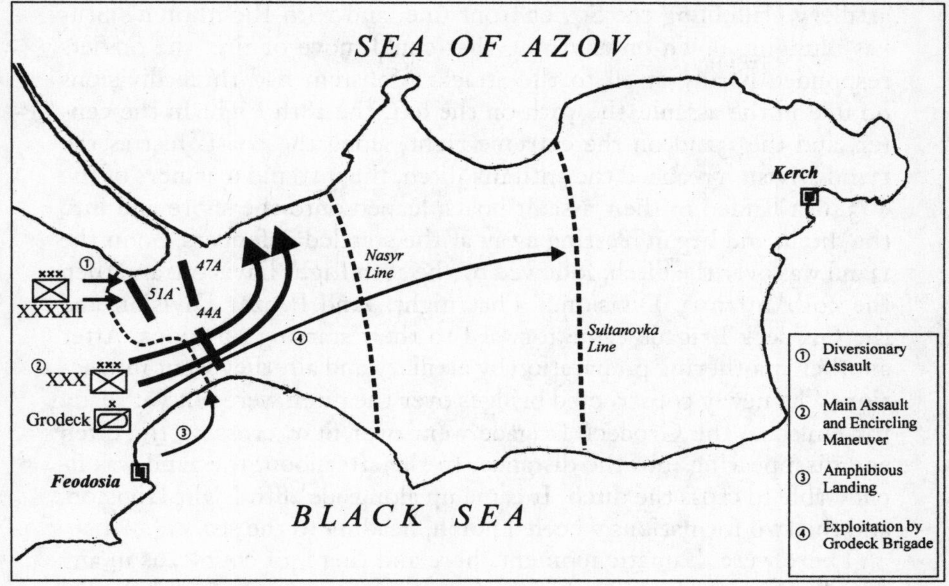

Map 3. *Bewegungskrieg* in the Kerch peninsula: Manstein's drive on Kerch, May 1942.

breakthrough sector, shooting up rear areas' installations, and slashing its way toward Kerch. Manstein's confidence that the Soviets would crumble once the damage had been done to their front was evident in the Grodeck Brigade's tiny size: all told, it amounted to barely more than a reinforced regiment in German terms, and it would be taking on forces the size of an army.

Finally, there was an unexpected and crafty opening, reminiscent of the glider assault on Eben Emael in the 1940 campaign. Early in the morning of May 9, a composite infantry battalion (the Vth of the 346th Infantry regiment) left the harbor of Dalniy Kamyshi, embarked on thirty assault boats. Its objective was a landing just behind the main Soviet defensive position, the great tank ditch running north-south through Parpach. As they disappeared into the night, an immense artillery barrage opened up along the entire front. It was 3:15 in the morning.[72] Ten minutes later, the ground attack started as wave after wave of German aircraft screamed overhead.

The actual operation was, in some sense, an anticlimax to the planning process, another hallmark of the way that German armies had traditionally made war. With a massive concentration of German artillery crumbling the Soviet front line, and with Richthofen's Stukas plunging down on anything that could move or fire, the Soviets responded hardly at all to the attack. Manstein had three divisions on line in the assault, the 50th on the left, the 28th Light in the center, and the 132nd on the extreme right, along the coast. Just as the 132nd Division reached the antitank ditch, the intrepid mariners of the V/346th landed in their assault boats, leaped onto the shore and into the ditch, and began blasting away at the startled defenders. Soon the 132nd was over the ditch, followed by the 28th Light Division, and then the 50th Infantry Division.[73] That night, 22nd Panzer Division and the Grodeck Brigade came forward to their starting positions. After another smothering preparation by artillery and air, they went into action. The newly constructed bridges over the ditch were not yet ready for tanks, so the Grodeck Brigade went over first, crossing the ditch and disappearing into the distance. In the afternoon, the 22nd was finally able to cross the ditch. It came up alongside 28th Light Division, and the two formations wheeled north, heading to the sea.

There were dramatic moments here and there, of course, as in any grand offensive. Just two hours after it got under way, 22nd Panzer came to a screeching halt as a sudden and immense downpour halted all movement across the front. It is events like these that surely have generals everywhere pondering the uncertainty of war. The 123rd Infantry Regiment (50th Infantry Division), on the extreme left of the attack, had been making good progress until the rains came and "turned the terrain into a quagmire within a few hours": "The Russian trenches and foxholes, where our troops and command posts were now located, abounded in knee-deep liquid mire. The swampy meadows in particular were so wet, that the companies located in craters and foxholes were actually lying in the water. . . . Everything was covered with wet clay: maps, telephone cranks, rations, etc. Everybody was covered with a thick layer of clay from head to toe."[74] The mud was more than an inconvenience: it rendered radios inoperable, and because the tanks had "destroyed almost all the telephone wires and had scattered them in the muck," more than a few units spent that evening out of command and control.

It finally stopped raining on the afternoon of the third day, however, and 22nd Panzer Division could finish its epic armored thrust into the rear of two Soviet armies. Indeed, the mud had held them tightly in place as much as it had gripped the Wehrmacht. A short left hook, and it was over. In two days, 22nd Panzer had covered perhaps seven miles, and yet it was one of the most successful Panzer drives of the war. With the Luftwaffe flying thousands of sorties per day over this relatively constricted battlefield, the *Kessel* became literally that: a seething cauldron of fire and destruction. The Germans soon took the surrender of thousands of men within the pocket.

As dramatic as these events had been, none of them can compare with the epic of the Grodeck Brigade. Even as its more pedestrian comrades were systemically closing the trap on 51st and 47th Armies, the brigade had already set out on one of the great pursuit drives of all time. Weaving its way through traffic, avoiding whatever it couldn't destroy and destroying whatever it could, Grodeck and his tiny mechanized column headed east. Blasting through the Nasyr Line and then the Sultanovka, it played a role in Trappenjagd out of all proportion to its tiny size. Campaign histories have a way of making pursuits sound like a simple drive in the country, but in fact the brigade was involved in numerous exchanges of fire, and overrunning rear installations is not without a certain danger to a force of thin-skinned vehicles. When it crossed the Nasyr line, it was simply lucky to come up against a portion of it that happened to be unoccupied; we know today that other sectors of the line were occupied at great strength. It ran out of luck once it crossed the Sultanovka line. It had arrived there quickly, late in the day on May 10, just the second day of the operation. It was low on fuel and out of ammunition. Air support proved to be a mixed blessing. It was so far out in front of the rest of the army that prowling Stukas mistook it for a hostile, bombed it, and severely wounded Colonel Grodeck; he would die several days later. Now under the command of the Romanian Colonel Korne, it got stuck once again in the mud, and there it sat as transport aircraft of Luftflotte 4 brought it ammunition by airdrop on May 11. It did not reach Kerch first, but it had paved the way for the rest of the army.[75]

By now, the entire 11th Army was in pursuit. Mattenklott's XXXXII Corps (with the VI Romanian Corps attached) liquidated the northern pocket and marched across its remains toward Kerch. XXX Corps did the same along the southern route. The Soviet Crimean Front had come apart. Those outside the pocket were running for the rear, trampling anything in their path, which often happened to be units being pushed to the front. Kozlov had been paralyzed by the breakthrough—and perhaps by the presence of one of Stalin's henchmen hovering over his shoulder—but he had proven himself utterly incapable of fighting a battle of maneuver. Of course, it didn't help that the initial German bombardment and air attacks had broken communications between his headquarters and the forward units, literally in the first minute of the offensive. Nor did it help when, minutes later, the Stukas pounded his own forward headquarters. The Luftwaffe, often unfairly tagged as a purely "tactical" air forces, here played the role for which it had been designed: fighting air war on the operational level (*operativer Luftkrieg*).[76]

Finally, what was Kozlov to make of orders from the Stavka on May 10 calling for him to pull 51st and 47th Army back behind the Sultanovka line? By that time, the two armies had already been trapped and the Grodeck Brigade was already over the Sultanovka. As to Mekhlis, he was beyond worthless; his presence was probably worth an army corps to the Germans. One historian described the battle as "Manstein versus Mekhlis," a fair assessment, and also no contest.[77] Stalin would demote him after the battle, but Mekhlis may well have deserved worse. Certainly, Stalin shot men on lesser pretexts during his bloody career.

By the time 11th Army got to the coast, it was witness to an amazing scene: the remnants of three modern armies huddled in masses on the shore, desperately trying to get aboard a vessel, any vessel, and make it to the far shore. The Germans dispatched weak Soviet rear guards one by one and clawed their way closer and closer to the beaches. If ever there was a time for the Luftwaffe, the moment when that incredible concentration of air power would truly justify itself, this was it. Unfortunately, it was also a moment in which disaster had apparently struck the Wehrmacht far to the north, where Marshal S. K. Timoshenko had just launched his huge armored offensive out of the Izyum bulge against German-held Kharkov. As a result, Hitler had recalled some of Richthofen's best units. German air activity in the Kerch peninsula slackened perceptibly, down from thousands to only hundreds of sorties. Richthofen himself was looking on, fuming, as one of the richest targets an airman could desire seemed poised to escape: "One isn't sure whether to cry or curse," he lamented.[78] It appeared the Soviets might slip the trap.

Fortunately for the Germans, Manstein still had his artillery. He wheeled the guns up to the cliffs, from which they had a clear line of sight to the port of Kerch and the waters below. He then laid on barrage after barrage against the evacuation fleet. With such a dense concentration of Soviet forces, vehicles, and ships, no round could be without effect. The slaughter was terrific, one of the most terrifying and decisive moments in the long history of the "King of Battle." Kerch itself would fall to the 170th Infantry Division on May 16. The mopping up in the city lasted another two days.

Operation Trappenjagd was over. There were still groups of Red Army soldiers in the caves along the peninsula's eastern coast. German and Romanian security units would hunt them down and root them out over the next months, part of a general antipartisan effort that the Axis had to mount in the coming months all over the Crimea, with all its attendant cruelties and atrocities.[79] Rapid victories in the German style always left such loose ends, as we have seen in Yugoslavia. Nevertheless, this had been one of the most decisive victories in the history of the German army. When all was said and done, Soviet losses had been in the range of 1941's great encirclement battles: 170,000 men, over 1,100 guns, and 250 tanks. It had taken just ten days to dismantle three Soviet armies. German losses were much lighter: 7,588 casualties total.

Although firepower had been essential from beginning to end—from cracking open the Soviet position at Parpach to engulfing the evacuation flotilla in a hail of fire—the real key to the German victory had been the operational maneuver. It used only a single Panzer Division, but then again, it didn't have all that far to go. Once the short left hook had taken place and the main Soviet force in the peninsula was marching into captivity, the Wehrmacht showed that it still possessed the traditional virtues of the German army: an officer corps that could be depended on to think for itself, manpower with a great deal of drive and energy, and a level of aggression that had served it well over the centuries. The lightning pursuit to Kerch had been an impressive thing, taking its place with Blücher's pursuit to the gates of Paris after Waterloo. Both times, calling on the troops for maximum exertion over a short distance had led to maximum reward.

Sevastopol, Again

All that remained was the fortress of Sevastopol, upon which Manstein could now concentrate the full weight of his massive artillery and airpower. He had gotten a good taste of the fortress's defenses last November (in the failed attempt to rush it), and last December (in the failed deliberate assault), and he had every expectation that the third round would be even tougher. Russian skill at siege and field fortification was proverbial, and that army of 106,000 men inside Sevastopol (the 1st Independent Coastal Army under General I. E. Petrov) hadn't been sitting idle for six months. New strongpoints, bunkers, tank traps, and minefields had sprung up in droves around the perimeter, comprising three distinct lines of fortification. The first stretched from

Balaklava on the Black Sea Coast in the south to the Belbek heights in the north; it ran through difficult, rough, and nearly trackless terrain. A second ran from Ljubimovka, bending sharply south along the Zapun Heights through a position known as Windmill Hill down to the sea. The third was a massive tank ditch protected by numerous strongpoints. Calling them "lines," however, does not do justice to their density. Some sectors of the front—the northern shore of Severnaya Bay, for example—were saturated with a bewildering number of heavily fortified concrete blockhouses and gun positions. With the entire defensive position tried together by underground tunnels, Sevastopol was as much labyrinth as fortress. Moreover, the Soviet Black Sea Fleet, under the command of Admiral F. S. Oktyabrsky, would play an extremely active role in the upcoming fighting—bringing in desperately needed supplies, lending its gunfire to the defense, and at times, as in December, contributing marine infantry to the defense of threatened strongpoints. Superlatives are always difficult things to prove in military history, but Sevastopol may indeed have been the "strongest fortress in the world" in 1942.[80]

Manstein knew what he needed to crack it open: a blast of "annihilation fire." By early June, Richthofen had his entire complement of air power back on line, the emergency at Kharkov having been mastered, as we shall see, and artillery pieces of every shape and size were pouring into the now-secure Crimea. They included the real monsters of the German arsenal: batteries of 305mm, 350mm, and 420mm howitzers. And, of course, there were the "big three," pieces so large that they fascinate even today: two 600mm guns code-named Karl, along with Dora, the world's largest artillery piece at 800mm. To say that Big Dora wasn't a mobile piece is to understate the matter considerably. It was a dinosaur. With a barrel ninety feet long and a bore of 31.5 inches, it could be transported only by rail, and to do so required twenty-five trainloads of equipment and a crew of 2,000. Its immense target profile to air attack made it unemployable under conditions of anything but absolute air superiority, and once emplaced, it wasn't likely to be moved all that often: it took up to six weeks to assemble. Although we might say that it made up in kick what it lacked in versatility, its entire operational career would be the thirteen days it spent in front of Sevastopol and the 48 rounds it actually fired in anger. It is probable that we shall not see its like again.[81]

There are few lessons to be learned from the attack on Sevastopol, Operation Störfang ("Sturgeon"), other than the obvious one: concentrating the firepower of an entire modern air force and artillery park against a relatively small target like Sevastopol can overcome even the toughest defenders and the most heavily fortified positions. We call it a "siege," but that is a misnomer. Instead, it was a large-scale assault. Since the advent of modern weaponry, armies had learned to use cities as strongpoints, unflankable and impossible to bypass, upon which they could base their defenses. Plevna in the Russo-Turkish War of 1877–1878, Port Arthur in the Russo-Japanese War, and Adrianople in the First Balkan War are all classic examples of the type.[82] In such a battle, neither side maneuvers, at least in the operational sense. Given enough firepower on the part of the attackers, the city will fall, as did all three of the above named. But with infantry having to go in and root the defenders out of each of their fortified positions, the casualties on both sides will always be enormous.

So it was with Sevastopol. The bombardment opened up on June 2. Richthofen's Fliegerkorps VIII had been beefed back up to over 600 ground support aircraft, and there were 611 artillery pieces crammed into a front of just twenty-one miles, for a density of twenty-nine guns per mile. It was by a considerable margin the greatest concentration of fire the Germans had yet managed to achieve. It turned Sevastopol and environs into a flaming ruin, and it kept going nonstop for much of the next month. "The scene before us was indescribable,"[83] wrote Manstein, and Richthofen would later call describe it as a "sea of flames."[84] Individual Soviet positions and bunkers, to which the Germans gave names like "the Bastion," "Molotov," and "Siberia," might have been as strong as the modern art of fortification and Russian genius could make them, but they were also stationary, and very large, targets for German fire. The same might be said for the two monstrous forts known as Maxim Gorky I (three miles north of Sevastopol) and Maxim Gorky II (a mile and a half to the south of the city), each of which consisted of two heavily armored turrets housing two 305mm guns apiece.[85] A single shell from Dora, for example, seems to have destroyed an entire ammunition dump constructed out of ninety feet of rock on the north shore of Severnaya Bay. Even the comprehensive system of underground tunnels and bunkers that linked these positions together, and that housed the civilian population of the city during the fighting, offered limited protection against the storm unleashed by the Germans.

The issue was therefore never in doubt. Once again, as in December, the main attack came from LIV Corps in the north, leading off on June 7 and driving toward Severnaya Bay, while XXX Corps mounted a secondary thrust in the southeast. Between them, the Romanian Mountain Corps was to carry out a holding operation in the center and guard the inner flank of each of the neighboring German corps. The divisions of LIV Corps ground their war forward during June against tenacious Soviet resistance. By June 13, forward elements of the German 22nd Infantry Division had reached the north shore of the bay, clearing a number of the fortifications in this area, including Fort Stalin, the same position that had held up its attack in December. Its neighbors on the right, 24th and 132nd Infantry Divisions, would clear the entire shore by June 2. Meanwhile, in the south, XXX Corps had successfully fought its way up to its first objective, the Zapun heights, the second of Sevastopol's three defense lines.

The stage was now set for the climax of the Sevastopol campaign. The orthodox solution at this point would have been for Manstein to shift the weight of his artillery and aerial bombardment to XXX Corps in the south, allowing it to close up with LIV Corps and invest the inner ring of Sevastopol's fortifications. That would take time, however. Because of the poor state of lateral communications in the area, it might require as much as two weeks. This was time that 11th Army simply didn't have, not with Operation Blue revving up to the north.

Manstein's solution was a classically German one: an elegant operational maneuver designed, in his words, to "unhinge" the entire Zapun line. Just after midnight on June 28–29, elements of 50th Infantry Division (LIV Corps) carried out a daring amphibious crossing of Severnaya Bay on one hundred assault boats, seizing the steep southern bank in their initial rush.[86] The landing came as a complete surprise to defenders of the fortress, and resistance, for once at Sevastopol, was light. By daybreak, 50th Division lay just outside the town, well inside the Zapun position. In the course of the day, it would overrun the Inkerman Ridge and the old Malakov bastion, positions that had been so crucial to the defense of the city in 1855. Meanwhile, to the south, XXX Corps launched its assault on Zapun Heights. Honors here have to go to the 170th Infantry Division, which achieved the decisive breakthrough, rolled up the Soviet line to north and south, then thrust far to the west against an increasingly demoralized defense.

Manstein's stroke had fatally compromised Sevastopol's innermost defensive ring and sealed the fate of the city. With 11th Army outside the gates, and with air and artillery continuing to chew up the already pulverized rubble, the Soviet commanders in Sevastopol received Stalin's orders late on June 30 to evacuate the city. The men of the 1st Independent Coastal Army, who had done their duty and then some in the previous month against monstrous odds, weren't so lucky. Their orders were to evacuate to the west, to the wedge-shaped Chersonese peninsula, and there await evacuation by sea. With German troops and artillery batteries crawling all over the coast, however, the promised ships never came, and as wave after wave of German attack aircraft appeared overhead, Soviet casualties were monstrous. Over 30,000 men would go into captivity here, along with another 60,000 captured within Sevastopol itself. The German 11th Army entered the city on July 1, and General Manstein heard on the radio that same evening the satisfying news that the Führer had decided to promote him to field marshal. He had done everything that Hitler had commanded. He had fought a brilliant battle of annihilation, he had reduced a powerfully defended enemy fortress, and, not incidentally, he had overseen the slaughter of the vast majority of the Crimea's Jewish population. By Nazi lights, Manstein was a model field marshal.

The Great Spring Recovery

The fighting in the Crimea was over, although there were the typical loose ends. Many Soviet soldiers were in still in the underground system of catacombs that linked the city to the various defensive bastions and had to be dug out. Although these engagements have barely made the history books, they could be surprisingly fierce, and it would be months before they were over. Soviet casualties in the fight for Sevastopol had been nearly 100 percent: 90,000 prisoners and perhaps another 50,000 battle casualties out of a total strength on the eve of the battle of some 150,000 men. German casualties, too, were extremely heavy. The Germans admitted at the time to a total of 24,000 casualties (4,000 killed, 18,183 wounded, 1,591 missing), with another 8,000 or so Romanian, but almost no specialist in the field believes this figure. The Soviets claimed 150,000 Germans dead; one reliable source says 75,000, another highly respected authority puts it at 100,000, and still another mentions 25,000—a high cost indeed for a field marshal's baton and the special campaign shield ("Krim," Crimea) awarded to participants in the fighting.[87]

The cost, although high, certainly didn't come as a surprise to German officers. If the Kriegsakademie had taught one thing to its graduates over the years, it was that a *Stellungskrieg*, a static war of position without maneuver by either side, would by definition be a slow, bloody, and attritional struggle. That's why German armies had traditionally tried to avoid them over the centuries, and why German officers believed that relatively few useful lessons could be drawn from them. Indeed, one might say that the single element of *Bewegungskrieg* employed in the Sevastopol fighting, the small nighttime crossing of Severnaya Bay by a mere handful of battalions, had been the decisive factor in German success, cracking open a position that had held up an entire army for a month.

Far more noteworthy to the German military mind was the Kerch campaign, Manstein's bustard hunt. Here the Wehrmacht had launched an offensive according to its predilections and its training, employing operational-level maneuver to bring decisive victory to a numerically inferior force in record time and with relatively few casualties. It was a classic example of *Bewegungskrieg*, the war of movement, and worth including in any list of the German army's greatest triumphs, along with Rossbach, Leuthen, and Königgrätz. It tore apart no fewer than three Soviet armies, took a huge bag of prisoners, and forced the rest into a hasty, Dunkirk-style evacuation on the fly—just the sort of improvised operation that caused the Red Army and Navy, not to mention the entire paranoid Soviet system, the most trouble. The Soviet armies at Kerch joined a long list of armies opposing the Wehrmacht, mainly the British, who had been booted off a mainland position while under fire.

The Wehrmacht had not only been reborn, so soon after its near-death experience of the previous winter, but it had reestablished contact with its most fundamental tradition. It proved that it could still launch rapid and decisive campaigns of movement and maneuver; it could still attack in the grand style. Its default setting was *Bewegungskrieg*, an inherently aggressive method of warmaking. "Establishing a secure line is only to be regarded as a temporary step on the way back to an aggressive war of movement," wrote the *Militär-Wochenblatt* in early 1942, while German armies in the east were still fighting for their lives. Even at the time, German formations were expected to conduct defensive actions in the spirit of the offensive, "characterizing them by a series of successful counterattacks."[88] The Wehrmacht might lose the war in the Soviet Union, but it was going to do so in a war of maneuver, not sitting in trenches or hunkering down behind a fortified line.

Within the army, the exultation over Kerch rivaled in some ways that of the campaigns in Poland and France, or the great victories in the opening phase of Barbarossa. There was the same sense of exhilaration, along with a certain smugness at having been proven right after all. The May 22 issue of the *Militär-Wochenblatt*, published even before the full extent of Manstein's victory at Kerch was clear, called it nothing less than a "great breakthrough battle." In this "first great victory of the spring," the Wehrmacht had done in a week what the

Soviet Army couldn't do in months of combat: break through the Parpach bottleneck. It had destroyed the "hopes of our enemies that the long, hard winter had disturbed the offensive strength" of the German army. Even though it was hiding behind "thousands of mines and a wide antitank ditch," a massive Soviet force had been "surrounded and utterly annihilated" (*eingekesselt und restlos vernichtet*) at Ak Monaj. The haul—68,000 men, 235 tanks, and 864 guns—recalled the "great *Kesselschlachts* of the autumn."[89]

The usually rather staid journal was just getting started, however. By the time the next issue had arrived, on May 29, the great breakthrough at Kerch had become "the first annihilation battle of the spring." The use of the term *Vernichtungsschlacht* is significant. It had a particular meaning in German military circles and could be safely applied to perhaps a half-dozen battles in German history. Only now had more precise reports come in, detailing "the full extent of the annihilation that had fallen in on the enemy": 170,000 men, 284 tanks, and 1,397 guns. The Soviet command would never have crammed such an immense force into such a tiny space unless it had big plans for it: a breakthrough, a drive north to Perekop, a death blow to the entire German southern front. Now most of that force was gone, encircled almost effortlessly. Those who escaped immediate destruction had been ordered to retreat. "It was too late, however." Pursued tirelessly by the victorious attackers, the Soviet armies in Kerch had been completely destroyed, although the Soviet had apparently made every effort to save "their heavy artillery—and their commissars."[90]

Kerch, then, was nothing less than a moral tonic for the Wehrmacht, at the precise moment one was most needed. As another staff officer put it, "Kerch had been in German hands in 1941. Unfortunately it was lost again. The tough winter, with its thousandfold hardships and pitiless cruelties, permitted us no opportunity to retake this highly valuable region. At the same time, the unified propaganda of our enemies bellowed ceaselessly to the whole world, 'Germany is at the end of its strength! No more German offensives! The initiative now lies with the Russians!'" That was then, however. Now, "suddenly, the German soldier has stood up in all the shining brilliance of his old combat strength." In preparing and conducting the attack, the German command been in "classic form": "It was exemplary: the extraordinary concentration of strength on the right wing, where the Schwerpunkt lay; the immediate exploitation of the breakthrough to envelop surround one wing and roll up the other; the rapid formation of a *Kessel* and at the same the tireless pursuit by mobile forces. With the best staff work and first-rate troops, the attack went off like a precision watch." The result was that "a force of vastly inferior numbers smashed the mass of three Russian armies." The western allies had to be drawing Conclusions from what they had just seen, especially the German display of air superiority. The Wehrmacht had had a hard winter, it was true, but Kerch showed that it had regained its old moral strength. At the start of a year that promised to be decisive, that was good news for Germany, but "a bitter lesson" for its foes.[91]

In the grand scheme of things, the Kerch offensive was not the largest battle on the eastern front, nor did it decide the war one way or another. Even on its own terms, any objective analysis has to admit that a crucial factor in the victory was what one modern authority has called the "bureaucratized, ideological, and unprofessional" nature of the Soviet command structure.[92] Still, viewed within the context of its time and not from hindsight, the struggle for this small peninsula within a peninsula on the extreme southern end of the front takes on new significance. Screened through the *mentalité* of the German officer corps, the real meaning of the Kerch operation is plain. As the summer of 1942 arrived, the Wehrmacht had given dramatic proof to the world that it could still bring it. It could still speak its own "unique language." The war might already have been lost, but it was far from over.

Kerch had made that point strongly, but for those who were perhaps not listening, there would be another, even greater, demonstration. For at the very moment that Manstein and the German General Staff were toasting their decisive victory at Kerch, a vicious tank battle was raging to the north, near the German-occupied city of Kharkov.

3

The Wehrmacht Reborn

Annihilation at Kharkov

The prehistory of the battle of Kharkov—the why, when, and where it was fought—is one of the most interesting episodes in the entire history of the war. In the spring of 1942, the two dictators on the eastern front, the small circle of advisors around each man, and both sets of highly trained professionals on the rival general staffs, were all staring at the same map. On it, they could study the roughly 1,700 miles of front over which their armies were then in contact, running from the port of Murmansk in the Arctic to the Crimea, a vast stretch divided into "army groups" for the Germans and "strategic directions" for the Soviets.

It was an extremely complex picture. The front was not a smooth one, anchored on natural terrain features like rivers or mountains. It was instead a jagged sawtooth, replete with salients, protrusions, and panhandles of every description. The Wehrmacht, for example, occupied a hooked salient of such extreme severity at Rzhev that fairly large forces had to hold a front facing westward—that is, toward Germany.[1] Southwest of Rzhev, there was a needle-thin German penetration into Soviet-held territory ending at the town of Belyy, an interesting defensive problem indeed. There was even a pocket of German troops surrounded at Demyansk, southeast of Lake Ilmen, although the Germans had been able to run enough supplies into the pocket by air and the situation seemed stable enough on the ground that there was little panic in German headquarters.[2] South of Leningrad, the Germans, too, had put a noose around Soviet 2nd Shock Army. Things looked bad here, but in April, the Soviet high command would send one of its few proven talents, General A. A. Vlasov, into the pocket to take charge, so there was some confidence that it, too, could hold out.[3] This ragged line was not a result of calm reflection or scientific strategy. No rational commander would have chosen such positions. Instead, it simply happened to be where two tottering armies had collapsed at the end of their long and bitter struggle during the winter of 1941–1942.

As they surveyed the map, interestingly enough, the leaders of both armies were looking for the same thing: an opportune place in which to launch an offensive. Both weighed the possibility of a grand operation into or around Leningrad, and rejected it: too little room for maneuver; too many swamps; too many forests; too many forces already encircled by the enemy. You couldn't breathe in that theater. Moscow? After the experience of the last winter, the Germans certainly weren't biting. One suspects that they were ready to attack anywhere but Moscow, although the Soviets still believed that they would take one more lunge and had placed large forces in readiness to meet it. The south? Perhaps, thought Stalin. Here there was open room for the massive armies he was beginning to deploy, terrain that was nice and flat, and limited possibilities for the Germans to anchor a defense, the result of the conformation of the great river bends of the Dnieper, Donets, and Don. Although many on his staff were urging caution, Stalin also had a fire-breathing commander: General S. K. Timoshenko, who was begging him for another crack at the Wehrmacht.

On the other side of the hill, it is interesting to note that we can say virtually the same things about Hitler. The south was where the mass of the Soviet Union's natural resources were, and perhaps *Lebensraum* for German colonists. The latter was a long-term project, something that could be dealt with after the war, whereas the former was much more urgent. For Hitler, the coal and industry of the Donets Basin (or "Donbas") and the oil of the Caucasus seemed to be the key to smashing Soviet resistance. Seize them, he argued, and the Soviet Union would collapse, while Germany could use the resources to fight the western allies indefinitely. He wasn't alone in this notion. His chief of the General Staff, General Franz Halder, supported it, as did officers up and down the chain of command. For the Wehrmacht, the south had something to offer beyond industry and oil: good tank country, wide-open spaces where a Panzer commander could roam, if not completely free, then at least relatively unfettered. Whatever the position of the staff, Hitler surely knew that he could also count on the generals in the field. Fire-breathing commanders chomping at the bit for permission to launch an offensive? Hitler had a stable full of them. That had been the hallmark of the German officer corps for a long, long time.

For both sides, the south it was. But where, exactly? The answer that each military establishment produced in May 1942 was a sign, perhaps, of how congruent all western armies had become since the Industrial Revolution. It might also be a reflection of similarities in the professional curriculum and training regimen for staff officers in both the Red Army and Wehrmacht. It may simply have been obvious. At any rate, the brain trust of these two great mechanized armies stared at the incredibly convoluted map in front of them, with all of its twists and turns, and uttered the same obscure phrase: "the Izyum salient."

We might also note that the Germans and the Soviets were in agreement on a number of other things at this point in the war. Both felt that the enemy had been badly mauled in the previous campaigns. Both were certain that the other side had been down, quite literally, to his last battalion, and that they themselves had come within an inch of his utter overthrow. All that had been required was one well-timed blow. Most German officers, staff and field alike, felt that victory had been there for the taking in the late fall. They would fill the memoir literature of the postwar era with that view, arguing vehemently of how they could have grasped it, if it were not for this or that wrong-headed decision by Hitler. For the Soviets, the opportunity had come during the winter, during Stalin's first strategic offensive. Of course, each side was badly underestimating the recuperability and strength of the other. Finally, both felt that 1942 would see the end of the war, that it would be a year of decisive and complete triumph. Indeed, Halder, had already called it "the great year of decision" (*der grosse Entscheidigungsjahr*).[4] So much for current buzzwords about warfare's "asymmetry." Sometimes it seems all too symmetrical.

Mutual Planning for Kharkov

The Izyum salient was another of those strange eruptions in the front as the 1942 campaigning season got under way.[5] A salient usually appears on the map as a rounded bulge jutting into the enemy line, but this one was much more extreme than that. In fact it was nearly square, 60 miles wide and 60 miles deep. Soviet forces in the bulge were facing simultaneously south (from Bogorodichnoye heading west to Lozovaia), west (from Lozovaia heading north to Bereka), and north (Bereka heading back to the Donets at Lekowka). The German-held towns of Balakleya in the north and Slavyansk in the south formed the shoulders of the bulge in the north and south, respectively, and the industrial city of Izyum on the northern Donets was centrally located along its base.[6]

The origins of the salient were to be found in Stalin's decision to expand his Moscow counteroffensive in early 1942 to a general, theaterwide offensive designed to smash the entire Wehrmacht once and for all. On January 18, three Soviet armies crashed into the increasingly tenuous German defenses near Izyum. It was a sharp blow, with Soviet 6th Army on the right, 57th Army in the center, and 9th Army on the left, and it tore open a great hole in front of the German XI Corps defending the Donets River line.[7] It also sliced open the seam between the German 6th and 17th Armies. For the German high command, this was just another in a series of apparently endless emergencies. Both German armies were still passing through the winter crisis, and behind them there were no reserves—not a single fresh formation in the order of battle to plug the hole. Halder's diary conveys the dark mood of those days:

> *January 19th:* The great attack that had been predicted against Kharkov has flared up against the northern front of the 17th Army and at several places along 6th Army's front. The most difficult position is on the seam of the 6th and 17th armies. There are going to be difficult days ahead until the tension is overcome.
>
> *January 20th:* The attack against Army Group South (17th Army) is leading in part to a very difficult situation. Above all, we have no answer to the enemy's tanks.
>
> *January 21st:* 17th Army in a terrific mess (*grosse Schweinerei*). In three days of fighting, front broken at two places (Izyum and the border with 6th Army). These two partial breakthroughs have now united into one great one.[8]

By January 21, the Soviet advance was threatening the entire position of the German army in the south. The defenders were, in the words of one German participant, "fought out, incapable of maneuver, not outfitted for the winter, hungry, and freezing. They had only one thing to throw against the enemy: their bravery. By itself, it wasn't enough."[9] By January 23, the Soviets had created a fifty-mile hole in the German defenses along the Donets. Two days later, they overran the 17th Army's main supply depot at Lozovaia (although the pickings here were fairly meager by this point in the winter fighting), and by January 28, their spearhead was a mere twelve miles from Dnepropetrovsk, the railhead for all three German armies over the Dnieper.[10]

Like all of the Soviet operations that first winter, however, the exploitation of this breakthrough was ultimately unsatisfying. Two factors in particular worked against the Red Army in virtually every one of these winter battles: the limited mobility of the exploiting formations, and the underdeveloped state of its logistical net. The second echelon in this offensive was a motley collection of units with varying degrees of mobility, consisting mainly of ski troops and three cavalry corps (the 6th, 5th, and 1st).[11] It was able to make local gains, but the Soviets found that even severely mauled German units were able to form enough platoon- and battalion-sized battle groups (*Kampfgruppen*) to reform a tenuous but cohesive defensive line.[12] They held long enough for mobile formations of the 1st Panzer Army, especially the III Panzer Corps, to rush to the north and slam into the southern flank of the Soviet offensive. Simultaneously, the German XI Corps launched an offensive of its own out of Dnepropetrovsk with a motley collection of newly arrived units, including security formations, several Romanian divisions, and a handful of German regiments that were in the process of reorganizing.[13] It pushed the Soviet spearhead back from Dnepropetrovsk and ended the crisis. The fighting died down by October 2. The principal result of this "Barvenkovo-Lozovaia operation," as the Soviet high command would eventually call it, was typical: yet another salient protruding into German lines to no real strategic effect.

In common with all salients, the Izyum bulge offered both sides temptations and opportunities, dangers and advantages. Stalin and Timoshenko could view it as a great sally port jutting far inside German lines. For an army obsessed with fighting "deep battle," Izyum had to seem like a perfect place from which to launch an offensive: Red Army formations deployed inside the salient were already well into the depth of Army Group South, threatening the German-held city of Kharkov. Even a short breakthrough and a hop to the west, to Krasnograd for example, might well have strategic impact. Once again, we can say the same for Hitler and his General Staff. To an army that sought, above all, to fight the *Kesselschlacht*, Izyum had to have been an especially tempting target. Even before the shooting started, Soviet forces within the salient were already kesseled on three sides.

It is no surprise, therefore, that March 1942 saw both armies planning an operation in the area. Timoshenko, the commander of both the Southwestern Strategic Direction and the Southwestern Front, managed to convince Stalin that there was great potential to a bold offensive stroke by the entire direction. It would smash Army Group South in its entirety, drive for the middle Dnieper, and recover the cities of Gomel, Kiev, and Cherkassy. All he needed, he told the dictator in a

March 22 report, were a few reinforcements: thirty-odd rifle divisions (amounting to 250,000 fresh troops) and twenty-seven or twenty-eight tank brigades.[14] Stalin liked the first part of Timoshenko's argument, the one about a dramatic offensive smashing the entire German position in the Ukraine, but he probably laughed when he read the second. If he had twenty-eight fresh tank brigades sitting around unused, the war would have been over and he'd be sitting in Berlin. He ordered Timoshenko instead to seek opportunities for limited operations within the region, part of a series of local offensives that Stavka was encouraging up and down the entire front: a plan for Leningrad and Volkhov Fronts to relieve the 2nd Shock Army, kesseled by the Germans south of Leningrad, for example, or one by Northwest Front to liquidate the German II Corps, cut off in the Demyansk Pocket.

It was at that point that Timoshenko and his chief of staff, General I. K. Bagramyan, began considering an offensive out of the Izyum salient. A smaller operation would be a prudent response to Stalin's request, and it could be carried out with a more realistic commitment of force. It still offered the possibility for a decisive victory, however, and was intended as such from the start. It was no simple spoiling attack. The operational plan, drawn up first on March 30 and then finalized on April 10, described the intent of the operation quite explicitly: to "encircle and destroy the enemy Kharkov grouping."[15]

To that end, Southwestern Front would undertake concentric operations aiming at a double envelopment of German forces at Kharkov.[16] The northern wing of the encirclement would consist of 28th Army (General D. I. Riabyshev), attacking out of the Volchansk bridgehead over the Donets River, a convenient bulge in the lines northeast of Kharkov. Riabyshev would mass his shock group, consisting of six rifle divisions and four tank brigades on a narrow front, just twenty kilometers wide, against isolated portions of the German XVII Corps (German 6th Army). Once 28th Army had smashed through the German lines and opened a breach, a second echelon consisting of 3rd Guards Cavalry Corps would exploit the gap, wheel left, and encircle Kharkov from the north. At the same time, in the south, the eight rifle divisions and four tank brigades of Soviet 6th Army (General A. M. Gorodniansky), along with an ad hoc unit that was designated "Group Bobkin," would crash through the defenses of the German VIII Corps. Group Bobkin was a mixed formation consisting of two rifle divisions and a cavalry corps, named for its commander, General L.V. Bobkin, who had distinguished himself in just this sort of mobile action in the winter fighting. As in the north, mobile units would stand ready to exploit.

Once 6th Army and Bobkin had penetrated the German position, the 21st and 23rd Tank Corps were to pour through the hole, wheel sharply to the right, and link up with 3rd Guards Cavalry Corps coming down from the north, completing the encirclement. Exploiting through the hole punched by the Bobkin group would also be 6th Cavalry Corps, its mission to head due west, seize Krasnograd, and form the outer ring of the encirclement, defending the newly formed Kharkov pocket against any German relief attempts from the outside. Meanwhile, Timoshenko's third large formation, the Southern Front, would have the mission of defending the left (southern) flank of the advance against any German attacks. To that end, it had 57th Army in front of Lozovaia and 9th Army guarding Barenkovo, both facing south.

As always, both Stalin and the Stavka tinkered with Timoshenko's original conception. There were some, including the Chief of the Soviet General Staff, Marshal B. M. Shaposhnikov, who thought he was mad, cramming such large forces into such a constricted region and attacking out of "a sack." Others, such as the commander of 28th Army's neighbor on the right, General K. S. Moskalenko of the 38th Army, were dubious about Timoshenko's choice of army to lead the northern attack. The 28th Army was green, newly formed and absolutely untried in combat. There had once been another 28th Army, but it had been encircled and destroyed south of Smolensk, courtesy of Panzer Group Guderian, in August 1941. The newly reconstituted 28th Army had been formed in November, but it had been sitting in the reserve since then. Moskalenko's divisions, by contrast, had been in contact with the Germans for months and knew a great deal about their routines, procedures, and fighting techniques. As deputy commander of the Soviet 6th Army, he had helped to plan the successful Barenkovo-Lozovaia operation in January. His protests to Timoshenko seemed to have an effect, resulting in a broadening of the original attack in the north. Rather than launch the assault alone, 28th Army would now be supported on either flank, with 21st Army on its right and 38th Army on its left. Likewise, the timetable changed as planning went forward. Timoshenko originally scheduled the offensive for May 4, but the ever-present difficulty of assembling assault forces over such vast distances led him to push it back to May 12.[17]

While all these preparations were going forward, the Germans were formulating their own offensive plans for the salient. By March, Hitler and the German General Staff were deeply involved in the planning process for Operation Blue, the great offensive in the south planned for June. It aimed to strike a killing blow at twin targets: the Soviet war economy and Soviet forces in the south. It would drive into the Donbas, seize the great bend of the Don River, cross it, and take the city of Stalingrad, then wheel right and drive deep into the oilfields of the Caucasus. Before the mass of Army Group South could launch its drive to the east, however, the Wehrmacht had to clear up two annoying situations: first of all, 11th Army had to conquer the Crimea; second, 6th Army and 1st Panzer Group had to flatten out the Izyum salient. The latter action would move the start line for the offensive up to the Donets River line, thus easing problems of deployment and supply. It would also free up large numbers of German formations that were presently tied down around the perimeter of the bulge.

This was the rationale behind Operation Fridericus ("Frederick"), first conceived in March, and then worked and reworked over the next two months. It, too, was a response to the unique allure of a salient. In the case of the Izyum bulge, all the Wehrmacht had to do was launch two relatively short operations against the base of the salient. While a thrust from the northern anchor at Balakleya drove to the south, one from the southern anchor at Slavyansk would head north. The two simultaneous thrusts would meet in the middle, seal off the bulge, and trap all Soviet forces inside. The southern thrust would be the mission of "Army Group von Kleist" (Field Marshal Ewald von Kleist). This was a temporary command comprising both 1st Panzer Army (also under Kleist's command) and 17th Army (General Richard Ruoff); it had originated during the winter crisis when it looked like the two formations were about to be cut off by Soviet forces driving on Dnepetrovsk. The northern drive would be in the hands of Paulus's 6th Army, attacking southward out of Balakleya, and reinforced with several Panzer divisions for the purpose.

Like Timoshenko's plan, Operation Fridericus went through several iterations before it was finalized. The original plan, soon to be known as Fridericus I, emerged from the staff of Army Group South, commanded now by Field Marshal Fedor von Bock.[18] Hitler had sacked the former commander of Army Group Center after the Moscow debacle and brought him back, in a different but still decisive theater, just a month later. It must have been a bewildering sequence of events for this ambitious man. Although the jab from the south seemed eminently feasible, Bock was concerned about 6th Army's descent from the north. The principal problem here was the uncooperative geography of the Donets River, which described a small, sharp loop just west of Izyum. As a result, the German-Soviet front line in this sector meandered along both banks of the river. The straightest shot in operational terms would be for the two German pincers to drive deep into the Soviet position, with 6th Army heading southeast and 1st Panzer Army northeast, and then linking up somewhere on the far side of the Donets, perhaps along the Oskol River. Such a move would have the advantage of taking the Donets out of play early in the operation. Unfortunately, it practically invited a Soviet counterstroke along 6th Army's open eastern (left) flank as it wheeled to the south. Bock had been in charge of the German drive on Moscow last December, and he had no intention of leaving himself vulnerable to a blow from the flank. His plan, therefore, called for a much shorter strike, using the Donets itself as a flank guard, with 6th Army marching down along its western (right) bank. Even this course was not as simple as it sounded, however. Because of the twisting course of the river, following the riverbank would have doubled the length of what was a short hop as the crow flies, and to link up at Izyum would require both armies to cross a river that the Wehrmacht was, at least technically, already "over." Nevertheless, it seemed like the safer course: 6th Army would march with the Donets on its left at a time that the river was in full flood, and would thus block Soviet attempts to interfere.[19] Bock's plan envisioned a start date of April 22, when the flood was at its height.[20]

That date would come and go without an offensive, however. The Wehrmacht was in the midst of its preparations for Operation Blue and could devote precious little of its always precarious logistical net to a buildup for Operation Fridericus. Moreover, Hitler and Halder were subjecting Bock's original plan to a great deal of scrutiny and criticism. The day had long passed in the German army when a field commander could draw up an operational plan and show it to the high command afterward. The more they studied the map, the more Bock's plan seemed disappointing. They argued for taking the riskier course, the very one that Bock had rejected, and shifting the bulk of 6th Army to the eastern bank of the Donets before its attack. Such a move would be theoretically vulnerable to a Soviet flank attack, but only if the Red Army could react fast enough, a proposition that Hitler and Halder alike saw as doubtful. A deeper strike well over the Donets would mean a greater haul of prisoners and booty when the pincers met.[21] Bock had never been an easy subordinate, and he accepted this revision with extreme reluctance. Bowing to force majeure, however, he drew up a new plan as directed, although he muttered all the while. "The whole thing isn't pretty," he complained, "but it can't be changed as long as the Führer sticks to his demand."[22] The new operation, now known as Fridericus II, was scheduled to begin on May 18.

On the eve of the great confrontation, it is interesting to note that neither side saw the Izyum bulge as an end to itself. Stalin viewed it as an operation of limited scope, one of many similar strikes up and down the front, designed to whittle down German strength for what he expected to be another drive by the Wehrmacht on Moscow. Once that had been blunted, the Germans would be ripe for a killing blow later in the year. Hitler, too, viewed it as a necessary preliminary operation for Operation Blue, nothing more and nothing less.

Even so, once the machinery was set in motion, both of these powerful adversaries began to gather massive forces in and around the salient. For the immediate operation, Timoshenko would employ four full four armies supported by 925 tanks, 29 rifle divisions, 9 cavalry divisions, 1 motorized rifle division, 4 motorized rifle brigades, 19 tank brigades, and 4 independent tank battalions. Counting both the fronts under Timoshenko's command, the Red Army disposed of 640,000 men, 1,200 tanks, 13,000 guns, and 926 aircraft in this sector.[23] For their part, the Germans were concentrating the combined forces of Army Group South: the 6th, 17th, and 1st Panzer Armies, perhaps 500,000 men, some 600 tanks, and a major portion of the Luftwaffe formations then deployed on the southern front. The two opponents, then, were about to try conclusions with over 1 million men and nearly 2,000 tanks. Such was the state of an "attack with limited objectives"[24] in the spring of 1942 on the Russo-German front.

Once again, it is the symmetry of this situation that is most striking. Two mighty military forces were planning offensives for the same tiny spot on the map. The schedule called for them to begin within a mere six days of one another. The most powerful Soviet formation—the *Schwerpunkt* of the operation, as the Germans would have called it—was the 6th Army. Its operational target? The *German* 6th Army.

The Kharkov Offensive: Shocking the Wehrmacht

All the heated discussions within the German command over rival versions of Operation Fridericus turned out to be moot. On May 12, Timoshenko opened his offensive. German intelligence had predicted it almost to the day and time. Colonel Reinhardt Gehlen, head of the General Staff's Fremde Heere Ost (Foreign Armies East) organization, had been predicting an enemy "attrition attack" (*Zermürbungsangriff*) out of the Izyum salient for months.[25] As late as May 1, he had reiterated his warning. Four days later, Halder and Bock had a discussion of the possibility that "the Russians might beat us to it and attack on both sides of Kharkov."[26] As always, however, there seemed to be a wide gulf between the army's intelligence services and the forces at the front. The Germans were simply unprepared for what was about to hit them. The two armies in the line, the 6th and 17th, were thinly stretched and extremely light on infantry, with the former short at least 16,000 replacements.[27] The seam between the two armies was hardly covered at all. This was the mission of Group Koch, a light screening force of just two infantry regiments.[28] Moreover, a major portion of 6th Army's front line strength, the units that would have to bear the brunt of the initial Soviet offensive, consisted of Allied formations—the Hungarian 108th Light Infantry Division, for example. The 17th Army's front line covering the southwestern face of the salient, and thus also intimately involved in the breakthrough phase of Timoshenko's offensive, consisted mainly of the Romanian VI Corps, a pair of relatively underequipped divisions. Nowhere around the sixty-mile perimeter of the salient had the Germans echeloned their defenses in any sort of depth. The Wehrmacht lacked sufficient forces for that, and at any rate it had been preparing itself for an offensive, not for defense against a breakthrough attempt.

For all these reasons, Timoshenko's attack got off to a roaring start.[29] His shock groups achieved at least tactical surprise, and maybe more, and there was success practically everywhere. At 6:30 A.M., both the northern and southern fronts erupted in concentrated artillery barrages that lasted an hour, followed by a massive fifteen-minute air raid. Targets were the German artillery and positions in the main defensive belt. When the bombardment lifted, the Red Army went over to the attack and struck one of the heaviest and most effective blows that the Wehrmacht had yet sustained in this war. It would probably not be accurate to describe what happened to the German defenders in the front line as "panic," but it certainly resembled it. One analyst described the sense of shock as rivaling that in front of Moscow the previous December.[30] Initial reports from the German front to headquarters at all levels described a hurricane bombardment, a morning sky filled with Soviet aircraft, and an armored horde containing thousands of enemy tanks rumbling toward their lines out of the early morning fog. In fact, there were considerably fewer than that: perhaps 300 fronting 28th Army's shock group in the north and another 200 in 6th Army's attack in the south. To unprepared troops manning a sleepy sector of the front and stunned by a bombardment unlike anything they had ever experienced, however, it may well have looked like more.

That was especially true in the south, where General Gorodniansky's 6th Army spearheaded the attack. Consisting of eight rifle divisions and four tank brigades, and with two powerful mechanized formations in support (21st and 23rd Tank Corps), 6th Army was the *Schwerpunkt* of the operation. After the preparatory bombardment had lifted, the shock groups came forward in dense waves of armor, smashing through the first German defensive line, then the second. The unlucky recipient of this first great Soviet tank attack of the war was the 454th Security Division. It was a light unit, armed mainly with captured equipment, and obviously not configured for this kind of fight at all. Soviet T-34 tanks overran it almost without noticing and broke into open country to the northwest by noon. The next day, 6th Army widened the breach, smashing the 62nd Infantry Division and then doing the same to the Hungarian 108th Light Infantry. Gorodniansky was already ten to twelve miles from his start line and had torn open a great gash in the German lines some thirty miles wide.[31] Progress continued the next day, with the width of the operational breach now at least thirty-five miles wide, and penetrations up to thirty miles into the German defenses west of the Donets.[32] Moreover, every single one of the German and Axis divisions in the path of 6th Army had suffered crippling casualties.

Perched on Gorodniansky's left flank was Army Group Bobkin (two rifle divisions and the 6th Cavalry Corps). It too managed a clean breakthrough by noon of the first day, crashing through the right wing of the 454th Security Division, which deserved some sort of hazardous duty pay for this operation, and brushing aside the Romanian 1st Infantry Division. Every attempt by the Germans to reestablish a line in front of Bobkin failed in the face of timely action by Soviet mobile forces. With the road to Krasnograd, his objective, now open, Bobkin set out on a wild ride to the northwest, advancing into air and overrunning German rear area installations. He would take the city on May 15. By the next day his spearheads stood far to the west of Krasnograd, approaching Karlovka. The group was now just twenty-five miles from Poltava, the headquarters of both Army Group South and the German 6th Army.[33]

It is a lesson that is generally lost in the disastrous ending to this operation, but the opening hours of the Kharkov offensive formed a watershed for the Red Army. It had learned some hard lessons about modern warfare, its German enemy, and itself since 1941. As a result, this was a different Soviet army than the one the Germans had fought last fall and winter. The old one had relied on mass, especially massed assault by hastily trained levies of infantry. This new army relied on a smaller infantry component, but a dramatically expanded complement of the supporting arms: armor, air, and artillery.[34] We may date its origins to January 10, 1942, the day that Marshal G. K. Zhukov issued Stavka Directive No. 03, a document that would define Soviet operational methods for the rest of the war.[35] It emphasized the role of the "shock group" as the spearhead of offensive action on the army or front level. Commanders were to concentrate their strength on extremely narrow frontages, with the goal of achieving overwhelming superiority against a single weak German unit. A front-level attack would have a width of just thirty kilometers; an army, only fifteen. Huge artillery offensives were to precede each attack, with a density of up to eighty guns per kilometer. Targeting first the prepared defenses, they were then to shift to deeper targets to support the penetration, and then deeper still to support the exploitation, with ground support aircraft mirroring them. This style of fighting, which amounted to nothing less than a new Soviet way of war, would require a far higher level of training and coordination than the old army had possessed, and it certainly had not been perfected by the time of Timoshenko's offensive at Kharkov. Nevertheless, one suspects that a survey of the unfortunate defenders belonging to the German 454th Security Division's outpost line, or the reserves of the Hungarian 108th Light Division, inserted in the battle on its second day and almost immediately scattered to the four winds, would have given it high marks for effectiveness, mobility, and above all, shock. It may not yet have been "deep battle," but it was immensely effective.

In the north, progress was slower. The terrain was less open here, the units more densely packed. With the great city of Kharkov immediately in the German rear, moreover, it was much easier for the Wehrmacht to reinforce the front than it was in the south. After the same softening up by artillery and air, Riabyshev's 28th Army (six rifle divisions and four tank brigades) went over to the attack at 7:30 A.M. The assault had the good fortune of hitting the Germans just at the moment that they were relieving one of their front line regiments, with the 513th (of the 294th Infantry Division) taking over the sector of the line held by the 211th (of the 71st).[36] Progress was solid in this sector, especially by General A. I. Rodimtsev's 13th Guards Rifle Division on the army's left flank, but not spectacular. That may also have been a sign of the army's relative inexperience, one of the worries during preoperational planning; more likely it was an intelligence failure.

The Soviets thought they'd be fighting a lone German infantry division here, but it was soon obvious that they were fighting two (the 71st and 294th). On the flanks, the veteran 21st and 38th Armies did much better. The former, in particular, made the deepest initial penetration. Having seized a bridgehead over the Donets at Bezliudovka the previous evening, the 21st managed to penetrate six miles to the north and five miles to the northwest. There was similar progress in the 38th Army sector, with 226th Rifle Division leading the way on the army's extreme right wing.

It is interesting to note that by the end of the day, both sides were expressing concern about the situation in the north, a classic example of the fog of war. The Soviets had laid on an enormous artillery and air barrage and had something less than a clear breakthrough to show for it. On the German side, there was simply shock, the natural reaction of troops and commanders who had been hit by a hurricane of fire before their morning coffee and whose radio airwaves were even now blaring Timoshenko's strident propaganda broadcasts threatening them all with fiery destruction. There were heavy German casualties here, to be sure. The chief of staff of the XXIX Army Corps described the corps's 294th Division as having been "virtually annihilated."[37] Although the German line was still holding firm, this was by far the shortest route to Kharkov and would naturally demand a major portion of the available reserves from Paulus's 6th Army, as well as those of Army Group South. Indeed, by the end of that horrible first day, a shaky General Paulus was already demanding reinforcements from Bock.

The latter duly dispatched the 23rd Panzer Division, along with the 71st and 113th Infantry Divisions, the very units that he had earmarked for the Operation Fridericus spearhead.[38] They began arriving at the front early the next day, desperately trying to stabilize the situation and hold back the onrushing Soviet tanks. Particularly worrisome to Paulus was the threat in the attack sector of 38th Army, and it was here that he deployed the main body of 23rd Panzer Division. Even so, over the course of the next two days, the Soviets continued to make progress in the north. It was slow but steady, and by nightfall on May 14, 28th Army's advanced units (with Rodimtsev's 13th Guards Rifle Division once again taking the honors) were just ten miles from Kharkov. The northern shock group had torn a hole thirty miles wide and had advanced fifteen miles, but with German reinforcements arriving, it was equally clear that it no longer had freedom of movement. The

German line had held in the north, just a stone's throw from the Kharkov city limits.

The end of day three, therefore, was a time for taking stock. For Timoshenko, the time had come to insert his armored reserves: the 21st and 23rd Tank Corps. He had been holding them up till now in reserve behind 6th Army. Fresh and unbloodied, perhaps they could finish what Gorodniansky had started so effectively in the south: a penetration into the depth of the German position and a thrust toward Kharkov from the southwest. The Germans may have held in the north, but were still nowhere near to reestablishing a firm line in the south. The timely arrival of such massive Soviet reinforcements might have blown things wide open in this sector.

Unfortunately, Timoshenko hesitated, and the literature on Kharkov—what little exists today—spends an inordinate amount of time on the question, "Why?" The marshal left behind no memoirs, but as far as can be determined, it was a combination of factors: stronger than expected German resistance, the unexpected presence of an entire Panzer division on the German northern flank, and reports of a strong German armored force being assembled at Zmiev, north of the salient.[39] The first two were true, but the last was a mirage, although Soviet reconnaissance may well have mistaken one of the reserve regiments of the Hungarian 108th Light Infantry Division for a German unit. Such things are typical of warfare at all levels, and especially of mobile warfare on the operational level. Things happen quickly, and intelligence is always sketchy.

Finally, the assault had gone so well and advanced so rapidly that Timoshenko's reserves were too far to the rear for timely insertion into the battle. Getting them to the front through roads already clotted with tanks and trucks, roads that were already chewed up by bombardment and ground combat, was a serious and unexpected problem. The Soviet General Staff study on Kharkov makes this point explicitly:

> By the end of 14 May, the second-echelon tank corps (with 260 tanks) and rifle divisions were a long way from the front line. General Kuzmin's 21st Tank Corps was forty-two kilometers away from 6th Army's forward units; General Pushkin's 23rd Tanks Corps was twenty kilometers away, and the 248th and 103rd Rifle Divisions, which comprised 6th Army's second echelon, were twenty to forty kilometers away. Such a separation of second-echelon forces and

> forces of the echelon for developing success made difficult their timely commitment into battle, which was urgently dictated by the situation.[40]

It was the paradox of deep battle: how to keep feeding units into the fire along the same axis when the front line was drawing further away by the hour.

For the Germans, too, the time had come to make some basic decisions. Even though intelligence had provided some foreknowledge of the offensive, the Soviet assault had still hit hard. On the first day, with a great hole torn in the German line in the south and with masses of Soviet tanks just miles from Kharkov and driving hard, Bock and Halder had spoken by telephone. After listening to Bock's litany of bad news, including a demand for "the commitment of all available reserves" in order to restore the situation, the chief of the General Staff had urged his army group commander to get a hold of himself and stop worrying about every little "blemish" in the line. Bock blew up. This wasn't about local blemishes, he hissed, but about life or death for 6th Army—perhaps for the entire army group: "Our very existence is at stake."[41]

Here, too, fundamental decisions were at hand. Would Operation Fridericus, scheduled to open in just four days, still go forward? Hitler and Halder said yes; Bock wasn't so sure, at least as it was presently configured. How could it? The Soviets currently had the original northern wing of the pincer, 6th Army, pinned up against Kharkov in a gritty defensive battle. A single-wing movement by the south pincer alone, Kleist's 1st Panzer Army, wasn't really a pincer movement at all, and Bock worried that "the available forces could scarcely produce the desired success." If Kleist failed to make more than a dent in the base of the salient, Army Group South would be dealing with two failed operations at the same time. "If Kleist gets stuck half way, his attack will become a failure whose repercussions must weigh on all further plans for the eastern campaign," he argued. Unless reinforcements arrived, along with a massive commitment of airpower, he said, then all he could do was aim at a "smaller, therefore partial, solution": transferring Kleist's group to the west of the salient, where it could halt the Soviet 6th Army, push it back, and retake Krasnograd. It wasn't satisfying, and Bock himself said he suggested it "with a heavy heart," but it was the best he could do. Suggesting a "little solution" to Hitler was a nonstarter by definition, and in fact it seems to have been Bock's way of goosing the Führer into action. The moment he got off the phone

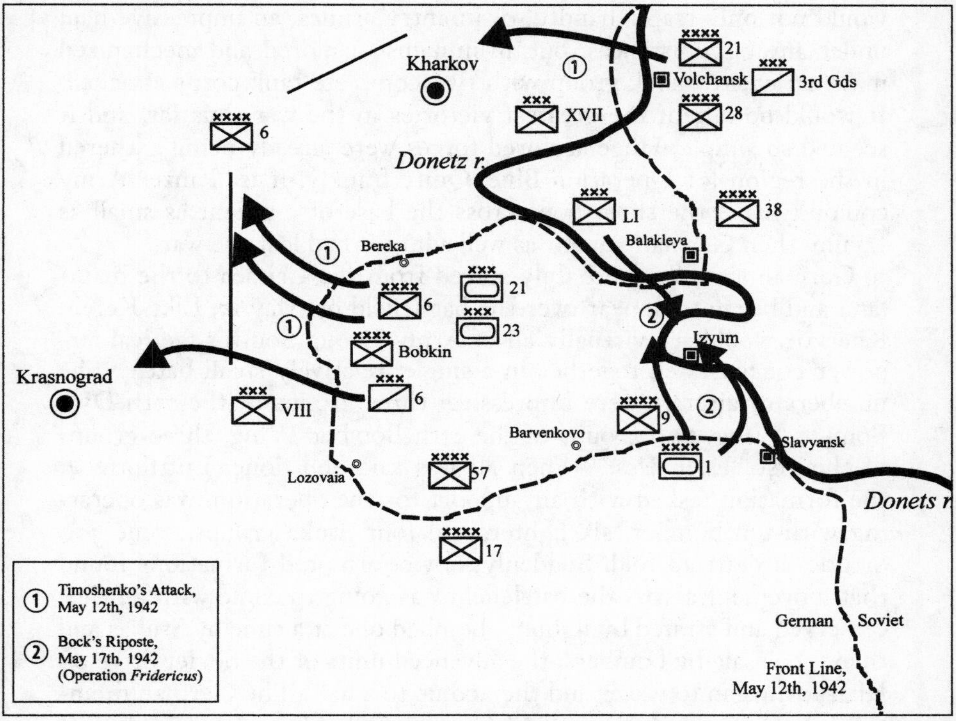

Map 4. Thrust and counterthrust in the Izyum salient: the battle of Kharkov, May 1942.

with Halder after having delivered his demands, he turned to his own chief of staff, General Georg von Sodenstern, and smirked, "Now the Führer will order the 'big' solution."[42]

In fact, the time was right for the big solution. With the winding down of the battle of Kerch, massive airpower assets were available for employment at Kharkov, and units of General Wolfram von Richtofen's VIII Fliegerkorps were already arriving in force. Likewise, Bock got his ground reinforcements: the 24th Panzer Division, the 305th Infantry Division, and elements of the 88th Division. The high command was not interested in simply holding Krasnograd. It had its eyes on much bigger game: the destruction of all Soviet forces in the bulge. The opportunity was simply too delicious to miss. Fridericus had originally called for a pincer movement to choke off whatever Soviet forces happened to be in the salient. With the rapid progress of Timoshenko's offensive to the west, a successful German offensive would not only trap a handful of infantry armies, an impressive haul under any circumstances, but an immense armored and mechanized mass: an entire shock group with two complete tank corps attached. It would be one of the greatest victories in the war thus far, and it seemed so simple. Huge armored forces were already being gathered in the region for Operation Blue. Quite frankly, if 1st Panzer Army couldn't make the short hop across the base of a salient as small as Izyum, then Germany might as well admit it had lost the war.

German air units were duly staged from the Crimea to the mainland and began to appear over the battlefield by May 15. Like Kerch, Kharkov would see virtually all of Army Group South's tactical airpower concentrated together in a single, relatively small battle. The numbers of aircraft were impressive: three groups of the 77th Dive Bomber Wing; two groups of the 27th Bomber Wing, three groups of the 51st "Edelweiss." When all was said and done, Luftflotte 4, the formation tasked with air support for the operation, was operating with ten bomber, six fighter, and four Stuka groups, some 500 or 600 aircraft all told. Suddenly, Soviet armored formations found that movement across the battlefield was going to come with a price. Observed and strafed by fighters, bombed one at a time by Stukas and then wholesale by bombers, the advanced units of the Soviet drive on Kharkov began to waver and then come to a halt. The German infantry, especially the hard-pressed formations holding the shoulders of the bulge at Balakleya and Slavyansk, sent back their share of requests for air support, and it usually arrived within twenty minutes.[43] Still generally unrecognized is the role played by Luftwaffe flak units, operating from airfields close to the front and using their 88mm guns as antitank weapons, in stopping the Soviet thrust. The T-34 was a lot for any German tank to handle, but it burned just like any other tank when drilled by an "88." General Halder was a commander who, in the words of one authority, "rarely paid attention to air activities" in his war diary,[44] but the relief he must have been feeling was palpable. "All in all," he wrote, "the force of the attack appears to have been broken by the efforts of our Luftwaffe."[45]

German Counterstroke: Operation Fridericus

There never was a time during the Kharkov operation when one could truthfully say that the situation had stabilized. As the Germans began preparing Fridericus for takeoff, with a start date of May 17, the Soviets were still hammering away in both north and south. In the north, they had lost whatever chance they had of a breakthrough. The shock group was engaged and thoroughly bloodied, and so was the second echelon, the 3rd Guards Cavalry Corps. The inability to stop, to recognize when an operation had gone bad and needed to be terminated, would be a problem for the Soviet command for the rest of the war. It was a pattern of "senseless, wild hammering"[46] that cost a great deal of blood. In the south, however, the Soviet 6th Army was still a body in motion, slowing down and taking a fierce pounding from the air, but nonetheless still rolling forward and over the weak formations the Germans had thus far managed to put in its way. It was certainly not a defenders' hall of fame: security divisions, formations of Germany's minor allies, a battalion from this division, a regiment from that one. Even on May 16, the eve of the German offensive, the Wehrmacht had not yet reestablished a firm line in this sector. Indeed, there are reports of Marshal Bock nervously staring at the map and wondering if he should junk Operation Fridericus at the last minute.[47]

He was talked out of it by the staff, but his jitters are instructive: Bock could see that he was dealing here with a new kind of Red Army, and he of all people knew how hard it was to handle the old one. The Wehrmacht, by contrast, had hardly changed at all. It was a little older and a little wiser perhaps, but it still knew what it did best. Operation Fridericus opened on May 17, supported by a massive commitment of air power, with hundreds of Stukas flying thousands of sorties, as well as a concentrated artillery barrage. As planned, it struck an extremely weak spot in the Soviet line: the 9th Army in the southern face of the original salient. This had been a quiet sector thus far, and it is fair to say that Kleist's attack came as much of a shock to the Soviet soldiers in the front line as Timoshenko's had been to the Germans just five days previously.

Kleist's 1st Panzer Army included three corps. On its extreme right stood LII Corps, consisting of two infantry divisions and the 101st Light Infantry Division; to its left, the XXXXIV Corps (three infantry divisions, 97th Light Infantry Division, and the 16th Panzer Division); and on the left of the army, its spearhead, the III Panzer Corps. As if to underline the historical continuity of German military operations, the commander of III Panzer Corps was none other than General Eberhard von Mackensen, the son of the great Field Marshal August von Mackensen, a commander who knew a thing or two about *Bewegungskrieg* himself.[48] The younger Mackensen's corps included 14th Panzer Division, 60th Motorized Division, 100th Light Infantry

Division, 1st Mountain Division, and the 20th Romanian Infantry Division. The 17th Army, to 1st Panzer Army's right, was also under Kleist's operational control for this battle, and in fact, it is technically correct to speak of "Army Group von Kleist" when discussing the fighting at Kharkov. It included a further two corps, the XI and VI Romanian Corps, containing five divisions between them. All told, then, Kleist was in command of eighteen divisions, including two Panzer divisions and one motorized division. By Wehrmacht standards, it represented a massive commitment of force.

The first day, as might be expected, brought overwhelming success. The point of Mackensen's spear was 14th Panzer Division, which sliced through the Soviet defenses and headed for Barvenkovo. Flanked by 1st Mountain Division on its left and 100th Light on its right, it "broke through the enemy's main defensive position in one bound,"[49] in Mackensen's phrase, and was in Barvenkovo by nightfall. That same day, 17th Army began its own drive from Slavyansk, the town holding the southern shoulder of the original bulge, with 16th Panzer Division attacking along the bank of the Donetz. The grueling, sticky heat, which hovered near 90°F for virtually all of the fighting, was an obstacle almost as tough as the Soviets here, and the terrain along the riverbank brought its own problems. The attack of the 101st Light Infantry Division, for example, which protected Kleist's eastern flank along the Donets, had to deal with a chain of lakes and a dense forest, along with numerous tiny villages, gardens, and orchards as it moved slowly to the north.[50] Indeed, by nightfall on May 18, Kleist's assault forces had caved in the entire southern face of the salient. As it had been at Kerch, Soviet command and control was the first victim of a mobile battle. With the Red Army employing unsecured communications centers and completely uncamouflaged headquarters, the Luftwaffe had its pick of targets. Indeed, virtually every Soviet division within the salient would fight the remainder of the battle out of contact with higher headquarters, the price of doing business under Luftwaffe attack.

A huge Soviet force lay far to the west. If it were not recalled immediately, it faced the certainty of being cut off from the rear. Once again, however, it appeared that setting the Red Army in motion was one thing, but that controlling it after that was something else again. Gorodniansky's 6th Army and the Bobkin Group actually continued their advance to the west and northwest for two days. Even if their rear had been secure, their own momentum was stalling by now in the face of stiffening ground opposition and the hailstorm being visited upon them from above by the Luftwaffe. As it was, with an iron trap about to sever their connections with the motherland, every step that they took to the west only put them further into trouble.

As in the case of Timoshenko's failure to insert his tank corps at the propitious moment, there are to this day arguments about whom to blame. Certainly, it was Timoshenko who issued those formations their orders to continue the advance. He had begged for the opportunity to launch the Kharkov offensive. He had planned it personally, and he knew that no matter what, it would forever be linked with his name. Calling it off would have represented a bitter personal defeat, with all the repercussions that might have in the Stalinist regime. Not only did he refuse to recall his attacking formations, he chose now, of all moments, to insert his two reserve formations (21st and 23rd Tank Corps) into the battle, setting them in motion to the west.

He was not a completely free agent, however. He could only have issued those orders after close consultation with Stalin and the Stavka. Most of the officers around Stalin, the deputy chief of the General Staff A. M. Vasilevsky, for example, could read a map as well as anyone, and by the end of May 17, the first day of the German offensive, it was clear to them that a disaster was about to overtake the Soviet 6th Army and the other forces in the salient. Stalin, however, remained optimistic. Just days before, he had been rejoicing in the good news coming out of the Izyum salient: the German line pried open, one enemy division after another mauled to the point of destruction; Kharkov about to be plucked like a ripe apple. He had even been doing a bit of gloating, mocking those on the staff who had been gloomy about the prospects of the operation during its planning stages. Processing what had happened in the few days since then may simply have been impossible for someone with his "preconceived notions and congenital optimism."[51] At any rate, Stalin refused to intervene to block Timoshenko, and in the Stalinist system, that meant that the advance would continue. It wasn't until the night of May 19, forty-eight hours after the start of the German thrust, that Timoshenko decided to face the facts and to recall 6th Army and Group Bobkin. By now, however, both formations were so far away from safety that they might as well have been an expeditionary force.

Certainly, human agency played a key role in the looming disaster. It is important, however, not to reduce something as large and as complex as the battle of Kharkov to a simple matter of personality. In the case of Soviet decision-making at Kharkov, the waters are even muddier than normal. Timoshenko's political commissar was one

Nikita Khrushchev, who would later ascend to Stalin's chair, and who would use Stalin's ineptitude at Kharkov as a effective club in his de-Stalinization campaign.[52] Given the course of the fighting up to now, and the capabilities of the engaged forces, it is entirely possible that none of the argument really mattered. The Germans had struck so rapidly and to such good effect that the Soviet grouping to the west may well have been doomed no matter what Timoshenko or Stalin did or did not do during the first two days of the German counterstroke. Although anyone reading an account of the battle of Kharkov will be tempted to cry, "Call off the offensive!," one must also recognize that doing so would have been far easier said than done. Timoshenko would have had to turn a great mechanized armada around on a dime, point it back the way it had come, rearrange its supply services and reorganize its rear areas, and then drive it at top speed to the east. The entire way, it would have been under assault from on onrushing 1st Panzer Army. All this would might well have constituted just another recipe for disaster. As to escaping, that had been out of the question since May 17: the mouth of the salient was shrinking inexorably, and with the Luftwaffe prowling over the increasingly narrow lifeline to the great mass of Soviet forces fighting to the west, even something as simple as running supplies into the pocket by truck had become a suicide mission. Running a large tank force out of the pocket at this point would have been a fantasy.

The fighting on May 20 saw the neck of the salient narrow to just twelve miles, as 14th Panzer Division continued to drive north and took the village of Protopovka. By the next day, it was only eight miles. One by one, the six bridges over the Donets upon which the Soviet forces to the west relied for their survival fell into German hands. That same day, Luftwaffe reconnaissance flights reported two dense Soviet columns of men and vehicles on the move. One was still moving toward the front through Alexeyevka; that would have been Timoshenko's two reserve tank corps. The other was heading in the exact opposite direction, from Krasnograd to the east: the original assault force. On May 22, the two columns collided, the precise moment that command and control within the Soviet army collapsed, paralyzing the entire immense force west of the Donets.

Opportunity was knocking, and the Wehrmacht was not the sort of army to ignore it. It was now time to tweak the plan. Originally, the role of 6th Army was to sit in place, defend itself in a broad arc around Kharkov, and passively receive the onrushing 1st Panzer Army. The stabilization of the situation in front of the city, however, as well as the signs of dissolution in the Soviet ranks, led the high command to order Paulus into action. Paulus now had the LI Corps (44th Division, 3rd and 23rd Panzer Divisions) launch a short thrust of its own to the south, out of Balakleya.[53] On May 22, the 14th Panzer Division (of Mackensen's III Panzer Corps) made contact with LI Corps just southwest of Balakleya, thus formally sealing off the pocket west of Izyum.

To be sure, there would be some hard fighting yet. For the Wehrmacht, closing off an encirclement was not an end in itself, but only the beginning of a concentric assault on the trapped forces. No sooner had the Panzer divisions met at Balakleya than they wheeled in unison to the left, slamming into the rear of Soviet forces still fighting to the west. For their part, the Soviet formations inside the *Kessel* did not sit passively and wait to surrender. They made a series of desperate attempts to break out of their constantly shrinking perimeter. It may well be that Soviet infantry inside the pocket *did* link arms, 1941 style, shout "Urraah!," and storm the nearest German outpost, only to be slaughtered by machine gun fire. At least one German report says so. What was certain is that this was a different kind of pocket from those of 1941, which were largely infantry. This one included a major force of uncommitted armor, two complete tank corps, which launched a series of breakout attempts in the course of the next few days. The most serious was probably the one heading due east toward Petrovskoye on May 25, which managed to smash its way through the encirclement, and was in turn vaporized by a combination of Stuka fire and Mackensen's Panzers. By the next day, all that was left was a pocket perhaps ten miles from north to south and two from west to east, seething with explosions, death, and destruction. Marshal Bock actually stood on a hilltop observation post and watched the whole thing through his field glasses. He was stunned by the destruction he was witnessing:

> The picture was the same everywhere; being squeezed ever harder, the enemy still made attempts to breakout here and there but was on the verge of collapse. I could see from a hill southeast of Lozovaia that the pounding the smoking pocket was taking from our batteries on all sides was being answered only weakly by the Russians. Masses of prisoners streamed to the rear, while our panzers and elements of the 1st Mountain Infantry Division passed them as they advanced to attack.[54]

It was, he said, "an overwhelming scene."[55]

By May 28, it was over. Another immense Soviet force had surrendered to the encircling Germans and marched off to a fate that is often called the "uncertainty of captivity," but which in Nazi Germany was all too certain. The mass of prisoners included virtually all of 6th and 57th Armies, Group Bobkin, and the 21st and 23rd Tank Corps: at least 240,000 men, over 1,200 tanks, and 2,600 guns. The clearest sign of the absolute nature of the German triumph, as well as the severity of the fighting, was the shocking number of Soviet commanders and staff who were among the casualties. They included General F. I. Kostenko, commander of the Southern Front, whose 9th Army bore the brunt of Kleist's assault; General K. P. Podlas, commander of the 57th Army, along with this chief of staff, his army commissar, and his chief of artillery; the commanders of the 47th, 150th, and 337th Rifle Divisions; General Bobkin—and the list goes on and on.[56] The most noteworthy, perhaps, given his role in this battle, was General Gorodniansky, the 6th Army commander and author of the great Soviet breakthrough on May 12. Just seventeen days after his greatest triumph, he apparently shot himself rather than fall into German captivity.[57]

Any postmortem on all this must admit that shoddy Soviet handling of the battle contributed to the slaughter. Indeed, a postwar German analysis recognized the "special characteristic" of this victory: "The operational maneuvers (*operativen Bewegungen*) that gave German forces the possibility of conducting an annihilation attack (*Vernichtungsangriff*), were by and large carried out by the enemy. After the difficult winter they had endured, the participating German formations would hardly have been able to carry out such maneuvers this early in the year." It had begun with the Soviet winter offensive, the Barenkovo-Lozovaia operation in January that had created the salient in the first place. It had continued with the Soviet double pincer toward Kharkov, and it had climaxed with "the tenacious continuation of the Russian attack even after May 17th," which "consumed so much of the striking power of the bulk of the enemy's forces, or drawn them so far away from the dangerous blow delivered by Army Group Kleist, that they were unable to intervene in sufficient time."[58]

Nevertheless, even allowing for this unexpected level of Soviet cooperation, Kharkov was one of the greatest triumphs in the long history of the German army. The peculiarities of a salient battle had assisted the Germans, but once again the Wehrmacht had demonstrated equal doses of operational skill and aggression. It had warded off at least one of the first massive Soviet blows, the drive on Kharkov out of the Volchansk salient to the north, which bought it enough time to concentrate a killing blow against the other. It had to junk the original plan for Fridericus for a two-prong drive into the salient and come up with another one on the fly. Kleist's drive from the south had to be quick, before the Soviets could concentrate against it. Luckily, he had in General von Mackensen and the III Panzer Corps one of the most aggressive commands in the German order of battle. Mackensen was a throwback, not simply in terms of his bloodlines (although they were significant); in terms of his aggression and drive, his ruthlessness to the enemy and his own men alike, he would have been as perfectly at home in the old Prussian army as his father had been. For the most part, Kleist let him do what he wanted in battle, and Mackensen almost always repaid the trust. The result was as neat and as simple a *Kesselschlacht* as any German army has ever fought. The cost had not been inconsequential, nearly 7,000 casualties from Mackensen's III Panzer Corps alone. Yet it was a price that was seemingly well within the limits for a battle of annihilation, and Kharkov fit that description as well as any battle in German history.

Within days of Kharkov, in fact, Mackensen was off to new adventure further east. The great *Kesselschlacht* did not end the fighting along the Donets line. There were still other preliminary operations to be carried out before the onset of Operation Blue. With another great victory in the books, it seemed to Hitler and Halder to be a propitious time to smash as many major Soviet formations as he could before the great drive to the Volga and Caucasus. First came Operation Wilhelm, aimed at encircling and destroying the Soviet 28th Army at Volchansk. It was scheduled for June 7, then pushed back because of the rain until June 10, and involved concentric attacks by VIII Corps coming down from the north and Mackensen's III Panzer Corps coming up from the north. They would meet on the Burluk River and seal off another impressive pocket. By now, Mackensen was carrying a particularly sharp sword: the 14th, 16th, and 22nd Panzer Divisions, plus 60th Motorized Division; he also had operational control of LI Corps (forming a temporary "Group von Mackensen"). The operation went smoothly, with Mackensen launching a night attack that took Soviet 28th Army completely by surprise. With his mobile formations slicing through the defenses in front of him and his infantry corps providing flank protection, he linked up with VIII Corps on June 13. The fighting ended only two days after that, with another 21,000 prisoners falling into German hands. The weather had been terrible and the roads awful, however, and it was clear that large elements of 28th Army were able to slip the trap.[59] Operation Wilhelm was a disappointment to the Germans and it continues to be treated as such, but that only shows how high the Wehrmacht's expectations had become, and how historians have tended to follow suit. In another time and place, an attack by limited forces that cleared a major portion of enemy territory and resulted in 21,000 prisoners would have been considered a signal victory.

Similar things might be said of the next operation. Hitler and Halder were still interested in a drive by 6th Army over the Donets—in other words, their original conception for Fridericus II—before Timoshenko had disrupted their plans. With Operation Wilhelm concluded, Soviet 38th Army now occupied a shallow salient of its own in front of the Oskol River, between Kupyansk in the north and Izyum in the south. By now, there was a certain anxiety on the part of the field commanders, Bock of Army Group South in particular, about these constant nibbling operations. The preparations for Operation Blue had gone on for so long now that the field formations were anxious to get it under way, with Bock warning that every day it was postponed was a loss, a "casualty"[60] that would never be replaced.

Nevertheless, on June 22, Operation Fridericus II began. Once again, it starred Mackensen's III Panzer Corps, which slashed its way into the Soviet bulge from the north toward Kupyansk and Gorochovatka. The southern pincer consisted of XXXXIV Corps, which crossed the Donets on both sides of Izyum. Two days later the spearheads met, with Mackensen having covered 80 percent of the distance. The fighting was over on June 26. The west bank of the Oskol had been cleared, and the fighting had been surprisingly easy. Soviet 38th Army had largely escaped, but Fridericus II still managed to trap another 13,000 men.[61]

Kharkov: The German View

Surveying the amazing scene of destruction in the Kharkov pocket just after the battle, Field Marshal von Kleist was wide-eyed: "The battlefield demonstrated the harshness of the struggle. In places of the heaviest fighting the ground is so thickly covered with the bodies of man and horses, as far as the eye can see, that it is only with difficulty that you can find a path for your tank."[62] The German official history of the Kharkov pocket, found in volume 6 of the series *Das Deutsche Reich und der Zweite Weltkrieg* (*The German Reich and the Second World War*), was not written until 1990. By that late date, the author purported to detect evidence of a certain "psychological shock"[63] in the field marshal's comments, a sense that perhaps things were starting to go wrong. Mackensen's observations that the enemy's conduct of operations was "more fanatic, more ruthless, more consistent" than it had been in 1941 gets the same treatment. Mackensen went on to say, "The Red leadership risked everything. It made big, clear decisions and then did everything it could to carry it out. Commanders and troops followed through far more than in the previous year. Red armor and cavalry displayed incredible guts (*Schneid*) and a willingness to fight to the death." It may have looked like an easy victory, Mackensen concluded, but those who were there knew that it had only been won "with our last strength."[64]

Both Kleist and Mackensen had been impressed by the fierceness and destructiveness of the battle, to be sure. Investing their comments with any sort of premonitory angst, however, is reading history backward. Not only do we know that the disaster of Stalingrad was looming just up the road, but we also live in a highly psychologized age, sensitive to all sorts of concerns and subtexts that once flew by completely unnoticed. Even the official history has to admit that the inner mood of the generals is "very difficult to fix from the sources."[65] In fact, we might say that Kleist was doing what many German commanders had done in different times and places: he was touring the site of his most recent annihilation victory and surveying the destruction, perhaps even reveling in such a vivid display of his own power. Although it might not be in harmony with current sensitivities, the tendency in 1942 would have been to exaggerate the mayhem and destruction within the pocket, not to minimize it, and there is really no evidence from his comment that Kleist was particularly disturbed by it one way or another. As to Mackensen's alleged forebodings, they were simply preamble to his discussion of the victory. He analyzed it, in fact, in traditional German terms, attributing it to low morale and bravery of the German troops, the independence of their leaders, the impact of surprise, and the massive level of dedicated air support.

Far from feeling a foreshadowing of doom as they hurtled ever deeper into the Soviet Union, then, German commanders must have been feeling ten feet tall. Reading opinions expressed at the time leaves a different impression from the emotional hand-wringing perceived by the official history. The officer corps may well have been shaken by Kharkov. All battle is traumatic, and the surprise with which this one began may have made it more traumatic than most. But drowning out those doubts was exultation at the way the battle had ended.

The *Militär-Wochenblatt*'s reportage on Kharkov may be taken as typical. The first mention of it, in the May 29 issue, presented it mainly as a tribute to the heroism of the German defenders. This was entirely in keeping with the uncertain mood at the front, where an outnumbered German defensive line was facing the first great Soviet tank attack of the war: "The heavy impact of the attack allowed the strength of the German defense to appear in all its brilliance." By holding off the Soviet thrust for six long days, the defenders gained time for the development of the German counterattack:

> It wasn't satisfied with simply throwing back the Soviets frontally and reestablishing the German front. Instead, it strove from the start for an encirclement [*Einkesselung*, literally, a "kettling"] and annihilation of the enemy. The decisive operation that led to the severing of the supply line to the main Bolshevist attack group succeeded by May 20th. At that point, a concentric attack [i.e., one directed against the mass of encircled forces] could begin.[66]

Just that simply, the battle of Kharkov, which Timoshenko had initiated with such high hopes, and which was seen "as the beginning of the end of the German campaign in the east," had morphed into a serious defeat for the Soviets.

By the next issue, the full impact of the fighting had made itself felt. It was nothing less than a "new German annihilation victory," the "*Kesselschlacht* of Kharkov."[67] A powerful blow had fallen on the enemy. Timoshenko, "once again facing his old enemy from last year, Marshal Bock," had lost three armies: twenty rifle divisions, seven cavalry divisions, and fourteen tank brigades. Soviet losses included 240,000 prisoners, 1,249 tanks, and an indeterminate number of battle casualties. Although the haul of prisoners was not as large as last year's encirclement battles, the number of tanks captured had been proportionally much higher. It was a sign of a new Soviet way of war, said the *Wochenblatt*, a sign that "even the Bolshevik reservoir of manpower is not inexhaustible." But the style of attack didn't matter. The German defenders managed to ward off Timoshenko's schematic "encirclement maneuvers and pincer movements" (*Umfassungsmanövern und Zangenbewegungen*), while the German high command was "making preparations to transform a would-be success into a Cannae."

While the Bolshevik main body was held fast by iron claws in north and south, hindering the expansion of the breach, the Panzers of General von Kleist broke through in lightning-quick fashion from Kramatorsk to Balakleya, linking up with the Panzers driving down from the north. They cut the lifeline of the penetrating forces and laid down an iron bolt on the door to his lines, one that resisted all attempts at relief. With German forces from Krasnograd going over to a counterattack, the Bolsheviks were encircled (*eingekesselt*) and handed over to destruction.[68] It was, said the *Wochenblatt*, a masterfully executed operation, one that "corresponded to its design and exceeded its own lofty expectations."

Another example of this literature of exultation appeared in *Die Wehrmacht*, a magazine aimed at the more general reader. In "With a Panzer Division at Kharkov: The Year's First Kesselschlacht,"[69] the well-known military correspondent Wilfried von Oven described his experience riding into the fighting with one of Kleist's mobile formations. He saw the battle as a sign to the world that the "harsh winter just past had robbed the German Wehrmacht of none of its striking power":

> The success was colossal. As if springing up from the ground, German Panzers had appeared in an area that the enemy had regarded as his own rear area of operations, and they had come not from the front, but from even further behind. The surprise was complete, and it completely upset the opponent's good judgment. . . . Confusion, even panic, gripped the opponent. He turned aimlessly to the north, then to the south and west. Where was the enemy?

Oven suddenly realizes that the Soviet armies opposite have no idea what is happening to them; they are unable to form any overall picture of the mobile German operation: "Just as fast as the German Panzers appeared, then they vanished again. The division had a new task, the third and last phase of forming the *Kessel*. A *Kampfgruppe*, formed from reconnaissance and armored elements, drove to the north, followed by the main body. It was to make contact with forces coming down from the north, from Kharkov." And then it happens, the moment of victory: "In the midst of a lively artillery engagement, we see flares rise in the north. They come from our own troops. A little later we make radio contact, and then comes an armored car with the commander of the detachment coming from the north. As he reaches out his hand to our general, the *Kessel* was symbolically closed." It was precisely six days after the division had gone into action. The German advantage, Oven wrote, had been leadership, which "towered high over that of the Bolshevist enemy." It was, he said, "sober and clear in its estimate of the enemy's situation and our own, bold in its planning, and lightning-quick in its execution."

Conclusion: Springtime for the Wehrmacht?

It is hard to argue with any of Oven's rhetoric, or even to see it as especially exaggerated. The battle of Kharkov was an exclamation point on an already amazing spring. At Kerch, Manstein had proved that a *Kesselschlacht* and a battle of annihilation were still possible against the Soviet army. At Kharkov, Bock and Kleist showed that it could still be easy—as easy as it had been in the summer of 1941, when the Wehrmacht had been tearing great chunks out of the Red Army seemingly at will. The two battles had accounted for a grand total of six Soviet armies and took no less that 410,000 prisoners; along with the fall of Sevastopol, the figure would rise to 500,000. After the shock in front of Moscow and the long winter doldrums, the German way of war, "bold in its planning and lightning-quick in its execution," once again seemed to be working to perfection.

The long winter was finally over, spring had returned, and it was apparent that the old truths still applied. An army armed and trained to fight *Bewegungskrieg*, "short and lively" campaigns ending in decisive operational-level victory with minimal friendly losses, had once again found its métier. Manstein in the Kerch peninsula and Kleist at Kharkov had both achieved the ideal of the German way of war: *Vernichtungsieg*, the annihilating victory. It was a particular kind of win, the kind in which you captured most of the enemy command staff and buried those you didn't, or where you ended the campaign blasting artillery rounds into helpless masses of enemy soldiers desperately trying to evacuate the mainland. They were victories in which you didn't simply beat the enemy army, but dismantled it into its component parts, then stood and surveyed its ruins.

Today, of course, it is possible to study the situation carefully and to see clear warning signs for the Germans. None of these victories would have been possible without the deployment of virtually the entire Luftwaffe on the southern front in three relatively constricted pieces of airspace: the Kerch peninsula, the Izyum salient, and the southwestern corner of the Crimea. How possible would it be to do that in Operation Blue, a campaign that intended to overrun the entire bend of the mighty Don River, then drive for the Volga River and the Causasus Mountains? The German supply situation, never a high priority for this army, was as abysmal as ever. Replacements of men and matériel were nowhere near the losses, and virtually every unit going into Operation Blue was starting the operation under its allotted strength. The situation of the railroad net, the lifeline of the German army in the east, could best be described as catastrophic. It is equally clear that the Soviets were learning a thing or two as well. There had been definite improvement in their use of combined arms, in particular the use of armor, air, and artillery. The opening moments of Timoshenko's mechanized offensive at Kharkov had thrown a scare into the Wehrmacht, soldiers and commanders alike. Things were likely to get a whole lot worse on that score as dismantled and reassembled Soviet industries began to gear up east of the Urals.

They were warning signs, certainly, although we must resist the temptation to see them as predictors of inevitable failure. The question is: could the Germans see them? Could military minds that were not simply the product of decades of education but centuries of tradition really break free of that context? Could they perceive the true nature of their predicament and devise alternative ways of proceeding? This was an army, after all, fighting operations named Frederick I, Frederick II, and Wilhelm. Its cutting edge of late, the tough III Panzer Corps, was commanded by a general named Mackensen. The formation that had driven south to meet Mackensen's and close the Kharkov pocket was LI Corps, commanded by a man with another famous Prussian name: General Walther von Seydlitz-Kurzbach. One can be forgiven for occasionally asking, "Which war is this, anyway?"

The answer is: it was a German war. It was proceeding along deeply traditional operational lines under the direction of a military caste whose roots ran deep into the history of Prussia-Germany, and it seemed to be going quite well at the moment. Indeed, as the German Panzers were fueling up for Operation Blue, more good news was arriving in what had already been a wonderful campaigning season. On the Führer's special train, where the Nazi leader was returning to Berlin from Munich after having attended a funeral of one of his "old fighters," this word of yet another in a long run of decisive victories was cause for rejoicing.[70] As was his wont of late, the Führer expressed his joy by handing out another field marshal's baton on the spot. In Washington, D.C., the news got a somewhat cooler reception. As two great men, rulers of empire and cornerstones of the anti-German coalition, were meeting in the White House to discuss their strategy for defeating Hitler, a shocking telegram suddenly arrived to upset their calculations and to trouble their counsels: Tobruk had fallen.

4

Battering the British

Gazala and Tobruk

More than any other theater of the war, North Africa has been the realm of myth. The desert was far more than mere "terrain" here, but an empty quarter where mechanized armies could roam free, liberated from towns and hills, choke points and blocking positions. It was a war of near-absolute mobility, especially for the tanks. The standard metaphor in the literature is "ships at sea": tanks could sail where they wished, set out on bold end runs around the enemy flank, then emerge out of the wastes to deal well-timed, devastating blows to their enemies.[1] Without the encumbrance of terrain features, it is often said, armored engagements had a purity to them, giving each battle the cut and thrust of a good chess match. Finally, in a landscape without civilians, the contending armies could fight cleanly, without having to worry about the moral ambiguities of occupation duty or the suppression of partisans in their rear. In our own day, in a fevered environment in which every last soldier in the Wehrmacht is routinely described as a racist and a war criminal, only the desert still has the reputation of being a "war without hate."[2]

In fact, this image of the desert war is an attractive construction, but little of it is true. The desert was not a thing of beauty or romance. It was a pain, for the most part, and fighting in it was a nightmare for both sides. Far from allowing tank fleets to roam free, the desert chained them inexorably to their supply lines; this was, after all, a theater in which not only ammunition and food, but every single drop of water, had to be shipped in from the outside.[3] A single failed supply convoy or a waylaid column of trucks could stop a division dead in its tracks. As to the mobility of desert warfare, both sides would spend far more time in static positions—often quite elaborate ones—with trenches, rifle pits, barbed wire, and hundreds of thousands of mines, than they did in motion. The British "fortified box" on the Gazala line may well be a more characteristic feature of desert war than the tank charge. Finally, there certainly were civilians in the desert, thousands of them scattered all over and around the various battlefields. They were on the radar screen of neither contending army, and even today, they remain all but invisible in the story of a war that took place in their homes.

The desert war gave rise to one other undying myth: that of Erwin Rommel. Sixty years later, he remains one of the stars of World War II. The "Desert Fox" has had countless biographies written about him, and there are more movies about him than all the other German generals put together. For those who grew up in a certain generation, indeed, his physiognomy will forever be conflated with that of British actor James Mason.[4] Every student of the war knows the Rommel myth. He was a brilliant, thoroughly apolitical soldier. He was no Nazi, and he fought a good, clean fight in the desert, earning a well-deserved reputation as one of history's greatest commanders. After belatedly realizing the demonic nature of the regime he served, he took an active part in the plot to kill the Führer, was discovered, and committed suicide in return for a promise not to harm his family.

In fact, not one of these statements is really true.[5] Rommel was hardly apolitical. His entire career was based on Hitler's favor, and his attitude toward the Führer might reasonably be described as worshipful. He was very much Hitler's fair-haired boy, a young officer who was repeatedly promoted over more senior (and sometimes more deserving) candidates thanks to Hitler's intervention. His exploits at the head of the Afrika Korps were exciting, to be sure, but there are many good analysts who reckon them as an ultimately valueless sideshow. His disinterest in the dreary science of logistics, his love of action, his tendency to fly off wherever the fighting was hottest—all these may make a good movie, but they are disastrous in an army commander under modern conditions, and they all contributed materially to his ultimate failure in the desert.

Still, Rommel fascinates us, doubtless because he was such a modern figure. Everything about him—his rugged good looks, his just-so poses, even his designer goggles—stamp him as someone we instinctively recognize: the media creation. Nazi propaganda painted him not only as a garden-variety hero, but as a model National Socialist and Aryan, a man who could overcome materially stronger enemies through sheer force of will. He was not merely a passive bystander to the creation of his own myth; he was an active accomplice. He loved nothing better than having a camera crew along with him while on campaign, and he would regularly order scenes to be reshot if his posture was insufficiently heroic or the lighting had not shown him to his best advantage.[6] As with many in his position, his relationship to the media was both self-serving and ultimately self-destructive. During the years of victory, the German propaganda machine used him as an example to the nation. When things went sour, he became a diversion from the increasingly bad news on other, more important fronts. Finally, when he was no longer useful for any purpose at all, the regime dropped him altogether and eventually killed him.

Beneath the veneer of modernity, however, Rommel's story is an old one, and the man himself in many ways a throwback who would have felt right at home in the old Prussian army. His dash and drive, his instinctive distrust of any higher authority save the liege lord (formerly a Hohenzollern, now Hitler), even the distrust he engendered among so many fellow officers: all these traits fit into the well-tried Prussian historical pattern. Frederick the Great's top cavalrymen, Hans-Joachim Ziethen for the hussars and Friedrich Wilhelm Seydlitz for the battle cavalry, also won few friends over the course of their careers, but they always had the confidence of the one man they needed. We may see Rommel, in fact, as the last of one of the oldest Prussian traditions of all: the ambitious and energetic outsider (he was not Prussian, but a Württemberger of Swabian ancestry[7]), the gifted foreigner without a pedigree who decided to throw in his lot with the King of Prussia and offer his talents to the "army of the Mark." It is a long and distinguished list, beginning with Brandenburg's first great field marshal, Georg von Derfflinger. The hero of Fehrbellin was an Austrian, a journeyman tailor, and a young man so poor "he couldn't afford to pay the boatman for passage over the Elbe."[8] His military career began in the Swedish army, and he only joined the Prussians when he was in his sixties. Field Marshal Blücher came from a long line of soldiers from the principality of Mecklenburg. He joined the Swedish army as a cavalry officer in 1758 during the Seven Years' War, and he entered Prussian service only after being taken prisoner in 1760.[9] The Prussian state had always prided itself on opening its doors to foreigners, provided they had talent. The presence of so many obviously non-German names within the officer corps, Du Moulin[10] and Heinrici[11] and François,[12] emphasizes the point. Typically, these men took eagerly to Prussian ways, and in fact they spent their entire careers trying to "out-Prussian" their colleagues—that is, displaying unusually high levels of aggression and drive even within an army where both traits were already highly pronounced.

"He's Gone Insane": Rommel in Africa

When Rommel arrived in Africa, he brought with him a fully realized art of war. This was the same man who had earned a Pour le Mérite for a series of nail-biting mountain exploits in the Caporetto campaign in 1917,[13] and who had commanded the 7th Panzer Division during Case Yellow. The French campaign saw Rommel behaving not so much like a traditional divisional commander as an 18th century hussar cut loose on a raiding mission. Historians typically concentrate on his personal brio in helping his assault troops cross the Meuse at Dinant on May 14. In fact, his characteristic moment of the campaign was the drive into Avesnes on the night of May 16–17. With the high command getting increasingly jittery about the separation between the armored forces and their supporting infantry, and trying hard to rein in the Panzer divisions, Rommel deliberately turned off his divisional radios to avoid recall. He was present with his lead elements as they embarked on a bold nighttime joyride that actually caught elements of the French 5th Motorized Division in bivouac. With its vehicles lined up along both sides of the road like "targets in a shooting gallery," Rommel's troopers drove into, over, and through them, firing wildly "from all barrels." He later commented, "The method that I have ordered, of driving into the enemy with all guns firing . . . has worked magnificently. It costs us a lot of ammunition, but it saves tanks and lives. The enemy have not found any answer to this method yet. When we come up on them like this, their nerves fail."[14]

It was an amazing moment, described by one German source as "apocalyptic," the death of a division caught completely flat-footed—and like so many highlights of Rommel's career, a seemingly made-for-cinema moment. Consider this description by one German soldier at Avesnes:

> I have never seen anything like the scenes along Rommel's route of advance. His tanks had run into a French division coming down the same road, and they had just kept on advancing right on past it. For the next five or six miles, there were hundreds of trucks and tanks, some driven into the ditches, others burned out, many still carrying dead or injured. More and more Frenchmen came out of the fields and woods with abject fear written on their faces and their hands in the air. From up front came the short, sharp crack of the guns of our tanks, which Rommel was personally directing—

> standing upright in his ACV [armored command vehicle] with two staff officers, his cap pushed back, urging everybody ahead.[15]

For the rest of the night, Rommel simply drove up to clumps of French men and tanks, commanding them to surrender: "He indicated to the French by sign language that they were to lay their weapons down and that the war was over for them."

Before the night was out, the French II Corps had melted in away in panic, the 1st Armoured Division was completely destroyed, and elements of at least five other divisions fell into German hands. Rommel's own losses in the Avesnes raid were forty killed in action and seventy-five wounded. The raid on Avesnes earned 7th Panzer the French nickname "the ghost division" (*la division fantôme*) for its tendency to drop off the situation maps and reappear where least expected. There were many in the German high command, up to and including General Franz Halder, who didn't much like having a "ghost division" in their order of battle, one that tended to drop off German situation maps from time to time, too. As for the commander himself, "it was impossible to court martial such a successful general, so Rommel instead got the Knight's Cross."[16]

Rommel in Africa would look a great deal like Rommel in France: the hussar on the prowl. His orders, from Hitler, from the General Staff, and from his nominal superior, General Italo Gariboldi, commander of the North African theater, were unanimous and explicit. Until he had a significant force under his command, he was not to seek a decisive action against the British.[17] His force was merely to function as a *Sperrband*, a blocking force to bolster the Italians and prevent them from withdrawing to Tripoli without a fight.[18] It was a reasonable request. Rommel's initial force was tiny, consisting of little more than the reconnaissance battalion and an antitank detachment of the 5th Light Division. The rest of the division was still en route, and the 15th Panzer Division would not arrive until the end of May. This was a campaign for which no advance planning had been done. Before 1939, there was hardly a soul in the German General Staff who had envisioned a major war outside of Europe. The German army had fought colonial campaigns, including, for example, the brutal suppression of the Hereros in Southwest Africa in 1904[19] and General Paul von Lettow-Vorbeck's guerrilla war in German East Africa during World War I.[20] But the colonies were gone now, and no one of any importance in German planning circles envisioned a repeat performance. There were hardly even any maps,[21] and Rommel would command a fair share of the campaigns to come on the basis of the compass and the odometer.

Nevertheless, Rommel arrived in Africa looking for an opening to launch an attack. It was a critical moment in the desert. After the signal British victory over the Italian army at Beda Fomm in February, General Richard O'Connor might have booted the Italians out of Tripoli altogether. Instead, he got canceled, with London stripping him of his best units and sending them off to Greece. British Middle Eastern command disbanded O'Connor's XIII Corps and replaced it with a static Cyrenaica Command under General Sir Philip Neame. O'Connor, one of Britain's only proven field commanders, moved upstairs to an administrative post, commander of British troops in Egypt. The unit with the most experience in the desert, the 7th Armoured Division, went back to Egypt, where it was scattered all over the country on various duties. Taking its place in the British line at El Agheila was the inexperienced 2nd Armoured Division. One of the division's brigades was armed with a number of captured Italian tanks, M 13/40s. Their performance in the campaign thus far could hardly have been a confidence booster for the British, but at least their sturdy FIAT engines made them more mechanically reliable than the British Crusader.

Rommel was an aggressive fighting general. He was facing green troops, a green commander, and a static command. He had his orders, but he had ignored orders in the past and been decorated for it. After linking up with his Italian partners (Ariete armored division and the infantry divisions of X Corps, Bologna and Pavia) and carrying out a rudimentary personal reconnaissance, he decided to strike. It began on March 24, with 3rd Reconnaissance Battalion probing the British defenses at El Agheila. The defenders pulled out without a fight. Continuing on to Mersa el Brega on March 31, the Germans met British tanks for the first time. This was a tough little fight. Rommel combined a frontal assault with a carefully reconnoitered flanking movement to the north (that is, between the British position and the sea) and hit the infantry in the Mersa el Brega defile with a concentric attack. A final rush by 8th Machine Gun Battalion cracked open the British position, captured thirty trucks and fifty Bren gun carriers, and sent the survivors scooting back up the Via Balbia toward Agedabia.[22] Rommel pursued them here, pausing only to take a number of phone calls and radio messages from both Berlin and Rome warning him not to do anything rash. At Agedabia, Rommel once again fought a battle of maneuver: he hit the defenders frontally with 5th Light Division's infantry and machine gun units, then sent his Panzers on a ride around their open desert flank to the south.[23] In the course of the fighting, he mauled 5th Royal Tank Regiment, destroying about twenty-five enemy tanks.

The Germans entered Agedabia on April 2. These had been three tiny encounters, barely more than regimental sized, but it was now clear to Rommel that he had unhinged the entire British defensive position in Cyrenaica. His "reconnaissance in force," the phrase he used to sell his move to his superiors, now became a general offensive. There were three simultaneous thrusts. On his left, the Italian Brescia Division and the 3rd Reconnaissance Battalion drove along the coastal road, harrying the British retreat. On the far right, elements of 5th Light Division and the reconnaissance battalion of the Ariete armored division made a wide sweep into the open desert, across the base of the great Cyrenaican bulge, heading toward Derna on the coastal road in order to cut off the British retreat. In between them, the main body of Rommel's armor (5th Panzer Regiment, elements of 5th Light Division, and Ariete) drove for the British supply depots at Msus and Mechili.[24]

In the face of the onslaught, the British front in Cyrenaica crumbled. There was hardly a single battle in the advance. The left column took Agedabia on April 2; Benghazi on the 4th; Derna on the 7th. The central tank-heavy column reached Msus and Mechili on April 6. Here it captured a mountain of British supplies and stores of all types, including the gasoline that would fuel the rest of the German drive eastward, as well as the commander of the 2nd Armoured Division and his entire headquarters staff. The next day, the head of the column reached Gazala. The British rear was in chaos. On April 6, a German motorcycle patrol stopped a car wandering in the dark, obviously lost. Inside it was the British commander in Cyrenaica, General Neame, as well as General O'Connor himself, both of whom went into German captivity.[25] The capture of the generals heralded the complete collapse of the British command structure in Cyrenaica, just one week into the fighting. By April 11, the Germans had surrounded the coastal fortress of Tobruk while smaller formations pressed on to the east, taking Bardia and reaching the Egyptian border at Sollum and Fort Capuzzo. This was top-speed maneuver, and the distances involved far exceeded the European conditions with which Rommel was familiar. Indeed: he had come over 600 miles in less than two weeks.

But 600 miles to where? Rommel had lunged to the Egyptian border in one great bound, but now he had an unconquered fortress sitting at his rear, a serious threat to his lines of communication and supply. His attempts to storm Tobruk went badly wrong. In the Easter battle (April 10–14) and the battle of the salient (April 30–May 4), the defenders from the 9th Australian Division hung tough. Minefields channeled the German attack, while direct fire from artillery, antitank guns, and supporting tanks shot up the assault force quite badly and killed General Heinrich von Prittwitz, commander of 15th Panzer Division. Like all great German generals of the past, Rommel excelled at the war of movement. But a grinding *Stellungskrieg* like this could make any commander look mortal.[26]

Tobruk not only remained unconquered, but its very presence rendered Rommel's drive across the desert pointless. Indeed, for all the fame it had brought Rommel outside of Germany, this first campaign won him few friends among the command echelons in Berlin. He had proven himself to be a master of space and time, able to drive wherever he wished at top speed, generating enormous excitement—and headlines—back home. Beyond that, what had he accomplished? At the end of April, General Halder sent his quartermaster general, General Friedrich Paulus, down to North Africa. His mission: meet with Rommel, who had apparently "gone insane,"[27] to try to talk some sense into him. It is difficult to disagree with the chief of the General Staff in that assessment, nor in the following comments:

> Rommel hasn't given us a clear report for days. I have the feeling something's wrong. All the comments I read in the officers' reports or in personal letters indicate that Rommel is in no way up to his leadership task. He storms around all day long with formations strewn all over the place, launches reconnaissance missions, fritters away his troops. Not one person has an overall view of the deployment of the troops or their battle-worthiness.[28]

Although it is easy to see Halder's kvetch as the complaint of a conservative and perhaps envious desk jockey against an overly bold man in the field, there was more going on here. It wasn't simply that Rommel was ignoring his logistics. Running mobile operations on a logistical shoestring was the way the Prusso-German army had done business for centuries, and it is instructive to note that Halder's complaint never even mentions the subject. Those devout soldiers who had just won the dramatic victory at Leuthen in 1757, and who camped afterward on the battlefield singing the traditional hymn, "Nun danket alle Gott," were doing so on empty stomachs.[29] The same was true for the victorious host at Königgrätz in 1866: same hymn, same hunger.[30] "Logistics" was a problem that the clerks were supposed to solve as best they could, freeing the operational genius to concentrate on his maneuver scheme. In fact, the Germans didn't even use the word. This was still an army that relied on good old-fashioned "supply" (*Nachschub* or *Versorgung* in German), a much narrower concept that implied little beyond "keeping forward units' haversacks, ammunition pouches, nosebags, and gas tanks reasonably full."[31]

The Wehrmacht's problem with Rommel went beyond logistics. It touched on the nature of the operations themselves. By the long-term standards of German warmaking, Rommel's opening blow was hardly the triumphal parade portrayed in the popular histories. It had featured no real breakthrough; there had been no enemy position to break. There had been no *Kesselschlacht;* the tiny force commitment on both sides had rendered it impossible. Because he had threatened no vital British interest, the British saw no need to throw an army in front of him in order to defend it. The absence of this dynamic, the motor of decisive Germans operations for centuries past, meant that there couldn't be any real *Vernichtungssieg,* no "victory of annihilation."[32] Rommel's pocket-sized force had overrun a vast wasteland, but it hadn't destroyed anything. The Afrika Korps had advanced 600 miles from El Agheila (900 miles from its supply base at Tripoli) and now sat precariously on the edge of nowhere. In that sense, although Rommel had shown a satisfying level of aggression, something the entire officer corps understood, most of them saw his drive to the Egyptian border as a misfire. Halder was simply speaking for many.

Subsequent operations deserve the same critical eye. As a relative calm settled over the theater, it was clear to both sides that Rommel had conquered himself into an impasse, unable to take Tobruk and equally unable to advance any further into Egypt without it. His forces had by now grown to three German divisions: the original 5th Light Division was upgraded to 21st Panzer Division in October 1941; along with 15th Panzer Division, it formed half of the famous "Afrika Korps." Rommel also had 90th Light Division (also called the Afrika Division), with specialized equipment and training for desert conditions. Unfortunately, the British had been reinforcing even faster than he had, which would be a recurring pattern in the desert war, the result of British command of the sea and the Suez Canal. Where Rommel had a corps, the British had an army.

On November 18, 1941, British 8th Army (General Alan Cunningham) launched its first great offensive against Rommel: Operation Crusader.[33] It was a two-corps operation. A heavy armored force (XXX Corps) would swing around Rommel's southern flank and occupy Gabr Saleh. There it would wait for Rommel to approach and precipitate a great clash of the two armored fleets. Once the British had smashed the mass of German armor, another force (XIII Corps, consisting of the infantry formations) would attack the Axis positions at Sollum frontally, breaking through and moving on to the relief of Tobruk.[34]

It worked, to a point. The flank drive by XXX Corps soon ran into trouble. The armored brigades rolled forward to Gabr Saleh and got no response. As a result, there was much milling about and confusion within the British ranks. When 22nd Armoured Brigade, on the extreme left, finally did contact tanks at Bir Gubi, they were not Germans at all, but Italians of the Ariete Division. Soon a full-fledged tank melee was under way here, sucking in virtually all of 22nd Armored and keeping it from its appointed round with the Afrika Korps. Moreover, 22nd Armored was new to the desert and suffered heavy losses, both to the Italians and to mechanical breakdown. With the 4th Armoured Brigade deployed in a protective role, that left the attack in the hands of a single brigade, the 7th Armoured. It rolled on to Gabr Saleh and beyond, heading toward the airfield at Sidi Rezegh.

As 7th Armoured Brigade approached the airfield on November 20, Rommel ambushed it, slamming into its rear with virtually the entire strength of the Afrika Korps. German tanks handled their British counterparts, mainly thin-skinned, undergunned "cruiser tanks" and U.S. M-3 Stuart cavalry tanks ("Honeys" to the British) roughly, inflicting heavy casualties. In the course of the fighting, the other two British armored brigades arrived on the scene. November 22 was a day of particularly heavy carnage around the airfield, with the smoke of hundreds of burning tanks raising the level of confusion.[35] Superior German training eventually told, however, and by the end of the day, the remnants of all three British brigades were retreating from the melee. As darkness fell, the Germans landed a last blow when 15th Panzer Division inadvertently overran the headquarters of the 4th Armoured Brigade.[36] The fighting climaxed the next day, *Totensonntag*, the German memorial day for the dead of World War I. Just south of Sidi Rezegh, Rommel forced the British back into a pocket, with 7th Armoured Division and the 1st South African Division under concentric attack from the south (Ariete), west (21st Panzer Division), and east (15th Panzer Division).[37] A significant portion of the British force was able to escape, however, with the assistance of an attack by 6th New Zealand Brigade, lying outside the pocket to the east. Losses were heavy on both sides. A *Kesselschlacht* under normal European conditions meant blocking perhaps two or three major roads. In the desert, it really did require 360-degree coverage, and no army of the day was capable of it—certainly not Rommel's already well-blooded force.

Nevertheless, the experience had apparently been unsettling enough for Cunningham. He began drafting orders for a general withdrawal of the army back into Egypt. Both his corps commanders (General A. R. Godwin-Austen for XIII Corps and General Willoughby Norrie for XXX Corps), however, recommended continuing the offensive. Seconding their opinion was the imperturbable commander in chief, Middle Eastern Command, General Claude Auchinleck.[38] The frontal assault by XIII Corps had overrun much of the Axis line from Sollum to Halfaya Pass ("Hellfire," in the British vernacular), and it was clear that Rommel, too, had lost heavily in the Sidi Rezegh battles. The thing to do now, they all felt, was to continue the offensive in conjunction with a breakout attack by the Tobruk garrison. Even Rommel would have trouble dealing with three simultaneous threats.

Rommel, by contrast, felt that *Totensonntag* had been a great victory, and all that remained was to deliver the killing blow. On the morning of November 24, he scrounged up every vehicle he could find and accompanied them in person to begin his famous "dash to the wire," a daring motorized strike deep into the British rear, aiming at the barbed wire entanglements on the Egyptian frontier. In the course of this wild ride, he overran, in quick succession, the headquarters of the XXX Corps, the 7th Armoured Division, the 1st South African Division, the 7th Support Group, and the 7th Armoured Brigade, unleashing panic as he went. He even came close to picking up another British commander for his collection, as Cunningham happened to be visiting XXX Corps headquarters. The drive finally stopped, unbeknownst to the Germans, less than fifteen miles short of 8th Army headquarters, and the entire store of water for four full divisions.[39]

Although it is hard to read all this and not be caught up in the excitement, the dash to the wire was another of those famous moments in Rommel's career that proved to be pointless. British transport scattered and the headquarters personnel got the shock of their lives, but the fighting troops stayed where they were, taking supply from two forward dumps. Even worse, with Rommel away, the Tobruk garrison had broken out over the Duda escarpment to the south and linked up with the New Zealanders of the relief force. By December 4, Rommel had no choice but to retreat back to the Gazala line, west of Tobruk. The British pursuit was none too vigorous but still persistent. With his supplies gone and his own losses heavy, Rommel now decided to go all the way back to the point at which his offensive had started back in March, El Agheila.

Once again, the mobility of the desert war is stunning, with routine advances of hundreds of miles on both sides. The Afrika Korps usually did it faster than the British, but both sides had enjoyed their moments of riding free. There was a certain iron logic at work here, however, and neither side could escape its grip. Long advances did not simply take you away from your railhead, they took you several time zones from it. Supply became not just a problem, but *the* problem. Rommel was far more dangerous at El Agheila, relatively close to Tripoli, than he was on the Egyptian wire 600 miles to the east. Likewise, the British were never more dangerous than when they were fighting with Egypt at their back, and never more helpless than when they had just overrun Cyrenaica. Before anyone was completely safe in this theater, one side or the other would have to be destroyed.

Gazala

It should not be surprising, then, that once he was back at El Agheila, Rommel turned the tables on the Allies one more time. In January 1942, after spending a few short weeks sorting out his forces after their long trek to the west, Rommel went back onto the offensive.[40] Once again, in an eerie repeat of the 1941 campaign, the British had stripped their front before him. Last year it had been the Balkans; this year it was to shore up Britain's collapsing position in the Far East, which was then reeling under a series of Japanese hammer blows. For both sides, it seemed, there was always someplace more important than Africa.

Rommel's second offensive quickly bore fruit. Once again, the British had rotated their most experienced units back to Egypt and had placed yet another green unit (1st Armoured Division) in his path. Rommel's opening blow tied it in knots. A regimental-sized task force, Group Marcks, got around the British right flank near the coast. The mass of Afrika Korps, coming up around the enemy left, had more trouble. It got mired in the deep dunes of the interior and failed to arrive in time. Group Marcks wound up riding clear around the British force.[41] Although there were immense gaps in the attempted *Kessel*, having German mobile units prowling around in the rear was enough to send 1st Armoured reeling back in utter disarray. In the next two weeks, Rommel reconquered Cyrenaica. It was even easier than the first time, perhaps the greatest hussar raid of all time. This was low-intensity fighting without a fully formed division in sight; it included few battles and generated minimal casualties. Spearheading the drive for the last 200 miles, in fact, were two tiny task forces, Group Marcks and Group Geissler.[42] By February 6, Rommel was back on the Gazala line, just east of the Cyrenaican bulge and thirty-five miles west of Tobruk.

Here, the hypermovement of the desert war ground to a halt. Both sides had wasted themselves racing back and forth and were, for the moment, incapable of further hostilities—or even movement. For nearly four months, Axis and British forces would sit facing each other. The Gazala position came to bear all the hallmarks of *Stellungskrieg*, adjusted for desert conditions. There were trenches, rifle pits, barbed wire, and machine gun nests. On the British side, fortified "boxes,"[43] dense 360-degree concentrations of tank obstacles and antipersonnel mines, came to dominate the front, with contact between them protected by great "mine marshes." As in all the desert lulls, it was a time of feverish activity behind the lines as both sides frantically attempted to reinforce and resupply. Rommel knew, however, that this was a game that the British would win in the long term.

But what of the short term? Here, on the Gazala line, Rommel would finally win a real victory, not the ultimately meaningless ones of the so-called Benghazi sweepstakes.[44] Here he would maul an actual British field army. In the process, he would open tempting operational vistas further to the east. Not only would the victory at Gazala finally unlock the door to Tobruk, but it would place Rommel within reach of one of the most tempting strategic targets to beguile the Wehrmacht in the entire war: the Suez Canal. For a few weeks in the summer of 1942, the fate of the British Empire seemed to hang in the balance. Rommel's win at Gazala, in other words, was a victory that even General Halder could love.

Planning: Operation Theseus

Certainly the balance of forces did not seem to recommend an Axis offensive. The British 8th Army, now commanded by General Neil Ritchie, numbered some 100,000 men deployed along a thirty-five-mile front and in similar depth back to Tobruk.[45] Supporting it were at least 900 tanks, and each formation in the army was fully motorized.[46] There were also new faces in the British arsenal: 316 American tanks shared between the 1st and 7th Armoured Divisions, 149 Stuart light tanks, and 167 M-3 Grant mediums. The Stuart was a speedy little machine, useful within clearly defined limits of scouting and reconnaissance. The Grant, however, was the best piece of armored hardware to hit the desert.[47] It had been rushed into production in early 1942 to meet America's suddenly pressing need for a medium tank, and it had all the design elegance of a boxcar. It was not particularly maneuverable, and its tall-as-a-house target profile (nine feet, three inches)[48] rendered it incapable of going "hull down" to protect itself from enemy fire. On the plus side, however, its thick armor made it impervious to just about anything but a direct hit from an 88mm antiaircraft gun. It was also one of the most heavily armed tanks of the day, packing two forms of main armament: a short-barreled 75mm gun in a fixed mounting, or sponson, in the hull, and a 37mm gun in the turret.

Facing this formidable array of manpower and material was a force that had recently been upgraded to the status of Panzerarmee Afrika. Its numbers barely reflected the new moniker. It was still small, fewer than 90,000 men. Its armored force consisted of just 561 tanks, but even that number was deceptive.[49] Over 200 of them were inferior Italian models, M 13/40s or M 14/41s—"rolling coffins," as their crews joked nervously.[50] Moreover, the mass of Rommel's armor was just then beginning to fall behind the British in terms of quality. The main battle tank was still the Pzkw Mark III, armed with the short-barreled 50mm (40 caliber) gun; only nineteen tanks in the entire theater had received the much more useful 50mm long (60 caliber). There were also forty Pzkw Mark IV models with the short-barreled 75mm gun. It could destroy a Grant tank, but only if it could reach it, and the Grant far outranged it. German designers were even then working on a new model Mark IV with a longer-barreled gun, which would have been able to battle the Grant on something like equal terms. Unfortunately only four of them had arrived in the theater, and these did not yet have the correct ammunition.[51]

Although the material situation looked bad, Rommel felt that he had an equalizer. The British way of war was to fight a carefully controlled, systematic battle based on tight schedules and phase lines. He had to find a way, therefore, try to force them out of their game and plunge them into a fight for which they were not suited: a battle of maneuver in the open desert (*das Manövrieren in der offenen Wüstenschlacht*).[52] Here the qualitative superiority of his troops, "who were not only superlatively trained in a tactical sense, but were also used to improvising," would come to the fore. As always in the German operations, man would be expected to overcome matériel.

Rommel's plan, Operation Theseus,[53] aimed at smashing the British army in North Africa with a single blow. He would do it with an extreme version of a maneuver that had worked for German armies many times before, and that in fact bore a strong resemblance to Frederick the Great's move against the Austrians at the battle of Leuthen[54]: one force would launch a convincing diversionary attack against the center and right of the British position, fixing the enemy's attention to his front. Meanwhile, in the dead of night, an immense mobile force would drive southeast into the open desert, bypass the British army's left flank south of Bir Hacheim, and then wheel back to the north, driving hard for the sea. The defenders in the British front line would awake to find themselves encircled by a dense mass of German armor bearing down on them from behind. British command staff, rear area administrators, and supply personnel would have it even worse. If all went well with Rommel's plan, they would start out their day running for their lives.

The offensive would begin in the north. Facing the northern stretch of the Gazala position were two Italian corps: XXI Corps to the north, with the German 15th Rifle Brigade along the coast and two Italian infantry divisions abreast (Sabratha on the left and Trento on the right); to the right of XXI Corps lay X Corps (divisions Brescia and Pavia, left to right). Rommel intended to accompany the mobile flanking maneuver to the south, so he had placed this diversionary wing under the command of General Ludwig Crüwell (Group Crüwell) and provided it with much of the Panzerarmee's artillery. Crüwell's mission was to open the battle with a strike into the heart of the British line along the most direct route to Tobruk. The more attention, fire, and tanks the Italians could lure to the north, the better it would be for maneuver in the south. Crüwell's orders, in fact, instructed him to make as much noise and dust as possible "by driving tanks and trucks around in circles" just behind his front.[55]

The business end of the Gazala maneuver was a powerful concentration of armor, certainly the largest strike force that Rommel had ever led. From left to right, it included the Italian XX Motorized Corps (Trieste motorized division on the left, Ariete tank division on the right), and the Afrika Korps under General Walther Nehring, with 21st Panzer Division on the left (General Georg von Bismarck) and 15th Panzer Division to its right (General Gustav von Värst). Finally, on the extreme right of the Axis advance stood 90th Light Division (General Ulrich Kleemann). Reinforcing it were three reconnaissance battalions, the 3rd, 33rd, and 580th, whose task was to form a thick screen ahead of the main body during its risky maneuver onto the British rear.[56]

Five complete divisions, then, containing virtually every tank that Rommel possessed, would drive around the British southern flank. There have been few more vivid demonstrations of the German concept of the *Schwerpunkt*, that "point of main effort" that generations of students at the Kriegsakademie had been taught was essential to a successful operation. "A battle without a *Schwerpunkt*," General Paul von Hindenburg had once remarked, "is like a man without a personality, who leaves everything to chance."[57] If that is so, then Rommel had definitely imprinted a personality on this battle; it would employ a combination of mobility, speed, and shock to smash a larger, more powerful, and entrenched enemy army.

The British position facing him was something new: an attempt to create an unshakeable line in the desert, and thus to force Rommel into a frontal attack no matter what his inclinations might be. Even if the Germans got around the southernmost defensive box at Bir Hacheim, held by a Free French Brigade under General Marie-Pierre Koenig, they would still be facing a series of unflankable British brigade boxes that they would have no choice but to assault. Their losses would be high in the attempt, and British armor would have an easy path into their rear as they attacked the boxes. The firmness of the British front line, in addition, would make any sort of bold drive to the wire extremely problematic in terms of supply, which Ritchie had already identified as the weakest arrow in Rommel's quiver.

Although General Ritchie's deployment has been the subject of controversy to the present day, it certainly seems sensible enough. He had two corps abreast: XIII Corps on the right and XXX Corps on the left, with the demarcation line between them the east-west track known as the Trigh Capuzzo. The XIII Corps (General W. H. E. Gott) was an infantry formation, containing 1st South African Division and 50th Infantry Division in the front line. Its mission was to defend the Gazala position from the Mediterranean coast down to the Trigh. The XXX Corps (General Norrie) was the mobile wing. Norrie had two armored divisions: the 1st (General Herbert Lumsden) and the 7th (General Frank Messervy), both placed well south of the Trigh Capuzzo. Ritchie had to guard against two possible German approaches: a frontal slam through his right and center toward Tobruk, or an end run around his left. Virtually all intelligence reports pointed to the former, and Ritchie's own superior, General Auchinleck, agreed. Ritchie deployed to meet the other eventuality, quite rightly, as things turned out, and placed his armor to meet it.[58] More difficult to justify is the layout of the British front line. The two infantry divisions of XIII Corps were firm, certainly, but south of them lay a wide gap between 150th Infantry Brigade (in the box at Got al Ualeb) and the southern anchor of the Bir Hacheim box. Covering the gap was an immense minefield, but one essentially uncovered by friendly forces.[59]

The problems here ran deeper than Ritchie's eye for the terrain. On the surface, the position of 8th Army seems relatively simple: a straight line, backed up by reserves, facing west. In fact, there wasn't a single formed division on the battlefield. As always, British formations lay strewn about the battlefield in a high state of operational dispersion.[60] Perhaps it was a vestige of its regimental tradition, but the British army, and especially its tanks, always seemed most comfortable when fighting in the smallest units possible. The result was a waste of resources and a needlessly complicated and unresponsive chain of command that would be inadequate to handle the brutal pace of the upcoming battle.

The high-mobility XXX Corps, for example, was all over the place between Knightsbridge, Bir Hacheim, and Bir Gubi, sprawled out across the desert with no real center of gravity. The 7th Motor Brigade and 3rd Indian Motorized Brigade were deployed south of Bir Hacheim, dangling out on a precarious limb. The 4th Armoured Brigade sat to the east of Bir Hacheim, while 22nd Armoured Brigade was far to the north at Knightsbridge. As a result, Rommel was able to concentrate a fist of tanks, five fully formed divisions, against a British force dispersed into a brigade here and a brigade there, with British divisional commanders trying to figure out how to defend themselves in two or three places at once and never being able to call upon their full, concentrated strength.

Consider, for example, the 7th Armoured Division. During the Gazala battle, it consisted of the following units: 4th Armoured Brigade, 7th Motor Brigade, 3rd Indian Motorized Brigade, 29th Indian Brigade, and 1st Free French Brigade. The first three units were mobile formations, deployed on the open left (south) flank of the Gazala position and ready to fight a maneuver battle with the Panzerarmee. The last two, however, were positional units, deployed in boxes and intended to function as static formations in the upcoming battle. The 1st Free French Brigade was well to the left front, in the Bir Hacheim box. The 29th Indian Brigade was far to the rear, in the box at Bir Gubi.[61] Coordinating three mobile brigades and two static ones would have taxed the ability of commanders far more gifted than General Messervy.

On the eve of the battle, then, it is possible to see a rout in the making. On the one side lay one of the century's most energetic and wily battlefield commanders, who had finally found an operational target worthy of his aggression. Rommel was seeking, in his own words, a decisive battle in Africa, "the destruction of the British in the Marmarica."[62] He was aware that the situation in this global conflict, with its heavy demands on other fronts, might not give him another chance. Under him was a thoroughly professional and extremely loyal staff. His chief of the General Staff, General Alfred Gause; his operations chief (his "Ia," in German parlance), Colonel Siegfried Westphal; his intelligence chief (his "Ic"), Colonel Friedrich Wilhelm von Mellenthin; Colonel Fritz Bayerlein, the chief of the General Staff the Afrika Korps—all of them were among the best in the business, smart, thoroughly professional, and not afraid to say whatever was on their minds. Above all, he had a battle-hardened army that justifiably feared no one at this point in the war. It was, more or less, undefeated; few of the men here had been in front of Moscow last winter. Rommel had a massive and concentrated mass of armor well in hand, a bold plan, and an enemy who had thus far proved himself utterly inept at fighting the war of movement, especially on the operational level.

As to the British, there weren't so much concentrated for battle as they were thrown down haphazardly in the desert. Their commander, Ritchie, was by all accounts a good and honest man, although "rather slow,"[63] and utterly unprepared for what Rommel's Panzerarmee was about to throw at him. In that sense, he was typical of enemy commanders that the Germans had met in the first three years of the war. If the men of 8th Army had gotten good at anything, it was giving a good account of themselves even through the disasters visited on them by their own commanders. They were going to need a lot of that in the days ahead.

Theseus: The Approach March

On May 26, at 2:00 P.M., the offensive opened in the north. A massive artillery barrage, strong air attacks against British airfields and installations, and an infantry assault by the Italian divisions against the British line running from Gazala to Got el Mahata. It certainly looked

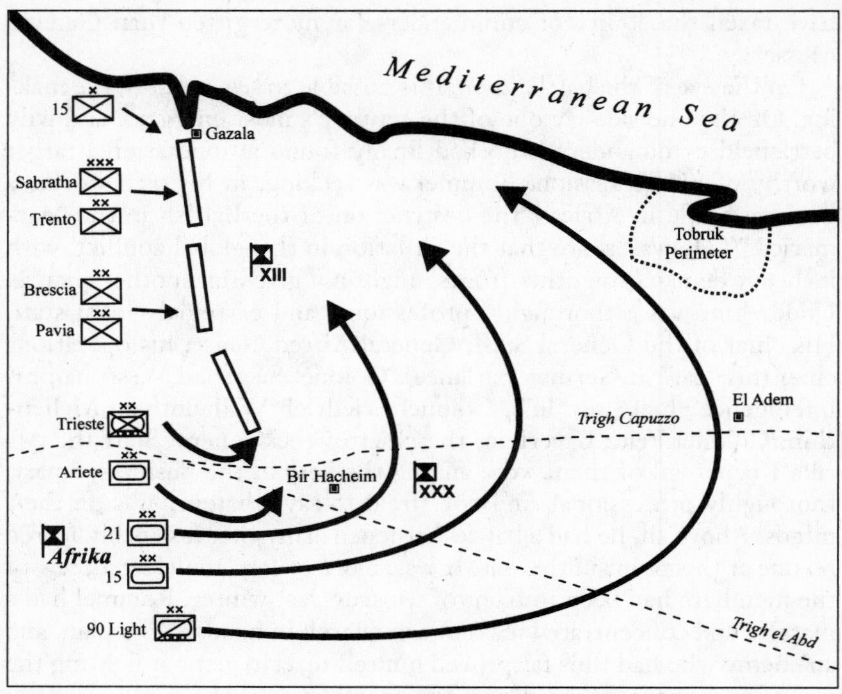

Map 5. Operation Theseus: Rommel's plan for Gazala, May 1942.

real enough and it unfolded exactly according to plan. It contacted British reconnaissance units ahead of the line and drove them back slowly onto the main position. As if on cue, a great desert storm, the *khamsin*, blew up in the late afternoon. To the British, the situation would have appeared exactly like a deliberate attack that had run afoul of the weather.[64] To keep them thinking that, Crüwell had his divisions make as loud a racket as possible, revving truck engines, driving captured British tanks in circles behind Italian lines, and keeping up a random shelling all evening.

It apparently worked well enough to keep British eyes averted for several crucial hours from what was happening in the south. All that day, Rommel was assembling his armored phalanx behind the German lines. The sandstorm hid his movements from the British, even if they had known where to look. With visibility reduced to just ten meters, however, it also played havoc with German march columns. Absolute radio silence, required for an operation of this sort, didn't help either, and more than a few German units briefly got lost. The mobile group got under way in the afternoon and reached its assigned Deployment Area A by early evening, around 6:00 P.M. for the 90th Light Division and 7:00 P.M. for the XX Motorized Corps and Afrika Korps. A mass of some 10,000 vehicles now stood just southwest of the British Gazala line. From here it moved southeast toward Deployment Area B, almost due south of Bir Hacheim. It was not a "line" or a "column" of troops in the classical sense, but a great square that was, according to several German officers involved, "only possible in the desert":

> The tanks were in the lead (deployed in wings or waves) with attached engineer units, behind them the light artillery, so that it could take part in any engagements which might develop, even at great distances. There were antitank units on the flanks as security troops. The divisional operations staff with signal facilities was directly behind the tank wave, behind them the signal battalion and combat columns. There was one armored infantry battalion as a rear covering force.[65]

This was desert warfare at its most developed, an entire army coming up in waves, without having to worry about forming road column or enemy obstructions: "The order of march did not follow any set form, but could be changed at will at any time without difficulty."[66] The only potential hiccup had taken place an hour earlier, when the considerable reconnaissance assets attached to 90th Light Division had detected strong British armored forces behind the left (southern) flank of the British line. The single radio code word "Venezia" now went out to all German formations on the flank march: the command to swing the march even deeper to the south before the turn into the British rear.[67]

Like so much that night, it seemed to go off without a hitch. When all was said and done, at around 3:00 A.M. on May 27, a solid block of armor nearly fifteen miles on a side stood on the British flank. The "armored phalanx" is a cliché of military history, but this was the real thing: XX Motorized Corps in the north; German Afrika Korps behind it; and 90th Light Division in the rear, all perched on the British right flank, as close to the perpendicular as a round earth and uneven ground would allow. In the final preparation for the attack, XX Motorized Corps now came up out of the column, falling in on Afrika Korps's left while 90th Light Division did the same onto its right, the entire maneuver analogous to an infantry column deploying into line.

Given its immense complexity, it was as smooth an approach march as any in the long history of the German army, rivaled only by Leuthen. The maneuver deserves special credit simply for the smooth arrangement of the two refueling stops (one each for Deployment Areas A and B, the latter topping off the gas tanks just before the great confrontation). Also deserving of mention was the idea to equip 90th Light, on the right flank, with dust-creating machines, essentially ground-mounted airplane propellers, kicking up a storm of their own to simulate the dust cloud of a much larger force, helping to deceive the British as to the exact location of the Afrika Korps.[68] Even the German official history, published in 1990 and hardly renowned for its enthusiasm for the Wehrmacht's art of maneuver, couldn't help but gush: "This nighttime cross-country march (*Flächenmarsch*)—with an actual width of almost 50 kilometers!—of such large formations through the desert, 'the great march,' as Mellenthin called it, was something new in the history of war," it exclaimed.[69]

Indeed, it had required careful and systematic preparation. Prebattle orders had to prescribe precise compass bearings, distances, and a march rate of ten kilometers per hour by moonlight. Pioneers placed blacked-out lights in gasoline cans to mark the way for the troops. Overall it is hard to argue with Colonel von Mellenthin's contention that the march moved "with the smoothness of a well-oiled machine."[70] The favorable weather conditions and suitability of the ground allowed the army to exceed the march rate. The inevitable snafus and anxious moments came and went. Some units lost sight of one another in the dark and smoke, and at one point the follow-on forces got well and truly separated from the armored wave going on ahead, but there were no serious mishaps.

Precision and planning may have been there in abundance, but Rommel would not remember it that way. He would later look at that night as one of almost unbearable uncertainty. His mind was racing. "I was filled with tension and impatiently awaited the coming day," he wrote. "What would the enemy do? What had he already done? These were questions that were going through my head."[71] He would soon have all the answers he needed.

Theseus: The Apotheosis of Erwin Rommel

At 7:00 A.M., it began. The British garrison in the Retma box—an unfinished one, naturally—saw it first. While sitting out in the sunshine of a beautiful May morning, the men looked on with curiosity as a dust cloud appeared on the horizon, some ten miles due east of Bir Hacheim. By now, every man among them had seen strange weather patterns and storms blow up out of nowhere. This one, however, clarified itself with awful suddenness into something they had never seen. There were tanks and vehicles of every description—hundreds, thousands, who could tell?—sailing out of the dust. It was "the whole of Rommel's command," one of them later remembered vividly, "in full cry straight for us."[72]

The same thing happened on both flanks of the Retma box. To the east, near Bir Gubi, lay the main body of the 7th Motor Brigade (7th Armoured Division). Half the unit had been given some well-earned rest and recreation time; at least one source has them swimming in Tobruk on that fateful May morning. West of Retma, 3rd Indian Brigade was caught similarly unprepared. Its commander, General A. A. E. Filose, radioed 7th Armoured Division in excited tones that there was "a whole bloody German armored division"[73] bearing down on him. It was, in fact, Italian tanks of the Ariete division, but it was early in the morning. Both brigades, along with the Retma box itself, were overrun with hardly any fighting in the opening moments of Operation Theseus. The final entry in the war diary of the 3rd Indian said it all: "Positions completely overrun with enemy tanks in the box."[74]

Next came the turn of the rest of 7th Armoured Division. Deployed in bits and pieces all over the battle area, its 4th Armoured Brigade proved to be little more than a speed bump to the Germans. The onrushing 15th Panzer Division caught it flat-footed and simply scattered it. By the time 22nd Armoured Brigade got its orders to ride to the relief of its sister formations, there was little left to relieve. The Germans had smashed the division, and 22nd Armoured rode into a disaster of its own.

So it went. By now, the British, and especially the XXX Corps command, were aware that things had gone badly wrong. General Norrie, the commander, was desperately trying to bring back some semblance of order to his corps, but with minimal effect. Scholars today see the issue of command and control to be central to success on the modern battlefield. Consider, then, the problem of command and control of the 7th Armoured Division, especially the trials and tribulations of its commander, General Frank Messervy. With 4th Armoured Brigade essentially crossed off his order of battle while many of its officers and men were still eating breakfast, Messervy and his divisional headquarters staff tried to escape to the north from their advance headquarters near Bir Beuid. However, they were run down by the armored cars of a German reconnaissance detachment, and Messervy, his chief of staff, and two other staff officers were all taken prisoner. The news did not reach XXX Corps headquarters until that evening, and it took a while to get them to believe it in 8th Army headquarters the next day.

The story did not end here. Messervy convinced his captors that he was a mere batman, so he was guarded half-heartedly, which permitted him to escape the next day. A little while later, while leading his division in a counterattack, he was captured again. He would escape again and be back at his post within another day. A few days after that, while reporting in person to 8th Army headquarters, he came within an ace of being captured a third time. He escaped from a patrol of 90th Light Division only by hiding for the better part of a day in a dry well. Each one of these was not just a brush with personal disaster; it meant an entire British armored division, one of only two at Gazala, going without orders for days on end. Near the end of the battle, his army commander, General Ritchie, would decide to remove him from his post. "Well, Frank, I'm afraid I've lost confidence in you—you seem to be out of luck," said Ritchie. "Nothing seems to be going right with you."[75]

The same could have been said of the entire British army at this point. By noon on May 27, Rommel had erupted suddenly and unexpectedly into the rear of the Gazala position. The entire southern wing of the British position was in shreds. One of 8th Army's armored divisions had been dispersed; the command structure of the entire army had momentarily collapsed. The army commander was out of the loop; the division and corps commanders were either in captivity or desperately trying to find a secure spot from which to reestablish control over their formations, which was a far harder task in desert conditions than it would be in European terrain. Here, commanders essentially plied their trade out in the open, completely vulnerable to whatever might drive by or fly over. Finally, XIII Corps's front line (1st South African Division and 50th Division) had four German divisions sitting astride its line of communications back to Tobruk and Egypt. The operational situation already had all the ingredients of a disaster.

In fact, however, although it was not yet obvious, a great deal was already going wrong for the Panzerarmee. In prebattle planning, Rommel and staff had considered a number of possibilities about where they might meet the British armored divisions. Hitting them in the first minute of the attack had not been part of the plan. The German armored thrust was supposed to head north to the Mediterranean coast and kessel the entire British army to the west. That plan had now come apart. On the left, the Italian attack (XX Motorized Corps) was in danger of misfiring altogether. Motorized division Trieste had apparently not received the "Venezia" signal. It therefore failed to make its flanking maneuver deep enough, swung north too soon, and blundered directly into the British minefields on the southern edge of the Gazala line. Armored division Ariete had crashed into the box at Bir Hacheim rather than go around it, and consequently had gotten nowhere.[76] On the right, 90th Light Division was far to the east, completely isolated and soon under attack from every direction. In the center, the Afrika Korps was no longer barreling toward the coast, but grinding its way forward against serious opposition and a great deal of British armor, led by the tallest and strangest-looking tank any of the German tanks crews had ever seen, which drilled one Panzer after another from impossible ranges.

Within hours, Afrika Korps too was under attack from the north and east. Neither Acroma nor El Adem, the first day's objectives, was yet in German hands. The commander of the 15th Panzer Division, General von Gustav von Värst, had already been seriously wounded by a shell splinter, and Colonel Eduard Crasemann, commander of the division's 33rd Artillery Regiment, had to take over the division. Running the 15th was hazardous business, apparently; Värst's predecessor, General Prittwitz, had been killed at Tobruk. Various members of Rommel's staff were scattered hither and yon, wherever British fire had happened to pin them down, and the forward fighting elements had completely lost contact with their supply columns. By 6:00 P.M., Rommel had to admit that the original plan had failed, and he sent Afrika Korps the signal: "Form up. Dig in. All around defense."[77] It could not have been a pleasant moment for such a hard-driving commander. "I won't deny," he later wrote, "that I was very nervous that first night."[78]

It is an interesting thing to contemplate, but if this were 1939 or 1940, the British might have melted away. This time, however, XIII Corps had not been "surrounded" in any real sense. It was sitting quite comfortably in a series of strong fortified boxes, sited for all-around defense and well stocked with ammunition and supply. Although the British couldn't hold them forever, neither was there any pressing need to abandon them at the moment. Curiously, being cut off from command was probably the best thing that could have happened to XIII Corps at this moment. With higher headquarters in a state that can only be described as momentary panic, the orders that would have come out of them would almost certainly have further destabilized an already shaky British position. Likewise, 1st Armoured Division in the British rear had been free to take its own counsel, without having to worry about hysterical orders that would almost certainly have had it patching holes all over the battlefield. It was the formation whose Grant tanks had blunted the German spearhead.

By the second day, therefore, Rommel was in the tightest spot of his career. His mobile formations were sitting deep in the enemy rear, and thus cut off from their own supply lines. They had a fully intact British defensive line behind them, and they were under nonstop British armored assault from their front and flanks. Supplies of all sorts were running out, and certain units, 15th Panzer Division foremost among them, were actually immobilized for lack of fuel. Rommel had fought a *Kesselschlacht* all right, but the wrong side had wound up in the soup. The British knew it, and would in fact refer to his position as "the cauldron," the English equivalent of *Kessel*. They may have lacked the doctrinal tradition, but they knew when they had an enemy force trapped and ripe for destruction. All day long, they kept up their attacks. For the most part, these consisted of uncoordinated runs against the cauldron by single brigades, but they were bad enough: a British brigade has as many tanks as an entire German division.[79] The two sides exchanged casualties, large numbers of them, and by the end of May 28, Rommel was barely hanging on.

Clearly, the Panzerarmee could not simply stay where it was. On May 29, Rommel personally escorted a supply column from Bir el Harmat through a gap in the British lines, one of the long "mine marshes" that connected the main position in the north to Bir Hacheim to the south, but that was not covered by any troops. Condemned by some of fellow officers as a "hussar's trick"[80] unworthy of an army commander, it was also a definite morale booster to his hard-pressed tank crews fighting on the eastern side of the British wire. In the next two days, further small convoys made it through two gaps cleared by the Italians along the Trigh Capuzzo and the Trigh El Abd. Escorted by the Panzers and shepherded to the east, they brought in just enough fuel to keep the mobile formations in motion.

These were quick fixes, however. With his mobility restored, if only temporarily, Rommel needed a permanent solution. He now made another of the war's most audacious decisions. With the Panzerarmee's antitank units forming a great defensive crescent facing to the east, bristling with 50mm and 88mm guns, Rommel concentrated his tanks and infantry for a fierce concentric attack against the box at Got al Ualeb and its garrison, the 150th Brigade. This was an attack to the *west*—that is, with the Panzerarmee driving toward its own original position. The 15th and 21st Panzer Divisions hit the box from the east and northeast, the Italian Trieste Division from the south and southwest, and the 90th Light Division from the southeast, all supported heavily by Stukas. By the end of the day, there was a hole in the British position where 150th Brigade had been, and 3,000 prisoners, 90 tanks, and 100 guns had fallen into German hands.[81] More importantly, Rommel had reestablished a regular supply line from the west, and the truck columns could now come without requiring a Panzer escort. The British armor to the east had sat passively that day, licking its wounds from the fierce fighting of the previous days, and the army command still seemed at sea. As one divisional commander put it, "150th Brigade was down and out before Ritchie realized it."[82]

There was more fierce fighting to come, to be sure, but the issue was no longer in doubt. The British never did consolidate what could have been a decisive superiority, while Rommel kept his armor in a concentrated mass even through the worst times. The cauldron was admittedly a strange formation, but it had proved its utility as a base for launching attacks to the north and east, and it defended itself against anything the British could throw at it, which was usually a regiment or brigade at a time. When they tried to coordinate larger operations, they ran into disaster. Their major counterattack against the cauldron southwest of Knightsbridge on June 5 was a classic example, a combination of an overly complex plan that bore all the hallmarks of being designed by committee (which it had); failed coordination between the attack elements; and tactical imbecility, featuring yet another unsupported tank charge. Consider the following description by the British official history, one of the great examples of its genre (courtesy of I. S.O. Playfair):

> It was to be in two phases. In the first phase the 10th Indian Infantry Brigade (of Major-General H. R. Briggs's 5th Indian Division) was to capture the first objective in the early hours of 5th June after a really heavy artillery bombardment. The 32nd Army Tank Brigade (of 13th Corps), with 7th Green Howards under command, was then to capture the Sidra ridge. In the second phase the leading role would pass to General Messervy's 7th Armoured Division with the 9th Indian Infantry Brigade (of 5th Indian Division) under command, its object being to destroy the enemy in the Cauldron. The

> 1st Armoured Division, whose reorganized 22nd Armoured Brigade was now in the 7th Armoured Division (replacing the rather battered 4th Armoured Brigade), was to prevent the enemy breaking out to the north or north-east and was to be ready to exploit success westwards.[83]

There was therefore no single commander for this counterattack; General Briggs and Messervy had to coordinate things as best they could. Moreover, orders mandated a separation, not a cooperation, of the armor and infantry: "In case of armoured action infantry are self-protecting. They will not hamper the movement of 22nd Armoured Brigade."[84]

Is this the voice of confidence speaking? Mellenthin called it, justifiably, "one of the most ridiculous attacks of the campaign."[85] The preliminary bombardment landed on empty desert, having misjudged the exact position of the German front line. The assault, spearheaded by the infantry of the 10th Indian Brigade, went in at 2:50 A.M. and, contrary to expectations, crashed frontally into the Ariete Division. The Italians gave a typically good account of themselves despite equipment deficiencies, and Ariete held up the British strike force just long enough for 15th Panzer Division to get around its left flank and 21st Panzer to get around its right. According to one tanker of the 22nd Armoured Brigade, the plan was "to mop up the enemy *en route* and be at [map coordinate] B 104 for breakfast," but soon ran into what Playfair calls "the concentrated fire of the most of the German artillery."[86] A counterattack against the spearhead of the 10th Indian, the 2nd Highland Light Infantry, soon led to a crisis, especially because the infantry had orders *not* to come to its assistance. In the north, along the Sidra ridge, the attack by 32nd Army Tank Brigade was a fiasco, coming to ruin against a wall of German antitank fire and an unmarked minefield, and leaving behind fifty of the seventy infantry tanks that made the assault. Finally, a small mobile detachment, drawn by Rommel out of his army reserve around Bir Hacheim, slipped around the British rear, completing the chain. In fighting throughout the next day, the British lost over 4,000 prisoners and 200 tanks, and with them the last, slim chance at rescuing anything out of the debacle.

The next day, Rommel launched a counterattack that was another one of the signal moments of the campaign. The 21st Panzer Division, along with Ariete, struck to the east, while 15th Panzer Division came up from the south, both attack columns heading toward Knightsbridge. In the course of what was truly a wild ride, the latter overran the Duke of Cornwall's Light Infantry, stationed at Bir el Harmat, and then, "joined by other units from Bir Hacheim and by Rommel himself, dispersed in confusion the Tactical Headquarters of both British divisions, the Headquarters of the 9th Indian Infantry Brigade and two of its battalions (the third, 3/9th Jats, had been sent to reinforce the 2/4 Gurkhas), the Headquarters of the 10th Indian Infantry Brigade and the survivors of the 2nd H.L.I."[87] By this time, "communication and control broke down completely," and the headquarters that had not been overrun were fleeing for their lives: 7th Armoured Division to Knightsbridge, the 5th Indian Division to El Adem. It was as complete a rout as the desert war had seen.

With the threat from British armor ended for the time being, Rommel was now able to clear up one last problem in his rear: the Free French box at Bir Hacheim. It had been driving him to distraction since the battle began by launching harassing raids on the Panzerarmee's already overworked supply columns coming from the west. A first assault on the night of June 1 had failed, and a second on June 6 had barely dented the perimeter. Both times, significant forces had to deploy against relief attempts from the outside. That was no longer the case, and Rommel was free to concentrate overwhelming combat power against the box. The decisive attack on Bir Hacheim opened on June 10, with 90th Light Division, Trieste motorized division, and a task force built around the 115th Infantry Regiment of the 15th Panzer Division (Group Baade) hitting the box concentrically, supported by nearly 400 aircraft: Stukas, Ju-88 bombers, and ME 109 fighters. Even now, it was a tough struggle, perhaps the finest feat of French arms in the entire war. For all the romance invested in the battle, however, there was no chance that a lone brigade box was going to stop Panzerarmee Afrika where the might of an entire British 8th Army had failed. That night, much of the garrison evacuated Bir Hacheim, slipping through German lines to the east as best it could.[88]

By June 14, it was clear to the British that they had lost the battle of Gazala. The original defensive position had fallen apart, and the British were desperately trying to form some sort of east-west line to protect Tobruk from the hard-driving Panzerarmee coming up from the south. The British offered battle one more time, a last-gasp tank attack between Knightsbridge and El Adem on the night of June 11. Afrika Korps and 90th Light, by now as exhilarated as the British were deflated, smashed it easily. The British command was still only tentatively in control of the battle. General Ritchie was commanding 8th Army, but Auchinleck was "advising" him hourly, an impossible situation that led to numerous contretemps and misunderstandings. Auchinleck, for example, thought that he and Ritchie were still discussing the possibility of a retreat long after Ritchie had already ordered it.

It is easy to look at Gazala and see the things that had gone wrong. The plan hadn't taken into account the full range of possible British deployments, and Rommel had to abandon it early. The diversionary attack in the north had achieved little, and it seems to have barely registered on the British. Another full day might have rendered it more useful in drawing off British reserves. Once the two sides clinched, the German and Italian armored divisions drove themselves into a pocket on day 1 and ran out of gas on day 2. Attacking backward toward your own lines to reopen a supply path was a fascinating tactical expedient, but it will probably never make the textbooks at most staff colleges. If the British had made even the slightest effort to concentrate their armor against the cauldron instead of feeding it in a brigade at a time, the Panzerarmee might well have gone down to its doom on day 3 or 4. Rommel had shown immense personal bravery throughout the battle, as he always did, but he wasn't always as easy to find as an army commander should be.

In assessing this battle, however, there is something more important than adding up the brilliance and the blunders. Gazala was a classic example of the German way of war: *Bewegungskrieg*. Its historic bloodlines are obvious, easily traceable to the maneuver tradition first established by Frederick the Great: the risky night march around the Austrian flank at Hohenfriedeberg in 1745; the combination of a diversion against the Austrian front, followed by a deep flank march around the left, at Leuthen in 1757; the march around the Russian army to attack it in the rear at Zorndorf in 1758. Most histories describe the opening maneuver at Gazala in a sentence or two, as if it were the most natural thing in the world, but there wasn't another commander around who would have risked such a dramatic maneuver onto the rear, nor another army in the world who could have pulled it off so smoothly.

Rommel had made his share of mistakes. In his memoirs, he adopted an extraordinarily defensive tone about the entire operation. He had evidently heard the whispers within the officer corps about Gazala, and he spent a great deal of time explaining the exact difference between boldness (*Kühnheit*) and a gamble (*militärische Hazardspiel*).[89] In the end, this subtle distinction mattered little. He had won the battle of Gazala in the first half-hour. It was the peak of his career, the only time that he welded his penchant for maneuver to truly destructive ends. Moreover, in the course of the fighting, the Desert Fox had, perhaps unwittingly, discovered a new truth of operational-level warfare. Call it Rommel's Rule No. 1: erupting into the enemy's rear with an entire tank army in the first moment of battle covers a multitude of operational sins.

It was a fairly familiar sight in the desert war by now: a long line of British vehicles of every description, all careening east at top speed. Rommel let them go. He had learned by now that a true "encirclement" probably wasn't possible in the desert. No matter how large an army was, it couldn't block every road, trigh, or avenue of approach in this open terrain. And besides, it was time, once again, for Tobruk.

Tobruk Again

Like so much in this theater of war, a great deal of mythology about Rommel's second attempt to take Tobruk continues to color the literature of World War II. When Rommel first attacked the fortress in 1941, he did so with barely a division, a force that had just made a high-speed lunge from El Agheila clear across the Cyrenaican desert. It had no real heavy weapons, little air support, and barely enough supply to eat, let alone fight. On that occasion, Rommel had failed to penetrate even the outpost line of the 9th Australian Division, and he suffered heavy losses. He then proceeded to "invest" Tobruk for the next six months. Given his small force commitment, it was an investment in name only—hence the disquiet of Halder and the General Staff about the entire Egyptian venture. Tobruk continued to receive supplies and reinforcement by sea, and certainly no one was starving there in the summer of 1941. The "siege of Tobruk," however, its presence "behind enemy lines," impelled the British command to do something to "relieve" the "besieged garrison." These were the traditional categories in which Winston Churchill viewed twentieth-century war. Hence the launching of Operation Crusader in November 1941, a bloodbath that relieved Tobruk at the coast of massive casualties on the German side and, unfortunately, on the British as well.

Since then, the British command in Africa had deliberately defortified Tobruk. In 1942, Ritchie and Auchinleck saw Tobruk not as a symbol of Britain's indomitable will, but as a man trap. They did not want to be forced, at some future point, to launch another Operation Crusader to relieve it. This time, they vowed, if circumstances forced

8th Army to retreat to Egypt, it would abandon Tobruk, a town of no real military value. At the very least, such a policy would free troops for mobile operations who would otherwise be stuck defending it. By the time of Gazala, Tobruk had neither the antitank ditch nor the extensive minefields of 1941. The British had destroyed them to improve access to the port.

Rommel's 1942 attack hit not a fortress, therefore, but a small, indifferently defended town. There was a single division, the 2nd South African, plus the 11th Indian Brigade and a small complement of armor (the 201st Guards Brigade and the 32nd Army Tank Brigade, the former with a single regiment, the latter equipped with slow-moving infantry tanks, Valentines and Matildas). In addition, there was the detritus of the British retreat from Gazala, portions of the 1st South African Division, for example, and whatever other units, subunits, or even individual soldiers who happened to be caught there when Rommel closed the ring. The morale of all these forces was low. Like all soldiers in all wars, they knew a great deal more than they are usually given credit for. They knew all about the rout from Gazala; some of them had just taken part in it. They also knew that the town was hardly prepared for defense and that, with Rommel already driving far to the east in pursuit of 8th Army, a relief column wasn't going to be riding to the rescue anytime soon.

Rommel, by contrast, had an entire Panzer army. It was pumped full of adrenaline and fully confident in its commanders. He had two Panzer divisions of the Afrika Korps as his main strike force, able assistance in the mobile realm from 90th Light Division, as well as the Italian duo of Ariete armored division and Trieste motorized, and, as backstops, the Italian infantry divisions. Almost always maligned in popular accounts of the fighting (and, unfortunately, too many of the scholarly ones as well), the soldiers of the Sabratha, Trento, Brescia, and Pavia Divisions had done everything that Rommel had asked them to do in this campaign, and more. He also had massive support from the Luftwaffe, once again concentrated against a single small target, and as much supply as he could use, much of it taken as booty from the various British fortified boxes captured in the course of the fighting. It was a rare combination of operational riches for German forces in the desert.

So great was the disparity in strength that Rommel could probably have taken Tobruk any way he wanted—with a simple rush, for example. But German generals from time immemorial had always led off great battles with a signature maneuver, and Rommel's second try for

Tobruk was no exception. The endgame of Gazala had seen his mobile divisions lunging far to the east, all the way to the Egyptian border. The maneuver was designed to lull the garrison into thinking that this was a repeat of 1941, that there would be a fairly leisurely investment of the city, and that there just might be time to prepare its defenses.

But this time would be different. On June 19, Rommel suddenly turned his Panzer divisions around with lighting speed and sent them careening back to Tobruk. The maneuver began in the late afternoon and was mostly completed by the early morning hours. The men of the Tobruk garrison awoke, therefore, to a new shock: the Afrika Korps had somehow materialized out of nowhere against the southeastern face of the perimeter. With awful suddenness, they realized that they were facing an assault.

The "second battle of Tobruk" would be something of an anticlimax, then. Only one side was in any shape to fight. Although sometimes analyzed, even by German sources, as a concentric attack, it was nothing of the sort. There was a ring around Tobruk, to be sure: XXI Italian Corps in the west, XX in the south; Afrika Korps to the southeast and east, 90th Light Division in reserve to the south. But in fact, few of these units fought. After a stupendous Stuka bombardment, soon joined by the combined weight of the Italian and German artillery, the Afrika Korps (15th Panzer on the left and 21st on the right, with Group Menny, mainly infantry elements from the 90th Light Division, deployed between them) launched its assault against a single narrow sector in the southeast. This was the sector of the 11th Indian Brigade, although Rommel was able to form a mighty *Schwerpunkt:* the full might of a German Panzer corps against a single battalion of the brigade, the 2/5th Mahratta Light Infantry. It cracked almost immediately, but who could blame it?

Consider this timetable: the first Stukas arrived overhead at 5:20 A.M.; by 7:00, Group Menny had taken an entire company from the 2/5th Mahratta prisoner; and by 7:45, a wide breach had been made in the assault sector. By 9:30, the tanks of the Afrika Korps were inside the perimeter and fanning out. There was some fighting here or there, and this or that artillery battery or tank unit made a stand, but they were speed bumps. In the operational sense, the Germans were already in the mop-up phase, with 21st Panzer Division driving for Tobruk and 15th Panzer attacking along the Pilastrino ridge, parallel and to the south of the town. Conspicuous throughout the entire operation was the presence of the German commanders. Rommel was in the forefront as always, directing the entire assault personally, but at his side were General Nehring in command of Afrika Korps and General Bismarck of 21st Panzer.

By noon, 21st Panzer Division stood on the Via Balba, as much of a downtown as this little town possessed. Joining it a couple of hours later was the 15th Panzer Division. The Tobruk defenses had been smashed, with individual soldiers and vehicles that had been cut off from their units by the speed of the German advance streaming to the west, just ahead of the conquering Germans. That night, responding to 8th Army's inquiries as to how things were going, General H. B. Klopper, the young and thoroughly overwhelmed commander of the 2nd South African Division, radioed back what may have the understatement of the century: "Situation not in hand."[90]

Not at all, in fact. Klopper formally signed the surrender the next morning. The whole thing had been workmanlike, and as predictable an outcome as an inherently unpredictable venture like war has to offer. The Germans took another great haul of prisoners: 33,000 men, including five generals; their own casualties were negligible. By now, British casualties in the Gazala-Tobruk campaign were nearing the 100,000 mark, including some 60,000 prisoners. Axis casualties were just about a third of that total, and most them were Italian. The victors had also seized a whole series of supply dumps filled nearly to bursting with food, clothing, and ammunition, as well as, most importantly, some 1,400 tons of fuel. British gasoline would be the propellant for the Panzerarmee's next great campaign: the one that would carry it over the wire, into Egypt.

The Wehrmacht: Present and Past in the Summer of 1942

The following description of a British counterattack at Gazala comes from the commander of the 9th Indian Brigade, General C. W. Ridley:

> On our way the Brigadier explained the position as given out at his earlier conference. In the middle of the mine marsh, which went from Gazala, on the coast, all the way to Bir Hacheim, there was a large belly sticking out the west. "The Germans," he said, "had managed to clear a way through the mines into this belly and were sending their supply vehicles through this gap to their panzer forces which had made the big advance round our south flank. We were to close the gap and stop this. . . ."

> Verbal orders were then given. First 7th Armoured Division would make a "swanning" attack in the belly, moving around it in an anti-clockwise direction. During this the Germans would have to send out what armor they had left back here to attack us. As we had more tanks here than they had we should defeat them. This part of the operation would be controlled by General Messervy. Then the 9th Infantry Brigade (ours) would move in clockwise and would set up three battalion boxes in the belly. This part of the operation would be commanded by General Briggs. Brigadier Fletcher asked that the armour should do a clockwise, not an anti-clockwise move. Otherwise his battalions would meet the armour coming out as they were going in and this would be bad for morale.[91]

The passage reads like a caricature, going out of its way to include every failing of the British army in Africa. There was the command muddle, with shared responsibility and handoffs during battle. There was the overly precious maneuver scheme, rotating this way and that. There was service parochialism, with the infantry and the armor wary of each other. Indeed, on the way back after the briefing, Fletcher actually told Ridley, "If we had made a plan like that at the Staff College, we would have been sent down, what!"[92]

While the British had been contemplating the advantages of clockwise and counterclockwise rotations, the Germans had been methodically preparing a merciless assault on Tobruk from land and air. The tanks had been the star of the show, but as in the other grand victories of that happy spring, the Luftwaffe had been able to concentrate overwhelming power against a small target. German aircraft flew nearly 600 hundred sorties against Tobruk on June 20 alone, along with 177 more by the Italian Regia Aeronautica. There were only 145 serviceable aircraft available, so each of them flew three or four missions on that single day. Overall, Fliegerkorps X, employing aircraft brought into the theater from Greece and Crete, flew no fewer than 7,035 missions in the month of June.[93]

Along with sheer weight of metal, there had been Rommel's opening flourish, remarkable even for a figure so intensely self-dramatizing. The lunge to the Egyptian border, looking for all the world as if he intended to ignore Tobruk altogether; the dramatic pause, as if the Afrika Korps were a great beast of prey considering its next victim; the 180-degree turn, accelerating into a top-speed drive for Tobruk, followed seamlessly by the assault: it was one of the most tightly and deliberately choreographed examples of *Bewegungskrieg* in history.

Consider this German description, from the pages of the *Militär-Wochenblatt:*

> If the previous year of war taught the British anything about the need to incorporate wonder and astonishment into their emotional lives, then the events of the past week should have further educated them. It was a remarkable night, when Rommel suddenly ordered his Panzer and motorized divisions, then rolling full speed to the east, to turn around. In the early hours of Sunday morning, when the German armored wedge broke into Tobruk's fortified ring, the Tommies in their trenches and along the route of attack could do nothing but shake their heads and utter words of astonishment, as if they had recognized that they lost the game.[94]

Indeed, every game has rules, and the rules here said that an army that had struck blows as hard as Rommel's would need some time to recover its cohesion before launching an assault.

Tobruk was just the latest example, but all the German campaigns of this period were essentially similar. In Kerch, Kharkov, Gazala, Tobruk, and Sevastopol, the Wehrmacht had won five of the most decisive victories in its entire history.[95] It was an amazing run that represented a climax for the German way of war as it had developed since the 1600s. It had taken nearly 600,000 prisoners in that stretch, its own casualties had been low—almost nonexistent if we exclude Sevastopol. It had fought each of these battles from a position of numerical inferiority. If the highest military accomplishment is the ability to "fight outnumbered and win," the Wehrmacht seemed to have the market cornered by 1942.

It achieved this enviable record of triumph by conducting its operations in the time-honored Prusso-German tradition. All were carefully prepared, highly aggressive, and centered around an operational-level maneuver designed to get onto the opponent's flank and rear with a significant portion of the available force. From that point on, the intent was always the same: to kessel most or all of the enemy's main body, subject it to concentric attack in the classic style, and destroy it. The breakthrough against the carefully chosen left wing of the Soviet line at Kerch; the maneuver at Kharkov, finding the deep left flank of the Soviet position and driving it in relentlessly; Rommel's drive into the British rear at Gazala, landing a first-round blow from which the enemy never recovered; the Afrika Korps's drive far to the east of Tobruk, followed by the sudden turnabout; Manstein's nighttime crossing of Severnaya Bay, bypassing the still unbroken Soviet defensive line in front of Sevastopol: again and again in this period, it was the surprising operational-level maneuver that delivered a shock to the adversary and brought victory even against unfavorable numerical odds.

None of this was new. Tanks and aircraft had given it a more modern sheen, but the essence was historical. It was an operational approach that had been burned into the German officer corps since Frederick the Great. As one German officer wrote in July 1942: "When we think of the decisive sources of strength that make up the concept of German soldiering, not the last among them is tradition. The military fabric of our day is not the result of a single deed. It has formed itself organically by a difficult, centuries-long process." Here is the authentic voice of the German officer corps, one that had emerged from an old and traditional historical matrix: "Tradition is bound up with memory of all the warlike events that have played themselves out on all the battlefields of the centuries. Leuthen and Kunersdorf, Jena and Auerstädt, Leipzig and Waterloo, Königgrätz and Sedan, Tannenberg and Gorlice-Tarnów: all the victories and battles that German soldiers have sealed with their blood arise before our eyes."[96] In other words, the great victories at Kerch and Kharkov, Gazala and Tobruk did not emerge from nowhere. They were instead part of a tradition, and they owed as much to the legacy of Frederick the Great and Moltke as they did to the genius of a Manstein, Kleist, or Rommel.

The decisive nature of these triumphs notwithstanding, they had been mere preliminaries to the upcoming main event. As spring yielded to the high summer of 1942, the Wehrmacht would return once again to the grand offensive. Operation Blue would take the army to many places that it had never dreamed of before: to the industrial city of Stalingrad on the Volga River, to the oil fields of Maikop in the Caucasus Mountain region, to forbiddingly remote places like the Kuban and the Taman and the Kalmuk—and, for the first time, to a place that was truly terra incognita to officers and men of the Wehrmacht alike: an annihilating defeat in a campaign of maneuver.

5

Debacle

The 1942 Summer Campaign

Was Stalingrad really necessary? Did the Wehrmacht have no other choice in the summer of 1942 but to ride to its doom in the ruins of a dying city? The decision to launch Operation Blue (*Unternehmen Blau*) has garnered its share of criticism from analysts, and certainly there is a strong strategic case to be made against it. If ever there was a campaign that seemed to mismatch its means and ends, it was the Wehrmacht's "second campaign" of 1942.[1] The drive to the Volga River, Stalingrad, and the Caucasus Mountains would be the campaign that finally stretched the Wehrmacht beyond its limits.

It is no exaggeration to say that the Germans began this offensive short of everything. The near-collapse of the previous winter had left scars that had not yet healed, and there is for the connoisseur a smorgasbord of statistics from which to choose. For some, it might be the 1,073,066 casualties that the Wehrmacht had suffered in its first nine months in the Soviet Union.[2] For others, it might be the General Staff's estimated replacement deficit of 280,000 men by October 1942, a minimum figure valid only if things went well and operations succeeded with relatively light casualties.[3] The 179,000 horses lost in the Soviet Union in the first year were not going to be replaced anytime soon,[4] and the figures for motor transport were dismal. An OKH (High Command of the Army) report in May put the figure at 85 percent of the trucks required for the mobile divisions of the spearhead.[5] A report from the Army Organization Section warned that it was more like 80 percent,[6] and those at the sharp end thought the situation was a great deal worse. Field Marshal Ewald von Kleist's 1st Panzer Army, which had played such a key role at Kharkov, entered the summer combat about 40 percent of its allotted strength.[7]

By 1942, in fact, there were two Wehrmachts: a high-powered strike force built around the Panzer and motorized divisions, and a low-grade infantry army, useful for little else beyond static positional defense. Another OKW report, written in June and entitled *War Potential 1942*, went so far as to warn that the army's mobility was going to be "seriously affected" in the upcoming campaign, and that "a measure of demotorization" was inevitable—dark words indeed for an army that lived and died by operational-level maneuver.[8] It was an ominous sign: on the verge of its great confrontation with a revived and rapidly mechanizing Red Army, the Wehrmacht was in the process of reequipping its reconnaissance battalions with bicycles. Historians often speak of the Germans scraping the bottom of the manpower barrel in 1944–1945, but in fact they had had already started that process in 1942. The class of 1923 had already been drafted in April 1941, eighteen months ahead of time, and eighteen- and nineteen-year-olds would play a crucial role in filling out the rosters of the new divisions being formed for Operation Blue.[9]

Perhaps the best symbol of Germany's new military economy of scarcity is this unhappy thought: of the forty-one new divisions arriving in the south for Case Blue, fully twenty-one of them would be non-German: six Italian, ten Hungarian, and five Romanian.[10] It was a sure sign that the Germans were having difficulty with the enormity of the front, which by now stretched some 1,700 miles from Murmansk in the north to Taganrog in the south. It hardly bodes well for the course of a major operation when you have to separate your allies to keep them from fighting each other. Operation Blue took into account the historical animosity between the Romanians and Hungarians by slipping the Italians, apparently neutral in this quarrel, between them. It also bodes ill when an allied commander, in this case the Italian general Giovanni Messe, states that the only way he knew of to deal with his German comrades in arms was to "punch them in the stomach."[11]

There were other problems beyond the Wehrmacht's lack of resources. Like so many great military operations of the German past, this one was based on an intelligence fiasco, in particular the failure to draw up an accurate portrait of enemy strength. The Germans estimated available Soviet aircraft at 6,600 planes; the reality was 21,681. They estimated they were facing 6,000 tanks; the actual number was 24,446. The German estimate of Soviet artillery (7,800 guns) was also off by a factor of four (the actual number was 33,111).[12] All in all, the intelligence failure of 1942 was one of the worst in German history, rivaled only by the failure of these same agencies during the run-up to Operation Barbarossa.

It is tempting to label the entire enterprise as hopeless, and many historians have. We must also remember, however, that this was not a military caste that historically spent a lot of time cautiously adding up the odds and only then daring to move. Rather, it had always relied on action as much as theory. One of its greatest twentieth-century soldiers, a man of no mean intellect himself, summed it up in a pithy sentence: "The essential thing is the deed" (*Das Wesentliche ist die Tat*).[13] Its manual for field operations, *Die Truppenführung*, took pains to stress this very point, in italics, no less: "*The first criterion in war remains decisive action. Everyone, from the highest commander on down to the youngest soldier, must constantly be aware that inaction and neglect incriminate him more severely than any error in the choice of means.*"[14] Certainly, it had put deep thinkers like Scharnhorst, Gneisenau, and Moltke on their respective pedestals over the years, but alongside them it had also enshrined an entire stable of hard-charging types like Georg von Derfflinger, General Gebhard Lebrecht von Blücher, and Frederick Charles, the "Red Prince" of the Wars of Unification. Derfflinger, one of the Prussian army's first great captains, had an art of war that boiled down to a simple demand: "No one advances ahead of me."[15] He kept his vigor well into his sunset years, and his career climaxed with the hard ride through the Thuringian Forest in 1675, the maneuver that resulted in the triumph over the Swedes at Fehrbellin, when he was a young man of sixty-nine.

Likewise, there are those who worked alongside Blücher who claimed that he never did learn how to read a map properly. He certainly never mastered basic written German; it often seemed as if his speech consisted of nothing but curse words, a rare thing for an officer in this more refined era, and he was not shy about describing his hallucinations to his comrades.[16] He had solid chiefs of staff to handle the more intellectual aspects of the job, however, Scharnhorst first, then Gneisenau. Blücher's aggression was proverbial, as was his burning hatred for the French enemy he faced. These were the attributes he brought to the table of a successful career as a commander. As to the Red Prince, it is fascinating to note how even complimentary pieces on him have to include the phrase, "The Prince was certainly no genius."[17] Indeed, it is probably fair to say that he had no more understanding of Moltke's art of war in the 1866 campaign than did Field Marshal Ludwig von Benedek, the unfortunate Austrian commander whom the Prussians trounced at Königgrätz.

All three of these men, however, shared certain attributes that continued to shape the German officer corps even in 1942. Their aggression, their inclination to reduce the art of war to making a beeline for the nearest enemy force and launching an attack, their distrust of anything that smacked of an overly cerebral approach to warfare—in all these, they were examples for later generations. This was an army that really did believe in "the offensive exploitation of any opportunity that presents itself,"[18] and that even in tough times, "the crisis was to be solved by offensive means,"[19] in the well-chosen words of Field Marshal Bock. Thinking too much beyond that could get you into trouble, they all felt.

Blücher, a hero at the battle of Kaiserslautern, would later criticize the generalship of the Prussian commander, Prince Hohenlohe, by remarking, "It would have been better if he had thought less and fought more" (*weniger kalkuliert und mehr geschlagen*). He continued: "For Prussian troops, the most appropriate course is to attack the enemy when he is near. It strikes me that a general who has a chance to destroy an entire enemy corps with such few losses, and does not grasp it, deserves nothing but reproach."[20] Blücher rarely missed an opportunity to attack anyone. As a 1942 memorial article to him in the OKW's own official journal, the *Militärwissenschaftliche Rundschau* (Military Science Review), put it, old "Marshal Forward" rarely stopped to ask, "How strong is the enemy?" He preferred instead a much simpler question: "Where is he?"[21]

A little later, the same journal highlighted the life and career of Frederick Charles, a commander who once declared that a "bold commander will get more out of Prussian soldiers than theory ever will." He was a man who viewed even the most difficult battles—Mars-la-Tour in August 1870, for example—solely in terms of his own willpower. "You've never lost a battle if you don't have the feeling you're beaten—and I didn't have that feeling," he would later say. He really did believe that a bold leader could "force History to name you the victor," no matter how bleak things happened to look at the moment. He was also the man who uttered the immortal words at the battle of Le Mans in 1871, just when things were getting sticky and some of his staff officers were advising retreat: "I've never turned around before and I'm not going to do it now."[22]

This was an important part of the mentality of the German officer corps in 1942, perhaps not even consciously formulated, but felt nevertheless. The Prusso-German military tradition had churned out dozens of commanders like Blücher and Frederick Charles over the centuries, tough types who ran fast and hard, but who never gave a lot of thought to where they were running. It was all a matter of will, they felt. If you didn't think you were beaten, you weren't, and if you didn't think you were going to be beaten, you wouldn't be. The stronger will could vanquish even the larger battalions. Those who coldly add up the numbers and try to think things through rationally—historians, for example—may have trouble understanding such an actionist point of view, and they may well see inevitability in the German defeat in the 1942 campaign. Certainly some German officers agreed with that gloomy prognosis. It might have been a long shot, driving to the Volga and to the Caucasus, remote spots that most of them knew only dimly from maps. But there was really nothing else to be done. As one staff officer put it, it was "the last year, perhaps, in which the mass of the Wehrmacht can be put into action undisturbed on a single front."[23] Although some of them may have had doubts, they had never turned around before, and they weren't about to start now. However unprofessional, even irrational, Hitler's orders may appear to us today, perhaps his commanders felt that they had finally found a leader they could admire, one "who thought less and fought more."

In his fine scholarly biography of the chief of the General Staff, General Franz Halder, historian Christian Hartmann notes the persistent tendency on the part of Hitler, Halder, and the staff to overrate German capabilities and to underrate the Soviets: "Wherever the German leadership and the German solder go over to the attack with concentrated strength, they are far superior to the enemy," as one staff officer put it. Hartmann notes that such rhetoric was partly a "propagandistic façade," typical of a regime addicted to its own press notices. He also argues that it played an important "psychological function,"[24] which allowed German planners to ignore unpleasant realities like the balance of forces or Germany's manpower crisis, a form of whistling past the graveyard. But there is a third possibility to explain such rhetoric, a simpler one that requires reference neither to propaganda nor psychology. Perhaps Hitler, Halder, and the officers really believed it.

Operation Blue: Planning

On April 5, 1942, Hitler issued Directive 41, the outline for the coming summer offensive. The Führer, working from a draft submitted to him by his operations staff, had rewritten much of it himself. What emerged was a curious document. "The winter battle in Russia is coming to an end," it began, and the German soldier could congratulate himself on "a defensive success of great magnitude."[25] Not only had enemy forces suffered serious losses in men and matériel, Hitler claimed, they had also burned up the reserves that they had intended to use for later operations. As soon as weather and terrain allowed, it was time to get back to business, exploiting German superiority in officers and men to dictate to the foe, to destroy the remaining fighting power of his army, and to seize the areas most important to his military economy. These included Leningrad in the north and the Caucasus region in the south. Because of the limited availability of forces and transport, however, the Wehrmacht would have to go for these one at a time, and here there was no ambiguity: "Therefore, all available forces are to unite immediately for the main operation in the southern sector, with the goal of destroying the enemy in front of the Don, in order to seize the oil fields in the Caucasus area, as well as the passes through the mountains themselves."[26] Army Group North, in the Leningrad sector, would have to wait for its day of reckoning until developments elsewhere freed up enough forces for the operation. Army Group Center, meanwhile, would essentially hold its positions.

The operational plans for the summer offensive were in many ways a departure from past military practice. They were exceedingly complex, containing a series of partial operations that would take place sequentially, rolling across the front on a strict timetable:

> Since many of the formations will still be in the process of arriving, the operation can only take place in a series of related and complementary attacks, sequenced so that they take place one after the other. They are to be timed so carefully from north to south that it will be possible to achieve the highest measure of concentration of land and especially air forces against the decisive points.[27]

For a military establishment that had always prided itself on keeping its orders short and sweet, that preached, per Clausewitz, that "In war everything is very simple, but the simplest thing is difficult,"[28] and that always deferred questions of timing to the commander in the field, those were strange words indeed.

But perhaps there was no choice. The high command designed Blue the way it did, operational complexity and all, in order to allow the Luftwaffe to concentrate on one relatively small operation at a time. This had been the most important lesson of the successful preliminary operations of the spring. Success was assured only if the high command could mass most or all of the air assets for an entire theater—an entire

Luftflotte, for example, in a single battle. Moreover, the remoteness of the front, the underdeveloped state of the road and rail networks, and the Wehrmacht's serious transport shortage meant that it would be impossible to assemble the entire force for Blue at the start of the operation. Thus, the first, limited offensive strokes could be under way while the formations tasked with the later, grander ones were still detraining in the southern Ukraine.

This, too, was a remarkable break with the past. The Prussian-German tradition had always placed greater emphasis on deployment (*Aufmarsch*) than on any other aspect of the operation. As Moltke had famously put it, "Even a *single* error in the original assembly of the armies can hardly ever be made good again during the entire course of the campaign."[29] In a complicated age of mass armies, railroads, and telegraphs, he also felt that the initial deployment was the only part of an operation that was subject to relatively high levels of organization and control, two things that deteriorated inevitably once the contending armies had locked horns. "No plan survives contact with the enemy's main body,"[30] Moltke believed. Once that had happened, strategy became little more than a "system of expedients,"[31] with the commander on the spot having a great deal to say about what happened next.

But that characteristic of Prussian-German war making also seemed endangered by the plans for Blue. The operation was to unfold as a series of relatively small but airtight *Kessels*. To achieve them, the field commanders received two strict operational guidelines:

> *What must be avoided:*
>
> Closing in too late with the enveloping formations and thus leaving open to the enemy the possibility of escaping destruction.
>
> *What must not be allowed to happen:*
>
> That the Panzer and motorized formations, through overly rapid or far-flung advances, lose contact with infantry following them. Equally, the Panzer and motorized formations must not miss possible opportunities to help the advance of the hard-fighting infantry forces by immediate action against the rear of the encircled Russian armies.[32]

For an army whose very identity was bound up with the notion of "the independence of the subordinate commander,"[33] this new directive was not so much an operational guideline for a free-thinking officer corps. It was more like a detailed instruction manual from the Führer to the hired help. It certainly appeared that way to German staff officers trained in the art of turning out short, sharp orders. General Walter Warlimont, deputy chief of operations for the OKW, read it and was appalled. "It was long and repetitive; it jumbled up operational instructions and universally known strategic principles; in general it was unclear and in detail it was complicated," he complained.[34]

The smaller encirclements, too, were a departure, and a different approach from the large-scale encirclements at Bialystok, Minsk, Smolensk, and Kiev at the start of Barbarossa. Those operations, as successful as they had been in the end, had experienced a number of serious problems that both Hitler and his staff wanted to avoid. In their race to seal off such monstrous pockets, the mobile formations had typically thrust far ahead of their accompanying infantry, often hundreds of miles. As a result, lone Panzer divisions sometimes found themselves tied up for weeks holding the outer ring of the encirclements. On more than a few occasions—at Yelnya during the battle of Smolensk, for example—they had to fight for their lives in grinding positional battles against powerful Soviet relief attempts, which was not at all a suitable mission for a Panzer division. Finally, in almost every one of those vast *Kessels*, which were typically the size of good-sized cities, large numbers of Soviets had managed to escape the pocket. Directive 41 went so far as to suggest that Soviet armies had thus far proven that they were unsuitable candidates for "large operational encirclements" (*operativen Einschliessungen*), and that a new approach was needed, one aiming for a series of closer and tighter ones (*enger Umklammerungen*).[35]

Smaller encirclements, Hitler believed, offered a number of advantages. They would trap and destroy a higher proportion of Soviet forces, even if the absolute number of prisoners in each was smaller. They would be close enough to the start line to be manageable, allowing the infantry to catch up quickly and freeing the Panzers to do what they did best: roar off to the next mobile battle down the line. In addition, because so much of this new eastern army (Ostheer) consisted of young draftees, it was crucial that the first moves go well. Smaller maneuver schemes would help in that regard. "The operation must begin with success; young troops mustn't suffer any setbacks," Hitler told the staff on March 28, during a long planning conference for the summer offensive. "Young troops need special support. The operation must proceed in such a way that our young divisions get used to the enemy."[36]

Blue would therefore unfold in four successive operations, eventually designated Blue I, II, III, and IV. As of June, detailed directives existed only for the first three. Blue IV would be the offensive into the Caucasus itself, the *raison d'être* for the entire operation. An actual plan for this most far-flung of German campaigns would not appear until July 23, nearly a month into Operation Blue. The complexity of this tripartite-plus structure would also necessitate a change in the chain of command, a potentially troublesome thing to do in the midst of a major operation. Marshal Fedor von Bock's Army Group South would oversee the operation at the start, but would then split into separate bodies: Army Group B (still under Bock) and Army Group A (Marshal Wilhelm von List). Add in the difficulties caused by integrating no fewer than four non-German armies into the operation (2nd Hungarian, 8th Italian, 3rd and 4th Romanian), and the complexities and uncertainties multiply. The non-German armies were not simply along for the ride. They would be responsible for absolutely essential tasks, guarding and reducing the expected encirclements as well as holding a long, stationary front along the Don south of Voronezh, a front that would grow in length with each bound forward by the Panzers.

Even the simplest operational description of Blue is enough to demonstrate its complexity, and that should have been a warning sign to everyone concerned. Bock's Army Group South had five German armies arrayed on a nearly straight line from Orel in the north to the Sea of Azov in the south: 2nd Army (General Maximilian von Weichs), 4th Panzer Army (General Hermann Hoth), the ill-fated 6th Army (General Friedrich Paulus), 1st Panzer Army (Field Marshal Ewald von Kleist), and 17th Army (General Richard Ruoff). Field Marshal Erich von Manstein's 11th Army was just finishing up in the Crimea and would soon be available as well.[37] Rather then simply blow the start whistle and allow all five of the front line armies to charge forward, seeking opportunities for encirclement of the Soviet defenders in front of them, the typical German approach in the past, Hitler and the high command opted for a carefully choreographed and tightly controlled approach. With its phase lines and timetables, in fact, Blue looked much more like a historically British or French operation than a German one, which is not paying it a compliment. The problem as Hitler and Halder saw it was that they had tried the more traditional approach in 1941, highlighting *Auftragstaktik* and the initiative of individual army and army group commanders, and it had degenerated into a mess. This time, all the commanders involved would be on a much shorter leash.

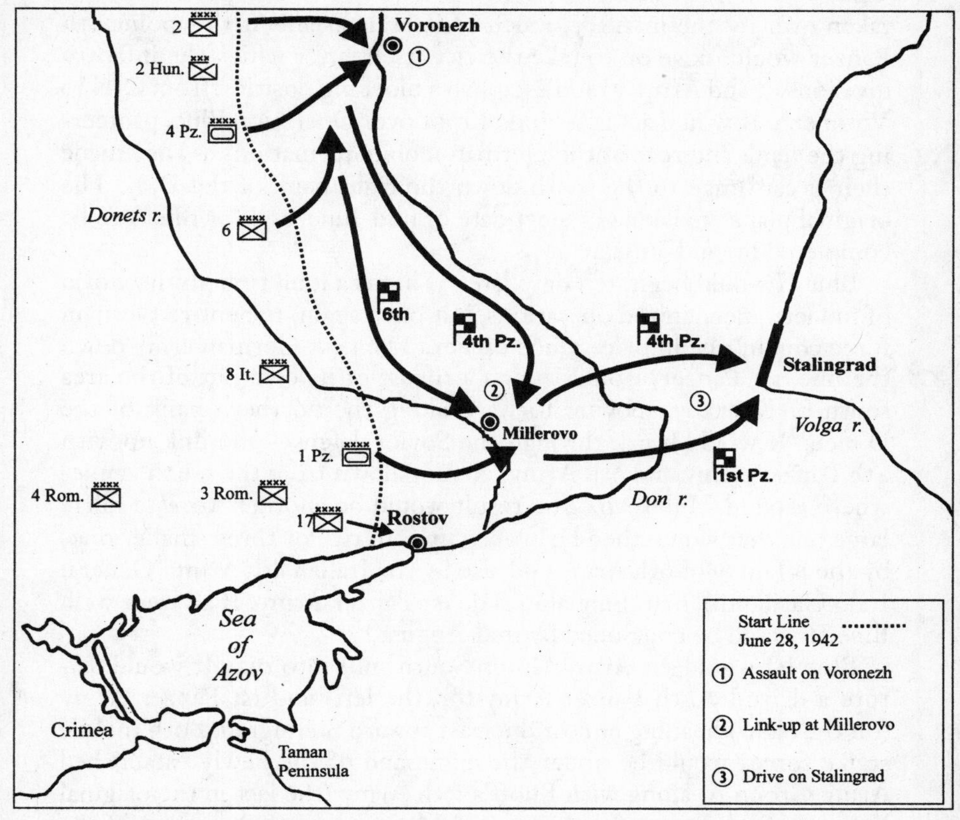

Map 6. Operation Blue: German summer offensive, 1942 (as conceived).

Blue would begin in the north. The first phase (Blue I) would include the top three armies (2nd, 4th Panzer, and 6th), along with an allied army (2nd Hungarian under General Gustav von Jany, inserted between 4th Panzer and 6th). Its operational objective would be the great city of Voronezh over the Don River.[38] The 2nd, 4th Panzer, and 2nd Hungarian armies (put together temporarily under the commander of 2nd Army as Army Group Weichs) would erupt out of their deployment area just south of Orel, cross the Oskol River, and thrust directly east toward Voronezh. At the same time, the mechanized formations of 6th Army (XXXX Panzer Corps) would be coming up from the Kharkov region to the southwest. The result would be a tight *Kessel* of Soviet forces in front of Voronezh, close enough to be quickly taken over by the infantry, much of it Hungarian. At this point 4th Panzer would move on to take the city itself, after which the infantry divisions of 2nd Army would establish a blocking position from Orel to Voronezh. It would act as a kind of roof over Operation Blue, protecting the flank and rear of the German mobile formations as they made their great lunge to the south down the right bank of the Don. The original plans envisioned a start date of mid-June, and for Blue I to be completed by mid-July.

Blue II would begin ten days later. That is a long time in the world of modern mechanized operations, but once again, the entire German force couldn't be in place much earlier. The next German army down the line, 1st Panzer, would launch a thrust of its own out of the area south of Kharkov, moving forward along the northern bank of the Donets. It would break through the Soviet defenses and link up with 4th Panzer Army and 6th Army, coming down from the north, somewhere around Millerovo. The result would be another *Kessel*, a fairly large one that would then be broken up into two or three smaller ones by the infantry of 6th Army and also by the Italian 8th Army (General Italo Gariboldi), marching alongside 1st Panzer Army. If all went well, Blue II would be concluded by mid-August.[39]

Blue III would see Army Group South split into two. It would feature a drive by 4th Panzer Army (on the left) and 1st Panzer Army (on the right) heading almost due east toward Stalingrad. Both mobile strike forces would be under the command of the newly established Army Group A, along with Ruoff's 17th Army (the last in the original lineup of five), Italian 8th Army, and Manstein's 11th Army out of the Crimea. The mission of Army Group B was essentially defensive and static. It would extend toward Stalingrad along the right bank of the Don. When Blue III was completed, Army Group B would occupy a solid defensive line running from Orel through Voronezh to Stalingrad, protecting the rear of Army Group A as it prepared for its drive into the Caucasus (the as-yet-unplanned Blue IV).

Needless to say, this was not a simple operational prospectus. Blue had five major German maneuver elements, plus three allied armies, all of them burdened with enough hairpin turns, precisely timed linkups, and tight bottlenecks to try the patience of any commander, even one schooled in the fine art of *Bewegungskrieg*. The rendezvous between 4th Panzer Army, 6th Army, 1st Panzer Army, and Italian 8th Army at Millerovo in the tight corridor between the Donets and the Don, the signature move of Blue II, promised to be an adventure if it were not handled with finesse. The Germans were having a hard enough time getting supplies to all these armies when they occupied their own discrete sectors. Supplying no fewer than four of them (650,000 men, let us say, and over 1,000 tanks) in a single crowded neighborhood might just overthrow the system completely.

Along with Blue's sheer complexity lay the problem of its destination. In the original plans as outlined in Directive 41, Stalingrad was no more or less important than Voronezh or Rostov or a half-dozen other key cities in the region. Its name appears in just two paragraphs in over five single-spaced pages of text. It certainly didn't appear to be any sort of mad Hitlerian obsession. The operational language did not even call for taking the city. The first reference mentions "the Stalingrad area" (*im Raum um Stalingrad*) as a rendezvous point for those German forces thrusting down the Don from the northwest and those advancing from the Taganrog area over the Donets and the lower Don. The second reference is not much more specific, saying only that "every effort must be made to reach Stalingrad itself or at least to bring it within the effective range of our heavy weapons, so that it ceases to be a center for armaments production or transportation."[40] Directive 41 left many unanswered questions. Was Stalingrad to be masked? Bombarded into submission by artillery and/or air power? Taken and held as the eastern anchor of a German defensive position? Although it called for Stalingrad to be "reached," it did not contain any hint whatsoever that the city was the principal objective of Operation Blue, or that its capture was worth the sacrifice of Germany's largest field army in the theater.

Even under the best of circumstances, Blue would have been difficult to coordinate. A thousand things can go wrong in any military operation, and this was more like running three of them at once. Moreover, even if it succeeded, with the Soviet armies smashed west of the Don, the enormous bend of the river cleared out with relatively low casualties, the Don crossed and the Volga reached at Stalingrad, it was only a prelude to what Hitler and the staff considered the main attraction, an operation that as yet had not been devised: the thrust into the Caucasus. It all added up to a need for a zero-defect summer, and that was something that even the Wehrmacht had never achieved in any previous campaign.

Is it possible to detect a certain hesitancy on the part of the German command to take the plunge and get Blue started? The preliminary operations of the spring (Trappenjagd in the Kerch peninsula, Störfang in Sevastopol, Fridericus I at Kharkov, Wilhelm and Fridericus II at Volchansk and Kupyansk) had all taken far longer, and tied up far more resources, than anticipated. June was slipping away, and Hitler had still not given the army a start date for the big operation. The original target had been June 15, but fierce fighting was still raging in Sevastopol on that day. Operation Fridericus II was waiting for a break in the heavy seasonal rains in the Kupyansk region; it didn't begin until June 22. As each day ticked past, nerves were on edge, for Hitler, staff, and field alike.

That is the backdrop to an event that caused a blowup within the command structure on the eve of this delicate operation. On June 19, a plane carrying the chief of the General Staff for the 23rd Panzer Division, Major Joachim Reichel, flew off course and landed in Soviet territory.[41] Contrary to standing orders, Reichel was carrying important official papers, including a complete set of the orders and situation maps for Blue I. Students of the 1940 campaign may remember a similar event: a forced landing in Belgium of a German aircraft carrying a staff officer, the so-called Mechelen incident. The documents seized in that affair had been fairly small potatoes: a general evaluation of the military situation (*Beurteilung der Lage*) and deployment instructions for Luftlotte II. They might have served as tea leaves revealing the shape of Case Yellow, but only if they were read correctly and carefully by a trained eye, and in any case, the Belgians were still neutral at the time. Nevertheless, the loss of those papers had led to a complete redesign of the German operational plan, as well as to new security measures that were still in place in 1942.[42]

The documents in what became known as the "Reichel case" were far different: a detailed set of plans for Blue I, placed directly into the hands of the Soviet enemy. Reactions to the security breach varied. There were some in the command who felt that the entire operation had to be shelved, or at least radically transformed. Others, Marshal Bock and most of the OKH among them, felt that it was urgent to start the operation as soon as possible. By the time the leaked information, no matter how detailed, worked its way up the chain of command to Stalin, Bock felt that it would be moot: the Wehrmacht would be halfway to Stalingrad. Indeed, OKH seemed to agree with this assessment, and informed Bock to have the operation ready to go on June 26. All that was needed now was the word from Hitler.

For Hitler, the Reichel case touched on something more serious than a security breach. It was yet another sign that the generals were not taking the war, or his own leadership, as seriously as they should. "The generals don't obey,"[43] he had hissed on numerous occasions, and now he had one more in a long list of grievances. As a result, the German army marched off to its appointment with destiny in the summer of 1942 in the midst of a nasty command shakeup. The commander of the 23rd Panzer Division, General Hans von Boineburg-Lengsfeld, was sacked. So was the commander of the XXXX Panzer Corps to which it belonged, General Georg Stumme, and his chief of staff (Colonel Franz). Stumme had committed a particularly egregious error by discussing the operations of a neighboring formation (in this case, 4th Panzer Army) in some detail in a memorandum to his divisions, also part of the haul of captured papers.[44] The formations affected by this affair were not peripheral ones; they were at the heart of the opening maneuvers. For a time, it seemed that General Paulus, commander of the 6th Army, might follow them. He briefly considered putting himself in for a court-martial, but was ordered to snap out of it by his superior, Marshal Bock, in classic, clipped Prussian terms: "Point your nose forward!" (*Nehmen sie jetzt die Nase nach Vorne!*).[45]—in other words, stop talking and get moving.

Operations Blue I and II

Blue I

Blue I opened on June 28 with the planned assault in the north against Voronezh. After a short bombardment, which drew almost no response from the Soviets, Army Group Weichs went over to the assault, 2nd Army on the left, 4th Panzer Army on the right, the infantry divisions of 2nd Hungarian Army covering their southern flank. In what was to become the pattern for all of Blue's early attacks, the Germans broke through virtually everywhere and almost immediately. Soviet resistance was sporadic in a few places, nonexistent in most others. It was clear that the Wehrmacht had at last achieved tactical surprise. In fact, we now know that Stalin had viewed the captured Reichel documents as deliberate German disinformation designed to strip forces away from the defense of Moscow. As in 1941, Stalin once again chose to ignore numerous intelligence reports, coming this time from his western allies, that correctly predicted a German attack in the south. He and virtually the entire Soviet brain trust felt that the capital had to be the Wehrmacht's true objective, perhaps even a thrust *behind* Moscow toward Gorky, and had deployed massive forces to meet it.[46] Confirming them in that belief had been an apparently successful German ruse operation known as Operation Kreml (Kremlin), which issued fake orders, documents, and radio traffic indicating an imminent drive on Moscow.[47]

By noon on day 1, 4th Panzer's armored spearhead (XXIV Panzer Corps on the left, XXXXVIII Panzer Corps on the right) had made ten miles, and would advance another twenty by evening. In the course of that hectic first day, XXXXVIII Panzer Corps, with 24th Panzer Division in the lead, crossed two rivers (first the Tim and then the Kshen), captured an intact railroad bridge over the former, and sliced through the junction between Soviet 13th and 40th Armies. It was a surprisingly smooth performance after all the doubts of recent days, and the Soviet defenders seemed stunned by the speed and ferocity of the assault.[48]

A heavy rain soaked the battlefield on June 29, but even that didn't slow things down appreciably. Hoth kept driving forward and overran Soviet 40th Army headquarters. The staff managed to escape but had to abandon their equipment, leaving 40th Army out of command and thus easy prey for the assault.[49] With the Panzers rolling forward and Richtofen's VIII Fliegerkorps patrolling overhead—Bf 109 fighter planes sweeping the skies clear of Soviet aircraft, Stukas functioning as a highly lethal mobile artillery, HE-111s bombers going deep against Soviet airfield and installations—it must felt like a replay of Kerch or Kharkov, only on a much larger scale. One historian has called it "the Wehrmacht at high tide,"[50] and that is no doubt how it must have felt.

By July 4, 4th Panzer Army had reached the Don in numerous places, over 100 miles away from its start line, and established several bridgeheads over the river. To its left, 2nd Army was keeping pace, occupying the intended defensive position from Livny to Voronezh. It had to ward off a series of heavy Soviet counterattacks from the north that had not been foreseen in the German plan, but the situation was stable.[51] On the right, 2nd Hungarian Army was advancing toward the Don, although much more slowly than its neighbors. A more deliberate operational doctrine, fewer heavy weapons, lack of air cover: it was a familiar pattern for all the allied armies, one that the Germans should have known well by now.[52] Nevertheless, with the rapid demise of Soviet 40th Army opening up some space, 2nd Hungarian did fulfill its mission of protecting the right flank of Army Group Weichs in the breakthrough phase.

Over 100 miles to the south, 6th Army was also supposed to get under way on June 28, but rains had turned the roads into a mess. Paulus did not move until June 30, but he too crashed through the Soviet defenders in front of him, principally the Soviet 21st Army, in record time. Almost everywhere, Soviet forces seemed to be in disarray, and in some places they had dissolved. Certainly this was nothing like what the field commanders had been expecting. This was, after all, a breakthrough battle from a standing start, without the great strategic surprise of Barbarossa. That had been a bolt out of the blue that literally caught the defenders napping. Blue, they had felt, was going to require some tough fighting at the outset, a brief *Stellungskrieg*, they hoped, before the Panzer divisions reached open ground for operational-level maneuver.

That had been the expectation. But Paulus saw nothing but daylight from the start, making as clean a breakthrough as the Wehrmacht had experienced in this war. With XXXX Panzer Corps (under its new commander, General Geyr von Schweppenburg) in the van, 6th Army drove toward the Oskol River nearly fifty miles away. The corps spearhead, 3rd Panzer Division, arrived at the river by the afternoon of the third day, July 1.[53] Extending its mobile columns to the north, 6th Army made contact with 4th Panzer Army along the rail line twenty-five miles to the east of Stary Oskol on July 2. Soviet 40th Army was now in a German pocket: a neat and shallow one that was, as planned, easily contained by the follow-on infantry formations.

To pause here would be to see a decisive German victory in the making. The machine seemed to be humming, the plan unfolding as scheduled. Bock could see the possibilities. With the Soviet defenders in front of Voronezh now in a pocket, it was to time to move. "Straight for Voronezh, don't look right or left," he told General Hoth of 4th Panzer Army on July 1.[54] Hoth crossed the Don and reached the outskirts of the city on July 4. He'd been held up by mud and congested roads more than anything else. There were the inevitable hiccups: a handful of "workers' battalions" hastily formed in the city appeared in German reconnaissance reports as Soviet infantry formations. A number of "field fortifications," always worthy of respect when fighting the Soviets, proved to be unmanned. Probing cautiously on July 5—Hoth well knew the dangers of embroiling a tank army in city fighting—4th Panzer Army entered the nearly undefended city the next day.[55] On his left, 2nd Army was holding firm against Soviet attacks that seemed to be gradually ebbing in intensity; on his right the Hungarians had come up to the Don alongside him. Further south, 6th Army had just kesseled an entire Soviet army. Hoth himself was over the Don, but most of the Red Army was still west of the river. The Soviet high command seemed befuddled, responding most aggressively to a nonexistent German threat to Moscow. On the actual battlefront, Soviet command and control, which was never this army's strong suit, seemed even weaker than usual. In fact, in many places it seemed to be breaking down altogether, and consequently Blue had not yet met anything like the organized resistance it had expected. Perhaps Hitler was right. "The Russian is finished," he told Halder at the time.[56]

Blue II: Operational Collapse

As happened so often in this war, it was at this very moment, with the Wehrmacht apparently on the verge of seizing its greatest trophy, that things began to fall apart. They did so for many reasons: fate, as always; uncertainty and waffling in the high command; and a great deal of command friction between the staff and the field. The behavior of the enemy had something to do with it too, something that is all too easy to lose sight of. But most of all, things fell apart under the iron logic of trying to conduct a great campaign of maneuver over vast distances while short-handed, undersupplied, and "demotorized."

Because Operation Blue had such a narrow margin of error, seemingly insignificant details—tiny events in the opening days, for example—could have serious negative repercussions. In this case, the problems started in the north, in the first days of 4th Panzer Army's drive on Voronezh. Hoth was as competent a Panzer commander as the army had, but he also had a reputation as something of a pessimist, one who "viewed everything darkly."[57] The Voronezh operation was not entirely to his liking. He could get there easily, but who knew what he might find there? Hence the concentration of his entire Panzer army on the target, as well as the two days he took to prepare a massive ground assault into a city that turned out to be nearly undefended.

His army group commander, Bock, also had a reputation: he was known as a man who gave a great deal of leeway to his army commanders, one who "made himself dependent on them," in Halder's words.[58] Both of these concepts (Hoth's notion of the independence of command, Bock's tolerance of it) had once been virtues in the German army, but they were now regarded as defects. Bock had no problems with the Voronezh assignment. Conquering cities was a path to historical fame, and Bock was as interested in glory as any German officer in the field. He did have reservations about the shape of the northern sector, however. Perhaps he had been absorbing some of Hoth's caution, but events played a role. No sooner had Bock deployed 2nd Army on the flank than it came under repeated and insistent Soviet attacks, including a great deal of armor. This was not 1941's Red Army, but the new model, a Kharkov-style force. It may still have been clumsy and rigid in its approach, but it had enough tanks and heavy weapons to give anyone a fright. Likewise, reconnaissance spoke of Soviet forces massing over the Don, presenting a potentially serious threat to Hoth's southern flank.

It was time for Blue II, but suddenly Bock wasn't so sure. Did he really want to send Hoth's 4th Panzer Army shooting down to the south, with its rear protected only by 2nd Army and its flanks protected by the Hungarians? Given his unhappy experience in 1941, he knew as well as anyone the danger of leaving large Soviet forces intact on his flank to be dealt with later. All too often, they weren't dealt with at all. He had also been there at Kharkov, and he knew what a massed attack by Soviet armor could look like, and what kind of panic it could induce. The 2nd Army would probably hold; the Hungarians probably would not. The field marshal now hesitated. Instead of the entire 4th Panzer Army, Bock decided to send down a corps at a time until the situation clarified itself.

In the Wolfsschanze, Hitler's East Prussian headquarters, Bock's hesitation led to an explosion. A battle was being fought here as well. Although it is usually portrayed as a struggle between Hitler and his staff officers, it was actually something more fundamental. The contending forces were, on one side, the traditional German system of command, which was based on the independence of the officer in the field and represented by the army commanders; on the other side was the new dispensation of tight control from the center, represented by Halder and Hitler.

In the opening days of Blue, both Hoth and Bock had made decisions that were well within the traditional parameters: driving forward when possible and pulling up when necessary had never before required orders from above. The number of German commanders over the centuries who had decided independently to take their corps, even entire armies, on questionable and even risky maneuvers could fill a book: the Red Prince during the Königgrätz campaign; General Karl von Steinmetz at the start of the Franco-Prussian war; General Hugo von Kirchbach before the battle of Wörth in 1870; and perhaps the classic example, the incorrigible General Hermann von François during the Tannenberg campaign. The number of them fired for acting as if an army formation were their personal property, to do with as they wished, is much easier to calculate: zero. It was far more typical to see them promoted for displaying initiative and aggression.

There was a new regime, however, and it had been born in pain: the harsh Moscow winter of 1941. Smashed frontally and with powerful Soviet forces probing deep into its flank, nearly immobilized by the weather and lack of supply, the Wehrmacht's very survival stood on the knife's edge. Its commanders had momentarily lost their nerve, and there was a great deal of confusion about how to proceed. Hitler had stepped into this void with his famous *Haltbefehl* and had retrieved the situation. It worked, of course, and a vindicated Hitler celebrated his own brilliance by firing a whole host of his field commanders.

The story of Hitler versus the generals is well known. What is less well known is the fact that at Hitler's side in that fracas stood the General Staff, in particular the figure of General Franz von Halder. In a set of directives to the chiefs of staff of the army groups and armies on January 6, 1942, he stressed that the time had come for a stricter system of command, one based firmly on Hitler's will. Handing down a mission whose means were the choice of the lower commander had led not only to a flouting of the high command's intentions, but to "serious disadvantages for the overall situation." It was time for clear and unambiguous orders, he told them. "The duty of soldierly obedience leaves no room for the sensibilities of lower headquarters. On the contrary it demands the best and most rapid execution of orders in the sense that the one issuing them intended."[59] Moreover, as long as the German army was engaged in the hard process of reestablishing a cohesive front, he warned that orders from the high command would be dealing with the most minute tactical details.

This was the background to the tension between headquarters and field in 1942. To Hitler and Halder, the course of operations was already looking troublesome. Blue depended more than anything on speed, in particular the rapidity with which 4th Panzer Army could get down from the north. It did not depend on taking Voronezh, which posed the danger of getting the Panzers stuck in positional fighting. Neither Halder nor Hitler could understand what they saw as Hoth's senseless, head-down charge for the city; they actually called it a "stampede."[60] Halder and Bock spoke on July 2, day 6 of the operation. Bock was stunned by what he heard: "I learned that the supreme command no longer places any decisive importance on the capture of Vorohezh!" he wrote that evening. "That is new."[61]

Indeed it was, and all Bock had to do was to point to the pertinent passage in Directive 41, which spoke of "the occupation of Voronezh." Clearly, there was some confusion about how to proceed, and it resulted from the simple fact that the plan had not taken into account any sort of Soviet counterthrust in the Voronezh region. Hitler himself decided to fly east to Bock's headquarters at Poltava on July 3 for a face-to-face meeting on this issue. He warned the field marshal not to get embroiled too deeply in Voronezh. The meeting was apparently cordial, and Bock would later describe a fairly reasonable conversation: "Talk of Voronezh ended with me saying to the Führer, 'I understand what was just said to mean that I am to take Voronezh if I can get it easily or without fighting, but that I am not to allow myself to become engaged in a major battle to capture the city.' The Führer confirmed this with a nod of his head."[62] Bock felt he had stayed faithful to that charge. Voronezh was in German hands on day 10 of the operation, with minimal fighting. This was not a minor town or a frontier post. It was a major city over 100 miles from Hoth's start line.

Hitler, by contrast, believed that he'd been had. It seemed as if Bock had simply ignored him, tying up a major portion of Army Group South's Panzers on a slow ride into Voronezh. He would later look back on those days and complain to his aides of the critical "forty-eight hours lost at Voronezh."[63] Neither Hitler nor Halder could understand Hoth's caution in finally taking the city, or Bock's reluctance to leave it to the infantry and dispatch Hoth's army—all of it, not just parts—on its assigned mission to the south.

Upon careful analysis, it was not the particulars, the drive to Voronezh or the turnaround of the Panzers afterward, that were at issue here. In some sense, all four of these figures were correct, at least in terms of putting forth defensible arguments. The question of how much force to leave for strategic protection at Voronezh, and for how long, did not have a simple answer. Hitler and Halder were justified in asking Bock to get a move on. Time is always precious in military operations, but particularly in this one. For their part, Hoth and Bock had no understanding of a new way of war that required them to get permission slips for each minor operational decision. They had come up in a different school. Tight control at the center was the way other armies fought, and the "independence of the lower commander," for all the problems it generated, had certainly paid for itself in past wars. Whether XXIV Panzer Corps spend a day more or a day less at Voronezh was not going to decide the war one way or another; at any rate, it was a decision for the commander on the spot. What was at stake in the argument was something much larger than Voronezh: Who fought Germany's wars: the man in the field, or the staff?

Sharpening this conflict was its immensely dramatic backdrop: the apparent collapse of the Soviet army in the east. The opening blow toward Voronezh had sliced open the Soviet position easily, Bock's fears about a counterattack notwithstanding. Hoth's ride had evinced hardly any opposition at all, and had found a nearly undefended city at its close, although there was strong Soviet pressure to the north and even within the eastern portions of the city. It was 6th Army's blow, however, that indicated that something startling was taking place: the Soviet armies in front of Paulus did not so much give way as simply dissolve. Paulus cut through a defensive position that the Soviets had been working on for six months, involving the labor of millions of soldiers, almost without noticing. From one end of the immense front to the other, German reconnaissance flights could see long columns of men, vehicles, and equipment scurrying to the east.

At first, Bock was ecstatic: "The enemy opposite 6th Army and 4th Panzer Army is defeated," he wrote. There was nothing left: "The enemy has not succeeded in organizing a new defense anywhere. Wherever he was attacked his resistance collapsed quickly and he fled. It has been impossible to discern any purpose or plan in his retreats. At no point thus far in the campaign in the East have such strong evidences of disintegration been observed on the enemy side."[64] Staff and field often clashed in those days, but on this point at least, Halder felt the same way:

> The actual picture of the enemy is not completely clear. There are two possibilities. Either we have overestimated the enemy and our attack has completely destroyed him, or he is retreating according to plan, or is at least attempting to avoid final destruction in the year 1942. The Führer holds to the opinion, based on foreign intelligence reports, that Timoshenko is fighting an "elastic" defense. I doubt it. He can't just "elastically" withdraw from his heavily fortified area in front of Army Group A, not without a serious shock.[65]

What was needed, he went on to say, "was to drive 6th Army and to get 1st Panzer Army ready, both at the highest possible tempo." These were indeed heady times in German headquarters, perhaps for the last time in this war.

It was, to put it mildly, highly uncharacteristic Soviet behavior. Historians today speak of the Red Army's "strategic retreat" in response to Operation Blue, ordered either by the new chief of the Soviet General Staff, Marshal A. M. Vasilevsky, or by Stalin himself. It makes so much sense. Remove yourself from the shockwave of a front-loaded German operation. Survive the worst—the first two weeks, let's say, or a month—and then prepare to administer a counterblow. Those who were on the scene, however, describe something else: utter confusion, a breakdown of Soviet command and control, large-scale desertions, abandonment of equipment. "Strategic retreat" (or "elastic defense," another often-used phrase) may have simply been a case of employing a euphemism to hide an unpleasant reality: many Red Army men of all ranks had decided that they were still not ready to go toe to toe with the Wehrmacht on hard ground in good weather. They knew just how quickly it could happen: the sudden and unexpected eruption of German Panzer forces into an apparently secure flank or rear, the horrors of encirclement. They had no intention of joining the millions of their comrades who had been taken prisoner in the previous year, and they were voting with their feet for a new strategy.

It is hard to reconcile these two points of view: strategic withdrawal or breakdown. Indeed, there were probably elements of both. It is clear that higher Soviet command echelons had indeed ordered some sort of retreat as an initial response to the German onslaught. It is equally clear, however, that lower levels of command, perhaps division on down, had been unable to maintain their control over the process, and that somewhere there had been a complete command failure. At least, that was the German view. According to General Carl Wagener, chief of the General Staff for the XXXX Panzer Corps (and later for Army Group B), "The manifestations of a disorderly retreat only appeared as a consequence of the deficiencies in the subordinate command structure. It was a complicated method of operations that lower commanders had not mastered. In no way, however, had the Russians lost command and control on the operational level (*die operative Führung*)." On the higher level, there did seem to be an operational plan: "not to give battle with their main forces, but to remove them systematically from a decisive encounter."[66]

Indeed, it hardly seems consonant in the context of a calmly ordered withdrawal for the Soviet high command to issue an order threatening to shoot deserters and malingerers. That's just what it did on July 28, however. Stalin's famous Order 227, "Not a step back!" (*Ne shagu zapad!*) captured the flavor of the moment: it promised summary execution for cowards, set up penal battalions for those caught shirking their duty, and established "blocking units" whose task it was to keep shaky units in the line, with gunfire and bayonet if necessary (joining the thousands of NKVD troops who had been doing just that since 1941).[67] For Stalin, these were tough times, and he reacted to them about as one would expect on the basis of his past performance.

Although a disappearing enemy is usually good news in the context of offensive military operations, the rapid Soviet flight to the east threatened Blue's entire operational conception. The Wehrmacht could hardly fight a series of encirclement and destruction battles if the enemy refused to cooperate. In 1941, the Soviets had not only deployed hard up along the border, but they had charged forward against the Germans wherever they could, and they had paid the price by entering prisoner of war camps in truly record numbers. Now, on the verge of Operation Blue II, the entry into the fray of 1st Panzer Army, the danger existed that there would be no enemy formations left to kessel. Bock could see what was about to happen: two great Panzer armies, 4th and 1st, would lurch forward in a bold concentric maneuver, involving most of the German armor on the front, and close on nothing at all. It would be what the Germans called a *Luftstoss*, a blow into the air. Indeed, it is almost possible to sympathize with Bock's plaintive cry, being asked to "encircle (*Einkesseln*) a foe who is longer there."[68] On July 8, staring at a map that just a single week ago had looked so favorable, he was not at all happy with what he saw: "At noon I submitted a telex to Halder, in which I said that the enemy without any doubt was retreating in front of the 6th Army's entire front and also south of it and that as presently deployed by the Army Command the double-sided envelopment will probably hit nothing." Indeed, he concluded, "In my opinion, Operation Blue II is dead."[69]

That remained to be seen. With the operation already careening out of control and the Soviets on the verge of slipping the noose, Hitler and Halder ordered Blue II into action. It was far earlier than originally intended—by a full two weeks, in fact. On the morning of July 9, Marshal Kleist's 1st Panzer Army crossed the start line on both sides of Lisichansk, hurtling over the Donets and swinging sharply to the northeast.[70] With Kleist's entry, new command arrangements had come into place. Army Group South had now been split into two: Army Group B (under Field Marshal Bock, originally intended to play a relatively static role of flank protection) and Army Group A (under Field Marshal List, handling the mobile thrust to Stalingrad and the Caucasus).

What happened over the course of the next few days, in any other context but war, could only be described as a comedy. The original orders were for a linkup with 6th Army and 4th Panzer Army in the vicinity of Vysochanovka, but they were obsolete as soon as Halder wrote them. With 6th Army advancing far more rapidly than anticipated, its spearhead XXXX Panzer Corps would be south of Vysochanovka long before 1st Panzer Army got there. The next day, new orders arrived: Kleist was to head due east for Millerovo, in order to effect a linkup further to the south. That didn't happen either: 4th Panzer

Army was having troubles of its own by now, especially keeping its forward elements fueled. It had been in action for twelve straight days, had covered nearly 250 miles, and had a couple of divisions actually immobilized for lack of fuel. Late on July 11, therefore, 1st Panzer Army received its third new set of operational objectives in three days.[71] This time it was to shift slightly to the right, aiming its left at Millerovo and its right at Kamensk, a key river crossing over the Donets.

For Kleist, the opening of Blue II was a nightmare of shifting objectives, constantly chattering teletypes bearing new orders, and a sense that he was not really the commander of the 1st Panzer Army. It was pretty clear to all the men in the field by now—Bock, List, and their army commanders alike—that the only result from a maneuver on Millerovo would be a traffic jam of immense proportions. If there had been any sizable Soviet formations in the vicinity, of course, their presence would have kept the German armies at a respectable distance from each other. But their refusal to play the allotted role robbed the German maneuver of its operational meaning. On July 15, the spearheads of the three armies duly met around Millerovo. In the course of their concentric drives, they had come across one Soviet column after another hurtling at top speed to the east and southeast. These were not encirclement battles, but a series of armies cutting across each other's perpendicular lines of march, and were replete with scenes of chaos. General Wagener, XXX Panzer Corps chief of staff, described what he saw:

> While the heads of the divisions smashed unhindered through numerous retreating enemy columns, all the movements of the corps suffered under ever stronger enemy attacks against its flanks and rear, where the Russians were seeking to break through from the west to the east. The main arteries (*Rollbahnen*) were broken over and over again, and supply was only possible through armed convoys. This was the reason that the fighting troops began to experience fuel shortages. Telephone communications were cut constantly and command was only possible by radio. The commanding general could visit his troops only by *Storch* (light airplane).[72]

Because the Panzer divisions of XXXX Corps (3rd and 23rd) were all alone and out front on the drive to Millerovo, they were unable to stop the stream of Soviet formations that passed them. The actual haul of prisoners at Millerovo, as it had been for last two weeks, was minuscule, perhaps 40,000.[73]

In any other military universe, what the Wehrmacht had achieved in the last two weeks—an enormous swath of extremely valuable enemy territory overrun and perhaps 100,000 prisoners taken—would have represented a famous victory. German military operations had historically aimed not at seizing territory, however, but at the destruction of armies, and the number of prisoners had been far below expectations. It was now clear to everyone that the entire operational scheme for Blue, with its highly elaborate juxtaposition of staggered starts, concentric maneuvers, and large-scale encirclements chopped up into smaller ones, had failed miserably. Indeed, in its current operational shape, it could only be described as a mess. There were huge armored forces, two Panzer armies and a mechanized corps from 6th Army (the XXXXth), concentrated into a dense mass around Millerovo, while weaker and far less mobile infantry armies stood off to the flanks. Field Marshal Bock registered a complaint with the OKH on precisely this point.[74] It was, more a less, a negative image of the way the Wehrmacht had fought the war up to now. In all previous campaigns, mobile forces had deployed on the wings, prepared to turn on the enemy's flank and rear, while the infantry had handled the frontal assaults. Something had clearly gone wrong, and it was time to take stock—or find scapegoats.

The first casualty was Bock himself. He was blamed for tying up his armor too long at Voronezh, a dubious charge at best, and "resigned" on July 17. It was his second dismissal of the war; the last time was just seven months ago, in front of Moscow. Command of Army Group B went to General Weichs, who had, interestingly enough, been equally firm in the need to seize and hold Voronezh. Moreover, the entire maneuver scheme for what was to have been Operation Blue III, a three-army drive (4th Panzer, 6th, and 1st Panzer) toward Stalingrad, was now scrapped. The original intent of the operation had been to firm up a defensive position to screen the rear of a German drive into the Caucasus. It was only to proceed, however, after the destruction of the mass of the Red Army west of the Don bend, and that was no longer a possibility. Blue had collapsed. If we date it from June 2 to the closing of the "Millerovo *Kessel*," it had lasted precisely eighteen days.

To Rostov and Beyond

With so much at stake, what happened in the weeks after Millerovo was all the more shocking. The Wehrmacht went from bad to worse, losing its way in the vastness of the Don bend in a vain search for Soviet forces to destroy. It was not a pretty sight: a huge and still immensely powerful army flailing around on a fruitless hunting expedition. It turned east and southeast, then south and southwest. Each new direction yielded nothing, and resulted in a decision to go even deeper in search of its prey.

The beginning of this second operational sequence was a sketchy intelligence report that large Soviet forces had slipped over the lower Don, east of Rostov. With the Wehrmacht's armored forces so tightly massed at Millerovo, unpacking them for mobile operations to the south was not as easy as it sounds. New directives eventually emerged from the Führer's headquarters, directing 1st Panzer Army to pursue. Incredibly, that meant actually recrossing the Donets River in order to drive on Rostov from the north. At the same time, 4th Panzer Army, also now reassigned to List's Army Group A, received orders to drive south and southeast toward the Don crossings at Konstantinovka and Zymlyanskaya, sixty-five and ninety miles northeast of Rostov, respectively. Hoth would cross the Don, wheel to his right (that is, to the west) and encircle Soviet forces south of the river. General Ruoff's 17th Army and the 3rd Romanian Army (grouped into one command as "Army Group Ruoff") would slog in from the west and complete the encirclement.[75]

It should be no surprise that the new scheme of maneuver worked to perfection. The Wehrmacht had been doing this sort of thing for nearly three years now, and they really did have it down to a science. Kleist recrossed a river he had conquered by assault just weeks before, Hoth added another 150 miles to his army's already impressive résumé by crossing the Don and establishing a series of bridgeheads on the south bank, and Ruoff's multinational force drove to the east from his start line along the Mius River. It was a classic concentric operation, an "operation with separate portions of the army," of the sort that had been seen many times before in German military history. Rostov fell to the Germans on July 23, the second time in a year they'd conquered it.[76] The fighting was light—too light, unfortunately. And well it should have been: most of the Soviet formations defending the city had fled.[77]

Once again, the intelligence had been faulty. There were no major Soviet formations south of the Don, at least not this far west. It was a second painful misfire, and it is a shame that the operation never did receive an official code name so that it could be studied more carefully in modern staff schools. It was nothing less than a second *Luftstoss*, another empty encirclement. It was a classic example of an army clinging to its historical pattern of operations even as the evidence was mounting that it was no longer valid.

General Eberhard von Mackensen's III Panzer Corps had once again served as Kleist's spearhead, and his description of the operation toward Rostov reads more like a travelogue than a battle report.[78] Still bloodied from Fridericus II, the strike at Kupyansk, III Panzer Corps was rushed back into combat after it was clear the Soviets were withdrawing from 1st Panzer Army's front. As a result, the corps (14th and 22nd Panzer Divisions, with the 1st Mountain Division, the XI Corps headquarters, and 76th and 295th Infantry Divisions attached) went into combat on July 9 seriously under strength and badly in need of a refit. Much of 14th Panzer Division, in particular, was still back at Stalino getting patched up when the call came to cross the start line. All along Mackensen's front, there was nothing but a few Soviet rear guards, and the entire corps closed up to the Donets on the third day, crossing it on either side of Lisichansk. From here, the corps headed east for the next four days, a mad drive that saw it crossing the Aidar and Derkul Rivers and also tangling constantly with Soviet columns that seemed to be pouring down from the north.[79] The pace was so fast that the divisions of XI Corps were soon out of sight far to the rear, and 1st Mountain Division went back into army reserve. On the 14th came new orders: turn to the southeast, back toward the stretch of the Donets between Kamensk and Forschstadt.

This new heading brought it across the Glubokaya River and put the corps athwart the important north-south railroad in the river valley. Train after train was running a fairly desperate gauntlet by this time, heading south, and III Panzer Corps picked up its share of prisoners and booty, including an airfield with fifteen intact aircraft that had apparently been forgotten in the mad Soviet flight. By July 15, Mackensen had closed up to the Donets—again. Crossing the river a second time wasn't as easy as it sounded. It was twice as wide as III Corps's intelligence had reported, the Soviets had managed to destroy every bridge in sight, and the bridging column, the slowest of all the traditional impedimenta, lay too far to the rear to arrive in time. An emergency bridge (*Kriegsbrücke*) at Kalitwenskaya had to suffice, which was strengthened sufficiently for the two Panzer divisions on July 16. It took time, however. There was only enough bridging material on hand to improve one crossing, and 14th Panzer had to line up behind 2nd Panzer and wait its turn. The divisions recrossed the Donets on the 17th, but soon found themselves bogged down in heavy rains that

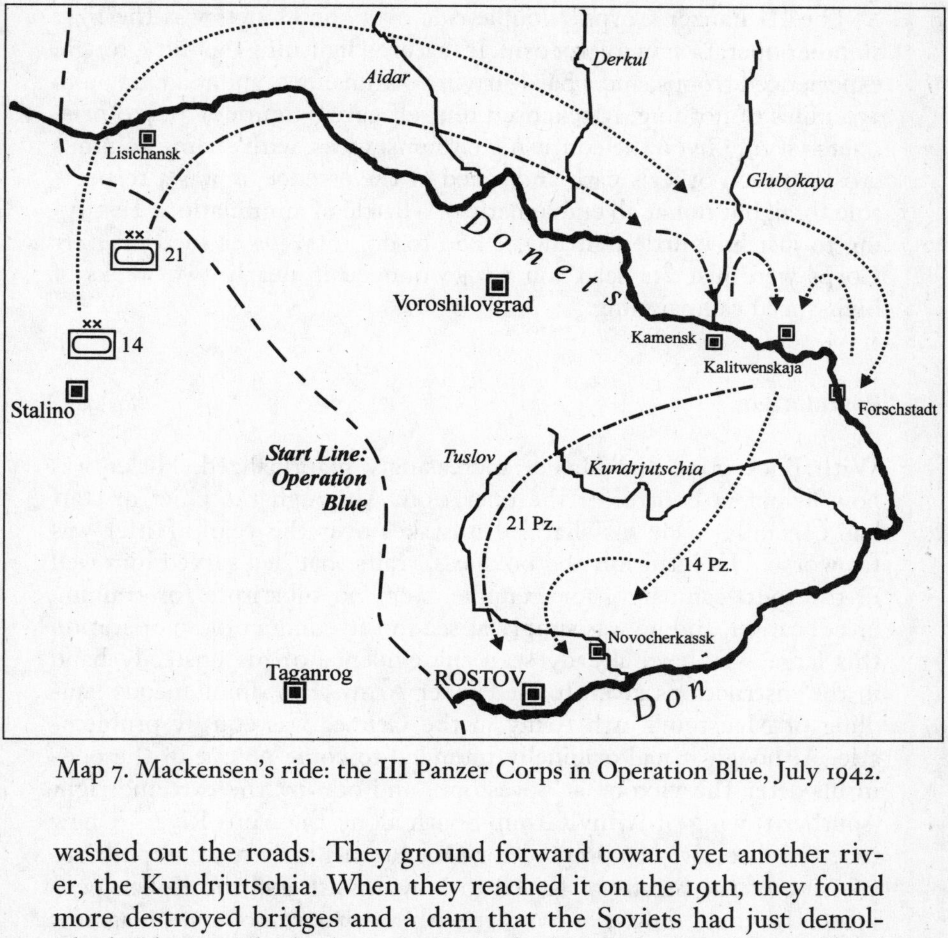

Map 7. Mackensen's ride: the III Panzer Corps in Operation Blue, July 1942.

washed out the roads. They ground forward toward yet another river, the Kundrjutschia. When they reached it on the 19th, they found more destroyed bridges and a dam that the Soviets had just demolished. Along with the heavy rains, it had brought the river to flood stage.

Mackensen got across the river on July 20 and headed southwest toward Rostov. He had to cross one more river, the Tuslov, on the 21st. A neat little maneuver levered the Soviet defenders out of their last defensible position to the northeast of Rostov, at Novocherkassk, with 14th Panzer Division feinting against the city frontally, than driving around it and encircling it on the left. The 22nd Panzer Division would play a role in the Rostov fighting, along with 17th Army coming in from the west and 4th Panzer Army from the south. It was not only the second time that the Wehrmacht had conquered Rostov, but the second time that Mackensen had done it personally.

The III Panzer Corps's double ride over the Donets was the 1942 summer operation in microcosm. It featured lightning mobility, tough, experienced troops, and a hard-driving commander, and it added up to 250 miles of nothing. Mackensen himself gave a figure of 33,450 prisoners taken. Given the confusing circumstances, with enemy columns crossing each other's path and speed of the essence, it was a respectable total, but not at all emblematic of a battle of annihilation. Testifying to just how little fighting he had to do, total losses to III Panzer Corps were just 251 dead and 1,134 wounded in nearly two weeks of high-speed campaigning.[80]

Postmortem

With Bock gone and Halder increasingly marginalized, Hitler was now firmly in control of the operation. Although the chief of staff had certainly made his share of mistakes over the years, Hitler was far worse. His intuition and boldness, traits that had served him well in the 1940 campaign, for example, were no substitute for training or education, and he was simply at sea in the conduct of an operation this large. We have already seen the evidence of his unsteady hand in the instructions given to 1st Panzer Army. His simultaneous handling of Manstein's 11th Army in the Crimea was equally problematic. Although it had originally intended to come up out of the peninsula after the victory at Sevastopol and occupy the extreme right (southern) wing of Army Group South along the Mius River, it now received directives to prepare for Operation Blücher, an amphibious crossing of the Straits of Kerch to Novorossisk and the Kuban peninsula. It would unfold in concert with an airborne operation against the oil city of Maikop. Once landed, it could form the extreme right wing of German forces moving down into the Caucasus. A great deal of preparatory staff work went into Blücher, but in the end it came to nothing. Hitler decided at the last moment to send the 11th Army north, to take part in yet another abortive attempt to capture Leningrad.[81]

This inability to concentrate on a single objective would be characteristic of the next few weeks, but blaming the Führer for what was to come is far too easy. It is not as if Hitler, or Halder, or the ghost of General Blücher himself could have conjured a magic solution to the operational problem now facing the Wehrmacht. It had overrun a great deal of territory and eaten up a large chunk of its limited supplies of fuel and transport. It could not stay where it was, in the great flat plain between the Donets and the Don; it certainly had no intention of retreating to a more defensible position. Before it lay a yawning void, apparently empty of Soviet troops as far as the Don itself. The only realistic choice was to go forward.

Viewed against the long history of the German army, Blue was the greatest operational misfire of them all. It had won a victory of sorts, but what German staff officers called an "ordinary" one. It had overrun a great deal of the enemy's territory, but it had not crushed his army. It was the sort of triumph described in the old German military proverb: "After the victory, tie your helmet tighter" (*Nach dem Siege binde den Helm fester*)[82]—the kind of victory that meant that there was a lot more fighting to come.

The disaster had resulted not from this or that individual decision, or the back-and-forth between the commanders that takes place in every great operation.[83] It had little to do with Hoth lingering at Voronezh or Bock's fears about the security of 2nd Army's flank guard. It had little to do with Hitler's anger at Bock or his decision to tinker with 1st Panzer Army's advance in Blue II. Indeed, the polished professional Halder had acquiesced in both of those. The Soviet flight, whether it was intentional or simply a mass collective impulse, had certainly played a role. Operation Blue had not accounted for it, and the newly centralized German system of top-down command was no longer nimble or responsive enough to deal with it. Having to wait for the word from the *Wolfsschanze*, or even from Hitler's new operational headquarters in Vinnitsa (code-named Werwolf), before any major move could proceed would have been familiar to the commanders of other armies in the world, but it was a new experience for men like Bock, Hoth, and Kleist.

Command and control problems seemed even worse than they were because of lack of hardware. There were too few mobile formations to do all the things the Wehrmacht needed to have done. It was, to be sure, a formidable list. The Panzer divisions had to make a rapid lunge toward Voronezh, then secure the city as a defensive cornerstone of the northern flank. They had to hurtle down to the south, creating a series of small *Kessels* along the way. Once they had destroyed the Soviet army in the Don bend, they had to launch a coordinated multi-army drive to the east, toward the Volga. Finally, once Stalingrad had either been taken or screened, they had to turn on a dime to roll down into the Caucasus. The distances involved would have been formidable even without Soviet resistance.

Hoth's 4th Panzer Army, in particular, had been overburdened. It had driven 100 miles east to Voronezh before the rest of the armies had even gotten under way. Its thrust toward Millerovo had taken it another 200 miles. Moving a tank army 300 miles in two weeks is an impressive feat under any circumstances, and we must give it all due credit. Unfortunately, most of this movement had been straight to the south, not to the east, where the enemy lay. Hoth had spent a great deal of his army's kinetic energy on a great drive across the face of the Wehrmacht's long defensive front in the east. He had begun on the extreme left flank of Army Group South, and he had ended on the extreme right flank. It had been an epic in its own way, but an empty one.

Or consider the case of XXXX Motorized Corps in the opening phase of Blue I. Not only was it under the command of officers who had just taken up their posts the day before, but it was vastly under strength at the start of the operation. Its two Panzer divisions, 3rd and 23rd, had ninety tanks apiece, and its 29th (Motorized) Division just fifty. The 23rd Panzer was unlucky enough to hit one of the few heavily defended portions of the front, complete with dense minefields and tanks dug in on the high ground opposite the start line, and after five days of combat, it possessed just thirty-five tanks. By the end of the first week, this "Panzer" corps contained fewer than 100 serviceable tanks.[84] Once across the first river line, the Oskol, part of the corps had to wheel left to make contact with Hoth, its original mission; another part was heading east and southeast along the Don on orders from 6th Army; Hitler and the high command had ordered a third to wheel south toward Millerovo. "Even if orders said that the Schwerpunkt was now in the south, the corps was aiming at goals in three directions at once, and was running the risk of not reaching any of them,"[85] wrote General Wagener, its chief of staff. The multidirectional maneuver soon became a moot point anyway: the corps ran out of gas.

Could Operation Blue have been better formulated? Certainly. Could the Wehrmacht have executed it more effectively? Undoubtedly; all campaigns look better on paper than they do in real life. In the end, however, this operation died of nothing more than a severe case of arithmetic. For all the ink spilled over its fundamental deficiencies, there was nothing wrong with Blue—its complexity, its size, its maneuver scheme—that a thousand or so extra tanks would not have fixed. But that was precisely the problem.

Young German infantry on the long march to the Don. Often accused of scraping the bottom of the manpower barrel in 1945, the Wehrmacht was already doing it by 1942: a large portion of the infantry in Operation Blue were 18-year-old draftees (Robert Hunt Library).

German antitank gun in action against a Yugoslavian bunker near Prevalje (from the Wehrmacht-published *Unterm Edelweiss in Jugoslawien*).

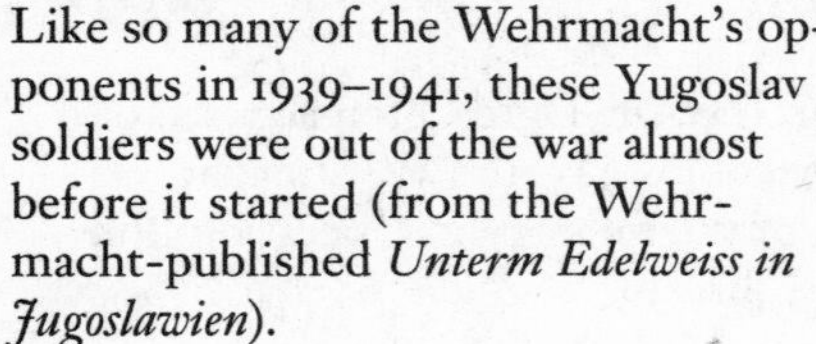

Like so many of the Wehrmacht's opponents in 1939–1941, these Yugoslav soldiers were out of the war almost before it started (from the Wehrmacht-published *Unterm Edelweiss in Jugoslawien*).

(above and below) *Bewegungskrieg* 1941. German troops smashing their way into the Soviet Union. Above, motorized troops of the Leibstandarte Adolf Hitler heading for Stalino. Below, infantry hitching a ride on a Panzer Mark III fire on Soviet positions during Operation Typhoon (Robert Hunt Library).

The Germans would crown the successful fighting in the Crimea with the storming of Sevastopol. A Wehrmacht captain, decorated with the Iron Cross, in a posture of command during the assault on the fortress (Robert Hunt Library).

German assault troops on the north shore of Severnaya Bay, June 1942 (from the OKW-published *Wir erobern die Krim*, p. 172).

Wehrmacht infantry enjoying some badly needed downtime in the Belbek valley, Sevastopol 1942 (from the OKW-published *Wir erobern die Krim*, p. 141).

The two adversaries at Kharkov, May 1942. Left, Marshal S. K. Timoshenko, commander of the Soviet thrust toward Kharkov. Right, Field Marshal Fedor von Bock, commander of Army Group Center in 1941 and Army Group South in 1942 (Robert Hunt Library).

A well-drilled German machine gun team in position at Kharkov (Robert Hunt Library).

General Erwin Rommel in the field in June 1942, inspecting the incomplete Tobruk fortifications after his greatest victory and no doubt awaiting the arrival of his field marshal's baton (Robert Hunt Library).

Forgotten armies. Top, elite Italian Bersaglieri moving toward the front. Often treated with contempt by their German allies, these formations more than did their duty. Below, the Free French defenders of Bir Hacheim, June 12, 1942. Note the mascot (Robert Hunt Library).

Margin of survival. The ungainly US M-3 was the great equalizer in the desert. Without it, the British 8th Army would almost certainly have been destroyed at Gazala. Seen here in its original "Lee" configuration, with commander's cupola (U.S. Army TACOM).

Margin of victory. In armament, speed, and armor, the M-4 Sherman was more than a match for anything Rommel could throw at it (Robert Hunt Library).

Rolling toward its doom. A German Panzer Mark III going into action at El Alamein, October 1942 (Robert Hunt Library).

In a desert landscape lacking even rudimentary terrain cover, matériel losses were always going to be high. Above, a knocked-out German Mark III being inspected by the British. Opposite page top, a knocked-out British Matilda being inspected by the Germans (Robert Hunt Library).

A hardy British Matilda tank, captured by the Germans, and then recaptured by the British. It remained operable the entire time (Robert Hunt Library).

The war of matériel: an all-night British bombardment, El Alamein front, June 1942 (Robert Hunt Library).

6

Coming to a Halt

North Africa

It would have made so much sense for Rommel to stop on the Egyptian border after storming Tobruk.[1] He desperately needed a period of rest, and so did the entire Panzerarmee. It had won the victories at Gazala and Tobruk, but only "by harnessing its last reserves of strength," he later wrote. It had been "weeks of the most difficult struggles against an enemy superior in manpower and materiel."[2] One can read these passages today and play armchair general with Rommel. Pull up at the Sollum position, await reinforcements, replacements, and resupply. Be patient until your convoys have arrived. Fill your units up to strength. Take a bit of time to incorporate the infantry and armor replacements. Let the airborne boys in Berlin and Rome finally carry out their long-planned strike against Malta (Operation Herkules, a companion to 1941's Operation Merkur against Crete).[3] Then, when you've replenished your forces and secured your seaborne supply lines, invade Egypt.

Good advice, as it turned out. In fact, it was such good advice that virtually every command echelon above Rommel had already decided on it. His orders, both from OKH (High Command of the Army) and from the Italian Commando Supremo, called for him to follow up the victory at Tobruk by halting on the Egyptian border and going over the defensive along a line from Sollum to Sidi Omar.[4] There he was to wait for the combined Italo-German airborne operation against Malta, an undertaking that would require most of the airpower and shipping available to the Axis in the Mediterranean. Only then, with secure supply lines permitting a steady buildup of men and equipment, was he to undertake an invasion of Egypt. Indeed, Field Marshal Albert Kesselring flew to Africa on June 21 to meet with Rommel and to make sure that he still remembered the correct order: Malta first, Egypt second. Kesselring wasn't above a little arm twisting. If Rommel refused to cooperate, he might wake up one morning to find those Luftwaffe units in North Africa redeployed to Sicily.[5]

In fact, Rommel had already made his decision. At the apogee of his career both personally and professionally, a man "at the height of his powers,"[6] he had just administered one of the worst thrashings of the war to the British 8th Army and was still flushed with victory. Gazala had not been a replay of the "Benghazi stakes," not another pointless run by light forces back and forth across the Cyrenaican bulge, but a crushing operational victory that saw him lever the British out of a tough defensive position, scatter them to the four winds, and storm Tobruk in a single day. Now he stood on the Egyptian border, a newly minted field marshal, the youngest in the army by a considerable margin,[7] surveying what must have seemed like glittering prospects. In front of him lay weighty strategic targets: Alexandria, the Nile River delta, and the Suez Canal. In between there was nothing, apparently, but the ruins of a defeated army. Rommel had apparently shattered the equilibrium of the desert war, the one that had stopped each side short of its objectives in the past two years.

In fact, even as he had been conferring with Kesselring, he had already drawn up orders to launch the Panzerarmee into Egypt. He had already telegraphed the decision in his message of congratulations to his victorious troops. "Fortress of Tobruk has capitulated," he had written at 9:45 A.M. on June 21. "All units will reassemble and prepare for further advance."[8] That evening, he sent Mussolini a telegram, explaining that "the state and morale of the troops, the present supply position owing to captured dumps, and the present weakness of the enemy, permit our pursuing him into the depths of the Egyptian area."[9] Hitler rated a personal liaison officer from Rommel, who put forth the same case in person.

It seemed to work. Hitler told Mussolini on June 23 that the fall of Tobruk had been a turning point. The British 8th Army "was as good as destroyed," he said, and it was time for "the most rapid and ruthless exploitation."[10] For a commander, "The Goddess of military fortune only knocks once."[11] If he knew how to do anything, Hitler knew how to talk to Mussolini. Both dictators now agreed to put off Malta until September—that is to say, forever. The original orders calling for a halt at the border had been sound and reasonable, but anyone who actually expected Rommel to obey them hadn't been paying much attention.

The German official history tends to adopt a modern perspective on all these questions, as indeed is only appropriate for a work published in 1990. On the issue of Rommel's decision, however, it has things exactly right: "Rommel was relying therefore on a general military experience, one based on the Prussian-German tradition of leadership. A momentarily weaker force could overcome its inferiority against a stronger opponent, up to a certain point, through a surprising blow, skillful operations, well-coordinated and agile leadership, a good knowledge of the enemy, and superior arms."[12] It is true that the desert was ideal terrain for modern Panzer tactics, and that the British army, with its "heterogeneous armor" and its "hesitant and methodical nature" was in many ways an ideal opponent. But the nature of the terrain and the fighting qualities of the British were both irrelevant. The decision to launch the drive into Egypt went deeper than the talent or ambition of Erwin Rommel. Behind it lay 300 years of German military history.

Into Egypt: Prelude at Mersa Matruh

On the evening of June 23, the Panzerarmee crossed the wire into Egypt on a broad front between the sea and Fort Maddalena. It was wasn't exactly a juggernaut by this point. According to Rommel, the two divisions of Afrika Korps shared a total of just fifty tanks between them.[13] His intelligence chief, Mellenthin, perhaps more precisely places the "ominously low figure" at forty-four.[14] The principal allied formation, the Italian XX Motorized Corps (Ariete and Littorio divisions) had fourteen tanks and only some 2,000 infantrymen in all. His logistics were a mess. June had been a bad month, with just 3,000 tons crossing the Mediterranean (against a budgeted requirement of 60,000 tons, a figure that was never achieved during the entire period of the North African war).[15] The immense store of booty from Tobruk had helped to fill the gap, especially in terms of fuel, but that was a cow Rommel could milk only once. A greater commitment of Axis air power might have kept Malta neutralized and the supply lanes open, but by June 1942, there were other fronts in far greater need of airpower—the Wehrmacht was just about to launch Operation Blue. At any rate, there was nothing to be done about his supply problem, and it probably occupied a far more important role in his post-Africa memoirs than it did in his decision making at the time.

With the British still in flight, the first few days of the Egyptian campaign saw rapid progress. The Italian infantry divisions of X and XXI Corps drove along the coastal road on the left. The Italian XX

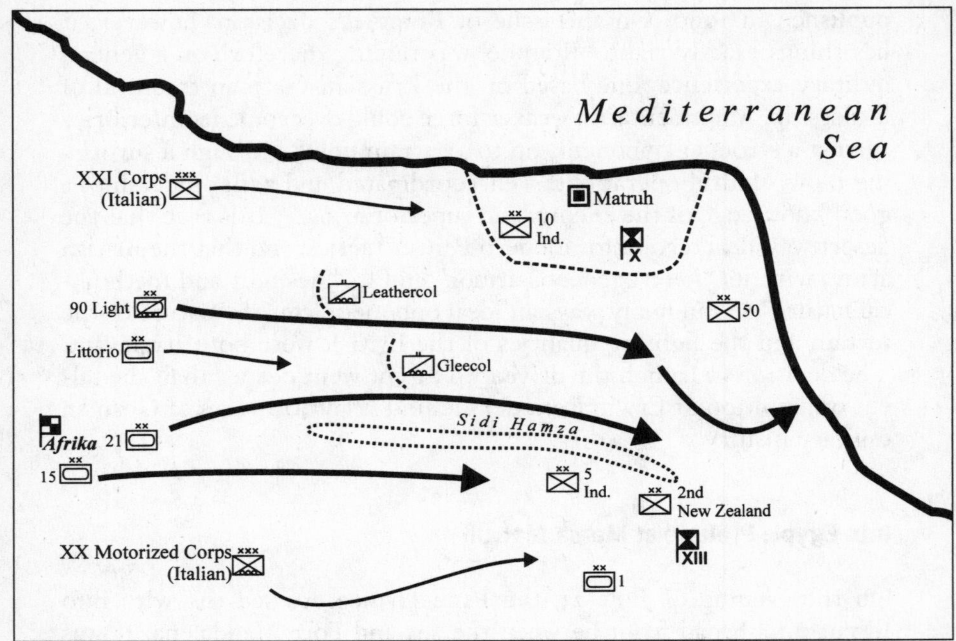

Map 8. Smashing the center: the Panzerarmee at Mersa Matruh, June 26–27, 1942.

Motorized Corps (Trieste motorized infantry and Ariete armored divisions) came in on the desert flank. Afrika Korps (15th and 21st Panzer Divisions) occupied the center, and 90th Light Division rode on ahead of the main body.[16] It made sensational time, no less than 100 miles on that first day. There were no formed British units to the front, although Rommel did notice a perceptible increase in attacks from the Desert Air Force. He was riding like the wind, as always, but among the many positive results of such speed was the negative one of outrunning his own fighter cover. The damage from the air might well have been worse but for an unusual aspect of this phase of the campaign. Rommel had so many British vehicles in his army by now—perhaps as many as 85 percent of his trucks—that British bombers often mistook his columns for friendlies and spared them. The pilots weren't the only ones fooled. British stragglers still in retreat from Gazala and Tobruk found that it was dangerous to venture too close to such a "British" vehicular column, and more than a few of them went into captivity as a result. There was the occasional friendly fire incident, especially from the Italians, as one of these foreign-looking columns whizzed by. As Rommel himself remarked bemusedly, "You couldn't tell friend from foe, for both sides were using British vehicles."[17]

Just two days into the invasion, the Panzerarmee stood in front of its first operational objective: the fortress of Mersa Matruh. After a reconnaissance so hasty it barely deserves the name, Rommel told his staff to prepare for an assault the next day, June 26. He had taken the measure of the British by now, and thought he had a pretty good idea of how they intended to fight. There was little doubt that the main body (four divisions, the 5th and 10th Indian Divisions, 2nd New Zealand, and 50th British), would deploy in the fortifications, while 1st Armoured would be protecting the desert flanks, probably somewhere around the Sidi Hamza escarpment. His plan, therefore, called for using Afrika Korps to drive off the 1st Armoured, then surround the infantry divisions in Matruh itself.[18]

As so often in the desert war, Rommel's notion of what the British intended to do was absolutely incorrect. There are many ways to deploy oneself for a defensive encounter: a balanced line, with reserves in the center, or a weighted or refused flank with reserves arranged accordingly. At Mersa Matruh, the British pioneered a new one: two strong flanks with hardly any forces deployed in the center at all other than a thin minefield.[19] It is still difficult to know exactly what the British intended here, and in fact the bungled deployment is only explainable as an example of the confusion then reigning in the British command. General Claude Auchinleck had just sacked General Ritchie and had taken over command of 8th Army himself. The force was in the midst of a hasty and disordered retreat, perhaps even a rout, and expecting rational planning, sensible deployment, and resolute defense is perhaps asking too much.

Contrary to Rommel's expectations, then, the Ritchie-Auchinleck command team deployed X Corps (consisting of 10th Indian and 50th Divisions) in the north, within the heavily mined perimeter of Mersa Matruh itself. Some ten miles to the south, on the far side of the Sidi Hamza escarpment, sat XIII Corps (2nd New Zealand, 5th Indian, and 1st Armoured Division). The area between these two sectors was hardly covered. There was a hastily laid minefield in the front, and two weak mobile columns patroled the gap behind it, "Leathercol" and "Gleecol," both formed around battalions of the 29th Infantry Brigade.[20] Again, what Mellenthin called the British "craving for dispersion"[21] was evident here in all its glory, a mark of many earlier battles. Also familiar were the confused, even contradictory, orders given to each corps. What Ritchie intended originally as a defensive stand, a "decisive action"[22] at Mersa Matruh, now turned into a delaying action. A position that he had been preparing for static operations, minefields and all, now suddenly became an example of "fluid defense."[23] Auchinleck's aim was "to keep all troops fluid and mobile, and strike at [the] enemy from all sides."[24] To that end, all divisions were reformed into so-called brigade groups, essentially truck-borne infantry organized around a battery or two of artillery, for use as a mobile arm against German armored breakthroughs.[25] The confusion was boundless. Each corps had orders to come to the assistance of the other if it were needed, by "rapidly and boldly attacking the enemy in the flank," the mark of a decisive battle.[26] At the same time, both had orders to retreat together rather than allow themselves to be encircled, the classic characteristic of a delaying action; 8th Army, Auchinleck ordered, was not to be "pinned down at Matruh."[27]

Processing such a confused set of directives was beyond British ability at this point in the war.[28] Perhaps it was beyond anyone's ability in any war. Rommel opened the attack with the 90th Light Division probing its way carefully, "nose to tail,"[29] through the minefield. An intelligence summary from British XIII Corps, however, noted that the Germans were simply passing through the minefield, without bothering to look for gaps, and that the mines were failing to explode.[30] It is hard to reconcile these two contradictory reports. At any rate, during its advance, 90th Light swatted away Leathercol, almost without noticing it. Coming up behind was the 21st Panzer Division, which did the same thing to Gleecol. Rommel had struck the British at their weakest point, smashing through the thinly held center of the line and interposing two of his divisions between the separated wings of the British defense. Mellenthin described the blow as being "purely by chance,"[31] and in a sense he was correct because there had been no detailed reconnaissance. It is equally correct to say, however, that the British command shuffle had resulted in a deployment that was likely to be weak in all sorts of crucial places, like the center.

Once again, as in all of Rommel's greatest battles, the Panzerarmee had triumphed in the first few hours, and it had done so through bold maneuver on the operational level. The next day, June 27, the German exploited the advantage. The 90th Light Division drove eastward, scattering small British columns and then wheeling left for the coast, while 21st Panzer worked its way around the right flank of 2nd New Zealand Division's position at Minqar Qaim on the Sidi Hamza escarpment. It eventually got into its rear and launched an attack on it from the east.[32] With German forces sitting squarely athwart their communications with Cairo, both British corps now appeared to be encircled.

Or were they? By this period of the desert war, the British had all but won the battle of matériel, and just as at Gazala, the next few days would see some hard fighting. Rommel had initiated this battle with a force worn down from earlier operations. He had sent it into Egypt without any respite and with a patchy supply chain, and it had been under bombardment for much of the past three days. It was showing the strain. The 21st Panzer Division, for example, possessed a grand total of "twenty three tanks and six hundred very tired infantry.[33] Rommel was with them in person, so they were acting with the aggression of a much larger force, but such ruses only went so far. To the east of Mersa Matruh, 90th Light Division had encircled British X Corps, but only in the barest sense: the German division could muster barely 1,500 infantrymen by this time. Perhaps it was simply the confusion of having major German formations show up where they ought not to be; perhaps it was paralysis induced by previous defeats; or perhaps it was fear of Rommel, but the British did little at this battle except sit and shoot at whatever happened to be in front of them. They did shoot well, however. The Germans still hadn't devised any sort of answer to the Grant tank, which was enjoying its moment in the sun and was present in abundance with the 1st Armoured Division. In the south, 15th Panzer Division spent much of day two hammering away at the 1st Armoured's position south of the escarpment. It made no dent and suffered huge losses in the process. In fact, as we survey the Mersa Matruh battlefield on the end of day 1, we might say with equal justice that Rommel's two forward divisions had just encircled themselves, exactly as they had done at Gazala.[34]

Fortunately for the Germans, the British were even more in the dark about Rommel than he was about them. By the afternoon of June 27, General William Gott, the commander of XIII Corps, had seen enough. Gott was a tired man by this point, a good officer who had seen too many defeats.[35] He knew that he had a German force, apparently an entire Panzer Division, moving east and lapping around his flank and rear, and he had firm orders in his pocket from General Auchinleck to retreat rather than allow himself to be encircled. He now ordered a retreat back to the position being established another fifty miles to the rear, at Fuka.[36] Gott's three divisions, including the 1st Armoured Division, duly began pulling out. The thin German screen in their rear was composed of the 21st Panzer Division, by now the size of a battle group, and it was completely overwhelmed: 1st Armoured disengaged and went around it to the south, 5th Indian skirted it to the north, and 2nd New Zealand ran over it. The New Zealanders caught segments of 21st Panzer sleeping, quite literally, and it came to hand-to-hand fighting in the dead of night. It was a wild scene. Later, there would be allegations, apparently true, that the division had overrun a German field hospital in the course of the breakout and slaughtered a number of wounded with bayonets.[37] Still, with Rommel on the scene, 21st Panzer managed to reform itself relatively quickly and to spend the next day pursuing the fleeing British all the way to the Fuka line. Here it halted on the escarpment, overlooking the construction of what looked like the next British defensive position.

By the morning of June 29, Gott's XIII Corps had succeeded in slipping away. Unfortunately, even though Auchinleck's orders had explicitly called for both corps to retreat together, the news had not yet reached X Corps. There had been a complete communications breakdown, replete with carelessly unsigned orders,[38] ambiguous operational language,[39] and radio equipment failure.[40] The X Corps, therefore, was still holding firm at Mersa Matruh. It had received neither the news of its neighbor's retreat nor the code word for the withdrawal, "Pike," until early the next morning. It was one of the war's classic "left in the lurch" moments and has generated a great deal of controversy ever since. Whatever X Corps's commander, General W. G. Holmes, originally had in mind, he now had no choice but to follow suit. That evening, X Corps launched its own breakout to the south and east. The weak encircling screen, a mere handful of battalions from 90th Light Division, was once again unable to keep any sort of containment around Mersa Matruh, and much of X Corps managed to slip away during the night. Still, this was as bad a moment as the British had experienced in the desert war. Here is how the 361st Infantry regiment (90th Light Division) saw the British retreat:

> Columns of trucks, full to bursting with infantry, were trying to escape down the road, which was barely 500 meters away. A ghastly butchery ensued. The "88," field guns, and machine guns poured their fire down at the trucks. The first one skidded and turned over, Others crashed into it. Vehicles stuck fast in the jam; others tried to drive around the wrecks.
>
> Eventually the officer commanding the AA gun said, "Cease fire!" He looked as if he might be sick. Down on the road a solid mass of vehicles was burning below a black pall. One man after another let

go of his machine gun. Down below, survivors were running eastwards; small scout cars picked their way through the country.

The regimental commander, Colonel Marcks, came up, apparently puzzled at the cease-fire. "Had enough?," he asked one of his men. "Look for yourself, Herr Oberst," came the response. Marcks looked down at the mess on the road. "See what you mean," he said, and walked off.[41]

Another British column did a little better, accidentally overrunning the battle headquarters of the Panzerarmee and forcing staff officers to wield their sidearms. Mellenthin had to pick up a submachine gun,[42] and Rommel himself had come far too close to the action. The firefight "swelled to an extraordinary level," he wrote:

> Within a short time my own command post was surrounded by burning vehicles and came under sustained British fire. After a while I had had enough. I ordered my staff to withdraw to the southwest. It is impossible to imagine the chaos that reigned in that night. The RAF bombed its own troops, both sides were firing at friendly forces, and tracer shells were falling on all sides.[43]

The madness continued when some of the retreating units ended their dash by running into a new trap set by 21st Panzer Division, which was already far to the east in front of Fuka. The 10th Indian Division, for example, lost 1,600 prisoners and a great deal of its transport, although the rest of the corps succeeded in barging directly through 21st Panzer, the second time it had been overrun in two days.[44]

The last act of Mersa Matruh was the Axis assault on the fortress itself. The first attempt, on June 28, stalled. The second, the next day, saw a concentric attack by 90th Light Division in the east and the XXI Italian Corps in the west. Much of the British X Corps had already packed up and gone in the night, but a sizable force remained to go into German captivity, about 6,000 men, along with the usual massive amount of stores and equipment. During the entire battle, the Germans took a total of 8,000 British prisoners. Their own losses had been negligible, although the increasingly small size of the force meant that any losses at all were becoming intolerable.

When the dust settled at Mersa Matruh, the British had been routed again and were steaming away in confusion to the east; the Panzerarmee had smashed through another prepared position and had once again proven its mastery of operational-level maneuver. The British were clearly improving in some areas, especially in terms of matériel, and their air and armor were both taking a much higher toll on the Germans than in previous battles. Rommel was riding the Panzerarmee so hard that at times it seemed it might fall apart on its own. But if 8th Army didn't want to be run out of Africa altogether, at some point it was going to have to remain in possession of a battlefield.

Heading to El Alamein

Even for a theater that had a reputation for slashing maneuver and lightning-quick advances, the pace was now dizzying. The British decided not to make a stand at Fuka and moved back even further, to the El Alamein position. Within two days, nipping hard at their heels the entire time, Rommel arrived. He had a reputation for commanding from the front as often as possible during the desert war, but never was that tendency as pronounced as it was now. Perhaps he was caught up in the excitement, or perhaps he sensed that time was short. At any rate, it was often difficult to tell who was the leader and who the led: "We heard from a radio broadcast," he wrote, "that the British were clearing out of the fortress of Haneish":

> I immediately gave orders for the retreating Tommies to be rounded up. We took a considerable number of prisoners. Several kilometers southeast of Fuka, the 90th Light Division suddenly took fire from British artillery from the southeast, for which an armored car was spotting. We quickly brought several guns into position and drove away the enemy's armored vehicle. The artillery fire slowly died down. The march went on. After several kilometers, we bumped into several mine-blocks located in the middle of the minefields beside the road. After I and several other men had removed them, our column got moving again. At dusk we were only ten kilometers away from El Daba. We could hear gigantic explosions to the east. The British had blown up their dumps, much to our annoyance, because we could have put them to good use.

"There are always moments," he concluded, "in which the commander's place is with the troops rather than with the staff." The notion that "the battalion commander alone is supposed to keep up the morale of the troops is sheer nonsense. The higher the rank, all the greater will be the effect of the example."[45] By June 30, Rommel had reached the western edge of the British position at El Alamein. As he had at Mersa Matruh, he planned to take the new position on the run, attacking from the march and crashing through in a single bound. It had worked before, and he had little doubt that it would work again.

This time, however, it didn't work. Some of the problem was the result of the vagaries of geography, which had provided Auchinleck with a made-to-order bottleneck, the forty-odd miles between the sea and the Qattara Depression. But stopping Rommel at El Alamein was not simply a matter of geographical determinism. Just last month, in fact, the Wehrmacht had levered a much larger Soviet army out of the Parpach position in front of Kerch, almost exactly the same breadth as the El Alamein line. The lesson of that battle had been that a well-handled armored force of sufficient strength and supported by enough air power could simply create its own flank by crashing through a carefully chosen sector of the front and then wheeling right or left. Rommel had performed that very act four days previously at Mersa Matruh. Moreover, outside of its narrowness, the El Alamein position offered almost no protection for the defender. It was as close to a flat plain as existed anywhere on earth. The "hills" and "ridges" that feature in so many accounts of the fighting here hardly registered as such: Deir el Shein, for example, was only 40 meters above sea level; the Ruweisat ridge just 66 meters, and Alam Halfa only 132.[46] Certainly there was nothing intrinsically worrisome about the terrain from the German point of view. It was the very embodiment of "good tank country," and thus, presumably, good hunting grounds for the Panzerarmee.

A much more important factor in the stability of the El Alamein position was the men who were manning it. This was the beginning of 8th Army's great recovery. It had just carried out one of the wildest retreats of the war, covering 350 miles in ten days.[47] Such an ordeal would have finished a force with less internal cohesion, but the British would have lost the war a long time ago were it not for an impressive ability to recover from disaster. Dunkirk, Norway, Greece, Crete—for a while, the rumor was that "BEF" stood for "back every fortnight."[48] Now it had fallen apart at Gazala, Tobruk, and Mersa Matruh. Auchinleck thought that the force assembling for action at El Alamein was not so much demoralized as "bewildered,"[49] a sentiment that Churchill would come to share: "The troops were very cheerful, and all seem confident and proud of themselves, but bewildered at having been baulked of victory on repeated occasions."[50] Later, his view would turn into the euphonious Churchillian expression of "brave but baffled."[51] The men knew that their weaponry, the Grant tank and the six-pounder antitank gun, was finally up to snuff, and things were only getting better on that score. They could see the impressive stream of new formations and equipment coming up to the front. Some of them had already heard the rumors of an emergency American convoy hurriedly being readied for Suez. The convoy, intended originally for the 1st U.S. Armored Division, contained 300 brand-new M-4 Sherman tanks and 100 self-propelled 105mm howitzers (another ungainly but effective American vehicle, known as the "Priest" for the pulpitlike compartment in which the machine gunner stood). There was also talk of U.S. B-24 Liberator bombers being sent to Palestine.[52] All of this was battlefield largesse beyond the wildest dreams of the 8th Army veterans, and they had been in the field long enough to know what such firepower could mean against the Afrika Korps.

The force that would make the stand at El Alamein was an unusual one. It consisted of two different streams of manpower and formations. Some of them, the 51st (Highland) Division, the 44th (Home Counties) Division, or the 18th Indian Brigade, for example, were brand new to the theater. That was a problem in that they were inexperienced in the intricacies of desert warfare. It was also a benefit, however: they were as yet unaffected by the Rommel mystique. Another new arrival, the 9th Australian Division, had already met the Germans once before, in the 1941 Tobruk fighting. There were also some retreating units, 1st Armoured Division and 50th Division, for example, which had been badly mauled at Gazala and which was going to need some time to sort itself out. Others, the 2nd New Zealand Division in particular, marched smartly into its place in the new line. It didn't feel all that defeated. It had, after all, recently done something that few divisions had done in this war: it had overrun a German Panzer division. Rommel himself regarded the New Zealanders as an elite unit and regretted allowing them to escape from Mersa Matruh: "I would much preferred to have had this division in our prison camps than once again before our front," he wrote.[53]

It was Auchinleck's job to mold these two streams together. The 8th Army's commander had never lost his spirit, or the respect of most of his subordinate officers. He also had some solid ideas about how to meet the Germans on a more equal footing. Probably the most important one, at least in terms of the upcoming clash, was to concentrate virtually all the artillery in 8th Army under his own centralized control.[54] It was something that Rommel had done a long time ago, and it had always seemed to give the Panzerarmee a superiority of fire at the decisive spot, even when it was vastly outnumbered in terms of batteries and guns.

What of the other side? It is tempting to say that the Panzerarmee was simply fought out by this point in the campaign, and indeed, many historians have. It had been in motion for so long that the men were ready to drop and the equipment was falling apart, and there were many men in the ranks who distinctly remembered hearing Rommel say that they were going to get a month or two of rest once they'd taken Tobruk and hit the Egyptian border.[55] For his first attack on the El Alamein position, he could muster about fifty tanks in total, a strange number indeed for a formation that styled itself a Panzerarmee. The manpower situation was even worse, with 15,000-man divisions down to 1,500 to 2,000 men apiece. As to air power, the Panzerarmee had outrun it a long time ago, one of the casualties of making a 300-mile advance in a single week. More of everything was on the way, of course, but it would have to make the long run from Tobruk or the even longer run from Tripoli. Clausewitz may or may not have been right when he said that each campaign had a "culmination point," when the attackers have gone as far as they can and can go no further, but if there is such a thing, Rommel had reached it in late June.

And yet even Clausewitz can be wrong. He certainly had never taken a situation like this into account. Since Gazala, the Panzerarmee had carried out one of the swiftest pursuits of all time, one that had seen it overrun dozens of the enemy's supply dumps. As it approached El Alamein, the Panzerarmee had about 6,000 captured British trucks in its possession, most of them Canadian Fords. Captured British 25-pounder field guns and ammunition were filling out a number of artillery formations; the soldiers were eating British rations, and the trucks were drinking British gasoline. Perhaps captured supply could postpone the culmination point indefinitely. In fact, Rommel, like most German field commanders, "lived permanently on the wrong side"[56] of the culmination point, in the words of a modern authority, and the German official history, looking back in 1990 on those fateful days, concurs: "Rommel was convinced of the correctness of his decision. He rejected any arguments against it and once again pledged himself to the rule by which he had lived for the past year and a half and which was backed by the German high command: to attack, in order not to be attacked, and perhaps to win in the end." Stopping here would have meant "renouncing the victory at Tobruk and giving away the initiative—Rommel's greatest advantage."[57]

At any rate, all these questions of the culmination point, troop exhaustion, and logistical problems were really beside the point. Historically, few German army commanders would go on the defensive in this situation. Their training and conditioning usually impelled them to launch themselves at any obstacle within reach, particularly if it carried strategic weight or the potential of glory. Generals tend to get points from military historians for displaying aggression in any and all circumstances, and those who take a more cautious approach tend to be cast out into the darkness. Rommel's career reputation, still so high today in the literature, rests largely on his habit of attacking no matter what the circumstances. Even within the most aggressive officer corps in the world, he was a special case, perhaps an example of the outsider trying to outdo those who belonged to the inner circle. He had arrived in Africa in early 1941 with barely more than a regiment. He attacked. He had been beaten badly in Operation Crusader, driven back across the Cyrenaican bulge, and apparently crushed in January 1942. He attacked. He had faced a fortified British line at Gazala. He attacked. Tobruk. Mersa Matruh. No matter what question the operational situation posed, Rommel always had the same answer. While he had worn down his own force, men and machines alike, he had also administered a series of stinging blows to the British armies facing him, and there was no reason to think that El Alamein would be any different. If the men were tired, well, they could rest when they reached Cairo.

The End of Movement: The First Battle of El Alamein (July 1942)

Rommel's plan of attack was not a particularly original one. He had run it by the British just days ago. Once again, there was a rudimentary reconnaissance followed by an immediate assault. It would open with 90th Light Division penetrating the center of 8th Army's defensive position, skirting around to the south of the El Alamein box, then wheeling left and driving to the sea to isolate it. The rest of the Panzerarmee (Afrika Korps, with Italian XX Motorized Corps coming up behind) would follow, wheel right, and encircle the mass of the British armor. Rommel knew well the size of the force he was commanding and its chances of actually smashing a fortified line. He entered battle on July 1 with a total of fifty-two serviceable tanks, virtually all of them Mark IIIs. Still, he felt that once he had pierced the main British line and gotten astride British communications, the defense would

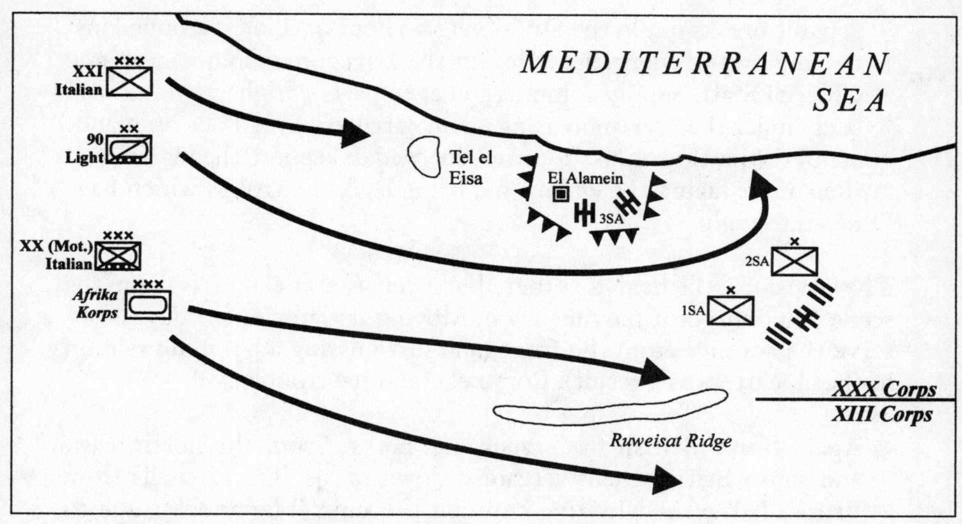

Map 9. First Alamein (Ruweisat Ridge): a surprise for the 90th Light Division.

collapse, and 8th Army would go into "headlong flight" as it had at Mersa Matruh.

In fact, virtually none of these things actually took place. The assault went in at 3:15 A.M. on July 1 and broke down almost immediately. Far from making a smooth slide past the El Alamein box to the coast, 90th Light advanced much more slowly than anticipated through shifting dunes and then ran into a hornet's nest of massed British artillery fire. It was emanating from a crescent of positions held by the 1st, 2nd, and 3rd South African Brigades, and its careful coordination spoke well for Auchinleck's new system of concentrating the guns under army control. It also came as a complete surprise to the Germans, who believed that El Alamein itself was held only by weak remnants of the 50th Division, one of the formations they had pounded so mercilessly at Gazala. In fact, 50th Division was even now back in reserve in the Nile delta, refitting.

By 7:30, the advance had come to a halt under this fearsome pounding. An attempt to slide to the south at about noon lasted just long enough for the British guns to register the range once again. Again there was a rain of shells, and this time there were some unusual scenes within the ranks of 90th Light Division's hardened veterans:

> A panic breaks out in the Division (1530 hours) which is stopped just in time by the energetic action of the Divisional Commander and Chief of Staff. Supply columns and even parts of fighting units rush back under the ever-increasing enemy artillery fire. The commanders of the battle groups, however, succeed in keeping the majority of their units facing the enemy and bring back the troops which have taken to flight.[58]

The division still held together, but even Rommel's arrival on the scene couldn't get it moving again. Moving up later in the day to observe the advance from the front (and just missing a bombing raid on his headquarters as a result), Rommel could see trouble:

> Again heavy British fire struck our ranks. From the north, east, and south British shells screamed down on us. Tracer-shells from British flak went whizzing through the unit. The attack came to a standstill in the heaviest possible fire. As quickly as we could we spread out the vehicles around us and got under cover. One British shell after another burst near us.[59]

For two hours, in fact, he and Colonel Fritz Bayerlein, his staff officer, lay pinned to the ground, unable to move. Rommel had always made a habit of leading from the front, but this was truly a rare occurrence for an army commander in World War II.

The main blow by Afrika Korps was a fiasco. Both of its divisions arrived three hours late at their start line, thanks to a sudden sandstorm and an unexpectedly rough series of escarpments that forced both of them onto the same trail for a time. The attack did not begin until 6:00 A.M., but that was only the first in a series of problems. An expected enemy position at Deir el Abyad wasn't there. A position expected to be unoccupied at Deir el Shein, a few miles to the east, was actually held in strength by the 18th Indian Brigade, newly arrived and absolutely green in the way of desert warfare. The commander of Afrika Korps, General Walther Nehring, opted to storm the box. His divisions were already late out of the gate, and now this. The assault succeeded—indeed, there were no cases in the desert war of an isolated British box *not* falling to German assault—and took some 1,200 prisoners. The Germans suffered extremely heavy losses, however: eighteen tanks, 35 percent of Rommel's total armored strength of fifty-two.[60]

The first day had ended with Rommel having penetrated deeply into a strong British position. Given his inferiority in numbers, that was an achievement.[61] From left to right, he had XXI Italian Corps along the west face of the El Alamein box; 90th Light Division to its southeast, Afrika Korps to the right of 90th Division, and on the extreme right of the Panzerarmee, the Italian XX (Motorized) Corps. Nevertheless, the advance had stopped well short of a breakthrough. Rommel and staff alike knew that this was a battle that could only be won by maneuver, rather than superior weight or firepower. Now the maneuver had failed. It had achieved neither of the two planned envelopments, and the battle already showed signs of turning into a shooting match—a battle of attrition that the Panzerarmee would surely lose. Better reconnaissance could have eased some of the day's worst problems, such as the presence of the Indians at the Deir el Shein box or the strength of the defenders in El Alamein itself, but it would also have given the British more time to prepare their defenses. There was no easy solution to the problem—indeed, no solution at all.

The next day, Afrika Korps tried to resume its advance, "to widen the break-in into a breakthrough" (*den Einbruch zum Durchbruch zu erweitern*) in the classic German military formulation.[62] But rather than follow the original plan to swing sharply to the southeast to encircle XIII Corps, it now had orders to head due east about five miles along the Ruweisat Ridge and then wheel north. In cooperation with 90th Light Division, it would drive for the coastal road and thus cut off the defenders in El Alamein. While Rommel and the Afrika Korps were heading north, the Italian XX Motorized Corps (Ariete, Littorio, and Trieste divisions), would hold the Panzerarmee's southern wing.

This plan, too, failed utterly. The Panzer divisions had hardly moved out before they ran squarely into the 1st Armoured Division. From its position on the Ruweisat Ridge, the 1st Armoured stopped the Germans cold with tank fire. Also playing a conspicuous role here was a small British mobile column, known as Robcol, made up of a handful of guns and infantry from various detachments of 10th Indian Division. It was a sign that the 8th Army was working, however tentatively, toward Auchinleck's more mobile ideal.[63] Afrika Korps managed to grind forward about four miles, but never did wheel north. The 90th Light Division stayed under murderous artillery fire all day and made no progress at all.

Rommel made one last try on July 3. There was nothing subtle here. The Panzerarmee concentrated its entire mobile force of five divisions (15th and 21st Panzer, 90th Light, and the Italian Ariete and Littorio armored divisions) as a battering ram to get around the El Alamein box. The attempt came to grief early. With Rommel and the Afrika

Korps driving east and north, the 2nd New Zealand Division, still in its untouched box at Qaret el Abd to the south, sent up a series of mobile columns to harass his southern flank. Two of them managed to hit Ariete division on the Panzerarmee's far right wing, taking it in the front and the flank and scattering it. In a single hour's action, the New Zealanders overran virtually all of Ariete's divisional artillery and put most of its tanks out of action.[64] The Afrika Korps fared little better. It ran once again into a brick wall on Ruweisat (1st South African Brigade and 22nd Armoured Brigade), and although it did manage to take and hold the westernmost extension of the ridge, it once again failed utterly in achieving the breakthrough that Rommel needed.

It was a signal moment, perhaps the signal moment, in the desert war. With strong British forces to his north, east, and south, and with the skies above filled with British aircraft, it was time for the Panzerarmee to halt the advance, dig in, and go over to the defensive. Three days of assault had won the Axis forces nothing but a dangerous salient jutting into the British defenses between the El Alamein and Qaret el Abd boxes, or in operational terms, between British XXX Corps to the north (the El Alamein defenses) and XIII Corps in the south (the mobile wing). Under cover of night, Rommel now extricated his armor (all twenty-six tanks that were still running, at any rate) and replaced them with the Italian infantry divisions. The presence of the latter at the front could mean only one thing: the war of movement had come to a halt.

For the next two weeks, there would be a to and fro across these same positions: El Alamein, Ruweisat Ridge, Qaret el Abd. Essentially, it was a contest between two operational plans. Rommel was attempting to get his drive to the east restarted, with the *Schwerpunkt* in the center or south of the British position. Once through, he could head directly east or revive the original plan to swing to the coast. Auchinleck, by contrast, had identified the Panzerarmee's weak spot: the Italian divisions holding the line west of El Alamein. Using the newly arrived 9th Australian Division as his shock troops, Auchinleck launched an attack early on the morning of July 10 directly along the coastal road and rail line. The formation holding the line here was the Italian Sabratha division. A combination of hurricane bombardment and the traditional fighting qualities of the Australian infantry soon cracked it wide open. It was a rare thing in the desert, even for the Italians: an entire division destroyed in a single stroke. Long columns of Italian infantry were soon streaming to the rear, abandoning their equipment and throwing off all discipline. The Australians pursued them, driving west and south, overrunning Sabratha's artillery and occupying the Tel el Eisa ridge, a commanding height on the western approaches to the El Alamein box.[65]

Tel el Eisa was a real crisis for the Germans: if the Australians broke out of El Alamein and got onto the coast road, the Panzerarmee was finished. Indeed, the army's headquarters were on the coastal road, just a few miles behind the line, and once again, staff officers had to form what Mellenthin called "a rough battle line,"[66] strengthened with 88mm antiaircraft guns and small units of infantry that had been approaching the front. Rommel was finally able to master the threat, but only by hurrying north with 15th Panzer Division in order to plug the gap. Later in the day, German reinforcements began to arrive: the main body of 382nd Infantry Regiment (164th Infantry Division). Earmarked originally for the renewal of the attack, they now had to be plugged into the hole in the line where Sabratha had been.[67]

Auchinleck would play this game skillfully for the next few weeks. There would be a series of confused engagements, but they were all essentially variations on the theme. On July 11, the Australians hit the Italian Trieste division; on the night of July 14–15, 2nd New Zealand Division and 5th Indian Brigade did the same to the Brescia and Pavia divisions (Italian X Corps), who were holding the line on Ruweisat ridge. The attack, known to the British as "First Ruweisat," smashed both Italian divisions and took some 2,000 prisoners, a number that represented most of the infantry of X Corps. Bit by bit, Rommel had to give up his breakthrough plans in order to rescue the Italians from destruction.

This is not to say that the 8th Army had suddenly mastered the fine art of maneuver warfare. The intent of these attacks was not so much a breakthrough or encirclement as it was to force Rommel to come to the rescue of the Italians. The strokes were short, sharp, and merciless, and backed up by massive amounts of artillery and air. Occasionally they reverted, either by design or by accident, to hitting German positions head-on, and that almost always had disastrous results. A July 22 attack code-named Operation Splendour (or "Second Ruweisat"), for example, was supposed to be a coordinated assault by 6th New Zealand Brigade, 161st Indian Brigade, and 23rd Armored Brigade, recently arrived in the desert from Britain. It went bad early. The New Zealanders failed to receive the promised armored support, went in unsupported, and fell victim to a nighttime concentric counterattack by 15th and 21st Panzer Divisions. The fire, New Zealand official history said, seemed to come from everywhere but the front:

> Some men thought it was deliberate, aimed fire; that the Germans carefully picked out the liaison officers' tanks, the six-pounders and the two-pounders, and then the mortars and the machine guns. That could not have been so. The target area was still in the dark and, even when burning trucks lighted the scene, it was next to impossible to choose particular targets within the mass. It was sufficient from the German point of view to fire into the area. Each bullet and shell was almost certain to hit something.[68]

The Germans would round up much of the 6th Brigade as prisoners, including the commander, Brigadier George Clifton.[69]

Operation Splendour was a "succession of disasters,"[70] in the words of the New Zealand official history. When the tanks of the 23 Armored Brigade finally did arrive, they too went in alone. It was a "real Balaklava,"[71] a senseless charge without infantry or artillery support. With two regiments abreast (40th Royal Tank Regiment on the right and 46th RTR on the left), it motored straight into a German minefield, then went to its doom in a murderous hail of German antitank and artillery fire. The tanks of the brigade were Mark III infantry (or "I") tanks, called Valentines. With a top speed of just fifteen miles per hour and a main armament consisting of the long obsolete two-pounder gun, they had no business being used in this sort of action. Of 106 tanks in the brigade, an even hundred were lost in just four hours of combat, nine of them to a single German 76.2mm antitank gun of captured Russian provenance.[72] The British were winning the battle of supply and matériel, and even more American aid was on the way. They had learned how to smash the Italians, and how to use that tactic to probe Rommel's vulnerability. But this was no way to win a war.

One More Time: Alam Halfa

Rommel was fighting with his old accustomed skill, and the troops under him were doing all that a commander could ask, but his mood was increasingly gloomy. A whole range of sources from these days—staff meetings, discussions with Luftwaffe General Albert Kesselring or the high command, his correspondence with his wife and confidant, Lu—testify to the frustration, even depression, he was feeling. It wasn't simply the proximity of the Nile or Suez, or a personal sense of failure. It was also operational frustration, the inability to fight the kind of war demanded both by his personal inclination and by his training. He described it in standard German military language:

> The front had now solidified. In operational terms, the British were in their element, for their strength was in conducting a method of warfare that corresponded to the modern forms of infantry battle and *Stellungskrieg*. Local attacks that took place under the protection of infantry tanks and artillery were their specialty. . . . Since we couldn't go around the El Alamein–*Stellung*, the war took on a shape in which both sides possessed a great deal of experience and theoretical knowledge, but neither side could bring forth anything that would be revolutionary or completely new to the other. In this *Stellungskrieg*, the decision went to the side that fired off more ammunition.[73]

The word *Stellung*, "position," has always had a vulgar ring in classical German military writing. It is possible to detect here the wounded tone of a portrait artist forced to paint houses for a living, or a concert musician reduced to writing commercial jingles to make ends meet. To any German commander, but especially to Rommel, fighting a *Stellungskrieg* was simply beneath him.

For most of August, the desert war went into hiatus, one of its periodic lulls when the parties had fired off all their ammunition and had to wait for resupply. There was no doubt in anyone's mind this time as to who was winning the logistical battle. The Germans had reports of one convoy after another leaving America and steaming around the Cape of Good Hope toward the Suez Canal, the tip of a massive wave of U.S. aid to the 8th Army stimulated by Rommel's drive into Egypt. The Panzerarmee, too, was recovering, a bit more slowly perhaps, but perceptibly. By mid-August, Rommel could call on the services of 229 German and 243 Italian tanks, unimaginable riches just a month before, when the entire army had been down to a dozen serviceable vehicles.[74] Provisions, equipment, and ammunition, he knew, were probably about as good as they were going to get relative to the enemy.

To Rommel and his staff, there seemed to be a window of opportunity. It would take at least another month or two for those American convoys to arrive, offload their matériel, and ready it for the front. By mid-September, the British would have an overwhelming superiority in the African theater. "We still had a space of several weeks," Rommel wrote, "before the gigantic reinforcements, promised to 8th Army after the fall of Tobruk, arrived on African soil."[75] The odds still weren't good. The staff felt that it was looking at a 3–1 British superiority in tanks (an overestimation of British armored strength) and a 5–1 superiority in aircraft (which was spot on). Nevertheless, they were the best odds the Panzerarmee was going to see.

Rommel therefore decided on an offensive. It was a characteristic, both of his own personality and of the historical tradition he represented. He was outnumbered in everything. He would have to crash through a fortified position in the face of vast British superiority in air, armor, and artillery, the only arms that mattered in the desert. Lack of fuel was almost certainly going to affect mobility if the operation were not short, sharp, and victorious. He had a guarantee from Luftwaffe Field Marshal Albert Kesselring that he could fly in 90,000 gallons of fuel per day, but even Rommel must have had his doubts about that figure, and his staff definitely did. Finally, as always, he was working under severe time constraints. Besides spending August preparing for the new offensive, he was peppering Berlin with demands for more equipment: more Pzkw III "special" tanks, with the long 50mm gun; twenty 100mm guns; one hundred 50mm antitank guns; a thousand trucks. These were "dreams," in the words of the recently written German official history; the Wehrmacht was sending everything it had to the east.[76]

Neither Rommel nor the staff was delusional. They could see the reality of the situation. "I should stress that as a matter of sober military appreciation," Mellenthin later wrote, "the general staff of the Panzerarmee did not believe that we could break through to the Nile."[77] But neither could it simply sit at El Alamein and be bombed night and day by the RAF. The staff discussed a voluntary retreat, perhaps of the infantry formations, while the armored and motorized units remained at the front. This would allow Rommel to do what he did best: fight mobile operations while robbing the British of their newly discovered trump card, hammering away at the Italian divisions. But voluntary retreat wasn't in the cards either. It rarely was in this army, even when it might have made perfect sense to do so. Moreover, 1st Panzer Army's drive into the Soviet Caucasus, and thence perhaps to Persia, had just gotten under way. This was a bad time to ask permission from Hitler for a retreat from a strong forward position in the Middle East.

Finally, although "sober military appreciation" indicated that an offensive would fail, *Bewegungskrieg* had evolved over the centuries precisely to short-circuit such rational calculation. For this operation, Rommel would refight Gazala. The entire army, or at least its mobile complement, would pass around the allegedly impassable southern flank of the El Alamein position and drive deep into the British left flank and rear. The operational maneuver would begin with a number of diversionary assaults against the face of the British position. The work of the 164th Infantry Regiment, as well as the Trento and Bologna Italian infantry divisions, they would recreate the frontal assaults of Mersa Matruh and the first battle of El Alamein in the mind of the British command, and were intended to fix British attention to the west. Deep on the southern end of the German line, however, the business end of the operation would be assembling. From north to south, 90th Light Division, the Italian XX (Motorized) Corps (Ariete and Littorio armored, Trieste motorized divisions), the Afrika Korps (21st and 15th Panzer Divisions), and a "Reconnaissance Group" (two reconnaissance detachments, the 3rd and 33rd *Aufklärungsabteilungen*) would crash through the minefields on the extreme left of the British line, drive forward into the British rear, then perform a great wheel to the left.

Now there would be a powerful line of Axis mechanized formations, stretching from 90th Light on the extreme left to the Reconnaissance Group on the extreme right, heading north-northwest. The Panzerarmee would pass to the east of the Alam Halfa ridge, then drive to the sea, interposing itself between the 8th Army and Cairo. Although Rommel didn't expect to encircle the entire 8th Army in one sweep, he thought that the threat was sure to generate British opposition, especially from the armored divisions. Once the Afrika Korps had engaged and destroyed them, the battle would be won. The rest of 8th Army would have no choice but to retreat, and the Panzerarmee would begin the pursuit: 21st Panzer Division toward Alexandria, 15th Panzer and 90th Light to Cairo.[78] It was an ambitious plan, one based on "the long reaction time of the British command and troops," in Rommel's words. Superior German mobility would present the British with "the *fait accompli* of a finished operation."[79]

Facing Rommel was the new commander of the 8th Army, General Bernard Law Montgomery.[80] Despite the claims of so much of the historiography, it is difficult to see any significant change in the army as a result of the change in command. Indeed, Montgomery had only been on the scene for two weeks when Rommel struck. His defensive position was almost exactly the same as Auchinleck's had been on July 1: a nearly straight line from El Alamein in the north to the Qattara Depression in the south, except for the balcony jutting out to the west of El Alamein where the Australians had taken Tel el Eisa in the first

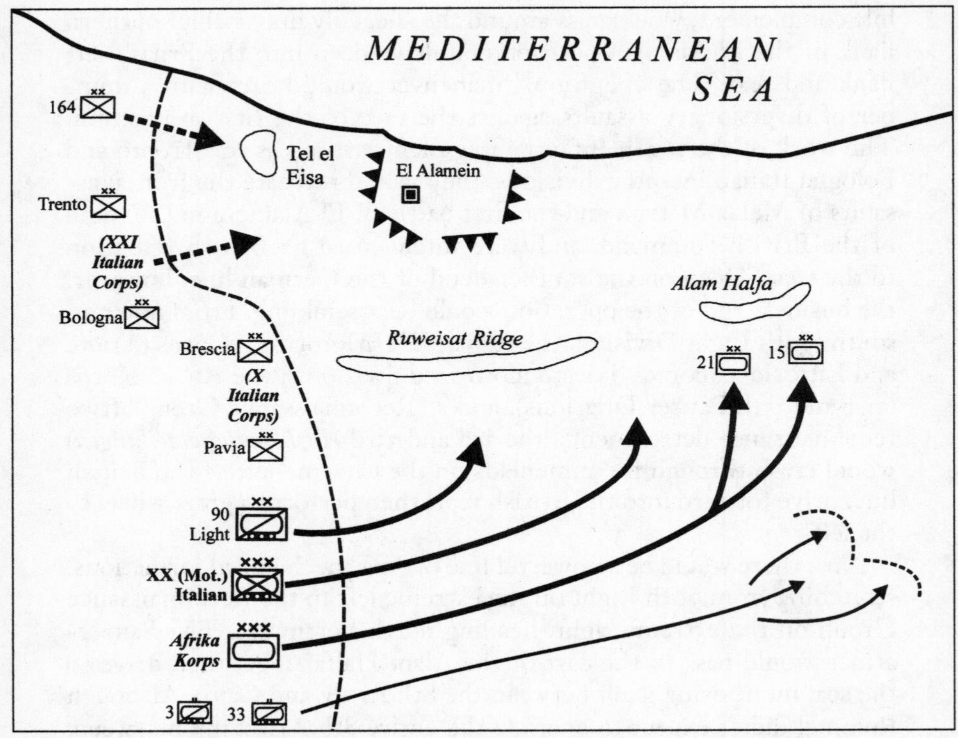

Map 10. Last gasp in the desert: the Panzerarmee at Alam Halfa, August 30, 1942.

battle. There was the same division into an infantry-based XXX Corps in the north and a mobile XIII Corps in the south. The divisional sectors, running north to south, belonged to 9th Australian, 1st South African, 5th Indian, 2nd New Zealand, and 7th Armoured. The biggest difference from the first battle was the maintenance of a good sized reserve, consisting of 10th Armoured Division and 44th Division. It was a result both of Britain's newfound wealth in men and matériel and of Montgomery's ultracautious nature.

The comparison to the earlier battle includes one last, hasty German reconnaissance, and thus a sketchy idea on Rommel's part of exactly what he was facing. Some things never change. He believed that the southern sector of the British position was covered only by "weakly mined defenses."[81] In fact, the minefield was much wider and the defenses behind it, made up of 7th Motor Brigade (of 7th Armoured

Division) and the armored cars of the 4th Light Armoured Brigade, much stronger than he had anticipated. The more carefully the Wehrmacht worked out its maneuver schemes, the less time it devoted to these less glamorous tasks. It was not Rommel's personal failing, or poor staff work, but a systemic problem of German war-making over the centuries.

The battle of Alam Halfa (or "second El Alamein") began on the evening of August 30. Under cover of darkness, the mobile divisions assembled, line abreast, along an eight-mile stretch in the southern portion of the front, between the left of the New Zealanders and Qaret el Himeimat. The "offensive group," as Rommel called it (90th Light, XX Motorized Corps, Afrika Korps), would be operating on what one authority has called a "ruthless timetable,"[82] leading off at 10:00 P.M., cutting their way through the minefields in the night, and slashing twenty-five or thirty miles to the east (nearly halfway to Alexandria) by dawn. Southwest of El Hammam, the wheel would turn and the Afrika Korps would make its lunge for the coast. It was all to take place in one bound, in a "mad rush"[83]—an extraordinary maneuver indeed.

Or at least, it would have been. In fact, almost none of the above actually took place. The Germans found the British minefields much tougher going than anticipated. The full moon provided a great deal of light for the German mine-clearing parties, but it also made them much more distinct targets for the artillery of the 2nd New Zealand Division (to the north) and the 7th Armoured Division (to the east). Both seemed to be zeroing in on the German assault force with uncanny accuracy, as though they'd been preregistered. Once again bearing the brunt of the incoming fire was the 90th Light Division. It took three tries by the engineers and infantry to clear the first gaps through the minefields, and the Panzerarmee lost time and men doing so. Once the mobile divisions entered the gaps, they came under heavy bombardment from the RAF. By 3:00 A.M. on August 31, Rommel received his first reports from the front. Although the details were still unclear, it was evident that the offensive group was nowhere near its timetable. Rather than being thirty miles from its point of departure, it wasn't even ten. British fire was growing in intensity, and losses had been heavy. The commander of the 21st Panzer Division, General Georg von Bismarck, was dead, and both the 90th Light Division commander (General Ulrich Kleemann) and the commander of the Afrika Korps (General Nehring) had been badly wounded.[84]

Rommel knew that the maneuver had failed. The attack no longer had the benefit of surprise. "The British now knew where we stood,"[85] he wrote, and they would be able to take effective countermeasures. In fact, he briefly considered breaking off the assault altogether and going over to the defensive. Before doing such a distasteful thing, however, he decided to see the situation on Afrika Korps's front for himself. He conferred with the temporary commander, Colonel Bayerlein, the chief of the General Staff for the corps. Bayerlein had been through a bad night. He'd been shelled and bombed, and he'd seen his commander badly wounded. He had also gotten through the wire, however, and he saw no need to break off anything. After a short conversation, Rommel ordered the operation to continue.

There would have to be changes, however. The intended width of the original German sweep was no longer possible. It relied on a sleeping 8th Army, not the awake and presumably alert one it now faced. A shorter sweep would have certain disadvantages, of course. It would lack the shock effect of an armored force driving unmolested into the British rear. It would compress the battlefield into a much smaller area, and that was going to be a problem in light of British air superiority. Finally, it would force the German mobile formations to drive directly over the Alam Halfa ridge, not around it, and the British were certain to have strongly garrisoned such a dominant terrain feature.

There was nothing to be done, however. In fact, most of the German force didn't crack the minefield until 9:30 the next morning. On the left of the offensive group, 90th Light Division did little more than pivot in place to the north. In the Italian XX (Motorized) Corps, mine-clearing equipment was both obsolete and in short supply, and the soldiers were often reduced to probing the sand with their bayonets.[86] They came up against the left of the 2nd New Zealand Division, never did make any sort of clean breakthrough, and played little role in the decisive action to the east. Both divisions of the Afrika Korps did manage to get moving again, aided by the inevitable random sandstorm that blew up suddenly and shielded their movements from British ground and air interference. They never did get back onto the original schedule, however. It was not until the late in the afternoon that Bayerlein was ready to execute his wheel, and not until evening that Afrika Korps started heading north toward Alam Halfa.

What it found there was a big problem: a firm defensive position on the ridge manned by the 44th Infantry Division and the 22nd Armoured Brigade. It was bristling with artillery, six-pounder antitank guns, and even fifty or so Grant tanks that had been dug into bulldozed emplacements in the ridge. This was quite an engineering feat when one considers the immensely tall target profile offered by a Grant. The confrontation, when it came, might have been a scene in a film. It was around 5:00 P.M. Emerging suddenly out of a sandstorm, with twenty or so of the new Mark IV "special" tanks in the lead, their long-barreled 75mm guns spitting out fire, the Germans came forward against Alam Halfa, with 21st Panzer Division on the left and 15th Panzer on the right. As the cream of the Panzerarmee approached Hill 132 on the western extension of the ridge, the British position suddenly erupted in fire of all sorts—tank, antitank, artillery. The German charge halted and broke up into individual tanks maneuvering for a better shot. Soon the two sides were trading nearly equal losses, which went on for nearly two hours. The Germans got their own licks in, especially with the new Mark IVs, and only the timely arrival of the Royal Scots Greys, thundering over the ridge and plugging a gaping hole in the British line, managed to stabilize the situation.[87] As night fell, with a breakthrough nowhere in sight, the Germans broke off the engagement, after having lost twenty-two tanks of 100 engaged. What was to have been a classic example of the war of movement at its boldest had instead turned into a one-act *Stellungskrieg*. In the historical lexicon of the German army, "trading losses" meant the same thing as defeat. Indeed, the whole point of German maneuver was to avoid having to trade losses with a numerically superior opponent.

There would be more fighting at Alam Halfa. On the morning of the next day, September 1, Rommel ordered another attack on Hill 132, but fuel shortages meant that it could be mounted by the 15th Panzer Division alone. Once again, the attack broke down in the face of tough British resistance. By now, both the 8th and 23rd Armored Brigades were on the ridge, ranged alongside the 22nd. It had taken over a year, but an entire British tank division, the 10th Armoured, was finally fighting as a concentrated unit. For the rest of that day and all of the next, September 2, lack of fuel nearly immobilized the Panzerarmee. Its Panzer divisions stayed in a tight hedgehog just south of Alam Halfa, still some fifteen or twenty miles behind the British positions, under nonstop bombardment from the air.[88] The night bombing, in particular, was terrifying: magnesium flares illuminated the darkness, followed by highly accurate high explosives. The Germans, lying in a nearly featureless plain, could barely find cover outside of the occasional slit trench. Rommel's visit to the Afrika Korps on the evening of September 2 nearly ended in tragedy. Between 10:00 P.M. and midnight, British bombers appeared overhead no fewer than six times. One explosion shot an eight-inch-long shell splinter clean through a spade that happened to be lying on the ground, sending it hurtling into

Rommel's improvised trench and showering the field marshal with red-hot metal.

We usually define war in terms of "fire and movement," but this was fire alone. Movement had broken down completely:

> There was one low-flying attack after another by British fighter bombers against my troops, causing them extraordinary losses. A mass of vehicles stood burning in the desert.
>
> In the afternoon I shifted my command post and considered once again whether I should break off the battle, especially in light of the terrible supply conditions. All day long, there were ceaseless attacks by British bomber formations on the battlefield. The enemy artillery fired off a great mass of ammunition, at least ten times the amount we were firing. A maneuver by large formations, the establishment and coordination of march schedules—these things seemed no longer possible.[89]

The next day Rommel decided on a retreat. It took place in stages, and by September 6, the Axis forces were back on their start line, more or less, although they were still in many places on the east side of the original British minefield. It had been, German soldiers said, a "six-day race" (*Sechs-Tagerennen*, from the famous Berlin bicycle race), a top-speed charge that had gotten them all back to their starting point.[90]

It might have been possible to sweep away the remnants of the German army in Africa at this point, particularly on September 1 and 2. Montgomery was satisfied to sit there and pound his adversary, however, rather than risk any sort of assault and needlessly throw away the victory he had won. On September 3, with all the signs pointing to a retreat by the Panzerarmee, he simply let it go. Enjoying massive material superiority while defending oneself in a fortified position was the easiest play in the book, but Montgomery was taking no chances. At Alam Halfa, the 8th Army fought as defensively as any force in history. It did not maneuver if not absolutely necessary, and certainly did not maneuver on the operational level. There would be activity by patrols and columns, in the south for example, where mobile battle groups from 7th Armoured Division harassed German supply columns coming through the minefield gaps for the entire duration of the battle. Larger units like the 10th Armoured Division, however, simply set themselves up in a defensible spot with a good field of fire and blazed away. In the end, it proved to be enough.

Failure in the Desert

Alam Halfa presented the Wehrmacht with a new and unpleasant experience: the hopelessness of having to operate under a constant and nearly unopposed attack from the air. Rommel himself identified the "third dimension" as a crucial point of Allied superiority. "The offensive misfired," he wrote,

> because of the unbroken heavy attacks by the RAF, which practically dominated the air space and literally nailed my army to the ground, making impossible any smooth deployment or timely thrust. . . .
>
> During these operations, we have been able to gain an important experience, one that should influence all later planning, perhaps the entire method of our conduct of operations. The operational and tactical possibilities are all too small, if the enemy has a strong force in command of the air, which can employ heavy bombers in mass raids, unmolested by our own defenses.

Fighting an enemy with control of the air, Rommel said, was akin to "a force of natives from the bush fighting modern European troops, under the same conditions and with the same chances of success."[91]

Air power seems to lend itself to numerical indices better than land conflict, and for Alam Halfa, there are many. Perhaps it was the thirty-eight tons of high explosive and incendiaries dropped on the Panzerarmee in the first night alone,[92] or the seven straight hours of bombing on the night of September 2.[93] Perhaps it was the 15,600 bombs dropped from August 31 to September 4 on a target just twelve to fifteen kilometers wide and eight to ten kilometers deep, an average of 100 bombs for every square kilometer.[94] Or perhaps it was the numeral "3," as in the number of German generals lost in the opening hours of the operation to British bombing and artillery: Bismarck, Kleemann, and Nehring. Rommel came within an inch of losing his life, which would have meant that the British had run the table. There were only four German field commanders present.

Whichever number one chooses, the Wehrmacht went to school at Alam Halfa in a new Allied way of war. Here the traditional German operational pattern met the Grand Alliance for the first time: sound British battlefield management married to nearly unlimited American industrial production. Besides winning the battle of matériel, the Allies had also won a decisive victory in the war of intelligence. Rommel didn't know it, but every radio message he sent in this period was being decoded, read, and handed to Montgomery within hours of its transmission. The British commander had used this intelligence windfall to help him make a number of decisions in this battle—where to place his reserves, for example. Those strong British forces on Alam Halfa ridge had not been there purely by accident, nor had the recent extraordinarily successful bombing raids on Axis shipping been purely random strikes. ULTRA had, indeed, gone to war.

All of these things were a formidable combination, and one well beyond the ability of any maneuver scheme, no matter how elegant, to handle. German losses had been fairly light compared with many of the war's battlefields, just 3,000 in all: 570 dead, 1,800 wounded, and 570 prisoners, along with 55 tanks and 700 other vehicles. These numbers do not tell the tale, however. What the Wehrmacht had lost, lying helplessly out in the middle of nowhere under a ceaseless stream of Boston and Albacore and Wellington bombers that "literally nailed it to the ground," was something far more precious, something that went to the heart of its historical identity and to the core of its ability to function as a military force: its ability to maneuver.

7

Coming to a Halt

The Caucasus and Stalingrad

For all the interest the desert war continues to hold for us today, it stood quite low on the German priority list in 1942. Hitler knew that nothing happening in Africa could directly threaten Germany, and he would occasionally crack jokes at the expense of the British armies there.[1] The editors of the *Militär-Wochenblatt*, always a reliable guide to opinion within the army, treated the theater with similar lack of respect. After a brief flurry of excitement over the storming of Tobruk and the drive into Egypt, it could hardly be bothered with Rommel in the late summer of 1942. The campaign had obviously stalled, degenerating into what the magazine disdainfully called "local engagements" and "artillery and sporadic patrol activity."[2] Rommel's last, great assault on Alam Halfa, it is interesting to note, did not even earn a reference in the *Wochenblatt*'s weekly reportage.

Not so with regards to the war in the east. Here, the Wehrmacht was writing a new, epic chapter in its history. In the rough triangle formed by the Don, the Volga, and the Caucasus Mountains, the Wehrmacht would have one last opportunity to make right the puzzling misfire of Operation Blue. The first two phases of the summer campaign (Blue I and II) had each ended in a *Luftstoss*, a blow into the air, one at Millerovo and then another at Rostov. It had been a professional embarrassment for officers trained in the art of the "concentric operation" and the *Kesselschlacht*. Perhaps the Soviets were fighting in a new, more *elastisch* style,[3] as Hitler had suggested, cleverly avoiding the first blow in order to regroup for a counterstroke at some future point. Perhaps the Red Army had simply fallen apart at the first German blow and was fleeing rather than wait to be surrounded, as Stalin's order "Not a step back!"[4] seemed to imply. At any rate, with the Red Army making itself scarce in the opening phases, the entire operational underpinning of Blue had vanished, and for a week or two, the Wehrmacht appeared to be in free fall. Hitler had already fired the theater commander, Field Marshal Fedor von Bock of Army Group South, just two weeks into the operation, supposedly over his unsteady handling of the armored forces.

Blue had failed, but the Wehrmacht could still right itself. Nothing was yet ordained. Its supply and transport situation was horrible, to be sure, but that was the way it had been in every great German military operation of the past 300 years. It was facing an enemy who vastly outnumbered it, who would eventually deploy some twenty armies along the Don and in the Caucasus, but that experience, too, was nothing new. German intelligence had vastly underestimated enemy strength, another standard feature of wars past. But its tank formations, consisting of nine Panzer divisions, were still intact; the internal cohesion of its fighting units as high as ever, its skill at combined arms undimmed. It could do one of two things: it could fight a battle of annihilation somewhere in this vast theater, and perhaps win the war; or it could fail, and certainly lose it. After the disappointing events of the summer, the autumn of 1942 was do or die time in the east.

The Campaign Continues: The Dual Offensive

On July 23, with Operation Blue lying in ruins, Hitler issued Directive 45.[5] Drawn up personally by the Führer and his small personal staff on the Oberkommando der Wehrmacht (OKW, the high command of the armed forces) it began on a wholly inappropriate triumphal note: "In a campaign that has lasted a little over three weeks, the broad objectives I outlined for the southern wing of the Eastern front have largely been achieved. Only weak enemy forces from Timoshenko's armies have succeeded in avoiding encirclement and reaching the southern bank of the Don."[6] It was plain, he stated, that the Soviet command was likely to reinforce these surviving armies from the Caucasus, and because a "further concentration of enemy force was underway in the Stalingrad area," the Wehrmacht would now have to solve both of these problems simultaneously. Army Group A would drive into the Caucasus in Operation Edelweiss, while Army Group B would head for Stalingrad (Operation Fischreiher, or "Heron").

Although the original Operation Blue had aimed at an eventual thrust into the Caucasus, it had left that operation for another day, and in fact had listed two prerequisites before it could begin. First, the Wehrmacht would have to destroy the main body of Soviet forces

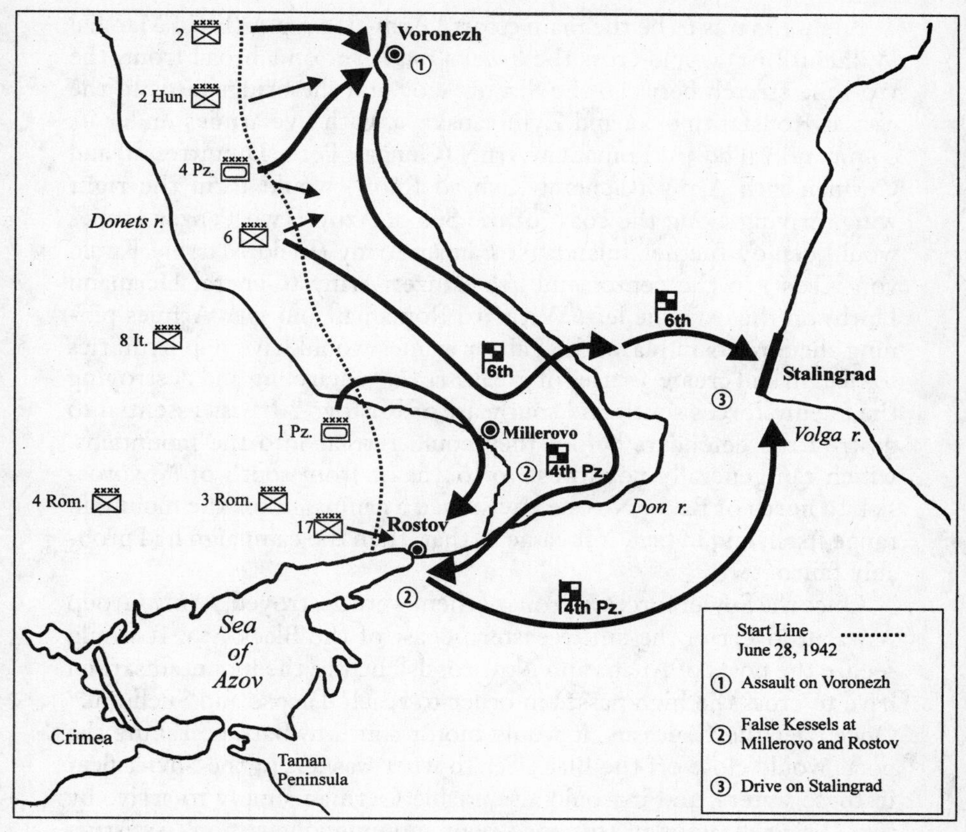

Map 11. Operational chaos: the Wehrmacht's summer offensive, 1942.

west of the Don River. Second, it would have to establish a blocking position along the Volga River, either at or near Stalingrad. To General Walther von Seydlitz, the hard-nosed commander of the LI Corps in the Stalingrad battle, "the order of the two operations was clear: first Stalingrad, then the Caucasus."[7] In fact, the Germans had achieved neither one of those prerequisites in the first month of the operation. The Soviets had fled rather than face destruction, and 6th Army hadn't even gotten over the Don yet, let alone reached the Volga. Hitler was therefore ordering the Wehrmacht to go for Stalingrad and the Caucasus at the same time, when it had already failed to achieve the relatively simpler objectives of Operation Blue. It meant splitting up the original operation into two (the German word is *Aufspaltung*),[8] thus dividing the Wehrmacht's already meager resources.

Edelweiss was to be the main effort.[9] Army Group A (Field Marshal Wilhelm List) would cross the lower Don River on a broad front, the 120-mile stretch between the Sea of Azov and the bridgeheads to the east at Konstantinovka and Zymlyanskaya, with five armies under its command.[10] The 3rd Romanian Army (General Petre Dumitrescu) and German 17th Army (General Richard Ruoff) would form the right wing, driving along the coast of the Sea of Azov. Two Panzer armies would deploy further inland: 1st Panzer Army (Field Marshal Ewald von Kleist) in the center and 4th Panzer Army (General Hermann Hoth) on the extreme left. With 3rd Romanian and 17th Armies pinning the Soviets in place, the Panzer armies would have opportunities to turn in and create a series of great *Kessels*, "encircling and destroying the enemy forces south and southeast of Rostov."[11] It was essential to destroy the defenders before they could retreat into the mountains, which ran generally northwest to southeast from south of Novorossisk to north of Baku. No one envisioned a campaign for the mountain range itself, and in fact, if it came to that, then the campaign had probably failed.

Once the Soviet forces in front of them were destroyed, Army Group A was to overrun the entire eastern coast of the Black Sea. It would secure the ports of Anapa and Novorossisk before the mountains, then have to cross the high passes in order to reach Tuapse and Suchumi.[12] Once over the Caucasus, it would motor south to Batum. Taking the ports would close off the Black Sea to what was left of the Soviet fleet in these waters, and it would also enable German supply to arrive by sea, a crucial factor in this road-poor mountainous region. Assisting in this last phase would be Field Marshal Erich von Manstein's 11th Army, which would cross the Straits of Kerch and land on the Taman peninsula. With all five armies assembled in the theater, Army Group A would be ready for a drive deep into central Asia, occupying the oil fields of Maikop in the west and Grozny far to the east. It would seize the Georgian and Ossetian Military Roads, the only two passes over the high Caucasus that were usable by motor vehicles,[13] and then complete Edelweiss by taking the third of the great oil cities, Baku on the Caspian coast.

The scale here was immense. Baku was some 700 miles from Rostov (about the same distance between Rostov and Warsaw),[14] and once the campaign had ended, the Wehrmacht would be holding a front 4,100 kilometers long.[15] The Caucasus region was roughly the size of pre-*Anschluss* Germany, with extreme variations of climate, rainfall, and temperature.[16] Although oil was the principal reason all these armies were there, the region also contained some of the Soviet Union's richest agricultural territories (along the Kuban River), not to mention the fifth and the ninth largest cities in the entire Soviet Union (Baku and Tbilisi, respectively).[17] For all these reasons, it promised to be stoutly defended.

While Army Group A was driving south, Army Group B (General Maximilian von Weichs) would be moving east toward Stalingrad. With most of the mobile forces concentrated in Army Group A, the Stalingrad operation would start out on a shoestring. It would essentially involve a single army, the 6th (General Friedrich Paulus). It was oversize, to be sure, consisting of six corps, two of them mechanized (XIV and XXIV Panzer Corps). Considering the work it had to do, however, it was hardly large enough. First, it had to clear the Don bend of Soviet forces, then cross the great river onto the land bridge between the Don and Volga. After approaching Stalingrad from the west, it was "to smash the enemy forces concentrated there, occupy the town, and block the land-bridge between the Don and the Volga, as well as the Don itself," in the words of Directive 45.[18] The rest of Army Group B (2nd Army, 2nd Hungarian Army, and 9th Italian Army) would play a static role, protecting the increasingly long flank left behind by 6th Army as it drove to the Volga.

Once again, seizing a major city at the end of a thousand-mile supply line would have been assignment enough, but Directive 45 went even further. Army Group B's final goal lay south, beyond Stalingrad, on the Caspian Sea: "In connection with this, mobile formations will drive along the Volga with the task of breaking through to Astrakhan and blocking the main artery of the Volga in the same way."[19] Stalingrad was 175 miles from 6th Army's position along the Don when the order was issued. Astrakhan was another 250 miles. If 6th Army ever did reach Astrakhan, Paulus would be approaching 1,000 miles in a single campaigning season. It promised to be an interesting ride.

Operations in the Caucasus: The Great Lunge

List's Army Group A barely paused to catch its breath at Rostov before plunging into the Caucasus. With two Panzer armies in tow, as well as a large portion of the available German truck transport in the east, Operation Edelweiss was able to explode out of the box. Viewed simply as a "miles per hour" exercise, the opening three weeks may well been have the most successful in the history of the German army.

Edelweiss began on July 26, broke through a thin crust of Soviet forces in some places and didn't even need to do that in others, and was soon running at top speed over open ground. Virtually every account of the campaign emphasizes the blazing heat as the main obstacle—day after day of 100°F-plus temperatures, rather than the strength of the Soviet defenders. In the west, the Romanian 3rd and German 17th Armies pushed down the coast of the Sea of Azov. They made good progress, closing up to the Eja River and establishing a bridgehead at Kushchevskaya on August 1. By August 9, the Romanians took the town of Ejsk, their first operational objective.[20] On their immediate left, 17th Army's spearhead, V Corps, lunged past Pavlovskaya all the way down to the rail junction at Krasnodar on the Kuban River, over 150 miles from its start line, in the first week.

This was impressive enough for an infantry force, but the opening bound of Kleist's 1st Panzer Army (three Panzer, two infantry, and one mountain corps) was simply incredible. Advancing to the south on a front over a hundred miles wide, it crossed the Manych River into Asia on the first day in three great columns. Kleist's right column (LVII Panzer, III Panzer, and XXXXIV Corps), closed up to the Kuban by August 3, then crossed it between Kropotkin and Armavir on August 6. Heading southwest now, the three corps converged on Maikop and took the oil city on August 9. The army's central column (XXXXIX Mountain Corps and XXXX Panzer Corps) drove toward the upper Kuban. The mountaineers crossed the river at Cherkessk on August 11 and then headed south, aiming for the high Caucasus and for Mount Elbrus, the highest peak in the chain. After advancing out of its bridgehead at Zymlyanskaya, XXXX Panzer Corps made the greatest leap of all: it tore across the steppe, making thirty miles a day and more, passed through Proletarskaya and Voroshilovsk, and reached Piatigorsk on August 10, heading toward the Terek River, the last defensible line before another great oil city, Grozny. It was nearly 300 miles from its start line.[21] Finally, LII Corps covered the army's left flank, advancing southeast along both sides of the Manych into the loneliness of the Kalmuk Steppe. By August 1, it had reached Divnoe and Elista, nearly 200 miles away.

In the course of this initial lunge, the Wehrmacht had to slice through the Soviet armies of the disintegrating South Front defending the line of the Don (18th, 12th, 37th, 51st, 56th). The Stavka then reorganized the region's defenses into a "North Caucasus Front" on July 28 under Marshal S. M. Budenny. Combining the tattered remnants of defeated armies with an influx of hastily trained manpower, it never

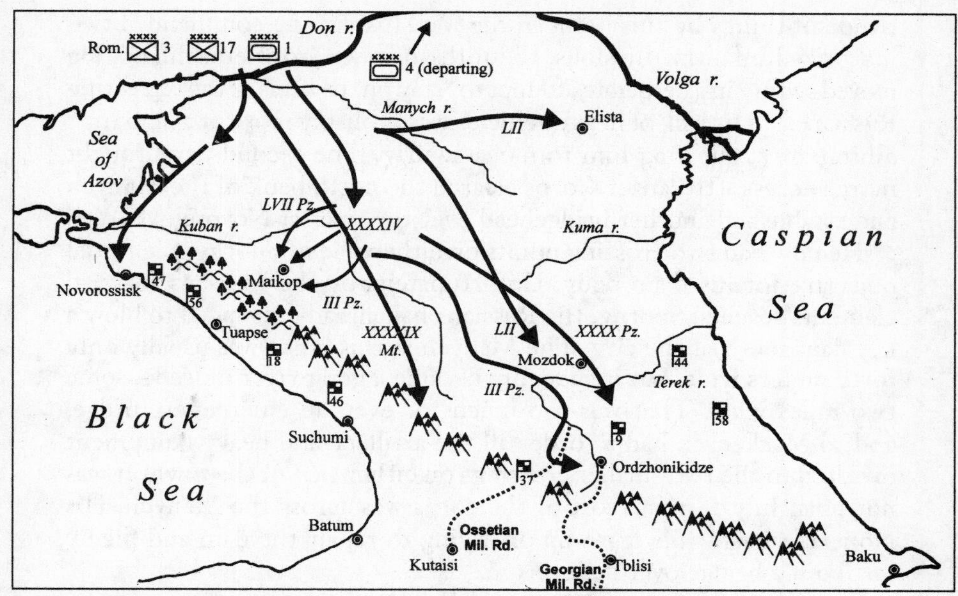

Map 12. Oil war: Army Group A's lunge into the Caucasus.

did cohere in battle, and its commander's incompetence didn't help. It was pounded in the course of August and disbanded on September 3.[22] The Red Army had improved to the point that it could avoid German encirclements, but in fact the Germans tried few of them in this opening phase, preferring instead to drive forward as hard and as fast as they could. The approach certainly seemed to be working, and Marshal List, for one, thought that the opening blow had landed so hard that Edelweiss had already entered the mopping-up and pursuit phase. "A fast thrust to the southeast with sufficient mobile forces," he said at the time, "will not encounter serious resistance anywhere forward of Baku."[23]

A closer look at the opening mechanized blow reveals both the difficulty and the exhilaration of those opening weeks. The spearhead of 1st Panzer Army was III Panzer Corps under General Eberhard von Mackensen, who was his old ebullient self, slashing out of his bridgehead on the Don and crossing the Manych River near the village of Swoboda, west of the town of Sporny, on day 1.[24] He was therefore the first German commander in Asia in this war.[25] Mackensen had no actual Panzer divisions; the term "Panzer Corps" could mean a multitude of things by this point in the war. Instead, he commanded two motorized infantry divisions, the 16th and the Grossdeutschland. He moved swiftly in a desperate attempt to "stay on the heels of the retreating Russians."[26] His lack of heavy vehicles was probably more of a help than a hindrance, allowing him to move swiftly. The second day brought more success: III Panzer Corps cleared the north bank of the Manych and established another bridgehead over the river at Novoselovka.

He now had two crossing points on either side of Sporny, the initial objective for his main body. Unfortunately, by the time his forward elements reached Sporny, the Russians had already managed to blow a key dam south of the city. The Manych at this point was usually only forty meters wide, but it suddenly became a great river indeed—some two miles wide. That was too much for even an emergency bridge, and so Mackensen had to order all the artillery and heavy equipment diverted to the two smaller crossings on either side of the town. It was not until July 28 that most of the corps was across the Manych. His pioneers, meanwhile, gave up on trying to repair the dam and finally just built a bridge over it.

In the early hours of July 31, III Panzer Corps got moving again. The 16th Motorized Infantry Division was again in the lead, and it managed "a great spring forward," in Mackensen's words. At first, he said, he was "pursuing a withdrawing enemy," but his forward troops soon had a shock, running into a blizzard of artillery and heavy weapons.[27] This was typical of the entire Caucasus campaign in this phase. With the Soviet army seemingly poised between its urge to flee and its desire to shoot, uncertainty attended virtually every encounter. Nevertheless, 16th Motorized moved swiftly forward, heading through the immense collective farm known as Gigant[28] toward the key communications center of Ssalsk. The seizure of Ssalsk would cut the principal rail line between the Caucasus and Stalingrad. The high command had by this time taken away Grossdeutschland, retaining it north of the Manych, and on August 1, Mackensen's "old and proven" 13th Panzer Division (General Traugott Herr) rejoined the corps.[29]

The two divisions closed in on Ssalsk, taking the town on August 1 and immediately establishing bridgeheads over yet another set of rivers, the Ssandata and Rassypnaya. The drive continued the next day. With 13th Panzer leading and 16th Motorized following close behind, III Panzer Corps captured Novo-Alexandrovskaya, cutting the railway through Kropotkin and Voroshilovsk and seizing large amounts of supplies and ammunition. On August 3, III Panzer Corps reached the Kuban River at Armavir. After some gritty fighting, it seized the town, a nearby airfield, and fifty operational aircraft.[30] It was now poised as the left pincer of a three-corps, concentric drive on Maikop, alongside XXXXIV Corps in the center and LVII Panzer Corps on the right.

There was some interesting action along the way, however. As the tip of 13th Panzer's assault group was smashing though a hastily erected defensive position just north of Armavir, the Russians succeeded in blowing the road bridge over the Kuban. The demolition left a single German tank all alone on the south bank of the river. Mackensen called it "a bridgehead in embryo."[31] That lonely tank crew sitting south of the Kuban, quite literally riding point for the entire German army in the Caucasus, would no doubt have chosen different, sharper words. A few more men and tanks were ferried across the river, however, and by evening, the crisis was past and Mackensen had his bridgehead.

By now, Mackensen was able to see a new dynamic to the fighting. The Soviets were growing in confidence and strength and were finally beginning to contest the German advance. His forces north of the Kuban were coming under heavy Soviet artillery fire and air attack, and the defenders were making good use of the dense overgrowth along the riverbank. The fighting was bitter over the next few days, and losses were high. Mackensen knew that this was no time for an improvised lunge across the river. Things would have to proceed "systematically" (*planmässig*), he said. The next day, August 4, was therefore devoted to building a bridge over the Kuban strong enough for his tanks. It was not an easy task, given the relatively small amount of equipment, the swift current of the river, and the increasingly worrisome level of Soviet resistance. Still, the next day, 13th Panzer Division blasted out of its bridgehead, driving southwest toward the next in an apparently unending series of river crossings. This time it was the strongly flowing Laba, reached on August 6 at Kurgannaya; 16th Motorized Division, coming up on the corps's left wing, reached the same river at Labinskaya. The Soviets had destroyed all the bridges over this river too, so once again, the corps found itself delayed. Scouting parties from the 13th Panzer Division spent the next forty-eight hours searching for fords and usable roads, 16th Motorized Division discovered an intact railroad bridge a few miles to the south at Ssassovskaya, and III Panzer Corps was able to get moving again on August 8.[32]

Mackensen crowned an eventful fifteen days by taking part in the assault on Maikop on August 9. It was a well-handled operation, displaying both stealth (small teams of German soldiers in NKVD uniforms broadcasting contradictory orders within the city, as well as a platoon of "Brandenburger" special forces driving Soviet trucks) and by muscle (the massed artillery of the army group and intense, nonstop Stuka attacks).[33] General Herr's 13th Panzer Division played a crucial role by storming the iron road bridge just before the Soviets could blow it. There was hard fighting in the streets of the city that night, and the corps's rear elements were in nearly constant and bloody combat with Soviet columns that were still desperately trying to withdraw to the south and southeast. Resistance in Maikop ceased on August 10. Mackensen's corps had come nearly 250 miles since the start of the operation seventeen days ago. It was not a fast pace in terms of the theoretical capability of a mechanized unit over flat ground. In light of the actual terrain over which it had passed, however, it was nothing short of spectacular. The Wehrmacht was in the oil fields.

Mackensen himself recognized Maikop as a kind of culmination point, the end of the mobile phase of operations. In its push out of the city in the next few days, 16th Motorized Division was already hitting the mountains. "By now, the motorized formations were advancing forward very slowly in the difficult and densely forested mountains. They could no longer bring their unique qualities to bear." It was time for lighter units, Jäger battalions and mountain troops, to take over. Their arrival would free up III Panzer Corps "for other, more suitable employment."[34]

Perhaps it is time to pause and pay respect where it is due. Maikop was the only one of the original strategic objectives of the 1942 campaigns that specified the destruction of the Soviet armies in the Don bend, the conquest of Stalingrad, and seizure of the oil cities, that the Germans actually achieved. It is customary at this juncture in the narrative to point out that Maikop had been thoroughly demolished by the retreating Soviet forces. It wasn't just a case of the refineries and tank farms being set on fire, as memorable a sight as that had been to the advancing Germans.[35] The destruction of Maikop was the work of highly trained engineers and technicians. The works above ground been subjected to a thorough trashing; demolition teams had even poured concrete down the wellheads. It was "a classic example of fundamental demolition," according to one German official.[36] As distressing as it must have been to its new overlords, however, getting Maikop pumping again was an engineering problem, not some sort of mystery, and engineering had always been a German specialty. Specialists from the Reich, a 6,500-man-strong Petroleum Technical Brigade, arrived on the scene almost immediately and could have put Maikop back online, given enough heavy equipment and time.[37] Unfortunately, there would not be nearly enough of either.

Nevertheless, the Wehrmacht had taken one oil city and seemed poised to take a second one, gathering forces on the Terek River less that 100 miles from Grozny. The roads in the Caucasus were filled with columns moving south: German Panzers, retreating Soviet columns, and the poignant site of hundreds of thousands of civilian refugees crowding the roads, heading south and east.[38] Moreover, one entire German army had not yet even made its appearance in the theater. Field Marshal Erich von Manstein's 11th Army was still in the Crimea, preparing to cross the Straits of Kerch. A concentric drive by five armies, even with all the attendant supply difficulties, would have put immense pressure on the Soviet defenses in this isolated region, and might have overloaded them altogether. Historians have tended to treat the Caucasus operation as an inevitable failure. It would be interesting to go back in time to mid-August 1942 and sample Soviet opinion on that point. Indeed, it looked very much like the Caucasus might be about to get new ownership.

Operations in the Caucasus: The Brake

In late August, things suddenly changed. During the second phase of the Caucasus operation, it was as if the god of war had suddenly reached down and applied a brake all along the front. German formations that were moving at top speed one moment suddenly found themselves slowed to a crawl the next. It is the swiftness of the transition from maneuver to positional and in some cases static warfare that continues to define this campaign. In German terms, *Bewegungskrieg* yielded all too quickly to *Stellungskrieg*.

There were a number of causes. The first was the strange nature of the dual operation that the Wehrmacht was running. While List's armies had been hurtling southward toward the mountains, the drive on Stalingrad had stalled. With most of the available fuel and transport earmarked for the Caucasus, Army Group B was suffering from serious logistical problems, and it was also crashing into increasingly larger Soviet forces. Faced with this serious operational problem, Hitler and the high command decided on August 1, less than a week into Operation Edelweiss, to reverse their operational priorities and make the drive to Stalingrad the new *Schwerpunkt*.[39] It was a decision that had immediate ramifications on the German order of battle. Hoth's 4th Panzer Army changed army groups, moving from "A" to "B," departing the Caucasus and heading north for Stalingrad.[40]

This was indeed a signal moment, a complete reversal of course less than a week into a major operation. Although Hitler usually gets the blame for this gaffe, the decision was not his alone. Halder and the General Staff had never been enamored of the Caucasus operation in the first place and had spent an entire week since the appearance of Directive 45 arguing that the Wehrmacht should aim first for Stalingrad. The drive to the east would feature better terrain, they argued, and would also be far easier to supply than a strike into the mountains. Given the tense relationships within the German high command, a suggestion to shelve Hitler's pet Caucasus project in favor of the more orthodox strike against Stalingrad received a chilly reception when Halder first raised it on July 24. Only when it became obvious that something had to be done about the extremely large Soviet buildup at Stalingrad did Hitler acquiesce. As always, he then tried to make it look like it had been his idea all along. On July 30, General Jodl, Hitler's operations chief in the OKW, announced in dramatic tones, "The fate of the Caucasus will be decided at Stalingrad."[41] Halder's annoyance at all this was palpable. He had been saying the exact same thing for a week.

With Hoth departing for Stalingrad and Manstein's 11th Army boarding rail transport for the Leningrad front, Army Group A had become a shadow of its former self. It had been envisioned in Directive 45 as a behemoth of five armies, but now it had just three: 1st Panzer, 3rd Romanian, and 17th. It would soon lose the Romanians as the never-ending flank of the Stalingrad operation became longer and the city itself became a furnace demanding ever more fresh formations. Five had thus become two, and the entire multiarmy thrust into the Caucasus had now been simplified, perhaps oversimplified: 17th Army in the west, heading for the Black Sea ports of Novorossisk, Tuapse, and Suchumi, and 1st Panzer Army in the east, heading for the Terek River and the oil fields of Grozny. They were separated by almost 300 miles, unable to give one another even the barest hint of support, and were running into increasingly tough Soviet resistance by the third week.[42]

Loss of *Schwerpunkt* status also meant a lower priority status for supplies, ammunition, replacements, and especially fuel. After the seizure of Maikop, for example, 1st Panzer Army was shifted to the east. Mackensen's III Panzer Corps was to head toward the town of Ischerskaya, a crossing point on the Terek and a suitable position from which to launch a drive on Grozny. Mackensen received his orders on August 16 and tore off at high speed, apparently the only speed this great Panzer leader knew. He made good progress on August 16 and 17 and then ran out of gas completely, early on day 3. Although his commander, Kleist, arranged for rapid resupply, Mackensen's corps would sit for four full days, a crucial period in which the civilian population of Grozny was feverishly digging defensive positions around the city: fortifications, gun emplacements, antitank ditches. On August 22, enough fuel arrived to get one division forward for a single day, and 13th Panzer Division finally made it to Ischerskaya. "Lack of fuel made any further movement of the corps impossible," wrote Mackensen. "And how much we might have achieved!"[43]

In addition to its fuel, Edelweiss also lost much of its airpower. It is no real surprise that the German drive slowed to a crawl just at the moment that most of the Luftwaffe was sent north to bases in the Stalingrad sector. Moreover, with the Wehrmacht lunging hundreds of miles away from its few serviceable airfields and already overworked infrastructure, the effectiveness of the air units still remaining in the south was greatly diminished. As it had proved repeatedly in this period, the Luftwaffe could be a fearsome instrument if massed in strength against one *Schwerpunkt*, but not two widely separated ones. As German air strength faded, moreover, the Soviet Air Force (VVS) was moving in the opposite direction. By mid-August, German reports from the field began to mention the presence of Soviet ground attack aircraft. The heavily armored Il-2, known as the Sturmovik, would become an increasingly common sight in the Caucasian skies during the weeks ahead.[44]

Consider, for example, the case of V Corps, the extreme right wing of 17th Army. Its first objective was the oil-refining city of Krasnodar on the Kuban River. The corps got to the outskirts easily enough, then had to endure several days of tough fighting with the Soviet 56th Army before capturing the city on August 9. Its next assignment called for V Corps to drive southwest across the Kuban, and in cooperation with Romanian 3rd Army, seize the Black Sea ports of Anapa, Novorossisk, and Tuapse. From the start, V Corps found the going much harder. With the bridges in Krasnodar destroyed by the retreating Soviets, it took the corps five full days to establish bridgeheads over the Kuban on either side of the city. When it got across the river, it found itself facing a deeply echeloned defense made up of reserves coming up from Novorossiisk, as well as a situation that Field Marshal List called "absolute enemy superiority in the air."[45] The V Corps duly began to chew through Soviet defenses, aiming for Krymskaya, but the combination of Soviet power, an increasingly feisty Red Air Force, and some of the most difficult terrain the Wehrmacht had ever seen all conspired to bring the war of movement to an end in this sector.

Indeed, no discussion of the Caucasus campaign can omit the natural conditions, especially the weather and the terrain. Local temperatures that August continued to top 100°F. The great Soviet Sturmovik pilot Vasily Emelianenko was from the region, and even he described the heat as "unbearable." The armored portions of his aircraft were too hot to touch, and the water in the radiator was boiling by the time he taxied out to the runway.[46] On the dirt roads of the region, the oppressive heat churned up great clouds of dust, a fine, choking mist that seemed to hover in the air and that coated everything—men, machines, horses, food—that was not carefully protected.

As for the terrain, the only campaign that rivaled Edelweiss in terms of similar operational difficulties would be the Italian conquest of Ethiopia in 1935–1936. As the Wehrmacht headed south, it seemed to be leaving civilization. It was a world of "mountainous primeval forest, never harvested and crossed only by a few beaten footpaths," in the words of the German official history. "Streams and rivers, when they weren't flooded by the rains, had to serve as the major routes for the troops."[47] The tactical problems can be imagined, but the difficulties the terrain caused in the areas of supply and transport are almost unimaginable. Field kitchens, for example, couldn't get far enough forward to deliver the food without long, grueling marches and climbs. Food rarely arrived on time, and it never seemed to arrive hot. Ammunition trucks were out of the question, and we have the unusual sight of a highly mechanized army bringing its artillery and mortar ammunition forward on horses, not for the last time in this war, as the Allied campaign in Italy would attest. The poor overloaded animals soldiered on and died in droves in the course of the campaign. So did wounded men. The roughness of the roads meant that the badly wounded simply could not be transported: if their injuries didn't kill them, the ride certainly would.[48] Lightly wounded men weren't much better off. They had to take a long and painful nightmare journey to the rear, replete with stops, starts, bumps, and jostling, and once the fighting had reached the mountains, they often had to be carried out of harm's way on the back of their comrades or by Soviet prisoners of war.[49] With the few and infrequent towns in the region being used as headquarters and concentration areas for the assault, most of the front-line soldiers slept under the stars, the rain, and eventually the snow. And of course, there were the Russians to be dealt with. Resistance began to stiffen as the front line reached the foothills of the mountain range. The terrain was ideal for the defense, for hidden gun emplacements and sudden ambushes with fire, and the Germans were beginning to see a lot of both.

Burdened by all these difficulties, then, Army Group A's advance slowed to a crawl in late August and then stopped altogether. The Black Sea port of Anapa fell to the Romanians on August 31, an operation conducted by General Radu Korne, the hero of the pursuit to Kerch in May 1942. As in Operation Trappenjagd, Korne was once again commanding a "detachment," a mobile battle group consisting of the motorized elements of the 5th and 9th Romanian Cavalry Divisions. The Anapa operation was an interesting one that saw Korne seize two batteries of Soviet 150mm guns on the Nassurovo heights overlooking the city and then turn them on the port itself, providing crucial fire support for his assault units.[50]

On September 2, a greatly reduced landing operation, Blücher II, finally took place along the Taman peninsula, with elements of the German XXXXII Corps making the crossing in the teeth of strong Soviet coastal artillery fire. By September 5, the peninsula was in German hands. The next day, German V Corps and the Romanian Cavalry Corps launched a drive against the key Black Sea port of Novorossiisk, smashing the Soviet defenses outside the city and seizing the port.[51] Once again, however, the Soviets refused to surrender the center of the city itself, and there would be four days of bitter street fighting. Even after the Germans took the town proper, the Soviets remained in possession of one shore of the bay and the mountains to the south, the beginning of the Caucasus chain proper in this sector.

By the end of August, the German position in the Caucasus was an enormous salient, a bulge stretching from the Lower Don across the Kuban to the mountains. The Germans had made enormous progress in the center, but 17th Army's drive had stalled altogether, and there were large stretches of the Black Sea coastline, including the key ports of Tuapse and Suchumi, still in Soviet hands. From right to left, 17th Army had Vth Corps in Novorossiisk, LVII Panzer Corps and XXXXIV (Jäger) Corps arrayed against Tuapse, and XXXXIX Mountain Corps against Suchumi. On the map, it might have appeared as if the Wehrmacht could simply reach out and snatch either port by a simple lunge to the coast. That certainly was how it seemed to Hitler, and in mid-August, Hitler ordered 17th Army to do just that. Rather than a lightning assault, the attack turned out to be a tough, slow grind. Tuapse and Suchumi may have only been thirty kilometers or so as the crow flies, but this was mountainous country. The drive on Tuapse had to pass through what the Germans called the *Waldkaukasus* (the forested mountains), while the mountain corps's attack on Suchumi had to negotiate the torturous passes of the *Hochkaukasus* (the high mountains). The latter entailed debouching from a number of high mountain passes; there was bitter fighting from the start, and German losses were heavy. It was clear to the men on the ground that the Red Army, so unsteady earlier in the open field, had now recovered its equilibrium in the mountains. Moreover, time was running short. By the end of September, the snows would close most of these passes.[52]

The slow pace of the operations, especially compared with the first two weeks, fed into the already high level of tension at Hitler's Vinnitsa headquarters. The result was, as always with the Führer, a great deal of pointless static for the man in the field: Field Marshal List. After surveying his map, his fuel situation, and his shrinking manpower levels, List argued for shortening the line by pulling back XXXXIX Mountain Corps, leaving small detachments guarding the high passes, and launching one concentrated thrust toward Tuapse. It is what we might call a little solution to the problem.[53] Characteristically, Hitler wanted an attack on both Tuapse and Suchumi at the same time, a decision that had 17th Army spread all over the place; indeed, XXXXIX Mountain Corps itself was holding a front of nearly 200 miles. An increasingly hard-pressed 4th Mountain Division had already had to pull back in the face of increased Soviet pressure.[54]

Hitler reacted to these command disagreements in his characteristic fashion. Because he believed that his own decisions could not be at fault, it must be his generals and their "half-hearted leadership."[55] There were stormy scenes in the Führer's Vinnitsa headquarters, the tension only increased by the stifling heat.[56] The entries in Halder's war diary became increasingly sarcastic, and Hitler returned the favor, one time mocking Halder openly for having spent all of World War I in an office, "sitting on that same swivel stool," while others (himself included) had been out doing the fighting,[57] another time flying into a rage at news that a unit of volunteers from the 1st Mountain Division had gone out of their way to scale Mount Elbrus, the tallest peak in the Caucasus range, a harmless photo op that happened to take place at the very moment that he had ordered every last man and weapon concentrated for the drive on Suchumi.[58] On September 9, Hitler relieved List of his command and took over Army Group A himself. He followed it up just a few weeks later on September 24 by dismissing Halder as chief of the General Staff and replacing him with General

Kurt Zeitzler, a much more enthusiastic Nazi but also a man of some ability.[59]

Not surprisingly, the new command team found that it could no more crack open the front and reestablish mobile conditions than List could. Even after Hitler followed List's advice and narrowed the attack to Tuapse alone, the assault came to a halt in the mountains anyway, just as List had warned. There would be, quite literally, no more movement on this front for the next three months. It was *Stellungskrieg* with a vengeance, a mechanized army caught fast in a great mountain range. For the Germans, concentrating sufficient attacking power was almost impossible in such rugged terrain. The Soviets, deployed in the coastal plain to the south and west, had much more operational freedom, not to mention easier and more secure supply lines.

By the end of September, the German armies in the Caucasus were facing a solid wall of Soviet formations. The Transcaucasus Front (General I. V. Tyulenev) contained no fewer than eight armies, although the massive nature of the force and its vast geographical sprawl required a further subdivision into a Black Sea Group and a North Group of four armies each. The former included the 47th, 56th, 18th, and 46th Armies, all crammed into the tiny coastal cockpit from just south of Novorossiisk through Tuapse to Suchumi, and all arrayed against a lone German formation, the 17th Army.[60] The latter contained the 37th, 9th, and 44th Armies defending along the line of the Terek River and 58th Army in reserve at Makhachkala on the coastline of the Caspian Sea. Once again, all four were in line against a single German army, the 1st Panzer. It was a typical *Stellungskrieg*. There was no real Soviet flank to be had, and before the Panzer divisions could even think about operational-level maneuver, they were first going to have to punch a hole somewhere.

Despite a balance of forces that had gone bad and a logistical situation that edged ever closer to disaster, the Wehrmacht still showed occasional flashes of the old fire. As the summer turned into fall, with the Black Sea front frozen in place, the focus of the Caucasus campaign shifted to the east, along the Terek, the last of the major rivers in the region. It was deep and swiftly flowing, with steep, rocky banks that sheltered a number of key targets: the cities of Grozny and Ordzhonokidze, as well as the Ossetian and Georgian Military Roads.[61] The roads were the only two routes through the mountains capable of bearing motor traffic, and possession of them would give the Wehrmacht effective control of the Caucasus. Indeed, the Russian czars had built them for just that purpose in the nineteenth century, and

Ordzhonikidze's original name had been Vladikavkaz ("master of the Caucasus"). The Georgian Road was especially important. It ran from Ordzhonikidze down to Tbilisi, and it would give the Germans the potential for a high-speed drive through the mountains to the rich oil fields of Baku, the greatest potential prize of the entire campaign.

By October, 1st Panzer Army had concentrated what was left of its fighting strength along the Terek. Mackensen's III Panzer Corps was on the right, LII Corps in the center, and XXXX Panzer Corps on the left, at Mozdok. On October 25, III Panzer Corps staged one of the last great set-piece assaults of the Caucasus campaign, aiming for an envelopment of the Soviet 37th Army near and east of Nalchik.[62] Mackensen had 2nd Romanian Mountain Division on his right, and much of his corps's muscle (13th and 23rd Panzer Divisions, plus 370th Infantry Division) on his left. The Romanians would lead off, punch a hole in the Soviet defenses, and fix their attention to their front. The next day, an attack group of two Panzer divisions would blast into the Soviet right, encircling the Soviet defenders and ripping open a hole in the front. Once that was done, the entire corps would wheel to the left (east), heading toward Odzhonikidze.

It went off just as planned. Even a badly weakened Wehrmacht, one that was short of fuel, men, and tanks and that operated in the thin mountain air, could still occasionally fight *Bewegungskrieg*. Its allies also more than held their own. The Romanians opened the attack on October 25, along with a German battalion (the 1st of the 99th Mountain Jäger Regiment).[63] Together they smashed into Soviet forces along the Baksan River and penetrated the front of 37th Army, driving toward Nalchik across three swiftly flowing rivers, the Baksan, Chegem, and Urvan. German Stukas supported the attack, achieving one of the war's great victories by destroying the 37th Army's headquarters near Nalchik, a blow that left the army leaderless in the first few crucial hours of the attack.[64] The next evening, the two Panzer divisions attacked by moonlight, crossing the Terek and achieving complete surprise. Soon they had blocked the roads out of Nalchik, and the Wehrmacht had achieved one of its few *Kessels* in the entire Caucasus campaign, although once again it took a day of hard street fighting in Nalchik itself to finish off Soviet resistance. The number of prisoners was somewhere around 11,000 in the opening days of combat.

The operation thus far was "working like a precision watch," the Wehrmacht's favorite operational metaphor.[65] Some survivors of the 37th Army limped back toward Ordzhonikidze; others apparently threw off discipline and fled to the mountains directly to the south.

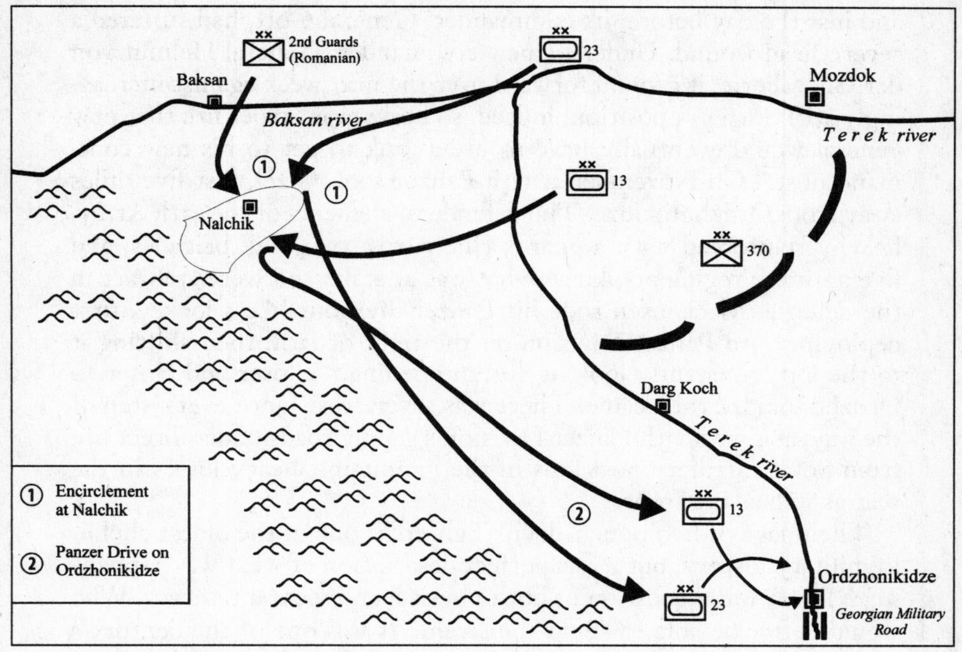

Map 13. End of the line in the Caucasus: Mackensen's drive on Ordzhonikidze.

The Panzer divisions now wheeled left, heading due east, with the mountains forming a wall directly on their right. With 23rd Panzer on the right and 13th on the left, it was reminiscent of the days when the Wehrmacht was still strong enough to form an operational *Schwerpunkt*. During October 27 and 28, the Panzer columns crossed one river after the other—the Lesken, the Urukh, the Chikola—with the Soviets either unwilling or unable to form a cohesive defense in front of them.

By October 29, they had reached the Ardon River, at the head of the Ossetian Military Road. Kleist saw it as "a chance that will never come again,"[66] and he was determined to seize it. On November 1, the 23rd Panzer Division took Alagir, closing the Ossetian Road and offering the Wehrmacht the possibility of access to the southeastern Caucaus through Kutais to Batum.[67] At the same time, 13th Panzer Division was driving toward the corps's objectives: Ordzhonikidze and the Georgian Military Road. Kleist ordered the division to take the city on the run. That evening, 13th Panzer's advance guard was less than ten miles from Ordzhonikidze. It had been through some tough fighting, and just the day before, its commander, General Gott, had suffered a severe head wound. Under its new commander, General Helmut von der Chevallerie, it ground forward over the next week against increasingly stiff Soviet opposition; indeed, so heavy was Soviet fire that new general would eventually have to use a tank to get to his new command post.[68] On November 2, 13th Panzer took Gizel, just five miles away from Ordzhonikidze. The defenders, elements of the 37th Army, heavily reinforced with a guards rifle corps, two tank brigades, and five antitank regiments, knew what was at stake and were stalwart in the defense. Mackensen rode his Panzer divisions like a jockey, first deploying 23rd Panzer Division on the right of 13th, then shifting it to the left, constantly looking for an opening.[69] Closer and closer to Ordzhonokidze they came. There was severe resistance every step of the way, and with 13th Panzer Division's supply roads under direct fire from Soviet artillery positions in the mountains, heavy losses in the rear as well as the front.

The image of two punch-drunk fighters is one of the oldest clichés in military history, but it is a perfect description of what was happening here. It was a question of both physical and mental reserves: Who would better be able to stand the strain? It was one of the century's great *mano a mano* ground combats. It had it all: bitter cold, swirling snowstorms, and a majestic wall of mountains and glaciers standing watch in the background. The road network sufficed for neither side, and so columns often had to crowd themselves onto minor branch roads where they were easy prey for enemy fighter-bombers.[70] Rarely have Stukas and Sturmoviks had more a more lucrative target set, and the losses on both sides were terrible.

By November 3, 13th Panzer Division had fought its way over the highlands and was two kilometers from the city. By now, a mere handful of battalions was carrying the fight to the enemy, bearing the entire weight of the German campaign in the Caucasus. For the record, they were the 2nd of the 66th Regiment (II/66th) on the left, II/93rd on the right, with 1/66th echeloned to the left rear. Deployed behind the assault elements were the I/99th Mountain Jägers, the 203rd Assault Gun Battalion, and the 627th Engineer Battalion.[71] The mission of the last formation was crucial: to rush forward and open the Georgian Military Road the moment Ordzhonikidze fell.

Over the next few days, German gains were measured in hundreds of meters—six hundred on November 4, a few hundred more on November 5. By now, it had become a battle of bunker busting, with the German assault formations having to chew their way through dense lines of fortifications, bunkers, and pillboxes. Progress was excruciatingly slow, but then again, the attackers didn't have all that far to go. Overhead the Luftwaffe thundered, waves of aircraft wreaking havoc on the Soviet front line and rear, and pounding the city itself. Mackensen's reserves had been used up a week ago, and it was inconceivable to him that the Soviets were not suffering as badly or worse.

But he was wrong. On November 6, the Soviets launched a counterattack, their first real concentrated blow of the entire Terek campaign, against 13th Panzer's overextended spearhead.[72] Mixed groups of infantry and T-34 tanks smashed easily through the paper-thin German flank guards and began to close in behind the mass of the division itself, in the process scattering much of its transport and cutting off its combat elements from their supply lines. Supporting attacks against the German left tied up the 23rd Panzer Division and 2nd Romanian Mountain Division just long enough to keep them from coming to 13th Panzer's assistance. There were no German reserves to restore the situation, and for the next three days, heavy snowstorms kept the Luftwaffe on the ground. Indeed, 13th Panzer only had the strength for one last blow: to the west, to break out of the threatened encirclement. After some shifting of units, including the deployment of the S.S. Division *Wiking* in support, the order went out on November 9. The first convoy out of the pocket contained tanks to punch a hole, followed by a convoy of trucks filled with the wounded. Within two days, a badly mauled 13th Panzer was back where it belonged, on the German side of the lines. The drive on Ordzhonikidze had failed, as had the drive on the oil fields of Grozny—and the Caucasus campaign itself.

But how close it had been! Consider these numbers. Take a German army group of five armies and reduce it to three, and then to two. Give it an absurd assignment, let us say a 700-mile drive at the end of a 1,200-mile supply chain, against a force of eight enemy armies in the worst terrain in the world. Wear down its divisions to less than 50 percent of their normal effective strength, both in terms of men and tanks. Then make it 33 percent. Feed them a hot meal perhaps once a week. Remove them from the control of their professional officer corps and throw them into the hands of a lone amateur strategist. Throw them into subzero temperatures and two feet of snow. Add it all up, and what do you get? Not an inevitable defeat, but a hard-driving Panzer corps stopped, but still churning its legs, less than two kilometers away from its strategic objective. Clausewitz was right about one thing: "War is the realm of uncertainty."[73]

The Drive on Stalingrad: Clearing the Don

Compared with the complexity of the struggle in the Caucasus, the drive on Stalingrad is far easier to comprehend.[74] It started as a straight shot to the east by a single German army, the 6th. As a secondary operation, it was undermanned and undersupplied, and it soon found itself facing nothing but frustration en route to Stalingrad. The commander, General Friedrich Paulus, had barely gotten started when fuel shortages forced him to call a halt. Moreover, the large buildup of Soviet forces in front of him, and the threat they posed to the entire German position in the east, led to an immediate change of priorities within the high command. Stalingrad became the main target, and now it was the commanders in the Caucasus who were bemoaning lack of fuel, transport, and attention.

The manner in which the city had suddenly become the center of the entire combined operation, the key to the Caucasus, the "hinge on which the entire future campaign depended,"[75] as one staff officer put it, was pregnant with irony. In the original plans for Operation Blue, Stalingrad was of decidedly secondary importance. Field Marshal von Kleist, commander of 1st Panzer Army, commented after the war, "The capture of Stalingrad was subsidiary to the main aim. It was only of importance as a convenient place, in the bottleneck between the Don and the Volga, where we could block an attack on our flank by Russian forces coming from the east. . . . At the start," he added with some bitterness, "Stalingrad was no more than a name on the map to us."[76]

Indeed, virtually all of the participants agree that the Germans could have taken Stalingrad in late July, had they so desired. The Soviets were just then in the process of forming a new Stalingrad front, but they had hardly begun to assemble their reserve armies or construct their defenses.[77] Hoth's 4th Panzer Army would have had a clear shot at the city—a long one, admittedly, but a clear one, and Hoth could move as fast as any army commander in the business when he was in the mood. Again, Marshal von Kleist:

> The 4th Panzer Army was advancing on that line, on my left. It could have taken Stalingrad without a fight, at the end of July, but was diverted south to help me in crossing the Don. I did not need its aid, and it merely congested the roads I was using. When it turned north again, a fortnight later, the Russians had gathered just sufficient forces at Stalingrad to check it.[78]

Instead, by the middle of July, Hoth, Kleist, and Paulus alike were tied up in the second great armored knot (a *Zusammenballung*, Halder called it[79]) of this campaign: the one around the empty Rostov pocket. No one was going anywhere for the time being.

When Paulus finally did get under way, he was driving east inside the Don bend with his force deployed in two spearheads. On his left (north), he had the XIV Panzer Corps (General Gustav von Wietersheim), skirting the southern bank of the Don with 16th Panzer Division, 3rd Motorized, and 60th Motorized Divisions. On the right (south) lay the army's *Schwerpunkt*: XXIV Panzer Corps (General Willibald von Langermann), with the 24th Panzer Division, 76th and 295th Infantry Divisions; and LI Corps (General Walther von Seydlitz-Kurzbach), containing the 4th and 71st Divisions. The southern group was coming up past Morozovsk and heading toward the confluence of the Chir and Don Rivers.

In between these two thrusts lay two defending Soviet armies still fighting to the west of the Don, 62nd and 64th, deployed right to left. They held a substantial bridgehead on the right bank some forty miles wide by twenty miles deep, stretching from Kalach in the north to Nizhne Chirskaya in the south. Whatever problems they might have been having in late June, they certainly seemed to be solidifying by now, and the going was slow. Paulus ground forward, but even that wasn't easy considering his supply situation. He was on the phone hourly in that last week of July, begging for more tanks, more ammunition, more fuel. A particular worry of his was his lack of infantry; there was nowhere near enough if it came down to a battle for the city of Stalingrad itself.[80]

By July 26, 6th Army was dead in the water. Its forward units had not been refueled for two days, and there were no promises coming from the high command about when it intended to put the situation right. Paulus would be immobilized for nearly ten days for lack of fuel, a time in which the Soviets were feverishly strengthening their defenses in the Don bend and at Stalingrad. These were some uncomfortable moments for 6th Army, and they got worse when the Soviets launched one of their first real counterattacks of the 1942 campaign. It involved the 1st and 4th Tank Armies, neither of which was as yet fully deployed.[81] It had strong air support, however, and there was a day or two of crisis as a nearly immobilized XIV Panzer Corps found itself locked in a tough defensive struggle against an overwhelming number of Soviet tanks. The Germans managed to beat back the assault, but only by using every drop of gas.[82] Stalingrad was only about eighty miles away, but it might as well have been on the moon at 6th Army's current pace.

The decision to make Stalingrad the new operational *Schwerpunkt*, manifested in the first place by the arrival of the 4th Panzer Army, transformed the situation. Although it would be nice to picture Hoth riding like the wind to Paulus's assistance, storming across the featureless plain of the Kalmyk steppe toward Stalingrad, that was not the case. Hoth's army was third of three on the priority list for fuel, behind 6th Army (newly prioritized) and 1st Panzer (newly demoted). His ability to maneuver was far below what it had been earlier in the summer, and it would stay that way for the rest of the campaign. Nevertheless, with 6th Army advancing on the city from the west inside the Don bend and Hoth now part of the Army Group B team, coming up from the south and southwest, the two armies were finally launching a concentric attack of sorts against Stalingrad.

It was not until August 7 that a newly refueled 6th Army was once again ready for action. First on the agenda were those Soviet forces, now considerable, still inside the Don bend. Paulus placed his two Panzer Corps, XIV and XXIV, in the van. With the former skirting the Don on its left and wheeling south and the latter skirting the river to its right and turning to the north, the two armored wedges drove deep into the flank and rear of the Soviet bridgehead over the Don. Massive support from the Luftwaffe destroyed every single bridge behind the defenders, sealing off their path of retreat. The two armored thrusts met early in the morning of August 8 just southwest of the Don crossing at Kalach. In the process, they trapped large parts of the 62nd and 1st Tank Armies in a tight *Kessel*. Over the course of the next two days, concentric ground attack and massive Luftwaffe support inexorably reduced the pocket. The roads inside it were filled with endless columns of Soviet vehicles heading east, desperately trying to reach the Don crossings, only to find the bridges destroyed. It was a hard target for the German bombers and Stukas to miss: the better part of two Soviet armies was herded into a zone less than four miles wide. There were nightly Soviet breakout attempts on all the compass points of the encirclement—southwest, east, and northeast—supported by artillery on the east bank of the Don. They came to naught, however, smashed by a combination of ground and air power. The carnage was horrible, as it had to be, given the force density in this tiny area.[83]

The Kalach *Kessel*, almost forgotten today, was the first real encirclement of the 1942 campaign and led to high hopes in Hitler's headquarters. By the time they had liquidated the Kalach pocket on August

11, the Germans had captured another 35,000 prisoners and accounted for 270 tanks and 560 guns. Total Soviet casualties were certainly much higher, given the density and ferocity of the German air assault over the pocket. Added to the totals for the previous week's battles in the Don bend, the Germans had taken a total of 57,000 prisoners and destroyed or captured nearly 1,000 tanks.

To Stalingrad

Although it is often claimed that the battle of Kalach had finally cleared the Don bend, that was not the case. There were still a number of pesky Soviet bridgeheads on Paulus's northern (left) flank, with those at Serafimovich, Kletskaya, and Kremenskaya being the most notable. Half-hearted attempts to reduce them came to nothing.[84] He had neither the time nor the forces to spare against each one, and he had more important business to the east. One lesson that the Wehrmacht would learn and relearn repeatedly in this war was that failing to crush a Soviet bridgehead almost always had deleterious consequences later on.[85] This would be no exception.

Still, with major operations in the Don bend completed, Paulus now had to cross the river and get to Stalingrad. The direct route would be eastward out of Kalach, but since the Soviets were expecting a thrust here, Paulus felt that it would probably be strongly manned. Instead of crashing through on the obvious route, he chose to maneuver. Shifting XIV Panzer Corps to the northeastern corner of the Don bend, he had it cross the river at Vertyachiy on August 21.[86] Over the course of the next two days, it drove across the thirty-five-mile-wide land bridge between the Don and the Volga. Supporting it every step of the way were the massed aircraft of Fliegerkorps VIII, now under the command of General Martin Fiebig. "Since early morning, we were constantly over the panzer spearheads, helping them forward with our bombs and machine guns," said the commander of one Stuka squadron.[87] By the afternoon of August 23, 3rd Panzer Division under General Hans Hube had lunged clear to the banks of Volga, arriving in the northern suburbs of Stalingrad. It was an impressive achievement, but not without a certain element of danger. Hube held not a defensible position so much as a narrow corridor to the Volga. Indeed, Soviet counterattacks soon sealed him off in an isolated pocket all his own. It was a nearly disastrous turn of events that required massive intervention by the Luftwaffe, which inflicted punishing losses on the Soviet formations assailing Hube's rear, softening them up for successful relief operations by LI Corps.

The same night that Hube reached the Volga, the Luftwaffe appeared over Stalingrad in force. It was the heaviest strike it had mounted since the first day of Operation Barbarossa.[88] Nearly 600 bombers, virtually the entire complement of German air power on the southern front, took part, with many planes flying two and even three sorties. The massive use of incendiaries started fires that could be seen forty miles away, gutted immense portions of the city, and inflicted a huge death toll. Estimates in the popular literature of 40,000 deaths are almost certainly too high, but it is probably best to say simply that they were high enough.[89] It was a calling card, a city-breaking blow by night, announcing to Stalingrad and to the world that the Wehrmacht was at the gates.

While Paulus was advancing on the city from the Don, Hoth was coming up from the south. As Paulus had already discovered, approaching Stalingrad wasn't a free ride. In the case of 4th Panzer Army, the obstacles were a combination of meager supplies of fuel and ammunition, along with the stubborn resistance of Soviet 57th Army. Following the line of the Ssalsk-Stalingrad railway across the otherwise featureless steppe, Hoth crossed the Aksai River heading northeast and managed to push to a point about thirty miles south of the city. Here, between the Aksai and the Mishkova Rivers, the Soviets successfully delayed him, then brought him to a halt a few days later along a line of fortified hills just north of Tinguta. It was a serious problem because the whole point of the two-army advance was to arrive at Stalingrad at more or less the same moment, and pose the defenders with an impossible dilemma.

Like Paulus, Hoth decided to use operational maneuver to achieve what brute force could not. Beginning on August 29, he shifted VI Romanian Corps to cover his front at Tinguta, then withdrew his mobile elements (XXXXVIII Panzer Corps, IV Corps) far to the rear. Sending them out on a wide flanking movement to the northwest, ten miles around the offending bottleneck, he then had them wheel back to the northeast, toward Stalingrad. Getting across the Karpovka River at Gavrilovka, he drove north, making contact with the formations of 6th Army on September 2. As they had for Paulus's arrival, German bombers proclaimed the coming of Hoth with yet another massive bombing raid over Stalingrad on September 3, a "twenty-four hour, relentless raid against the already ruined city" that churned up a great deal of rubble, killed thousands more civilians, and nearly bagged the

Soviet commander in Stalingrad, General V. I. Chuikov of the reconstituted 62nd Army.[90]

The two German armies had met, reestablishing a continuous front directly in front of Stalingrad. The question was, now what? Outside of the *Kesselschlacht* at Kalach two weeks ago, they had failed to trap any substantial Soviet forces outside of the city. The remnants of 62nd and 64th Armies were in Stalingrad, the former defending in the north, the latter the south. If the point of the air attacks had been to crack the morale of the defenders and the civilian population alike, it was soon obvious that that had not happened. One recent arrival in the theater was General G. K. Zhukov, Stalin's deputy supreme commander. He immediately set about planning a counterstroke. It opened on September 5, with 24th Army, 1st Guards Army, and 66th Army slamming into the northern flank of the still narrow German penetration to the Volga. It failed to achieve its aim due to a variety of reasons: shortages of heavy weapons; poor coordination of the arms, in particular of the massive initial barrage with the infantry and tank assault; and slipshod planning that forced the rifle divisions to move straight to the attack off of a thirty-mile march. Nevertheless, it did distract 6th Army from attacking Stalingrad, and it gave Chuikov and the 62nd Army one more crucial day to put its defenses in order.

It was a time for decisions. In front of the German armies lay a great city with a population of 600,000 and a large, heavy industrial base. Just a few months ago, the Germans had suffered some 75,000 casualties reducing the much smaller city of Sevastopol, the bloodiest encounter of the spring by a considerable margin. Stalingrad, moreover, presented an unusual set of geographical problems. Rather than a collection of neighborhoods radiating out of some central point, the city was one long urbanized area stretching along the right bank of the Volga for nearly thirty miles, as straight as a railroad tie. In operational terms, therefore, it was not so much a city as a long, fortified bridgehead on the western bank of the river. The Germans could never put it under siege. Behind it lay a great river, behind the river a huge force of artillery that could intervene in the battle at will, and behind the artillery a vast, secure, and rapidly industrializing Soviet hinterland.

Not for the first time in this war, the Wehrmacht had conquered its way into an impasse. It could not go forward without sinking into a morass of urban fighting. The high command, from Hitler on down through Halder, the staff, and the field commanders, all knew what a city fight would mean. The preferred way of war, *Bewegungskrieg* (the war of movement on the operational level) would inevitably degenerate into *Stellungskrieg* (positional, or static, warfare), and finally into a *Festungskrieg* (fortress war): the slow and bloody reduction of a heavily fortified area. Indeed, Hitler and the staff had designed the entire convoluted operational sequence in 1942 for the very purpose of avoiding this prospect. No one, certainly not General Paulus, relished the possibility of having to dig an entire Soviet army out of a built-up area. At the same time, however, the Germans could not simply go around Stalingrad, and there was no possibility of simply staying put—not with Paulus and Hoth both sitting out on the end of a long and vulnerable limb.

Given a choice of three unpalatable alternatives, the Wehrmacht made the only decision consonant with its history and traditions, dating back to Frederick the Great, Blücher, and Moltke. On September 5, the big guns roared, the Panzers stormed forward, and the Stukas screamed overhead. The assault on Stalingrad had begun.

In the City

The first great thrust saw bitter fighting on all sectors.[91] It was five full days before the spearhead of Hoth's 4th Panzer Army (XXXXVIII Panzer Corps) reached the Volga near Kuporosnoye, splitting Stalingrad in two parts: the industrial districts and city center on the one hand, and the southern suburbs on the other. More importantly, Hoth's assault tore open the seam between 62nd Army to the north and 64th Army to the south, leaving Chuikov's army to fight it out alone in Stalingrad. On September 13, the Wehrmacht renewed the assault, with two assault groups, XXXXVIII Panzer Corps (now transferred to Paulus's 6th Army, in order to unify the assault under a single commander) attempting to smash into the city from the south and LI Corps doing the same from the north and west. That two-corps battle array would remain a constant, and in operational level terms, it is probably all the description that the battle of Stalingrad requires.

But this was no longer operational level warfare. It was a battle not of corps or divisions, but of squads, with small arms and the machine gun predominant, and even that rarest of modern military actions, hand-to-hand combat. Here, a German army that in the summer had hurtled hundreds of miles at a bound had to figure out a way to get from one side of a street to the other without being cut down by a hail of hostile fire. Individual positions or buildings, not whole provinces or mountain ranges, became the focus: the Dzerzhinsky Tractor Works, the grain elevator, the vodka works, or the ancient burial mound hill known to the Soviets as the Mameyev Kurgan (appearing more prosaically on German maps as "Hill 102"). Stalingrad's most famous literary trope belongs to General Hans Doerr, the chief of the General Staff of the LII Corps. In Stalingrad, he wrote, "the meter replaced the kilometer as a measure of distance, and the city plan replaced the General Staff's map."[92]

With the use of tanks ruled out, at least en masse, Stalingrad was by necessity an infantry battle. The major mobile formation, XXXXVIII Panzer Corps, soon receded in importance, and Seydlitz's LI Corps eventually became an infantry army in its own right. At its height, it contained no fewer than nine divisions, becoming perhaps the largest "corps" of the entire war.[93] Stalingrad was indeed a *Festungskrieg*, but with both sides occasionally using the sewer system as a relatively secure means of movement within the city, perhaps it is better to use the term coined by an anonymous German grunt: *Rattenkrieg* ("war of the rats").[94]

For the next two months, both sides fought, bled, and died in the streets of a ruined city, one of the most apocalyptic scenes of a bloody century. Chuikov's orders were simple, at least in concept. He was to hold the city at all costs while expecting minimal reinforcement. He did just that, keeping his grip on an ever-narrower strip of the city along the Volga, protecting the ferry sites (actually small boats, cutters, and barges—anything that would float) on which his reinforcements and supplies depended. The Volga bank was not a sandy beach but an enormous and steep escarpment into which 62nd Army tunneled for its very life, and it presented the Germans with yet another tactical problem that was unique to this battle.[95]

That is not to say there were no scares for the defenders. Indeed, there was at least one a week for the entire two months. On September 14, for example, during the first great assault, German assault troops took the crest of the Mameyev Kurgan and swept toward the Volga, taking the central landing site under fire. At one point they were within 800 yards of 62nd Army headquarters—longer than it sounds in a city fight, but still far too close for comfort. Chuikov managed to restore the situation, but only by committing his last tactical reserve, an understrength tank brigade, and also by summoning the 13th Guards Division under its battle-tested commander, General A. I. Rodimtsev, from across the Volga. Rodimtsev's men crossed the river under murderous fire and went into the fight piecemeal. In its first day in action, the division took 30 percent casualties, throwing back the Germans from the Mameyev Kurgan.[96] Within a week, the number had risen to 80 percent. Chuikov, at least, was certain: "Let me say frankly," he later wrote, "that had it not been for Rodimtsev's division the city would have fallen completely into enemy hands approximately in the middle of September."[97]

Likewise, there was another great German assault on October 14, aimed at the Dzerzhinsky Tractor Works.[98] Although the name may conjure up a single facility or building, it was an immense industrial complex on the scale, let us say, of the Ford River Rouge plant outside of Detroit. The assault, which involved units of the 14th Panzer Division, the 305th, and 389th Infantry Divisions, ground forward a grand total of one mile. Chuikov's entire position hung by a thread, however, because the distance between the front line and the Volga was only two miles. His entire army, headquarters included, was taking a merciless hammering from German air. The Luftwaffe flew 1,250 sorties that day, although it seemed like a lot more, and Chuikov himself claimed the figure was more like 3,000.[99] Over the next few days, the Germans smashed Soviet resistance nests in the tractor factory building by building, then turned south toward their next set of objectives, the Barrikady gun factory, the bread factory, and the Krasnyi Oktyabr metallurgical plant. A lone four-story apartment complex along the river, known for the Red Army captain whose troops were defending it as Pavlov's House, played a crucial role in preventing the Germans from breaking through to the Volga, but the margin was about as thin as it could get.

The Germans had superior firepower, but the Soviet infantry countered it with a great deal of imagination. Chuikov's men had to use every advantage of terrain and concealment, forcing the Wehrmacht into a style of fighting for which it was simply not prepared, either by training or by inclination: close assault. The most important tactical innovation was to hug the Germans—to hold positions in such close proximity to the Germans that they would hesitate to call in air and artillery strikes for fear of bombing their own positions.[100] Under such conditions, losses were enormous on both sides. Moreover, the Germans soon found that many of the forward objectives they had seized in the daytime were untenable at night. With stealthy Soviet combat groups infiltrating through the city's many gulleys and ravines and threatening to cut them off, German infantry had to abandon many a hard-won position, only to retake them the next day.

By mid-November, the 6th Army had "practically conquered" Stalingrad, in the words of General Jodl.[101] It had also taken about four miles of the Volga bank, mainly in the northern industrial districts. It had driven 62nd Army relentlessly back to the fortified riverbank, and in the course of the fighting it had sliced Chuikov's command into three pieces. It had also expended its last ounce of strength. One by one, Paulus had to cross divisions off his list of formations that were still "capable of attack" (*angriffsfähig*): the 79th, 94th, and 305th Infantry Divisions, the 14th and 24th Panzer.[102]

Nevertheless, the Wehrmacht still had one last throw of the dice. In early November, the Volga began to freeze. Ice floes in the river were a real problem to navigation, and thus to the type of small craft that were ferrying supplies and reinforcements to Chuikov's army. It seemed to the Germans a propitious time for another assault, one final operation in the northern factory district aimed at the Lazur Chemical Works and the large railway loop (the Tennis Racket) in which it sat. Operation Hubertus would include eight pioneer battalions, although like every formation in the German Ostheer, many were well under strength.[103] They were not infantrymen in the purest sense, in that they weren't trained in the coordination of fire and movement. Instead, their specialties were the art of demolition and the use of explosives, heavy equipment, and flamethrowers. They would blaze a trail, and behind them would come a veteran but motley assemblage of infantry and infantry-like troops: any able-bodied men, essentially, that Paulus and Seydlitz could scrounge from the broken-down divisions now littering the order of battle.

The attack went in on November 11. Under the overall command of Major Josef Linden, 6th Army's chief of pioneers, the engineers blasted, demolished, and torched one Soviet position after another with relentless efficiency. They were masters of destruction. What they couldn't do, however, was achieve an operational breakthrough. Loaded down with heavy equipment, they weren't configured for rapid maneuver, and even when they did open a narrow path through a fortified zone, there wasn't enough infantry to pass into the breach. On the night of November 15, a broad-front counterattack by 62nd Army placed all the gains of the previous days in jeopardy, and Seydlitz beat it back only by inserting his last infantry battalions. All told, Hubertus traded meager gains for massive casualties—the battle for Stalingrad in microcosm.

The Wehrmacht had indeed broken Stalingrad, but in the process it had broken itself. Chuikov was badly battered, but his army was still in being, entrenched along sixteen miles of the Volga bank. The next day, November 16, the first snow fell in the city. The day after that,

Hitler sent Paulus an official *Führerbefehl* ("Führer order") to be read to all commanders in Stalingrad down to the regimental level:

> I am aware of the difficulties of the fighting in Stalingrad and of the decline in combat strengths. The difficulties for the Russians are even worse, however, due to the ice floes on the Volga. If we make good use of this period of time, we will save a great deal of blood later.
>
> I expect, therefore, that the leadership and the troops will once more, as they often have in the past, devote the same energy and spirit (*Schneid*) that they have shown in the past to fight their way through to the Volga at the gun factory and the metallurgical plant and to take those sections of the city."

Paulus promised that he would try: "I am convinced," he responded, "that this order will give our brave troops new encouragement!"[104]

Just two days after that, on November 19, all hell broke loose on the southern front.

Conclusion: The Dual Campaign of 1942

After all the sound and fury and lightning-quick maneuver, the conquest of mighty peaks and the smashing of entire cities, the final operational result of the 1942 campaigns was a "vast bulge." It stretched clear across the southern portion of the front "from the Black Sea to the snowy peaks of the Caucasus to the rivers that carry the life blood of the Soviet Union, the Volga and Don."[105] The Wehrmacht had driven forward nearly a thousand miles, but outside of Maikop, it had not seized a single one of its original objectives. It had taken 625,000 prisoners (the figure given in a *Fremde Heere Ost* report for July and August, fairly early into the dual offensives), destroyed or captured 7,000 tanks, and captured the princely sum of 416 aircraft, roughly the equipment for another Luftflotte. Nevertheless, the figures were far lower than the nearly 4 million men captured in 1941, and they barely made a dent in the Soviet manpower reserves. Indeed, that same report ended with the ominous point: "The summer and fall campaigns have closed with losses that had not exceeded Russian estimates, and as a result the Russian army will enter the winter campaign weakened, but not fatally so."[106] In inflicting these losses on the enemy, the Germans had suffered a devastating blow of their own: 200,000 casualties in

August alone. It was a new and ghastly high point during more than two years of war in the east. As a result, the Wehrmacht currently held a position that was certainly not defensible with the resources it had at its disposal. Indeed, it was clear that the survival of the German army in the southern Soviet Union increasingly depended not on the strength of the Reich, but on that of the allied and satellite states—the Italians, Hungarians, and Romanians.

Yes: Germany's survival now depended on Romania and Hungary. The traditional analysis of the 1942 campaign lays the entire mess at Hitler's feet. The simultaneous drives toward two widely separated objectives, Stalingrad and the Caucasus, bore all the hallmarks of a military dilettante. Hitler, lacking even the barest understanding of strategy, had marched the Wehrmacht off in multiple directions at the same time, had tried to do everything at once instead of one thing at a time, and had fired his professional staff officers when they tried to talk sense into him. One authoritative source has Hitler committing "the cardinal tactical sin"[107] of splitting up his forces, a violation of war's sacred and inviolable laws, and another states that he "unintentionally came to Stalin's rescue"[108] with Directive 45 at a time when Soviet fortunes looked darkest.

To Halder and the General Staff, Directive 45 was more than a blunder. Its problems were more fundamental because it violated one of the traditional canons of German operational-level war making. It was a term that staff officers used so often that it had become a kind of *Schlagwort*, or buzzword, for all of them: operations had to be "concentric" (*konzentrisch*), with "separated portions of the army" (*getrennter Heeresteile*)[109] maneuvering toward one another at all times. The goal of concentric maneuver was to find the opponent, fix him, then attack him simultaneously in the front, flanks, and rear. It was a difficult and tricky operational doctrine, requiring armies to deploy in a widely dispersed fashion and then to link up on the battlefield itself. As Moltke had once put it, one had to "march separately and strike united,"[110] and the training of German field officers and staff alike had made it an obsession over the centuries. If the timing were even slightly off, if one army dawdled while the other hurried, if the weather failed to cooperate, or if a crucial bridge were washed out unexpectedly, the result could be a misfire or worse. The 1914 campaign in the west, especially the fighting in and around Namur, where the Germans squandered their best chance at a decisive victory, was a classic example of what could go wrong.[111] When it worked, however, as at Sedan in 1870, it could win a war in an afternoon.

The pair of operations initiated by Directive 45, however, violated this canon. They were not concentric. In fact, they were the exact opposite: *exzentrisch* (used in a more technical sense than the English cognate, "eccentric").[112] According to the dictates of Hitlerian strategy, the main bodies of the German army, in this case Army Group A and Army Group B, were marching away from one another. The drive on Stalingrad and the thrust into the Caucasus were not mutually supporting. They bore no relationship to one another at all, except to steal each other's resources and fuel. As the gap between the operations grew wider and wider, the danger was obvious. Indeed, even one unschooled in strategy can see it on a map: long, vulnerable flanks stretching for hundreds of miles on either side. At one point in the upcoming autumn, there was a yawning 200-mile gap between the two army groups, patrolled, in the loosest possible sense of the term, by a single division, the 16th Motorized, from its lonely perch at Elista in the middle of the Kalmuk Steppe. It was this operational disconnect, far more than the matériel or logistical factors, that marked the subsequent operations as unique in German military history.

Although it is tempting to blame Hitler, such a personalist interpretation is ultimately simplistic. These problems were not so much the result of individual decisions as they were of systemic problems. They were the price of conducting a war with limited resources inside the vast reaches of the Soviet Union. The distances involved were so great that there were bound to be problems. The same trend toward *exzentrisch* operations had already happened at least twice in this war. Operation Barbarossa had begun with three army groups packed tightly into their assembly area in Greater Germany and Poland. Within weeks of the start, however, the front had broadened to nearly twice its original size, as Army Group North headed almost due north toward the Baltic littoral and Leningrad and Army Group South passed through the Carpathian-Pripet bottleneck into the broad fields of the Ukraine. The yawning gaps that opened between the army groups had led to serious problems in the course of the fighting. Hitler's diversion of armored forces toward the northern and southern flanks in the middle of August was a response to what the entire staff recognized as a problem. The great *Kessel* at Kiev in September was the result.

Likewise, the initial stages of Operation Typhoon in October 1941 saw a similar series of eccentric operational maneuvers. In a general sense, Army Group Center was aiming at Moscow, but it certainly failed to achieve anything like a decisive concentration of force. In the south, Guderian's 2nd Panzer Army was supposed to be driving on Tula, the crucial railway town almost due south of Moscow. At the same time, however, he had to tie up much of his strength maintaining the massive pocket at Bryansk. He also had to drive southeast and take Kursk as means of protecting the operation's flank. Guderian was a resourceful, perhaps brilliant, Panzer leader, but even he couldn't devise a sound way to maneuver in three directions at once. On the other wing of the army group, a strong battle group of 9th Army and 3rd Panzer Group received orders to shift the axis of their advance almost due north, to make contact with the open southern wing of Army Group North.

The same thing happened in the late summer of 1942. One can read Halder's war diary from those days and actually feel him overheating. He had had his disagreements with Hitler before, but his reaction to Directive 45 on July 23 was something else, condemning the "senseless pile-up of mobile formations around Rostov, obvious even to the eyes of a layman like Hitler": "The ever-present underestimation of the enemy's possibilities is gradually assuming grotesque forms and is becoming dangerous. It is more and more unbearable. No one can say there's any serious work being done around here. The mark of this so-called 'leadership' is a pathological response to the impressions of the moment and a complete lack of judgment regarding the command mechanism and its limitations."[113] A few days later, he was referring to General Jodl and Führer's personal staff in OKW in mocking tones as that "illuminated society" and rejecting Hitler's tactical decisions in the opening phase of the Caucasus campaign as "nonsense, and he knows it."[114]

Indeed, "so-called leadership," "pathological," and "nonsense" are all perfectly valid phrases to describe Hitler's art of war. In the words of the German official history, his operational decisions were not simply "unconventional," which might have carried certain advantages, as in 1940, but also "unprofessional and defective."[115] But for all of Halder's objections to them, both at the time and after the war, it is clear that he had nothing to put in their place. He had shared Hitler's disastrous underestimation of the fighting abilities of the Red Army in both 1941 and 1942—the same judgment he now described as "grotesque" and "dangerous." He really had thought that the Wehrmacht had won Barbarossa in the first fourteen days, and he had agreed enthusiastically with Hitler's assessment that the "Russian is finished" a week into Operation Blue. He had played a key role in conceiving the summer offensive in the first place, he bore a great deal of responsibility for planning it, and he had presided over its first two disastrous weeks. Now he was trying to tinker with a disaster. Certainly his suggestions, essentially that the Wehrmacht concentrate on Stalingrad first and worry about the Caucasus second, made sense in terms of an ideal textbook solution. By this time, however, there was probably no textbook that could have rescued the Wehrmacht.

No matter who was in command or what orders were proceeding from the staff to the front, the Soviet Union was still going to be as large as it was. The resources of the German army in men, supplies, and equipment were still going to be as limited as they were. It was patently impossible for a force the size of the German Ostheer to seize every objective, guard every approach, and protect every threatened flank on the approaches to Moscow, Stalingrad, or the Caucasus oil fields. At some time, whether Hitler or Halder—the amateur or the trained professional—was in control, operations were going to have to verge into the *exzentrisch* simply because of the geography involved. Any operation that started along the Donets and intended to head for the Don bend and beyond was, by definition, going to forfeit the possibility of a concentration of force against a single objective. Hitler's dual campaign was a poor response, but Halder's single thrust to Stalingrad would also have been pregnant with disaster, with gigantic dangling flanks in both north and south to be covered by the Romanians, Italians, and Hungarians. To put it another way, the impending disaster was not simply the result of a series of individual decisions in the summer of 1942. It was more fundamental and systemic. By this point, the war with the Soviet Union had placed burdens on the Wehrmacht that were far heavier than the traditional German way of war could bear.

Operation Blue: German motorized column heading east (Robert Hunt Library).

Operation Blue: SdKfz 251/10 halftrack of the XIV Panzer Corps on the way to Stalingrad (Robert Hunt Library).

Having crossed the Don and reached the Volga, German infantry found tougher fighting on the outskirts of Stalingrad than they had expected (Robert Hunt Library).

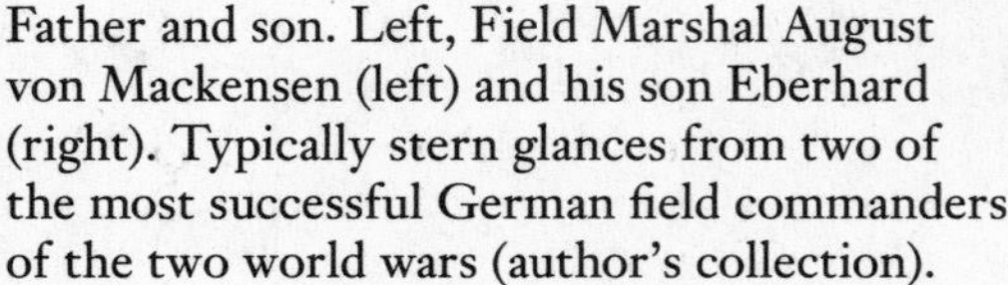

Father and son. Left, Field Marshal August von Mackensen (left) and his son Eberhard (right). Typically stern glances from two of the most successful German field commanders of the two world wars (author's collection).

General Friedrich von Paulus having a word with his gunners outside of Stalingrad. His admittedly pedestrian leadership was not the only reason for the German catastrophe (Robert Hunt Library).

City fight in Stalingrad. A German noncommissioned officer giving a section briefing before battle in the northern industrial district (Robert Hunt Library).

The Wehrmacht conquers yet another factory in Stalingrad, although the battle for the city rages on, October 1942 (author's collection).

Plunging into the Caucasus. Right, lead elements of the 1st Panzer Army over the Don, southeast of Rostov (Robert Hunt Library). Opposite page top, an exultant German tank crew, XXXX Panzer Corps (author's collection).

The war of movement comes to a halt. A German soldier in a prepared position in the *Waldkaukasus*. Note the personal photos on left (Robert Hunt Library).

Even within a war noted for its detailed photographic record, these images of German mountain troops in the *Hochkaukasus* are still striking. Top, lone German sentry patrolling the Ssantsharo Pass on the way to Suchumi (author's collection). Below, machine gunner scanning the horizon (Robert Hunt Library).

The death of the Wehrmacht. Top, German prisoners march into captivity at El Alamein under New Zealander guard. Rommel had a great deal of respect for the Kiwis. "I would much preferred to have had this division in our prison camps," he later wrote, "than once again before our front." Middle, a German graveyard near the El Alamein battlefield (Robert Hunt Library).

Left, memorial stone to the Afrika Korps in the Western Desert (Robert Hunt Library).

Death of the Wehrmacht. Final resting place of German mountain troops en route to the Black Sea port of Tuapse (author's collection).

The Wehrmacht's nemesis in the last years of the war: a U.S. M-4 Sherman tank with an apparently inexhaustible supply of ammunition (Joanna Vecchiarelli Scott Collection).

8

The End

El Alamein and Stalingrad

By the late fall of 1942, the Wehrmacht's great drive forward had ground to a halt. It sat now, motionless and relatively harmless, on three separate and far-flung fronts: El Alamein, Stalingrad, and the Caucasus. It had fought itself out. Its supplies were spent; its last reserves of manpower and equipment were gone; and its opponents were deep in the planning stages of counterstrokes that it would be unable to withstand. No doubt there were German officers, both staff and field, who were looking at the map, shaking their heads and smiling ruefully at the morass into which they had driven. All of them had passed through the same schools and had benefited from same military education. All of them had read the works of the great Prussian military philosopher, Karl von Clausewitz, particularly his epic, *On War*.[1] No doubt certain phrases from those long-ago classroom days were surfacing in their minds, as their applicability to the three failed campaigns on the situation maps in front of them became obvious. Perhaps they were wishing they had paid closer attention.

There was, for example, the concept of "friction,"[2] the process that grinds down even the best-laid operational plans and frustrates even the best-trained armies. For an army on campaign, little things go wrong, which soon add up to big things, making even the simplest thing seem difficult. The 1942 campaigns had seen friction aplenty, from the so-called Reichel incident to the disagreements between Hitler and Bock over Voronezh down to the piece of shrapnel that caught General Herr in the back of the head near Nalchik. There was the "fog of war,"[3] the basic uncertainty of any military enterprise, leading to surprises and sudden turnarounds. The Wehrmacht had predicated its entire summer offensive in the Soviet Union on the notion that the Red Army would stand and fight. It decided not to, preferring flight to the possibility of encirclement, and the German operational scheme never did recover. There was the "superiority of the defense,"[4] which allowed even inferior forces to triumph against stronger and bolder ones. In a mythical, terrain-free universe, Rommel and the Afrika Korps would have made short work of the British 8th Army, but so what? War is not decided on style points. In the tight, close terrain over which the armies were now actually fighting, the British were doing just fine. There was the single most famous trope in the entire book, Clausewitz's claim that war was "the continuation of policy by other means,"[5] and thus had to be waged within a certain political context. This was an area in which it was obvious to many German officers by 1942 that the Reich was failing. American aid and equipment had already steadied the British in Africa, and it was now clear that there was a lot more of it on its way.

Finally, one last phrase from Clausewitz would have popped into the mind of any German officer studying the maps of North Africa, the Volga, and the Caucasus in October 1942. It was a phrase that they knew well, even if they hadn't read Clausewitz recently. It had appeared repeatedly in the army's professional literature during the interwar period, especially in studies on the 1914 campaign, the one that ended in disaster on the Marne.[5] For that reason, it had an ominous ring to most members of the officer corps. It was the "culmination point."

The Culmination Point—and Beyond?

Discussion of the culmination point (*Kulminationspunkt*) appears late in *On War*, in the seventh of eight books, "The Attack."[6] Like so much of Clausewitz, it is a concept that seems perfectly obvious, one that can be explained in a single phrase, which the author then subjects to the most rigorous analysis possible. In this case, we might state it simply: All offensives wear down eventually, and the further they advance, the more rapidly it happens. Every offensive operation, Clausewitz explained, carried within itself the probability of its own destruction. No run of victories could go on forever, and it was not always possible "for the victor to overthrow his enemy completely."[7] In the course of a campaign, the strength of the armies on both sides was constantly changing as a result of battles won or lost, casualties relative to those of the opponent, the addition or subtraction of key allies, fluctuations in morale, and many other factors. At some point, the initial superiority of the victorious side, the "greater aggregate of physical and psychological strength," would wear down. At this point, the advantages that had fueled the initially successful advance would fall away, and the once promising campaign would grind to a halt. Obviously, it would be a good thing for a commander to be able to recognize a culmination point when he saw one. It would be a good time to halt the advance and consolidate the position, or perhaps even pull back to more defensible terrain. Otherwise, an army ran the risk of running itself into the ground in pursuit of objectives that it could no longer reach.

Unfortunately, like everything in Clausewitz, recognizing the culmination point was not as easy as it seemed. Many variables are in play. Certain factors tended to lead to an increase in the attacker's strength, and certain others diminished it. Clausewitz listed seven of the former and five of the latter. Among those accruing to the attacker's benefit, for example, were the following: the victor typically suffered far fewer losses than the defeated and routed defender; the defender had to abandon valuable "fixed assets" such as magazines, depots, and bridges; he also lost ground and resources to the advancing enemy; the attacker not only seized enemy terrain, but valuable resources that he could use to a supply basis for further operations. Clausewitz warned that it took time for lost or looted resources to transform the situation on either side: "In connection with these last two points, it should be noted that they seldom have an immediate effect on troops in action. Their work is slow and indirect. Therefore one should not on their account make too great an effort and so place oneself in too dangerous a situation."[8] The defender might also lose allies as his situation became desperate and they were trying to cut their losses. Finally, the continuing defeats might discourage and disarm the defender. He might begin to lose his cohesion as an invading force advanced deeper into the country, but here too, the advantage only began to tell "after an army had advanced some distance, and when the configuration of the enemy's country provided an opportunity to isolate certain areas from the rest. Like tightly constricted branches, these will then tend to wither away."[9]

All of this is eerily descriptive of the German offensives of 1942. The Germans inflicted punishing losses on the British and Soviet armies in the spring and summer of 1942, far higher than they themselves suffered. They seized numerous "fixed assets" in both North Africa and the Soviet Union, from Tobruk to the Donbas to the oil city of Maikop. They also laid hands on numerous resources and did indeed supply themselves to a considerable extent from the wealth of their foes: British gasoline, Canadian Ford trucks, Russian 76.2mm antitank guns. Even Clausewitz's admonition that stolen resources don't often have an "immediate effect" at the front seems completely apposite with regards to the seizure of Caucasus oil. So, too, does his warning "not to place oneself in too dangerous of a situation" on their account, and his observation that "in general, deliveries from enemy resources are neither so prompt nor so reliable as those from one's own."

His analysis of the causes for an attacker's loss of strength in particular seems prophetic. The invader, says Clausewitz, will find a number of pressing assignments. He might have to besiege or assault enemy fortresses, for example, which would drain away forces from his main field armies. He would be marching deeper into enemy territory, where the "nature of the operational theater" changes: "It becomes hostile. It must be garrisoned, for the invader can control it only to the extent that he has done so; but this creates difficulties for the entire machine, which will inevitably weaken its effectiveness."[10] Every step the invader took into the enemy country was another step away from his supply bases, while the defender was falling back on his own. Not only were the distances longer, but the lines of communications, and therefore the strategic flanks, became extended and vulnerable. The longer the advance, the worse the problem: "All this contributes to place a new burden on an advancing army with every step it takes; so unless it started with exceptional superiority, it will find its freedom of action dwindling and its offensive power progressively reduced." The result, he argued, was an increasing feeling of insecurity, as the army becomes "nervous about its situation."[11]

Even if things went so well for the attacker that the enemy seemed on the verge of total overthrow, there was still the possibility that "the danger threatening the defender will bring allies to his aid." Moreover, the defender might react to the danger by making the "greater effort," while "the efforts of the victor slacken off": "Sometimes, stunned and panic-stricken, the enemy may lay down his arms, at other times he may be seized by a fit of enthusiasm: there is a general rush to arms, and resistance is much stronger after the first defeat than it was before." Determining which was which was not easy, he argued. It required careful study of the "character of the people and the government," as well as "the nature of the country and its political affiliations."[12]

Clausewitz was at his best in the discussion of the most delicate question of all: when to continue and when to halt an offensive campaign. There was much to judge, many things for a commander to weigh:

> He must *guess*, so to speak: guess whether the first shock of battle will steel the enemy's resolve and stiffen his resistance, or whether,

> like a Bologna flask, it will shatter as soon as its surface is scratched; guess the extent of debilitation and paralysis that the drying up of particular sources of supply and the severing of certain lines of communication will cause in the enemy; guess whether the burning pain of the injury he has been dealt will make the enemy collapse with exhaustion or, like a wounded bull, arouse his rage; guess whether the other powers will be frightened or indignant, and whether and which political alliances will be dissolved or formed.[13]

Indeed, it is for that very reason that most generals "prefer to stop well short of their objective rather than risk approaching it too closely, and why those with high courage and an enterprising spirit will often overshoot it and so fail to attain their purpose."

It was the great paradox, and one might say a particularly appropriate one for 1942: an advancing army could march from victory to victory, smashing every enemy concentration in his way, but it had to recognize that every step forward dulled its fighting edge, robbing it of precisely those qualities that had made it formidable in the first place. When to stop? Clausewitz admitted that no one saw a warning sign that was clearly labeled "culmination point," but he also suggested an intriguing possibility: "It is even possible that the attacker, reinforced by the psychological forces peculiar to attack, will in spite of his exhaustion find it less difficult to go on than to stop—like a horse pulling a load uphill."[14]

One of the men driving that horse in 1942 was General Carl Wagener, chief of the General Staff for the XXXX Panzer Corps. In October 1942, his corps had crossed the Don and Nikolajewka at the end of July and then hurtled southward at top speed, crossing one river after another: the Manych, Kuban, Kuma, and finally the Terek, forming a bridgehead over the last at Ischerskaya. Nothing could stand before it, and it seemed as if victory were at hand. As we have seen, the front soon solidified, with supplies drying up, air support vanishing as the Luftwaffe flew north to Stalingrad, and the Soviets moving up huge reinforcements. The first bound made four hundred miles in a month; the next four months saw the contending forces hardly move an inch in XXXX Panzer Corps's sector. Wagener could read the signs:

> An ever sparser flow of supply, and then only filling the barest minimum requirements; increased jumbling of formations; their dispersion over a wide area; the immobilization of entire units; ever growing enemy resistance, including the assumption of air superiority;

> diminished fighting strength, equipment breakdowns, a loss of combat spirit among the troops, who are hit hard by the transition from the previous rapid successes to a slow and methodical way of fighting. In connection with all these, the command becomes nervous and makes mistakes, it worries about its rear and flanks, it makes empty appeals to the valor of the troops, without placing the necessary combat resources at their disposal.

Indeed, Wagener wrote, "if the leadership can only count on the valor of the troops, then it has done something wrong."[15] That was precisely the situation by the fall of 1942. Something had gone wrong. Like a horse pulling a load uphill, the Wehrmacht was still moving long beyond the point when it should have stopped.

Even Clausewitz, however, would have been amazed at the situation in the fall of 1942. How could one possibly reckon with a mechanized campaign of mass armies, with millions of men and thousands of tanks and aircraft in an intricate waltz in time and space over hundreds of thousands of square miles, which grinds to a halt within a single mile of Ordzhonikidze, or 400 yards from the Volga, or a mere fifteen miles of open desert from Alexandria? In all three campaigns, the Wehrmacht stuttered and even stopped a half-dozen times, mainly because of fuel shortages. It rolled through any number of potential culmination points, but it somehow found the reserves to keep driving forward. Even at the end, during Operation Hubertus in Stalingrad, after having virtually run out of foot soldiers and using combat engineers in their place, it was still grinding it out.

It is the task of the military theorist to draw up universal principles whenever possible, and Clausewitz's attempt to compose a "metaphysic of war" was arguably the grandest and most profound of them all. The actual course of the 1942 campaigns, however, should warn us against making a fetish of *On War*, or turning a concept as complex as the culmination point into a simplistic buzzword. If the Wehrmacht had proven anything in 1942, it was that even an army that was past its culmination point could still be extremely dangerous.

The British Way of War: Planning for El Alamein

In late October, the British 8th Army launched a grand offensive of its own at El Alamein. Montgomery's historical reputation has tended to emphasize his cautious and systematic nature. The pantheon of great

World War II commanders tends to be dominated by fire breathers, and he is surely the only one who once described his art of war as containing an "infinite capacity for taking pains and preparing for every foreseeable contingency." Indeed, he said, it was "the foundation of all success in war," and those without it were destined to fail.[16] It is easy to mock this fussy attention to detail, but in his defense, caution was a prerequisite for a British commander by this point in the war. Another disaster, another half-baked operational plan, could well have been disastrous.

Even though he enjoyed an overwhelming superiority in men, tanks, planes, trucks, and artillery, Montgomery planned Operation Lightfoot as a slow, methodical battle of attrition. He has taken a great deal of fire for it over the years from popular writers and military historians who prefer the thrills of daring maneuver, but the fact remains that the terrain—the sea to the north, the Qattara Depression to the south, and wall-to-wall Axis divisions in between—hardly permitted any other approach, at least in the battle's opening stages. The many analysts who criticize Montgomery for his formulation and handling of the El Alamein battle have never come up with any better suggestions. Sitting opposite him was the master of maneuver himself, Erwin Rommel, who knew the problem of breaking through here as well as anyone. Here is the Desert Fox himself on the nature of the fighting in this particular bottleneck:

> In all the other positions in the western desert, it was possible to drive around the southern flank with motorized units into the enemy's rear, in order to seek a decision through a mobile battle. The existence of the open flank in our theater of war had again and again created completely novel situations. On the Alamein front it was different. The opponent first had to strive for the breakthrough, which gave the defender the possibility of holding the position long enough for the mobile reserves to come up and enter the battle. The defender had a certain tactical advantage, because he could dig himself in and protect himself with mines, while the attacker was vulnerable to the fire of the dug-in defender. In other positions, as in Sollum in 1941–42 and Gazala in 1942, the battle took place in a purely mobile form that offered an advantage to neither attacker nor defender. The tanks and vehicles of both sides had stood equally open in the desert.[17]

Indeed, Rommel had tried maneuver twice in this sector and had failed, and if the Panzerarmee had been unable to solve the Qattara conundrum through maneuver, 8th Army was almost guaranteed to fail. It is interesting to note that Montgomery described the problem in almost exactly the same way. His objectives for Lightfoot were "*First*—to punch a hole in the enemy positions. *Second*—to pass X Corps, strong in armour and mobile troops, through this hole into enemy territory. *Third*—then to develop operations so as to destroy Rommel's forces." It promised, he knew, to be "an immense undertaking."[18]

As a result, like so many great British operations of both world wars (the great tank breakthroughs at Cambrai and Amiens come to mind), Lightfoot barely requires a map to explain. The British had gone from deploying two corps, as at Gazala, to three: XXX Corps (General Oliver Leese) in the north, with five infantry divisions deployed from the sea to just south of Ruweisat Ridge; XIII Corps (General Brian Horrocks), with two divisions in the south from Ruweisat to the Qattara Depression; and X Corps (General Herbert Lumsden), containing two armored divisions in reserve directly behind XXX Corps. The main blow would fall in the north, where the four assault divisions of XXX Corps (9th Australian, 51st Highland, 2nd New Zealand, and 1st South African) would carry the weight. They would attack on an extremely narrow front, with massive support by air, artillery, and infantry tanks, and chew their way through Rommel's front line, some five miles of minefields, wire, and strongpoints. This was the "break-in" phase, as Montgomery called it, and its goal was "to punch two corridors through the enemy defenses and minefields."[19]

After the break-in would come the second phase: the "breakthrough," although the term needs careful parsing in this context. The tank divisions of X Corps (1st and 10th Armoured) would pass through the two recently opened corridors into the German rear. Montgomery was not seeking a decisive armored battle here. Indeed, the main point of the armored thrust was to prevent Rommel from unleashing the Afrika Korps against the British infantry formations while the latter took their time destroying one Italian infantry division after another. Phase 2 was going to take a long time. Montgomery predicted it would be a "dogfight" lasting at least a week, within an overall battle of ten to twelve days. He also emphasized that he intended to destroy the Panzerarmee not in a great encirclement, but slowly and methodically. "Crumbling" it was the term he used. The plan "was to hold off, or contain, the enemy armour while we carried out a methodical destruction of the infantry divisions holding the defensive system. These unarmored divisions would be destroyed by means of a 'crumbling' process, the enemy being attacked from the flank and rear and cut off from their supplies."[20] Indeed, he was on to something here. Montgomery wanted to force Rommel into a *Stellungskrieg*. The German commander couldn't simply stand by while the British smashed the Italians. He would have no choice but to launch an attack to come to their aid, and in the process would have to run a gauntlet of British armor, air, artillery, and antitank fire, the same combination that had crushed him at Alam Halfa.

While these events were transpiring in the north, the XIII Corps (50th Division, 44th Division, 1st Free French Brigade, 7th Armoured Division) was to launch an attack of its own further to the south. There seems to have been some conceptual confusion here, much of it of Montgomery's making. The assault's operational target was the Taqa Plateau, behind the right rear of the Axis position. At the same time, however, XIII Corps had orders not to suffer heavy casualties, with 7th Armoured Division told to keep itself "in being," to be available for mobile operations at some later point in Lightfoot. Adding weight to the diversionary nature of the mission here was a thorough disinformation effort, Operation Bertram. On October 18, the entire X Corps moved, quite openly, into position south of the Ruweisat Ridge, a maneuver picked up immediately by German intelligence. Over the next four nights, however, X Corps moved north again in secret, leaving behind canvas replicas of virtually every vehicle in the corps, 400 tanks and 2,000 trucks, along with a comprehensive system of fake supply dumps, and even a dummy pipeline twenty miles long. Finally, there was a constant stream of radio reports to and from bogus headquarters, with the 7th Armoured Division, in particular, leaving behind an easily detected trail of nonstop chatter.[21]

The plan, then, emphasized "methodical progress" in order to destroy the foe "part by part, slowly and surely."[22] It is fair to say, however, what was to come next, after the "break-in," the "breakthrough," and the "crumbling," received hardly any thought at all. Montgomery had told more than one officer that he intended to unleash the armored divisions of X Corps as a pursuit corps (a *corps de chasse*) to exploit far into the German rear.[23] Exactly what they would do when they got there, where they would be headed, and how they would be refueled went largely unexplained. In Montgomery's defense, there was no reason to spend a lot of time planning details of the exploitation if the first three phases failed.

In the end, Operation Lightfoot arose out of a matrix that was deeper and more complex than the unique terrain of the El Alamein position or Montgomery's own caution. Great Britain had faced Germany alone for the first two years of the war, and by 1942 it was feeling the pinch: lack of energy, lack of resources, and above all, lack of men. It would fight the last three years of the war knowing that if it lost another army, it probably wouldn't be able to replace it. Doctrine had to reflect these facts. The British had once worked out a successful tactical approach against the German army back in World War I. Now, it seemed, they were returning to it unconsciously. They had learned that they could not outmaneuver the Wehrmacht; even attempting to do so was a recipe for disaster. El Alamein would be a set-piece battle, a careful attack undertaken only with both sides in relatively static positions, with a careful schedule and strict phase lines, an approach designed to make sure that things unfolded slowly and methodically. The 8th Army would undertake carefully prepared attacks in which the infantry received massive support from tanks, air, and artillery. Once the infantry divisions had taken a bite into the German line, they would hold it, securing it against the inevitable German counterattack and then repeating the entire process.[24] The approach lacked flair, perhaps, but it made perfect sense for the most population and resource poor of the wartime powers. At El Alamein, therefore, 8th Army was not simply launching an offensive; it was returning to a distinctively British way of war.

The Panzerarmee at El Alamein

Facing this massive, if unimaginative, onslaught, was Panzerarmee Afrika, now drawn up in a linear and well-constructed defensive position behind an ocean of mines. Rommel was temporarily out of the picture. After eighteen months in Africa, his health—perhaps above all his emotional health—was shot. He had departed for Europe on September 23 in order to take the cure (but also, characteristically, to give a press conference stating that the Germans would soon be in Alexandria).[25] He would not return until he had received some distressing news: the opening of the British offensive on October 23.

In fact, for all his undeniable brilliance, his presence probably wouldn't have made a difference one way or another. There was little he could have done. The Panzerarmee was in a waiting game at the moment, and waiting had never been one of Rommel's specialties. His substitute commander, General Georg Stumme, was no ball of fire, but he was a solid professional who seems to have followed Rommel's instructions regarding defensive preparations. He was also a man under a cloud. He had been in command of the XXXX Panzer Corps (6th Army) in June 1942, at the time of the Reichel incident. He had been dismissed and condemned by a court-martial and was now in North Africa on a kind of probation. He needed to prove himself to Hitler in order to restore his "lost honor."[26]

It wasn't going to be easy, and the overall situation may well have been hopeless. Current levels of supply were barely covering the minimum requirements, an identical complaint on all three of the Wehrmacht's static fronts in the fall of 1942. Moreover, no matter how much supply arrived, it was unlikely to include spare parts for the British and American trucks that were now such a major portion of the Panzerarmee's transport. The manpower situation was little better. Before Alam Halfa, Rommel had estimated the four German divisions in the theater (15th and 21st Panzer Divisions, 90th Light Division, and 164th Division) to be about 33 percent below their established strength; the four of them could muster only 34,000 men between them. Moreover, the most recent arrivals, the German 164th Division and Ramcke Parachute Brigade, were leg infantry. They had arrived with no vehicles at all, resulting in serious strain on the transport columns of its sister formations.

The travails of coalition warfare were at work here too. When Rommel was winning, differences among the allies receded. Now that he was stuck, they reappeared. In terms of the muster rolls, the army's Italian divisions constituted just one-third of the manpower of the Panzerarmee (82,000 Germans to 42,000 Italians). With control of Mediterranean shipping in the hands of the Italian *Commando Supremo*, however, the Italians were receiving three times the amount of supply the Germans were. The Pistoia Division, for example, had arrived in North Africa at the beginning of August. It was intended for safe rear-area security duty in Libya, not for the front, but its complement of vehicles, some 400 of them, tied up a major portion of the available shipping for weeks. Units like the German 164th Division, meanwhile, which were already in the line, barely received a thing—just sixty vehicles for the entire month of August.[27]

A victory at Alam Halfa would have solved these supply problems, of course, but they had only gotten worse since the defeat. Rommel himself estimated during the first eight months of 1942 that the Panzerarmee had received only 120,000 tons of supply, just 40 percent of its "absolute minimum needs."[28] His own demands to Rome and Berlin for 30,000 tons of supplies in September and another in October, what he called an "indispensable condition for a successful defense against the forthcoming British attack,"[29] were a pipe dream by this point in the war. He had presented them to Hitler at an inauspicious time: at the very moment that things seemed to be slowing down in Stalingrad.

By now, fatigue, lack of supply, and bad rations were also beginning to make serious inroads into the Panzerarmee's health. It wasn't just Rommel. There was a chronic shortage of potable water, putting thousands of men onto the sick rolls. Most needed rest and recuperation in Europe at a time when they simply could not be spared. The officers were suffering apace: Westphal was yellow with jaundice, like many others; Mellenthin was wasting away with amebic dysentery.[30] Rommel seemed to be suffering from a little bit of both, and he also had a serious blood-pressure problem (no doubt induced by stress), as well as chronic and bothersome sinusitis.[31]

Serious supply problems, a shaky alliance, a line of communications 1,200 miles long, organ failure—this was the face of the Panzerarmee before El Alamein. This couldn't be a mobile battle. Neither the men nor the machines were in shape for it, and the British had no desire to fight one. They preferred a systematic, methodical, and grinding approach, as Rommel recognized: "It was utterly clear to us that the British military machine was well-suited to the task, for its entire program of training rested on the battles of materiel (*Materialschlachten*) of the First World War. Technical developments had certainly had an effect on this form of warfare, but they had brought about no revolution." The well-known British deficiencies in mobile warfare would be beside the point in this "upcoming battle of position and breakthrough," because the tanks would be acting as infantry support anyway. Such a battle would bring to the fore "the outstanding qualities of the Australian and New Zealand infantry, and the British would be able to get the most out of their artillery."[32]

There was only one way that Rommel could see to counter what was about to happen. The infantry formations in the main line of defense (the *Hauptkampflinie*, or HKL) had to hold the position in strength and defend it as long as they could, even against the strongest British attacks. Their goal was not just to die in place, but to provide the mobile reserves time to enter the battle and seal off the penetration. Although that might be an hour or two under normal conditions, these mobile counterattacks would be taking place under an umbrella of enemy aircraft, and they consequently were going to take a lot longer to get under way. To buy the front line more time, the Panzerarmee constructed the deepest defense it could. The front line was held by light outposts only, while the HKL was located one to two kilometers behind, and would itself be two to three kilometers in depth. Directly behind it were the Panzer divisions, which were positioned so as to be able to lend their direct fire to the defense. Once the enemy attack had developed a clearly defined *Schwerpunkt*, the mobile divisions in north and south would close up as quickly as they could in order to beat it back.

Holding the entire position together was an enormous sea of mines. It was a perfect solution: a poor man's weapon for a starving army. Nearly 500,000 mines were placed in front of, around, and in some cases even behind the main German positions. They were grouped into enormous *Minenkästen* ("mine boxes") designated on the map by letters (A through L, south to north).[33] Despite their name, they were not the equivalent of the British "fortified boxes" in the Gazala position, which had possessed garrisons and an all-around defense capability. They were simply passive delay mechanisms designed to slow down the attackers and allow the mobile formations time to get into place. No defensive position is impregnable, and this one certainly wasn't, but the mines made sure that the Axis *Stellung* wasn't going to be rushed in a single bound, no matter how strong the attacker might be. It was about as effective a posture as the Panzerarmee could have taken at the time.

There is little to say about the actual Axis deployment. In a battle of position, one has to deploy in a line, and that was the case here. The front line was in the hands of the infantry: XXI Corps (Italian Bologna and Trento Divisions, German 164th Infantry Division, half of the Ramcke Parachute Brigade) in the northern sector and X Corps (Brescia Division, Trieste Motorized Division, Folgore Parachute Division, the other half of the Ramcke Brigade) in the south. In all these forward infantry positions, the habit of "corseting" Italian units with German ones had reached its peak. Now, wherever possible, each and every Italian battalion had a German one on both of its flanks, even though they all still reported back to their regular parent formations. Although it definitely solidified the defense, it was a command-and-control nightmare, and with each army still dependent on its own supply train, it was a logistical problem as well.[34]

Behind the front line lay the mobile formations of Afrika Korps and XX (Motorized) Corps: 15th Panzer and Littorio Armored Divisions in the north; 21st Panzer and Ariete Armored Divisions in the south. Their task was to respond to an enemy breakthrough as aggressively as possible, in General Stumme's words, "to hold him frontally and use the armored formations to launch pincers counter attacks against him, surround him and destroy him. It may become necessary . . . for battle groups of Afrika Korps and XX (Motorized) Corps to move east through our minefields to launch a concentric attack, in order to make the pincer movement as effective as possible."[35] The 90th Light Division lay along the coast in the north, guarding against British landings, a key concern since a series of abortive commando landings at Tobruk, Benghazi, and Barce on September 13–14. The artillery was not deployed en masse, which would have presented a huge target to enemy aircraft, but was split up behind the front as equally as possible. There was no defensive *Schwerpunkt*, no attempt to guess on which sector of the front the British might be attacking. The Panzerarmee would simply have to wait and see, and then react accordingly. Allied strength in the air wouldn't allow it to do much more than that.

If Rommel and the entire Axis command in Africa were looking nervously at the sky, it is hard to blame them. Indeed, their weakness in this area was already on full display even before Montgomery launched his offensive. Taking advantage of good flying weather on October 19, the Anglo-American air force began another round-the-clock bombing campaign. Axis landing grounds at Fuka and El Daba were the principal targets, as were forward bases. Although they did not necessarily destroy many enemy planes, they kept Axis ground crews up all night long and seriously affected serviceability rates of Axis aircraft. The results: on day 1 of the offensive, not a single Axis aircraft appeared over the positions of the 8th Army. Air superiority had become air supremacy.

The Battle: Lightfoot and Supercharge

Any participant in this "third battle of El Alamein," especially a German or Italian soldier, could be forgiven for forgetting everything about it except the explosions.[36] That was the principal impression it left on anyone who was there. It began on the moonlit night of October 23, 10:40 P.M. German time, with a massive artillery barrage. The traditional description in the literature on this battle describes a "1,000 gun barrage."[37] The actual number was 892,[38] but it may well have seemed like 10,000 to those under it. The British had scheduled the firing of each gun precisely, not so that they would all *fire* the same time, but that all the shells would *land* on the defenders' positions at exactly the same instant, the reference point being a series of BBC time signals. Montgomery, who by his own accounts was either sleeping during the entire thing or at the front watching his handiwork in action—apparently he could not decide which was more heroic—described it as "a wonderful sight, similar to a Great War 1914–18 attack. . . . Suddenly the whole front burst into fire, it was beautifully timed and the effect was terrific."[39] General Lungerhausen, commander of the German 164th Division, was more poetic: it was, he said, "as though a giant had banged his fist down on a table."[40]

The first fifteen minutes of fire was counterbattery, and it dealt the Axis guns a blow from which they never recovered. Each group of four German guns received a monstrous deluge of a hundred shells apiece (4.5 or 5.5 inch). The bombardment destroyed its share of German guns, but an even more important effect was to disrupt signals communications between the army command and the gunners, as well as to administer a severe dose of shock to anyone on the receiving end. "We had never yet experienced a drum-fire (*Trommelfeuer*) of this sort in Africa," Rommel wrote, "and it would stay like this throughout the entire action at El Alamein."[41] Within a few minutes, the intensity rose to fever pitch as British air power joined the fray. For the next six hours, flights of Wellingtons took to the sky, dropping another 125 tons of bombs on known Axis gun positions.

The German reaction to this rain of explosives was curiously passive. Although part of it was the confusion and shock of the moment, which temporarily ripped apart the Panzerarmee's command and control, part of it was deliberate. General Stumme, conscious of the serious shortages in gun ammunition of all calibers, deliberately withheld his fire at this moment. The guns did not even open up on preregistered British assembly areas, as they might have. Rommel himself, who was still in Europe as this was going on, would label Stumme's decision a mistake, a judgment in which the German official history concurs.[42] They may well be correct. As much as this battle seems to us like a forgone conclusion, 8th Army had never yet won a clear-cut offensive victory over the Panzerarmee, and a few well-chosen rounds might well have made a major dent in the morale of the attackers. In Stumme's defense, however, he had no idea exactly what was happening. Reports both from the front and from the gun positions were sparse at first; those under the barrage had bigger problems than reporting back to headquarters. Moreover, eating through a major chunk of the army's limited supply of artillery ammunition in the first half-hour or so wouldn't have helped over the long term, and it is hard to criticize Stumme for refusing. The villain here is not the decision to shoot or not to shoot, but the ammunition shortage that made such a decision necessary in the first place.

After the first quarter hour, the guns had switched to targets in the front line, and they stayed there for the rest of the night. It was the signal for the first wave of the infantry assault. The frontages were unbelievably narrow: four full divisions crammed into a sector of front less than six miles wide. Two hours later, the British added a brace of armored divisions to the assault, as Montgomery inserted X Corps. There was no subtlety here, no real rush, just one army giving an impression, even if only a momentary one, of overwhelming strength while its opponent sat paralyzed. The uninterrupted shelling had shredded the Panzerarmee's telephone lines and radio sets, and specially equipped bombers loaded with electronic equipment were jamming those radio transmissions that did get on the net. Pounded from above and bulldozed from the front, waiting helplessly for orders on a dead phone line or smashed radio equipment, the units in the main line of defense had no real chance. The carnage was terrific, and Rommel's description, "Our outposts fought to the last round and then either surrendered or died,"[43] is as eloquent as it is laconic. Some units, the Italian 62nd Infantry Regiment (Trento Division), for example, were already streaming to the rear. They had put up with a great deal over the past six months since Gazala—the battles against odds, Rommel's impossible demands, the rotten food—but they hadn't signed up for this. Others, like the II Battalion of the German 382nd Grenadier Regiment (164th Infantry Division), fought to the end, meaning in this context they vanished in a concentric barrage from hundreds of British guns.

By the next morning, large sections of the HKL in the north were in British hands. Unmolested by German artillery and barely noticing the German outposts they overran, the Australian 9th and the 51st Highland Divisions smashed their way into and through boxes J and L. In the process, they scattered or overran the remnants of the battalions broken by the bombardment. There had already been a local counterattack in the north by 15th Panzer and Littorio Divisions. Passing through a blizzard of British artillery fire and bombs, it cut its way through to another one of the battalions of the 382nd Grenadiers that had been encircled in the night's fighting, and temporarily restored the situation in the sector. The cost had been immense, however. By October 25, only 31 of its 119 tanks were still in service. Given that there were only 234 German tanks in the force at the start of the battle, those 88 destroyed tanks represented disastrous losses of some 40 percent of the Afrika Korps's total.

Command and control continued to be the real problem for the Germans. Even on the morning of October 24, the overall situation remained unclear. The Germans knew that an attack had occurred, and that it had received an extraordinary level of artillery support. But specific reports from the HKL were still sparse. Stumme, therefore, decided to pull a "Rommel" and go up to the front for a closer look. Thoughts of personal and professional rehabilitation may well have been on his mind here. The army's headquarters were on the coastal road, just a few miles behind those of 90th Light Division, but his temporary chief of staff, General Westphal, advised him to travel with an armored escort vehicle and a signals truck, as per Rommel's custom. Stumme didn't think it was necessary. Traveling light, accompanied only by his intelligence officer, Colonel Büchting, and driver, Corporal Wolf, he set out for what should have been an hour-long round trip. Somewhere during that short drive the car came under fire, either an attack by British fighter-bombers or an ambush by infantry of the 9th Australian Division. A shot to the head killed Büchting instantly. Wolf turned the car around in a wild 180-degree turn that apparently threw Stumme from the car without the driver being aware of what had happened.[44] When the general's body was later recovered, it was found that he had died of a heart attack, suffered either during the attack or as a result of the accident.

The situation was still unclear enough, with Stumme still listed as missing and the Panzerarmee under the temporary command of General Wilhelm Ritter von Thoma, commander of the Afrika Korps, that Rommel did not receive orders to return to Africa until late in the day on October 24. He did not reach his headquarters until dusk on October 25, almost forty-eight hours into the fighting. The sources do indicate that his reappearance gave a morale boost to the entire army. One British prisoner remembers his German captors telling him that the battle was as good as won: Rommel was back.[45] In general, however, it was too late to reverse the process already under way. Montgomery was well into the "crumbling" stage of his operation, German armor had failed to land any kind of decisive blow in the north, and the entire army was already well into the process of dissolution. Although it was now obvious to Rommel and the entire staff that the *Schwerpunkt* of the British assault was in the north, there was not much they could do about it. The original plan—concentrating the armor for a massed counterblow—was impossible due to lack of fuel.

Near midnight on October 25, Rommel made his one significant operational decision of the entire battle. He summoned 21st Panzer Division from its positions behind the southern portion of the line to the north.[46] He knew, and undoubtedly the crews of those tanks

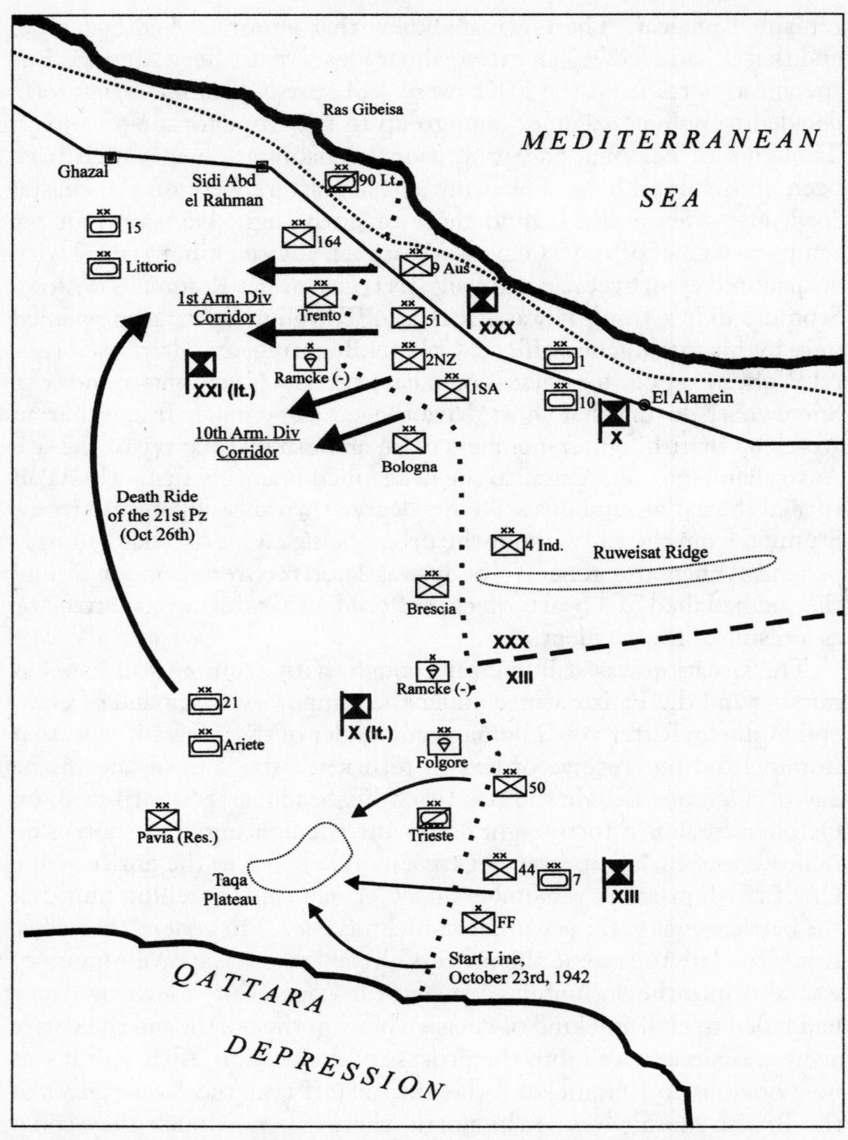

Map 14. Death of the Wehrmacht I: the Allied attack at El Alamein, October 1942.

did as well, that this was a one-way journey. They barely had enough fuel to get there, let alone do much maneuvering or fighting once they'd arrived. As for a retreat, should it become necessary: that would clearly be impossible. Well-schooled German officers like Rommel or Thoma knew what they were asking: a death ride (*Totenritt*) for the 21st Panzer.[47]

By now, the fighting was concentrated around a number of tiny terrain features in the northern sector: Hill 28 ("Kidney Ridge" to the British), and the positions around it, labeled on British maps as "Snipe" and "Woodcock."[48] Although accounts of El Alamein tend to focus on the murderous details of the close-in fighting, the picture on the operational level receives much less attention. Here, the issue was never in doubt. It really was, in Rommel's famous phrase, a "battle without hope."[49] Four infantry divisions and two armored divisions, well armed with brand-new M4 Sherman tanks, were chewing their way through a carefully selected portion of the Panzerarmee's defense line. Resistance was futile in the face of well-coordinated, nonstop shelling and round-the-clock bombing. There were high levels of material destruction as the two sides traded casualties, but the British assault formations were moving inexorably, if slowly, westward. This was the way the Germans viewed the fighting. Even the British operational pause, a cessation of the assault on October 28–29 did nothing to reverse the process. The shelling and the bombing never stopped, and it was clear that Montgomery was simply reorganizing his assault units for the final blow. Rommel, for his part, was already ordering a reconnaissance of the Fuka position about fifty miles in the rear, for what was beginning to look like an inevitable retreat.

This view of inevitability and hopelessness runs contrary to British histories of the battle. They tend to focus on the problems that 8th Army experienced. The "break-in" by XXX Corps was far slower than it might have been, mainly because of the unexpected thickness and density of the German mine boxes. As a result, the insertion of the armored divisions of X Corps led not to a breakthrough that first night but to nearly unimaginable levels of chaos, with men and tanks milling around in confusion. If the Germans did have any air power that first night, or a concentrated and well-stocked artillery, they would have had a target-rich environment indeed: six divisions packed into a small box, perhaps five miles by five miles. With London pressing him for a breakthrough, Montgomery's well-known sangfroid began to crumble just a bit. He had to light a fire under his armor commander, General Lumsden, in order to get him moving on that first night, and his diary entry for October 29 finds him reaching the perhaps startlingly obvious conclusion that "It is becoming essential to break through somewhere."[50] This sense of urgency is what lay behind his decision to reconcentrate his armor, with 7th Armoured now thrown into the mix, for an all-out assault in the north, Operation Supercharge.

It began at 1:00 A.M. on the night of November 1–2 in what was by now the accustomed pattern: seven hours of air attack and three hours of relentless pounding by the artillery. And now on they came, the combined forces of three complete armored divisions on both sides of Hill 28, just northwest of mine box J, with the infantry of the New Zealand Division accompanying. Two massive columns advanced behind a steel curtain of high explosives, protected on the flanks by thick clouds of artificial smoke. The original plan called for them to attack to the northwest and break through to the coastal road, but when intelligence reports indicated that the mass of the 90th Light Division was deployed in the area, Montgomery shifted the axis of advance to the southwest. The German official history has British armor overrunning battalions of the 155th Regiment (90th Light Division), elements of the Italian Bersaglieri Regiment, the 65th Italian Infantry Regiment (Trieste Division), and a battalion of the German 155th Grenadier Regiment (15th Panzer Division), all in quick succession.[51]

The next two days were filled with dramatic moments, a fitting emotional climax to eighteen months of combat in this theater. On November 2, Rommel summoned the Italian XX (Motorized) Corps and the armored division Ariete to the northern sector. The defense of the south was now in the shaky hands of the infantry divisions of X Corps: immobile, nearly unsupplied, and already beginning to filter out of their positions to the rear. The Afrika Korps was down to just thirty working tanks and could no longer hold the north on its own. The Panzerarmee stood on the brink of destruction, and Rommel began to pull parts of it out of the line in order to begin his retreat.

He had no sooner given the orders to begin the retreat than another kind of bomb exploded in his headquarters. On 1:30 P.M., an order from Hitler arrived, forbidding even a tactical retreat. He commanded the Panzerarmee "to stand fast, to take not one step backwards, and to throw every gun and every man who you can free up into the battle." The order continued, "Despite his superiority, your enemy must also be at the end of his strength. It would not be the first time in history that a strong will has triumphed over the bigger battalions of the enemy. As to your troops, however, you can show them no other road than the one that leads to victory or death."[52]

Rommel now stopped his retreat in midstream, which we may take as the moment that the Panzerarmee fell apart. Caught flat-footed, not retreating but certainly not prepared to receive an attack, the Afrika Korps fell victim to a massive blow by British 1st Armoured Division on the afternoon of November 4 near Tel el Mansfra, which overran the right wing of 15th Panzer Division and smashed what was left of 21st Panzer Division. By now, both formations were "Panzer" in name only; 21st Panzer Division had just twenty operational tanks, which would be destroyed in the next two days. To the left of 1st Armoured, British 7th Armoured Division overran the Italian XX (Motorized) Corps, which was already in an advanced state of collapse. Further to the south, the Bologna infantry division had begun its retreat per the original order, then either failed to translate or willfully ignored the stand-fast order on November 3. Attempts that evening by its officers to get it back in the line were fruitless, and the division simply dissolved. The final blow on that awful day landed on the Italian Ariete armored division. Fuel shortages had forced it to come north by stages. It did, finally arriving on November 3, just in time for the onrushing armored formations of 8th Army to encircle and destroy it.[53] The battle was over.

The stand-fast order is a good point to end this discussion. Rommel professed to be shocked at it: "It was like we had all been hit over the head," he later wrote, "and for the first time in the African campaign I didn't know what I should do."[54] But surely he must have known by now that such rigid commands had become a common feature of the war in the east. Moreover, he had certainly heard this kind of rhetoric before. It had been a central feature of the propaganda campaigns that had made him a household name in Germany in 1940 and 1941. The Nazi propaganda machine had always portrayed Rommel as "a man of willpower, not much given to cool calculation," in the words of his most recent biographer, who could "triumph over, or at least stand up to, materially superior enemies." In that sense, he had been the "prototype of the National Socialist army leader."[55] It was this very reputation as Hitler's favorite that led to so much of the animus directed against the field marshal by his fellow officers, from Halder's exasperated claim that he had "gone crazy" in Africa to Jodl's postwar mockery (at the Nuremberg Tribunal) of the entire campaign as "Rommel's little shooting expedition in North Africa."[56]

The stand-fast order, in fact, represented the last gasp of one of the strongest Prussian-German military traditions of all: the elevation of will over all other factors on the road to victory. From the very earliest moments in the history of the Prussian army—its victory in coalition with the Swedes over a much larger Polish force at Warsaw in 1656, for example—this was a force the mocked the probabilities, that ignored the traditional calculus, and that disregarded the numerical balance.[57] Frederick the Great had made a career of it. He wouldn't have fought, much less won, any of his great battles if he had been wedded to a rational calculation of the odds. Hohenfriedeberg, Rossbach, Leuthen: the Roi-Connétable had fought and won all these signal victories against enemies that vastly outnumbered him and could call on many times his own meager resources. The successful crossing of the Elbe by General Yorck in 1813, the maneuver that more than any other led to Napoleon's defeat at Leipzig, was an especially senseless move when viewed against the probability that Napoleon would turn and crush him. Had the great Moltke been wedded to actuarial tables in 1866, he almost certainly would have fought the campaign in a far different way, rather than invading Bohemia with three widely separated armies, each of which was numerically inferior to the Austrian North Army he was facing.

Perhaps there really is an explanation for each of these improbable victories, hidden factors that rendered them safer bets than they looked. The point is that this is how the Prussian, and later the German, army viewed its own history: a series of victories over the odds, resulting above all from the indomitable will of the commander. In rejecting that notion on November 3, 1942, describing it as "one of the most remarkable days in history,"[58] Rommel was not simply showing his ignorance of Prussian history—understandable, after all, in a Württemberger. He was bringing down the curtain on the oldest tradition in German military history. The army had not changed, Rommel had. He had stood helpless under the irresistible mark of western allied power, the round-the-clock attack from the air. He had seen well-trained and battle-hardened troops panic and flee under its effect. He had seen what a seven-hour bombardment by artillery could do when it didn't have to worry about where its next consignment of shells might be coming from. North Africa marked a new era: the first time that the traditional German way of war, grounded in handiwork, tradition, and old-world craftsmanship, encountered a new one, one that had emerged from a different matrix of industrial mass production and a boundless confidence in technology. At El Alamein, the German way of war found itself trapped in the grip of the Machine.

The Soviet Way of War: Planning for Operation Uranus

The ink was barely dry on Hitler's stand-fast order to Rommel when the Red Army landed the gravest blow suffered by the Wehrmacht during the entire war: Operation Uranus, the Stalingrad counteroffensive north and south of Stalingrad.[59] Just as El Alamein faced the Wehrmacht with a way of war for which it had no effective answer, so too did the Soviet counteroffensive at Stalingrad. Here, too, was a distinctive operational culture at work. The Red Army was a curious amalgam of old and new. It had drawn much of its first wave of commanders from the ranks of the old czarist army. It had also inherited two separate operational traditions, both of which stemmed from the enormous size of the country. One featured massed infantry formations carrying out broad-front offensives, in the style of 1916's Brusilov offensive, on discrete operational sectors, or "fronts." At the same time there was a more mobile heritage of deep strikes, utilizing long-range cavalry as a *corps volant*.[60]

Overlaid on this legacy, however, were a number of new traditions. The interwar era had been a time of great intellectual ferment in the armed services, with the revolution clearing the decks for new ideas and new faces in equal measure—Marshal M. N. Tukhachevsky and G. S. Isserson, for example. They derived a new set of lessons largely taken from the Bolshevik experience in the Russian Civil War: an emphasis on offensive operations as opposed to defensive ones; an openness to new technology; and, perhaps most importantly, a theory of "consecutive operations." Modern mass armies were simply too large and too durable to destroy a single climactic battle, à la Napoleon or Moltke. Rather, one had to pound them repeatedly in a series of nonstop large-scale offensive operations, one after the other.[61] Tukhachevsky envisioned using powerful "shock groups," mixed groups of infantry, tanks, and artillery, to make the breakthrough on extremely narrow frontages. Highly mobile groups of armor and cavalry in second and third waves (echelons) would then exploit far into the enemy's rear areas, constantly feeding fresh new units along the breakthrough axis, aided by airpower and airborne troops. It was a new doctrine, a mobile yet tightly choreographed vision called "deep battle." Perhaps most importantly, Isserson, one of the leading lights at the Frunze General Staff Academy in the 1930s, argued for linkage between the two concepts of deep battle and consecutive operations: "Future deep operations," he argued, "will appear not as single links of a series of interrupted engagements, but as an unbroken chain extending for the entire depth of military activities."[62]

Since then, deep battle had had it ups and downs. Tukhachevsky had run afoul of Stalin and disappeared in the purges, and so had a sizable percentage of the Red Army's higher officer corps. The first six months of the war had seen the virtual dismemberment of the force at the hands of the Wehrmacht, a horrible story that ended, miraculously, in survival. Stavka Directive 03 in January 1942 had now resurrected Tukhachevky and Isserson's ideas, but except for the disastrous offensive at Kharkov in May, it had not actually tried them out. Since then, the Red Army had spent a great deal of time running, then successfully defending in place. What it had not done was launch any sort of grand offensive.

Zhukov and the other commanders would find that their new doctrine rarely worked as smoothly as it did on the drawing board. The Red Army hardly ever achieved the desired degrees of concentration called for in the directives. Still, the numbers are impressive enough. For the Stalingrad counteroffensive, for example, Southwest Front concentrated half of its rifle divisions, all of its tank and cavalry corps, 85 percent of its artillery, and all its rocket launchers and air power along less than 10 percent of its line. Artillery concentrations within the attack sector reached a density of seventy tubes per kilometer. The front's shock force, the 5th Tank Army (General P. L. Romanenko), deployed along a frontage of thirty-five kilometers. Twenty-five of it was guarded by a pair of rifle divisions. Along the army's narrow ten-kilometer *Schwerpunkt*, 5th Tank Army deployed a first echelon of two rifle divisions up and two back; a second one was made up of a tank brigade and two tank corps, along with a cavalry corps in reserve.[63] This was the new face of Soviet operational art: massive strength deployed in echelons, prepared to penetrate, exploit, and keep exploiting.

Of course, it didn't hurt Soviet chances that they were aiming this enormous concentration of force mainly at the Romanians. Operation Uranus was a response to an unusual operational situation. The splitting up (*Aufspaltung*) of the German offensive, first noted by Field Marshal Fedor von Bock, had ended in absurdity. Two arrowheads were firmly embedded deep inside the Soviet Union, one at Stalingrad and the other far into the Caucasus. Along the flanks of these arrowheads sat the armies of the Axis satellites. It is a long voyage from Voronezh to Stalingrad, but one could have taken it in November 1942 and seen precious few Germans, and virtually no major German formations. Moving left to right, this was the operational sector of the Hungarian 2nd Army (General Gustav von Jany), the Italian 8th (General Italo Gariboldi), and the Romanian 3rd (General Petre Dumitrescu).[64] The Romanians held a front almost a hundred miles in length, "tactically disadvantageous, scarcely improved, and almost devoid of cover." The situation on the right of 4th Panzer Army was even worse. Here the Romanian 4th Army (General Constantin Constantinescu) was sitting out in a flat plain, unanchored and holding a line that simply petered out in the Kalmuk Steppe. Along much of its front there were no formed units, only light reconnaissance troops, and some divisional frontages were as broad as fifty miles. The entire army had only thirty-four heavy antitank guns.[65]

All these satellite armies had some tough soldiers and decent commanders, and in good times, all of them might have been capable of static defense.[66] By now, however, months into a long and grueling campaign, they were utterly "threadbare,"[67] in the words of one expert. Largely unmotorized, undersupplied with artillery and antitank weapons, and possessing only the barest complement of air power, they were unprepared for the crucial role thrust upon them by the Wehrmacht. "German commands which have Romanian troops serving under them must reconcile themselves to the fact the moderately heavy fire, even without an enemy attack, will be enough to cause the troops to fall back," wrote General Hoth on September 30, and it seems a fair assessment.[68] The German high command made some half-hearted moves to do something about it, forming so-called emergency units (*Alarmeinheiten*) out of troops not immediately engaged in the front and preparing them for "auxiliary duty in times of difficult fighting," the reference here being to Soviet breakthrough of one of the satellite armies. The new Luftwaffe "field divisions," badly trained and barely equipped, were also starting to arrive in the theater.[69]

More to the point, the high command stationed XXXXVIII Panzer Corps (General Ferdinand Heim) in reserve behind the Romanian 3rd Army. It offered theoretical security, but like so much of the German Panzer force by now, was in truth barely armored. Consisting of 22nd Panzer Division, 1st Romanian Armored Division, and elements of the 14th Panzer Division, it could scarcely muster a regiment of tanks all told. The 22nd Panzer, for example, had just forty-five tanks, most of them light. It had been in the reserve, and thus had gone without fuel for weeks, sitting immobilized. Those who live in the north and try to start their car during the winter will sympathize with its plight when it went into action against the Soviet breakthrough.[70] The 1st Romanian Armored Division was, if possible, in even worse shape; it had only forty tanks, all of them older Czech models.

The Soviet operational plan was a fairly simple one. Two pincers would emerge from north and south of Stalingrad, drive toward one another, and meet on the Don River, thus encircling German 6th Army and perhaps some of 4th Panzer Army as well.[71] Although the Red Army was in the process of resurrecting deep operations, this one didn't aim all that far. Forming the northern pincer was Southwestern Front under General N. F. Vatutin. He had two armies, 5th Tank (Romanenko) and 21st (under the command of General I. M. Christiakov), deployed abreast in the Serafimovich and Kletskaya bridgeheads over the Don, respectively. Once their infantry shock groups had crashed through the thin screen of Romanian 3rd Army, mobile units would pass through the breach. The 1st and 26th Tank Corps (from 5th Tank Army) and the 4th Tank Corps and 3rd Guards Cavalry Corps (from 21st Army) would then wheel sharply to the southeast, heading toward the Don and encircling Stalingrad from the north and west. A final mobile unit (8th Cavalry Corps, from 5th Tank Army) was to peel off to the southwest, to protect the newly formed pocket against relief attempts. The southern pincer would consist of the Stalingrad Front (General A. I. Eremenko). Here, Soviet 51st and 57th Armies were to blow through the Romanian 4th Army. Mobile units (13th Tank Corps and 4th Mechanized Corps) would wheel sharply to the right (northwest) and link up with 5th Tank Army coming down from the north. The meeting place of the two arms was to be the town of Kalach on the Don River. A last cavalry corps, the 4th, would provide the outer layer of the encirclement in this sector.

Nothing in war is ever a sure thing, and Uranus was hardly the forgone conclusion that appears in the history books. This was the same region in which the Wehrmacht had been having so much difficulty: poor in resources and materials, badly served by roads, and nearly devoid of rail lines. Two single-track railways had to suffice for all three fronts involved in the undertaking (Southwestern, Stalingrad, and between them, the Don Front). This meant, among other things, that some of the formations taking part had to make approach marches of 200 to 250 miles just to get to the theater.[72] The operational timetable was a brutal one. Although the Red Army was confident that it could vaporize the Romanian formations along both fronts, such things have a way of taking longer in reality than they do on paper. Uranus called for 5th Tank Army (Southwest Front) to reach Kalach on the third day of the operation, a drive of seventy miles; 4th Mechanized Corps (Stalingrad Front) had to go only fifty miles, but it had only two days. Moreover, because of the disparity in distances, the operation had to stagger its start times, with Southwest Front leading off a day earlier than its partner.

When it finally came, Operation Uranus was anything but a surprise to the German high command. There is today a great deal of interest in the Soviet skill at *maskirovka* (deception): fake radio traffic, shuttling of reserves to nondecisive sectors as though they were preparing for an attack, keeping operational details even from the assault formations until the last moment. None of that seemed to have much effect this time. Any German officer could see the danger that might erupt along the long Don flank. Hitler and Halder had discussed the very point back in August, in reference to Stalin's generalship along the lower Don in the Russian civil war. Soviet preparations were obvious and noted in the German records.[73] Forewarned, however, did not seem to translate to forearmed in this case, and the Wehrmacht hardly took preparations to meet the threatened Soviet attack.

Much of the problem resulted from what had become by now a German fixation on Stalingrad. The night before the Soviet offensive, Paulus was still planning further attacks inside the city. Perhaps there was also a certain fatalism within the high command, Hitler concluded, a sense that the current situation had to play itself out to the end. But there was another reason for lack of German counterpreparations: the options were limited by this time. Exactly how could the Wehrmacht have met this threat? Free up more infantry from 6th Army and transfer it to the flanks? There was none. Retreat from Stalingrad altogether? Not in the cards politically and, given the limited mobility of 6th Army, much more difficult to carry out than most people think. Free up the mobile formations to fight a battle of maneuver? There was hardly enough fuel left for tactical movement. Perhaps in some operational situations, there is simply nothing to be done.

Operation Uranus: Forming the Stalingrad *Kessel*

The Soviet counteroffensive opened at 5:00 A.M. on November 19, with a massive barrage against the entire front of the Romanian 3rd Army.[74] Fifty minutes later, elements of Southwestern Front's 5th Tank Army on the right and 21st Army on the left erupted out of their bridgeheads over the Don. Within hours, they had ruptured the front of the 3rd

Romanian Army beyond repair. The 5th Tank Army directed its attack against the town of Bolshoi, directly into the heart of the Romanian II Corps (9th and 14th Infantry Divisions, left to right, with 7th Cavalry Division in reserve). The initial wave of infantry slashed open the seam between the front-line divisions. Soon both of them were streaming away in confusion, as 5th Tank Army's mobile formations (I Tank Corps and 26th Tank Corps) slashed through the gaps opened by the assault infantry and overran the Romanian artillery positions. By the evening, there was a gash twelve miles wide and twenty miles deep where Romanian II Corps had once stood.

The 21st Army had similar success, thrusting out of the Kletskaya bridgehead and ripping open the front of the Romanian IV Corps (13th Infantry and 1st Cavalry Divisions, left to right, with 15th Infantry Division in reserve). It too was into the artillery positions before lunchtime. A counterattack by the 15th Division, aiming to seal the breach, came to nothing. Between II and IV Corps, the unfortunate Romanian V Corps (5th and 6th Infantry Divisions) was now trapped between the two converging armies. Containing elements of the broken units on both flanks, the pocket managed to hold out for a few days under the energetic leadership of General Mihail Lascar, commander of the Romanian 6th Infantry Division. When "Group Lascar" finally surrendered on November 23, the Soviets took some 27,000 prisoners, although elements of the pocket did manage to break out to the south.

Although the Romanians bore the brunt of the initial assault, the Germans were having a difficult time formulating a response. In both Soviet attack sectors, the weather was bad enough to ground the Luftwaffe, a factor that played no small role in the rapid success of the assaults. The only real move that day involved the XXXXVIII Panzer Corps, in reserve behind Romanian 3rd Army.[75] Its commander, General Heim, had recognized the severity of the attack quite early. The first reports highlighted the Soviet threat from the Kletskaya bridgehead, and by 9:30 A.M., he had decided on a thrust to the northeast to seal it off. The orders went out to his divisions at 10:35 A.M.. The maneuver had hardly begun when new orders came from the army group. They pointed out that the main Soviet thrust lay to the northwest, near Bolshoi, and quite rightly ordered him to counter it. Heim dutifully changed his axis of advance, a difficult left wheel that split up the two divisions in this desolate and nearly roadless region. A corps that already had serious problems in cohesion (pairing off a German Panzer and a Romanian armored division) and hardly any fuel reserves at all was thus split up in two divergent directions. Heim had the German

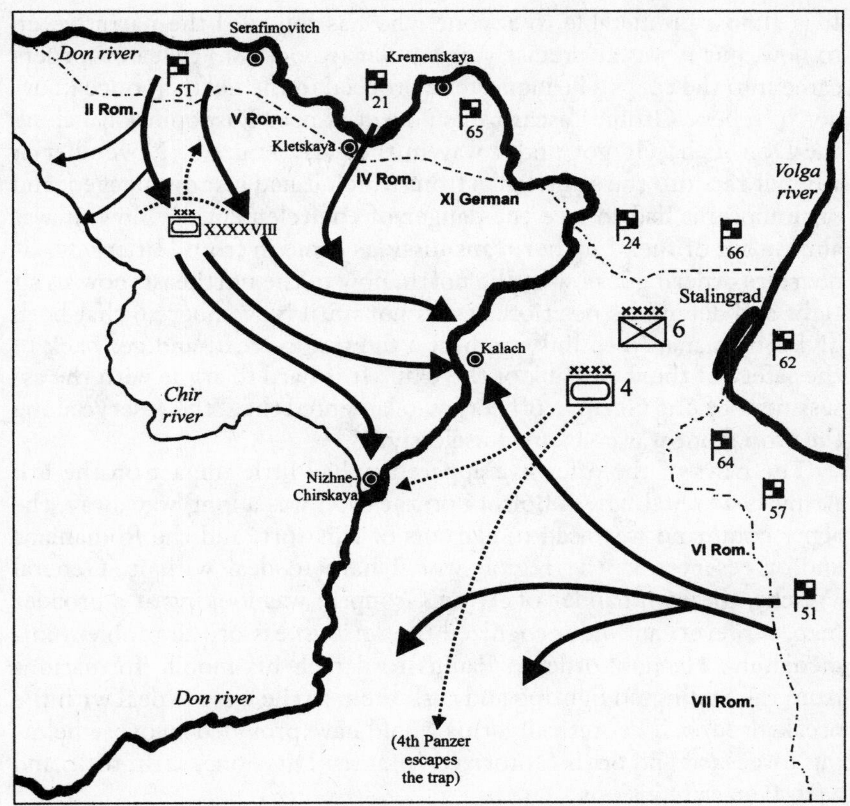

Map 15. Death of the Wehrmacht II: Operation Uranus, November 1942.

division in hand, but 1st Romanian Armored Division simply fell off his situation map. He lost radio contact with it, and try as he might, he could not reestablish it. German sources tend to attribute this failure to a lack of fighting spirit on the part of the Romanians; the Romanians point to the weather and the bad atmospheric conditions. Viewed objectively, it was probably a mixture of both.

The corps duly set off, slipping and sliding on the icy roads. By nightfall, both divisions had driven into an attack by the concentrated forces of 5th Tank Army in full stride. With Soviet tanks creating a seam between them and lapping around their flanks, both divisions were now in serious danger of being encircled. They spent the next whole day, November 20, warding off repeated Soviet tank attacks, and they only managed to cut their way through to the south by nightfall.

It is almost predictable to anyone who has followed the narrative up to now, but it was at precisely this point (10:00 P.M.) that new orders came into the corps's headquarters: proceed to the north at once in order to relieve Group Lascar in its pocket at near Raspopinskaya along the Don. It barely got under way in the early hours of November 21 when it ran into the same tanks from which it had just disengaged, and once more, it had to face the danger of encirclement. By now, it was almost out of fuel. Further transmissions came in from Hitler's headquarters ordering it now to the north, now to the northeast, now to sit tight and defend its position. It was not until November 26 that both divisions managed to link up, beat a fighting retreat, and get back to the safety of the west bank of the Chir. It is hard to argue with the assessment of one German officer, who lamented that "the reserve along the Don front was consumed uselessly."[76]

The news of the offensive apparently had little impact on the 6th Army inside Stalingrad. Bolshoi on the Don was a long way away, the army command was used to alarums of this sort, and the Romanians and/or reserves in the region would have to deal with it. General Weichs, the commander of Army Group B, was looking at a broader map, however, and he recognized the seriousness of the problem immediately. He now ordered Paulus to detach his mobile formations from the Stalingrad fighting and rush them to the west to deal with the breakthrough. Theoretically, this would have provided an overwhelming force: 3rd and 60th Motorized Infantry Divisions, 14th, 16th, and 24th Panzer Divisions.

As the 6th Army staff studied the situation, however, it was clear that fuel shortages would prevent any of these mobile units from intervening in the threatened zones in a timely fashion—that is, in anything less than three to four days.[77] Unfortunately, things were happening a lot faster than that. Over the course of the next two days, the mobile corps of the two Soviet armies drove hard, wheeling to the southeast and heading for Kalach. After the first day's breakthrough, they put the pedal down and were soon motoring in high gear against minimal opposition. By making an average of thirty-five miles per day (with some units topping forty), and by simply bypassing any potential resistance, they were on the outskirts of Kalach by November 22. Meanwhile, 8th Cavalry Corps was successfully clearing the line of the Chir River in the west, preparing the outer ring of the anticipated encirclement at Stalingrad. It must have been an amazing ride for 8th Cavalry. It was perhaps 150 miles in the rear of the German forces at Stalingrad, but the region was—outside of the usual rear-area installations such as supply dumps, hospitals, map depots, and the like—quite empty of hostile forces.

The breakthrough of the Stalingrad Front in the south reads in a similar way. Touching off a day later, it simply blew away the Romanian 4th Army. The formation directly in the way of the Soviet attack was Romanian VI Corps, which consisted of five weak infantry divisions strung out in the open in a long, thin line. There was a chain of shallow lakes here, south of Beketovka, but they barely slowed down 51st Army (General N. I. Trufanov) and 57th Army (General F. I. Tolbukhin) at all. The operation in this sector featured the same overwhelming preliminary bombardment, the same initial assault by infantry shock groups, and the same exploitation by a powerful mechanized second echelon. The attack began at 6:00 A.M., and within hours, it had broken through the seam of the infantry divisions in the center of VI Romanian Corps: the 18th (on the left) and 1st (on the right). The axis of attack here was due west until the Soviet tanks hit Plodovitoe, where they wheeled sharply to the right. Now the Soviet 4th Mechanized Corps smashed through the gap, overrunning the Romanian artillery and then wheeling to the northwest toward Kalach. Meanwhile, 4th Cavalry Corps peeled off to the southwest to form the encirclement's outer ring.

There was even less resistance here than in the north, the result of the absence of significant German forces in the sector. Technically, Romanian 4th Army was under the command of 4th Panzer Army. By now, however, Hoth's command was in a sorry state. Its component formations consisted of three corps: two Romanian and one German (the IV); the latter included three divisions, although one of them was also Romanian (the 20th Infantry Division). Hoth also had two motorized divisions: the 29th and the 16th, neither of which were truly motorized by now, and which could probably call on twenty tanks between them. His 4th Panzer Army no longer contained a single Panzer division.

The next two days saw a great deal of action on the front, but almost all of it was Soviet. German forces were pinned down in Stalingrad or so low on fuel that they might as well have been moving in slow motion. On November 22, the vanguard of the Soviet 5th Tank Army, the 26th Tank Corps, rolled into Kalach. Concerned lest the Germans succeed in demolishing the crucial road bridge over the Don, which would have seriously set back the Soviet operational timetable, the corps commander, General A. G. Rodin, sent a small detachment into the city: a pair of motorized infantry companies fronted by precisely five T-34 tanks. They entered Kalach with headlights blazing, rushed the bridge, and reached it just before the befuddled German garrison could react. The next day, the spearheads of 26th Tank Corps, coming down, and 4th Mechanized Corps, coming up, met on the Karpovka River, formally sealing off the Stalingrad encirclement. Appropriately enough, the name of the village where this signal event took place was Sovietsky.

German 6th Army was now in deep trouble inside Stalingrad. There is some dispute as to whether it was actually "encircled" (*eingeschlossen*)[78] at this point, the term that Paulus used in his report to Army Group B on the evening of November 22. It certainly was ringed round with enemies (*umstellt*), however.[79] Likewise, there were differing ideas within the army as to how to proceed, a debate ended by a pair of Hitler's transmissions to Paulus that same day: 6th Army was to stay put.[80] Within days, it had formed a front to the west in addition to the one to the east. In German parlance, it had "hedgehogged" itself, and now it sat to contemplate its options: the first a potential breakout attempt from within the pocket, the second a relief offensive from outside, linked with a risky effort to supply it from the air.

The End: Winter Storm

Neither one of these options was particularly attractive. Outside of Paulus's twenty-one-division force (315,000 men at the start of operations, but well below that now), there was a horde of other, personnel-rich formations inside the Stalingrad *Kessel*: an army headquarters and five corps headquarters; substantial portions of 4th Panzer Army (its German IV Corps and 29th Motorized Division); two complete Romanian divisions; a Croat unit (the 369th Reinforced, or Verstärkte, Infantry Regiment); no fewer than 149 independent units, including army artillery detachments, construction battalions, and police units; and finally about 20,000 Soviet civilian "volunteers" (*Hilfswilligen*) who were performing the army's menial chores, and who had to know the fate that awaited them at the hands of the NKVD if the pocket were to be liquidated. One more person needs to be mentioned: General Paulus himself, perhaps the only German officer to fly into the pocket and stay there, which he did from his headquarters at Nizhne Chirskaya on November 22.

The sheer size of the *Kessel*, which was much larger than the 90,000 or so that Soviets planners had envisioned, immediately began to foreclose on the available German options. A breakout was the first choice of the Wehrmacht leadership: Chief of Staff General Kurt Zeitzler; Paulus himself; General Richtofen and the other competent Luftwaffe authorities[81]; the fiery commander of LI Corps inside the pocket, General Seydlitz.[82] There were only two choices, Seydlitz told his assembled divisional commanders at the time. It was either going to be "a Brzeziny or a Cannae."[83] Likewise, the first major German operational study of the campaign, written in 1955, recommended it, and it still surfaces in the literature today.[84] It would have been a far more difficult operation than many analysts allow, however. Not only was virtually all of 6th Army's fighting strength embedded in Stalingrad, but the army's supply, fuel, and transport situation was bordering on the disastrous.[85] Paulus had long ago sent away the horses, for example, the backbone of 6th Army's transport. There were, moreover, two crucial voices raised against a breakout attempt: one was Hitler's, and the other, a crucial one because it broke the monopoly of professional military opinion in favor of the breakout, was the newly appointed theater commander, Field Marshal Erich von Manstein.[86]

For all these reasons, the breakout soon receded in favor of a relief offensive, with the pocket surviving on air supply until a land corridor to it could be opened. But here too difficulties soon came to the fore. According to a report from 6th Army headquarters on December 18, the ration strength of the troops in the pocket was 246,000 men. At the time, there wasn't an air force in the world with the transport capacity to ship enough food to feed a quarter-million mouths per day, let alone the ammunition and replacement parts to allow a modern army to fight a sustained, 360-degree battle against encircling forces. This was also precisely the moment that the Wehrmacht was in the process of rushing units to North Africa by air, reinforcing what Hitler was promising would be a "Tunisian bridgehead." Air transport assets, always at a premium, were therefore scarcer than ever. Moreover, as fresh Soviet attacks continued to push back the front, the Luftwaffe had to abandon airfield after airfield, with the round trip flight to the pocket increasing proportionally, from 200 miles to 500 or more. When Soviet attacks on the pocket overran the airfields at Pitomnik, Gumrak, and Stalingradskiy, the Luftwaffe continued its supply runs, dropping its cargo from the air. The entire airlift suffered from lack of adequate fighter cover and took place under punishing Soviet air attack. According to one Soviet source, the Germans lost 672 Ju-52 transport aircraft[87] in the course of the airlift; the Germans gave a figure of 266.[88] Taking either number or splitting the difference, the

Luftwaffe, too, suffered a major defeat at Stalingrad. Even the lower German number represented one-third of the Luftwaffe's total transport complement. At any rate, the airlift itself was an affair of constantly shrinking numbers. The daily requirement of 6th Army was at least 500 to 750 tons per day.[89] Luftwaffe chief Hermann Göring, or perhaps it was Luftwaffe Chief of Staff General Hans Jeschonnek, promised some 350 tons.[90] Chief of Staff Zeitzler called that promise a "lie,"[91] and Richtofen warned that the daily figure would hardly reach 300.[92] Over the course of the siege, the actual figure was a little over 117 tons per day.[93]

Even that might have been enough if the Wehrmacht had been able to mount a swift relief operation. In late November, the high command dissolved Army Group B and created a new command in its place, Army Group Don. At its head, Hitler placed one of the most gifted operational minds in the army, Field Marshal Erich von Manstein, a commander who had proven himself over and over again in the first three years of the war. But even Manstein could not manufacture formations that weren't available, or fashion a relief offensive out of the miserable *Alarmeinheiten* and Luftwaffe divisions that the high command offered as his reinforcements. The only real operational reserve in the region had been XXXXVIII Panzer Corps, torn apart by Soviet action and German indecision in the opening days of Uranus.

It is a sign of how low German fighting strength in the theater had sunk that out of the entire Wehrmacht, Manstein could assemble a single corps, just two divisions, for the relief offensive, code-named Operation Winter Storm (*Wintergewitter*).[94] This was LVII Panzer Corps under General Friedrich Kirchner. Placed under 4th Panzer Army, the corps concentrated at Kotelnikovo in early December, some ninety miles southwest of Stalingrad, by which time the Soviets had drawn the ring around 6th Army tightly indeed. It contained 23rd Panzer Division, which had seen too much hard fighting in the Caucasus and was badly in need of refit; and 6th Panzer Division, whose refit in France was actually cut short by orders to proceed at once to the east. There doesn't seem to have been a single responsible individual on site who felt that this force would suffice for a ninety-mile drive against strong frontal opposition and with the by now customary open flanks. There was some talk of including a second thrust by the 17th Panzer Division (part of "Army Detachment Hollidt"), which would launch a secondary attack across the Don and hit the Soviets in the deep right flank after the operation got moving, but the worrisome level of Soviet pressure along the line of the Chir rendered its entry into the battle problematic at best.

The offensive, which touched off on December 12, began well enough. There was no real surprise, outside of the usual tactical variety, and no real maneuver, either. The two divisions drove northeast, straight up the rail line out of Kotelnikovo, 6th Panzer to the left of the line and 23rd to the right. The initial assault penetrated the Soviet defenses (302nd Rifle Division on the right and 126th on the left) and breeched the first river line (the Aksai) that evening. Under the command of one of the most experienced and savvy tank men in the army, General Eberhard Raus, 6th Panzer Division formed the corps's spearhead and gave a typically good accounting of itself in the fighting.[95] From the start, however, 23rd Panzer was good for little else except flank protection; it had only thirty tanks to its name.

Not surprisingly, then, the pace slowed down after that promising start. The Soviets rushed reinforcements to the sector, mostly units of the 2nd Guards Army, and began hammering against the flanks of the penetration on the second day of the offensive. With two complete Soviet mechanized corps on the scene (IV on the right and XIII on the left), there would be nearly a week of hard positional fighting around the village of Verchne Kumskiy. It was the type of engagement for which the infantry-poor German formations were singularly unsuited. The weather went from good to terrible, German formations had to fight with one eye on their fuel gauges at all times, and Soviet resistance was fierce. While 6th Panzer was fighting forward slowly, 23rd Panzer nearly lost its bridgehead on the Aksai on December 17. The 17th Panzer Division joined the fray on the 18th, falling in on 6th Panzer's left and helping it break the Verchne Kumskiy position the next day. The Panzers now motored north toward the next river line, the Mishkova, but were unable to get across it in strength.

Although Winter Storm was just thirty-five miles from Stalingrad, it had also broken down. Soviet strength was growing daily, German losses were rising apace, and strong armored counterattacks were threatening both flanks of the German penetration. The decision a few days later (December 23) to transfer 6th Panzer Division to the north ended Winter Storm. It is sometimes portrayed as wasting the last chance to save Stalingrad, and Raus certainly saw it that way, but there was no real choice.[96] He and his Panzers had business in the north, dealing with a new emergency: the crushing of yet another satellite force, the Italian 8th Army, in the Soviet operation known as Little Saturn.

The Red Army had finally turned the tables. For three years, the Wehrmacht had been a harsh, demanding schoolmaster, dealing out dozens of unwanted lessons to neighboring armies on the subject of *Bewegungskrieg*, and giving virtually all of them failing grades. Now it suddenly found itself going to school. There were no electives here, no real choice of course or major. Like many new students, it was having trouble keeping up with the professor. It was an unfamiliar area of study, one that the Soviet army had pioneered and that seemed utterly baffling to the Wehrmacht. It was called "consecutive operations."

9

Conclusion

The Death of the Wehrmacht

Sometimes it seems as if history really does have a Musè, some poetic and divine force that guides it into ever more improbable and dramatic paths. Even Clio at her most whimsical, however, could not have written a stranger plotline for the campaigns of 1942. For the Wehrmacht, the campaigning season began with some of the greatest operational victories in the entire history of German arms: Kerch, Kharkov, and Gazala. All of them took place within weeks of one another in May 1942. Then, in June, the Wehrmacht placed an exclamation point on this successful season with the reduction of the great fortress of Sevastopol. After providing all the participants with enough nail-biting moments to last several lifetimes, the year's fighting ended, just six months later, with the Germans suffering two of the most decisive defeats of all time: El Alamein and Stalingrad. Again, these two signal events took place within weeks of one another. Field Marshal Erwin Rommel's Panzerarmee (now restyled, in its death throes, the "German-Italian Panzerarmee") was still streaming across North Africa in some disarray, heading toward its fate in Tunisia, at the very moment that the Soviet 5th Tank Army was smashing through the thin Romanian line along the Don.

These two events, and especially their almost exact confluence, represented more than a simple military failure. German armies had failed to achieve their objectives in past wars, and the great distances involved to reach Stalingrad, the Caucasus, or the Suez Canal could act as salve on that point. Nor was it simply defeat: German arms had suffered innumerable defeats in the past—so many that you could fill a book with them: Kolin and Kunersdorf for Frederick the Great; Jena and Auerstädt for the Prussian army in the age of Napoleon; Verdun and Amiens in World War I. Nor was the El Alamein–Stalingrad nexus simply the "turning point" of World War II. This war, more than any other before it, was a vast and sprawling conflict on land, sea, and air. It involved hundreds of millions of human beings from the freezing cold of the Arctic to the sweltering heat of the Burmese jungle, and the notion that there was a single discrete moment that "turned" it is problematic, to say the least.[1]

What had happened in the summer and fall campaigns of 1942 was something far more significant. In those brief six months, an entire way of war that dated back centuries had come to an end. The German traditions of maneuver-based *Bewegungskrieg*, the notion that "war is an art, a free and creative activity,"[2] the belief in the independence of the subordinate commander within his own sphere of competency: each and every one of these bedrock beliefs had taken a pounding in the past six months, and in fact had revealed themselves to be no longer valid. The war of movement as practiced by the German army had failed in the wide open spaces of the Soviet Union; the southern front, especially, presented it with challenges that it was not designed to handle. The notion of war as an art was difficult to maintain in the face of what had happened in North Africa and on the Volga. Here, enemy armies looked on calmly as the Wehrmacht went through its ornate repertoire of maneuver, then smashed it with overwhelming material superiority: hordes of tanks, skies filled with aircraft, seventy artillery gun tubes per kilometer. German defeat in both theaters looked far less like an art than an exercise in an industrial shop class: helpless raw materials being torn to shreds in a drill press.

To the German officer corps, those small encirclements at the start of the summer campaign, and then again on the Don and in the Caucasus in the fall, had seemed disappointing: 20,000 prisoners? 30,000? Those figures used to represent a morning's work to the German Panzers earlier in the war. In fact, had the Wehrmacht only been able to peer into the future, it would have savored them like a fine wine. As insignificant as they might have seemed, they were the last in a long line of German operational-level triumphs, stretching back 300 years from the Great Elector to Marshal Fedor von Bock. No one knew it yet, but 1942 marked the end of an era in German military history: the death of the *Kesselschlacht*, a way of war that no longer corresponded to modern conditions.

Another aspect of *Bewegungskrieg*, independent command, also died in 1942. At both El Alamein and Stalingrad, it had been conspicuous by its absence. The new communications technology, an essential ingredient in the Wehrmacht's earlier victories, now showed its negative face. Radio gave the high command a precise, real-time picture of even the most rapid and far-flung operations. It also allowed staff and political leaders alike to intervene in the most detailed and, from the perspective of field commanders, the most obnoxious way possible. As one German staff officer put it,

> Thanks to modern means of communication and information, an exchange of ideas between the highest command echelons of the army and the lower ranking commanders was possible on an almost uninterrupted basis. This technical advantage had psychological disadvantages, however. Specifically, it caused the supreme command to interfere too often with the leadership of the armies under it. It also caused many army commanders to substitute the opinions of the high command for their own decisions. This was not a plus for the art of war.[3]

Indeed, the new face of German command, 1942-style, was evident in the absurd *Haltbefehl* to Rommel in the desert and the incessant debates between Hitler and Field Marshal List about how to seize the relatively minor Black Sea port of Tuapse. Georg von Derfflinger, the first field marshal in the history of Brandenburg-Prussia, would probably have started a fistfight with his lord, the Great Elector, rather than suffer such indignity. Likewise, at the crisis of the battle of Zorndorf, Frederick the Great ordered his cavalry commander, Friedrich Wilhelm von Seydlitz, to launch an immediate counterstroke on the left of the hard-pressed Prussian infantry. When it seemed late in coming, the king sent a messenger to Seydlitz with orders to march immediately, and with threats if he did not do so. Seydlitz was a commander who moved only when he judged the moment ripe, however. His response was one of the most famous moments in the history of the Prussian army, known to every cadet who had passed through the Kriegsakademie, and certainly part of the mental lexicon of every German commander in the field in 1942: "Tell the king that after the battle my head is at his disposal," Seydlitz told the king's messenger, "but meantime, I hope he will permit me to exercise it in his service."[4]

Those days were evidently long gone by 1942. Hitler took a number of heads in this campaign while the fight was still raging: Bock, List, Halder, not to mention poor General Heim of the XXXXVIII Panzer Corps. The new dispensation was most evident in the attenuated struggle within the Stalingrad *Kessel.* Paulus and the 6th Army may have been cut off from supply, but they certainly weren't cut off from communication. From Hitler's first intervention (his orders of

November 22 that "6th Army will hedgehog itself and await further orders") to the last (the January 24 refusal of permission to surrender), the Führer had been the de facto commander of the Stalingrad pocket. This is not to exculpate Paulus's admittedly pedestrian leadership before the disaster and his curious mixture of fatalism and obsequiousness to the Führer once he had been encircled. "You're talking to dead men here," he had once hissed at a Luftwaffe officer trying to explain the difficulties of the air transport problem.[5] Indeed, Paulus may actually have welcomed Hitler's interventions as a way of evading his own responsibility for the disaster. Hitler did not kill the concept of flexible command, whether one calls it "the independence of the subordinate commander" or *Auftragstaktik.* Radio did. It is unfortunate when a general on the spot may no longer order a retreat, but things have reached an absurd pass when a commander no longer has the authority to surrender his army without permission from someone a thousand miles away.

Like any deep-rooted historical phenomenon, however, *Bewegungskrieg* died hard. It resisted both the foibles of Hitler's personality as well as the more complex systemic factors that were working against it. Those haunting arrows on the situation maps will remain, fixed permanently to the map of our historical consciousness, as a reminder of what a near-run thing it was: the 13th Panzer Division, operating under a brand-new commander, just a single mile outside of Ordzhonikidze and still driving forward; Hube's 3rd Panzer Division slashing out of its Don bridgehead and lunging to the Volga in a single bound, reaching the northern edge of the Stalingrad suburbs; German pioneers, bristling with flamethrowers and satchel charges, blasting one Soviet defensive position after another to smithereens and driving grimly for the riverbank just a few hundred yards away; Rommel's right wing at Alam Halfa, a mere half hour's ride by armored car from Alexandria. Rarely have the advance guards of a defeated army ever come so tantalizingly close to their strategic objectives.

In the end, the most shocking aspect of 1942 is not Hitler's own foolishness in splitting his armies or the obvious inadvisability of *exzentrisch* operations.[6] It is how absurdly close the Wehrmacht came to taking not one, but all of its objectives for 1942: splitting the British empire in two at Suez and paving the way for a drive into the Middle East, seizing the Soviet Union's principal oil fields, its most productive farmland, and a major share of its industries. Would it have meant ultimate victory in the war? Probably not. There was still the United States and the Manhattan Project to worry about. Would it have meant serious trouble for the Grand Alliance? Absolutely.

* * *

In its lead article for its first issue of 1944, the editorial staff of the *Militärwissenschaftliche Rundschau* (the "Military Science Review," the journal edited and published by the Wehrmacht's high command, made a startling admission. The magazine would no longer be carrying articles on the current war: "At the end of our issues for the war year 1943, the *Militärwissenschaftliche Rundschau* raised the question of whether and how it was possible to keep publishing this magazine despite all the difficulties of the war. It will be clear from the contents of this first issue of 1944 what we have decided to do."[7]

Indeed it was. Beginning with Hitler's 1930 article, "Reichswehr und deutsche Politik" ("The Army and German Politics"),[8] the magazine was filled with older historical material, often reprinted from other sources. It was quite a decline for a journal that had been on the cutting edge of military developments for a century, and never more so than in the 1930s when it was conceiving of new and interesting ways to integrate the new technologies of tank, aircraft, and radio on the modern battlefield.

According to the editors, the decision arose not only from the obvious difficulties of a General Staff magazine trying to publish material on a currently ongoing war. Articles on individual battles or campaigns of the war had "found only limited interest amongst our readers," especially because the journal did not presently find it possible to deal with these subjects in any sort of critical or controversial way. The journal, therefore, had decided that, "in future issues of the *Militärwissenschaftliche Rundschau*, the treatment of military historical subject matter will be a more conscious characteristic than ever before."[9] The readers had spoken, and what they seemed to be saying was this: as things stood, "history" was a good place for the Wehrmacht to be. There it could debate traditional and comfortable issues like the "independence of the subordinate commander"[10] (along with the precise limits thereof);[11] the importance of recognizing the "culmination point" in a campaign (and the German failure to do so in the Marne campaign of 1914)[12]; the role that Blücher's optimism had played in bringing the Prussian army through the dark days after the battle of Jena ("Blucher and Gneisenau had lived through their fatherland's darkest hours before holding high office in wartime. Their souls, too, had been hardened in the school of misfortune. But men with great hearts learn indifference to the irrelevant and the trivial . . . ");[13] the necessity for persistence and tenacity (*Beharrlichkeit*) in the assault[14]—all the things that, according to its own traditional analysis, had made the Prussian and German army great over the centuries.

We might also add this: in early 1944, history was certainly a friendlier place to be than the present, where a reader would have to confront any number of troubling issues: the Wehrmacht's defensive posture in the Ukraine or Byelorussia, where it faced ever larger Soviet armies that were certain to land a heavy blow in the upcoming year; the likelihood that a vast Anglo-American army was about to land in western Europe; an Allied bombing campaign against the Reich's major cities that had now begun in earnest. There certainly were 1,001 things to worry about if you were a German commander or staff officer in 1944. Perhaps the only article in the entire issue that actually corresponded to the German army's current plight was a short piece by Emperor Napoleon himself, describing the correct handling of forces inside an encirclement.[15] It is not unfair to wonder whether copies of the issue were flown into the Korsun pocket southwest of the Dnieper, where XI and XXXXII Corps were even then struggling for their lives against Soviet forces hammering them from all directions.

On another level, however, it seems fitting that the high command had reacted to this drastic turn in Germany's military fortunes by retreating into its own history. This was a war that had been fought from the start along traditional lines. Despite all the trappings of modern technology, the operational principles were old ones, and their roots lay deep within the history of Prussia and the second Reich. Rommel may have been one of the most modern of the Wehrmacht's generals, in terms of recognizing the weaknesses of the traditional German way of war, but it is interesting to hear him describe himself and his own operational art: "The time of a Seydlitz and Ziethen has returned. We have to see war from a cavalry perspective—lead tank units like squadrons. Give commands from a moving tank as one used to from the saddle."[16] These names—Seydlitz and Ziethen and Blücher and Moltke and a dozen others—appear again and again in German analyses of the war they were fighting. When Rommel wasn't comparing himself to Seydlitz, there were others who were happy to do it for him. His own intelligence officer, Colonel Mellenthin, once described him as "the Seydlitz of the Panzer corps,"[17] and so did a June 1940 radio broadcast from the African theater: "The personal motto of the Führer, 'What does not defeat me only makes me stronger,'" it said, was also "the battle cry of this Seydlitz who led here and his gallant band."[18]

This same linking of past and present was evident in an encomium published in the Luftwaffe magazine for the Mediterranean region, *Adler im Süden* ("Eagle of the South"): "What would Sedan have been without Moltke, Tannenberg without Hindenburg, Waterloo without

Blücher and Gneisenau . . . What would the fight in North Africa be without the brilliant fencing artistry of General Rommel?"[19] Or there is Hitler, on the very night that he returned to East Prussia after having been notified of the Stalingrad encirclement. Was he discussing the possibilities of a breakout? The modalities of the upcoming air supply effort? The potential order of battle for the relief offensive? It turned out to be none of these things. He wasn't contemplating the future, but thinking of history: "We must show firmness of character in misfortune," he told Chief of General Staff General Kurt Zeitzler. "We must remember Frederick the Great."[20]

Indeed, there may have been more at work than playacting in that dramatic moment late in the war when Hitler first heard of the death of President Franklin Roosevelt. History seemed to be repeating itself. Just as the death of Czarina Elizabeth II had saved Frederick the Great's Prussia at the last moment, so too might Roosevelt's death save Hitler's Germany. Hitler was many things in the course of his life: a starving artist, the idol of millions, an ideologue, a mass murderer. In that split second, however, when a last glimmer of hope flashed through the Führerbunker, he was nothing other than the last of the Hohenzollerns.

Historian Omer Bartov has described a "demodernization" of the Wehrmacht that took place in the course of the fighting in the east.[21] Within the specific limits of his thesis, he is correct. The severity of the fighting tore apart the bonds of modern social and relational life inside the army, a vacuum that was filled by Hitler worship and by National Socialism's murderous racialist ideology. Speaking strictly of the army's operational characteristics, however, it is not an appropriate term. The Wehrmacht never demodernized operationally. In its bedrock conceptions of battle and campaigns, in its emphasis on the genius and the will of the commander over material factors, it wasn't all that modern to begin with.

Notes

Introduction

1. Within the historiography of World War II, there is no more common phrase than "turning point." For its use in connection with the year 1942, see, among many others, Geoffrey Jukes, *Stalingrad: The Turning Point* (New York: Ballantine, 1968); Alan Wykes, *1942—The Turning Point* (London: Macdonald, 1972); and the commercial war game ("conflict simulation" to the *grognards* who play them), *Turning Point—Stalingrad* (Baltimore: Avalon Hill Game Company, 1989), designed by Donald J. Greenwood. The concept is also implicit in the periodization used in the two-volume series on the Russo-German war in the U.S. Army Historical Series: Earl F. Ziemke and Magna E. Bauer, *Moscow to Stalingrad: Decision in the East* (Washington, D.C.: Center of Military History, 1987); and Earl F. Ziemke, *Stalingrad to Berlin: The German Defeat in the East* (Washington, D.C.: Center of Military History, 1968); and the two-volume history of the eastern front by John Erickson, *The Road to Stalingrad* (New York: Harper & Row, 1975) and *The Road to Berlin: Continuing the History of Stalin's War with Germany* (Boulder, Colo.: Westview Press, 1983). For a careful and nuanced German point of view, see Andreas Kunz, "Vor sechzig Jahren: Der Untergang der 6. Armee in Stalingrad," *Militärgeschichte*, no. 4 (2002): 8–17, especially the sidebar on 13, "Stalingrad—Wendepunkt des Zweiten Weltkrieges?"

2. See Winston S. Churchill, *The Second World War*, vol. 4, *The Hinge of Fate* (Boston: Houghton Mifflin, 1950). For a sophisticated analysis of the origins, composition, and historical context of Churchill's six-volume masterwork (1948–1953), see David Reynolds, *In Command of History: Churchill Fighting and Writing the Second World War* (New York: Random House, 2005).

3. Winston S. Churchill, *The Second World War*, vol. 3, *The Grand Alliance* (Boston: Houghton Mifflin, 1951). For Churchill's survey of the career of his illustrious forebear, see also *Marlborough: His Life and Times* (Chicago: University of Chicago Press, 2002), which combines the four original volumes, issued from 1933 to 1938, into two.

4. For a discussion of this point, see Robert M. Citino, *The German Way of War: From the Thirty Years' War to the Third Reich* (Lawrence: University Press of Kansas, 2005), esp. 4–5.

5. See, for example, Major Bigge, "Über Selbstthätigkeit der Unterführer im Kriege," in *Beihefte zum Militär-Wochenblatt* (Berlin: E. S. Mittler, 1894), 17–55; and General von Blume, "Selbstthätigkeit der Führer im Kriege," in *Beihefte zum Militär-Wochenblatt* (Berlin: E. S. Mittler, 1896), 479–534. For a discussion of the issue, see Citino, *German Way of War*, 308.

6. For the nearly forgotten battle of Langensalza, see Geoffrey Wawro, *The Austro-Prussian War: Austria's War With Prussia and Italy in 1866* (Cambridge: Cambridge University Press, 1996), 75–81. Wawro is a meticulous scholar and a fine writer, one of the best working today; his work has largely superseded the earlier standard on the 1866 war, Gordon A. Craig's *The Battle of Königgrätz: Prussia's Victory over Austria, 1866* (Philadelphia: Lippincott, 1964). See also the still useful older sources, such as Oscar von Lettow-Vorbeck, *Geschichte des Krieges von 1866 in Deutschland*, vol. 1, *Gastein-Langensalza* (Berlin: E. S. Mittler, 1896), an analysis by a General Staff officer accompanied by excellent maps; and Theodor Fontane, *Der deutsche Krieg von, 1866*, vol. 2, *Der Feldzug in West- und Mitteldeutschland* (Berlin: R. v. Decker, 1871), a popular account from one of Prussia's best known writers and novelists. For a synthesis, see Citino, *German Way of War*, 153–60.

7. Once again, today's historian of record for the Franco-Prussian War is Geoffrey Wawro. See *The Franco-Prussian War: The German Conquest of France in 1870–1871* (Cambridge: Cambridge University Press, 2003), which has now largely superseded the earlier standard work by Michael Howard, *The Franco-Prussian War* (New York: Macmillan, 1962). For the reaction of the Prussian high command to Steinmetz's near debacle, see Wawro, *Franco-Prussian War*, 110. Dennis Showalter's *Wars of German Unification* (London: Arnold, 2004) places all three wars firmly into their historical contexts in often surprising ways and continues the tradition he began with *Wars of Frederick the Great* (London: Longman, 1996) in devoting unparalleled attention to the question of soldierly motivation. Arden Bucholz, *Moltke and the German Wars, 1864–1871* (New York: Palgrave, 2001), is also indispensable, an operational history that is firmly grounded in issues of organizational and management theory. The primary source is Helmuth von Moltke, *The Franco-German War of 1870–71* (New York: Howard Fertig, 1988). See also Daniel J. Hughes, ed., *Moltke on the Art of War: Selected Writings* (Novato, Calif.: Presidio, 1993), an indispensable selection of Moltke's works, smoothly translated and incisively annotated.

8. Hermann von François deserves a military biography in English. Until then, Randy R. Talbot, "General Hermann von François and Corps-Level Operations during the Tannenberg Campaign, August 1914" (master's thesis, Eastern Michigan University, 1999), offers solid operational-level analysis. On the Tannenberg campaign generally, the standard work is Dennis E. Showalter, *Tannenberg: Clash of Empires* (Washington, D.C.: Brassey's, 2004), exhaustively researched, a delight to read, and perceptive in its insight (the true strength of all Showalter's operational histories) into just what makes officers and men tick under stressful conditions. Norman Stone, *The Eastern Front, 1914–1917* (London: Hodder and Stoughton, 1975), is still indispensable for any inquiry into the war between the Central Powers and Russia, and so is Holger H. Herwig, *The First World War: Germany and*

Austria-Hungary, 1914–1918 (London: Arnold, 1997). A detailed German account of operations, with essential maps, is to be found in an article by Lieutenant Colonel Ponath, "Die Schlacht bei Tannenberg 1914 in kriegsgeschichtlicher, taktischer, und erzieherischer Auswertung," *Militär-Wochenblatt* 124, no. 8 (August 18, 1939): 476–82.

9. For Kolin, see Citino, *German Way of War*, 69–71.

10. Showalter, *Wars of Frederick the Great*, 186. For the Rossbach campaign, start with the official history by the German General Staff, *Die Kriege Friedrichs des Grossen*, pt. 3, *Die siebenjährige Krieg*, vol. 5, *Hastenbeck und Rossbach* (Berlin: Ernst Mittler, 1903); and the useful summary in Curt Jany, *Geschichte der königlich preussischen Armee bis zum Jahre 1807*, vol. 2, *Die Armee Friedrichs des Grossen 1740 bis 1763* (Berlin: Karl Siegismund, 1928), 426–45. Hugo Freiherr von Freytag-Loringhoven, *Feldherrengrösse: Von Denken und Handeln hervorragender Heerführer* (Berlin: E. S. Mittler, 1922), 65–67, provides another view from the German General Staff. See also Citino, *German Way of War*, 72–82. As with any topic dealing with the career of Frederick the Great, one should also consult the works of Christopher Duffy, who has spent a long and fruitful career analyzing the life and times of the king. See especially *The Army of Frederick the Great* (London: David & Charles, 1974) and *Frederick the Great: A Military Life* (London: Routledge and Kegan Paul, 1985).

11. For the German view of "inner" and "outer" lines, see General Ludwig, "Die Operation auf der inneren und der äusseren Linie im Lichte underer Zeit," *Militär-Wochenblatt* 126, no. 1 (July 4, 1941): 7–10.

12. For Prince Henry, once praised by his brother as "the general who never made a mistake," see Richard Schmitt, *Prinz Heinrich als Feldherr im Siebenjährigen Kriege*, 2 vols. (Greifswald: Julius Abel, 1885–1899). For a more modern look at the prince, an important figure due for an updated biography, see Chester V. Easum, *Prince Henry of Prussia: Brother of Frederick the Great* (Westport, Conn.: Greenwood Press, 1971), a reprint of the original 1942 work.

13. For the Jena campaign, as for everything Napoleonic, begin with the magisterial work by David G. Chandler, *The Campaigns of Napoleon* (New York: Macmillan, 1966), esp. 479–88 and 502–6. Robert B. Asprey, *The Reign of Napoleon Bonaparte* (New York: Basic Books, 2001), 20–34, is also useful. See also Citino, *German Way of War*, 109–19. Much of the work on Jena is now old, although it is by no means obsolete. See the early twentieth-century works by Colonel F. N. Maude, *1806: The Jena Campaign* (London: Swan Sonnenschein, 1909), reprinted as *The Jena Campaign, 1806* (London: Greenhill, 1998); and F. Loraine Petre, *Napoleon's Conquest of Prussia, 1806* (London: John Lane, 1914). For the campaign after Jena, see Colmar Baron von der Goltz, *Jena to Eylau: The Disgrace and the Redemption of the Old-Prussian Army* (New York, E. P. Dutton, 1913).

14. For Königgrätz, see Wawro, *Austro-Prussian War*, 208–73, stressing both "Benedek's stand in the Bystrice pocket" and "Moltke's envelopment." See also Craig, *Battle of Königgrätz*, 87–164; Robert M. Citino, *Quest for Decisive Victory: From Stalemate to Blitzkrieg in Europe, 1899–1940* (Lawrence: University Press of Kansas, 2002), 21–25; and Citino, *German Way of War*, 160–73.

15. The work of Terence Zuber has been instrumental in revising hoary old clichés about the Schlieffen Plan. See especially his book *Inventing the Schlieffen Plan: German War Planning, 1871–1914* (Oxford: Oxford University Press, 2002), and the seminal article on which it was based, "The Schlieffen Plan Reconsidered," *War in History* 6, no. 3 (July 1999): 262–305; and most recently, his edited sourcebook, *German War Planning, 1891–1914: Sources and Interpretations* (Rochester, N.Y.: Boydell Press, 2004). Zuber argues that the "Schlieffen Plan" is a postwar construction. He notes that there is no printed reference to the plan until 1920, and that the first operational history of the war, Swiss historian Hermann Stegemann's *Geschichte des Krieges* (Stuttgart: Deutsche Verlags-Anstalt, 1918), didn't even mention it at all. It was, in fact, a myth created by the postwar officer corps to help explain the German defeat. Schlieffen had a perfect plan for victory, they claimed, which his successor, the inept General Helmuth von Moltke (the Younger), had unfortunately "watered down." Zuber's work is convincing but controversial. Because he is attempting the always difficult task of proving a negative, he necessarily has to base the argument not on documents, but on the lack thereof. It is possible today to speak, as one scholar does, of "a *Schlieffenstreit* of sorts." See Antulio J. Echevarria II's review of Zuber's *German War Planning* in *Journal of Military History* 69, no. 4 (October 2005): 1228–29, as well as the prickly back and forth between Echevarria and Zuber in the "Letters" section of the April 2006 issue (70, no. 2, 584–85).

16. For the Romanian campaign, see the primary source, General Erich von Falkenhayn, *Der Feldzug der 9. Armee gegen die Rumänen und Russen, 1916/17* (Berlin: E. S. Mittler, 1921). Other German sources include "Truppen-Kriegsgeschichte, Beispiel 9: Turnu Severin 1916," 2 parts, *Militär-Wochenblatt* 123, no. 17–18 (October 21, 1938; October 28, 1938): 1078–81, 1146–50; Lieutenant Colonel Ponath, "Feuerüberfälle gegen lohnende Augenblicksziele: Kämpfe der Abteilung Picht (verst. I./I.R. 148) vom 20.11. bis 6.12. 1916 bei Turnu-Severin und am Alt in der Schlacht in Rumänien," *Militär-Wochenblatt* 112, no. 35 (March 18, 1928): 1344–46; and by the same author, "Aus grosser Zeit vor zwanzig Jahren: Der Einbruch in die rumänische Ebene," *Militär-Wochenblatt* 121, no. 21 (December 4, 1936): 1101–3. For a modern synthesis, see Jacob Lee Hamric, "Germany's Decisive Victory: Falkenhayn's Campaign in Romania, 1916" (master's thesis, Eastern Michigan University, 2004).

17. For an overview of the planning, execution, and collapse of Operation Blue, see Robert M. Citino, *Blitzkrieg to Desert Storm: The Evolution of Operational Warfare* (Lawrence: University Press of Kansas, 2004), 83–93.

18. For Hitler's "zweiter Feldzug," see the German official history of World War II, written under the auspices of the Militärgeschichtliches Forschungsamt (Military Historical Research Office), *Das Deutsche Reich und Der Zweite Weltkrieg*, vol. 6, *Der Globale Krieg: Die Ausweitung zum Weltkrieg und der Wechsel der Initiative, 1941–1943* (Stuttgart: Deutsche Verlags-Anstalt, 1990), esp. 761–815, written by Bernd Wegner. It is unfair to label this an "official history," with all the connotations of special pleading, silence on controversial matters, and protection of both personal and institutional reputations that the term usually implies. The German

official history is the product of teams of some of Germany's most noted scholars, and it rarely pulls a punch. It is *Kriegsgeschichte* ("war history") in its broadest form, with the most comprehensive treatment imaginable of every topic from the tactical details of submarine warfare to precise calculations of Soviet manganese production. It is also an excellent campaign history. It deserves wider distribution and readership.

19. For more on this point, see Showalter, *Wars of Frederick the Great*, 1, a marvelous discussion of the two conflicting schools of traditional military historiography, which he calls "Whigs" and "Calvinists." The former analyzes war as "a contest between progress and obscurantism," while the latter sees "victory and defeat as judgments on the militarily righteous."

20. For arguments on behalf of the continued relevance of operational history, see Bernd Wegner, "Wozu Operationsgeschichte?" and Dennis E. Showalter, "Militärgeschichte als Operationsgeschichte: Deutsche und amerikanische Paradigmen," both in *Was ist Militärgeschichte?*, ed. Benjamin Ziemann and Thomas Kühne (Paderborn: Ferdinand Schöningh, 2000).

Chapter 1. From Victory to Defeat: 1941

1. For Case White, begin with the belated "official history" commissioned by the Militärgeschichtliches Forschungsamt, *Das Deutsche Reich und Der Zweite Weltkrieg*, vol. 2, *Die Errichtung der hegemonie auf dem Europäischen Kontinent* (Stuttgart: Deutsche Verlags-Anstalt, 1979), especially "Hitler's Erster 'Blitzkrieg' und seine Auswirkungen auf Nordosteuropa," 79–156. Labeling this "official history" is misleading; it is far more a meticulously researched critical history by a team of crack scholars. Robert M. Kennedy, *The German Campaign in Poland, 1939*, Department of the Army Pamphlet 20-255 (Washington, D.C.: Department of the Army, 1956), continues to dominate the field; and Matthew Cooper, *The German Army, 1933–1945* (Chelsea, Mich.: Scarborough House, 1978), 169–76, is still useful. Pat McTaggart, "Poland '39," *Command*, no. 17 (July–August 1992): 57; and David T. Zabecki, "Invasion of Poland: Campaign that Launched a War," *World War II* 14, no. 3 (September 1999): 26 ff., are written for the popular audience, but are no less insightful for that. See also the memoir literature: Heinz Guderian, *Panzer Leader* (New York: Ballantine, 1957), 46–63; Erich von Manstein, *Lost Victories* (Novato, Calif.: Presidio, 1982), 22–63; and Friedrich Wilhelm von Mellenthin, *Panzer Battles: A Study of the Employment of Armor in the Second World War* (New York: Ballantine, 1956), 3–9. Steven Zaloga and Victory Madej, *The Polish Campaign* (New York: Hippocrene, 1991), is indispensable, still the only work in English based on the Polish sources. For a blow-by-blow account while it was happening, see "Deutschlands Abwehrkrieg von 1939," pt. 1, "Die Ereignisse im Osten vom 1. bis 9. September," *Militär-Wochenblatt* 124, no. 12 (September 15, 1939): 729–33; pt. 2, "Die Ereignisse im Osten vom 9. September bis 16. September," *Militär-Wochenblatt* 124, no. 13 (September 22, 1939): 769–74; and pt. 3, "Die Ereignisse in Polen vom 17. bis 24. September," *Militär-Wochenblatt* 124, no. 14 (October 1, 1939): 809–13. A most recent scholarly

work melds German army operations and Hitler's murderous racial designs on Poland into a single chilling account; Alexander B. Rossino, *Hitler Strikes Poland: Blitzkrieg, Ideology, and Atrocity* (Lawrence: University Press of Kansas, 2003).

2. For *Weserübung*, Adam R. A. Claasen, *Hitler's Northern War: The Luftwaffe's Ill-Fated Campaign, 1940–1945* (Lawrence: University Press of Kansas, 2001), remains the definitive portrait of this triphibious (air, land, and sea) campaign. James S. Corum offers another excellent contribution to his already impressive list of works on the German army with "The German Campaign in Norway as a Joint Operation," *Journal of Strategic Studies* 21, no. 4 (1998): 50–77, which compares the record of German interservice cooperation with that of the Allies, much to the disadvantage of the latter. Erich Raeder's memoir, *Grand Admiral* (New York: Da Capo Press, 2001), is a new edition of a venerable primary source; see esp. 300–318. For a fine operational summary of the Danish campaign, see Major Macher, "Die Besetzung Dänemarks," *Militär-Wochenblatt* 125, no. 45 (May 9, 1941): 1791–93, written on the occasion of the campaign's first anniversary.

3. For Case Yellow, the best scholarly work is Karl-Heinz Frieser, *The Blitzkrieg Legend: The 1940 Campaign in the West* (Annapolis: Naval Institute Press, 2005), a welcome English-language edition of the 1995 work *Blitzkrieg-Legende: Der Westfeldzug 1940*. Not only was it a detailed and comprehensive look at this most successful of modern military campaigns, but it also staked out bold revisionist terrain that called into question all of the received wisdom about Case Yellow. Hardly the inevitable victory of a *Blitzkrieg*-oriented army, Frieser's vision of the 1940 campaign was instead filled with chance and contingency and the fog of war on both sides. It wasn't simply a victory of German armor, virtually all of which was vastly inferior to that of the Allies, but rather a victory for superior doctrine. Frieser therefore moved the discussion from hardware factors to areas of software: planning, command and control, logistics, and information. The author is a *Bundeswehr* officer-scholar publishing under the auspices of the official Military History Research Institute in Potsdam. He had access to the complete documentary record, stored in archives with which he is intimately familiar. For the planning of the offensive, see the crucial article by Hans-Adolf Jacobsen, "Hitlers Gedanken zur Kriegführung im Westen," *Wehrwissenschaftliche Rundschau* 5, no. 10 (October 1955): 433–46. All subsequent work on the topic has been a commentary on this article, including Hans-Adolf Jacobsen, *Fall Gelb: Der Kampf um den deutschen Operationsplan zur Westoffensive 1940* (Wiesbaden: F. Steiner, 1957). See also the official history, Militärgeschichtliches Forschungsamt (Military Historical Research Office), *Das Deutsche Reich und der Zweite Weltkrieg*, vol. 2, *Die Errichtung der Hegemonie auf dem Europäischen Kontinent* (Stuttgart: Deutsche Verlags-Anstalt, 1979), especially the portions written by Hans Umbreit, "Der Kampf um die Vormachtstellung in Westeuropa" (233–327). The standard works in English are Jeffrey A. Gunsburg, *Divided and Conquered: The French High Command and the Defeat in the West, 1940* (Westport, Conn.: Greenwood, Press, 1979); and especially Robert A. Doughty, *The Breaking Point: Sedan and the Fall of France, 1940* (Hamden, Conn.: Archon, 1990). For the role of Guderian's Panzers in the campaign, see the monograph by Florian K. Rothbrust, *Guderian's XIXth Panzer Corps and the*

Battle of France: Breakthrough in the Ardennes, May 1940 (Westport, Conn.: Praeger, 1990). Finally, even with all these scholarly riches, there will always be those who turn to the fine popular account by Alistair Horne, *To Lose a Battle: France, 1940* (Boston: Little, Brown, 1969).

4. There is an immense literature on the Crete campaign. The best scholarly account is Ian McDougall Guthrie Stewart, *The Struggle for Crete 20 May–1 June 1941: A Story of Lost Opportunity* (London: Oxford University Press, 1966), a book that has aged well in the thirty-six years since it was published. The text is lucid and the criticism of both the German attackers and the Commonwealth defenders is judicious. See, in particular, the discussion on 481–83. The best short introduction, probably still the most widely read account of the campaign, is Hanson Baldwin, *Battles Lost and Won: Great Campaigns of World War II* (New York: Harper & Row, 1966), 57–113 ("Crete—The Winged Invasion"). See also D. M. Davin, *Crete: Official History of New Zealand in the Second World War, 1939–45* (Wellington, N.Z.: War History Branch, 1953), still an authoritative voice, and particularly so when discussing the unfortunate role of the 5th New Zealand Brigade during the Maleme fighting; Baron Friedrich August von der Heydte, *Daedalus Returned: Crete, 1941* (London: Hutchinson, 1958), the account by a German airborne battalion commander; and Hans-Otto Mühleisen, *Kreta, 1941: Das Unternehemen Merkur, 20. Mai–1. Juni 1941* (Freiburg: Rombach, 1968), a trenchant account published by the Federal Republic of Germany's Militärgeschichtliches Forschungsamt, including a great deal of primary documentation from the German side. Finally, for a postwar analysis by German officers (part of the German Report Series), see "Airborne Operations: A German Appraisal" (Washington, D.C.: Center of Military History, 1989). One still little-used German primary source is the unpublished manuscript by Conrad Seibt, *Einsatz Kreta Mai 1941*, German Report Series B-641 (Headquarters United States Army, Europe: Foreign Military Studies Branch, n.d.), by the quartermaster of the XI Fleigerkorps during the campaign. A copy of the report, along with the rest of this immense series, is on file in the U.S. Army Military History Institute in Carlisle, Pa.

5. The term *blitzkrieg*, usually credited to American journalists, can actually be found here and there in the professional literature of the prewar period. It signified any rapid and complete victory, although the Germans never did use it in any precise sense. For the earliest printed use of the term that I have found, see Lieutenant Colonel Braun, "Der strategische Überfall," *Militär-Wochenblatt* 123, no. 18 (October 28, 1938): 1134–36, although the sense here is that the word has been already been in use: "Nach dem Zeitungsnachrichten hatten die diesjährigen französischen Manöver den Zweck, die Bedeutung des strategischen Überfalls—auch 'Blitzkrieg' genannt—zu prüfen" (1134). For later uses, see Lieutenant Colonel Köhn, "Die Infanterie im 'Blitzkrieg.'" *Militär-Wochenblatt* 125, no. 5 (August 2, 1940): 165–66, where "blitzkrieg" is used only in quotation marks and is described as a "buzzword" (*Schlagwort*); and Colonel Rudolf Theiss, "Der Panzer in der Weltgeschichte," *Militär-Wochenblatt* 125, no. 15 (October 11, 1940): 705–8, which likewise uses the term in quotes. By 1941, German usage in literature had dropped the quotation marks, although the word was still not used in any sort of

precise technical sense. See Lieutenant Colonel Gaul, "Der Blitzkrieg in Frankreich," *Militär-Wochenblatt* 125, no. 35 (February 28, 1941): 1513–17.

6. For the best scholarly discussion of the Experimental Mechanized Force, see Harold R. Winton, *To Change an Army: General Sir John Burnett-Stuart and British Armored Doctrine, 1927–1938* (Lawrence: University Press of Kansas, 1988), 72–94. Robert H. Larson, *The British Army and the Theory of Armored Warfare* (Newark: University of Delaware Press, 1984), 133–47; and J. Harris, *Men, Ideas, and Tanks: British Military Thought and Armoured Forces, 1903–1939*. Manchester: Manchester University Press, 1995), 217–19, continue to be useful.

7. Looking back on his service in the interwar German army (*Reichswehr*), Captain Adolph Reinicke described the training of the officers as focusing on two principles: "*Bewegungskrieg* and the close cooperation of the arms." Adolf Reinicke, *Das Reichsheer, 1921–1934: Ziele, Methoden der Ausbildung und Erziehung sowie der Dienstgestaltung* (Osnabrück: Biblio Verlag, 1986), 220.

8. For the origins of the Panzer division, see two works by Robert M. Citino, *Armored Forces: History and Sourcebook* (Westport, Conn.: Greenwood Press, 1994), 50–57, and *Quest for Decisive Victory: From Stalemate to Blitzkrieg in Europe, 1899–1940* (Lawrence: University Press of Kansas, 2002), 193–210. For the 1937 Fall Maneuver, the first to feature a Panzer division in action, see Citino, *The Path to Blitzkrieg: Doctrine and Training in the German Army, 1920–1939* (Boulder, Colo.: Lynne Rienner, 1999), 236–42. The works of Richard M. Ogorkiewicz are also indispensable, especially *Armoured Forces: A History of Armoured Forces and Their Vehicles* (New York: Arco, 1970). Virtually the entire body of interwar German writings about armor stresses the importance of the cooperation of all arms with the tanks. To give just one example of hundreds from the pages of the *Militär-Wochenblatt*, see Helmut Burckhardt, "Grosstanks oder Massenangriff mit unzureichend gepanzerten Tanks," *Militär-Wochenblatt* 122, no. 3 (July 16, 1937): 143–44: "Schließlich kämpfen die Panzer ja nicht allein . . . , sondern werden von allen möglichen Waffen unterstützt" (143). See also the writings of Heinz Guderian, both from the day and later. *Achtung—Panzer! The Development of Armored Forces, Their Tactics, and Operational Potential* (London: Arms and Armour Press, 1992) is a translation of Guderian's seminal work from 1937; Guderian's *Panzer Leader* is his postwar retelling of the tale. See also the two articles that formed the basis for *Achtung—Panzer!*: "Kraftfahrtruppen," *Militärwissenschaftliche Rundschau* 1, no. 1 (1936): 52–77; and "Die Panzertruppen und ihr Zusammenwirken mit den anderen Waffen," *Militärwissenschaftliche Rundschau* 1, no. 5 (1936): 607–26. Guderian was just one of many German officers discussing these concepts, however. See, for example, General Ludwig von Eimannsberger, "Panzertaktik," pt. 1 *Militär-Wochenblatt* 120, no. 23 (December 18, 1935): 981–85; and pt. 2, *Militär-Wochenblatt* 120, no. 24 (December 25, 1935): 1027–30; and the body of work by Colonel Walter Spannenkrebs, especially *Angriff mit Kampfwagen* (Oldenburg: Gerhard Stalling, 1939) and "Infanterie und Panzer," *Militär-Wochenblatt* 123, no. 7 (August 12, 1938): 402–4. Finally, for the importance of radio communications to the Panzer division, see Friedrich Bertkau, "Die nachrichtentechnische Führung mechanisierter Verbände," *Militär-Wochenblatt* 120, no. 15 (October 18, 1935): 611; and an unsigned

article, "Divisionsführung und Befehlstechnik," *Militär-Wochenblatt* 116, no. 44 (May 18, 1932): 1540–42.

9. *Auftragstaktik* has had a convoluted history. Seen by scholars as a type of wonder weapon in the German arsenal, and coveted by operators in modern western militaries, especially the U.S. Army, it is, like the term *blitzkrieg*, one of those German terms that has had more of a life outside of Germany than inside it. For the record, it appears hardly at all in the professional literature of the twentieth-century German army. For the derivation of the term, see Antulio J. Echevarria II, *After Clausewitz: German Military Thinkers before the Great War* (Lawrence: University Press of Kansas, 2000), 32–42 and 94–103, who warns that "The term *Auftragstaktik* has been greatly abused in military publications in recent years." See also the blizzard of articles in the late 1980s in *Military Review*, the journal of the U.S. Army Command and General Staff College at Fort Leavenworth, Kans., the U.S. equivalent of the *Militär-Wochenblatt* or the *Militärwissenschaftiche Rundschau:* Roger A. Beaumont, "On the Wehrmacht Mystique," *Military Review* 66, no. 7 (1986): 44–56; Antulio J. Echevarria II, "*Auftragstaktik:* In Its Proper Perspective," *Military Review* 66, no. 10 (October 1986); Daniel J. Hughes, "Abuses of German Military History," *Military Review* 66, no. 12 (December 1986): 66–76; and Martin van Creveld, "On Learning from the Wehrmacht and Other Things," *Military Review* 68, no. 1 (1988): 62–71. The Hughes article, especially, is essential on the difficulty of borrowing terms from other tongues when the U.S. officer corps has so little knowledge of foreign languages. For more, see Robert M. Citino, *The German Way of War: From the Thirty Years' War to the Third Reich* (Lawrence: University Press of Kansas, 2005), 32–33, 61–62, 170–72, and 306–11.

10. See the memorial article on the 200th anniversary of the Marshal's birth. Eberhard Kessel, "Blücher: Zum 200. Geburtstag am 16. Dezember," *Militärwissenschaftliche Rundschau* 7, no. 4 (1942): 303–13.

11. See especially the essay by the great and testy German military historian Hans Delbrück, "Prinz Friedrich Karl," in *Historische und Politische Aufsätze* (Berlin: Georg Stilke, 1907), 302–16. See also Lieutenant Foerster, "Prinz Friedrich Karl," *Militärwissenschaftliche Rundschau* 8, no. 2 (1943): 89–94.

12. "Seitdem mit dem Ende des Winters die deutschen Waffen wieder ihre vernehmliche Sprache zu reden begonnen haben," in *Grossdeutschlands Freiheitskrieg*, pt. 145, "Die deutsche Frühjahrsoperation auf der Krim," *Militär-Wochenblatt* 126, no. 47 (May 22, 1942): 1345–48. The quote is from 1345.

13. The Balkan campaign garnered its share of attention at the time and in the immediate postwar years, but it seems to have fallen off the historiographical radar screen since then. It is due for a modern, multilingual scholarly monograph. The best place to start, as always for the German army in World War II, is with the official history, commissioned by the Militärgeschichtliches Forschungsamt (Military Historical Research Office), vol. 3, *Der Mittelmeerraum und Südosteuropa: Von der "non-belligeranza" Italiens bis zum Kriegseintritt der Vereinigten Staaten* (Stuttgart: Deutsche Verlags-Anstalt, 1984), especially pt. 3, written by Detlef Vogel, "Das Eingreifen Deutschlands auf dem Balkan," 417–511. Janusz Piekalkiewicz, *Krieg auf dem Balkan* (Munich: Südwest Verlag, 1984), is useful in terms of both

text and photographs. In English, George E. Blau, *The German Campaign in the Balkans (Spring 1941)*, Department of the Army Pamphlet 20-260 (Washington, D.C.: Department of the Army, 1953), has of necessity been the go-to work for a long time now—perhaps too long. Part of the venerable German Report Series, it assembles the testimony of a number of German officers who took part in the campaign; the foreword mentions Helmut Greiner, General Burkhard H. Mueller-Hillebrand, and General Hans von Greiffenberg (iii). It has all the virtues (primary source testimony) and defects (the German officers being interviewed often did not have access to their war diaries, correspondence, or maps) that we associate with this series, which often matches excruciatingly detailed testimony with surprisingly superficial analysis. It needs to be supplemented with other sources. For the German Report Series and its impact on the postwar U.S. Army, see Kevin Soutor, "To Stem the Red Tide: The German Report Series and its Effect on American Defense Doctrine, 1948–1954," *Journal of Military History* 57, no. 4 (October 1993): 653–88. For a German wartime view of "this wonderful operation, which in its excellence can stand beside the summer 1940 campaign in France," see General von Tieschowitz, "Der Feldzug im Südosten," and the anonymously authored "Olymp—Thermopylen—Athen," both in Oberkommando der Wehrmacht, ed., *Die Wehrmacht: Um die Freiheit Europas* (Berlin: Verlag "Die Wehrmacht," 1941), 154–67 and 186–97, respectively; and the pertinent articles in the ongoing wartime series *Grossdeutschlands Freiheitskrieg*, pt. 88, "Eine Woche der Siege," *Militär-Wochenblatt* 125, no. 42 (April 18, 1941): 1705–9; pt. 89, "Kapitulation Jugoslawiens. Kroatien selbständig. Durchbruch durch die Front in Griechenland," *Militär-Wochenblatt* 125, no. 43 (April 25, 1941), 1731–36; pt. 90, "Kapitulation der griechischen Hauptarmee. Athen und Korinth besetzt," *Militär-Wochenblatt* 125, no. 44 (May 2, 1941), 1759–64; and pt. 91, "Abschluss der Kämpfe in Griechenland," *Militär-Wochenblatt* 125, no. 45 (May 9, 1941), 1787–91. For the use of specialist troops in the campaign, see Lieutenant Günther Heysing, "Pionere auf dem Balkan," and Hans Rechenberg, "Fallschirmjäger im Sudösten," both in *Die Wehrmacht*, 168–74 and 198–207, respectively, as well as Egid Gehring, ed., *Unterm Edelweiss in Jugoslawien: Aus den Erlebnissen einer Gebirgsdivision* (Munich: Franz Eher, 1941). For a journalistic account by two German war correspondents, sensationalist yet still helpful on the mood of the times, see Heinz Hünger and Ernst Erich Strassl, *Kampf und Intrige um Griechenland* (Munich: Franz Eher, 1942). For the German view of Yugoslav operations, see "Ein Überblick über die Operationen des jugoslawischen Heeres im April 1941 (Dargestellt nach jugoslawischen Quellen)," pt. 1, "Die Mobilmachung und die Kämpfe vom 6. bis 8. April," in *Militärwissenschaftliche Rundschau* 7, no. 3 (1942): 276–88; and pt. 2, "Die Kämpfe vom 9. April bis zum Abschluss des Waffenstillstandes am 17. April," *Militärwissenschaftliche Rundschau* 7, no. 4 (1942): 387–99. For the German view of Greek operations, see "Ein Überblick über die Operationen des griechischen Heeres und des britischen Expeditionskorps im April 1941," pt. 1, "Die griechischen Verteidigungspläne, die Mobilmachung und der Aufmarsch der verbündeten Streitkräfte," in *Militärwissenschaftliche Rundschau* 8, no. 1 (1943): 67–87; and pt. 2, "Die Operationen der verbündeten Streitkräfte bis zum Rückzuge des britischen

Expeditionskorps aus Griechenland," *Militärwissenschaftliche Rundschau* 8, no. 2 (1943): 167–78. The memoirs of the Greek supreme commander are indispensable: General Alexander Papagos, *The Battle of Greece, 1940–1941* (Athens: Hellenic Publishing, 1949); so is the abridged volume of the Greek official history, Hellenic Army General Staff, *An Abridged History of the Greek-Italian and Greek-German War, 1940–1941: Land Operations* (Athens: Army History Directorate, 1997).

There was a great deal of interest in the campaign within West German military circles after 1945. See, for example, General Kurt von Tippelskirch, "Der deutsche Balkanfeldzug 1941," *Wehrwissenschaftliche Rundschau* 5, no. 2 (February 1955): 49–65; Leo Hepp, "Die 12. Armee im Balkanfeldzug 1941," *Wehrwissenschaftliche Rundschau* 5, no. 5 (May 1955): 199–216; Sigfrid Henrici, "Sarajevo 1941: Der raidartige Vorstoss einer mot. Division," *Wehrwissenschaftliche Rundschau* 10, no. 4 (April 1960), 197–208; and Edgar Röhricht, "Der Balkanfeldzug 1941," *Wehrwissenschaftliche Rundschau* 12, no. 4 (April 1962). See also the short piece on the occasion of Field Marshal List's eightieth birthday, Hermann Foertsch, "Generalfeldmarschall List 80 Jahre Alt," *Wehrwissenschaftliche Rundschau* 10, no. 5 (May 1960): 235–36.

English-language works tend to focus on the British intervention in Greece and ignore the Yugoslavian campaign altogether. Robin Higham, *Diary of a Disaster: British Aid to Greece, 1940–1941* (Lexington: University Press of Kentucky, 1986), is the best book on the topic, carefully researched (the narrative is in diary form, and often goes down to the level of minutes) and nuanced in its argument. It largely superseded the previous standard account, Charles Cruickshank, *Greece, 1940–1941* (London: Davis-Poynter, 1976), although the latter is still useful on certain details. See also Christopher Buckley, *Greece and Crete, 1941* (London: H. M. Stationery Office, 1952), part of the series The Second World War, 1939–1945, "a popular military history by various authors in eight volumes," which has the attraction of offering a comparative discussion of both the failed intervention in Greece and the fighting on Crete. Matthew Willingham, *Perilous Commitments: The Battle for Greece and Crete, 1940–1941* (Staplehurst, Kent: Spellmount, 2005), is another perfectly serviceable and well-written popular account. An exception to the rule of Greek campaign particularism in the Anglo-Saxon historical community is John F. Antal's "Operation 25: The Wehrmacht's Conquest of Yugoslavia," in *Maneuver Warfare: An Anthology*, ed. Richard D. Hooker Jr. (Novato, Calif.: Presidio, 1993), 391–404.

14. Tippelskirch, "Der deutsche Balkanfeldzug 1941," 54; Hepp, "Die 12. Armee," 54.

15. "Ein Überblick über die Operationen des jugoslawischen Heeres im April 1941 (Dargestellt nach jugoslawischen Quellen)," pt. 1, "Die Mobilmachung und die Kämpfe vom 6. bis 8. April," *Militärwissenschaftliche Rundschau* 7, no. 3 (1942): 276–78; Blau, *German Campaign in the Balkans*, 36–37.

16. Nis Petersen, "Polens Vernichtung als Vorschule für den genialen Durchbruch der deutschen Panzerwaffe im Westen," *Militär-Wochenblatt* 125, no. 10 (September 6, 1940): 377.

17. See, for example, John Keegan, *The Second World War* (New York: Penguin, 2005): "But no country has perhaps ever as irrationally dispersed its forces as the Yugoslavs did in April 1941, seeking to defend with ancient rifles and mule-borne mountain artillery one of the longest land frontiers in Europe against Panzer divisions and 2000 modern aircraft" (155).

18. "Ein Überblick über die Operationen des jugoslawischen Heeres im April 1941 (Dargestellt nach jugoslawischen Quellen)," pt. 2, "Die Kämpfe vom 9. April bis zum Abschluss des Waffenstillstandes am 17. April," *Militärwissenschaftliche Rundschau* 7, no. 4 (1942): 392, speaks of "mutiny" (*Meuterei*) among Croat units of the Yugoslav 7th Army.

19. For the vexed question of the relationship between the Balkan campaign and Operation Barbarossa, especially whether the former delayed the latter, see the thoughtful study by Andrew L. Zapantis, *Hitler's Balkan Campaign and the Invasion of the USSR* (Boulder: East European Monographs, 1987). His answer: "Marita and Merkur, Hitler's Balkan campaign and in particular his invasion of Greece and the attack on Crete, delayed the start of the attack on the Soviet Union by about five weeks" (205).

20. For detailed orders of battle of the German *Luftwaffe*, the Italian *Regia Aeronautica*, and the Yugoslav *Kraljevsko Ratno Vazduhoplovstvo* (or JKRV), see Christopher Shores and Brian Cull with Nicola Malizia, *Air War for Yugoslavia, Greece and Crete, 1940–41* (London: Grub Street, 1987), 180–90. Shores and Cull list the attack formations for the Belgrade strike as follows: "74 Ju87s from StG77 were approaching between 8,000 and 10,000 feet, with 160 He111s of II/KG 4 and Do17Zs from KG 2 and 3, with escorting Bf110s at 11,000–12,000 feet, 100 Bf109Es (including 56 aircraft from Stab, II and III/JG 77) providing top cover at 15,000 feet" (195). Piekalkiewicz, *Krieg auf dem Balkan*, lists aircraft of "KG 2, KG 3 und KG 51 der Luftflotte 4," for 486 machines in all (100).

21. Blau, *German Campaign in the Balkans*, 50.

22. See, for example, Antal, "Operation 25," 397.

23. Tippelskirch, "Der deutsche Balkanfeldzug 1941," 60–61.

24. Vogel, "Das Eingreifen Deutschlands auf dem Balkan," 479; Blau, *German Campaign in the Balkans*, 59–60.

25. "Ein Überblick über die Operationen des jugoslawischen Heeres im April 1941," pt. 2, 389.

26. Henrici, "Sarajevo 1941," 205–6.

27. Friedrich Wilhelm von Mellenthin, *Panzer Battles: A Study of the Employment of Armor in the Second World War* (New York: Ballantine, 1956).

28. The phrase is from Alan Palmer, "Operation Punishment," *History of the Second World War*," no. 14 (1978): 374–91. The quote is from 391.

29. "Kapitulation Jugoslawiens," 1731.

30. See Klaus Schmider, *Partisanenkrieg in Jugoslawien, 1941–1944* (Hamburg: E. S. Mittler, 2002), a fascinating portrait of a tail, in this case the Croatian Ustasha movement, wagging the dog of German strategic policy. The standard work in English on German antipartisan operations in Yugoslavia is still Robert M. Kennedy, *German Antiguerrilla Operations in the Balkans, 1941–44*, Department of

the Army Pamphlet 20-243 (Washington, D.C.: Department of the Army, 1954). A great deal of work has come out of late on the antipartisan war in the Soviet Union, especially as it relates to the brutalization of the fighting and the Wehrmacht's slide into mass murder. See, for example, Ben Shepherd, *War in the Wild East: The German Army and Soviet Partisans* (Cambridge, Mass.: Harvard University Press, 2004); and Edward B. Westermann, *Hitler's Police Battalions: Enforcing Racial War in the East* (Lawrence: University Press of Kansas, 2005).

31. For the origins of "Lustre" and "W," see Cruickshank, *Greece, 1940–41*, 105–17, as well as Higham, *Diary of a Disaster*, 94–117.

32. Mellenthin, *Panzer Battles*, 39.

33. Hellenic Army General Staff, *Abridged History*, 173, speaks of "a deployment of all Greek-British forces at the fortified area of Beles [Veles]-Nestos"—far north indeed. The British, by contrast, "supported the abandonment of the Beles-Nestos area and proposed the occupation of the Vermio [Vermion] line instead." See also Sketch Map 21, facing 164. On this question, see also Papagos, *Battle of Greece*, 322–23 and 325–26.

34. Tippelskirch, "Der deutsche Balkanfeldzug 1941," 54–55.

35. Willingham, *Perilous Commitments*, 73–74.

36. Tieschowitz, "Der Feldzug im Südosten," 158–59.

37. Willingham, *Perilous Commitments*, 74. See also Papagos, *Battle of Greece*, 355–56.

38. Blau, *German Campaign in the Balkans*, 86–87.

39. For the retreat, there is no better guide than British armored commander Robert Crisp, *The Gods Were Neutral* (London: Frederick Muller, 1960), a less famous companion piece to his classic on combat in the Western Desert, *Brazen Chariots* (New York: Ballantine, 1961). See esp. 138–56.

40. Willingham, *Perilous Commitments*, 90–91. For a detailed account of the Thermopylae fighting, see the New Zealand Official History, W. G. McGlymont, *To Greece* (Wellington, N.Z.: War History Branch, 1959), esp. 384–99. For the German tanks coming up single file, see 390–93.

41. For the Corinth airdrop, see Piekalkiewicz, *Krieg auf dem Balkan*, 110–11. The account includes a chilling photograph taken by a war correspondent moments before the bridge exploded, killing him and all the paratroopers on it.

42. Crisp, *Gods Were Neutral*, 142–43.

43. The title of an article by German war correspondent Gert Habedanck, "Wir fegten den Tommy vom Kontinent," in *Die Wehrmacht*, 175–85.

44. A classic statement along these lines is Wilhelm Deist, "The Road to Ideological War: Germany, 1918–1945," in *The Making of Strategy: Rulers, States, and War*, ed. Williamson Murray, MacGregor Knox, and Alvin Bernstein (Cambridge: Cambridge University Press, 1994), 352–92. Germany's military leaders "simply ignored" the kind of war they were fighting under Hitler, he argued. "For them, war remained limited to actual combat, and the political and strategic aspects of industrialized warfare were of very limited interest" (392). See also Eric Dorn Brose, *The Kaiser's Army: The Politics of Military Technology in Germany during the Machine Age, 1870–1918* (Oxford: Oxford University Press, 2001), which accuses

the officer corps of technological backwardness and obscurantism. Isabel V. Hull, *Absolute Destruction: Military Culture and the Practices of War in Imperial Germany* (Ithaca, N.Y.: Cornell University Press, 2005), is a more complex work that takes on certain aspects of military culture. Hull condemns what she calls the "hegemony of the operative" (168) within the German military, by which the General Staff tended to boil the complexities of war down to a single, highly destructive battle. In doing so, she argues, it had to train itself to ignore material realities—matters like the balance of forces, the importance of changing technology, and logistical difficulties—and substitute instead specious notions of "will, extreme daring (*Kühnheit*), optimistic recklessness, and one-sided actionism." As a cultural study of the officer corps, the text is first rate. But the text hardly deals with operations at all, and its discussion of military doctrine in the late nineteenth century may make the specialist wince. It also credits all these deleterious operational tendencies solely to the age of Moltke and Schlieffen; Frederick the Great merits a single, unrelated mention in the index. Finally, both Brose and Hull have to portray the Schlieffen Plan as an inevitable failure in order to clinch their arguments—a sense of certainty that might not sit well with all operational historians. Terence Zuber, for example, has argued recently that there was no Schlieffen Plan. Likewise, German operations came far closer than historians have generally realized to a decisive victory at Namur. See Citino, *German Way of War*, 208–18. Also, for an argument that is in many ways the exact opposite of those put forth by Brose and Hull, see Antulio Echevarria II, *After Clausewitz: German Military Thinkers before the Great War* (Lawrence: University Press of Kansas, 2000).

45. Here the works of Williamson Murray and Geoff Megargee have been instrumental. The former has made a career out of puncturing notions of overarching German military excellence. See, for example, Williamson Murray, *The Luftwaffe, 1933–45: Strategy for Defeat* (Washington, D.C.: Brassey's, 1996). In *German Military Effectiveness* (Baltimore: Nautical & Aviation Publishing Company of America, 1992), he admits that the Germans did some things very well indeed (coordination of the combined arms, operational planning) and were horrid at others. In particular, they fought World War II, he argues, without any view of higher strategy. In his "May 1940: Contingency and Fragility of the German RMA," in *The Dynamics of Military Revolution, 1300–2050*, ed. MacGregor Knox and Williamson Murray (Cambridge: Cambridge University Press, 2001), 154–74, he cuts the German victory down to size, reminding us of the role that "contingency" (in this case, French operational ineptitude) played in the triumph. Murray's former student, Geoffrey Megargee, has continued the attack in two successful works of his own, *Inside Hitler's High Command* (Lawrence: University Press of Kansas, 2000) and *War of Annihilation: Combat and Genocide on the Eastern Front, 1941* (New York: Rowman & Littlefield, 2006), the former the book that can truly be said to have demolished the myth of an infallible German General Staff, and the latter a book that ties operational planning for war in the east firmly to Hitler's murderous racial policies.

There is by now a massive literature on the criminal behavior of the Wehrmacht during the war, especially on the eastern front. See, for example, Hamburger Institut für Sozialforschung, ed., *Verbrechen der Wehrmacht: Dimensionen des Vernichtungskrieges, 1941–1944* (Hamburg: Hamburger Edition, 2002), the massive printed catalog that accompanied the celebrated exhibition of the same name; and the collection of essays edited by Hannes Heer and Klaus Naumann, eds., *Vernichtungskrieg: Verbrechen der Wehrmacht, 1941–1944* (Hamburg: Hamburger Edition, 1995), available in English translation as *War of Extermination: The German Military in World War II, 1941–1944* (New York: Berghahn, 2000), although there is not an exact confluence of essays between the two volumes, and the interested researcher should consult both. In the English-language edition, see especially Jan Philipp Reemtsma, "The Concept of the War of Annihilation," 13–38; Manfred Messerschmidt, who more than any other German scholar has worked tirelessly to expose this aspect of the Wehrmacht's history, "Forward Defense: The 'Memorandum of the Generals' for the Nuremberg Court," 381–99; Omer Bartov, about whom the same could be said among American scholars, "Whose History Is it Anyway? The Wehrmacht and German Historiography," 300–416, which casts a critical eye on, among other things, the German official history of the war; and Klaus Naumann, "The 'Unblemished' Wehrmacht: The Soviet History of a Myth," 417–29. For the best synthesis of all these questions, see Wolfgang Wette, *The Wehrmacht: History, Myth, Reality* (Cambridge, Mass.: Harvard University Press, 2006): "In 1941 the generals of the Wehrmacht were prepared to wage an unprecedented kind of war against the Soviet Union, motivated by ideology and designed to exterminate specific ethnic groups within the population. Today these facts are no longer in dispute" (1).

46. F. W. Winterbotham, *The Ultra Secret* (New York: Dell, 1974); and Ronald Lewin, *Ultra Goes to War: The First Account of World War II's Greatest Secret Based on Official Documents* (New York: McGraw-Hill, 1978), were the works that first spilled the beans on this crucial aspect of wartime intelligence. The best account of how the allies cracked the Enigma machine, replete with all the technological details, is R. A. Ratcliff, *Delusions of Intelligence: Enigma, Ultra, and the End of Secure Ciphers* (Cambridge: Cambridge University Press, 2006). Ratcliff is useful in explaining how German institutional and organizational culture played into Allied hands. For an example of the Allies having to cover their tracks, see Niall Barr, *The Pendulum of War: The Three Battles of El Alamein* (New York: Overlook Press, 2005), in which he points out that before Ultra-directed bombers could strike a convoy, it first "had to be visually sighted by an aircraft" (223).

47. Hal Vaughan, *FDR's 12 Apostles: The Spies Who Paved the Way for the Invasion of North Africa* (Guilford, Conn.: Lyons Press, 2006).

48. For the incredible tale of "Garbo," see Hervie Haufler, *The Spies Who Never Were: The True Story of the Nazi Spies Who Were Actually Allied Double Agents* (New York: NAL Caliber, 2006), esp. 190–202.

49. Megargee, *Inside Hitler's High Command*, 93.

50. For a vivid portrayal of the staff at work in a period of crisis, see ibid., 142–69, esp. 168–69.

51. For Barbarossa and the campaigns that followed in the east, one must begin with the German official history, Militärgeschichtliches Forschungsamt (Military

Historical Research Office), *Das Deutsche Reich und Der Zweite Weltkrieg*, vol. 4, *Der Angriff auf die Sowjetunion* (Stuttgart: Deutsche Verlags-Anstalt, 1983), especially the sections authored by Jürgen Förster, "Das Unternhemen 'Barbarossa' als Eroberungs- und Vernichtungskrieg," 413–47; Ernst Klink, "Die Operationsführung: Heer und Kriegsmarine" (451–652); and Horst Boog, "Die Operationsführung: Die Luftwaffe," 652–712. For the state of the historiography in Germany, see Rolf-Dieter Müller and Gerd R. Überschär, *Hitlers Krieg im Osten, 1941–1945: Ein Forschungsbericht* (Darmstadt: Wissenschaftliche Buchgesellschaft, 2000). Two English-language works that profoundly influenced all those that followed are the volumes in the U.S. Army Historical Series: Earl F. Ziemke and Magna E. Bauer, *Moscow to Stalingrad: Decision in the East* (Washington, D.C.: Center of Military History, 1987); and Earl F. Ziemke, *Stalingrad to Berlin: The German Defeat in the East* (Washington, D.C.: Center of Military History, 1968). Both continue to be the best sources for German operational details. The two-volume history of the eastern front by John Erickson, *The Road to Stalingrad* (New York: Harper & Row, 1975) and *The Road to Berlin: Continuing the History of Stalin's War with Germany* (Boulder, Colo.: Westview Press, 1983), was the first to do likewise for the Soviet side. Erickson also deserves special mention for his readable, even inspiring, prose. Another extraordinarily influential book is George E. Blau, *The German Campaign in Russia—Planning and Operation, 1940–1942*, Department of the Army Pamphlet 20-261a (Washington, D.C.: Department of the Army, 1955), once again part of the German Reports Series, with all the pluses and minuses that it entails. The officers being channeled here are General Franz Halder, chief of the General Staff until 1942, General Gotthard Heinrici, "and others" (iii).

The memoir literature has been enormous, almost all of it from the German side. See, for example, Guderian, *Panzer Leader*; Erich von Manstein, *Lost Victories* (Novato, Calif.: Presidio, 1982); and Mellenthin, *Panzer Battles*. More recent additions are Erhard Raus, *Panzer Operations: The Eastern Front Memoir of Erhard Raus, 1941–1945* (New York: Da Capo, 2003), compiled and translated by Stephen H. Newton; and Peter G. Tsouras, *Panzers on the Eastern Front: General Erhard Raus and His Panzer Divisions in Russia, 1941–1945* (London: Greenhill, 2002).

In terms of modern scholarship, David M. Glantz is today the leading western authority, not only on the Soviet military, but also on the Russo-German war. He continues to ply his successful trade, exploiting former Soviet sources that most other historians haven't even heard of, knitting them together with tight prose and often brilliant analysis, and churning out books with frightening regularity. A partial list includes *When Titans Clashed: How the Red Army Stopped Hitler* (Lawrence: University Press of Kansas, 1995), written with Jonathan M. House, a welcome change from traditional analysis that saw Barbarossa strictly in terms of how the Wehrmacht lost it; *Stumbling Colossus: The Red Army on the Eve of World War II* (Lawrence: University Press of Kansas, 1998); *Colossus Reborn: The Red Army at War, 1941–1943* (Lawrence: University Press of Kansas, 2005); and for those unsatisfied with its nearly 800 pages of text, notes, and tables, *Companion to Colossus Reborn* (Lawrence: University Press of Kansas, 2005), which contains "a richer and more complete documentary foundation" than was possible in the earlier work.

Specific operational accounts include *The Battle of Kursk* (Lawrence: University Press of Kansas, 1999), again with Jonathan M. House; *Zhukov's Greatest Defeat: The Red Army's Epic Disaster in Operation Mars, 1942* (Lawrence: University Press of Kansas, 1999); and *The Battle for Leningrad, 1941–1944* (Lawrence: University Press of Kansas, 2002). Needless to say, there will be others.

52. Megargee, *War of Annihilation*, 24.

53. See Constantine Pleshakov, *Stalin's Folly: The Tragic First Ten Days of the World War II on the Eastern Front* (Boston: Houghton Mifflin, 2005), 2, a marvelously written book that skillfully straddles the line between scholarly and popular history, and is marred only by its subscription to the "preventive war" theory, the belief that Stalin was planning an attack on Germany in June 1941, intentions that were just barely forestalled by the German attack. It is a notion for which there is no real documentary evidence, as any number of scholarly works have now established. See the collection of articles in Gerd Überschär and Lev A. Bezymenskij, eds., *Der deutsche Angriff auf die Sowjetunion, 1941: Die Kontroverse um die Präventivkriegsthese* (Darmstadt: Primus, 1998). Especially helpful is the essay by Wolfram Wette, "Die NS-Propagandathese vom angeblichen Präventivkriegscharakter der Überfalls," 38–47, Nikolaj Romaničev, "Militärische Pläne eines Gegenschlags der UdSSR," 77–89, and Lev A. Bezymenskij, "Der sowjetische Nachrichtendienst und Kriegsbeginn von 1941," 103–15.

54. John Lukacs, *June 1941: Hitler and Stalin* (New Haven, Conn.: Yale University Press, 2006), 74–75.

55. Pleshakov, *Stalin's Folly*, 11.

56. The best look at the chaos of the opening phase of the war from the ground up is Catherine Merridale's *Ivan's War: Life and Death in the Red Army, 1939–1945* (New York: Metropolitan Books, 2006), esp. 82–115.

57. Pleshakov, *Stalin's Folly*, 216–17.

58. Ibid., 169–71.

59. For the drive of Army Group North on Leningrad, see the account by the chief of the General Staff of Panzer Group 4, General W. Charles de Beaulieu, *Der Vorstoss der Panzergruppe 4 auf Leningrad* (Neckargemünd: Kurt Rowinckel Verlag, 1961), vol. 29 in the indispensable series Die Wehrmacht im Kampf. A short translated version is available as "Drive to Leningrad: The Baltic States, June–September 1941," *History of the Second World War*, no. 23 (1978): 617–28.

60. The works of Richard L. DiNardo are essential to the importance of horses to German "mechanized" warfare. See *Mechanized Juggernaut or Military Anachronism? Horses and the German Army of World War II* (Westport, Conn.: Greenwood, 1991); and, with Austin Bay, "Horse-Drawn Transport in the German Army," *Journal of Contemporary History* 23, no. 1 (1988): 129–42. See also Megargee, *War of Annihilation*, 29.

61. The primary source for Army Group Center is Fedor von Bock, *Generalfeldmarschall Fedor von Bock: The War Diary, 1939–1945* (Atglen, Pa.: Schiffer Military History, 1996).

62. For Panzer Group 2's role in the opening phase of Barbarossa, see Guderian, *Panzer Leader*, esp. 120–52.

63. Citino, *German Way of War*, 293–94.

64. For Army Group South in the opening phases of Barbarossa, see the useful sourcebook by Werner Haupt, ed., *Army Group South: The Wehrmacht in Russia, 1941–1945* (Atglen, Pa.: Schiffer, 1998), esp. 7–108.

65. The famous passage is found in the July 3, 1941, entry in General Franz Halder, *Kriegstagebuch*, vol. 3, *Der Russlandfeldzug bis zum Marsch auf Stalingrad* (Stuttgart: W. Kohlhammer Verlag, 1964), 38–39.

66. For the Uman *Kessel*, see Haupt, *Army Group South*, 30–47.

67. See the August 11, 1941, entry in Halder, *Kriegstagebuch*, 3:170.

68. For these still little-known battles in front of Smolensk and their impact, see Glantz and House, *When Titans Clashed*, 58–61.

69. For the clash on the Desna, with especially helpful maps, see Pat McTaggart, "Smolensk-Yelnia: Blunting the Blitzkrieg," *Command*, no. 21 (March–April 1993): 52–59.

70. Raus, *Panzer Operations*, 26–33.

71. Hans Kissel, "Die ersten T-34," *Wehrwissenschaftliche Rundschau* 5, no. 3 (March 1955): 130–32.

72. Halder kept the figures meticulously in his war diary. See, for example, the entries in Halder, *Kriegstagebuch*, vol. 3, for August 4 (151), August 7 (161), and August 17 (182). The figure given on August 4: the Wehrmacht had already suffered 213,301 casualties in the east; by August 17, the number had risen to 318,333 (almost 10 percent of the total of the Eastern Army [Ostheer]).

73. Megargee, *Inside Hitler's High Command*, 123. The subject of logistics in the campaign deserves more attention than it has received. See Klaus A. Friedrich Schüler, *Logistik im Russlandfeldzug: Dsie Rolle der Eisenbahhn bei Planung, Vorbereitung und Durchführung des deutschen Angriffs auf die Sowjetunion bis zur Krise vor Moskau im Winter, 1941–42* (Frankfurt: Peter Lang, 1987), printed in typescript.

74. See de Beaulieu, *Der Vorstoss der Panzergruppe 4*, 75–76, 89–108.

75. For the Kiev *Kessel*, see Haupt, *Army Group South*, 48–86. Geoffrey Jukes, "Drive to Kiev: Ukraine, June 23–September 18, 1941," *History of the Second World War*, no. 22 (1978): 605–16, is a particularly good operational account

76. See, for example, one of the most interesting books ever written on Barbarossa, R. H. S. Stolfi, *Hitler's Panzers East: World War II Reinterpreted* (Norman: University of Oklahoma Press, 1992). Stolfi argues, with a great deal of documentation to back him up, that a drive on Moscow was certainly within the power of the Wehrmacht in August, that it had the logistics and the combat strength to get there, and that Hitler's "fundamental underestimation of the offensive capabilities of the German army" and his interpretation of the war as a "siege" were the real problems of the campaign. Hitler's turn to Kiev, for Stolfi, is nothing less than "the most important judgment" of the twentieth century (201).

77. For Operation Typhoon, see Citino, *German Way of War*, 297–301. For a penetrating discussion of Operation Typhoon's operational shortcomings, see Klink, "Die Operationsführung: Heer und Kriegsmarine," 575–79.

78. Bock, *War Diary*, entry for October 21 (337).

79. Ibid., entry for October 24 (340).

80. Ibid., entry for November 18 (362).

81. A good primary source for the battle of Moscow is Marshal Vasili Sokolovsky, "The Battle of Moscow," in *Battles Hitler Lost: First-Person Accounts of World War II by Russian General on the Eastern Front* (New York: Richardson & Steirman, 1986), 50–61. For the human side, see Rodric Braithwaite, *Moscow, 1941* (New York: Knopf, 2006), which uses memoirs, diaries, and interviews successfully to evoke the epic nature of those days.

82. For expert narration and analysis of the Moscow counteroffensive—no mean feat, considering its sprawl and confusion nature—see Glantz and House, *When Titans Clashed*, 87–97; and Megargee, *War of Annihilation*, 99–115.

83. For Stalin's attempt to widen the Moscow assault into a "strategic offensive," see Glantz and House, *When Titans Clashed*, 91–97.

84. *Grossdeutschlands Freiheitskrieg*, pt. 120, "Nach fünf Monaten Ostfeldzug," *Militär-Wochenblatt* 126, no. 22 (November 28, 1941): 595–98. The quote is from 595.

85. Colonel Däniker, "Zwei Jahre deutsche Strategie," *Militär-Wochenblatt* 126, no. 23 (November 25, 1941): 637–43.

86. *Grossdeutschlands Freiheitskrieg*, pt. 128. "Offensivgeist in der Defensive." *Militär-Wochenblatt* 126, no. 30 (January 23, 1942).

Chapter 2. The Wehrmacht Reborn: The Crimean Campaign

1. The phrase belongs to the OKW's Deputy Chief of Operations, General Walter Warlimont, *Inside Hitler's Headquarters, 1939–45* (Novato, Calif.: Presidio, 1964), 226–40.

2. For a good example of the genre, with some serious scholars (Charles Vasey, John Prados, David C. Isby, Paddy Griffith, Stephen Badsey, and others) considering scenarios that are more plausible than most, see Peter G. Tsouras, ed., *Hitler Triumphant: Alternate Decisions of World War II* (London: Greenhill, 2006). Griffith, for example, posits an airborne operation against the Caucasus oil fields in fall 1941 ("Wings over the Caucasus: Operation Leonardo," 169–88), while Prados describes a combined sea-air-land strike against Gibraltar in January 1941 ("The Spanish Gambit: Operation Felix," 58–86). Even here, however, some of the alternatives are more fanciful than others. See, for example, David M. Keithly, "Black Cross, Green Crescent, Black Gold: The Drive to the Indus," 124–67.

3. See, for example, Kathleen Broome Williams, *Secret Weapons: U.S. High-Frequency Direction Finding in the Battle of the Atlantic* (Annapolis: Naval Institute Press, 1996), which is instructive on "huff-duff," one of the crucial pieces of the technological puzzle that brought the Allies victory in the Atlantic.

4. On Nazi strategic bombing plans, ranging from the "America bomber" to the "atmosphere skipper," see James Duffy, *Target America: Hitler's Plan to Attack the United States* (Westport, Conn.: Praeger, 2004), as well as Manfred Griehl, *Luftwaffe over America: The Secret Plans to Bomb the United States in World War II* (London: Greenhill, 2004). For German plans to carry out a strategic bombing

campaign against the Soviet Union in 1943 (Operation Eisenhammer, "Iron Hammer"), see Richard Muller, *The German Air War in Russia* (Baltimore: Nautical and Aviation Publishing, 1992), 170–77.

5. On February 18, 1943, just weeks after the liquidation of the Stalingrad pocket, Nazi Minister of Public Enlightenment and Propaganda Josef Goebbels delivered a speech at the Berlin Sportpalast before a hand-picked audience of 14,000, a masterfully demagogic performance in which he posed a number of rhetorical questions to the audience, culminating in, "Do you want total war?" See Ian Kershaw, *Hitler*, vol. 2, *Nemesis* (New York: Norton, 2000), 561–77, for the disappointing results.

6. See Edward B. Westermann, *Flak: German Anti-Aircraft Defenses, 1914–1945* (Lawrence: University Press of Kansas, 2001). Richly detailed and cogently argued, it is unlikely ever to be superseded. See, in particular, the discussion of the costs of a "kill" (292–94) as well as the "lost divisions" argument—i.e., the notion that flak took too much manpower away from the army's replacement pool (294–95). The best book on the cost to Allied fliers of the dense concentration of German flak over urban targets—a truly chilling account in places—is Donald L. Miller, *Masters of the Air: America's Bomber Boys Who Fought the Air War against Nazi Germany* (New York: Simon & Schuster, 2006).

7. On the Crimea, one must start with the primary source, Erich von Manstein, *Lost Victories* (Novato, Calif.: Presidio, 1982), esp. 204–59. It has become axiomatic in the profession to advise caution in using the memoir literature generated by the German officer corps. This is particularly important with regard to the tendency of the authors to blame Hitler for everything that went wrong in the war, to exculpate themselves, and to invent disagreements with him, even to the point of describing bogus face-to-face arguments. There is, likewise, nary a word in any of them about "donations"—large grants of money and land from the Führer to his loyal commanders, which certainly puts a new spin on their determination to hold out to the last man. Manstein's memoir is no exception. However, all these books are arguably at their most reliable when they are actually discussing operations—orders of battle, troop movements, operational maneuvers, and the like—and that is how they are being used in the present work. Two other essential primary sources are General Friedrich Schulz, "Battle for Crimea," Foreign Military Studies Series (manuscript T-20); and General Hellmuth Reinhardt, "Selected German Army Operations on the Eastern Front (Operational)," Foreign Military Studies Series (manuscript P-143a), 187–212. A copy of each of these reports, along with the rest of this immense series, is on file in the U.S. Army Military History Institute at Carlisle Barracks in Carlisle, Pa.

There is no scholarly monograph dealing solely with the Crimean campaign, but there should be. The researcher should begin with the superb German official history, *Das Deutsche Reich und Der Zweite Weltkrieg*, vol. 6, *Die Ausweitung zum Weltkrieg und der Wechsel der Initiative, 1941–1943* (Stuttgart: Deutsche Verlags-Anstalt, 1990), especially pt. 6, "Der Krieg gegen die Sowjetunion, 1942–43," by Bernd Wegner, 840–52. The work that comes closest, because of its meticulous scholarship, is Joel S. A. Hayward, *Stopped at Stalingrad: The Luftwaffe and Hit-*

ler's Defeat in the East, 1943–1943 (Lawrence: University Press of Kansas, 1998). Although it focuses on air power, especially the activities of General Wolfram von Richtofen, it is expansive in its analysis, and deals well with the entire 1942 campaigning season on land, sea, and air. For Hayward's take on the Crimea, see 27–119. C. G. Sweeting, *Blood and Iron: The German Conquest of Sevastopol* (Washington, D.C.: Brassey's, 2004), is handsome and richly illustrated. It also contains just ninety-four pages of text, however—even less when one considers the number of photographs and maps. Padding out the volume to book length are numerous appendices, which are always interesting but not always especially relevant to the fighting in the Crimea. Among them might be mentioned appx. B, "Ranks, Uniforms."

8. Schulz, "Battle for Crimea," 1.

9. For a discussion of Romanian oil and its importance, see Hayward, *Stopped at Stalingrad*, 3–4, 7–9, 18–21, 29.

10. Manstein, *Lost Victories*, 204.

11. Schulz, "Battle for Crimea," 204.

12. Manstein, *Lost Victories*, 204.

13. The best source for the fall campaign, much more specific than Manstein's account, is Schulz, "Battle for Crimea," 1–18. Schulz was 11th Army's Chief of the General Staff (see Manstein, *Lost Victories*, 236).

14. Sweeting, *Blood and Iron*, 14.

15. See the article on General Staff officers by General William Voigts-Rhetz, "Erklärung," *Militär-Wochenblatt* 84, no. 37 (April 26, 1889): 1013.

16. For a military biography of Manstein, see Robert M. Citino, *Armored Forces: History and Sourcebook* (Westport, Conn.: Greenwood Press, 1994), 252–56.

17. Manstein, *Lost Victories*, 203.

18. The most recent research on German difficulties in forming a solid battlefield relationship with their Axis partners is found in Richard L. DiNardo, *Germany and the Axis Powers: From Coalition to Collapse* (Lawrence: University Press of Kansas, 2005). For 1941, see 109–15. See also Alesandru Dutu, "The Romanian Troops in the Siege of Sevastopol (October 1941–July 1942)." *Revue Internationale d'Histoire Militaire* 77 (1992).

19. Manstein, *Lost Victories*, 212–15.

20. Schulz, "Battle for Crimea," 3.

21. For eyewitness accounts of this tough fight, see Christopher Scheller, "Infanterie vor Perekop," and Captain Dittrich, "Tartaren-Graben and und Perekop," both in *Wir erobern die Krim: Soldaten der Krim-Armee berichten* (Neustadt: Pfälzische Verlagsanstalt, 1943), 14–19 and 29–22, respectively.

22. Werner Haupt, ed., *Army Group South: The Wehrmacht in Russia, 1941–1945* (Atglen, Pa.: Schiffer, 1998).

23. Sweeting, *Blood and Iron*, says the fifteenth century. See 34.

24. Haupt, *Army Group South*, 89–90.

25. Ibid., 90.

26. The "battle of the Sea of Azov," or the "Orekhov-Osipenko *Kessel*," has received little attention and deserves more, if based on nothing else than the sheer

number of Soviet prisoners. See Sweeting, *Blood and Iron*, 36–37, for a short introduction; Manstein, *Lost Victories*, 214–16; and Geoffrey Jukes, "Barbarossa: Drive to Kharkov: Ukraine, September–December 1941," *History of the Second World War*, no. 23 (1978): 634–40. For a good primary source, see Hans Steets, *Gebirgsjäger in der nogaischen Steppe* (Heidelberg: Kurt Vowinckel, 1956), vol. 8 in the Die Wehrmacht im Kampf series. The author was the chief of the General Staff of the 1st Mountain Division (XXXXIX Mountain Corps) during the campaign.

27. Manstein, *Lost Victories*, 214. Victor Nitu, "Manstein's Romanians in the Crimea," available at: http://www.feldgrau.com/articles.phpID=75), 1, includes the German 170th Division in those formations "pushed back" by the Soviet attack.

28. Manstein, *Lost Victories*, 214.

29. Steets, *Gebirgsjäger in der nogaischen Steppe*, 15–21.

30. Schulz, "Battle for Crimea," 5.

31. Sweeting, *Blood and Iron*, 36–37.

32. Nitu, "Manstein's Romanians," 1–2.

33. Manstein, *Lost Victories*, 219; Sweeting, *Blood and Iron*, 38.

34. Manstein, *Lost Victories*, 219–20.

35. Haupt, *Army Group South*, 96.

36. For 11th Army's headlong pursuit, see Schulz, "Battle for Crimea," 6–9.

37. For the flavor of the pounding march south, see Corporal Klümann, "Marsch ans Schwarze Meer," in *Wir erobern die Krim*, 62–64: "My comrade crosses the mole, laughs, and says, 'I am the right wing of the entire eastern front'!" (64).

38. Ibid., 6.

39. Sweeting, *Blood and Iron*, 43. The pioneers were there soon afterward, repairing blown bridges. See the anonymous article, "Als pioniere bei der Vorausabteilung," in *Wir erobern die Krim*, 62–64.

40. Schulz, "Battle for Crimea," 7.

41. John Erickson, *The Road to Stalingrad* (New York: Harper & Row, 1975), 256.

42. See Eberhard von Mackensen, *Vom Bug zum Kaukasus: Das III. Panzerkorps im Feldzug gegen Sowjetrussland, 1941–42* (Neckargemünd: Kurt Vowinckel, 1967), vol. 42, in the excellent Die Wehrmacht im Kampf series. For the taking and untaking of Rostov, see esp. 41–48.

43. Manstein, *Lost Victories*, 223.

44. General Hans von Sponeck had been the commander of the 22nd until days before the storming of Ishun; he would move on to command XXXXII Corps, handing over the division to Wolff. See Haupt, *Army Group South*, 96.

45. Manstein, *Lost Victories*, 223–24.

46. Sweeting, *Blood and Iron*, 45.

47. Erickson, *Road to Stalingrad*, 289–90.

48. The principal source on the Soviet offensive in the Crimea is David M. Glantz, "Forgotten Battles of the German-Soviet War (1941–45), Part 6: The Winter Campaign (5 December 1941–April 1942): The Crimean Counteroffensive and Reflections," *Journal of Slavic Military Studies* 14, no. 1 (March 2001): 121–70.

It is part of a long-term project in which Glantz is painstakingly reconstructing a historical narrative of numerous battles and campaigns that ended disastrously for the Red Army, and that were then systematically tossed down the Stalinist memory hole in the postwar years. His book, *Zhukov's Greatest Defeat: The Red Army's Epic Disaster in Operation Mars, 1942* (Lawrence: University Press of Kansas, 1999), may be seen as part of the same effort.

49. For a German view of Soviet order of battle and operations, see Colonel Gaul, "Kurze Darstellung der sowjetrussischen Kämpfe auf der Krim und um Sewastopol vom Oktober 1941 bis July 1942," *Militärwissenschaftliche Rundschau* 8, no. 2 (1943): 179–88, and the four accompanying maps.

50. Cited chapter and verse by Glantz, "Crimean Counteroffensive and Reflections," 122–40, including the operational report of January 1, 1942, from General D. T. Kozlov, commander of the Caucasus Front that had carried out the landings; the Stavka VGK directive of January 2; and the transcript of the telephone conversation between Kozlov, Stalin, and the chief of the Soviet General Staff, General A. M. Vasilevsky, on January 5, all of which speak of a decisive operation to liberate the entire Crimea.

51. Erickson, *Road to Stalingrad*, 291.

52. Hayward, *Stopped at Stalingrad*, 32.

53. For an effective period evocation of the German triumph at Eupatoria, see the article by war correspondent Herbert Ladda, "Der Aderlass der Kaukasusarmee," *Die Wehrmacht* 6, no. 5 (March 4, 1942): 16–17. See also Lieutenant Kolbe, ". . . ins Meer zurückzuwerfen," in *Wir erobern die Krim*, 88–90.

54. General Franz von Halder, December 29, 1941, entry in *Kriegstagebuch*, vol. 3, *Der Russlandfeldzug bis zum Marsch auf Stalingrad* (Stuttgart: W. Kohlhammer Verlag, 1964), 369. See Hayward, *Stopped at Stalingrad*, 33, who translates the passage more evocatively as "a *very* heavy day!"

55. See Gottlob Herbert Bidermann, *In Deadly Combat: A German Soldier's Memoir of the Eastern Front* (Lawrence: University Press of Kansas, 2000), 93–94. See also Sponeck's online biography of Sponeck at http://www.historic.de/, a site dedicated to "Militärgeschichte: Bremen und Umland."

56. Erickson, *Road to Stalingrad*, 329.

57. See Kozlov's operational orders to his front, in Glantz, "Crimean Counteroffensive and Reflections," 138.

58. The quote is from Konstantin Simonov, Soviet war correspondent. See Wegner, "Der Krieg gegen die Sowjetunion, 1942–43," 844.

59. Quoted in Glantz, "Crimean Counteroffensive and Reflections," 163. See also Catherine Merridale, *Ivan's War: Life and Death in the Red Army, 1939–1945* (New York: Metropolitan Books, 2006), 148. On Simonov generally, see Rodric Braithwaite, *Moscow, 1941* (New York: Knopf, 2006), esp. 92–93, and the dashing photo in the section after 240.

60. Manstein, *Lost Victories*, 207.

61. For Sonderstab Krim, see Hayward, *Stopped at Stalingrad*, 34–42; for Fliegerführer Süd, see 55–64. For German airpower at Kerch, see two journal articles by Hayward, "Von Richtofen's 'Giant Fire-Magic': The Luftwaffe's Contribution

to the Battle of Kerch, 1942," *Journal of Slavic Military Studies* 10, no. 2 (June 1997): 97–124; and "A Case Study in Early Joint Warfare: An Analysis of the Wehrmacht's Crimean Campaign of 1942," *Journal of Strategic Studies* 22, no. 4 (December 1999): 103–30.

62. Hayward, *Stopped at Stalingrad*, 58.

63. Bidermann, *In Deadly Combat*, 97–98.

64. For Nanshan, see Robert M. Citino, *Quest for Decisive Victory: From Stalemate to Blitzkrieg in Europe, 1899–1940* (Lawrence: University Press of Kansas, 2002), 72–76.

65. For Chatalja, see ibid., 125–27.

66. See the primary source, General Günter Meinhold, "123rd Infantry Regiment in the Breakthrough Battle for the Parpach Position, 8–11 May 1942," Foreign Military Studies Series (manuscript D-264), 2.

67. Hayward, *Stopped at Stalingrad*, 68–69.

68. Earl F. Ziemke and Magna E. Bauer, *Moscow to Stalingrad: Decision in the East* (Washington, D.C.: Center of Military History, 1987), 264.

69. Hayward, *Stopped at Stalingrad*, 67, is the only source to pick up on the humorous nature of the name.

70. For a discussion of XXX Corps, see Reinhardt, "Selected German Army Operations," 191–92.

71. Nitu, "Manstein's Romanians," 4–5.

72. Ziemke and Bauer, *Moscow to Stalingrad*, 266.

73. For the breakthrough battle in the Parpach position, see Captain Dittrich, "Einbruch in die Parpatsch-Stellung," and Corporal Kahlert, "Die Parpatsch-Stellung wird durchbrochen," both in *Wir erobern die Krim*, 102–5 and 123–27, respectively. See also Colonel Constantini, "Operations en Crimée de mai à juillet 1942," *Revue Historique de l'Armée* 21, no. 1 (1965).

74. Meinhold, "123rd Infantry Regiment," 4–5.

75. See Hayward, *Stopped at Stalingrad*, 81.

76. For the *operativer Luftkrieg*, see Muller, *German Air War in Russia*, chap. 1, "Preparations for a Proper War," 1–24. For its origins in the 1930s and the war's first year, see James S. Corum, *The Luftwaffe: Creating the Operational Air War, 1918–1940* (Lawrence: University Press of Kansas, 1997). See especially the review of literature on the Luftwaffe (10–12) and Corum's comments on Muller's work (11).

77. John Erickson, *Road to Stalingrad*, 349.

78. Hayward, *Stopped at Stalingrad*, 84.

79. For a sanitized version of combat with the "Banden," see Harry Kügler, "Gefecht mit Banden im Gebirge," and Klaus Döring, "Banden am Werk," both in *Wir erobern die Krim*, in 73–75 and 75–77, respectively. Not all of the cruelty was necessarily being dealt out by the Germans. In the Crimea, the Soviet regime identified Crimean Tatars as German sympathizers, and regional officials "accused the overwhelming majority of Tatars of actively collaborating." See Kenneth Slepyan, *Stalin's Guerrillas: Soviet Partisans in World War II* (Lawrence: University Press of Kansas, 2006), 207.

80. For a German usage of this term, see *Grossdeutschlands Freiheitskrieg*, pt. 152, "Der Fall von Sewastopol," *Militär-Wochenblatt* 127, no. 2 (June 19, 1942): 31–34. The quote is on 32.

81. For Karl and Dora, see Sweeting, *Blood and Iron*, 148–71.

82. For Port Arthur, see Citino, *Quest for Decisive Victory*, 76–83; for Adrianople, see 127–28.

83. Manstein, *Lost Victories*, 248.

84. Hayward, *Stopped at Stalingrad*, 109.

85. Sweeting, *Blood and Iron*, 74–75.

86. See the account from the regimental commander, Colonel von Choltitz, "Ein Brandenburgisches Regiment an der Ssewernaja-Bucht," and one of the soldiers in the second wave over the bay, Sergeant Grosser, "Die Ssewernaja-Bucht ist überquert," in *Wir erobern die Krim*, 217–20 and 207–10, respectively.

87. For the 75,000 figure, see Hayward, *Stopped at Stalingrad*, 117; for the 100,000 figure, see Gerhard Weinberg, *A World at Arms: A Global History of World War II*, 2nd ed. (Cambridge: Cambridge University Press, 2005), 413; for 25,000 German dead, see Wegner, "Der Krieg gegen die Sowjetunion, 1942–43": "allein auf deutscher Seite fielen fast 25,000 soldiers" (851).

88. *Grossdeutschlands Freiheitskrieg*, pt. 128, "Offensivgeist in der Defensive," *Militär-Wochenblatt* 126, no. 30 (January 23, 1942): 835–38. The quote is on 836.

89. See the exultant passages in *Grossdeutschlands Freiheitskrieg*, pt. 145, "Die deutsche Frühjahrsoperation auf der Krim," *Militär-Wochenblatt* 126, no. 47 (May 22, 1942): 1345–48.

90. *Grossdeutschlands Freiheitskrieg*, pt. 146, "Kertsch, die erste Vernichtungsschlacht des Frühjahrs," *Militär-Wochenblatt* 126, no. 48 (May 29, 1942): 1375–79.

91. M. Braun, "Die Schlachten auf Kertsch und im Korallenmeer in ihrer moralischen Bedeutung," *Militär-Wochenblatt* 126, no. 49 (June 5, 1942): 1412–14. See also Wilhelm Rossbach, "Kertsch—Charkow: Luftherrschaft aus dem Angriff und aus der Verteidigung," *Militär-Wochenblatt* 126, no. 52 (June 26, 1942): 1503–6.

92. Wegner, "Der Krieg gegen Die Sowjetunion, 1942–43," 844.

Chapter 3. The Wehrmacht Reborn: Annihilation at Kharkov

1. For the fighting at Rzhev, see two selections in the useful volume edited by Stephen H. Newton, *German Battle Tactics on the Russian Front, 1941–1945* (Atglen, Pa.: Schiffer, 1994). Otto Schellert, "Winter Fighting of the 253rd Infantry Division in the Rzhev Area, 1941–1942," 55–79 (written by the divisional commander), and Otto Dessloch, "The Winter Battle of Rzhev, Vyazma, and Yukhov, 1941–1942" (by a senior Luftwaffe commander), 81–108. The essays were originally part of the Foreign Military Studies Series. Newton is also responsible for the elegant translation from the German, a welcome development to anyone who has struggled with the hurried and often amateurish translations done by army personnel in the years after the war. See also Stephen H. Newton, *Hitler's Commander: Field Marshal Walther Model—Hitler's Favorite General* (Cambridge, Mass.:

Da Capo, 2005), for solid analysis and biography of the commander of German forces in the Rzhev salient.

2. See, for example, Franz Kurowski, *Demjansk: Der Kessel im Eis: 14 Monate Abwehrkampf im Nordabschnitt der Ostfront* (Wölfersheim: Podzun-Pallas, 2001).

3. David M. Glantz, *The Battle for Leningrad, 1941–1944* (Lawrence: University Press of Kansas, 2002), 183.

4. Christian Hartmann, *Halder: Generalstabschef Hitlers, 1938–1942* (Paderborn: Ferdinand Schöningh, 1991), 312.

5. There is no scholarly monograph dealing solely with the battle of Kharkov. It is no doubt a matter of timing: with Stalingrad looming just around the corner, Kharkov will probably always suffer in comparison. The researcher should begin with the few primary sources available. Pride of place goes to the Soviet Staff Study, edited by David M. Glantz, *Kharkov, 1942: Anatomy of a Military Disaster through Soviet Eyes* (Shepperton, Surrey: Ian Allan, 1998). Glantz presents this 1951 account warts and all, then brackets it with his own informed commentary. For the German side, there is the postwar account by the chief of the General Staff for the LI Corps, Hans Doerr, "Der Ausgang der Schlacht um Charkow im Frühjahr 1942," *Wehrwissenschaftliche Rundschau* 4, no. 1 (January 1954), 9–18. Doerr was the chief of the General Staff for the German LII Army Corps during the battle. There is also a report entitled "1942 Offensive (Strategic Survey)," Foreign Military Studies Series (manuscript T-14), which has a section dealing with the battle of Kharkov (90–107). A copy is on file in the U.S. Army Military History Institute at Carlisle Barracks in Carlisle, Pa. Written ostensibly by General Heinz von Gyldenfeldt in 1948, it reveals itself upon closer inspection to be an incomplete English version of Doerr's article, although the translation from the German is so inelegant that it is at times difficult to tell. The exact relationship between Gyldenfeldt's report and Doerr's journal article (which appeared six years later) will have to remain open for the time being, and it is another sign of the questionable provenance of so many of the documents in the series. Wherever possible, both documents will be cited in the notes. Fedor von Bock, *Generalfeldmarschall Fedor von Bock: The War Diary, 1939–1945* (Atglen, Pa.: Schiffer Military History, 1996), is essential in tracing the difficult birth and triumphant course of the battle. See also the German official history, Militärgeschichtliches Forschungsamt (Military Historical Research Office), *Das Deutsche Reich und Der Zweite Weltkrieg*, vol. 6, *Die Ausweitung zum Weltkrieg und der Wechsel der Initiative, 1941–1943* (Stuttgart: Deutsche Verlags-Anstalt, 1990), pt. 6, "Der Krieg gegen die Sowjetunion, 1942–43," authored by Bernd Wegner, 852–61.

Within the secondary literature, Kharkov usually receives brief treatment. Begin with the pertinent sections in John Erickson, *The Road to Stalingrad* (New York: Harper & Row, 1975), which are short (343–47) but typically excellent. For those of a certain scholarly generation, it was Erickson's prose that first captured the drama of the Russo-German war. Indeed, it will be tough for any future author to top passages like this one: "On the morning of 12 May, preceded by an hour of artillery and air bombardment, Timoshenko's northern and southern prongs jabbed into Paulus's Sixth Army which for three days and nights rocked and lurched in a highly dangerous situation as waves of Soviet riflemen and slabs of Soviet armour crashed down on it" (345). It certainly doesn't hurt that the scholarship is also meticulous.

See also the useful sections in Earl Ziemke and Magna Bauer, *Moscow to Stalingrad: Decision in the East* (Washington, D.C.: Center of Military History, 1987), 269–82. Ziemke and Bauer's judgments have stood the test of time, and the book is accessible to a wide audience, from scholars to soldiers to war-game buffs. Leading the way in today's secondary literature is Joel S. A. Hayward's *Stopped at Stalingrad: The Luftwaffe and Hitler's Defeat in the East, 1943–1943* (Lawrence: University Press of Kansas, 1998), which again disposes of Kharkov relatively quickly (120–28), but which is essential reading on the 1942 campaign. The book's title is in part deceiving; this is a fine history of operations on land as well as in the air (and even occasionally at sea).

6. There are few battles of the war that have a greater need of a map in order to follow the action. For the outlines of the complex evolutions of this front, see the maps in Doerr, "Der Ausgang der Schlacht um Charkow," 10–11.

7. The most cogent analysis of the Soviet offensive at Izyum is to be found in Glantz, *Kharkov, 1942*, 17–20, especially the map on 19.

8. See the entries for those three days in Franz Halder, *Kriegstagebuch*, vol. 3, *Der Russlandfeldzug bis zum Marsch auf Stalingrad* (Stuttgart: W. Kohlhammer Verlag, 1964), 387–89.

9. Doerr, "Der Ausgang der Schlacht um Charkow," 10; this passage is missing from "1942 Offensive (Strategic Survey)," Foreign Military Studies Series (manuscript T-14).

10. Doerr, "Der Ausgang der Schlacht um Charkow," 11; see also "1942 Offensive (Strategic Survey)," 92.

11. Glantz, *Kharkov, 1942*, 18.

12. For the Wehrmacht's success at employing mixed-arms "battlegroups" (*Kampfgruppen*), see James Lucas, *Battle Group! German Kampfgruppe Action of World War Two* (London: Arms and Armour Press, 1993).

13. Doerr, "Der Ausgang der Schlacht um Charkow," 12; see also "1942 Offensive (Strategic Survey)," 92.

14. For Soviet planning for the Kharkov offensive, see Glantz, *Kharkov, 1942*, 27, as well as Ziemke and Bauer, *Moscow to Stalingrad*, 269–70.

15. See the pertinent documents in appx. 1–3, Glantz, *Kharkov, 1942*, 252–58.

16. For a short operational précis, see Robert M. Citino, *Blitzkrieg to Desert Storm: The Evolution of Operational Warfare* (Lawrence: University Press of Kansas, 2004), 86–87.

17. Glantz, *Kharkov, 1942*, 31.

18. For the pertinent documents, see Bock, *War Diary*, entries for March 10, 1942 (442–43), and March 31, 1942 (460–61). For German planning in general, see Ziemke and Bauer, *Moscow to Stalingrad*, 272–73.

19. Ibid., entry for April 23, 1942 (465).

20. Ziemke and Bauer, *Moscow to Stalingrad*, 272.

21. Bock, *War Diary*, entry for April 25, 1942 (465–66).

22. Ibid., entry for April 30, 1942 (468).

23. Erickson, *Road to Stalingrad*, 344.

24. The German phrase is "Angriff mit begrenztem Ziel." For examples of contemporary usage, see Erwin Rommel, *Krieg ohne Hass* (Heidenheim: Heidenheimer Zeitung, 1950), 126, 177.

25. Erickson, *Road to Stalingrad*, 341–42.

26. Bock, *War Diary*, entry for May 5, 1942 (469–70).

27. Wegner, "Der Krieg gegen die Sowjetunion, 1942–43," 855–56.

28. Glantz, *Kharkov, 1942*, 42.

29. For the course of the original Soviet offensive and German counterblow, see ibid., 114–217, which interweaves the original Soviet General staff study with Glantz's commentary, and twenty-eight maps. For an overview of operations on both sides, see Stephen B. Patrick, "Kharkov: The Soviet Spring Offensive," *Strategy and Tactics* 68 (June 1978): 4–14, complete with a simulation game on the battle designed by Stephen B. Patrick and Redmond A. Simonsen.

30. Ziemke and Bauer, *Moscow to Stalingrad*, 273.

31. Glantz, *Kharkov, 1942*, 134.

32. Ibid.

33. Doerr, "Der Ausgang der Schlacht um Charkow," 14; see also "1942 Offensive (Strategic Survey)," 97.

34. The Germans recognized this immediately. See, for example, *Grossdeutschlands Freiheitskrieg*, pt. 147, "Abschluss der Kesselschlacht von Charkow," *Militär-Wochenblatt* 126, no. 49 (June 5, 1942): 1405–9. The Soviets were becoming stingier with their manpower than they had been in 1941, it argued, employing massed armor instead: "Man hat deshalb diesmal auf Massenagriffe in der bisherigen Form mehr verzichtet und statt dessen Kriegsmaterial, insbesondere Panzer, in ungewöhnlich hoher Zahl eingesetzt" (1405).

35. David M. Glantz and Jonathan House, *When Titans Clashed: How the Red Army Stopped Hitler* (Lawrence: University Press of Kansas, 1995), 99–101.

36. Glantz, *Kharkov, 1942*, 116–17.

37. Ibid., 121.

38. Ziemke and Bauer, *Moscow to Stalingrad*, 273.

39. Erickson, *Road to Stalingrad*, 345.

40. Glantz, *Kharkov, 1942*, 140–41.

41. Bock, *War Diary*, entry for May 12, 1942 (474–75). Hayward, *Stopped at Stalingrad*, 121, once again gives the more evocative translation: "It's neck or nothing!" Bock's actual words: "Hier handelt sich's nicht um Schönheitsfehler, sondern um's Dasein." See Walter Görlitz, ed., *Paulus: "Ich stehe hier auf Befehl!"* (Frankfurt: Bernard & Graefe, 1960), 177.

42. Bock, *War Diary*, entry for May 14, 1942 (477).

43. Doerr, "Der Ausgang der Schlacht um Charkow," 15; see also "1942 Offensive (Strategic Survey)," 101.

44. Hayward, *Stopped at Stalingrad*, 122–23.

45. See the entry for May 15, 1942, in Halder, *Kriegstagebuch*, 3:442.

46. The quote is from a German intelligence summary of the Rzhev fight-

ing in 1942 during Marshal G. K. Zhukov's failed Operation Mars. See David M. Glantz, *Zhukov's Greatest Defeat: The Red Army's Epic Disaster in Operation Mars, 1942* (Lawrence: University Press of Kansas, 1999), 301. See also the article on which the book was based, "Counterpoint to Stalingrad: Operation Mars (November–December 1942): Marshal Zhukov's Greatest Defeat," (Fort Leavenworth, Kans.: Foreign Military Studies Office, 1997).

47. See Bock, *War Diary*, entry for May 16, 1942 (479–80): "It is difficult to see how the attack by Army Group Kleist beginning tomorrow will be sustained." See also "1942 Offensive (Strategic Survey)," 99–100; there is no mention in Doerr, "Der Ausgang der Schlacht um Charkow," of Bock's last-second hesitation.

48. For the role of III Panzer Corps in the 1942 campaign, see Eberhard von Mackensen, *Vom Bug zum Kaukasus: Das III. Panzerkorps im Feldzug gegen Sowjetrussland, 1941–42* (Neckargemünd: Kurt Vowinckel, 1967), vol. 42 in the series Die Wehrmacht im Kampf. For Kharkov, see 68–75.

49. Ibid., 68.

50. See the testimony of the commander of the 101st Light Infantry Division, General Hans Kissel, *Angriff einer Infanteriedivision: Die 101.leichte Infanteriedivision in der Frühjahrsschlacht bei Charkow, Mai 1942* (Heidelberg: Kurt Vowinckel, 1958), vol. 42 in the series Die Wehrmacht im Kampf.

51. Glantz, *Kharkov, 1942*, 139. The phrase belongs to Glantz, not the staff study.

52. For the Khrushchev-Stalin angle on the Kharkov battle, see Dmitri Volgokonov, *Stalin: Triumph and Tragedy* (New York: Grove Weidenfeld, 1988), 431–32.

53. Doerr, "Der Ausgang der Schlacht um Charkow," 16; see also "1942 Offensive (Strategic Survey)," 103.

54. Ziemke and Bauer, *Moscow to Stalingrad*, 282, has "south of Lozovenka," a location that would have put Bock in harm's way just to the east of the pocket and thus squarely in the path of any Soviet breakout attempt.

55. See Bock, *War Diary*, entry for May 26, 1942 (488).

56. Glantz, *Kharkov, 1942*, 218–19.

57. Erickson, *Road to Stalingrad*, 347.

58. Doerr, "Der Ausgang der Schlacht um Charkow," 18; see also "1942 Offensive (Strategic Survey)," 106–7.

59. Operation Wilhelm has been largely missing in the historiography for all of the same reasons as the battle of Kharkov. For a good introduction and helpful map, see the pertinent section in the German official history, Wegner, "Der Krieg gegen die Sowjetunion, 1942–43," 861, 862; for a readable primary source by the armored spearhead, see Mackensen, *Vom Bug zum Kaukasus*, 76–80.

60. See Bock, *War Diary*, entry for May 26, 1942 (498); the English translation is "loss"; the original German is "Verlust."

61. Operation Fridericus II receives little mention in the standard works. Once again, see the German official history, Wegner, "Der Krieg gegen die Sowjetunion, 1942–43," 861–62, as well as Mackensen, *Vom Bug zum Kaukasus*, 81–84.

62. Quoted in the German official history, Wegner, "Der Krieg gegen die Sowjetunion, 1942–43," 860.

63. Ibid. The original German is "psychischen Erschütterungen."

64. Ibid.

65. Ibid.

66. *Grossdeutschlands Freiheitskrieg*, pt. 146, "Die Schlacht von Charkow: Aus der Abwehr zum Angriff," *Militär-Wochenblatt* 126, no. 48 (May 29, 1942): 1375–79. The quote is from 1377.

67. *Grossdeutschlands Freiheitskrieg*, pt. 147, "Abschluss der Kesselschlacht von Charkow," *Militär-Wochenblatt* 126, no. 49 (June 5, 1942): 1405–1409. The quotation is from 1405.

68. Ibid., 1406.

69. Wilfried von Oven, "Mit einer Panzerdivision bei Charkow: Die erste Kesselschlacht dieses Jahres," *Die Wehrmacht* 6, no. 13 (June 24, 1942): 8–9. See especially the dramatic photo displaying some of the quarter-million prisoners taken in the battle.

70. See Nicolaus von Below, *At Hitler's Side: The Memoirs of Hitler's Luftwaffe Adjutant, 1937–1945* (London: Greenhill, 2001), 149. The funeral was for Adolf Hühnlein, a veteran of the Beer Hall Putsch and the head of the NSKK (Nationalsozialistisches Kraftfahrkorps, the National Socialist Motor Corps), the driving and roadside assistance association.

Chapter 4. Battering the British: Gazala and Tobruk

1. See, for example, Correlli Barnett, *The Desert Generals* (Bloomington: Indiana University Press, 1982): "The desert war of 1940–43 is unique in history; it was fought like a polo game on an empty arena. With one exception, there were no roads, but as virtually the whole of the arena was good going, at least for tanks, movement was almost as free as that of a fleet. . . . The desert campaign was therefore war in its purest form" (23).

2. See Erwin Rommel, *Krieg Ohne Hass* (Heidenheim: Heidenbheimer Zeitung, 1950); and John Bierman and Colin Smith, *Alamein: War without Hate* (London: Viking, 2002).

3. See Barnett, *Desert Generals:* "Yet, equally, there was in this dusty arena no food and little water; all had to be imported. Supply was the major limit to movement" (23). See also Fred Majdalany, *The Battle of El Alamein: Fortress in the Sand* (Philadelphia: Lippincott, 1965): "The Western Desert is a desolate scorching emptiness; not the golden sand dunes of romantic imagination" (6).

4. Mason played Rommel in two films: *The Desert Fox* (1951), directed by Henry Hathaway, and *The Desert Rats* (1953), directed by Robert Wise.

5. For the best recent biography of Rommel, synthesizing much current research, see Ralf Georg Reuth, *Rommel: Das Ende einer Legende* (Munich: Piper, 2004), recently translated into English as *Rommel: The End of a Legend* (London: Haus, 2005). Equally good, as sophisticated in its interpretation as it is marvelous in its writing, is the comparative biography by Dennis Showalter, *Patton and Rommel: Men of the War in the Twentieth Century* (New York: Berkley Caliber, 2005).

For a short biographical profile of Rommel, see Robert M. Citino, *Armored Forces: History and Sourcebook* (Westport, Conn.: Greenwood Press, 1994), 266–69.

6. Reuth, *Rommel: The End of a Legend*, 123–24.

7. For the importance of Rommel's Swabian heritage, see Showalter, *Patton and Rommel*, 25–28.

8. For Derfflinger, see Ernst Fischer, "Georg Derfflinger: Bruchstücke seines Lebensbildes," *Beihefte zum Militär-Wochenblatt, 1894* (Berlin: E. S. Mittler, 1894), 397–451; and the fascinating personality profile in Rudolf Thiel, *Preussische Soldaten* (Berlin: Paul Neff, 1940), 15–37. For analysis of his career, see Robert M. Citino, *The German Way of War: From the Thirty Years' War to the Third Reich* (Lawrence: University Press of Kansas, 2005), 30–33.

9. See Rudolf Dahms, *Blücher, der Marschall Vorwärts* (Berlin: R. Hobbing, 1935); and Roger Parkinson, *The Hussar General: The Life of Blücher, Man of Waterloo* (London: P. Davies, 1975). For the view from professional German military circles, see Eberhard Kessel, "Blücher: Zum 200. Geburtstag am 16. Dezember," *Militärwissenschaftliche Rundschau* 7, no. 4 (1942): 303–13.

10. General Peter Du Moulin commanded Frederick the Great's advance guard at Hohenfriedeberg. See Citino, *German Way of War*, 54, 57, 58, 61–62; Richard Du Moulin served as German military attaché to Poland in the interwar era. See Robert M. Citino, *The Evolution of Blitzkrieg Tactics: Germany Defends Itself against Poland* (Westport, Conn.: Greenwood, 1987), 135–37, 152.

11. General Gotthard Heinrici commanded the XXXXIII Corps in the French campaign and in the early phases of Barbarossa. He commanded 4th Army during the horrible winter campaign of 1941–1942 and 1st Panzer Army in 1944. See Johannes Hürter, *Ein deutscher General an der Ostfront: Die Briefe und Tagebücher des Gotthard Heinricis, 1941–42* (Erfurt: Alan Sutton, 2001).

12. General Hermann von François was the commander of I Corps during the Tannenberg campaign and 8th Army during the fall campaign of 1914. See his story in his own words: *Marneschlacht und Tannenberg: Betrachtungen zur deutscher Kriegsführung der ersten sechs Kriegswochen* (Berlin: Scherl, 1920).

13. For the capture of Mount Matajur, see Erwin Rommel, *Infantry Attacks* (London: Greenhill Books, 1990), 218–27; for a vivid recreation of Rommel's exploits with the Württemberg Gebirgs-Battaillon (Württemberg Mountain Battalion), see Showalter, *Patton and Rommel*, 62–79.

14. For Avesnes, see Karl-Heinz Frieser, *The Blitzkrieg Legend: The 1940 Campaign in the West*. Annapolis: Naval Institute Press, 2005), 265–73. The quotes are from 268.

15. The comment of a German soldier. Ibid., 268–69.

16. Frieser's own comment. Ibid., 273.

17. A few years ago, the Desert War seemed to be tapped out as a field of new historiography. There were hundreds of books available, but they were aging and little new seemed to be coming up to replace them. Perhaps that is no longer true, as a number of new books on North Africa have recently appeared. Most of them are British or deal with events from the British point of view. See, for example, the wave of new El Alamein literature from 2002: Jon Latimer, *Alamein* (Cambridge,

Mass.: Harvard University Press, 2002); John Bierman and Colin Smith, *Alamein: War without Hate* (London: Viking, 2002); and Stephen Bungay, *Alamein* (London: Aurum, 2002). All are fundamentally similar works. All purport to be about the battle itself; all are in fact general histories of the entire North African campaign from the Anglo-Italian battles to Rommel's final retreat to Tunisia. None of them brings anything particularly new in terms of analysis, although they do use interviews with veterans to good effect. Latimer's work is the most scholarly. Bungay, and Bierman and Smith offer solid popular histories, including a huge amount of perhaps extraneous detail on matters as wide ranging as the identity of the real *English Patient* or a deconstruction of the desert war's greatest hit, "Lili Marlene" (Bierman and Smith, *Alamein*, 84–86). All three offer particularly vivid accounts of the crucial encounter at the position called "Snipe," where the 2nd Battalion of the Rifle Brigade, just 300 infantrymen in all, decisively blunted Rommel's largest armored counterattacks on October 26. For the later, post-Alamein period, there is Rick Atkinson's Pulitzer Prize–winning *An Army at Dawn: The War in North Africa* (New York: Holt, 2002), vol. 1 in Atkinson's Liberation Trilogy; and its British counterpart, James Holland, *Together We Stand: America, Britain, and the Forging of an Alliance* (New York: Hyperion, 2005). Robin Neillands, *Eighth Army: The Triumphant Desert Army that Held the Axis at Bay from North Africa to the Alps, 1939–1945* (Woodstock, N.Y.: Overlook, 2004), is an unusual history of a single army from campaign to campaign, and it too makes extensive use of interviews with veterans.

Next to these mostly popular works are sophisticated works of operational history: Niall Barr, *The Pendulum of War: The Three Battles of El Alamein* (New York: Overlook Press, 2005), which will likely be the standard work on British arms in the desert for some time to come. Also useful, especially for future research, is H. W. Wynter, *Special Forces in the Desert War* (London: Public Record Office, 2001). It includes, for the first time in print, two historical reports written by Brigadier Wynter for the Historical Section of the War Cabinet: "The History of the Long Range Desert Group (June 1940 to March 1943)," and "Special Service Troops in the Middle East and North Africa (January 1941 to April 1943)."

There is still a fine body of older literature to consult. For a good overview of the entire campaign, from operations to equipment, see George Forty, *The Armies of Rommel* (London: Arms and Armour Press, 1997). See also W. G. F. Jackson, *The Battle for North Africa, 1940–43* (New York: Mason, Charter, 1975); Roger Parkinson, *The War in the Desert* (London: Hart-Davis, MacGibbon, 1976); Ronald Lewin, *The Life and Death of the Afrika Korps* (London: Batsford, 1977); and Alexander McKee, *El Alamein: Ultra and the Three Battles* (Chatham, Kent: Souvenir, 1991). In the historiography of the field, the military biography has played a key role, not surprising given the force of the personalities at work in this theater. See Barnett, *Desert Generals*; Nigel Hamilton, *Monty*, 3 vols. (London: Hamish Hamilton, 1981–1986); John Keegan, ed., *Churchill's Generals* (New York: Grove Weidenfeld, 1991); Ronald Lewin, *Montgomery as Military Commander* (London: Batsford, 1971) and *Rommel as Military Commander* (London: Batsford, 1968); and Kenneth Macksey, *Rommel: Battles and Campaigns* (London: Arms and Armour Press, 1979).

The best among them manage to raise enough questions about their subject to make them worth reading. Often, however, they lapse into hagiography, and their format often prevents them from going beyond the issue of personalities. Other works worthy of consultation include the vast number of memoirs, by figures both great and small. See R. L. Crimp, *The Diary of a Desert Rat* (London: Leo Cooper, 1971); Robert Crisp, *Brazen Chariots* (New York: Ballantine, 1961), perhaps the finest book to come out of the war; Bernard Law Montgomery's *El Alamein to the River Sangro; Normandy to the Baltic* (London: Barrie and Jenkins, 1973), and Bernard Law Montgomery, *Memoirs of Field-Marshal the Viscount Montgomery of Alamein* (Cleveland: World, 1968).

Among the secondary literature, the body of literature by Field Marshal Michael Carver (chief of staff for the 7th Armoured Division during the campaign) is essential reading: *Tobruk* (London: Batsford, 1964), *El Alamein* (London: Batsford, 1962), and *Dilemmas of the Desert War: A New Look at the Libyan Campaign, 1940–1942* (London: Batsford, 1986). For two well-done pictorial works among the hundreds available, see A. J. Barber, *Afrika Korps* (London: Bison, 1977); and George Forty, *Desert Rats at War: North Africa* (London: Ian Allan, 1975). Finally, three books deserve special mention: Wolf Heckmann, *Rommel's War in Africa* (Garden City, N.Y.: Doubleday, 1981), for its vignettes of the desert war from the German perspective; Hans-Otto Behrendt, *Rommel's Intelligence in the Desert Campaign, 1941–43* (London: William Kimber, 1985), for being the only book to deal exclusively with this crucial problem; and Alan J. Levine, *The War against Rommel's Supply Lines, 1942–1943* (Westport, Conn.: Praeger, 1999), for the same reason.

From the German side, the primary source is still the most important one: Rommel, *Krieg ohne Hass. The Rommel Papers*, ed. B. H. Liddell Hart (New York: Harcourt, Brace, 1953), is the English equivalent, although it intersperses Rommel's letters to his wife Lu throughout the text, not always to good effect. It is a sign of the talent among Rommel's staff and subordinate commanders that virtually all of them became authors, producing an essential body of work on these campaigns. See the works by Alfred Gause (Rommel's chief of staff), "Der Feldzug in Nordafrika im Jahre 1941," *Wehrwissenschaftliche Rundschau* 12, no. 10 (October 1962): 592–618; "Der Feldzug in Nordafrika im Jahre 1942," *Wehrwissenschaftliche Rundschau* 12, no. 11 (November 1962): 652–80; and "Der Feldzug in Nordafrika im Jahre 1943," *Wehrwissenschaftliche Rundschau* 12, no. 12 (December 1962): 720–28; Siegfried Westphal, his operations officer, *Heer in Fesseln* (Bonn: Athenaum-Verlag, 1950), translated into English as *The German Army in the West* (London: Cassell, 1951), and *Erinnerungen* (Berlin: Von Hase & Koehler, 1975); his intelligence chief, F. W. von Mellenthin, *Panzer Battles: A Study of the Employment of Armor in the Second World War* (New York: Ballantine, 1956); his aide de camp, Heinz Werner Schmidt, *With Rommel in the Desert* (New York: Bantam, 1977); the commander of the Afrika Korps, Walther Nehring, *Die Geschichte der deutschen Panzerwaffe, 1916 bis 1945* (Berlin: Propyläen Verlag, 1969); and Nehring's chief of staff, Fritz Bayerlein, who not only helped edit Rommel's *Krieg ohne Hass* after the field marshal's untimely death, but actually wrote large parts of it, including the entire section on Crusader and Rommel's second offensive, pt. 2, "Duell der Panzer," 63–107 (chap. 8 of

Rommel, *Rommel Papers*, "The Winter Campaign 1941–2," 154–88). See also Bruce Gudmundsson, *Inside the Afrika Korps* (London: Greenhill Books, 1999), containing edited portions of the *History of the Campaign in North Africa*, "a multivolume set of reports assembled under the direction of General Walther Nehring for the U.S. Army Foreign Military Studies Program" (12). For a fine synthesis of this material, see two volumes of the German official history: *Das Deutsche Reich und Der Zweite Weltkrieg*, vol. 3, *Der Mittelmeerraum und Südosteuropa: Von der "non belligeranza" Italiens bis zum Kriegseintritt der Vereinigten Staaten* (Stuttgart: Deutsche Verlags-Anstalt, 1979), especially pt. 5, Bernd Stegemann, "Die italienische-deutsche Kriegführung im Mittelmeer und in Afrika," 589–682; and vol. 6, *Der Gobale Krieg: Die Ausweitung zum Weltkrieg und der Wechsel der Initiative, 1941–1943*, especially pt. 5, Reinhard Stumpf, "Der Krieg im Mittelmeerraum, 1942–43: Die Operationen in Nordafrika und im mittleren Mittelmeer," 567–757. And although there has as yet not been a flood of literature on the German effort in Africa to match the British outpouring since 2000, see two important new works of military biography: Showalter, *Patton and Rommel*; and Reuth, *Rommel: The End of a Legend*.

18. Rommel's orders from General Franz Halder, chief of the General Staff: "Hauptaufgabe ist, Graziani dazu zu Bringen, dass er nicht kampflos auf Tripolis ausweicht." Entry for February 7, 1941, in Franz Halder, *Kriegstagebuch*, vol. 2, *Von der geplanten Landung in England bis zum Beginn des Ostfeldzuges* (Stuttgart: W. Kohlhammer Verlag, 1964), 272. See also Christian Hartmann, *Halder: Generalstabschef Hitlers, 1938–1942* (Paderborn: Ferdinand Schöningh, 1991), 259–260.

19. For a recent look at Herero War (actually the German suppression of the Herero and Nama uprisings), see Isabel V. Hull, *Absolute Destruction: Military Culture and the Practices of War in Imperial Germany* (Ithaca, N.Y.: Cornell University Press, 2005), 5–90. Hull places the war in the context of what she calls "institutional extremism" (1), in which German planners and commanders on the spot needlessly, and almost thoughtlessly, imposed the traditional patterns of "concentric operations" and the "battle of annihilation" on a conflict for which they were manifestly unsuited, leading to the virtual extermination of the Herero. It was a phenomenon that emerged not so much from advance planning or the racism of the local commander, General Lothar von Trotha, as from German "military-institutional culture" (5)

20. For Lettow-Vorbeck, see the primary source, Paul von Lettow-Vorbeck, *Meine erinnerungen aus Ostafrika* (Leipzig: K. F. Koehler, 1920). For a popular work in English, see Edwin Hoyt, *Guerrilla: Colonel von Lettow-Vorbeck and Germany's East African Empire* (New York: Macmillan, 1981).

21. Siegfried Westphal, "Notes on the Campaign in North Africa, 1941–1943," *Journal of the Royal United Service Institution* 105, no. 617 (1960): 70–81. Westphal was on the Operations Section of the General Staff in Berlin in 1938 and personally turned down a request from another section for maps of North Africa. "None of us ever dreamed of the possibility of having to wage war in the desert," he later laughed (1).

22. German official history, Stegemann, "Die italienische-deutsche Kriegführung im Mittelmeer und in Afrika," 617.

23. Gause, "Der Feldzug in Nordafrika im Jahre 1941," 598.

24. A standard account of Rommel's opening offensive out of El Agheila is Mellenthin, *Panzer Battles*. For more recent works, see Forty, *Armies of Rommel*, 115–19; and Bruce Allen Watson, *Desert Battle: Comparative Perspectives* (Westport, Conn.: Praeger, 1995), 1–13.

25. Rommel, *Krieg ohne Hass*, 33–34; Rommel, *Rommel Papers*, 117–18.

26. For analysis of the fighting in front of Tobruk, see Robert M. Citino, *Blitzkrieg to Desert Storm: The Evolution of Operational Warfare* (Lawrence: University Press of Kansas, 2004), 52–53.

27. Halder's phrase is "diesen verrückt gewordenen Soldaten." Entry for April 23, 1941, in Halder, *Kriegstagebuch*, 2:377–78.

28. Ibid.

29. An unforgettable scene, rendered nicely by Dennis Showalter, *Wars of Frederick the Great* (London: Longman, 1996), 203.

30. See Gordon A. Craig, *The Battle of Königgrätz: Prussia's Victory over Austria, 1866* (Philadelphia: Lippincott, 1964), 164. The Prussian supply net virtually collapsed during the Königgrätz campaign. The bread supply for the entire 1st Army, for example, was being baked as far away as Berlin, and the Prussian authorities tended to give priority to items like weaponry and ammunition. See German General Staff, *Studien zur Kriegsgeschichte und Taktik*, vol. 6, *Heeresverpflegung* (Berlin: E. S. Mittler, 1913), 105.

31. *Logistik* would be a word imported into German military circles from the west after 1945. A trenchant observation from Showalter, *Patton and Rommel*, 234.

32. See for example, Helmuth von Moltke's planning for war with France in 1870, which referred to "several marches into the French interior in the general direction of Paris in order to bring about a battle with the enemy army." See Ernst Kabisch, "Systemlose Strategie," *Militär-Wochenblatt* 125, no. 26 (December 27, 1940): 1235.

33. The best account of Operation Crusader—cogent and clear throughout, no mean feat for such a confused operation—is still Barnett, *Desert Generals*, 83–120, seen through the experience of General Alan Cunningham. No account communicates the chaos of the battle better than Crisp, *Brazen Chariots*, especially the friendly fire incident on 147–48, and the hilarious discussion of the difference between a "demonstration" and a "reconnaissance in force," 141–42. For the German perspective, see Hermann Büschleb, *Feldherren und Panzer im Wüstenkrieg: Die Herbstschlacht "Crusader" im Vorfeld von Tobruk, 1941* (Neckargemünd: Kurt Vowinckel, 1966), vol. 40 in the series Die Wehrmacht im Kampf.

34. Barnett, *Desert Generals*, 88–89.

35. See Crisp, *Brazen Chariots*, 41–42. The entire thing, he said, was a "balls-up" (49).

36. Barnett, *Desert Generals*, 101–2.

37. For the *Totensonntag* battle, see Rommel, *Krieg ohne Hass*, "Die Panzerschlacht am Totensonntag," 74–77. *Nota bene*: the author of this section of the book is not Rommel, but the Afrika Korps chief of staff, Fritz Bayerlein. See the equivalent passages in Rommel, *Rommel Papers*, 160–62.

38. For a fine biographical portrait, see Philip Warner, "Auchinleck," in *Churchill's Generals*, ed. John Keegan (New York: Grove Weidenfeld, 1991), 130–47.

39. For the "dash to the wire," see Rommel, *Krieg ohne Hass*, "Der Raid nach Agypten," 77–81. For the provenance, see note 37. See also the equivalent passages in Rommel, *Rommel Papers*, 163–67. The accounts in the German official history, Stegemann, "Die italienische-deutsche Kriegführung im Mittelmeer und in Afrika," 669–73, and Barnett, *Desert Generals*, 113–16, are still the best in the secondary literature.

40. For the battle of Gazala, see Rommel, *Krieg ohne Hass*, 109–74, and the parallel passages in Rommel, *Rommel Papers*, 189–232; Mellenthin, *Panzer Battles*, 107–37; Gause, "Der Feldzug in Nordafrika im Jahre 1942," 659–67; Nehring, *Geschichte der deutschen Panzerwaffe*, 190–99; and Westphal, *Erinnerungen*, 158–65.

The official histories are superb: for the Germans, see Stumpf, "Der Krieg im Mittelmeerraum, 1942–43," especially "Der Feldzug nach El Alamein (Unternehman 'Theseus')," 595–647; for the British, see I. S. O. Playfair, *The Mediterranean and Middle East*, vol. 3, *British Fortunes Reach their Lowest Ebb* (London: Her Majesty's Stationery Office, 1960), esp. 197–252. In the secondary literature, see Samuel W. Mitcham Jr., *Rommel's Greatest Victory: The Desert Fox and the Fall of Tobruk, 1942* (Novato, Calif.: Presidio, 1998), a typically rousing account; Neillands, *Eighth Army*, 91–118, marred only by its inclusion of overlong passages of first-person testimony; and Barnett, *Desert Generals*, 121–76, marred only its obsessive focus on the figures of Auchinleck, whom he defends, and Ritchie, whom he condemns. For a more sophisticated approach, see Carver, *Dilemmas of the Desert War*, 62–105; for Carver's direct rejoinder to Barnett, calling his argument "naïve," see 62–65. For an example of a nearly unreadable map that needlessly tries to reinvent the wheel and gets into trouble as a result, do not miss John Keegan, ed., *Collins Atlas of the Second World War* (Ann Arbor, Mich.: Borders Press, 2003), 80b.

41. For Rommel's second campaign, see the German official history, Stegemann, "Die italienische-deutsche Kriegführung im Mittelmeer und in Afrika," esp. 573–88.

42. See the map in ibid., facing 580.

43. For a critical analysis of the box, calling it "the nadir of British tactics in the desert," see Barr, *Pendulum of War*, 64–65.

44. Or sometimes the "Msus stakes." See Carver, *Dilemmas of the Desert War*, 139.

45. For a biographical portrait of Ritchie, see Michael Craster, "Cunningham, Ritchie and Leese," in *Churchill's Generals*, ed. John Keegan (New York: Grove Weidenfeld, 1991), 200–224.

46. A point Rommel stresses repeatedly: "Alle diese Verbände waren voll kampfkräftig und motorisiert," *Krieg ohne Hass*, 117; "vollmotorisiert Briten," 119; "vollmotorisierten Gegnern," 127. See, for example, Rommel, *Rommel Papers*, 195.

47. For the Grant's power in combat, see Schmidt, *With Rommel in the Desert*, especially the chapter entitled "My Battalion is Overrun," 145–51. For technical details, see Eric Grove, Christopher Chant, David Lyon, and Hugh Lyon, *The*

Military Hardware of World War II: Tanks, Aircraft, and Naval Vessels (New York: Military Press, 1984), 52–54; and Armin Halle and Carlo Demand, *Tanks: An Illustrated History of Fighting Vehicles* (New York: Crescent, 1971), 86–87.

48. In its original incarnation as the "Lee," it had an additional machine gun in a cupola on top of the turret, giving it a height of ten feet, three inches. See the discussion in Douglas Niles, "Ruweisat Ridge: The First Battle of El Alamein," *Strategy and Tactics*, no. 105 (January–February 1985): 16–21, especially the sidebar, "US M3 Medium Tank," 21. Like all issues of *Strategy and Tactics*, this one came complete with a war game ("conflict simulation"), *Ruweisat Ridge*, designed by Niles.

49. Rommel, *Krieg ohne Hass*, 117; Rommel, *Rommel Papers*, 196. Mellenthin, *Panzer Battles*, 111, specifies 561, not 560 (Rommel's command tank?).

50. Rommel, *Krieg ohne Hass*, 117–18; Rommel, *Rommel Papers*, 197 (wherein "rollende Särge" is translated as "self-propelled coffins").

51. Rommel, *Krieg ohne Hass*, 117; Rommel, *Rommel Papers*, 196.

52. Rommel, *Krieg ohne Hass*, 114; Rommel, *Rommel Papers*, 194.

53. Not "Venezia," as virtually all English-language histories of the operation have it. See the German official history, Stegemann, "Die italienische-deutsche Kriegführung im Mittelmeer und in Afrika," 598 n. 16.

54. For an introduction to Leuthen, see Dennis Showalter, "Masterpiece of Maneuver and Resolution," *Military History Quarterly* 11, no. 3 (spring 1999): 6–17; and Citino, *German Way of War*, 83–90. Setting the standard in the secondary literature are Dennis Showalter, *Wars of Frederick the Great* (London: Longman, 1996), 192–206; Christopher Duffy, *The Army of Frederick the Great* (London: David & Charles, 1974), 176–79; and Duffy, *Frederick the Great: A Military Life* (London: Routledge and Kegan Paul, 1985), 148–54.

55. As in both Rommel, *Krieg ohne Hass*, 124, and Rommel, *Rommel Papers*, 201–2. The actual operational orders specify "captured tanks and heavy trucks" ("Beutepanzern und schweren Kraftfahrzeugen"). See the German official history, Stegemann, "Die italienische-deutsche Kriegführung im Mittelmeer und in Afrika," 601.

56. For detailed orders of battle, look no further than the German official history, Stegemann, "Die italienische-deutsche Kriegführung im Mittelmeer und in Afrika," 600–603, as well as the essential Panzerarmee deployment map facing 596. It is a milestone for the study of Gazala: the first truly accurate map of Rommel's intentions for Operation Theseus.

57. Quoted in Heinz-Ludger Borgert, "Grundzüge der Landkriegführung von Schlieffen bis Guderian," in *Handbuch zur deutschen Militärgeschichte, 1648–1939*, vol. 9, *Grundzüge der militärischen Kriegführung* (Munich: Bernard & Graefe Verlag, 1979), 543.

58. For criticism of the deployment, see Barnett, *Desert Generals*, 140–41, in which the author opines that Ritchie did his best, "but, as the French proverb has it, the most beautiful girl can only give what she has" (140–43); contra Barnett, see Carver, *Dilemmas of the Desert War*, 64–67, who points out the obvious: Ritchie correctly guessed Rommel's intentions and deployed his armor accordingly.

59. See the ever-sensible Playfair, *Mediterranean and Middle East*, 3:216, who argues that "these minefields were really a compromise solution to the problem of how far to extend the desert flank."

60. See Mellenthin, *Panzer Battles*, 114.

61. Playfair, *Mediterranean and Middle East*, 3:217–19.

62. Rommel, *Krieg ohne Hass*, 126; Rommel, *Rommel Papers*, 202–3.

63. The quote is from Ritchie's immediate superior in Cairo, where he was serving as Brigadier General Staff to Auchinleck as GOC Southern Command. Barnett, *Desert Generals*, 123.

64. German official history, Stegemann, "Die italienische-deutsche Kriegführung im Mittelmeer und in Afrika," 605.

65. See *German Experiences in Desert Warfare during World War II*, vol. 2, Fleet Marine Force Reference Publication (FMFRP) 12-96-II (Quantico, Va.: United States Marine Corps, 1990), A-8–20. The author is General Alfred Toppe, Chief of the Wehrmacht's Army Supply Department.

66. Ibid.

67. German official history, Stegemann, "Die italienische-deutsche Kriegführung im Mittelmeer und in Afrika," 605–6.

68. Rommel, *Krieg ohne Hass*, 125–26; Rommel, *Rommel Papers*, 202.

69. German official history, Stegemann, "Die italienische-deutsche Kriegführung im Mittelmeer und in Afrika," 606.

70. Mellenthin, *Panzer Battles*, 116.

71. Rommel, *Krieg ohne Hass*, 128; Rommel, *Rommel Papers*, 206.

72. Barnett, *Desert Generals*, 146, identified only as "the words of an eyewitness."

73. Playfair, *Mediterranean and Middle East*, 3:223

74. German official history, Stegemann, "Die italienische-deutsche Kriegführung im Mittelmeer und in Afrika," 609.

75. Barnett, *Desert Generals*, 164.

76. German official history, Stegemann, "Die italienische-deutsche Kriegführung im Mittelmeer und in Afrika," 609.

77. Ibid., 608.

78. Rommel, *Krieg ohne Hass*, 131–32; Rommel, *Rommel Papers*, 208.

79. See the discussion in Paddy Griffith, *Forward into Battle: Fighting Tactics from Waterloo to the Near Future* (Novato, Calif.: Presidio, 1990), 123–26.

80. This significant phrase is Field Marshal Albert Kesselring's. See Showalter, *Patton and Rommel*, 268.

81. Gause, "Der Feldzug in Nordafrika im Jahre 1942," 662.

82. Barnett, *Desert Generals*, 150.

83. Playfair, *Mediterranean and Middle East*, 3:232.

84. Ibid.

85. Mellenthin, *Panzer Battles*, 132–33.

86. Playfair, *Mediterranean and Middle East*, 3:232–33.

87. Ibid., 234.

88. See Gause, "Der Feldzug in Nordafrika im Jahre 1942," 663–64; and the German official history, Stegemann, "Die italienische-deutsche Kriegführung im Mittelmeer und in Afrika," 619–20.

89. Rommel, *Krieg ohne Hass*, 123; Rommel, *Rommel Papers*, 201.

90. Playfair, *Mediterranean and Middle East*, 3:272.

91. C. W. Ridley, "The Battle of the Cauldron," *Journal of the Society for Army Historical Research* 68, no. 274 (1990): 75–82; the passage is from 76.

92. Ibid.

93. See the German official history, Stegemann, "Die italienische-deutsche Kriegführung im Mittelmeer und in Afrika," 629.

94. *Grossdeutschlands Freiheitskrieg*, pt. 151, "Die Auswertung des Sieges von Tobruk," *Militär-Wochenblatt* 127, no. 1 (July 3, 1942): 1–5. The quote is from 1.

95. For a revealing comparative analysis from the German perspective, see General Dittmar, "Tobruk und Sewastopol," *Militär-Wochenblatt* 127, no. 1 (July 3, 1942): 10–13.

96. See Colonel Obermayer, "Gedanken zur soldatischen Tradition: Friedrich der Grosse—Moltke—Schlieffen—Seeckt," *Militär-Wochenblatt* 127, no. 3 (July 17, 1942): 63–66. The quotes are from 63.

Chapter 5. Debacle: The 1942 Summer Campaign

1. The battle for the city of Stalingrad has a huge body of literature devoted to it, and the Soviet offensive that ended it has not done badly, either. The complex campaign that led up to it, however (Operation Blue) has been underserved, rarely rating more than a clichéd sentence or two in the general histories. There are three essential works on the topic. The first is the primary source by Hans Doerr, *Der Feldzug nach Stalingrad: Versuch eines operativen Überblickes* (Darmstadt: E. S. Mittler, 1955). It is interesting to see the one passage from Doerr's book that appears in virtually every book on Stalingrad (the present one included): the description of the nature of urban combat within the city ("Der Kilometer als Masseinheit wich dem Meter, die Generalstabskarte dem Stadtplan," 52). In fact, urban combat is not the subject of the book at all. In the German tradition, Doerr is much more interested in the operational prehistory of the city fight (the *Vorgeschichte*, Doerr calls it, 15), the weeks of *Bewegungskrieg* in the open field that brought the Wehrmacht to Stalingrad (and to the Caucasus) in such bad shape. The second essential work is the German official history, Militärgeschichtliches Forschungsamt (Military Historical Research Office), *Das Deutsche Reich und der Zweite Weltkrieg*, vol. 6, *Die Ausweitung zum Weltkrieg und der Wechsel der Initiative, 1941–1943* (Stuttgart: Deutsche Verlags-Anstalt, 1990) (hereinafter GOH), pt. 6, "Der Krieg gegen Die Sowjetunion, 1942–43," authored by Bernd Wegner. See especially the sections on "Hitlers 'zweiter Feldzug': Militärische Konzeption und strategtische Grundlagen" (761–815) and "Der Beginn der Sommeroffensive" (868–98). The third essential work, and the best study of the topic currently

available in English, is Joel S. A. Hayward, *Stopped at Stalingrad: The Luftwaffe and Hitler's Defeat in the East, 1943–1943* (Lawrence: University Press of Kansas, 1998), a book that is ostensibly about air operations but that is also a careful analysis of the interplay between land, air, and sea. It is carefully researched, deftly written, and one of the ten or so most important books ever published on the war in the east.

Beyond these two, see the three earliest western works on the German-Russian war, written by a Pole, a Swiss, and a Frenchman, respectively: Wladyslaw Anders, *Hitler's Defeat in Russia* (Chicago: H. Regnery Co., 1953), 81–158, has sober operational analysis that has stood the test of time, and the same might be said for Colonel E. Lederrey, *Germany's Defeat in the East: The Soviet Armies at War, 1941–1945* (London: War Office, 1955). The third in the trio, however, General Augustin Guillaume, *The German-Russian War, 1941–1945* (London: War Office, 1956), must be used with caution because the numbers he quotes often seem absurd, e.g., the 1,500 tanks and 180,000 killed the Germans suffered at Stalingrad (22). The following continue to be useful: Earl Ziemke and Magna Bauer, *Moscow to Stalingrad: Decision in the East* (Washington, D.C.: Center of Military History, 1987), 283–397; John Erickson, *The Road to Stalingrad* (New York: Harper & Row, 1975), 343–93; Walter Kerr, *The Secret of Stalingrad* (Garden City, N.Y.: Doubleday, 1978). Less useful are Matthew Cooper, *The German Army, 1933–1945* (Chelsea, Mich.: Scarborough House, 1978), which devotes all of six pages (415–21) to the actual operation; and Alan Clark, *Barbarossa: The Russian German Conflict, 1951–45* (New York: Quill, 1985), 204–19, which offers a particularly disjointed account. German secondary sources include Karlheinrich Rieker, *Ein Mann verliert einen Weltkrieg: Die entscheidenden Monate des deutsch-russischen Krieges, 1942–43* (Frankfurt am Main: Fridericus-Verlag, 1955), which offers interesting operational analysis; and Guido Knopp, *Stalingrad: Das Drama* (Munich: Bertelsmann, 2002), a popular work with a surprising level of operational detail, authored by a historian/television personality.

2. Entry for March 25, 1942, in General Franz Halder, *Kriegstagebuch*, vol. 3, *Der Russlandfeldzug bis zum Marsch auf Stalingrad* (Stuttgart: W. Kohlhammer Verlag, 1964), 418.

3. GOH, Wegner, "Der Krieg gegen Die Sowjetunion, 1942–43," 6:779.

4. Ziemke and Bauer, *Moscow to Stalingrad*, 293.

5. See George E. Blau, *The German Campaign in Russia—Planning and Operation, 1940–1942*, Department of the Army Pamphlet 20-261a (Washington, D.C.: Department of the Army, 1955), 137. The book is part of the German Reports Series. Blau based his text on manuscripts written by the German generals in captivity, among them General Franz Halder, chief of the General Staff until 1942, General Gotthard Heinrici, "and others" (iii). It is good on the preparations for the offensive (the German authors apparently had use of their planning memoranda), but too general on the actual course of operations.

6. Ibid., 138.

7. Ibid., 149–50.

8. Walter Warlimont, *Inside Hitler's Headquarters, 1939–45* (Novato, Calif.: Presidio, 1964), 239–40. Warlimont was deputy chief of operations for the OKW from 1939 to 1944.

9. Ziemke and Bauer, *Moscow to Stalingrad*, 294; Warlimont, *Inside Hitler's Headquarters*, 240. See also Andreas Kunz, "Vor sechzig Jahren: Der Untergang der 6. Armee in Stalingrad," *Militärgeschichte*, no. 4 (2002): 8–17, especially the photo at the top of 10.

10. Blau, *German Campaign in Russia*, 126.

11. Count Galeazzo Ciano, quoted in Richard L. DiNardo, *Germany and the Axis Powers: From Coalition to Collapse* (Lawrence: University Press of Kansas, 2005), 136.

12. See the table entitled "Die deutsche Einschätzung der sowjetischen Industrieproduktion des Jahres 1942," in GOH, Wegner, "Der Krieg gegen Die Sowjetunion, 1942–43," 6:806.

13. The figure is General Hans von Seeckt, and the German is "Das Wesentliche ist die Tat!" See the cover of the *Militär-Wochenblatt* 125, no. 43 (April 25, 1941), a memorial on what would have been Seeckt's seventy-fifth birthday. The standard work on the general is James S. Corum, *The Roots of Blitzkrieg: Hans von Seeckt and German Military Reform* (Lawrence: University Press of Kansas, 1992). See also Robert M. Citino, *The Evolution of Blitzkrieg Tactics: Germany Defends Itself against Poland* (Westport, Conn.: Greenwood, 1987). For German opinion of Seeckt during the war, see Fritz Pohl, "Generaloberst von Seeckt und die Reichswehr," *Militär-Wochenblatt* 127, no. 25 (December 18, 1942): 673–78.

14. The German is "Untätigkeit belastet schwerer als ein Fehlgreifen in der Wahl der Mittel." See Bruce Condell and David T. Zabecki, *On the German Art of War: Truppenführung* (Boulder, Colo.: Lynne Rienner, 2001), paragraph 15, 19.

15. Robert M. Citino, *The German Way of War: From the Thirty Years' War to the Third Reich* (Lawrence: University Press of Kansas, 2005), 32.

16. On Blücher's inability to read a map, see the testimony of his Russian comrade, General Alexandre de Langeron. Eberhard Kessel, "Blücher: Zum 200. Geburtstag am 16. Dezember," *Militärwissenschaftliche Rundschau* 7, no. 4 (1942): 309–10.

17. "Der Prinz was überhaupt kein Genie." In Lieutenant Foerster, "Prinz Friedrich Karl," *Militärwissenschaftliche Rundschau* 8, no. 2 (1943): 89.

18. Entry for January 28, 1942, in Fedor von Bock, *Generalfeldmarschall Fedor von Bock: The War Diary, 1939–1945* (Atglen, Pa.: Schiffer Military History, 1996), 413.

19. Ibid., entry for January 31, 1942 (416).

20. Kessel, "Blücher," 305.

21. Ibid., 312.

22. All quotes taken from Foerster, "Prinz Friedrich Karl," 90–91.

23. The officer is Kurt von Tippelskirch. Quoted in GOH, Wegner, "Der Krieg gegen Die Sowjetunion, 1942–43," 6:776.

24. Christian Hartmann, *Halder: Generalstabschef Hitlers, 1938–1942* (Paderborn: Ferdinand Schöningh, 1991), 319.

25. For Directive 41, see Walther Hubatsch, *Hitlers Weisungen für die Kriegführung, 1939–1945* (Koblenz: Bernard & Graefe, 1983), 183–91.

26. Directive 41, "Allgemeine Absicht," Hubatsch, *Hitlers Weisungen*, 184.

27. Directive 41, "Die Hauptoperation an der Ostfront," Hubatsch, *Hitlers Weisungen*, 185.

28. Carl von Clausewitz, *On War*, ed. and trans. Michael Howard and Peter Paret (Princeton: Princeton University Press, 1976), book 1, chap. 7, "Friction in War," 119.

29. See the indispensable work by Daniel J. Hughes, ed., *Moltke on the Art of War: Selected Writings* (Novato, Calif.: Presidio, 1993), 91.

30. A standard translation. Hughes, *Moltke*, 92, has it, "Therefore no plan of operations extends with any certainty beyond the first contact with the main hostile force."

31. "Die strategie ist ein System der Aushilfen." See "Generalfeldmarschall Graf von Schlieffen über den grossen Feldherren der preussisch-deutschen Armee," *Militär-Wochenblatt* 125, no. 17 (October 25, 1940): 805–7. For a general discussion of this point, see in that same wartime issue General Ludwig, "Moltke als Erzieher," *Militär-Wochenblatt* 125, no. 17 (October 25, 1940): 802–4.

32. Directive 41, " Die Hauptoperation an der Ostfront," Hubatsch, *Hitlers Weisungen*, 185.

33. See Colonel Müller-Loebnitz, "Führerwille und Selbständigkeit der Unterführer," pt. 1, *Militär-Wochenblatt* 122, no. 22 (November 26, 1937), and pt. 2, *Militär-Wochenblatt* 122, no. 23 (December 3, 1937): 1431–34. See also the lead editorial by General Wetzell, "Vom Geist deutscher Feldherren," *Militär-Wochenblatt* 123, no. 20 (November 11, 1938): 1273–79.

34. Warlimont, *Inside Hitler's Headquarters*, 231. See also the comments of the deputy chief of the General Staff, General Günther Blumentritt, who bemoaned the "abundance and length of the orders—the very contrary to our training. Their often bombastic language and use of superlatives was against all the rules of the old style—with its pregnant shortness and concise phrasing." Basil Liddell Hart, *The German Generals Talk* (New York: Quill, 1979), 197.

35. Directive 41, " Die Hauptoperation an der Ostfront," Hubatsch, *Hitlers Weisungen*, 185.

36. Entry for March 28 in Halder, *Kriegstagebuch*, 3:420. See also Ziemke and Bauer, *Moscow to Stalingrad*, 290.

37. Operation Blue cannot be studied adequately without access to a series of maps, and not all are to be trusted. See the comprehensive set of twenty-three detailed *Skizzen* appended to Doerr, *Feldzug nach Stalingrad*. For the opening of the operation, see *Skizze* 1, "Plan gemäss Führerweisung Nr. 41 vom 5. April."

38. "The goal of this breakthrough is the occupation of Voronezh itself." Directive 41, " Die Hauptoperation an der Ostfront," Hubatsch, *Hitlers Weisungen*, 186.

39. Hayward, *Stopped at Stalingrad*, 22–25, contains a lucid explanation of this complicated operation; Ziemke and Bauer, *Moscow to Stalingrad*, 286–90, is also helpful.

40. Directive 41, "Die Hauptoperation an der Ostfront," Hubatsch, *Hitlers Weisungen*, 186.

41. For the Reichel case, see GOH, Wegner, "Der Krieg gegen Die Sowjetunion, 1942–43," 6:868–69. See also the cogent account in Geoffrey Jukes, *Hitler's Stalingrad Decisions* (Berkeley: University of California Press, 1985), 31–33.

42. Jean Vanwelkenhuyzen, "Die Krise vom January 1940," *Wehrwissenschaftliche Rundschau* 5, no. 2 (February 1955): 66–90, is still the best piece on the Mechelen incident.

43. GOH, Wegner, "Der Krieg gegen Die Sowjetunion, 1942–43," 6:868–69.

44. Entry for June 25, 1942, Bock, *War Diary*, 505–6.

45. Untranslatable. Ziemke and Bauer, *Moscow to Stalingrad*, has it literally: "Point your nose forward and follow it." The entry for June 28, 1942, in Bock, *War Diary*, gives it as, "Concern yourself with the business at hand!"

46. Erickson, *Road to Stalingrad*, 338–42; David M. Glantz and Jonathan House, *When Titans Clashed: How the Red Army Stopped Hitler* (Lawrence: University Press of Kansas, 1995), 105–6.

47. Ziemke and Bauer, *Moscow to Stalingrad*, 228–30, has virtually the only sustained discussion of Operation Kreml in the literature.

48. GOH, Wegner, "Der Krieg gegen Die Sowjetunion, 1942–43," 6:875. See also *Skizze* 2, "Durchbruch der Armeegruppe Weichs auf Woronesh und Abdrehen des XXXX. Pz Korps nach Süden," appended to Doerr, *Feldzug nach Stalingrad.*

49. Erickson, *Road to Stalingrad*, 356.

50. The title of the chapter on Operation Blue in Clark, *Barbarossa*, 204–19.

51. For Soviet counterblows at Voronezh, which began early and never really did stop, see David M. Glantz, "Forgotten Battles of the German-Soviet War (1941–1945), Part 7: The Summer Campaign (12 May–18 November 1942): Voronezh, July 1942," *Journal of Slavic Military Studies* 14, no. 3 (September 2001): 150–220.

52. On the travails of the Hungarian 2nd Army, see Heinz Helmert and Helmut Otto, "Zur Koalitionskriegsführung Hitler-Deutschlands im zweiten Weltkrieg am Beispiel des Einsatzes der ungarischen 2. Armee," *Zeitschrift für Militärgeschichte* 2, no. 3 (1963): 320–39.

53. For a primary source on the advance of 6th Army's spearhead, see Carl Wagener, "Der Vorstoss des XXXX. Panzerkorps von Charkow zum Kaukasus, July–August 1942," Part 1, *Wehrwissenschaftliche Rundschau* 5, no. 9 (September 1955): 397–407.

54. Entry for July 1, 1942, Bock, *War Diary*, 510.

55. Ziemke and Bauer, *Moscow to Stalingrad*, 339–340.

56. Quoted in Geoffrey Roberts, *Victory at Stalingrad* (London: Longman, 2002), 60.

57. Entry for July 6, 1942, in Halder, *Kriegstagebuch*, 3:474. For a short biographical sketch of Hoth, see Robert M. Citino, *Armored Forces: History and Sourcebook* (Westport, Conn.: Greenwood Press, 1994), 246–48.

58. Entry for July 6, 1942, in Halder, *Kriegstagebuch*, 3:474. For a short biographical sketch of Bock, see Citino, *Armored Forces*, 224.

59. See the discussion in Citino, *German Way of War*, 301–5.

60. The phrase is "das sture Losrennen Hoths auf Woronesh," entry for July 5, 1942, in Halder, *Kriegstagebuch*, 3:474.

61. Entry for July 2, 1942, in Bock, *War Diary*, 512.

62. Ibid., entry for March 22, 1943 (539).

63. Ibid., 540.

64. Quoted in Ziemke and Bauer, *Moscow to Stalingrad*, 339.

65. Entry for July 6, 1942, in Halder, *Kriegstagebuch*, 3:475.

66. Wagener, "Der Vorstoss des XXXX. Panzerkorps," pt. 1, 407.

67. Particularly good on the order is Richard Overy, *Russia's War: A History of the Soviet War Effort, 1914–1945* (New York: Penguin, 1998), 158–61.

68. "Einen gegner einzukesseln, der nicht mehr da ist." Entry for July 7, 1942, in Bock, *War Diary*, 520. See also GOH, Wegner, "Der Krieg gegen Die Sowjetunion, 1942–43," 6:881.

69. Entry for July 8, 1942, in Bock, *War Diary*, 520.

70. See Doerr, *Feldzug nach Stalingrad*, 19–20.

71. See Ziemke and Bauer, *Moscow to Stalingrad*, 346.

72. Wagener, "Der Vorstoss des XXXX. Panzerkorps," pt. 1, 405.

73. For the maneuver on Millerovo, see *Skizze* 3, "Lage beim Eintreffen des Führerbefehls vom 13. 7.," appended to Doerr, *Feldzug nach Stalingrad.*

74. Entries for July 12 and July 13, 1942, in Bock, *War Diary*, 525–26.

75. See *Skizze* 4, "Lage 13.7.," appended to Doerr, *Feldzug nach Stalingrad.*

76. For the fighting in Rostov, see Bernd Overhues, Günther Pilz, and Bruno Waske, "Über die Barrikaden: Der Sturm auf Rostow," *Die Wehrmacht* 6, no. 17 (August 19, 1942): 6–9.

77. For a contemptuous look at "Die 'Kesselschlacht' von Rostow," see Doerr, *Feldzug nach Stalingrad*, 22–24.

78. See the primary source, Eberhard von Mackensen, *Vom Bug zum Kaukasus: Das III. Panzerkorps im Feldzug gegen Sowjetrussland, 1941–42* (Neckargemünd: Kurt Vowinckel, 1967), especially "Zum zweiten Mal gen Rostow, 27.6.–25.7. 1942," 85–90.

79. Ibid., 86–87.

80. Ibid., 90.

81. For the subsequent "dismemberment" of the 11th Army, see the primary source, Erich von Manstein, *Lost Victories* (Novato, Calif.: Presidio, 1982), 260–61.

82. Quoted in Wagener, "Der Vorstoss des XXXX. Panzerkorps," pt. 1, 407.

83. Doerr, *Feldzug nach Stalingrad*, 24 n. 11.

84. Wagener, "Der Vorstoss des XXXX. Panzerkorps," pt. 1, 398–99.

85. Ibid., 405.

Chapter 6. Coming to a Halt: North Africa

1. See the German official history (hereinafter GOH), Militärgeschichtliches Forschungsamt (Military Historical Research Office), *Das Deutsche Reich und Der Zweite Weltkrieg*, vol. 6, *Der Globale Krieg: Die Ausweitung zum Weltkrieg und der Wechsel der Initiative, 1941–1943*, especially pt. 5, Reinhard Stumpf, "Der Krieg im

Mittelmeerraum, 1942–43: Die Operationen in Nordafrika und im mittleren Mittelmeer," 567–757; the phrase is found on 650.

2. " . . . unter Anspannung der letzten Kräfte." See Erwin Rommel, *Krieg Ohne Hass* (Heidenheim: Heidenheimer Zeitung, 1950). It is a memoir edited (and partially written by) the former Afrika Korps Chief of Staff Fritz Bayerlein. *The Rommel Papers*, ed. B. H. Liddell Hart (New York: Harcourt, Brace, 1953), is a translation of the English equivalent, although it intersperses Rommel's letters to his wife Lu throughout the text, which sometimes assists the reader's understanding and sometimes simply distracts.

3. One of the most controversial topics of the entire war was the Axis's decision against the invasion of Malta. British sources tend to argue the importance of the island in defeating Rommel; most German sources don't think that the Axis had sufficient forces to attack it; and historian Martin van Creveld has staked out revisionist terrain by arguing that it was the lack of transport within Africa that was Rommel's downfall, not British ships and planes prowling from Malta against Axis convoys. For a good discussion by a top-notch historian, see Douglas Porch, *The Path to Victory: The Mediterranean Theater in World War II* (New York: Farrar, Straus & Giroux, 2004), 281–82. For the pertinent literature, see GOH, Stumpf, "Der Krieg im Mittelmeerraum," 6:588–94 ("Der Kampf um Malta, Dezember 1941 bis 21. Mai 1942"), and 6:751–57 ("Das Nachschubproblem"); Martin van Creveld, *Supplying War: Logistics from Wallenstein to Patton* (Cambridge: Cambridge University Press, 1977), 195–96, 198–201; the British official history, I. S. O. Playfair, *The Mediterranean and Middle East*, vol. 3, *British Fortunes Reach their Lowest Ebb* (London: Her Majesty's Stationery Office, 1960), esp. 177–95 ("Malta's Greatest Trial, April–May 1942"); and F. H. Hinsley et al., *British Intelligence in the Second World War: Its Influence on Strategy and Operations*, 3 vols. (Cambridge: Cambridge University Press, 1979–1988), esp. 2:417–24.

4. Alfred Gause (chief of staff to Panzerarmee Afrika), "Der Feldzug in Nordafrika im Jahre 1942," *Wehrwissenschaftliche Rundschau* 12, no. 11 (November 1962): 652–80. See esp. 667–68.

5. F. W. von Mellenthin (the Panzerarmee's intelligence officer), *Panzer Battles: A Study of the Employment of Armor in the Second World War* (New York: Ballantine, 1956), 149–50.

6. Siegfried Westphal (Rommel's operations officer), "Notes on the Campaign in North Africa, 1941–943," *Journal of the Royal United Service Institution* 105, no. 617 (1960), 70–81. For the quote, see 77.

7. GOH, Stumpf, "Der Krieg im Mittelmeerraum," 6:636–37. His last promotion, to Generaloberst, had only been six months ago.

8. Mellenthin, *Panzer Battles*, 149.

9. Ibid., 150.

10. GOH, Stumpf, "Der Krieg im Mittelmeerraum," 6:634.

11. See Walter Warlimont (deputy chief of operations for the OKW from 1939 to 1944), *Inside Hitler's Headquarters, 1939–45* (Novato, Calif.: Presidio, 1964), 241. See also GOH, Stumpf, "Der Krieg im Mittelmeerraum," 6:634.

12. GOH, Stumpf, "Der Krieg im Mittelmeerraum," 6:644.

13. Rommel, *Krieg ohne Hass*, 167; Rommel, *Rommel Papers*, 236.

14. Mellenthin, *Panzer Battles*, 152.

15. Rommel, *Krieg ohne Hass*, 177; Rommel, *Rommel Papers*, 243. Gause, "Der Feldzug in Nordafrika im Jahre 1942," 668, gives a figure of 30,000 tons for May, when the Luftwaffe effort against Malta was at its height.

16. The best operational account is GOH, Stumpf, "Der Krieg im Mittelmeerraum," especially "Der Vorstoss nach El Alamein," 6:637–42, as well as the extremely useful maps facing 629. See also Playfair, *Mediterranean and Middle East*, vol. 3, especially "The Retreat to El Alamein," 277–97, and map 31, facing 283.

17. For British vehicles fooling the Desert Air Force and British columns, see Rommel, *Krieg ohne Hass*, 167; and Rommel, *Rommel Papers*, 236. For fooling the Italians, see Rommel, *Krieg ohne Hass*, 172; and Rommel, *Rommel Papers*, 240.

18. For the botched intelligence appreciation of the British deployment at Mersa Matruh, see the primary source, intelligence officer Mellenthin, *Panzer Battles*, 152–53.

19. For critiques of the British deployment at Mersa Matruh—there are no real defenders of it—see Playfair, *Mediterranean and Middle East*, 3:284–89; Correlli Barnett, *The Desert Generals* (Bloomington: Indiana University Press, 1982), 168–70; Niall Barr, *The Pendulum of War: The Three Battles of El Alamein* (New York: Overlook Press, 2005), 26–30; Barrie Pitt, *The Crucible of War: Year of Alamein, 1942* (London: Jonathan Cape, 1982), 115–29; and the always authoritative Michael Carver, *Dilemmas of the Desert War: A New Look at the Libyan Campaign, 1940–1942* (London: Batsford, 1986), 124–28. Otherwise, Mersa Matruh often gets lost, occurring as it did between the twin dramas of Gazala-Tobruk on the one hand and the battles of El Alamein on the other. It is missing, for example, in such standard works as John Bierman and Colin Smith, *Alamein: War without Hate* (London: Viking, 2002).

20. Barr, *Pendulum of War*, 26–27.

21. Mellenthin, *Panzer Battles*, 155 n. 22. See also Porch, *Path to Victory*, 299: "Ritchie and Auchinleck had failed to meld the Eight Army into a coherent force. The British generals had been too clever by half, shattering units and then reassembling them into 'brigade groups' and 'battle groups,' all in the name of flexibility."

22. Ritchie's orders from the Middle East Defense Committee. Quoted in Barr, *Pendulum of War*, 22.

23. Quoted in Playfair, *Mediterranean and Middle East*, 3:287.

24. Ibid., 286.

25. Ibid., 287.

26. Quoted in Barnett, *Desert Generals*, 186.

27. Quoted in Barr, *Pendulum of War*, 26.

28. See Pitt, *Crucible of War*, 119–20; Carver, *Dilemmas of the Desert War*, 127–28. The classic judgment on British preparation for Mersa Matruh, especially on Auchinleck's role, is found in Playfair, *Mediterranean and Middle East*, 3:287:

"Whether the fluid tactics were appropriate to the occasion or not, they were certainly new and entirely unpracticed. The British tactical doctrine for a withdrawal had for many years insisted that anything in the nature of a running fight must be avoided. Thus the 8th Army was facing a bewildering number of changes. Its Commander had been replaced; it was retreating before a thrusting enemy; it had barely prepared itself for one kind of battle when it was ordered to fight another; and in the midst of all this it was told to change its organization and its tactics. But before anything could be done in the way of reorganization, the enemy put an end to one uncertainty by starting to attack."

29. Playfair, *Mediterranean and Middle East*, 289.

30. Quoted in Barr, *Pendulum of War*, 28.

31. Mellenthin, *Panzer Battles*, 154.

32. See Pitt, *Crucible of War*, 121–22.

33. Mellenthin, *Panzer Battles*, 155.

34. For variations on the "who had encircled whom" theme, see Mellenthin, *Panzer Battles*, 156, who argues that 90th Light "was hardly capable of tackling the British X Corps, which it had 'cut off' so impudently." Pitt, *Crucible of War*, 122, notes that 21st Panzer Division's move against the 2nd New Zealand's flank had give the "paper impression" of having cut it off. Barnett, *Desert Generals*, 188: "Rommel's advance constituted only a fantastic imposture."

35. See the careful character study of Gott, blunt yet fair, in Carver, *El Alamein* (London: Batsford, 1962), 29–31.

36. Playfair, *Mediterranean and Middle East*, 3:290–92.

37. For a detailed discussion of this charge, see GOH, Stumpf, "Der Krieg im Mittelmeerraum," 6:640–41 n. 240.

38. There was a garbled message from XIII Corps and one to 2nd New Zealand Division. "Both are inexplicable, and there is no clue as to who sent them, other than that the use of the word 'I' in each suggests that it may well have been General Gott." Playfair, *Mediterranean and Middle East*, 3:292.

39. "Gott was in fact telling General Freyberg of the New Zealanders that he could withdraw if he so wished." Barnett, *Desert Generals*, 189

40. "Unfortunately, the transport for the [2nd New Zealand] division had been chased off by 21st Panzer Division and was unreachable by radio." Barr, *Pendulum of War*, 29.

41. For the unforgettable scene, see Wolf Heckmann, *Rommel's War in Africa* (Garden City, N.Y.: Doubleday, 1981), 289. Heckmann is a modern cynic who attacks Rommel, the Afrika Korps, and the entire Desert War in full demythologizing mode. The approach, designed for a German audience, is trenchant, funny, and infuriating—often all three at once. It is one of the few indispensable books on North Africa, if only because of is uniqueness.

42. Mellenthin, *Panzer Battles*, 157.

43. Rommel, *Krieg ohne Hass*, 170; Rommel, *Rommel Papers*, 238.

44. GOH, Stumpf, "Der Krieg im Mittelmeerraum," 6:641.

45. Rommel, *Krieg ohne Hass*, 172–73; Rommel, *Rommel Papers*, 240.

46. GOH, Stumpf, "Der Krieg im Mittelmeerraum," 6:651.

47. Porch, *Path to Victory*, 286; Gause, "Der Feldzug in Nordafrika im Jahre 1942," 671, gives a figure of 550 kilometers (341 miles) "from Tobruk to the front."

48. Porch, *Path to Victory*, 321.

49. Quoted in Barnett, *Desert Generals*, 192.

50. Winston S. Churchill, *The Second World War*, vol. 4, *The Hinge of Fate* (Boston: Houghton Mifflin, 1950), 459.

51. The name of a chapter in Carver, *El Alamein*, 27–40.

52. Barr, *Pendulum of War*, 30.

53. Rommel, *Krieg ohne Hass*, 171–72; Rommel, *Rommel Papers*, 230–40.

54. Barr, *Pendulum of War*, 51–56, is the most informative on this crucial topic.

55. Playfair, *Mediterranean and Middle East*, 3:331.

56. Porch, *Path to Victory*, 281.

57. GOH, Stumpf, "Der Krieg im Mittelmeerraum," 6:646–47.

58. Quoted in Barr, *Pendulum of War*, 81.

59. Rommel, *Krieg ohne Hass*, 182; Rommel, *Rommel Papers*, 246.

60. Barr, *Pendulum of War*, 80.

61. See map 1.-3.7.42, facing 180, in Rommel, *Krieg ohne Hass*. As crude as the maps are in this volume, they have the advantage of displaying these battles on the operational level (divisions and corps)—in other words, the way a German commander was trained to see things—and for that reason are more useful than the more ornate ones that accompany many other works. Compare, for example, the map facing 331 in Playfair, *Mediterranean and Middle East*, vol. 3.

62. GOH, Stumpf, "Der Krieg im Mittelmeerraum," 6:656.

63. For full details of Robcol's successful—if harrowing—fight, see Barr, *Pendulum of War*, 86.

64. The classic source on the routing of the Ariete is the New Zealand Official History, J. L. Scoullar, *Battle for Egypt: The Summer of 1942* (Wellington: War History Branch, 1955), chap. 16, "Defeat of Ariete Division," 167–77.

65. For the destruction of the Sabratha division at Tel el Eisa ("Jesus Hill"), see Barr, *Pendulum of War*, 105–17, especially his demolition of the claim by General Eric Dorman-Smith, the chief of staff, that the attack was somehow an expression of Basil Liddell Hart's "indirect approach" (109–11). See also Playfair, *Mediterranean and Middle East*, 3:345–46.

66. Mellenthin, *Panzer Battles*, 164–65.

67. One loss that the Panzerarmee could not make good was the capture of the 621st Radio Intercept Company, Rommel's principal source of intelligence regarding enemy intentions and deployments. The company, perched behind the Italians "at possibly too far advanced operations point near Tel el Eisa"—in fact perhaps only 6,000 to 7,000 yards west of the front line—was "overrun and annihilated" in the wake of the dissolution of the Sabratha Division. For the 621st in general, see Hans-Otto Behrendt (an intelligence officer himself), *Rommel's Intelligence in the Desert Campaign, 1941–43* (London: William Kimber, 1985). For the capture of the company, see 168–87.

68. Scoullar, *Battle for Egypt*, 353. See also the entire chapter on the operation in Barr, *Pendulum of War*, 151–74.

69. He would escape that evening, after disguising himself as a private and spending the whole day helping to tend the wounded, only to be captured again a month later at Alam Halfa. See Rommel, *Krieg ohne Hass*, 218–18; Rommel, *Rommel Papers*, 281–82.

70. The title of the chapter on Operation Splendour in Scoullar, *Battle for Egypt*, 352–63.

71. Mellenthin, *Panzer Battles*, 169.

72. For his actions on that day, the baby-faced nineteen-year-old gunlayer Günther Halm would receive the Knight's Cross. See Heckmann, *Rommel's War in Africa*, especially "The Destruction of the 40th Royal Tank Regiment," 299–303.

73. Rommel, *Krieg ohne Hass*, 190; Rommel, *Rommel Papers*, 254.

74. Mellenthin, *Panzer Battles*, 172.

75. Rommel, *Krieg ohne Hass*, 199–200; Rommel, *Rommel Papers*, 264.

76. GOH, Stumpf, "Der Krieg im Mittelmeerraum," 6:670.

77. Mellenthin, *Panzer Battles*, 172.

78. For German sources on Rommel's operational plan at Alam Halfa, see GOH, Stumpf, "Der Krieg im Mittelmeerraum," 6:678–80; Gause, "Der Feldzug in Nordafrika im Jahre 1942," 672–74; Mellenthin, *Panzer Battles*, 170–74; Rommel, *Krieg ohne Hass*, 207–10; Rommel, *Rommel Papers*, 272–75.

79. Rommel, *Krieg ohne Hass*, 209; Rommel, *Rommel Papers*, 274.

80. For a solid biographical profile, see Michael Carver, "Montgomery," in *Churchill's Generals*, ed. John Keegan (New York: Grove Weidenfeld, 1991), 148–65; and Robert M. Citino, *Armored Forces: History and Sourcebook* (Westport, Conn.: Greenwood Press, 1994), 258–61. Nigel Hamilton, *Monty*, 3 vols. (London: Hamish Hamilton, 1981–1986), is still the standard work. In English, Fred Majdalany, *The Battle of El Alamein: Fortress in the Sand* (Philadelphia: Lippincott, 1965), 46–48, is a good place to start. It is part of Lippincott's Great Battles of History series, which remains a readable collection of operational history, and which deserves to be reprinted in some form.

81. So Rommel, *Rommel Papers*, 273, has it; the German in Rommel, *Krieg ohne Hass*, 208 is perhaps more subtle: "nur verhältnismässig leicht zu überwindende Minenanlagen."

82. Majdalany, *Battle of El Alamein*, 48.

83. "Im rasanten Vorstoss," according to General Nehring. Quoted in GOH, Stumpf, "Der Krieg im Mittelmeerraum," 6:679.

84. Majdalany, *Battle of El Alamein*, 48–61; and Barr, *Pendulum of War*, 218–52, share honors for the description of Alam Halfa. Mellenthin, *Panzer Battles*, 174–77, has also been extraordinarily influential.

85. "Die Briten wussten nun, wo wir stehen." Rommel, *Krieg ohne Hass*, 212. Rommel, *Rommel Papers*, 277, has it, "The enemy now knew where we were."

86. Dennis Showalter, *Patton and Rommel: Men of the War in the Twentieth Century* (New York: Berkley Caliber, 2005), 283.

87. For the drama of the Royal Scots Greys, see Majdalany, *Battle of El Alamein*, 54–56. For a more detailed account, see Barr, *Pendulum of War*, 230–31.

88. For a well-researched overview of the role of air power in the desert, with a great deal of tabular data, see Michael Cunningham, "Air War North Africa, 1940–43," *Strategy and Tactics*, no. 198 (July–August 1999): 20–38.

89. Rommel, *Krieg ohne Hass*, 215; Rommel, *Rommel Papers*, 279.

90. For the institution of the Six Days' Race, see Gordon A. Craig, *Germany, 1866–1945* (Oxford: Oxford University Press, 1978), 496–97.

91. Rommel, *Krieg ohne Hass*, 219–20, 223; Rommel, *Rommel Papers*, 283, 285.

92. Barr, *Pendulum of War*, 226.

93. Siegfried Westphal, *Erinnerungen* (Berlin: Von Hase & Koehler, 1975), 170.

94. GOH, Stumpf, "Der Krieg im Mittelmeerraum," 6:685.

Chapter 7. Coming to a Halt: The Caucasus and Stalingrad

1. Including, incredibly, the following one: "In the discussion the Führer made fun of the English for sacking every general for whom something went wrong and thus undermining the freedom of decision in their army." Hitler's reference was apparently to General Neil Ritchie, recently relieved of the command of 8th Army. See the entry for July 3, 1942, in Fedor von Bock, *Generalfeldmarschall Fedor von Bock: The War Diary, 1939–1945* (Atglen, Pa.: Schiffer Military History, 1996), 513. The officer to whom he made this comment would himself be dismissed just ten days later.

2. For "local engagements" (*örtliche Gefechtstätigkeit*), see *Grossdeutschlands Freiheitskrieg*, pt. 154, "Die Lage in Ägypten," *Militär-Wochenblatt* 127, no. 4 (July 24, 1942): 83–86. The quote is from 86. For "artillery and sporadic patrol activity" (*Artillerietätigkeit und vereinzelter Spähtruppzusammenstösse*), see *Grossdeutschlands Freiheitskrieg*, pt. 157, "Die militärischen und politischen Ereignisse vom 2. bis 8. August 1942," *Militär-Wochenblatt* 127, no. 7 (August 14, 1942): 169–73.

3. See the entry for July 6, 1942, in Franz Halder, *Kriegstagebuch*, vol. 3, *Der Russlandfeldzug bis zum Marsch auf Stalingrad* (Stuttgart: W. Kohlhammer Verlag, 1964), 475.

4. See Catherine Merridale, *Ivan's War: Life and Death in the Red Army, 1939–1945* (New York: Metropolitan Books, 2006), 155–60.

5. For Directive 45, see Walther Hubatsch, *Hitlers Weisungen für die Kriegführung, 1939–1945* (Koblenz: Bernard & Graefe, 1983), 196–200. See also Hans Doerr, *Der Feldzug nach Stalingrad: Versuch eines operativen Überblickes* (Darmstadt: E. S. Mittler, 1955), 124–26.

6. Introduction to Directive 45, Hubatsch, *Hitlers Weisungen*, 196.

7. Walther von Seydlitz, *Stalingrad: Konflikt und Konsequenz: Erinnerungen* (Oldenburg: Stalling, 1977), 169.

8. See the German official history, Militärgeschichtliches Forschungsamt (Military Historical Research Office), *Das Deutsche Reich und der Zweite Weltkrieg*, vol. 6, *Die Ausweitung zum Weltkrieg und der Wechsel der Initiative, 1941–1943* (Stutt-

gart: Deutsche Verlags-Anstalt, 1990), hereinafter GOH, part 6, "Der Krieg gegen Die Sowjetunion, 1942–43," authored by Bernd Wegner, esp. 6:887, "Die Aufspaltung der Offensive." The term originally belongs to Field Marshal Fedor von Bock, although he was referring more to the breakup of Army Group South into Army Groups A and B early on in Operation Blue, a split that he understandably opposed as diminishing his own command authority. See entry for July 5, 1942, in Bock, *War Diary*, 517.

9. For a campaign of such earth-shaking importance—indeed, the first war for oil—the literature on Operation Edelweiss is thin. The geography is remote, the campaign lacks the distinguishing feature of a great, culminating battle, and the entire undertaking lives in the shadow of the dramatic events unfolding to the north at Stalingrad. It is, in the parlance of military history cliché, the "forgotten war." Two books that may be said to have been standard works among the popular reading public both barely mention the campaign: Ian Clark, *Barbarossa: The Russian German Conflict, 1951–45* (New York: Quill, 1985), originally published in 1965; and Matthew Cooper, *The German Army, 1933–1945* (Chelsea, Mich.: Scarborough House, 1978). Indeed, neither "Mailkop" nor "Caucasus" even appears in Cooper's index. The entire campaign earns a single paragraph in John Keegan, *The Second World War* (New York: Penguin, 2005).

The best current source in English is the chapter devoted to it in Joel S. A. Hayward, *Stopped at Stalingrad: The Luftwaffe and Hitler's Defeat in the East, 1943–1943* (Lawrence: University Press of Kansas, 1998), 152–82. Hayward's focus is on air operations, but he also interweaves a great deal of analysis of the fighting on land. Also essential is the short chapter "Operation Edelweiss" in Earl Ziemke and Magna Bauer, *Moscow to Stalingrad: Decision in the East* (Washington, D.C.: Center of Military History, 1987), 366–81; John Erickson, *The Road to Stalingrad* (New York: Harper & Row, 1975), 376–81, offers useful details on the complex Soviet command structure in the region. Wilhelm Tieke, *The Caucasus and the Oil: The German-Soviet War in the Caucasus, 1942–43* (Winnipeg: J. J. Fedorowicz, 1995), is big, sprawling, and, unfortunately, far too disorganized to be the definitive work on the topic. A translation of the original German-language work from 1970, it delves into tactical details of the fighting with such relish that anyone looking for a broader, operational-level view will be disappointed, and its lack of an index is a serious oversight. For German-language sources, begin with GOH, pt. 6, Wegner, "Der Krieg gegen Die Sowjetunion, 1942–43." See especially chap. 5, "Die Offensive in den Kaukasus," 6:927–61. See also Roland Kaltenegger, *Gebirgsjäger im Kaukasus: Die Operation "Edelweiss," 1942–43* (Graz: Leopold Stocker, 1997), a fine journalistic account. As the title implies, it focuses on the mountain troops rather than the mobile formations, the text includes immense portions of unadorned and unanalyzed first-person testimony (the war diary of Oberjäger Alfred Richter, for example, covers twenty-two pages from 110–32), and once again its lack of an index makes it far less useful than it ought to have been.

Beyond these few works, it is necessary to consult a fairly obscure body of German-language literature in order to fill out the picture of German operation in the Caucasus. Almost all of it, like Kaltenegger, focuses on the exploits of the mountain troops. Among the few published primary sources, Rudolf Konrad and E. W. Rümmler, *Kampf um den Kaukasus* (Munich: Copress, 1955), is a useful short introduction. Konrad commanded the XXXXIX Mountain Corps during the campaign, so the focus is necessarily limited to his sector and the battle for the Black Sea ports; Rümmler had been a war photographer, and he contributed the book's interesting selection of photographs. Equally helpful in terms of photographs is Alex Buchner, *Die deutsche Gebirgstruppe, 1939–1945: Eine Bilddokumentation* (Dorheim: Podzun, 1971). The most famous mountaineer of them all was Josef Martin Bauer, perhaps the single most famous German soldier who took part in the campaign. He was one of the small team of volunteers who scaled the highest peak in the Caucasus chain, Mount Elbrus, on August 21. His account of that signal moment, *Kaukasisches Abenteuer* (Esslingen: Bechtle, 1950), has remained popular in German until the present day. It is, however, about as relevant to an operational study of the campaign as the conquest of the mountain had been to the original operation. Bauer was also an essayist and novelist, and among his immense body of writings, see his wartime diary from the eastern campaign, *Die Kraniche der Nogaia: Tagebuchblätter aus dem Feldzug im Osten* (Munich: R. Piper, 1942), and *As Far as My Feet Will Carry Me* (Morley, Yorkshire: Elmfield Press, 1957), a reality-based novel about "Clemens Forell," a German soldier who escaped Soviet captivity by traveling on foot through Siberia. For the rest of the sprawling front covered by the nonmountain troops, one must rely on the fairly short passages in Eberhard von Mackensen, *Vom Bug zum Kaukasus: Das III. Panzerkorps im Feldzug gegen Sowjetrussland, 1941–42* (Neckargemünd: Kurt Vowinckel, 1967), especially "Nach Maikop," 91–95, and "Kämpfe im Terek-Gebiet," 96–111; and an article by the chief of the General Staff of one of the Panzer formations, Carl Wagener, "Der Vorstoss des XXXX. Panzerkorps von Charkow zum Kaukasus, July–August 1942," pt. 2, *Wehrwissenschaftliche Rundschau* 5, no. 10 (October 1959): 447–58. Two other works are partially helpful. See the relevant portions of Karlheinrich Rieker, *Ein Mann verliert einen Weltkrieg: Die entscheidenden Monate des deutsch-russischen Krieges, 1942–43* (Frankfurt am Main: Fridericus-Verlag, 1955), worth consulting for the overview. Finally, Joachim Hoffmann, *Kaukasien, 1942–43: Das deutsche Heer und die Orientvölker der Sowjetunion* (Freiburg: Rombach Verlag, 1991), contains interesting details of German policy toward the forty or so ethnic and religious groupings within the region, as well as the nearly 100,000 volunteers from the region who fought alongside the Germans, often in their own battalions, the 450th Turkestan or the 804th Azerbaidjani. For more on this topic, see Albert Jeloschek, Friedrich Richter, Ehrenfried Schütte, and Johannes Semler, *Freiwillige vom Kaukasus: Georgier, Armenier, Tschetschenen u. a. auf deutscher Seite: Der "Sonderverband Bergmann" und sein Gründer Theodor Oberländer* (Graz: Leopold Stocker, 2003).

In sum, the Caucasus campaign is deserving of an updated scholarly monograph in English, based on German-language sources, Russian-language sources, or both.

10. Hayward, *Stopped at Stalingrad*, 152.

11. Directive 45, "Ziele der weiteren Operationen," Hubatsch, *Hitlers Weisungen*, 197.

12. Konrad and Rümmler, *Kampf um den Kaukasus*, 19, has information, including a useful map, on the "high passes" (Hochpässe) in front of Tuapse and Suchumi.

13. For German military intelligence on the Georgian Military Road (Grusinische Heerstrasse) and the Ossetian Military Road (Ossetische Heerstrasse), see Tieke, *The Caucasus and the Oil*, 229–30. See also the recent article by Laurence Mitchell, "The High Road to the Caucasus: Exploring the Georgian Military Highway," *Hidden Europe*, no. 9 (July 2006): 2–7.

14. Hayward, *Stopped at Stalingrad*, 149.

15. Doerr, *Feldzug nach Stalingrad*, 27.

16. See "Kaukasien," *Militär-Wochenblatt* 126, no. 23 (December 5, 1941): 643–45.

17. Ibid., 645.

18. Directive 45, "Ziele der weiteren Operationen," Hubatsch, *Hitlers Weisungen*, 198.

19. Ibid.

20. GOH, Wegner, "Der Krieg gegen Die Sowjetunion, 1942–43," 6:930–31. See also the map facing 6:932, the most accurate operational map in print for Operation Edelweiss.

21. For XXXX Panzer Corps's great lunge to the Terek, see Wagener, "Der Vorstoss des XXXX. Panzerkorps," pt. 2, 447–53.

22. For the Russian command structure in the Caucasus, see Ziemke and Bauer, *Moscow to Stalingrad*, 367–68; Erickson, *Road to Stalingrad*, 376–77.

23. Quoted in Ziemke and Bauer, *Moscow to Stalingrad*, 370.

24. Mackensen, *Vom Bug zum Kaukasus*, 91.

25. A matter of great propaganda value to the Germans, as the sheer number of official photos of the crossings over the river testify. "Mit dem Schritt über den Unterlauf des Don und seine Nebenflüsse haben deutsche Soldaten zum erstenmal in diesem Kriege asiatischen Boden betreten." Caption to photo of "Manytsch—Damm: Grenze Europa Asien," *Die Wehrmacht* 6, no. 18 (September 2, 1942): 2. See also Mackensen, *Vom Bug zum Kaukasus*, 91; and Hayward, *Stopped at Stalingrad*, 155.

26. "Dem weichenden Russen auf den Fersen zu bleiben." Mackensen, *Vom Bug zum Kaukasus*, 91.

27. "Am 31. macht die 16. (mot) Inf. Div. einen gross Sprung vorwärts, zunächst weichendem Feind folgend, dann mit einem an Artl. und schweren Waffen starken Feind hart kämpfend." Mackensen, *Vom Bug zum Kaukasus*, 92.

28. A "model state farm," it had "three quarters of a million acres and its own laboratories, shops, and processing plants." Ziemke and Bauer, *Moscow to Stalingrad*, 366.

29. Mackensen, *Vom Bug Zum Kaukasus*, 92.

30. Tieke, *The Caucasus and the Oil*, 52.

31. "Die Hauptsache aber: ein Brückenkopf ist im Keim vorhanden." Mackensen, *Vom Bug Zum Kaukasus*, 92.

32. Ibid., 94

33. For the fighting in Maikop, see Tieke, *The Caucasus and the Oil*, 57–61.

34. Mackensen, *Vom Bug Zum Kaukasus*, 95.

35. Ziemke and Bauer, *Moscow to Stalingrad*, 370–71, have 1st Panzer Army "across the river in strength and bearing west toward Maikop, guided night and day by sheets of flame thousands of feet high."

36. Quoted in GOH, Wegner, "Der Krieg gegen Die Sowjetunion, 1942–43," 6:943.

37. The advanced guard of the Technische Brigade Mineralöl, "Advance Detachment Laad," actually came under attack along its march route by "enemy stragglers." See Tieke, *The Caucasus and the Oil*, 60–61. For the brigade in general, see GOH, Wegner, "Der Krieg gegen Die Sowjetunion, 1942–43," 6:942–43, and Hayward, *Stopped at Stalingrad*, 159–60.

38. Mentioned throughout the literature on the Caucasus. See, for example, Alexander Werth, *Russia at War, 1941–1945* (New York: Carroll & Graf, 1964), 565–66; Walter Kerr, *The Secret of Stalingrad* (Garden City, N.Y.: Doubleday, 1978), 99; and Erickson, *Road to Stalingrad*, 378.

39. The primary source for this great turnaround is Halder, *Kriegstagebuch*, vol. 3, especially the entries from July 23 to July 30, 488–94. See also Walter Warlimont, *Inside Hitler's Headquarters, 1939–45* (Novato, Calif.: Presidio, 1964), 248–50, for a good play-by-play, as well as Ziemke and Bauer, *Moscow to Stalingrad*, 362–65.

40. There were now two German armies in either thrust, an equalization that did not sit well with German staff officers trained to think in terms of a *Schwerpunkt*. For a fundamental criticism, see Doerr, *Feldzug nach Stalingrad*, 30 ("So war mit dem neuen Befehl Hitlers vom 30. 7. der letzte Rest operativer Konzeption über Bord geworfen").

41. Halder has Jodl making his pronouncement "mir grössen Tönen" ("in portentous tones"). Entry for July 30, Halder, *Kriegstagebuch*, 3:493.

42. For a good short introduction to the German brake and the Soviet recovery, see the pertinent pages in Gerhard Weinberg, *A World at Arms: A Global History of World War II*, 2nd ed. (Cambridge: Cambridge University Press, 2005), 415–17.

43. Mackensen, *Vom Bug zum Kaukasus*, 96 ("Zum Terek"), plus map.

44. For a primary source on VVS ground support in the Caucasus, see the memoirs of Sturmovik pilot Vasily B. Emelianenko, *Red Star against the Swastika: The Story of a Soviet Pilot over the Eastern Front* (London: Greenhiill, 2005).

45. Quoted in GOH, Wegner, "Der Krieg gegen Die Sowjetunion, 1942–43," 6:935.

46. Emelianenko, *Red Star against the Swastika*, 125.

47. GOH, Wegner, "Der Krieg gegen Die Sowjetunion, 1942–43," 6:938.

48. See the long extract from the report by General Gyldenfeldt, the operations chief of Army Group A, found in GOH, Wegner, "Der Krieg gegen Die Sowjetunion, 1942–43," 6:935–39.

49. Konrad and Rümmler, *Kampf um den Kaukasus*, 31.

50. Hayward, *Stopped at Stalingrad*, 168. For a good military biography of Korne, see the Web site "World War2.ro: Romanian Armed Forces in the Second World War," http://www.worldwar2.ro/generali/?article=102.

51. For the Novorossiisk fighting, see Erickson, *Road to Stalingrad*, 379–81.

52. Konrad and Rümmler, *Kampf um den Kaukasus*, 34.

53. The best discussion of this issue is Hayward, *Stopped at Stalingrad*, 170–71.

54. See General Konrad's (commander, XXXXIX Mountain Corps) interview with Hitler in Konrad and Rümmler, *Kampf um den Kaukasus*, 29–35.

55. Warlimont, *Inside Hitler's Headquarters*, 254.

56. For the "September crisis" in Vinnitsa and the shift to Zeitzler, see Geoffrey Megargee, *Inside Hitler's High Command* (Lawrence: University Press of Kansas, 2000), 179–89; Christian Hartmann, *Halder: Generalstabschef Hitlers, 1938–1942* (Paderborn: Ferdinand Schöningh, 1991), 329–42; and Warlimont, *Inside Hitler's Headquarters*, 252–64.

57. For this painful scene, see the diary entry for August 27, 1942, by Hitler's military adjutant, Gerhard Engel, *Heeresadjutant bei Hitler, 1938–1943: Aufzeichnungen des Major Engels* (Stuttgart: Deutsche Verlags-Anstalt, 1974), 124–25. Halder had been arguing that men were suffering and dying in the Caucasus because their commanders were not allowed to make even the simplest decisions to deploy them more sensibly. Hitler exploded: "Was wollen Sie, Herr Halder, der Sie nur, auch im ersten Weltkrieg, auf demselben Drehschemel sassen, mir über Truppe [*sic*] erzählen, Sie, der Sie nicht einmal das schwarze Verw(undeten)abzeichen tragen?" Warlimont, *Inside Hitler's Headquarters*, 252, offers slightly different language.

58. See Albert Speer, *Inside the Third Reich* (London: Spheere, 1971), 332; and Nicolaus von Below, *At Hitler's Side: The Memoirs of Hitler's Luftwaffe Adjutant, 1937–1945* (London: Greenhill, 2001), 150.

59. Hayward, *Stopped at Stalingrad*, 171, calls him "a fervent Nazi but also a dynamic leader with exceptional organizing abilities." Megargee, *Inside Hitler's High Command*, 183–84, is more critical, calling Zeitzler "confident and energetic to the point of impulsiveness" and arguing that his main qualifications were "his emphasis on the importance of will as well as overt allegiance to Hitler."

60. Ziemke and Bauer, *Moscow to Stalingrad*, 374, has the Black Sea Group containing 12th Army instead of 46th.

61. Hayward, *Stopped at Stalingrad*, 166–67.

62. For the Nalchik-Ordzhonkidze campaign, see the primary source, Mackensen, *Vom Bug zum Kaukasus*, 102–11; and Tieke, *The Caucasus and the Oil*, 221–37. The account in Hayward, *Stopped at Stalingrad*, 174–76, is particularly useful.

63. Mackensen, *Vom Bug zum Kaukasus*, 103.

64. Emelianenko, *Red Star against the Swastika*, 187.

65. Mackensen, *Vom Bug zum Kaukasus*, 103.

66. See Ziemke and Bauer, *Moscow to Stalingrad*, 453–54.

67. Mackensen, *Vom Bug zum Kaukasus*, 105.

68. Tieke, *The Caucasus and the Oil*, 234.

69. See the map in Mackensen, *Vom Bug zum Kaukasus*, 104.

70. See *Grossdeutschlands Freiheitskrieg*, pt. 170, "Bei Tuapse und am Terek Raumgewinn," *Militär-Wochenblatt* 127, no. 20 (November 13, 1942): 527–31, esp. 529–30.

71. Tieke, *The Caucasus and the Oil*, 230.

72. Mackensen, *Vom Bug zum Kaukasus*, 107–80; Hayward, *Stopped at Stalingrad*, 175–76.

73. Carl von Clausewitz, *On War*, ed. and trans. Michael Howard and Peter Paret (Princeton: Princeton University Press, 1976), 101.

74. The literature on Stalingrad is voluminous. Most of it deals with the fighting in the city and the Soviet counteroffensive afterward, rather than the German campaign in the open field that brought the Wehrmacht to Stalingrad. The three indispensable sources are: Hans Doerr, *Feldzug nach Stalingrad*, by the chief of the General Staff of the LII Corps during the campaign; GOH, Wegner, "Der Krieg gegen Die Sowjetunion, 1942–43," especially the sections "Vorstoss zur Volga" (6:962–76) and "Der Kampf um der Stadt" (976–97); and Hayward, *Stopped at Stalingrad.*

75. Warlimont, *Inside Hitler's Headquarters*, 250.

76. B. H. Liddell Hart, *The German Generals Talk* (New York: Quill, 1979), 199.

77. For Soviet defenses at Stalingrad in July and August, see Louis Rotundo, ed., *Battle for Stalingrad: The 1943 Soviet General Staff Study* (Washington, D.C.: Pergamon-Brassey's, 1989), 45–46.

78. Liddell Hart, *The German Generals Talk*, 204–5.

79. Entry for July 23, 1942, in Halder, *Kriegstagebuch*, 3:489.

80. The chief of the General Staff for 6th Army, General Schmidt, warned repeatedly, "dass für die Schlacht bei Stalingrad zu wenig Infanterie vorhanden ist." GOH, Wegner, "Der Krieg gegen Die Sowjetunion, 1942–43," 6:963.

81. David M. Glantz and Jonathan House, *When Titans Clashed: How the Red Army Stopped Hitler* (Lawrence: University Press of Kansas, 1995), 121.

82. Ziemke and Bauer, *Moscow to Stalingrad*, 357–58.

83. For maps and narrative of the Kalach *Kessel*, see "Die Schlacht im Don-Bogen westlich Kalatsch," *Die Wehrmacht* 6, no. 18 (September 2, 1942): 19. For what Doerr calls 6th Army's "last victory in the open field," see *Feldzug nach Stalingrad*, 40–41.

84. GOH, Wegner, "Der Krieg gegen Die Sowjetunion, 1942–43," 6:962.

85. For the Red Army's propensity to form "bridgeheads everywhere and at any time," which "are bound to grow into formidable danger-points in a very brief time," see F. W. von Mellenthin, *Panzer Battles: A Study of the Employment of Armor in the Second World War* (New York: Ballantine, 1956), 222–23. Mellenthin was appointed chief of the General Staff for XXXXVIII Panzer Corps in late November 1942.

86. For the lunge to the Volga, see Hayward, *Stopped at Stalingrad*, 187–88; Doerr, *Feldzug nach Stalingrad*, 44–45, along with *Skizze* 11, "Angriff der 6. Armee auf Stalingrad"; and Ziemke and Bauer, *Moscow to Stalingrad*, 384.

87. Captain Herbert Pabst, quoted in Hayward, *Stopped at Stalingrad*, 187–88.

88. The first great air raid on Stalingrad features prominently in every source on the battle. For the dramatic impact, see Alan Clark, *Barbarossa: The Russian German Conflict, 1941–45* (New York: Quill, 1985), 216–17: "The effect was spectacular. Nearly every wooden building—including acres of workers' settlements on the outskirts—was burned down, and the flames made it possible to read a paper forty miles away." For the operational details, see Hayward, *Stopped at Stalingrad*, 188–89.

89. This is particularly true in our modern environment, when the casualty statistics from Allied bombing raids on German cities—1,000 plane raids by B-17 and B-24 bombers—are being routinely revised downward. We have now reached a point where civilian deaths during the fiery destruction of Dresden are now said to be just 25,000. If that is so, then it is hard to imagine a much smaller German air force dropping a fraction of the payload of Allied bombers actually generating 40,000 civilian casualties in Stalingrad. The older literature on Dresden relied first on inflated estimates from Nazi propaganda that were then filtered through the lens of cold war concerns. Dresden lay in the eastern zone, and Soviet propaganda routinely portrayed the bombing, and the quarter-million casualties it was said to have generated, as an example of western and capitalist frightfulness. See, for example, David Irving, *The Destruction of Dresden* (London: Kimber, 1963); and the work by the *Bürgermeister* of the city, Walter Weidauer, *Inferno Dresden* (Berlin [Ost]: Dietz, 1966). By the 1980s, the number was shrinking. See Alexander McKee, *Dresden, 1945: The Devil's Tinderbox* (London: Souvenir, 1982), which estimates 35,000–40,000. For the latest word on Dresden, see Frederick Taylor, *Dresden: Tuesday, February 13, 1945* (New York: HarperCollins, 2004), especially appx. B, "Counting the Dead," 443–48. For a collection of scholarly essays reflecting new thinking on Dresden, see Paul Addison and Jeremy A. Crang, eds., *Firestorm: The Bombing of Dresden, 1945* (Chicago: Ivan R. Dee, 2006). Especially useful are the contributions by Sebastian Cox, "The Dresden Raids: Why and How," 123–42; and Donald Bloxham, "Dresden as a War Crime," 180–208. The 25,000 figure comes from Overy, "The Post-War Debate," 137. For the still-raging debate in Germany over the precise way to view both Allied bombing and its German victims, see Lothar Kettenacker, ed., *Ein Volk von Opfern? Die neue Debatte um den Bombenkrieg, 1940–45* (Berlin: Rohwohlt, 2003), especially the contributions of Horst Boog, "Kolossalgemälde des Schreckens," 131–36; Hans-Ulrich Wehler, "Wer sind sät, wird Sturm ernten," 140–44; and Hans Mommsen, "Moralisch, strategisch, zerstörerisch," 145–51. Hayward, *Stopped at Stalingrad*, 188, gives what seems like a reasonable estimate of some 25,000 dead in the Stalingrad raid.

90. Hayward, *Stopped at Stalingrad*, 191.

91. There is an immense literature on the fighting within Stalingrad. It comes in every shape and size, from novels to simplistic narratives of the fighting to serious scholarship, and there is every shading and gradation in between. Soviet primary sources, which should be read and consulted with care, include the testimony of Marshal G. K. Zhukov, *Marshal Zhukov's Greatest Battles*, ed. Harrison E. Salisbury (New York: Harper & Row, 1969); and V. I. Chuikov, *The Battle for Stalingrad* (New York: Holt, Rinehart and Winston, 1964), the latter one of the

most widely quoted books on the battle. See also Rotundo, *Battle for Stalingrad*, although it reads like what it is: an official, in-house military document, and many readers, even well-informed ones, will find it tough going. By way of contrast, see David M. Glantz, ed., *Kharkov, 1942: Anatomy of a Military Disaster Through Soviet Eyes* (Shepperton, Surrey: Ian Allan, 1998). It too is a Soviet General Staff study on the battle of Kharkov, but it contains much more of Glantz's comments and emendations as a reading guide, and is therefore much more useful overall. For the Germans, Hitler, Halder, Zeitzler, and Paulus never wrote full narrative accounts, for obvious reasons. Walter Görlitz, ed., *Paulus: "Ich stehe hier auf Befehl!"* (Frankfurt: Bernard & Graefe, 1960), is far more the work of editor Görlitz than of Paulus, although the former did have access to Paulus's "Nachlass, Briefen, und Dokumentation" as well as the cooperation of the field marshal's family. Nevertheless, it does reprint many of the pertinent documents and it is worthwhile for that reason alone. One can, with some diligent searching, find the unit histories of virtually every German formation in and around the city. Some are more useful than others, as is typical of the genre, but virtually all of them reprint enough documentation, orders, and after-action reports to make for worthwhile reading. See, for example, Rolf Grams, *Die 14. Panzer Division, 1940–1945: Herausgegeben im Auftrag der Traditionsgemeinschaft der 14. Panzer Division* (Bad Neuheim: Podzun, 1957); Wolfgang Werthen, *Geschichte der 16. Panzer Division, 1939–1945: Herausgegeben vom Kameradschaftsbund 16. Panzer- und Infanterie-Division* (Bad Neuheim: Podzun, 1958); and Jochen Löser, *Bittere Pflicht: Kampf und Untergang der 76* (Berlin-*Brandenburgischen Infanterie-Division* (Osnabrück: Biblio Verlag, 1988), with the last, in particular, being chock-full of operational detail, especially on the hard road from the Don to the Volga.

The journalistic and popular histories continue to be read. Begin with Alexander Werth, *The Year of Stalingrad: An Historical Record and a Study of Russian Mentality, Methods and Policies* (London: Hamish Hamilton, 1946), by the BBC and London Sunday Times correspondent. It bears the marks of its time, but its judgments are surprisingly valid after all these years. See, in particular, the "six main reasons" why the Germans were unable to take the city (196–97). Its counterpart from the German side is Heinz Schröter, *Stalingrad* (New York: E. P. Dutton, 1958), by a correspondent attached to the 6th Army during the battle. It is a translation of his *Stalingrad. . . . "Bis zur letzten Patrone"* (Lengerich: Kleins Druck- und Verlags-Anstalt, 1953). It is a gritty account, far from the *heroisch-pathetisch* style so beloved of German war writers. For that reason, Nazi propaganda minister Josef Goebbels forbade its publication during the war. It is, as one might expect, highly sensitive to the plight of German soldiers during the fighting: "They crouched in their holes, between the crumbly walls of frozen earth, in the ruins of pillboxes. They caught rats, awaited the inevitable, wrote letters, worried about their rations, observed the highly decorated pilots dog-fighting in the skies over them, and grieved when they saw German transport planes, heavily laden with wounded, shot down in flames by the Russian fighters" (112). A recent addition to the journalistic literature is Antony Beevor and Luba Vinogradova, eds., *A Writer at War: Vasily Grossman with the Red Army, 1941–1945* (New York: Pantheon, 2005), which restores Grossman to his rightful place as one of the most passionate eyewitnesses to the "ruthless truth of war" on the eastern front. For his accounts of the Stalingrad fighting, see 110–212.

Among the popular histories, Edwin P. Hoyt, *199 Days: The Battle of Stalingrad* (New York: Tor, 1993), is typical of this prolific author's highly readable narrative oeuvre, as is the chapter on Stalingrad in his *Stalin's War: Tragedy and Triumph, 1941–1945* (New York: Cooper Square Press, 2003). Hoyt may well have taught more Americans about World War II than all other authors in the country put together. A British equivalent is Ronald Seth, *Stalingrad: Point of No Return: The Story of the Battle, August 1942–February 1943* (New York: Coward-McKann, 1959), which is all narrative, little analysis, and no documentation. William Craig, *Enemy at the Gates: The Battle for Stalingrad* (New York: Reader's Digest Press, 1973), is still a fine and readable work, episodic rather than thematic or chronological, and one of its episodes (dealing with Soviet sniper ace Vasily Zaitsev) served as the basis for the 2001 film *Enemy at the Gates* (directed by Jean-Jacques Annaud), starring Jude Law, Ed Harris, and Rachel Weisz. More useful still, yet still necessarily classified as popular literature because of the insufficiency of citation and bibliography, are V. E. Tarrant, *Stalingrad: Anatomy of an Agony* (London: Leo Cooper, 1992); and the most recent word on the battle, Antony Beevor, *Stalingrad* (London: Viking, 1998). The latter, in particular, could well be a scholarly book were the scholarly apparatus more sophisticated: it is well researched enough to appeal to the scholar, with a great deal of information from newly available Soviet sources, and well written enough to have won a large audience of general readers. It will remain the standard narrative of the battle for many years. For photographs, see Heinz Bergschicker, *Stalingrad: Eine Chronik in Bildern* (Berlin [Ost]: Verlag der Nation, 1960).

The other popular literature is mixed bag. See for example, two comparative works: J. Bowyer Bell, *Besieged: Seven Cities under Siege* (Philadelphia: Chilton Books, 1966), is a largely unsuccessful work that places the fighting in Stalingrad within a strange grouping that includes Jerusalem during the First Arab-Israeli War and Berlin during the postwar Soviet blockade (not the Soviet assault in 1945); John Antal and Bradley Gericke, eds., *City Fights: Selected Histories of Urban Combat from World War II to Vietnam* (New York: Ballantine, 2003) is more focused. Eric M. Walters's essay on "Stalingrad, 1942: With Will, Weapon, and a Watch" (27–92) is a fine narrative of the city fighting, but it is marred by an overreliance on a few eclectic sources from within the war-gaming community. There are two sure signs that a topic holds a special place in western historical consciousness. The first is its upgrade to coffee-table book status. See Will Fowler, *Stalingrad: The Vital 7 Days: The Germans' Last Desperate Attempt to Capture the City, October 1942* (Staplehurst, Kent: Spellmount, 2005), a fine marriage of text, maps, and photographs, with sidebars and diagrams aplenty. Only one chapter deals with the October fighting (the "last desperate attempt"), and the book describes, rightly, a last assault in November, the pioneer-heavy Operation Hubertus. The second is a television special. See Guido Knopp, *Stalingrad: Das Drama* (Munich: Bertelsmann, 2002), the companion volume to the ZDF series of the same name.

Still the best scholarly account of Stalingrad, peerless in its attention to detail and its analysis, is Manfred Kehrig, *Stalingrad: Analyse und Dokumentation einer Schlacht* (Stuttgart: Deutsche Verlags-Anstalt, 1974), which also includes no fewer than sixty-eight of the most crucial documents pertaining to the battle (548–638). Other necessary sources are Janusz Piekalkiewicz, *Stalingrad: Anatomie einer Schlacht* (Munich: Südwest Verlag, 1977), in which the author successfully marries operational analysis, photographs, and documentary sources in much the same way as his companion works on the battle of Moscow and the German conquest of the Balkans. See also the pertinent chapters in Ziemke, *Moscow to Stalingrad*, 383–97 and 458–77; Erickson, *Road to Stalingrad*, 387–464; Hayward, *Stopped at Stalingrad*, 183–221; and GOH, Wegner, "Der Krieg gegen Die Sowjetunion, 1942–43," 6:976–97. A good summation of recent scholarship, written for a popular German audience, is Andreas Kunz, "Vor sechzig Jahren: Der Untergang der 6. Armee in Stalingrad," *Militärgeschichte*, no. 4 (2002): 8–17.

Within Germany, the 1980s saw the rise of new scholarly genres that were relatively uninterested in operational analysis, but that sought to place the battle of Stalingrad in its broader social context. A good place to start is the collection of essays edited by Wolfram Wette and Gerd R. Überschär, *Stalingrad: Mythos und Wirklichkeit einer Schlacht* (Frankfurt am Main: Fischer Taschenbuch Verlag, 1992), which brings to the fore issues of historical memory and *Alltagsgeschichte*. See, for example, the contributions of Wette himself, "Das Massensterben als 'Heldenepos': Stalingrad in der NS-Propaganda," 43–60; Rosemarie Papadopoulos-Killius, "Die Verarbeitung von Todesahnungen," 146–59; and Hans Joachim Schröder, "Alltag der Katastrophen," 168–77. More useful for the operational historian are the essays by Gerd R. Überschär, "Die Schlacht von Stalingrad in der deutschen Historiographie," 192–204; Manfred Kehrig, "Stalingrad im Spiegel der Memoiren deutscher Generale," 205–13; and Horst Giertz, "Die Schlacht von Stalingrad in der sowjetischen Historiographie," 214–20. A characteristic form of this new history of Stalingrad, with its aim to write an account "from below" is the published collection of letters written by German soldiers within the *Kessel*. See, for representative examples, Wido Spratte, ed., *Stalingrad: Feldpostbriefe des Oberleutnants Harald Bleker* (Osnabrück: Wennner, 2000); and Jens Ebert, ed., *Feldpostbriefe aus Stalingrad* (Göttingen: Wallstein, 2003). For the phenomenon in general, see Martin Humburg, "Die Bedeutung der Feldpost für die Soldaten in Stalingrad," in Wette and Überschär, *Stalingrad*, 68–79. Other examples of "kleiner Mann" Stalingrad literature include Wolfgang Haidin, *Stalingrad: Kampf und Gefangenschaft überlebt: Aus den Lebenserinnerungen des Josef Schönegger*. Steyr: Ennsthaler, 1995); and Carl Schüddekopf, *Im Kessel: Erzählen von Stalingrad* (Munich: Piper, 2002). Germany will never, for obvious reasons, produce a "greatest generation" literature, but works such as these—and there are hundreds of them circulating in Germany—serve much the same sort of purpose for a broad readership, humanizing the common *Landser* whose historical reputation is being pounded daily in more scholarly publications. For a typical contrary view of 6th Army, see Bernd Boll and Hans Safrian, "On the Way to Stalingrad: The 6th Army in 1941–42," in *War of Extermination: The German Military in World War II, 1941–1944*, ed. Hannes Heer and Klaus Naumann (New York: Berghahn, 2000), 237–71: "But closer examination reveals that tightly focusing on the topos of 'victim,' which has characterized discourse concerning Stalingrad until today, historically perpetuates National Socialist mythologizing" (237).

Finally, for a report on the "state of the Stalingrad question" at various times in the past 25 years, see Gerhard Förster, "Einige Fragen der Kriegskunst während der Stalingrader Schlacht," *Militärgeschichte* 22, no. 1 (1983): 5–15; Karl-Heinz Schmick, "Der Zweite Weltkrieg und Stalingrad: Sammelbesprechungen," *Politische Vierteljahresschrift* 34, no. 4 (1993): 700–16; and the short handbook by Bernd Ulrich, *Stalingrad* (Munich: C. H. Beck, 2005).

92. For Doerr's classic quotation, see *Feldzug nach Stalingrad*, 52.

93. For the activities of LI Corps, see the primary source, Walther von Seydlitz, *Stalingrad*, 160.

94. See the section in Tarrant, *Stalingrad*, 74–80, as well as the chapter in Beevor, *Stalingrad*, 145–65.

95. See the scene in Seydlitz, *Stalingrad*, 254–55, in which the German prisoners are brought for the first time to the Volga bank.

96. Beevor, *Stalingrad*, 135.

97. Chuikov, *Battle for Stalingrad*, 205. As is plain from the rest of Chuikov's account, however, he had tired of Soviet propaganda highlighting the role Rodimtsev's division alone, when so many other formations had perished in defending Stalingrad (205–6).

98. The best account of the October fighting is the richly illustrated account in Fowler, *Stalingrad*, 70–34.

99. Chuikov, *Battle for Stalingrad*, 180; Hayward, *Stopped at Stalingrad*, 211. Chuikov's contention that "some 180 tanks broke through the lines of Zholudev's [37th] division" is manifestly impossible, given the relatively small numbers of tanks the Germans could call upon at this point.

100. Glantz and House, *When Titans Clashed*, 122–23. The notion, expressed in Walters, "Stalingrad, 1942," 29, that Chuikov's concept "was to encourage the Germans to keep attacking, enjoying victory after tactical victory but consistently falling short of conquering all of Stalingrad," is absurd; it assumes a degree of command and control that simply did not exist in 1942, or perhaps in any era.

101. Quoted in GOH, Wegner, "Der Krieg gegen Die Sowjetunion, 1942–43," 6:994. Hitler went Jodl one better: "We have as good as got it," he told a group of his "old fighters" at the annual Bürgerbräukeller speech on November 8, the anniversary of the Beer Hall Putsch. "There are only a couple of small bits left." The army could be moving faster, Hitler added, but he wanted to avoid "a second Verdun." See Beevor, *Stalingrad*, 213.

102. GOH, Wegner, "Der Krieg gegen Die Sowjetunion, 1942–43," 6:995.

103. The published sources on Hubertus are thin, but there is an immense literature generated by buffs who are often conversant with the most minute details of the battle. The best source extant is Wolf Höpper, "Operation Hubertus: Ljudnikows Last Stand in Stalingrad," available at: http://www.flamesofwar.com/Article.asp?ArticleID=1032.

104. Reprinted with some bitterness in Seydlitz, *Stalingrad*, 167.

105. *Grossdeutschlands Freiheitskrieg*, pt. 173, "Sowjetangriffe vom Kaukasus bis zur Newa abgewiesen," *Militär-Wochenblatt* 127, no. 23 (December 4, 1942): 613–17. The quotes are from 613.

106. See the figures quoted in GOH, Wegner, "Der Krieg gegen Die Sowjetunion, 1942–43," 6:957.

107. Ziemke and Bauer, *Moscow to Stalingrad*, 359.

108. Glantz and House, *When Titans Clashed*, 120.

109. For the best available source, with a discussion rich in operational insight, see the four-part article by Lieutenant General Waldemar Erfurth, "Das Zusammenwirken getrennter Heeresteile," *Militärwissenschaftliche Rundschau* 4, nos. 1–4 (1939).

110. The German is "Getrennt marschieren, vereint schlagen." See General Ludwig, "Moltke als Erzieher," *Militär-Wochenblatt* 125, no. 17 (October 25, 1940): 802–4.

111. For the Namur fighting, see Robert M. Citino, *The German Way of War: From the Thirty Years' War to the Third Reich* (Lawrence: University Press of Kansas, 2005), 208–18.

112. See, for example, the memorial article on the occasion of Field Marshal List's eightieth birthday, Hermann Foertsch, "Generalfeldmarschall List 80 Jahre Alt," *Wehrwissenschaftliche Rundschau* 10, no. 5 (May 1960): 235–36: "Das Jahr 1942 stellte den Generalfeldmarschall List an die Spitze der Heeresgruppe A, die die politisch falsch gesehene und militärisch unzulänglich bedachte Aufgabe erhielt, in den Kaukasus vorzustossen, um Russland durch Eroberung der kaukasischen Ölquellen zur Entscheidung zu zwingen. Das Missverhältnis zwischen Raum und Kräftezuteilung und *der falsche exzentrische Ansatz der Operation* durch den militärischen Laien Hitler gab der ganzen Operation von vorherein kaum Aussicht auf Erfolg" (236). See also Weinberg, *A World at Arms*, 415–16, who uses the word in the German manner by referring to "Hitler's personal role in this eccentric set of operations."

113. Entry for July 23, 1942, in Halder, *Kriegstagebuch*, 3:489.

114. Ibid., entry for July 30, 1942 (3:493–94). The German phrase is "ausgekochter Unsinn."

115. See GOH, Wegner, "Der Krieg gegen Die Sowjetunion, 1942–43," 6:954. The German is "oft genug nicht nur unkonventioneller, sondern auch unprofessioneller und fehlerhafter operativer Entschlüsse Hitlers."

Chapter 8. The End: El Alamein and Stalingrad

1. For the best introduction to Clausewitz's thought, see two articles by Peter Paret: "Clausewitz and the Nineteenth Century," in *The Theory and Practice of War*, ed. Michael Howard (Bloomington: Indiana University Press, 1965), 21–42; and "Clausewitz," in *Makers of Modern Strategy From Machiavelli to the Nuclear Age*,

ed. Peter Paret (Princeton: Princeton University Press, 1986), 186–213. Still useful, despite its age, is Hans Rothfels, "Clausewitz," in *Makers of Modern Strategy: Military Thought from Machiavelli to Hitler*, ed. Edward Mead Earle (New York: Atheneum, 1966), 93–113. The last great Clausewitz wave took place in the early 1990s, due no doubt to the sudden and surprising end of the cold war, and the need for a new strategic outlook. See, for example, Martin van Creveld, *The Transformation of War* (New York: Free Press, 1991); Azar Gat, *The Origins of Military Thought: From the Enlightenment to Clausewitz* (Oxford: Oxford University Press, 1992); and Peter Paret, *Understanding War: Essays on Clausewitz and the History of Military Power* (Princeton: Princeton University Press, 1992). See also Brian R. Sullivan, "Intelligence and Counter-Terrorism: A Clausewitzian-Historical Analysis," *Journal of Intelligence History* 3, no. 1 (2003): 1–18, which places Clausewitz squarely in a post-9/11 context; and Jon Tetsuro Sumida, "The Relationship of History and Theory in *On War:* The Clausewitzian Ideal and its Implications," *Journal of Military History* 65, no. 2 (April 2001): 333–54, who argues that there was an instrumental purpose behind Clausewitz's synthesis of history and theory: helping an officer who had never served in a war "to grapple with the moral dilemmas that accompanied critical operational decision making and thus improve the person's ability to learn from actual experience." See also two works dealing with Clausewitz and the problems of interpreting his thought, Christopher Bassford, *Clausewitz in English: The Reception of Clausewitz in Britain and America, 1815–1945* (Oxford: Oxford University Press, 1994); and Beatrice Heuser, *Reading Clausewitz* (New York: Random House, 2002). For a discussion of the relationship between Clausewitz and traditional German military praxis, see Robert M. Citino, *The German Way of War: From the Thirty Years' War to the Third Reich* (Lawrence: University Press of Kansas, 2005), 143–47.

2. The standard English translation is Carl von Clausewitz, *On War*, ed. and trans. Michael Howard and Peter Paret (Princeton: Princeton University Press, 1976), with introductory essays by Paret, Howard, and Bernard Brodie. For "friction in war," see book 1, chap. 7, 119–21.

3. Clausewitz, *On War*, book 2, chap. 2, 140.

4. Ibid., book 6, chap. 1, 358.

5. Ibid., book 1, chap. 1, 87.

6. See ibid., book 7, chap. 4, "The Diminishing Force of the Attack," 527; chap. 5, "The Culminating Point of the Attack," 28, and chap. 22, "The Culminating Point of Victory," 566–73.

7. Ibid., book 7, chap. 22, 566.

8. Ibid., book 7, chap. 22, 567–68.

9. Ibid., book 7, chap. 22, 568.

10. Ibid., book 7, chap. 22, 567.

11. Ibid., book 7, chap. 22, 568–69.

12. Ibid., book 7, chap. 22, 569.

13. Ibid., book 7, chap. 22, 572–73.

14. Ibid., book 7, chap. 22, 572.

15. Carl Wagener, "Der Vorstoss des XXXX. Panzerkorps von Charkow zum Kaukasus, July–August 1942," pt. 2, *Wehrwissenschaftliche Rundschau* 5, no. 10 (October 1959): 447–58. The quote is from 458.

16. Bernard Law Montgomery, *Memoirs of Field-Marshal the Viscount Montgomery of Alamein* (Cleveland: World, 1968), 352. He was also on record as saying, "I know that I am regarded by many people as being a tiresome person. I think this is very probably true" (178).

17. "Denn die Panzer und Fahrzeuge beider Gegner standen gleich offen in der Wüste," Erwin Rommel, *Krieg ohne Hass* (Heidenheim: Heidenheimer Zeitung, 1950), 239–40; see also Rommel, *The Rommel Papers*, ed. B. H. Liddell Hart (New York: Harcourt, Brace, 297–98, with the usual attendant minor differences.

18. Montgomery, *Memoirs*, 116. For El Alamein in general, see also the helpful volume on "Al-Alamein" (as it is now transliterated) in Jill Edwards, ed., *Al-Alamein Revisited: The Battle of al-Alamein and Its Historical Implications* (Cairo: American University in Cairo, 2000). These proceedings of a symposium held on May 2, 1998, at the American University include introductory article by Michael Howard, "The Battle of al-Alamein," 3–12, and indispensable essays by Raimondo Luraghi, "Italian Forces at the Battle of al-Alamein: 'Ferrea Mole, Ferreo Cuore,'" 13–31, and Peter Liddle, "Rescuing the Testimony of the North Africa Campaign Experience," 32–42. See also the comprehensive analysis of the German perspective on the battle by Thomas Scheben, "The German Perspective of War in North Africa, 1940–42: Three-dimensional, Intercontinental Warfare," 55–98.

19. Montgomery, *Memoirs*, 118. For controversy over planning Lightfoot, especially Montgomery's decision to change the structure of the battle, see Niall Barr, *The Pendulum of War: The Three Battles of El Alamein* (New York: Overlook Press, 2005), 274–75.

20. Montgomery, *Memoirs*, 119.

21. For various details on this elaborate deception plan, code-named Operation Bertram, see Montgomery, *Memoirs*, 121–22; Michael Carver, *El Alamein* (London: Batsford, 1962), 93–95; Douglas Porch, *The Path to Victory: The Mediterranean Theater in World War II* (New York: Farrar, Straus & Giroux, 2004), 312–14; and Barr, *Pendulum of War*, 299–301, who quotes one British document to the effect that Bertram was a deception effort "unequalled in military history." Still, there is little evidence presented anywhere that it had much impact on the course of the battle itself.

22. See the notes Montgomery used in addressing his officers on October 19 (XIII and XXX Corps) and October 20 (X Corps), in Montgomery, *Memoirs*, 127.

23. Porch, *Path to Victory*, 300: "His [Montgomery's] one concession to Teutonic military organization was to create what he called a corps de chasse of three armored divisions and one infantry division equipped with the American Sherman tanks donated by Roosevelt," an innovation "obviously inspired by the *Afrika Korps*."

24. For the slow and painful, but ultimately successful, evolution of British tactics during World War I, see Shelford Bidwell and Dominick Graham, *Fire-Power: British Army Weapons and Theories of War, 1904–1945* (London: Allen and

Unwin, 1982); and the large body of work by Tim Travers, including *The Killing Ground: The British Army, the Western Front, and the Emergence of Modern Warfare, 1900–1918* (London: Allen and Unwin, 1987); "The Evolution of British Strategy and Tactics on the Western Front in 1918: GHQ, Manpower, and Technology," *Journal of Military History* 54, no. 2 (April 1990): 173–200; "Could the Tanks of 1918 Have Been War-Winners for the British Expeditionary Force?" *Journal of Contemporary History* 27, no. 3 (July 1992): 389–406; *How the War Was Won: Command and Technology in the British Army on the Western Front, 1917–1918* (New York: Routledge, 1992); and "Command and Leadership Styles in the British Army: The 1915 Gallipoli Model," *Journal of Contemporary History* 29, no. 3 (July 1994): 403–42. See also the discussion of "bite and hold" operations in Robin Prior and Trevor Wilson, *Passchendaele: The Untold Story* (New Haven, Conn.: Yale University Press, 1996), 197–98.

25. "Heute stehen wir hundert Kilometer vor Alexandria und Kairo," he told the assembled international press, "und haben das Tor Ägyptens in der Hand—and zwar mit der Absicht, hier zu handeln!" See Ralf Grog Reuth, *Rommel: Das Ende einer Legende* (Munich: Piper, 2004), 187.

26. The security breach that allowed planning documents from Operation Blue to fall into Soviet hands. See chap. 5, pt. 2, "Operation Blue: Planning." The German official history describes him as a "kriegsgerichtlich Verurteilter unter dem Zwang, sich vor den Augen Hitlers bewähren zu müssen." See the German official history (hereinafter GOH), Militärgeschichtliches Forschungsamt (Military Historical Research Office), *Das Deutsche Reich und Der Zweite Weltkrieg*, vol. 6, *Der Gobale Krieg: Die Ausweitung zum Weltkrieg und der Wechsel der Initiative, 1941–1943*, especially pt. 5, Reinhard Stumpf, "Der Krieg im Mittelmeerraum, 1942–43: Die Operationen in Nordafrika und im mittleren Mittelmeer," 6:567–757. The quote on Stumme is found on 6:691.

27. Rommel, *Krieg ohne Hass*, 202–4; Rommel, *Rommel Papers*, 266–7.

28. Rommel, *Krieg ohne Hass*, 227; Rommel, *Rommel Papers*, 287.

29. Found in Rommel, *Rommel Papers*, 294, but not in Rommel, *Krieg ohne Hass* (236, presumptively).

30. Carver, *El Alamein*, 101. See also F. W. von Mellenthin, *Panzer Battles: A Study of the Employment of Armor in the Second World War* (New York: Ballantine, 1956), 177.

31. Wolf Heckmann, *Rommel's War in Africa* (Garden City, N.Y.: Doubleday, 1981), 320, gives the diagnosis from Rommel's doctor: "*Generalfeldmarschall* Rommel suffers from the consequential symptoms of low blood pressure, with a tendency to fainting fits. His present condition can be traced back to stomach and intestinal complaints of fairly long standing, aggravated by the excessive physical and psychological strains of recent weeks, particularly in view of the unfavorable climactic conditions."

32. Rommel, *Krieg ohne Hass*, 241; Rommel, *Rommel Papers*, 298–9.

33. For the *Minekästen*, see GOH, Stumpf, "Der Krieg im Mittelmeerraum," 6:699; Barr, *Pendulum of War*, 276, gives a precise figure for Axis mines of 445,358.

34. Porch, *Path to Victory*, 311.

35. Barr, *Pendulum of War*, 305, brings forth a more robust an image of Stumme than in any previous literature: "The Panzerarmee was certainly not a passive force awaiting its doom."

36. Every history of World War II includes an account of El Alamein, of which John Keegan, *The Second World War* (New York: Penguin, 2005), 336–41, is a clear and concise example. Kenneth Macksey, *Tank Versus Tank: The Illustrated Story of Armored Battlefield Conflict in the Twentieth Century* (New York: Barnes & Noble, 1999), 102–4, offers food for thought on the armor involved; and Paddy Griffith, *Forward into Battle: Fighting Tactics from Waterloo to the Near Future* (Novato, Calif.: Presidio, 1990), 111–15, does the same thing for the infantry and antitank units.

For operational details, see the best currently available account of the battle in Barr, *Pendulum of War*, 307–405; one reviewer, Peter Stanley, in *War in History* 13, no. 2 (2006): 272–73, called Barr "a worthy successor to Barrie Pitt or Correlli Barnett," particularly for his use of the still relatively underconsulted Australian archives. The accounts by both Pitt, *The Crucible of War: Year of Alamein, 1942* (London: Jonathan Cape, 1982), 297–53, and Correlli Barnett, *The Desert Generals* (Bloomington: Indiana University Press, 1982), 249–313, are still extremely useful. The latter is highly critical of Montgomery's generalship at El Alamein, which is the book's principal thesis. Fred Majdalany, *The Battle of El Alamein: Fortress in the Sand* (Philadelphia: Lippincott, 1965), 46–48 is still worthwhile, part of Lippincott's readable Great Battles of History series. Michael Carver participated in the battle, and both his *Dilemmas of the Desert War: A New Look at the Libyan Campaign, 1940–1942* (London: Batsford, 1986) and *El Alamein* (104–94) are valuable, the former for the matrix of factors that generated Alamein and the latter for its reminder to be wary of "wisdom after the event" (195–205). Other worthy works are the "2002 wave" of Alamein literature, appearing during the sixtieth anniversary of the battle: Jon Latimer, *Alamein* (Cambridge, Mass.: Harvard University Press, 2002); John Bierman and Colin Smith, *Alamein: War without Hate* (London: Viking, 2002), and Stephen Bungay, *Alamein* (London: Aurum, 2002). Finally, Robin Neillands's *Eighth Army: The Triumphant Desert Army that Held the Axis at Bay from North Africa to the Alps, 1939–1945* (Woodstock, N.Y.: Overlook, 2004), is a popular history that makes good use of veterans' interviews.

From the German side, the classic account is Rommel, *Krieg ohne Hass*, including "Der Orkan bricht los," 244–54; "Ein Ringen um jeden Meter," 254–63, and ". . . zum Siege order zum Tode," 263–75; the corresponding passages in Rommel, *Rommel Papers*, are 300–334, plus two helpful tables on Luftwaffe sorties and German-Italian battle strength (335–36, respectively). Still invaluable are the following: Alfred Gause (the Panzerarmee's chief of staff), "Der Feldzug in Nordafrika im Jahre 1942," *Wehrwissenschaftliche Rundschau* 12, no. 11 (November 1962), 652–80, esp. 674–77; Siegfried Westphal (Rommel's operations officer), *The German Army in the West* (London: Cassell, 1951), 118–21, and *Erinnerungen* (Berlin: Von Hase & Koehler, 1975); 173–80, his aide de camp, Heinz Werner Schmidt, *With Rommel in the Desert* (New York: Bantam, 1977), 196–200; and the commander of the Afrika Korps, Walther Nehring, *Die Geschichte der deutschen Panzerwaffe, 1916 bis*

1945 (Berlin: Propyläen Verlag, 1969), 205–11. Mellenthin had by now departed the theater, so El Alamein unfortunately does not figure in his *Panzer Battles*.

It is also necessary to consult the official histories where appropriate. For precise location of units on down to battalion-level, see I. S. O. Playfair, *The Mediterranean and Middle East*, vol. 4, *The Destruction of the Axis forces in Africa* (London: Her Majesty's Stationery Office, 1966), esp. 31–79, including chap. 2, "El Alamein: The Break-In ('Lightfoot') and Dog-Fight," 31–52, and chap. 3, "El Alamein: the Dog-Fight Continued and the Break-Out," 53–79. For the German side, see GOH, Stumpf, "Der Krieg im Mittelmeerraum," especially "Die dritte Schlacht: Entscheidung bei El Alamein (23. Oktober bis 4. November 1942), 6:688–709.

37. Westphal, *German Army in the West*, 119.

38. See Barr, *Pendulum of War*, 276; Majdalany, *Battle of El Alamein*, had it right back in 1965, "just under 900 guns" (82).

39. Quoted in Barr, *Pendulum of War*, 309.

40. Bierman and Smith, *Alamein*, 276.

41. Rommel, *Krieg ohne Hass*, 245; Rommel, *Rommel Papers*, 302.

42. Rommel, *Krieg ohne Hass*, 246–47; Rommel, *Rommel Papers*, 303. The verdict of the German official history: "Ein schwerer Fehler, der es den britischen Verbänden ermöglichte, ziemlich ungestört zum Angriff anzutreten." GOH, Stumpf, "Der Krieg im Mittelmeerraum," 6:699.

43. "Die Gefechtsvorposten kämpften bis zur letzten Patrone und gerieten dann in Gefangenschaft oder fielen." Rommel, *Krieg ohne Hass*, 245; Rommel, *Rommel Papers*, 302.

44. Stumme's death is a set piece that few authors have been able to resist. See Majdalany, *Battle of El Alamein*, 92, for a representative example.

45. Bierman and Smith, *Alamein*, 287.

46. Rommel, *Krieg ohne Hass*, 252; Rommel, *Rommel Papers*, 308; Majdalany, *Battle of El Alamein*, 109.

47. The *Totenritt* was one of the most famous episodes in the history of the Prussian army: the cavalry charge by the 12th Cavalry Brigade under General Friedrich Wilhelm von Bredow at the battle of Mars-la-Tour, August 16, 1870. When ordered into action against the gun line of the French VI Corps, Bredow responded, "Koste es, was er wolle" ("Whatever it costs"). See Geoffrey Wawro, *The Franco-Prussian War: The German Conquest of France in 1870–1871* (Cambridge: Cambridge University Press, 2003), 138–63, 168; and Citino, *German Way of War*, 174–75, 190.

48. A certain amount of confusion still seems to exist about the exact nature of these barely noticeable terrain formations, with some identifying them as a slight depression, others as a ridge or hill. See Peter Stanley's review of Barr, *Pendulum of War*, in *War in History* 13, no. 2 (2006): 272–73.

49. "Schlacht ohne Hoffnung," the title of pt. 5 of Rommel, *Krieg ohne Hass*, 225–83; chap. 14 in Rommel, *Rommel Papers*, 287–326; chap. 16 in Barr, *Pendulum of War*, 332–58.

50. Barr, *Pendulum of War*, 369.

51. GOH, Stumpf, "Der Krieg im Mittelmeerraum," 6:704.

52. The full order is printed verbatim in Rommel, *Krieg ohne Hass*, 268; Rommel, *Rommel Papers*, 321, mentions "a shortened version of the order" that was found in Rommel's papers.

53. For the destruction of Ariete, see the account in Luraghi, "Italian Forces at the Battle of al-Alamein," 27–28.

54. "Wir waren alle wie vor den Kopf geschlagen und ich wusste das erste Mal während des afrikanischen Feldzuges nicht, was ich tun soll." Rommel, *Krieg ohne Hass*, 268; Rommel, *Rommel Papers*, 321

55. Ralf Georg Reuth, *Rommel: The End of a Legend* (London: Haus, 2005), 121–22. The German is *Willensmensch* ("man of will").

56. Ibid., 188.

57. For the nearly forgotten battle of Warsaw in 1656, see Robert I. Frost, *The Northern Wars: War, State, and Soviet in Northeastern Europe, 1558–1721* (Essex: Longman, 2000), 173–76; and Citino, *German Way of War*, 7–14.

58. "Einer der denkwürdigsten Tage in der Geschichte." Rommel, *Krieg ohne Hass*, 268; Rommel, *Rommel Papers*, 321.

59. Along with the street fighting, the Soviet counteroffensive has been the star of the show in the Stalingrad historiography. Until recently, however, few scholars had access to the Soviet documents. For that reason alone, even the relatively short account in David M. Glantz and Jonathan House, the chapter in *When Titans Clashed: How the Red Army Stopped Hitler* (Lawrence: University Press of Kansas, 1995), "Operation Uranus: The Destruction of 6th Army," 129–47, was a signal event in the literature, and it is still the place to start. One awaits a larger study from Glantz on Stalingrad to take its rightful place next to his works on Leningrad and Kursk. Two readily available primary sources from the Soviet side, still worth consulting, are Marshal G. K. Zhukov, *Marshal Zhukov's Greatest Battles*, ed. Harrison E. Salisbury (New York: Harper & Row, 1969), 105–94, especially chap. 10, "Stalingrad Strikes Back," 174–94; and Marshal Andrei Yeremenko, "Battle of Stalingrad," in *Battles Hitler Lost: First-Person Accounts of World War II by Russian General on the Eastern Front* (New York: Richardson & Steirman, 1986), 62–75. For the German side, the two indispensable sources are Hans Doerr, *Der Feldzug nach Stalingrad: Versuch eines operativen Überblickes* (Darmstadt: E. S. Mittler, 1955), 62–83, and Manfred Kehrig, *Stalingrad: Analyse und Dokumentation einer Schlacht* (Stuttgart: Deutsche Verlags-Anstalt, 1974), especially section 2, "Die Einschliessung der 6. Armee," 129–303. The best operational accounts in English are, in order of appearance, John Erickson, *The Road to Stalingrad* (New York: Harper & Row, 1975), 394–472; Earl Ziemke and Magna Bauer, *Moscow to Stalingrad: Decision in the East* (Washington, D.C.: Center of Military History, 1987), 468–77; Antony Beevor, *Stalingrad* (London: Viking, 1998), 239–65; and Joel S. A. Hayward, *Stopped at Stalingrad: The Luftwaffe and Hitler's Defeat in the East, 1943–1943* (Lawrence: University Press of Kansas, 1998), 222–33

60. See, for example, Bruce Menning, "The Deep Strike in Russian and Soviet Military History," *Journal of Soviet Military Studies* 1, no. 1 (April 1988): 9–28.

61. The best work on these doctrinal developments is Richard W. Harrison, *The Russian Way of War: Operational Art, 1904–1940* (Lawrence: University Press of Kansas, 2001), esp. 34–35, 157–68. For Tukhachevsky, see Sally Stoecker, *Forging Stalin's Army: Marshal Tukhachevsky and the Politics of Military Innovation* (Boulder, Colo.: Westview Press, 1998). For Soviet doctrinal and technological experimentation in the interwar era, see Mary R. Habeck, *Storm of Steel: The Development of Armor Doctrine in Germany and the Soviet Union, 1919–1939* (Ithaca, N.Y.: Cornell University Press, 2003).

62. The scholarly world needs a comprehensive biography of Isserson. For the importance of the critical figure to U.S. doctrinal debate in the 1990s, see the article by Frederick Kagan, "Army Doctrine and Modern War: Notes toward a New Edition of FM 100-5," *Parameters* 27, no. 1 (spring 1997): 134–51.

63. Kehrig, *Stalingrad*, 124 n. 390.

64. For the impact of coalition warfare on the battle of Stalingrad, see Richard L. DiNardo, *Germany and the Axis Powers: From Coalition to Collapse* (Lawrence: University Press of Kansas, 2005), 136–57; for the impact of Stalingrad on the Axis coalition, see Jürgen Förster, *Stalingrad: Risse im Bündnis, 1942–43* (Freiburg: Rombach, 1975).

65. See GOH, "Der Krieg gegen Die Sowjetunion, 1942–43," by Bernd Wegner, 6:1008–10.

66. For a fair assessment of the Romanian forces that goes well beyond the clichés of General Erich von Manstein, see Kehrig, *Stalingrad*, 62–63: "Der rumänische Soldat enstammte in der Regel dem Bauernstand und war gutmätig, ausdauernd und anspruchlos."

67. Glantz and House, *When Titans Clashed*, 130.

68. Ziemke and Bauer, *Moscow to Stalingrad*, 458.

69. See the assessment of the Luftwaffe field divisions and "deren geringeren Kampfwert" in GOH, Wegner, "Der Krieg gegen Die Sowjetunion, 1942–43," 6:1011–12.

70. Both Beevor, *Stalingrad*, 231, and Hayward, *Stopped at Stalingrad*, 227–28, tell the story of mice nesting in the tanks of the 2nd Panzer Division to escape the cold and chewing through the insulation of the electric cables, thus preventing a number of tanks from starting.

71. Glantz and House, *When Titans Clashed*, 132–34.

72. Kehrig, *Stalingrad*, 126–27.

73. Most notably in a November 12, 1942, report from Colonel Reinhardt Gehlen of Fremde Heere Ost that predicted "an attack in the near future against Romanian 3rd Army with the object of cutting the railroad to Stalingrad." Quote in Ziemke and Bauer, *Moscow to Stalingrad*, 457.

74. The best source for operational detail of the Soviet assault in north and south is Kehrig, *Stalingrad*, 131–48.

75. For the ordeal of General Heim and the XXXVIII Panzer Corps, see Doerr, *Feldzug nach Stalingrad*, 63–66; and Kehrig, *Stalingrad*, 132–33. DiNardo, *Germany and the Axis Powers*, 150–53, has a richly detailed and carefully researched account, perhaps the best available in English.

76. Doerr, *Feldzug nach Stalingrad*, 64.

77. Kehrig, *Stalingrad*, 136–37. Weichs's original order is reprinted in Doerr, *Feldzug nach Stalingrad*, 65.

78. See the beginning of Paulus's chilling dispatch, reprinted in its entirety in the appendices to Kehrig, *Stalingrad*, 559–60: "Armee eingeschlossen. Ganzes Zarizatal, Eisenbahn von Sowjetskij bis Kalatsch, ebendortige Donbrücke, Höhen auf Westufer Don bis Golubinskaja, Oskinskij and Krainij trotz heldenmütigen Widerstandes in Händen der Russen."

79. See Doerr, *Feldzug nach Stalingrad*, 70: "'Armee eingeschlossen.'—Das war nicht ganz richtig. Der Armee war umstellt."

80. Once again, Doerr, *Feldzug nach Stalingrad*, 70, gives the text of both Führer orders. First, "Der O.B. begibt sich mit seinem Stab nach Stalingrad. Die 6. Armee igelt sich ein and wartet weitere Befehle ab." The second, "6. Armee igelt sich und wartet Entsazt von Aussen ab."

81. For the opinion of Luftwaffe officials, see Hayward, *Stopped at Stalingrad*, 233–46.

82. For the tortured story of General Seydlitz, see his own memoirs, Walther von Seydlitz, *Stalingrad: Konflikt und Konsequenz: Erinnerungen* (Oldenburg: Stalling, 1977). Although at one time he was universally despised by fellow officers for collaborating with the Soviets after his imprisonment, he receives much gentler treatment at the hands of historians today. See Hans Martens, *General von Seydlitz, 1942–1945: Analyse eines Konflikts* (Berlin [Ost]: Von Kloeden, 1971); and Leonid Reschin, *General zwischen den Fronten: Walter von Seydlitz in sowjetischer Kriegsgefangenschaft und Haft, 1942–1955* (Berlin: Edition q, 1995).

83. That is, a breakout (Brzeziny was the site of the dramatic breakout of the encircled XXV Reserve Corps in the battle of Lodz in November 1914) or the complete destruction of the encircled army, as in the defeat that Hannibal had inflicted on the Romans at Cannae in 216 B.C. Seydlitz, *Stalingrad*, 189.

84. Doerr, *Feldzug nach Stalingrad*. To Doerr, writing as a traditionally trained staff officer, the real issue raised by Stalingrad was not so much breakout or relief, but the denial of "freedom of action" (*Handlungsfreiheit*) to the commanders within the *Kessel*, and General Paulus's acquiescence in that denial. See esp. 117–19.

85. See Glantz and House, *When Titans Clashed*, 134, for a reasoned counterargument to a breakout: "Quite apart from the problem of disobeying Hitler's wishes, this argument assumes a logistical strength that Paulus did not possess. The entire siege of Stalingrad had been conducted on a shoestring, and his forces lacked the fuel, ammunition, and transportation to break out unassisted. In addition, the Stavka possessed powerful reserves that could block relief of or breakout by the Stalingrad garrison."

86. The primary source here is Erich von Manstein, *Lost Victories* (Novato, Calif.: Presidio, 1982), especially chap. 12, "The Tragedy of Stalingrad," 289–366. Manstein blamed Hitler above him and 6th Army beneath him for the destruction of the *Kessel*. Paulus in particular comes under heavy fire for refusing to take the decision to cooperate with the relief offensive. Not everyone has been satisfied

with Manstein's explanation. See Joachim Wieder, *Stalingrad und die Verantwortung des Soldaten* (Munich: Nymphenburger, 1962); and the expanded and updated edition, Joachim Wieder and Heinrich Graf von Einsiedel, *Stalingrad: Memories of Hell* (London: Arms and Armour Press, 1993). Wieder survived the battle and Soviet captivity to write his memoirs in 1962; Einsiedel, a Luftwaffe lieutenant, was taken prisoner and joined the anti-Nazi Nationalkommitee Freies Deutschland. He helped edit a new edition of the book in 1993, which spends a great deal of time haranguing Manstein. See especially the section "Critical Assessments after Fifty Years," 134–78. For a good summation of these issues, see Manfred Kehrig, "Stalingrad im Spiegel der Memoiren deutscher Generale," in *Stalingrad: Mythos und Wirklichkeit einer Schlacht*, ed. Wolfram Wette and Gerd R. Überschär (Frankfurt am Main: Fischer Taschenbuch Verlag, 1992), 205–13.

87. Glantz and House, *When Titans Clashed*, 136.

88. Hayward, *Stopped at Stalingrad*, 310.

89. For this estimate, see Hayward, *Stopped at Stalingrad*, 235.

90. See GOH, Wegner, "Der Krieg gegen Die Sowjetunion, 1942–43," 6:1011–12, 6:1044; and Hayward, *Stopped at Stalingrad*, 234–35, who is highly critical of Jeschonnek's ill-considered promise. Doerr, *Feldzug nach Stalingrad*, 108–9, sees a more realistic figure of 946 tons per day.

91. See Johannes Fischer, "Über den Entschluss zur Luftversorgung Stalingrads: Ein Beitrag zur militärischen Führung im Dritten Reich," *Militärgeschichtliches Mitteilungen* 2, 1969): 7–67. The quote is from 12. V. E. Tarrant, *Stalingrad: Anatomy of an Agony* (London: Leo Cooper, 1992), 141.

92. Ziemke and Bauer, *Moscow to Stalingrad*, 477.

93. Hayward, *Stopped at Stalingrad*, 310. For the struggle to keep enough planes serviceable for the increasingly difficult daily flights, see Hans-Detlef Herhudt von Rohden, *Die Luftwaffe ringt um Stalingrad* (Wiesbaden: Limes, 1950), esp. 99–106.

94. For Winter Storm (*Wintergewitter*), see Horst Scheibert, *Nach Stalingrad—48 Kilometer! Der Entsatzvorstoss der 6. Panzerdivision, Dezember 1942* (Heidelberg: Kurt Vowinckel, 1956), vol. 10 in the series Die Wehrmacht im Kampf, and the expanded edition, *Entsatzversuch Stalingrad: Dokumentation einer Panzerschlacht in Wort und Bild: Das LVII. Panzerkorps im Dezember 1942* (Neckargemünd: Kurt Vowinckel, 1968).

95. For the adventure of 6th Panzer Division in the course of the relief operation, see two published versions of the memoir of the divisional commander, Erhard Raus, *Panzer Operations: The Eastern Front Memoir of Erhard Raus, 1941–1945* (New York: Da Capo, 2003), compiled and translated by Stephen H. Newton, 137–84; and Peter G. Tsouras, *Panzers on the Eastern Front: General Erhard Raus and His Panzer Divisions in Russia, 1941–1945* (London: Greenhill, 2002), 104–71. Both essentially present the same report that Raus presented to the U.S. Army in postwar interrogation. The former has a better translation of Raus's original reports for the U.S. Army; the latter has better maps. Both editors take him at his word, and neither treats his testimony, in which he presents himself as the greatest tank commander of the war, in any sort of critical way.

96. Raus, *Panzer Operations*, 183: "Right down to the most junior officer it was absolutely clear that this signified defeat at Stalingrad"; Tsouras, *Panzers on the Eastern Front*, 170 n. 30: "This move definitely sealed the doom of the German forces at Stalingrad."

Conclusion: The Death of the Wehrmacht

1. For an argument that treats the "turning point" of 1942 with some suspicion, see the German official history, Militärgeschichtliches Forschungsamt (Military Historical Research Office), *Das Deutsche Reich und Der Zweite Weltkrieg*, vol. 6, *Die Ausweitung zum Weltkrieg und der Wechsel der Initiative, 1941–1943* (Stuttgart: Deutsche Verlags-Anstalt, 1990), pt. 6, "Der Krieg gegen Die Sowjetunion, 1942–43," by Bernd Wegner, 1100–1102: "Das in der Literature unterschiedlichster Provenienz immer wieder kolportierte Urteil, die Stalingrader Schlacht stelle eine oder gar *die* Wende des Zweiten Weltkrieges dar, ist jedenfalls in mehrfacher Hinsicht problematisch," because it implies that a winnable war had suddenly become unwinnable. "Indessen kann gerade davon keine Rede sein" (1101).

2. The opening paragraph of the German manual *Truppenführung*. See Bruce Condell and David T. Zabecki, *On the German Art of War: Truppenführung* (Boulder, Colo.: Lynne Rienner, 2001), paragraph 1, 17.

3. Hans Doerr, *Der Feldzug nach Stalingrad: Versuch eines operativen Überblickes* (Darmstadt: E. S. Mittler, 1955), 117.

4. Robert M. Citino, *The German Way of War: From the Thirty Years' War to the Third Reich* (Lawrence: University Press of Kansas, 2005), 100. For all its telling and retelling, the story may well be apocryphal. Christopher Duffy, *Frederick the Great: A Military Life* (London: Routledge and Kegan Paul, 1985), 167, notes that it was first related only in 1797, in the fanciful biography by Blankenberg (*Karakter- und Lebensgeschichte des Herrn von Seydlitz*).

5. Quoted in Joel S. A. Hayward, *Stopped at Stalingrad: The Luftwaffe and Hitler's Defeat in the East, 1943–1943* (Lawrence: University Press of Kansas, 1998), 303.

6. See, among many references, Walther von Seydlitz, *Stalingrad: Konflikt und Konsequenz: Erinnerungen* (Oldenburg: Stalling, 1977), 171: "Die Sommeroffensive 1942 vefolgte zwei exzentrisch auseinanderlaufende Ziele, die aus Mangel an ausreichenden Stossdivisionen nur nacheinander erreichbar waren."

7. See the article by General Walter Scherff, "Geleitwort zum Kriegsjahrgang 1944," *Militärwissenschaftliche Rundschau* 9, no. 1 (1944): 1–2. Scherff was the Führer's official military historian (*Beauftrager des Führers für die militärische Geschichtsschreibung*) and was apparently held in low repute by a number of staff officers. See Walter Warlimont, *Inside Hitler's Headquarters, 1939–45* (Novato, Calif.: Presidio, 1964), 231 and 615 n. 10.

8. Adolf Hitler, "Reichswehr und deutsche Politik," *Militärwissenschaftliche Rundschau* 9, no. 1 (1944): 3–13.

9. Scherff, "Geleitwort zum Kriegsjahrgang 1944," 1.

10. Colmar Baron von der Goltz, "Der Feldherr und seine Unterführer," *Militärwissenschaftliche Rundschau* 9, no. 2 (1944): 98–100.

11. Erich Weniger, "Die Selbständigkeit der Unterführer und ihre Grenzen," *Militärwissenschaftliche Rundschau* 9, no. 2 (1944): 101–15.

12. General von Tschischwitz, "Der Kulminationspunkt des Angriffs im Landkriege," pt. 1, *Militärwissenschaftliche Rundschau* 7, no. 4 (1942): 3–13, and pt. 2, *Militärwissenschaftliche Rundschau* 8, no. 1 (1943): 15–35.

13. General Hugo Freiherr von Freytag-Loringhoven, "Optimismus im Kriege," *Militärwissenschaftliche Rundschau* 9, no. 2 (1944): 84–96.

14. Captain Beck-Broichsitter, "Über die Beharrlichkeit im Angriff," *Militärwissenschaftliche Rundschau* 9, no. 1 (1944): 57–64.

15. "Napoleon I. Über das Verhalten eingeschlossener Truppen," *Militärwissenschaftliche Rundschau* 9, no. 1 (1944): 65–66. Note that Walter Görlitz includes the same Napoleonic passages in his 1960 work on General Friedrich von Paulus and Stalingrad, *Paulus: "Ich stehe hier auf Befehl!"* (Frankfurt: Bernard & Graefe, 1960), 90–91.

16. "Die Zeit eines Seydlitz und Zieten ist wiedergekommen. Wir müssen den heutigen Krieg vom Kavallerie-Standpunkt sehen—Panzereinheiten wie Schwadronen führen. Befehle im fahrenden Panzer wie früher aus dem Sattel geben." Ralf Georg Reuth, *Rommel: Das Ende einer Legende* (Munich: Piper, 2004), 136. While on the subject of historical contextualization of contemporary military figures, see the report by General Han-Henning von Holtzendorff, "Reasons for Rommel's Success in Afrika [*sic*], 1941–1942," Foreign Military Studies Series (manuscript D-024), esp. 31–34, wherein Rommel's art of war is compared with that of Hannibal. A copy of this report, along with the rest of this immense series, is on file in the U.S. Army Military History Institute at Carlisle Barracks in Carlisle, Pa.

17. F. W. von Mellenthin, *Panzer Battles: A Study of the Employment of Armor in the Second World War* (New York: Ballantine, 1956), 51.

18. Reuth, *Rommel*, 156–57.

19. Quoted in Ibid., 172.

20. Quoted in Hayward, *Stopped at Stalingrad*, 245. For further reinforcement of the importance of Frederick the Great to German military planners during World War II, see the letter written in 1951 by the former chief of staff, General Franz Halder, to General Günther Blumentritt: "The question [put by an American historian], of when the last war had to be seen as lost, makes no sense. A war is a political act and can be militarily hopeless for the longest time while it still offers political chances. Such chances can even come up unexpectedly, as the Seven Years' War proved. So the correct answer remains: a war is only lost when one gives up." Quoted in Geoffrey Megargee, *Inside Hitler's High Command* (Lawrence: University Press of Kansas, 2000), 181.

21. See Omer Bartov, *The Eastern Front, 1941–45: German Troops and the Barbarisation of Warfare* (New York: St. Martin's Press, 1986), and his *Hitler's Army: Soldiers, Nazis and War in the Third Reich* (New York: Oxford University Press, 1991), especially the first two chapters, "The Demodernization of the Front" and

"The Destruction of the Primary Group" (12–58). See also Stephen G. Fritz, *Frontsoldaten: The German Soldier in World War II.* Lexington: University Press of Kentucky, 1995), especially chap. 8, "Trying to Change the World," 187–218, which locates new sources of combat cohesion in the Nazi ideology of the people's community (*Volksgemeinschaft*). For the seminal work on the issue of German combat performance, which located it within a matrix of soldier training and small-unit cohesion, see Martin van Creveld, *Fighting Power: German and U.S. Army Performance, 1939–1945* (Westport, Conn.: Greenwood, 1982): "The German army, in other words, was built upon the needs, social and psychological, of the individual fighting man" (164). See also Williamson Murray, *German Military Effectiveness* (Baltimore: Nautical & Aviation Publishing Company of America, 1992), a collection of previously published essays focusing largely on air power. For the broader picture, see "The Problem of German Military Effectiveness, 1900–1945" (1–38) and "Force Structure, Blitzkrieg Strategy, and Economic Difficulties: Nazi Grand Strategy in the 1930s" (217–28): "When the dust had settled in both 1918 and 1945 the German military had proven themselves inept politically and incompetent strategically" (31).

Bibliography

"1942 Offensive (Strategic Survey)." Foreign Military Studies Series. Manuscript T-14. On file at U.S. Army Military History Institute at Carlisle (Pa.) Barracks.

Addison, Paul, and Jeremy A. Crang, eds. *Firestorm: The Bombing of Dresden, 1945*. Chicago: Ivan R. Dee, 2006.

"Airborne Operations: A German Appraisal." Washington, D.C.: Center of Military History, 1989.

"Als pioniere bei der Vorausabteilung." In *Wir erobern die Krim: Soldaten der Krim-Armee berichten*. Neustadt: Pfälzische Verlagsanstalt, 1943.

Anders, Wladyslaw. *Hitler's Defeat in Russia*. Chicago: H. Regnery Co., 1953.

Antal, John F. "Operation 25: The Wehrmacht's Conquest of Yugoslavia." In *Maneuver Warfare: An Anthology*. Edited by Richard D. Hooker Jr. Novato, Calif.: Presidio, 1993.

Antal, John, and Bradley Gericke, eds. *City Fights: Selected Histories of Urban Combat from World War II to Vietnam*. New York: Ballantine, 2003.

Asprey, Robert B. *The Reign of Napoleon Bonaparte*. New York: Basic Books, 2001.

Atkinson, Rick. *An Army at Dawn: The War in North Africa*. New York: Holt, 2002.

Baldwin, Hanson. *Battles Lost and Won: Great Campaigns of World War II*. New York: Harper & Row, 1966.

Barber, A. J. *Afrika Korps*. London: Bison, 1977.

Barnett, Correlli. *The Desert Generals*. Bloomington: Indiana University Press, 1982.

Barr, Niall. *The Pendulum of War: The Three Battles of El Alamein*. New York: Overlook Press, 2005.

Bartov, Omer. *The Eastern Front, 1941–45: German Troops and the Barbarisation of Warfare*. New York: St. Martin's Press, 1986.

———. *Hitler's Army: Soldiers, Nazis and War in the Third Reich*. New York: Oxford University Press, 1991.

———. "Whose History Is it Anyway? The Wehrmacht and German Historiography." In *War of Extermination: The German Military in World War II, 1941–1944*. Edited by Hannes Heer and Klaus Naumann. New York: Berghahn, 2000.

Bassford, Christopher. *Clausewitz in English: The Reception of Clausewitz in Britain and America, 1815–1945*. Oxford: Oxford University Press, 1994.

Bauer, Josef Martin. *As Far as My Feet Will Carry Me*. Morley, Yorkshire: Elmfield Press, 1957.

———. *Kaukasisches Abenteuer*. Esslingen: Bechtle, 1950.

———. *Die Kraniche der Nogaia: Tagebuchblätter aus dem Feldzug im Osten*. Munich: R. Piper, 1942.

Beaumont, Roger A. "On the Wehrmacht Mystique." *Military Review* 66, no. 7 (1986).

Beck-Broichsitter, Captain. "Über die Beharrlichkeit im Angriff." *Militärwissenschaftliche Rundschau* 9, no. 1 (1944).

Beevor, Antony. *Stalingrad*. London: Viking, 1998.

Beevor, Antony, and Luba Vinogradova, eds. *A Writer at War: Vasily Grossman with the Red Army, 1941–1945*. New York: Pantheon, 2005.

Behrendt, Hans-Otto. *Rommel's Intelligence in the Desert Campaign, 1941–43*. London: William Kimber, 1985.

Bell, J. Bowyer. *Besieged: Seven Cities under Siege*. Philadelphia: Chilton Books, 1966.

Below, Nicolaus von. *At Hitler's Side: The Memoirs of Hitler's Luftwaffe Adjutant, 1937–1945*. London: Greenhill, 2001.

Bergschicker, Heinz. *Stalingrad: Eine Chronik in Bildern*. Berlin [Ost]: Verlag der Nation, 1960.

Bertkau, Friedrich. "Die nachrichtentechnische Führung mechanisierter Verbände." *Militär-Wochenblatt* 120, no. 15 (October 18, 1935).

Bezymenskij, Lev A. "Der sowjetische Nachrichtendienst und Kriegsbeginn von 1941." In *Der deutsche Angriff auf die Sowjetunion, 1941: Die Kontroverse um die Präventivkriegsthese*. Edited by Gerd Überschär and Lev A. Bezymenskij. Darmstadt: Primus, 1998.

Bidermann, Gottlob Herbert. *In Deadly Combat: A German Soldier's Memoir of the Eastern Front*. Lawrence: University Press of Kansas, 2000.

Bidwell, Shelford, and Dominick Graham. *Fire-Power: British Army Weapons and Theories of War, 1904–1945*. London: Allen and Unwin, 1982.

Bierman, John, and Colin Smith. *Alamein: War without Hate*. London: Viking, 2002.

Bigge, Major. "Über Selbstthätigkeit der Unterführer im Kriege." In *Beihefte zum Militär-Wochenblatt*. Berlin: E. S. Mittler, 1894.

Blau, George E. *The German Campaign in Russia—Planning and Operation, 1940–1942*. Department of the Army Pamphlet 20-261a. Washington, D.C.: Department of the Army, 1955.

———. *The German Campaign in the Balkans (Spring 1941)*. Department of the Army Pamphlet 20-260. Washington, D.C.: Department of the Army, 1953.

Bloxham, Donald. "Dresden as a War Crime." In *Firestorm: The Bombing of Dresden, 1945*. Edited by Paul Addison and Jeremy A. Crang. Chicago: Ivan R. Dee, 2006.

Blume, General von. "Selbstthätigkeit der Führer im Kriege." In *Beihefte zum Militär-Wochenblatt*. Berlin: E. S. Mittler, 1896.

Bock, Fedor von. *Generalfeldmarschall Fedor von Bock: The War Diary, 1939–1945*. Atglen, Pa.: Schiffer Military History, 1996.

Boll, Bernd, and Hans Safrian. "On the Way to Stalingrad: The 6th Army in 1941–42." In *War of Extermination: The German Military in World War II, 1941–1944.* Edited by Hannes Heer and Klaus Naumann. New York: Berghahn, 2000.

Boog, Horst. "Kolossalgemälde des Schreckens." In *Ein Volk von Opfern? Die neue Debatte um den Bombenkrieg, 1940–45.* Edited by Lothar Kettenacker. Berlin: Rohwohlt, 2003.

———. "Die Operationsführung: Die Luftwaffe." In Militärgeschichtliches Forschungsamt (Military Historical Research Office). *Das Deutsche Reich und Der Zweite Weltkrieg.* Volume 4. *Der Angriff auf die Sowjetunion.* Stuttgart: Deutsche Verlags-Anstalt, 1983.

Borgert, Heinz-Ludger. "Grundzüge der Landkriegführung von Schlieffen bis Guderian." In *Handbuch zur deutschen Militärgeschichte, 1648–1939.* Volume 9, *Grundzüge der militärischen Kriegführung.* Munich: Bernard & Graefe Verlag, 1979.

Braithwaite, Rodric. *Moscow, 1941.* New York: Knopf, 2006.

Braun, Lieutenant Colonel. "Der strategische Überfall." *Militär-Wochenblatt* 123, no. 18 (October 28, 1938).

Braun, M. "Die Schlachten auf Kertsch und im Korallenmeer in ihrer moralischen Bedeutung." *Militär-Wochenblatt* 126, no. 49 (June 5, 1942).

Brose, Eric Dorn. *The Kaiser's Army: The Politics of Military Technology in Germany during the Machine Age, 1870–1918.* Oxford: Oxford University Press, 2001.

Buchner, Alex. *Die deutsche Gebirgstruppe, 1939–1945: Eine Bilddokumentation.* Dorheim: Podzun, 1971.

Bucholz, Arden. *Moltke and the German Wars, 1864–1871.* New York: Palgrave, 2001.

Buckley, Christopher. *Greece and Crete, 1941.* London: H. M. Stationery Office, 1952.

Bungay, Stephen. *Alamein.* London: Aurum, 2002.

Burckhardt, Helmut. "Grosstanks oder Massenangriff mit unzureichend gepanzerten Tanks." *Militär-Wochenblatt* 122, no. 3 (July 16, 1937).

Büschleb, Hermann. *Feldherren und Panzer im Wüstenkrieg: Die Herbstschlacht "Crusader" im Vorfeld von Tobruk, 1941.* Neckargemünd: Kurt Vowinckel, 1966.

Carver, Michael. *Dilemmas of the Desert War: A New Look at the Libyan Campaign, 1940–1942.* London: Batsford, 1986.

———. *El Alamein.* London: Batsford, 1962.

———. "Montgomery." In *Churchill's Generals.* Edited by John Keegan. New York: Grove Weidenfeld, 1991.

———. *Tobruk.* London: Batsford, 1964.

Chandler, David G. *The Campaigns of Napoleon.* New York: Macmillan, 1966.

Choltitz, Colonel von. "Ein Brandenburgisches Regiment an der Ssewernaja-Bucht." In *Wir erobern die Krim: Soldaten der Krim-Armee berichten.* Neustadt: Pfälzische Verlagsanstalt, 1943.

Chuikov, V. I. *The Battle for Stalingrad.* New York: Holt, Rinehart and Winston, 1964.

Churchill, Winston S. *Marlborough: His Life and Times.* Chicago: University of Chicago Press, 2002.

———. *The Second World War*. Volume 3. *The Grand Alliance*. Boston: Houghton Mifflin, 1951.

———. *The Second World War*. Volume 4. *The Hinge of Fate*. Boston: Houghton Mifflin, 1950.

Citino, Robert M. *Armored Forces: History and Sourcebook*. Westport, Conn.: Greenwood Press, 1994.

———. *Blitzkrieg to Desert Storm: The Evolution of Operational Warfare*. Lawrence: University Press of Kansas, 2004.

———. *The Evolution of Blitzkrieg Tactics: Germany Defends Itself against Poland*. Westport, Conn.: Greenwood, 1987.

———. *The German Way of War: From the Thirty Years' War to the Third Reich*. Lawrence: University Press of Kansas, 2005.

———. *The Path to Blitzkrieg: Doctrine and Training in the German Army, 1920–1939*. Boulder, Colo.: Lynne Rienner, 1999.

———. *Quest for Decisive Victory: From Stalemate to Blitzkrieg in Europe, 1899–1940*. Lawrence: University Press of Kansas, 2002.

Claasen, Adam R. A. *Hitler's Northern War: The Luftwaffe's Ill-Fated Campaign, 1940–1945*. Lawrence: University Press of Kansas, 2001.

Clark, Alan. *Barbarossa: The Russian German Conflict, 1941–45*. New York: Quill, 1985.

Clausewitz, Carl von. *On War*. Edited and translated by Michael Howard and Peter Paret. Princeton: Princeton University Press, 1976.

Condell, Bruce, and David T. Zabecki. *On the German Art of War: Truppenführung*. Boulder, Colo.: Lynne Rienner, 2001.

Constantini, Colonel. "Operations en Crimée de mai à juillet 1942." *Revue Historique de l'Armée* 21, no. 1 (1965).

Cooper, Matthew. *The German Army, 1933–1945*. Chelsea, Mich.: Scarborough House, 1978.

Corum, James S. "The German Campaign in Norway as a Joint Operation." *Journal of Strategic Studies* 21, no. 4 (1998).

———. *The Luftwaffe: Creating the Operational Air War, 1918–1940*. Lawrence: University Press of Kansas, 1997.

———. *The Roots of Blitzkrieg: Hans von Seeckt and German Military Reform*. Lawrence: University Press of Kansas, 1992.

Cox, Sebastian. "The Dresden Raids: Why and How." In *Firestorm: The Bombing of Dresden, 1945*. Edited by Paul Addison and Jeremy A. Crang. Chicago: Ivan R. Dee, 2006.

Craig, Gordon A. *The Battle of Königgrätz: Prussia's Victory over Austria, 1866*. Philadelphia: Lippincott, 1964.

———. *Germany, 1866–1945*. Oxford: Oxford University Press, 1978.

Craig, William. *Enemy at the Gates: The Battle for Stalingrad*. New York: Reader's Digest Press, 1973.

Craster, Michael. "Cunningham, Ritchie and Leese." In *Churchill's Generals*. Edited by John Keegan. New York: Grove Weidenfeld, 1991.

Creveld, Martin van. *Fighting Power: German and U.S. Army Performance, 1939–1945*. Westport, Conn.: Greenwood, 1982.

———. "On Learning from the Wehrmacht and Other Things." *Military Review* 68, no. 1 (1988).

———. *Supplying War: Logistics from Wallenstein to Patton*. Cambridge: Cambridge University Press, 1977.

———. *The Transformation of War*. New York: Free Press, 1991.

Crimp, R. L. *The Diary of a Desert Rat*. London: Leo Cooper, 1971.

Crisp, Robert. *Brazen Chariots*. New York: Ballantine, 1961.

———. *The Gods Were Neutral*. London: Frederick Muller, 1960.

Cruickshank, Charles. *Greece, 1940–1941*. London: Davis-Poynter, 1976.

Cunningham, Michael. "Air War North Africa, 1940–43. *Strategy and Tactics*, no. 198 (July–August 1999).

Dahms, Rudolf. *Blücher, der Marschall Vorwärts*. Berlin: R. Hobbing, 1935.

Däniker, Colonel. "Zwei Jahre deutsche Strategie." *Militär-Wochenblatt* 126, no. 23 (November 25, 1941).

Davin, D. M. *Crete: Official History of New Zealand in the Second World War, 1939–45*. Wellington, N.Z.: War History Branch, 1953.

de Beaulieu, W. Charles. "Drive to Leningrad: The Baltic States, June–September 1941." *History of the Second World War*, no. 23 (1978).

———. *Der Vorstoss der Panzergruppe 4 auf Leningrad*. Neckargemünd: Kurt Rowinckel Verlag, 1961.

Deist, Wilhelm. "The Road to Ideological War: Germany, 1918–1945." In *The Making of Strategy: Rulers, States, and War*. Edited by Williamson Murray, MacGregor Knox, and Alvin Bernstein. Cambridge: Cambridge University Press, 1994.

Delbrück, Hans. *Historische und Politische Aufsätze*. Berlin: Georg Stilke, 1907.

Dessloch, Otto. "The Winter Battle of Rzhev, Vyazma, and Yukhov, 1941–1942." In *German Battle Tactics on the Russian Front, 1941–1945*. Edited by Stephen H. Newton. Atglen, Pa.: Schiffer, 1994.

"Deutschlands Abwehrkrieg von 1939." Part 1. "Die Ereignisse im Osten vom 1. bis 9. September." *Militär-Wochenblatt* 124, no. 12 (September 15, 1939).

"Deutschlands Abwehrkrieg von 1939." Part 2. "Die Ereignisse im Osten vom 9. September bis 16. September." *Militär-Wochenblatt* 124, no. 13 (September 22, 1939).

"Deutschlands Abwehrkrieg von 1939." Part 3. "Die Ereignisse in Polen vom 17. bis 24. September." *Militär-Wochenblatt* 124, no. 14 (October 1, 1939).

DiNardo, Richard L. *Germany and the Axis Powers: From Coalition to Collapse*. Lawrence: University Press of Kansas, 2005.

———. *Mechanized Juggernaut or Military Anachronism? Horses and the German Army of World War II*. Westport, Conn.: Greenwood, 1991.

DiNardo, Richard L., and Austin Bay. "Horse-Drawn Transport in the German Army." *Journal of Contemporary History* 23, no. 1 (1988).

Dittrich, Captain. "Einbruch in die Parpatsch-Stellung." In *Wir erobern die Krim: Soldaten der Krim-Armee berichten*. Neustadt: Pfälzische Verlagsanstalt, 1943.

———. "Tartaren-Graben and und Perekop." In *Wir erobern die Krim: Soldaten der Krim-Armee berichten*. Neustadt: Pfälzische Verlagsanstalt, 1943.

Dittmar, General. "Tobruk und Sewastopol." *Militär-Wochenblatt* 127, no. 1 (July 3, 1942).

"Divisionsführung und Befehlstechnik." *Militär-Wochenblatt* 116, no. 44 (May 18, 1932).

Doerr, Hans. "Der Ausgang der Schlacht um Charkow im Frühjahr 1942." *Wehrwissenschaftliche Rundschau* 4, no. 1 (January 1954).

———. *Der Feldzug nach Stalingrad: Versuch eines operativen Überblickes*. Darmstadt: E. S. Mittler, 1955.

Döring, Klaus. "Banden am Werk." In *Wir erobern die Krim: Soldaten der Krim-Armee berichten*. Neustadt: Pfälzische Verlagsanstalt, 1943.

Doughty, Robert A. *The Breaking Point: Sedan and the Fall of France, 1940*. Hamden, Conn.: Archon, 1990.

Duffy, Christopher. *The Army of Frederick the Great*. London: David & Charles, 1974.

———. *Frederick the Great: A Military Life*. London: Routledge and Kegan Paul, 1985.

Duffy, James P. *Target America: Hitler's Plan to Attack the United States*. Westport, Conn.: Praeger, 2004.

Dutu, Alesandru. "The Romanian Troops in the Siege of Sevastopol (October 1941–July 1942)." *Revue Internationale d'Histoire Militaire* 77 (1992).

Easum, Chester V. *Prince Henry of Prussia: Brother of Frederick the Great*. Westport, Conn.: Greenwood Press, 1971.

Ebert, Jens, ed. *Feldpostbriefe aus Stalingrad*. Göttingen: Wallstein, 2003.

Echevarria, Antulio J., II. *After Clausewitz: German Military Thinkers before the Great War*. Lawrence: University Press of Kansas, 2000.

———. "*Auftragstaktik:* In Its Proper Perspective." *Military Review* 66, no. 10 (October 1986).

———. "Review of Terence Zuber, *German War Planning*." *Journal of Military History* 69, no. 4 (October 2005).

Edwards, Jill, ed. *Al-Alamein Revisited: The Battle of al-Alamein and Its Historical Implications*. Cairo: American University in Cairo, 2000.

Eimannsberger, Ludwig von. "Panzertaktik." Parts 1 and 2. *Militär-Wochenblatt* 120, no. 23 (December 18, 1935), and *Militär-Wochenblatt* 120, no. 24 (December 25, 1935).

Emelianenko, Vasily B. *Red Star against the Swastika: The Story of a Soviet Pilot over the Eastern Front*. London: Greenhiill, 2005.

Engel, Gerhard. *Heeresadjutant bei Hitler, 1938–1943: Aufzeichnungen des Major Engels*. Stuttgart: Deutsche Verlags-Anstalt, 1974.

Erfurth, Waldemar. "Das Zusammenwirken getrennter Heeresteile." 4 parts. *Militärwissenschaftliche Rundschau* 4, nos. 1–4 (1939).

Erickson, John. *The Road to Berlin: Continuing the History of Stalin's War with Germany*. Boulder, Colo.: Westview Press, 1983.

———. *The Road to Stalingrad*. New York: Harper & Row, 1975.

Falkenhayn, Erich von. *Der Feldzug der 9. Armee gegen die Rumänen und Russen, 1916/17*. Berlin: E. S. Mittler, 1921.

Fischer, Ernst. "Georg Derfflinger: Bruchstücke seines Lebensbildes." *Beihefte zum Militär-Wochenblatt, 1894*. Berlin: E. S. Mittler, 1894.

Fischer, Johannes. "Über den Entschluss zur Luftversorgung Stalingrads: Ein Beitrag zur militärischen Führung im Dritten Reich." *Militärgeschichtliches Mitteilungen* 2, 1969.

Foerster, Lieutenant. "Prinz Friedrich Karl." *Militärwissenschaftliche Rundschau* 8, no. 2 (1943).

Foertsch, Hermann. "Generalfeldmarschall List 80 Jahre Alt." *Wehrwissenschaftliche Rundschau* 10, no. 5 (May 1960).

Fontane, Theodor. *Der deutsche Krieg von, 1866*. Volume 2. *Der Feldzug in West- und Mitteldeutschland*. Berlin: R. v. Decker, 1871.

Förster, Gerhard. "Einige Fragen der Kriegskunst während der Stalingrader Schlacht." *Militärgeschichte* 22, no. 1 (1983).

Förster, Jürgen. *Stalingrad: Risse im Bündnis, 1942–43*. Freiburg: Rombach, 1975.

———. "Das Unternhemen 'Barbarossa' als Eroberungs- und Vernichtungskrieg." In Militärgeschichtliches Forschungsamt (Military Historical Research Office). *Das Deutsche Reich und Der Zweite Weltkrieg*. Volume 4. *Der Angriff auf die Sowjetunion*. Stuttgart: Deutsche Verlags-Anstalt, 1983.

Forty, George. *The Armies of Rommel*. London: Arms and Armour Press, 1997.

———. *Desert Rats at War: North Africa*. London: Ian Allan, 1975.

Fowler, Will. *Stalingrad: The Vital 7 Days: The Germans' Last Desperate Attempt to Capture the City, October 1942*. Staplehurst, Kent: Spellmount, 2005.

François, Hermann von. *Marneschlacht und Tannenberg: Betrachtungen zur deutscher Kriegsführung der ersten sechs Kriegswochen*. Berlin: Scherl, 1920.

Freytag-Loringhoven, Hugo Freiherr von. *Feldherrengrösse: Von Denken und Handeln hervorragender Heerführer*. Berlin: E. S. Mittler, 1922.

———. "Optimismus im Kriege," *Militärwissenschaftliche Rundschau* 9, no. 2 (1944).

Frieser, Karl-Heinz. *The Blitzkrieg Legend: The 1940 Campaign in the West*. Annapolis: Naval Institute Press, 2005.

Fritz, Stephen G. *Frontsoldaten: The German Soldier in World War II*. Lexington: University Press of Kentucky, 1995.

Frost, Robert I. *The Northern Wars: War, State, and Soviet in Northeastern Europe, 1558–1721*. Essex: Longman, 2000.

Gat, Azar. *The Origins of Military Thought: From the Enlightenment to Clausewitz*. Oxford: Oxford University Press, 1992.

Gaul, Colonel. "Der Blitzkrieg in Frankreich." *Militär-Wochenblatt* 125, no. 35 (February 28, 1941).

———. "Kurze Darstellung der sowjetrussischen Kämpfe auf der Krim und um Sewastopol vom Oktober 1941 bis July 1942." *Militärwissenschaftliche Rundschau* 8, no. 2 (1943).

Gause, Alfred. "Der Feldzug in Nordafrika im Jahre 1941." *Wehrwissenschaftliche Rundschau* 12, no. 10 (October 1962).

———. "Der Feldzug in Nordafrika im Jahre 1942." *Wehrwissenschaftliche Rundschau* 12, no. 11 (November 1962).

———. "Der Feldzug in Nordafrika im Jahre 1943." *Wehrwissenschaftliche Rundschau* 12, no. 12 (December 1962).

Gehring, Egid, ed. *Unterm Edelweiss in Jugoslawien: Aus den Erlebnissen einer Gebirgsdivision*. Munich: Franz Eher, 1941.

"Generalfeldmarschall Graf von Schlieffen über den grossen Feldherren der preussisch-deutschen Armee." *Militär-Wochenblatt* 125, no. 17 (October 25, 1940).

German Experiences in Desert Warfare during World War II. Volume 2. Fleet Marine Force Reference Publication (FMFRP) 12-96-II. Quantico, Va.: United States Marine Corps, 1990.

German General Staff. *Die Kriege Friedrichs des Grossen*. Part 3. *Die siebenjährige Krieg*. Volume 5. *Hastenbeck und Rossbach*. Berlin: Ernst Mittler, 1903.

———. *Studien zur Kriegsgeschichte und Taktik*. Volume 6. *Heeresverpflegung*. Berlin: E. S. Mittler, 1913.

Giertz, Horst. "Die Schlacht von Stalingrad in der sowjetischen Historiographie." In *Stalingrad: Mythos und Wirklichkeit einer Schlacht*. Edited by Wolfram Wette and Gerd R. Überschär. Frankfurt am Main: Fischer Taschenbuch Verlag, 1992.

Glantz, David M. *The Battle for Leningrad, 1941–1944*. Lawrence: University Press of Kansas, 2002.

———. *Colossus Reborn: The Red Army at War, 1941–1943*. Lawrence: University Press of Kansas, 2005.

———. *Companion to Colossus Reborn*. Lawrence: University Press of Kansas, 2005.

———. "Counterpoint to Stalingrad: Operation Mars (November–December 1942): Marshal Zhukov's Greatest Defeat." Fort Leavenworth, Kans.: Foreign Military Studies Office, 1997.

———. "Forgotten Battles of the German-Soviet War (1941–45), Part 6: The Winter Campaign (5 December 1941–April 1942): The Crimean Counteroffensive and Reflections." *Journal of Slavic Military Studies* 14, no. 1 (March 2001).

———. "Forgotten Battles of the German-Soviet War (1941–1945), Part 7: The Summer Campaign (12 May–18 November 1942): Voronezh, July 1942." *Journal of Slavic Military Studies* 14, no. 3 (September 2001).

———. *Stumbling Colossus: The Red Army on the Eve of World War II*. Lawrence: University Press of Kansas, 1998.

———. *Zhukov's Greatest Defeat: The Red Army's Epic Disaster in Operation Mars, 1942*. Lawrence: University Press of Kansas, 1999.

———, ed. *Kharkov, 1942: Anatomy of a Military Disaster through Soviet Eyes*. Shepperton, Surrey: Ian Allan, 1998.

Glantz, David M., and Jonathan House. *The Battle of Kursk*. Lawrence: University Press of Kansas, 1999.

———. *When Titans Clashed: How the Red Army Stopped Hitler*. Lawrence: University Press of Kansas, 1995.

Goltz, Colmar Baron von der. "Der Feldherr und seine Unterführer." *Militärwissenschaftliche Rundschau* 9, no. 2 (1944).

———. *Jena to Eylau: The Disgrace and the Redemption of the Old-Prussian Army.* New York, E. P. Dutton, 1913.

Görlitz, Walter, ed. *Paulus: "Ich stehe hier auf Befehl!"* Frankfurt: Bernard & Graefe, 1960.

Grams, Rolf. *Die 14. Panzer Division, 1940–1945: Herausgegeben im Auftrag der Traditionsgemeinschaft der 14. Panzer Division.* Bad Neuheim: Podzun, 1957.

Greenwood, Donald J. *Turning Point—Stalingrad.* Baltimore: Avalon Hill Game Company, 1989.

Griehl, Manfred. *Luftwaffe over America: The Secret Plans to Bomb the United States in World War II.* London: Greenhill, 2004.

Griffith, Paddy. *Forward into Battle: Fighting Tactics from Waterloo to the Near Future.* Novato, Calif.: Presidio, 1990.

———. "Wings over the Caucasus: Operation Leonardo." In *Hitler Triumphant: Alternate Decisions of World War II.* Edited by Peter G. Tsouras. London: Greenhill, 2006.

Grossdeutschlands Freiheitskrieg. Part 88. "Eine Woche der Siege." *Militär-Wochenblatt* 125, no. 42 (April 18, 1941).

Grossdeutschlands Freiheitskrieg. Part 89. "Kapitulation Jugoslawiens. Kroatien selbständig. Durchbruch durch die Front in Griechenland." *Militär-Wochenblatt* 125, no. 43 (April 25, 1941).

Grossdeutschlands Freiheitskrieg. Part 90. "Kapitulation der griechischen Hauptarmee. Athen und Korinth besetzt." *Militär-Wochenblatt* 125, no. 44 (May 2, 1941).

Grossdeutschlands Freiheitskrieg. Part 91. "Abschluss der Kämpfe in Griechenland." *Militär-Wochenblatt* 125, no. 45 (May 9, 1941).

Grossdeutschlands Freiheitskrieg. Part 120. "Nach fünf Monaten Ostfeldzug." *Militär-Wochenblatt* 126, no. 22 (November 28, 1941).

Grossdeutschlands Freiheitskrieg. Part 128. "Offensivgeist in der Defensive." *Militär-Wochenblatt* 126, no. 30 (January 23, 1942).

Grossdeutschlands Freiheitskrieg. Part 145. "Die deutsche Frühjahrsoperation auf der Krim." *Militär-Wochenblatt* 126, no. 47 (May 22, 1942).

Grossdeutschlands Freiheitskrieg. Part 146. "Kertsch, die erste Vernichtungsschlacht des Frühjahrs." *Militär-Wochenblatt* 126, no. 48 (May 29, 1942).

Grossdeutschlands Freiheitskrieg. Part 146. "Die Schlacht von Charkow: Aus der Abwehr zum Angriff." *Militär-Wochenblatt* 126, no. 48 (May 29, 1942).

Grossdeutschlands Freiheitskrieg. Part 147. "Abschluss der Kesselschlacht von Charkow." *Militär-Wochenblatt* 126, no. 49 (June 5, 1942).

Grossdeutschlands Freiheitskrieg. Part 151. "Die Auswertung des Sieges von Tobruk." *Militär-Wochenblatt* 127, no. 1 (July 3, 1942).

Grossdeutschlands Freiheitskrieg. Part 152. "Der Fall von Sewastopol." *Militär-Wochenblatt* 127, no. 2 (June 19, 1942).

Grossdeutschlands Freiheitskrieg. Part 154. "Die Lage in Ägypten." *Militär-Wochenblatt* 127, no. 4 (July 24, 1942).

Grossdeutschlands Freiheitskrieg. Part 157. "Die militärischen und politischen Ereignisse vom 2. bis 8. August 1942." *Militär-Wochenblatt* 127, no. 7 (August 14, 1942).

Grossdeutschlands Freiheitskrieg. Part 170. "Bei Tuapse und am Terek Raumgewinn." *Militär-Wochenblatt* 127, no. 20 (November 13, 1942).

Grossdeutschlands Freiheitskrieg. Part 173. "Sowjetangriffe vom Kaukasus bis zur Newa abgewiesen." *Militär-Wochenblatt* 127, no. 23 (December 4, 1942).

Grosser, Sergeant. "Die Ssewernaja-Bucht ist überquert." In *Wir erobern die Krim: Soldaten der Krim-Armee berichten*. Neustadt: Pfälzische Verlagsanstalt, 1943.

Grove, Eric, Christopher Chant, David Lyon, and Hugh Lyon. *The Military Hardware of World War II: Tanks, Aircraft, and Naval Vessels*. New York: Military Press, 1984.

Guderian, Heinz. *Achtung—Panzer! The Development of Armored Forces, Their Tactics, and Operational Potential*. London: Arms and Armour Press, 1992.

———. "Kraftfahrtruppen." *Militärwissenschaftliche Rundschau* 1, no. 1 (1936).

———. *Panzer Leader*. New York: Ballantine, 1957.

———. "Die Panzertruppen und ihr Zusammenwirken mit den anderen Waffen." *Militärwissenschaftliche Rundschau* 1, no. 5 (1936).

Guillaume, Augustin. *The German-Russian War, 1941–1945*. London: War Office, 1956.

Gudmundsson, Bruce. *Inside the Afrika Korps*. London: Greenhill Books, 1999.

Gunsburg, Jeffrey A. *Divided and Conquered: The French High Command and the Defeat in the West, 1940*. Westport, Conn.: Greenwood, Press, 1979.

Habeck, Mary R. *Storm of Steel: The Development of Armor Doctrine in Germany and the Soviet Union, 1919–1939*. Ithaca, N.Y.: Cornell University Press, 2003.

Habedanck, Gert. "Wir fegten den Tommy vom Kontinent." In *Die Wehrmacht: Um die Freiheit Europas*. Edited by Oberkommando der Wehrmacht. Berlin: Verlag "Die Wehrmacht," 1941.

Haidin, Wolfgang. *Stalingrad: Kampf und Gefangenschaft überlebt: Aus den Lebenserinnerungen des Josef Schönegger*. Steyr: Ennsthaler, 1995.

Halder, Franz. *Kriegstagebuch*. Volume 2. *Von der geplanten Landung in England bis zum Beginn des Ostfeldzuges*. Stuttgart: W. Kohlhammer Verlag, 1964.

———. *Kriegstagebuch*. Volume 3. *Der Russlandfeldzug bis zum Marsch auf Stalingrad*. Stuttgart: W. Kohlhammer Verlag, 1964.

Halle, Armin, and Carlo Demand. *Tanks: An Illustrated History of Fighting Vehicles*. New York: Crescent, 1971.

Hamburger Institut für Sozialforschung, ed. *Verbrechen der Wehrmacht: Dimensionen des Vernichtungskrieges, 1941–1944*. Hamburg: Hamburger Edition, 2002.

Hamilton, Nigel. *Monty*. 3 volumes. London: Hamish Hamilton, 1981–1986.

Hamric, Jacob Lee. "Germany's Decisive Victory: Falkenhayn's Campaign in Romania, 1916." Master's thesis, Eastern Michigan University, 2004.

Harris, J. P. *Men, Ideas, and Tanks: British Military Thought and Armoured Forces, 1903–1939*. Manchester: Manchester University Press, 1995.

Harrison, Richard W. *The Russian Way of War: Operational Art, 1904–1940*. Lawrence: University Press of Kansas, 2001.

Hartmann, Christian. *Halder: Generalstabschef Hitlers, 1938–1942*. Paderborn: Ferdinand Schöningh, 1991.

Haufler, Hervie. *The Spies Who Never Were: The True Story of the Nazi Spies Who Were Actually Allied Double Agents*. New York: NAL Caliber, 2006.

Haupt, Werner, ed. *Army Group South: The Wehrmacht in Russia, 1941–1945*. Atglen, Pa.: Schiffer, 1998.

Hayward, Joel S. A. "A Case Study in Early Joint Warfare: An Analysis of the Wehrmacht's Crimean Campaign of 1942." *Journal of Strategic Studies* 22, no. 4 (December 1999).

———. *Stopped at Stalingrad: The Luftwaffe and Hitler's Defeat in the East, 1943–1943*. Lawrence: University Press of Kansas, 1998.

———. "Von Richtofen's 'Giant Fire-Magic': The Luftwaffe's Contribution to the Battle of Kerch, 1942." *Journal of Slavic Military Studies* 10, no. 2 (June 1997).

Heckmann, Wolf. *Rommel's War in Africa*. Garden City, N.Y.: Doubleday, 1981.

Heer, Hannes, and Klaus Naumann, eds. *Vernichtungskrieg: Verbrechen der Wehrmacht, 1941–1944*. Hamburg: Hamburger Edition, 1995.

———. *War of Extermination: The German Military in World War II, 1941–1944*. New York: Berghahn, 2000.

Hellenic Army General Staff. *An Abridged History of the Greek-Italian and Greek-German War, 1940–1941: Land Operations*. Athens: Army History Directorate, 1997.

Helmert, Heinz, and Helmut Otto. "Zur Koalitionskriegsführung Hitler-Deutschlands im zweiten Weltkrieg am Beispiel des Einsatzes der ungarischen 2. Armee." *Zeitschrift für Militärgeschichte* 2, no. 3 (1963).

Henrici, Sigfrid. "Sarajevo 1941: Der raidartige Vorstoss einer mot. Division." *Wehrwissenschaftliche Rundschau* 10, no. 4 (April 1960).

Hepp, Leo. "Die 12. Armee im Balkanfeldzug 1941." *Wehrwissenschaftliche Rundschau* 5, no. 5 (May 1955).

Herwig, Holger H. *The First World War: Germany and Austria-Hungary, 1914–1918*. London: Arnold, 1997.

Heuser, Beatrice. *Reading Clausewitz*. New York: Random House, 2002.

Heydte, Friedrich August von der. *Daedalus Returned: Crete, 1941*. London: Hutchinson, 1958.

Heysing, Günther. "Pionere auf dem Balkan." In *Die Wehrmacht: Um die Freiheit Europas*. Edited by Oberkommando der Wehrmacht. Berlin: Verlag "Die Wehrmacht," 1941.

Higham, Robin. *Diary of a Disaster: British Aid to Greece, 1940–1941*. Lexington: University Press of Kentucky, 1986.

Hinsley, F. H., et al. *British Intelligence in the Second World War: Its Influence on Strategy and Operations*. 3 volumes. Cambridge: Cambridge University Press, 1979–1988.

Hitler, Adolf. "Reichswehr und deutsche Politik." *Militärwissenschaftliche Rundschau* 9, no. 1 (1944).

Hoffmann, Joachim. *Kaukasien, 1942–43: Das deutsche Heer und die Orientvölker der Sowjetunion*. Freiburg: Rombach Verlag, 1991.

Holland, James. *Together We Stand: America, Britain, and the Forging of an Alliance*. New York: Hyperion, 2005.

Holtzendorff, Han-Henning von. "Reasons for Rommel's Success in Afrika [*sic*], 1941–1942." Foreign Military Studies Series. Manuscript D-024. On file at U.S. Army Military History Institute at Carlisle (Pa.) Barracks.

Höpper, Wolf. "Operation Hubertus: Ljudnikows Last Stand in Stalingrad." Available at: http://www.flamesofwar.com/Article.asp?ArticleID=1032.

Horne, Alistair. *To Lose a Battle: France, 1940*. Boston: Little, Brown, 1969.

Howard, Michael. "The Battle of al-Alamein." In *Al-Alamein Revisited: The Battle of al-Alamein and Its Historical Implications.* Edited by Jill Edwards. Cairo: American University in Cairo, 2000.

———. *The Franco-Prussian War*. New York: Macmillan, 1962.

———, ed. *The Theory and Practice of War*. Bloomington: Indiana University Press, 1965.

Hoyt, Edwin P. *199 Days: The Battle of Stalingrad.* New York: Tor, 1993.

———. *Guerrilla: Colonel von Lettow-Vorbeck and Germany's East African Empire.* New York: Macmillan, 1981.

———. *Stalin's War: Tragedy and Triumph, 1941–1945*. New York: Cooper Square Press, 2003.

Hubatsch, Walther. *Hitlers Weisungen für die Kriegführung, 1939–1945*. Koblenz: Bernard & Graefe, 1983.

Hughes, Daniel J. "Abuses of German Military History." *Military Review* 66, no. 12 (December 1986).

———, ed. *Moltke on the Art of War: Selected Writings.* Novato, Calif.: Presidio, 1993.

Hull, Isabel V. *Absolute Destruction: Military Culture and the Practices of War in Imperial Germany.* Ithaca, N.Y.: Cornell University Press, 2005.

Humburg, Martin. "Die Bedeutung der Feldpost für die Soldaten in Stalingrad." In *Stalingrad: Mythos und Wirklichkeit einer Schlacht.* Edited by Wolfram Wette and Gerd R. Überschär. Frankfurt am Main: Fischer Taschenbuch Verlag, 1992.

Hünger, Heinz, and Ernst Erich Strassl. *Kampf und Intrige um Griechenland.* Munich: Franz Eher, 1942.

Hürter, Johannes. *Ein deutscher General an der Ostfront: Die Briefe und Tagebücher des Gotthard Heinricis, 1941–42*. Erfurt: Alan Sutton, 2001.

Irving, David. *The Destruction of Dresden.* London: Kimber, 1963.

Jackson, W. G. F. *The Battle for North Africa, 1940–43*. New York: Mason, Charter, 1975.

Jacobsen, Hans-Adolf. *Fall Gelb: Der Kampf um den deutschen Operationsplan zur Westoffensive 1940*. Wiesbaden: F. Steiner, 1957.

———. "Hitlers Gedanken zur Kriegführung im Westen." *Wehrwissenschaftliche Rundschau* 5, no. 10 (October 1955).

Jany, Curt. *Geschichte der königlich preussischen Armee bis zum Jahre 1807*. Volume 2. *Die Armee Friedrichs des Grossen 1740 bis 1763*. Berlin: Karl Siegismund, 1928.

Jeloschek, Albert, Friedrich Richter, Ehrenfried Schütte, and Johannes Semler. *Freiwillige vom Kaukasus: Georgier, Armenier, Tschetschenen u. a. auf deutscher Seite: Der "Sonderverband Bergmann" und sein Gründer Theodor Oberländer*. Graz: Leopold Stocker, 2003.

Jukes, Geoffrey. "Barbarossa: Drive to Kharkov: Ukraine, September–December 1941." *History of the Second World War*, no. 23 (1978).

———. "Drive to Kiev: Ukraine, June 23–September 18, 1941." *History of the Second World War*, no. 22 (1978).

———. *Hitler's Stalingrad Decisions.* Berkeley: University of California Press, 1985.

———. *Stalingrad: The Turning Point*. New York: Ballantine, 1968.

Kabisch, Ernst. "Systemlose Strategie." *Militär-Wochenblatt* 125, no. 26 (December 27, 1940).

Kagan, Frederick. "Army Doctrine and Modern War: Notes toward a New Edition of FM 100-5." *Parameters* 27, no. 1 (spring 1997).

Kahlert, Corporal. "Die Parpatsch-Stellung wird durchbrochen." In *Wir erobern die Krim: Soldaten der Krim-Armee berichten.* Neustadt: Pfälzische Verlagsanstalt, 1943.

Kaltenegger, Roland. *Gebirgsjäger im Kaukasus: Die Operation "Edelweiss," 1942–43.* Graz: Leopold Stocker, 1997.

Keegan, John. *The Second World War*. New York: Penguin, 2005.

———, ed. *Churchill's Generals.* New York: Grove Weidenfeld, 1991.

———, ed. *Collins Atlas of the Second World War*. Ann Arbor, Mich.: Borders Press, 2003.

Kehrig, Manfred. *Stalingrad: Analyse und Dokumentation einer Schlacht.* Stuttgart: Deutsche Verlags-Anstalt, 1974.

———. "Stalingrad im Spiegel der Memoiren deutscher Generale." In *Stalingrad: Mythos und Wirklichkeit einer Schlacht.* Edited by Wolfram Wette and Gerd R. Überschär. Frankfurt am Main: Fischer Taschenbuch Verlag, 1992.

Keithly, David M. "Black Cross, Green Crescent, Black Gold: The Drive to the Indus." In *Hitler Triumphant: Alternate Decisions of World War II.* Edited by Peter G. Tsouras. London: Greenhill, 2006.

Kennedy, Robert M. *German Antiguerrilla Operations in the Balkans, 1941–44.* Department of the Army Pamphlet 20-243. Washington, D.C.: Department of the Army, 1954.

———. *The German Campaign in Poland, 1939.* Department of the Army Pamphlet 20-255. Washington, D.C.: Department of the Army, 1956.

Kerr, Walter. *The Secret of Stalingrad.* Garden City, N.Y.: Doubleday, 1978.

Kershaw, Ian. *Hitler.* Volume 2. *Nemesis.* New York: Norton, 2000.

Kessel, Eberhard. "Blücher: Zum 200. Geburtstag am 16. Dezember." *Militärwissenschaftliche Rundschau* 7, no. 4 (1942).

Kettenacker, Lothar, ed. *Ein Volk von Opfern? Die neue Debatte um den Bombenkrieg, 1940–45.* Berlin: Rohwohlt, 2003.

Kissel, Hans. *Angriff einer Infanteriedivision: Die 101.leichte Infanteriedivision in der Frühjahrsschlacht bei Charkow, Mai 1942.* Heidelberg: Kurt Vowinckel, 1958.

———. "Die ersten T-34." *Wehrwissenschaftliche Rundschau* 5, no. 3 (March 1955).

Klink, Ernst. "Die Operationsführung: Heer und Kriegsmarine." In Militärgeschichtliches Forschungsamt (Military Historical Research Office). *Das Deutsche Reich und Der Zweite Weltkrieg.* Volume 4. *Der Angriff auf die Sowjetunion.* Stuttgart: Deutsche Verlags-Anstalt, 1983.

Klümann, Corporal. "Marsch ans Schwarze Meer." In *Wir erobern die Krim: Soldaten der Krim-Armee berichten.* Neustadt: Pfälzische Verlagsanstalt, 1943.

Knopp, Guido. *Stalingrad: Das Drama.* Munich: Bertelsmann, 2002.

Knox, MacGregor, and Williamson Murray, eds. *The Dynamics of Military Revolution, 1300–2050*. Cambridge: Cambridge University Press, 2001.

Köhn, Lieutenant Colonel. "Die Infanterie im 'Blitzkrieg.'" *Militär-Wochenblatt* 125, no. 5 (August 2, 1940).

Kolbe, Lieutenant. " . . . ins Meer zurückzuwerfen." In *Wir erobern die Krim: Soldaten der Krim-Armee berichten*. Neustadt: Pfälzische Verlagsanstalt, 1943.

Konrad, Rudolf, and E. W. Rümmler. *Kampf um den Kaukasus*. Munich: Copress, 1955.

Kügler, Harry. "Gefecht mit Banden im Gebirge." In *Wir erobern die Krim: Soldaten der Krim-Armee berichten*. Neustadt: Pfälzische Verlagsanstalt, 1943.

Kunz, Andreas. "Vor sechzig Jahren: Der Untergang der 6. Armee in Stalingrad." *Militärgeschichte*, no. 4 (2002).

Kurowski, Franz. *Demjansk: Der Kessel im Eis: 14 Monate Abwehrkampf im Nordabschnitt der Ostfront*. Wölfersheim: Podzun-Pallas, 2001.

Ladda, Herbert. "Der Aderlass der Kaukasusarmee." *Die Wehrmacht* 6, no. 5 (March 4, 1942).

Larson, Robert H. *The British Army and the Theory of Armored Warfare*. Newark: University of Delaware Press, 1984.

Latimer, Jon. *Alamein*. Cambridge, Mass.: Harvard University Press, 2002.

Lederrey, Colonel E. *Germany's Defeat in the East: The Soviet Armies at War, 1941–1945*. London: War Office, 1955.

Lettow-Vorbeck, Oscar von. *Geschichte des Krieges von 1866 in Deutschland*. Volume 1. *Gastein-Langensalza*. Berlin: E. S. Mittler, 1896.

Lettow-Vorbeck, Paul von. *Meine erinnerungen aus Ostafrika*. Leipzig: K. F. Koehler, 1920.

Levine, Alan J. *The War against Rommel's Supply Lines, 1942–1943*. Westport, Conn.: Praeger, 1999.

Lewin, Ronald. *The Life and Death of the Afrika Korps*. London: Batsford, 1977.

———. *Montgomery as Military Commander*. London: Batsford, 1971.

———. *Rommel as Military Commander*. London: Batsford, 1968.

———. *Ultra Goes to War: The First Account of World War II's Greatest Secret Based on Official Documents*. New York: McGraw-Hill, 1978.

Liddle, Peter. "Rescuing the Testimony of the North Africa Campaign Experience." In *Al-Alamein Revisited: The Battle of al-Alamein and Its Historical Implications*. Edited by Jill Edwards. Cairo: American University in Cairo, 2000.

Liddell Hart, B. H. *The German Generals Talk*. New York: Quill, 1979.

Löser, Jochen. *Bittere Pflicht: Kampf und Untergang der 76. Berlin-Brandenburgischen Infanterie-Division*. Osnabrück: Biblio Verlag, 1988.

Lucas, James. *Battle Group! German Kampfgruppe Action of World War Two*. London: Arms and Armour Press, 1993.

Ludwig, General. "Moltke als Erzieher." *Militär-Wochenblatt* 125, no. 17 (October 25, 1940).

———. "Die Operation auf der inneren und der äusseren Linie im Lichte underer Zeit." *Militär-Wochenblatt* 126, no. 1 (July 4, 1941).

Lukacs, John. *June 1941: Hitler and Stalin.* New Haven, Conn.: Yale University Press, 2006.

Luraghi, Raimondo. "Italian Forces at the Battle of al-Alamein: 'Ferrea Mole, Ferreo Cuore.'" In *Al-Alamein Revisited: The Battle of al-Alamein and Its Historical Implications.* Edited by Jill Edwards. Cairo: American University in Cairo, 2000.

Macher, Major. "Die Besetzung Dänemarks." *Militär-Wochenblatt* 125, no. 45 (May 9, 1941).

Mackensen, Eberhard von. *Vom Bug zum Kaukasus: Das III. Panzerkorps im Feldzug gegen Sowjetrussland, 1941–42.* Neckargemünd: Kurt Vowinckel, 1967.

Macksey, Kenneth. *Rommel: Battles and Campaigns.* London: Arms and Armour Press, 1979.

———. *Tank Versus Tank: The Illustrated Story of Armored Battlefield Conflict in the Twentieth Century.* New York: Barnes & Noble, 1999.

Majdalany, Fred. *The Battle of El Alamein: Fortress in the Sand.* Philadelphia: Lippincott, 1965.

Manstein, Erich von. *Lost Victories.* Novato, Calif.: Presidio, 1982.

"Manytsch—Damm: Grenze Europa Asien." *Die Wehrmacht* 6, no. 18 (September 2, 1942).

Martens, Hans. *General von Seydlitz, 1942–1945: Analyse eines Konflikts.* Berlin [Ost]: Von Kloeden, 1971.

Maude, Colonel F. N. *1806: The Jena Campaign.* London: Swan Sonnenschein, 1909.

———. *The Jena Campaign, 1806.* London: Greenhill, 1998.

McGlymont, W. G. *To Greece.* Wellington, N.Z.: War History Branch, 1959.

McKee, Alexander. *Dresden, 1945: The Devil's Tinderbox.* London: Souvenir, 1982.

———. *El Alamein: Ultra and the Three Battles.* Chatham, Kent: Souvenir, 1991.

McTaggart, Pat. "Poland '39." *Command,* no. 17 (July–August 1992).

———. "Smolensk-Yelnia: Blunting the Blitzkrieg." *Command,* no. 21 (March–April 1993).

Megargee, Geoffrey P. *Inside Hitler's High Command.* Lawrence: University Press of Kansas, 2000.

———. *War of Annihilation: Combat and Genocide on the Eastern Front, 1941.* New York: Rowman & Littlefield, 2006.

Meinhold, Günter. "123rd Infantry Regiment in the Breakthrough Battle for the Parpach Position, 8–11 May 1942." Foreign Military Studies Series. Manuscript D-264. On file at U.S. Army Military History Institute at Carlisle (Pa.) Barracks.

Mellenthin, Friedrich Wilhelm von. *Panzer Battles: A Study of the Employment of Armor in the Second World War.* New York: Ballantine, 1956.

Menning, Bruce. "The Deep Strike in Russian and Soviet Military History." *Journal of Soviet Military Studies* 1, no. 1 (April 1988).

Merridale, Catherine. *Ivan's War: Life and Death in the Red Army, 1939–1945.* New York: Metropolitan Books, 2006.

Messerschmidt, Manfred. "Forward Defense: The 'Memorandum of the Generals' for the Nuremberg Court." In *War of Extermination: The German Military in World War II, 1941–1944*. Edited by Hannes Heer and Klaus Naumann. New York: Berghahn, 2000.

"Militärgeschichte: Bremen und Umland." Available at: http://www.historic.de.

Militärgeschichtliches Forschungsamt (Military Historical Research Office). *Das Deutsche Reich und Der Zweite Weltkrieg*. Volume 2. *Die Errichtung der hegemonie auf dem Europäischen Kontinent*. Stuttgart: Deutsche Verlags-Anstalt, 1979.

———. Volume 3. *Der Mittelmeerraum und Südosteuropa: Von der "non-belligeranza" Italiens bis zum Kriegseintritt der Vereinigten Staaten*. Stuttgart: Deutsche Verlags-Anstalt, 1984.

———. Volume 4. *Der Angriff auf die Sowjetunion*. Stuttgart: Deutsche Verlags-Anstalt, 1983.

———. Volume 6. *Der Globale Krieg: Die Ausweitung zum Weltkrieg und der Wechsel der Initiative, 1941–1943*. Stuttgart: Deutsche Verlags-Anstalt, 1990.

Miller, Donald L. *Masters of the Air: America's Bomber Boys Who Fought the Air War against Nazi Germany*. New York: Simon & Schuster, 2006.

Mitcham, Samuel W., Jr. *Rommel's Greatest Victory: The Desert Fox and the Fall of Tobruk, 1942*. Novato, Calif.: Presidio, 1998.

Mitchell, Laurence. "The High Road to the Caucasus: Exploring the Georgian Military Highway." *Hidden Europe*, no. 9 (July 2006).

Moltke, Helmuth von. *The Franco-German War of 1870–71*. New York: Howard Fertig, 1988.

Mommsen, Hans. "Moralisch, strategisch, zerstörerisch." In *Ein Volk von Opfern? Die neue Debatte um den Bombenkrieg, 1940–45*. Edited by Lothar Kettenacker. Berlin: Rohwohlt, 2003.

Montgomery, Bernard Law. *El Alamein to the River Sangro; Normandy to the Baltic*. London: Barrie and Jenkins, 1973.

———. *Memoirs of Field-Marshal the Viscount Montgomery of Alamein*. Cleveland: World, 1968.

Mühleisen, Hans-Otto. *Kreta, 1941: Das Unternehemen Merkur, 20. Mai–1. Juni 1941*. Freiburg: Rombach, 1968.

Muller, Richard. *The German Air War in Russia*. Baltimore: Nautical and Aviation Publishing, 1992.

Müller, Rolf-Dieter, and Gerd R. Überschär. *Hitlers Krieg im Osten, 1941–1945: Ein Forschungsbericht*. Darmstadt: Wissenschaftliche Buchgesellschaft, 2000.

Müller-Loebnitz, Colonel. "Führerwille und Selbständigkeit der Unterführer." Part 1. *Militär-Wochenblatt* 122, no. 22 (November 26, 1937). Part 2. *Militär-Wochenblatt* 122, no. 23 (December 3, 1937).

Murray, Williamson. "Force Structure, Blitzkrieg Strategy, and Economic Difficulties: Nazi Grand Strategy in the 1930s." In *German Military Effectiveness*. Baltimore: Nautical & Aviation Publishing Company of America, 1992.

———. *German Military Effectiveness*. Baltimore: Nautical & Aviation Publishing Company of America, 1992.

———. *The Luftwaffe, 1933–45: Strategy for Defeat.* Washington, D.C.: Brassey's, 1996.

———. "May 1940: Contingency and Fragility of the German RMA." In *The Dynamics of Military Revolution, 1300–2050*. Edited by MacGregor Knox and Williamson Murray. Cambridge: Cambridge University Press, 2001.

———. "The Problem of German Military Effectiveness, 1900–1945." In *German Military Effectiveness.* Baltimore: Nautical & Aviation Publishing Company of America, 1992.

"Napoleon I. Über das Verhalten eingeschlossener Truppen." *Militärwissenschaftliche Rundschau* 9, no. 1 (1944).

Naumann, Klaus. "The 'Unblemished' Wehrmacht: The Soviet History of a Myth." In *War of Extermination: The German Military in World War II, 1941–1944*. Edited by Hannes Heer and Klaus Naumann. New York: Berghahn, 2000.

Nehring, Walther. *Die Geschichte der deutschen Panzerwaffe, 1916 bis 1945.* Berlin: Propyläen Verlag, 1969.

Neillands, Robin. *Eighth Army: The Triumphant Desert Army that Held the Axis at Bay from North Africa to the Alps, 1939–1945.* Woodstock, N.Y.: Overlook, 2004.

Newton, Stephen H. *German Battle Tactics on the Russian Front, 1941–1945.* Atglen, Pa.: Schiffer, 1994.

———. *Hitler's Commander: Field Marshal Walther Model—Hitler's Favorite General.* Cambridge, Mass.: Da Capo, 2005.

Niles, Douglas. "Ruweisat Ridge: The First Battle of El Alamein." *Strategy and Tactics,* no. 105 (January–February 1985).

Nitu, Victor. "Manstein's Romanians in the Crimea." Available at: http://www.feldgrau.com/articles.phpID=75.

Oberkommando der Wehrmacht, ed. *Die Wehrmacht: Um die Freiheit Europas.* Berlin: Verlag "Die Wehrmacht," 1941.

Obermayer, Colonel. "Gedanken zur soldatischen Tradition: Friedrich der Grosse—Moltke—Schlieffen—Seeckt." *Militär-Wochenblatt* 127, no. 3 (July 17, 1942).

Ogorkiewicz, Richard M. *Armoured Forces: A History of Armoured Forces and Their Vehicles.* New York: Arco, 1970.

"Olymp—Thermopylen—Athen." In *Die Wehrmacht: Um die Freiheit Europas.* Edited by Oberkommando der Wehrmacht. Berlin: Verlag "Die Wehrmacht," 1941.

Oven, Wilfried von. "Mit einer Panzerdivision bei Charkow: Die erste Kesselschlacht dieses Jahres." *Die Wehrmacht* 6, no. 13 (June 24, 1942).

Overhues, Bernd, Günther Pilz, and Bruno Waske. "Über die Barrikaden: Der Sturm auf Rostow." *Die Wehrmacht* 6, no. 17 (August 19, 1942).

Overy, Richard. "The Post-War Debate." In *Firestorm: The Bombing of Dresden, 1945.* Edited by Paul Addison and Jeremy A. Crang. Chicago: Ivan R. Dee, 2006.

———. *Russia's War: A History of the Soviet War Effort, 1914–1945.* New York: Penguin, 1998.

Palmer, Alan. "Operation Punishment." *History of the Second World War*, no. 14 (1978).

Papadopoulos-Killius, Rosemarie. "Die Verarbeitung von Todesahnungen." In *Stalingrad: Mythos und Wirklichkeit einer Schlacht*. Edited by Wolfram Wette and Gerd R. Überschär. Frankfurt am Main: Fischer Taschenbuch Verlag, 1992.

Papagos, Alexander. *The Battle of Greece, 1940–1941*. Athens: Hellenic Publishing, 1949.

Paret, Peter. "Clausewitz." In *Makers of Modern Strategy From Machiavelli to the Nuclear Age*. Edited by Peter Paret. Princeton: Princeton University Press, 1986.

———. "Clausewitz and the Nineteenth Century." In *The Theory and Practice of War*. Edited by Michael Howard. Bloomington: Indiana University Press, 1965.

———. *Understanding War: Essays on Clausewitz and the History of Military Power*. Princeton: Princeton University Press, 1992.

Parkinson, Roger. *The Hussar General: The Life of Blücher, Man of Waterloo*. London: P. Davies, 1975.

———. *The War in the Desert*. London: Hart-Davis, MacGibbon, 1976.

Patrick, Stephen B. "Kharkov: The Soviet Spring Offensive." *Strategy and Tactics* 68, June 1978.

Petersen, Nis. "Polens Vernichtung als Vorschule für den genialen Durchbruch der deutschen Panzerwaffe im Westen." *Militär-Wochenblatt* 125, no. 10 (September 6, 1940).

Petre, F. Loraine. *Napoleon's Conquest of Prussia, 1806*. London: John Lane, 1914.

Piekalkiewicz, Janusz. *Krieg auf dem Balkan*. Munich: Südwest Verlag, 1984.

———. *Stalingrad: Anatomie einer Schlacht*. Munich: Südwest Verlag, 1977.

Pitt, Barrie. *The Crucible of War: Year of Alamein, 1942*. London: Jonathan Cape, 1982.

Playfair, I. S. O. *The Mediterranean and Middle East*. Volume 3. *British Fortunes Reach their Lowest Ebb*. London: Her Majesty's Stationery Office, 1960.

———. Volume 4. *The Destruction of the Axis forces in Africa*. London: Her Majesty's Stationery Office, 1966.

Pleshakov, Constantine. *Stalin's Folly: The Tragic First Ten Days of the World War II on the Eastern Front*. Boston: Houghton Mifflin, 2005.

Pohl, Fritz. "Generaloberst von Seeckt und die Reichswehr." *Militär-Wochenblatt* 127, no. 25 (December 18, 1942).

Ponath, Lieutenant Colonel. "Aus grosser Zeit vor zwanzig Jahren: Der Einbruch in die rumänische Ebene." *Militär-Wochenblatt* 121, no. 21 (December 4, 1936).

———. "Die Schlacht bei Tannenberg 1914 in kriegsgeschichtlicher, taktischer, und erzieherischer Auswertung." *Militär-Wochenblatt* 124, no. 8 (August 18, 1939).

———. "Feuerüberfälle gegen lohnende Augenblicksziele: Kämpfe der Abteilung Picht (verst. I./I.R. 148) vom 20.11. bis 6.12. 1916 bei Turnu-Severin und am Alt in der Schlacht in Rumänien." *Militär-Wochenblatt* 112, no. 35 (March 18, 1928).

Porch, Douglas. *The Path to Victory: The Mediterranean Theater in World War II*. New York: Farrar, Straus & Giroux, 2004.

Prados, John. "The Spanish Gambit: Operation Felix." *Hitler Triumphant: Alternate Decisions of World War II*. Edited by Peter G. Tsouras. London: Greenhill, 2006.

Prior, Robin, and Trevor Wilson. *Passchendaele: The Untold Story*. New Haven, Conn.: Yale University Press, 1996.

Raeder, Erich. *Grand Admiral*. New York: Da Capo Press, 2001.

Ratcliff, R. A. *Delusions of Intelligence: Enigma, Ultra, and the End of Secure Ciphers*. Cambridge: Cambridge University Press, 2006.

Raus, Erhard. *Panzer Operations: The Eastern Front Memoir of Erhard Raus, 1941–1945*. New York: Da Capo, 2003.

Rechenberg, Hans. "Fallschirmjäger im Sudösten." In *Die Wehrmacht: Um die Freiheit Europas*. Edited by Oberkommando der Wehrmacht. Berlin: Verlag "Die Wehrmacht," 1941.

Reemtsma, Jan Philipp. "The Concept of the War of Annihilation." In *War of Extermination: The German Military in World War II, 1941–1944*. Edited by Hannes Heer and Klaus Naumann. New York: Berghahn, 2000.

Reinhardt, Hellmuth. "Selected German Army Operations on the Eastern Front (Operational)." Foreign Military Studies Series. Manuscript P-143a. On file at U.S. Army Military History Institute at Carlisle (Pa.) Barracks.

Reinicke, Adolf. *Das Reichsheer, 1921–1934: Ziele, Methoden der Ausbildung und Erziehung sowie der Dienstgestaltung*. Osnabrück: Biblio Verlag, 1986.

Reschin, Leonid. *General zwischen den Fronten: Walter von Seydlitz in sowjetischer Kriegsgefangenschaft und Haft, 1942–1955*. Berlin: Edition q, 1995.

Reuth, Ralf Georg. *Rommel: Das Ende einer Legende*. Munich: Piper, 2004.

———. *Rommel: The End of a Legend*. London: Haus, 2005.

Reynolds, David. *In Command of History: Churchill Fighting and Writing the Second World War*. New York: Random House, 2005.

Ridley, C. W. "The Battle of the Cauldron." *Journal of the Society for Army Historical Research* 68, no. 274 (1990).

Rieker, Karlheinrich. *Ein Mann verliert einen Weltkrieg: Die entscheidenden Monate des deutsch-russischen Krieges, 1942–43*. Frankfurt am Main: Fridericus-Verlag, 1955.

Roberts, Geoffrey. *Victory at Stalingrad*. London: Longman, 2002.

Rohden, Hans-Detlef Herhudt von. *Die Luftwaffe ringt um Stalingrad*. Wiesbaden: Limes, 1950.

Röhricht, Edgar. "Der Balkanfeldzug 1941." *Wehrwissenschaftliche Rundschau* 12, no. 4 (April 1962).

Romaničev, Nikolaj. "Militärische Pläne eines Gegenschlags der UdSSR." In *Der deutsche Angriff auf die Sowjetunion, 1941: Die Kontroverse um die Präventivkriegsthese*. Edited by Gerd Überschär and Lev A. Bezymenskij. Darmstadt: Primus, 1998.

Rommel, Erwin. *Infantry Attacks*. London: Greenhill Books, 1990.

———. *Krieg ohne Hass*. Heidenheim: Heidenheimer Zeitung, 1950.

———. *The Rommel Papers*. Edited by B. H. Liddell Hart. New York: Harcourt, Brace, 1953.

Rossbach, Wilhelm. "Kertsch—Charkow: Luftherrschaft aus dem Angriff und aus der Verteidigung." *Militär-Wochenblatt* 126, no. 52 (June 26, 1942).

Rossino, Alexander B. *Hitler Strikes Poland: Blitzkrieg, Ideology, and Atrocity*. Lawrence: University Press of Kansas, 2003.

Rothbrust, Florian K. *Guderian's XIXth Panzer Corps and the Battle of France: Breakthrough in the Ardennes, May 1940*. Westport, Conn.: Praeger, 1990.

Rothfels, Hans. "Clausewitz." In *Makers of Modern Strategy: Military Thought from Machiavelli to Hitler*. Edited by Edward Mead Earle. New York: Atheneum, 1966.

Rotundo, Louis, ed. *Battle for Stalingrad: The 1943 Soviet General Staff Study*. Washington, D.C.: Pergamon-Brassey's, 1989.

Scheben, Thomas. "The German Perspective of War in North Africa, 1940–42: Three-dimensional, Intercontinental Warfare." In *Al-Alamein Revisited: The Battle of al-Alamein and Its Historical Implications*. Edited by Jill Edwards. Cairo: American University in Cairo, 2000.

Scheibert, Horst. *Entsatzversuch Stalingrad: Dokumentation einer Panzerschlacht in Wort und Bild: Das LVII. Panzerkorps im Dezember 1942*. Neckargemünd: Kurt Vowinckel, 1968.

———. *Nach Stalingrad—48 Kilometer! Der Entsatzvorstoss der 6. Panzerdivision, Dezember 1942*. Heidelberg: Kurt Vowinckel, 1956.

Scheller, Christopher. "Infanterie vor Perekop." In *Wir erobern die Krim: Soldaten der Krim-Armee berichten*. Neustadt: Pfälzische Verlagsanstalt, 1943.

Schellert, Otto. "Winter Fighting of the 253rd Infantry Division in the Rzhev Area, 1941–1942." In *German Battle Tactics on the Russian Front, 1941–1945*. Edited by Stephen H. Newton. Atglen, Pa.: Schiffer, 1994.

Scherff, Walter. "Geleitwort zum Kriegsjahrgang 1944." *Militärwissenschaftliche Rundschau* 9, no. 1 (1944).

"Die Schlacht im Don-Bogen westlich Kalatsch." *Die Wehrmacht* 6, no. 18 (September 2, 1942).

Schmick, Karl-Heinz. "Der Zweite Weltkrieg und Stalingrad: Sammelbesprechungen." *Politische Vierteljahresschrift* 34, no. 4 (1993).

Schmider, Klaus. *Partisanenkrieg in Jugoslawien, 1941–1944*. Hamburg: E. S. Mittler, 2002.

Schmidt, Heinz Werner. *With Rommel in the Desert*. New York: Bantam, 1977.

Schmitt, Richard. *Prinz Heinrich als Feldherr im Siebenjährigen Kriege*. 2 volumes. Greifswald: Julius Abel, 1885–1899.

Schröder, Hans Joachim. "Alltag der Katastrophen." *Stalingrad: Mythos und Wirklichkeit einer Schlacht*. Edited by Wolfram Wette and Gerd R. Überschär. Frankfurt am Main: Fischer Taschenbuch Verlag, 1992.

Schröter, Heinz. *Stalingrad*. New York: E. P. Dutton, 1958.

———. *Stalingrad. . . . "Bis zur letzten Patrone."* Lengerich: Kleins Druck- und Verlags-Anstalt, 1953.

Schüddekopf, Carl. *Im Kessel: Erzählen von Stalingrad*. Munich: Piper, 2002.

Schüler, Klaus A. Friedrich. *Logistik im Russlandfeldzug: Dsie Rolle der Eisenbahhn bei Planung, Vorbereitung und Durchführung des deutschen Angriffs auf die Sow-*

jetunion bis zur Krise vor Moskau im Winter, 1941–42. Frankfurt: Peter Lang, 1987.

Schulz, Friedrich. "Battle for Crimea." Foreign Military Studies Series. Manuscript T-20. On file at U.S. Army Military History Institute at Carlisle (Pa.) Barracks.

Scoullar, J. L. *Battle for Egypt: The Summer of 1942.* Wellington: War History Branch, 1955.

Seibt, Conrad. *Einsatz Kreta Mai 1941.* German Report Series B-641. Headquarters United States Army, Europe: Foreign Military Studies Branch, n.d.

Seth, Ronald. *Stalingrad: Point of No Return: The Story of the Battle, August 1942–February 1943.* New York: Coward-McKann, 1959.

Seydlitz, Walther von. *Stalingrad: Konflikt und Konsequenz: Erinnerungen.* Oldenburg: Stalling, 1977.

Shepherd, Ben. *War in the Wild East: The German Army and Soviet Partisans.* Cambridge, Mass.: Harvard University Press, 2004.

Shores, Christopher, and Brian Cull with Nicola Malizia. *Air War for Yugoslavia, Greece and Crete, 1940–41.* London: Grub Street, 1987.

Showalter, Dennis. "Masterpiece of Maneuver and Resolution." *Military History Quarterly* 11, no. 3 (spring 1999).

———. "Militärgeschichte als Operationsgeschichte: Deutsche und amerikanische Paradigmen." In *Was ist Militärgeschichte?* Edited by Benjamin Ziemann and Thomas Kühne. Paderborn: Ferdinand Schöningh, 2000.

———. *Patton and Rommel: Men of the War in the Twentieth Century.* New York: Berkley Caliber, 2005.

———. *Tannenberg: Clash of Empires.* Washington, D.C.: Brassey's, 2004.

———. *Wars of Frederick the Great.* London: Longman, 1996.

———. *Wars of German Unification.* London: Arnold, 2004.

Slepyan, Kenneth. *Stalin's Guerrillas: Soviet Partisans in World War II.* Lawrence: University Press of Kansas, 2006.

Sokolovsky, Vasili. "The Battle of Moscow." In *Battles Hitler Lost: First-Person Accounts of World War II by Russian General on the Eastern Front.* New York: Richardson & Steirman, 1986.

Soutor, Kevin. "To Stem the Red Tide: The German Report Series and its Effect on American Defense Doctrine, 1948–1954." *Journal of Military History* 57, no. 4 (October 1993).

Spannenkrebs, Walter. *Angriff mit Kampfwagen.* Oldenburg: Gerhard Stalling, 1939.

———. "Infanterie und Panzer." *Militär-Wochenblatt* 123, no. 7 (August 12, 1938).

Speer, Albert. *Inside the Third Reich.* London: Spheere, 1971.

Spratte, Wido, ed. *Stalingrad: Feldpostbriefe des Oberleutnants Harald Bleker.* Osnabrück: Wennner, 2000.

Steets, Hans. *Gebirgsjäger in der nogaischen Steppe.* Heidelberg: Kurt Vowinckel, 1956.

Stegemann, Bernd. "Die italienische-deutsche Kriegführung im Mittelmeer und in Afrika." In Militärgeschichtliches Forschungsamt (Military Historical Research Office). *Das Deutsche Reich und Der Zweite Weltkrieg*. Volume 3. *Der Mittelmeerraum und Südosteuropa: Von der "non belligeranza" Italiens bis zum Kriegseintritt der Vereinigten Staaten*. Stuttgart: Deutsche Verlags-Anstalt, 1979.

Stegemann, Hermann. *Geschichte des Krieges*. Stuttgart: Deutsche Verlags-Anstalt, 1918.

Stewart, Ian McDougall Guthrie. *The Struggle for Crete 20 May–1 June 1941: A Story of Lost Opportunity*. London: Oxford University Press, 1966.

Stoecker, Sally. *Forging Stalin's Army: Marshal Tukhachevsky and the Politics of Military Innovation*. Boulder, Colo.: Westview Press, 1998.

Stolfi, R. H. S. *Hitler's Panzers East: World War II Reinterpreted*. Norman: University of Oklahoma Press, 1992.

Stone, Norman. *The Eastern Front, 1914–1917*. London: Hodder and Stoughton, 1975.

Stumpf, Reinhard. "Der Krieg im Mittelmeerraum, 1942–43: Die Operationen in Nordafrika und im mittleren Mittelmeer." In Militärgeschichtliches Forschungsamt (Military Historical Research Office). *Das deutsche Reich und der zweite Weltkrieg*. Volume 6. *Der Globale Krieg: Die Ausweitung zum Weltkrieg und der Wechsel der Initiative, 1941–1943*. Part 5. Stuttgart: Deutsche Verlags-Anstalt, 1990.

Sullivan, Brian R. "Intelligence and Counter-Terrorism: A Clausewitzian-Historical Analysis." *Journal of Intelligence History* 3, no. 1 (2003).

Sumida, Jon Tetsuro. "The Relationship of History and Theory in *On War*: The Clausewitzian Ideal and its Implications." *Journal of Military History* 65, no. 2 (April 2001).

Sweeting, C. G. *Blood and Iron: The German Conquest of Sevastopol*. Washington, D.C.: Brassey's, 2004.

Talbot, Randy R. "General Hermann von François and Corps-Level Operations during the Tannenberg Campaign, August 1914." Master's thesis, Eastern Michigan University, 1999.

Tarrant, V. E. *Stalingrad: Anatomy of an Agony*. London: Leo Cooper, 1992.

Taylor, Frederick. *Dresden: Tuesday, February 13, 1945*. New York: HarperCollins, 2004.

Theiss, Rudolf. "Der Panzer in der Weltgeschichte." *Militär-Wochenblatt* 125, no. 15 (October 11, 1940).

Thiel, Rudolf. *Preussische Soldaten*. Berlin: Paul Neff, 1940.

Tieke, Wilhelm. *The Caucasus and the Oil: The German-Soviet War in the Caucasus, 1942–43*. Winnipeg: J. J. Fedorowicz, 1995.

Tieschowitz, General von. "Der Feldzug im Südosten." In *Die Wehrmacht: Um die Freiheit Europas*. Edited by Oberkommando der Wehrmacht. Berlin: Verlag "Die Wehrmacht," 1941.

Tippelskirch, Kurt von. "Der deutsche Balkanfeldzug 1941." *Wehrwissenschaftliche Rundschau* 5, no. 2 (February 1955).

Travers, Tim. "Command and Leadership Styles in the British Army: The 1915 Gallipoli Model." *Journal of Contemporary History* 29, no. 3 (July 1994).

———. "Could the Tanks of 1918 Have Been War-Winners for the British Expeditionary Force?" *Journal of Contemporary History* 27, no. 3 (July 1992).

———. "The Evolution of British Strategy and Tactics on the Western Front in 1918: GHQ, Manpower, and Technology." *Journal of Military History* 54, no. 2 (April 1990).

———. *How the War Was Won: Command and Technology in the British Army on the Western Front, 1917–1918.* New York: Routledge, 1992.

———. *The Killing Ground: The British Army, the Western Front, and the Emergence of Modern Warfare, 1900–1918.* London: Allen and Unwin, 1987.

"Truppen-Kriegsgeschichte, Beispiel 9: Turnu Severin 1916." 2 parts. *Militär-Wochenblatt* 123, no. 17–18 (October 21, 1938, and October 28, 1938).

Tschischwitz, General von. "Der Kulminationspunkt des Angriffs im Landkriege." Part 1. *Militärwissenschaftliche Rundschau* 7, no. 4 (1942). Part 2. *Militärwissenschaftliche Rundschau* 8, no. 1 (1943).

Tsouras, Peter G. *Panzers on the Eastern Front: General Erhard Raus and His Panzer Divisions in Russia, 1941–1945.* London: Greenhill, 2002.

———, ed. *Hitler Triumphant: Alternate Decisions of World War II.* London: Greenhill, 2006.

"Ein Überblick über die Operationen des griechischen Heeres und des britischen Expeditionskorps im April 1941." Part 1. "Die griechischen Verteidigungspläne, die Mobilmachung und der Aufmarsch der verbündeten Streitkräfte." *Militärwissenschaftliche Rundschau* 8, no. 1 (1943).

"Ein Überblick über die Operationen des griechischen Heeres und des britischen Expeditionskorps im April 1941." Part 2. "Die Operationen der verbündeten Streitkräfte bis zum Rückzuge des britischen Expeditionskorps aus Griechenland." *Militärwissenschaftliche Rundschau* 8, no. 2 (1943).

"Ein Überblick über die Operationen des jugoslawischen Heeres im April 1941 (Dargestellt nach jugoslawischen Quellen)." Part 1. "Die Mobilmachung und die Kämpfe vom 6. bis 8. April." *Militärwissenschaftliche Rundschau* 7, no. 3 (1942).

"Ein Überblick über die Operationen des jugoslawischen Heeres im April 1941 (Dargestellt nach jugoslawischen Quellen)." Part 2. "Die Kämpfe vom 9. April bis zum Abschluss des Waffenstillstandes am 17. April." *Militärwissenschaftliche Rundschau* 7, no. 4 (1942).

Überschär, Gerd R. "Die Schlacht von Stalingrad in der deutschen Historiographie." In *Stalingrad: Mythos und Wirklichkeit einer Schlacht.* Edited by Wolfram Wette and Gerd R. Überschär. Frankfurt am Main: Fischer Taschenbuch Verlag, 1992.

Überschär, Gerd, and Lev A. Bezymenskij, eds. *Der deutsche Angriff auf die Sowjetunion, 1941: Die Kontroverse um die Präventivkriegsthese.* Darmstadt: Primus, 1998.

Ulrich, Bernd. *Stalingrad.* Munich: C. H. Beck, 2005.

Umbreit, Hans. "Der Kampf um die Vormachtstellung in Westeuropa." In Militärgeschichtliches Forschungsamt (Military Historical Research Office). *Das Deutsche Reich und Der Zweite Weltkrieg.* Volume 2. *Die Errichtung der hegemonie auf dem Europäischen Kontinent.* Stuttgart: Deutsche Verlags-Anstalt, 1979.

Vanwelkenhuyzen, Jean. "Die Krise vom January 1940." *Wehrwissenschaftliche Rundschau* 5, no. 2 (February 1955).

Vaughan, Hal. *FDR's 12 Apostles: The Spies Who Paved the Way for the Invasion of North Africa*. Guilford, Conn.: Lyons Press, 2006.

Vogel, Detlef. "Das Eingreifen Deutschlands auf dem Balkan." In Militärgeschichtliches Forschungsamt (Military Historical Research Office). *Das deutsche Reich und der zweite Weltkrieg*. Volume 3. *Der Mittelmeerraum und Südosteuropa: Von der "non-belligeranza" Italiens bis zum Kriegseintritt der Vereinigten Staaten*. Part 3. Stuttgart: Deutsche Verlags-Anstalt, 1984.

Voigts-Rhetz, William. "Erklärung." *Militär-Wochenblatt* 84, no. 37 (April 26, 1889).

Volgokonov, Dmitri. *Stalin: Triumph and Tragedy*. New York: Grove Weidenfeld, 1988.

Wagener, Carl. "Der Vorstoss des XXXX. Panzerkorps von Charkow zum Kaukasus, July–August 1942." Part 1. *Wehrwissenschaftliche Rundschau* 5, no. 9 (September 1955).

———. "Der Vorstoss des XXXX. Panzerkorps von Charkow zum Kaukasus, July–August 1942." Part 2. *Wehrwissenschaftliche Rundschau* 5, no. 10 (October 1959).

Walters, Eric M. "Stalingrad, 1942: With Will, Weapon, and a Watch." In *City Fights: Selected Histories of Urban Combat from World War II to Vietnam*. Edited by John Antal and Bradley Gericke. New York: Ballantine, 2003.

Warlimont, Walter. *Inside Hitler's Headquarters, 1939–45*. Novato, Calif.: Presidio, 1964.

Warner, Philip. "Auchinleck." In *Churchill's Generals*. Edited by John Keegan. New York: Grove Weidenfeld, 1991.

Watson, Bruce Allen. *Desert Battle: Comparative Perspectives*. Westport, Conn.: Praeger, 1995.

Wawro, Geoffrey. *The Austro-Prussian War: Austria's War With Prussia and Italy in 1866*. Cambridge: Cambridge University Press, 1996.

———. *The Franco-Prussian War: The German Conquest of France in 1870–1871*. Cambridge: Cambridge University Press, 2003.

Wegner, Bernd. "Der Krieg gegen die Sowjetunion, 1942–43." In Militärgeschichtliches Forschungsamt (Military Historical Research Office). *Das deutsche Reich und der zweite Weltkrieg*. Volume 6. *Der Globale Krieg: Die Ausweitung zum Weltkrieg und der Wechsel der Initiative, 1941–1943*. Part 6. Stuttgart: Deutsche Verlags-Anstalt, 1990.

———. "Wozu Operationsgeschichte?" In *Was ist Militärgeschichte?* Edited by Benjamin Ziemann and Thomas Kühne. Paderborn: Ferdinand Schöningh, 2000.

Wehler, Hans-Ulrich. "Wer sind sät, wird Sturm ernten." In *Ein Volk von Opfern? Die neue Debatte um den Bombenkrieg, 1940–45*. Edited by Lothar Kettenacker. Berlin: Rohwohlt, 2003.

Weidauer, Walter. *Inferno Dresden*. Berlin [Ost]: Dietz, 1966.

Weinberg, Gerhard. *A World at Arms: A Global History of World War II*. 2nd ed. Cambridge: Cambridge University Press, 2005.

Weniger, Erich. "Die Selbständigkeit der Unterführer und ihre Grenzen." *Militärwissenschaftliche Rundschau* 9, no. 2 (1944).

Werth, Alexander. *Russia at War, 1941–1945*. New York: Carroll & Graf, 1964.

———. *The Year of Stalingrad: An Historical Record and a Study of Russian Mentality, Methods and Policies*. London: Hamish Hamilton, 1946.

Werthen, Wolfgang. *Geschichte der 16. Panzer Division, 1939–1945: Herausgegeben vom Kameradschaftsbund 16. Panzer- und Infanterie-Division*. Bad Neuheim: Podzun, 1958.

Westermann, Edward B. *Flak: German Anti-Aircraft Defenses, 1914–1945*. Lawrence: University Press of Kansas, 2001.

———. *Hitler's Police Battalions: Enforcing Racial War in the East*. Lawrence: University Press of Kansas, 2005.

Westphal, Siegfried. *Erinnerungen*. Berlin: Von Hase & Koehler, 1975.

———. *The German Army in the West*. London: Cassell, 1951.

———. *Heer in Fesseln*. Bonn: Athenaum-Verlag, 1950.

———. "Notes on the Campaign in North Africa, 1941–1943." *Journal of the Royal United Service Institution* 105, no. 617 (1960).

Wette, Wolfram. "Das Massensterben als 'Heldenepos': Stalingrad in der NS-Propaganda." In *Stalingrad: Mythos und Wirklichkeit einer Schlacht*. Edited by Wolfram Wette and Gerd R. Überschär. Frankfurt am Main: Fischer Taschenbuch Verlag, 1992.

———. "Die NS-Propagandathese vom angeblichen Präventivkriegscharakter der Überfalls." In *Der deutsche Angriff auf die Sowjetunion 1941: Die Kontroverse um die Präventivkriegsthese*. Edited by Gerd Überschär and Lev A. Bezymenskij. Darmstadt: Primus, 1998.

———. *The Wehrmacht: History, Myth, Reality*. Cambridge, Mass.: Harvard University Press, 2006.

Wette, Wolfram, and Gerd R. Überschär, eds. *Stalingrad: Mythos und Wirklichkeit einer Schlacht*. Frankfurt am Main: Fischer Taschenbuch Verlag, 1992.

Wetzell, Georg. "Vom Geist deutscher Feldherren." *Militär-Wochenblatt* 123, no. 20 (November 11, 1938).

Wieder, Joachim. *Stalingrad und die Verantwortung des Soldaten*. Munich: Nymphenburger, 1962.

Wieder, Joachim, and Heinrich Graf von Einsiedel. *Stalingrad: Memories of Hell*. London: Arms and Armour Press, 1993.

Williams, Kathleen Broome. *Secret Weapons: U.S. High-Frequency Direction Finding in the Battle of the Atlantic*. Annapolis: Naval Institute Press, 1996.

Willingham, Matthew. *Perilous Commitments: The Battle for Greece and Crete, 1940–1941*. Staplehurst, Kent: Spellmount, 2005.

Winterbotham, F. W. *The Ultra Secret*. New York: Dell, 1974.

Winton, Harold R. *To Change an Army: General Sir John Burnett-Stuart and British Armored Doctrine, 1927–1938*. Lawrence: University Press of Kansas, 1988.

"World War2.ro: Romanian Armed Forces in the Second World War." Available at: http://www.worldwar2.ro/generali/?article=102.

Wykes, Alan. *1942—The Turning Point*. London: Macdonald, 1972.

Wynter, H. W. *Special Forces in the Desert War*. London: Public Record Office, 2001.

Yeremenko, Andrei. "Battle of Stalingrad." In *Battles Hitler Lost: First-Person Accounts of World War II by Russian General on the Eastern Front*. New York: Richardson & Steirman, 1986.

Zabecki, David T. "Invasion of Poland: Campaign that Launched a War." *World War II* 14, no. 3 (September 1999).

Zaloga, Steven, and Victory Madej. *The Polish Campaign*. New York: Hippocrene, 1991.

Zapantis, Andrew L. *Hitler's Balkan Campaign and the Invasion of the USSR*. Boulder: East European Monographs, 1987.

Zhukov, G. K. *Marshal Zhukov's Greatest Battles*. Edited by Harrison E. Salisbury. New York: Harper & Row, 1969.

Ziemke, Earl F. *Stalingrad to Berlin: The German Defeat in the East*. Washington, D.C.: Center of Military History, 1968.

Ziemke, Earl F., and Magna E. Bauer. *Moscow to Stalingrad: Decision in the East*. Washington, D.C.: Center of Military History, 1987.

Zuber, Terence. *German War Planning, 1891–1914: Sources and Interpretations*. Rochester, N.Y.: Boydell Press, 2004.

———. *Inventing the Schlieffen Plan: German War Planning, 1871–1914*. Oxford: Oxford University Press, 2002.

———. "The Schlieffen Plan Reconsidered." *War in History* 6, no. 3 (July 1999).

Index